MOON • HANDBOOKS

D0348696

SANTA BARBARA
& THE CENTRAL COAST

STUART THORNTON

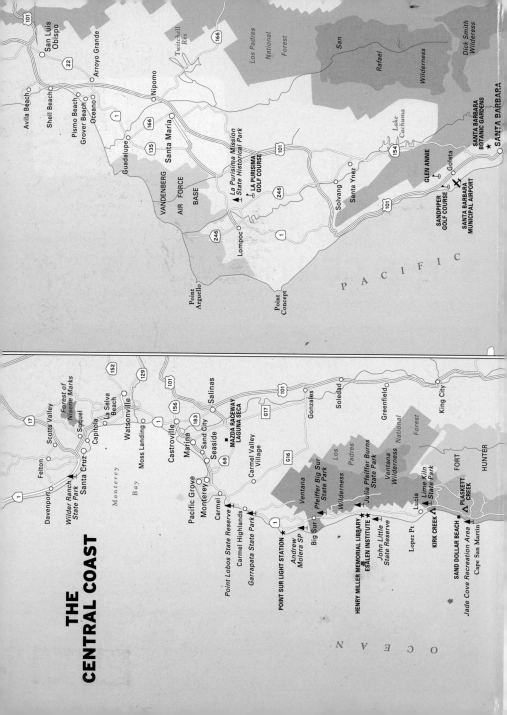

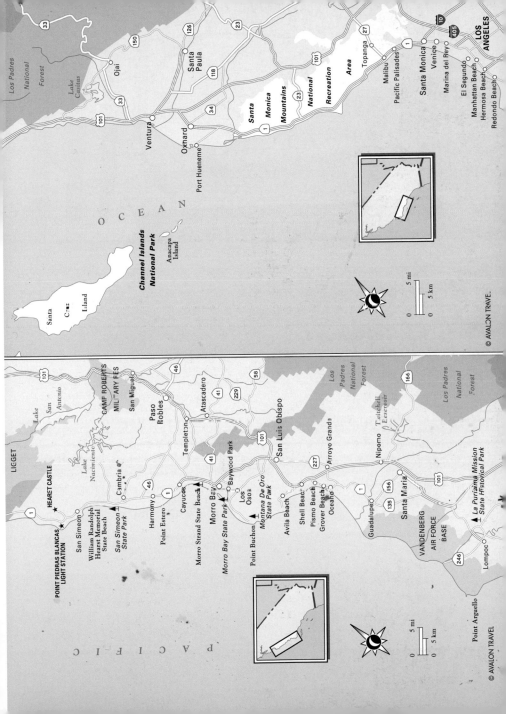

Contents

DISCOVER
Santa Barbara &
the Central Coast

With the crisp, blue ocean and a dramatic mountain range as backdrops, Santa Barbara is surrounded by beauty. Wildflowers color the landscape like artful daubs from a painter's palette. Towering palm trees decorate a skyline of stunning Spanish Colonial Revival architecture that features the most beautiful of the California missions.

With all of this natural and constructed beauty, people compare the coastal city to Old World destinations on the Mediterranean—but Santa Barbara could only exist in California. Its unique south-facing coastline is a magnet for sunshine, with close to 300 sunny days a year. Adjacent to the Santa Ynez Mountains and the relatively undeveloped Gaviota Coast, it's surrounded by the kind of open spaces that encourage both exploration and recreation. The topography of the coastline produces world-renowned surf breaks like Rincon as well as tranquil coves ideal for kayaking or stand-up paddleboarding. Easily accessible hiking trails braid the hillsides, binding the city to the backcountry. Offshore, the Channel Islands offer entry to a wild, natural world honeycombed with sea caves and teeming with wildlife.

Santa Barbara is also an easy place to spend time. The innovative local cuisine is fed by the bounty of the Pacific. Fresh ingredients from abalone to sea urchin will have your taste buds swimming. The vineyards striping the nearby Santa Ynez Valley keep the wine flowing. Spas and comfortable accommodations—from charming boutique hotels to luxury resorts—make relaxation easy to achieve.

Just 90 minutes north of Los Angeles, Santa Barbara is a day-tripper's dream. The surrounding area offers enough possibilities to fill several long weekends or an easygoing coastal road trip. Ventura is appropriately named "the city of good fortune," with an eclectic Main Street and a surf culture all its own. Dreamy Ojai is a place of spiritual retreat in the mountains. North along the coast you'll find a string of easy-to-love towns like Pismo Beach, Morro Bay, Cayucos, and Cambria—gateway to an opulent relic of another era, Hearst Castle. And San Luis Obispo and Paso Robles offer their own sunny mountain communities as well as another burgeoning wine industry.

On the Central Coast, the living is easy. It's an easy place to visit, an easy place to love, and an easy place to return.

Planning Your Trip

Where to Go

SANTA BARBARA

With an idyllic location between the sparkling Pacific Ocean and the rugged Santa Ynez
Mountains, Santa Barbara is the quintessen-
tial California getaway. Attractions include the
Santa Barbara Mission, the finest in the state, as
well as the underrated Santa Barbara Museum
of Art and Santa Barbara Museum of Natural
History. State Street provides an easy introduction to the unique local architecture as well as
shops, restaurants, and nightlife. But the biggest draw is the beauty of the coastline, which
can be experienced by sunning on wide, sandy
Leadbetter Beach, surfing the waves of Rincon
in nearby Carpinteria, or exploring the wild, undeveloped Gaviota Coast.

SANTA BARBARA WINE COUNTRY

Intimate tasting rooms and pleasant small
towns punctuate this wine region northwest
of Santa Barbara. Danish-themed Solvang
is famous for its European feel and authentic cuisine, but it can be overrun with visitors. The countryside around tiny Los Olivos
is spotted with vineyards and winery tasting
rooms. Farther north, Santa Maria is more
sprawling. It's also the birthplace of the famous Santa Maria tri-tip.

VENTURA AND OJAI

The surf vibe is strong in Ventura, thanks
in part to C Street, a world-renowned
wave that draws not only surfers and pad-
dle-boarders but recreation enthusiasts of
all stripes. Ventura also boasts an up-and-
coming arts community, a vibrant walkable Main Street, and a mission of its own,
Mission San Buenaventura. Ojai is a small
town that offers a retreat to anyone seeking

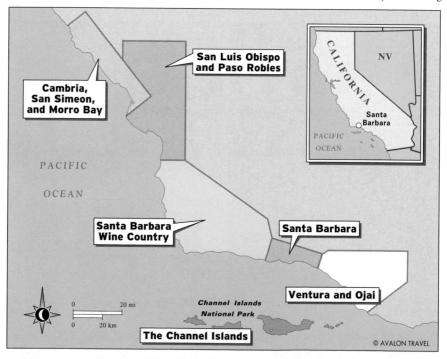

© AVALON TRAVEL

the historic well at Mission San Luis Obispo de Tolosa

an off-the-beaten-path experience, spiritual or otherwise. Contemplate the scenery at Meditation Mount or wander the surrounding mountains, striped with trails and hot springs.

THE CHANNEL ISLANDS

Channel Islands National Park offers a glimpse of the California coastline at is wildest and least developed. The most accessible islands, Santa Cruz and Anacapa, allow day-trippers to explore the natural world by kayaking, snorkeling, diving, and hiking. Inspiration Point provides a breathtaking view of the Pacific you can see nowhere else.

SAN LUIS OBISPO AND PASO ROBLES

The charm of San Luis Obispo is in its slow pace. Visit Mission San Luis Obispo de Tolosa for a touch of history and the over-the-top Madonna Inn for a taste of kitsch. You'll find appealing sands at Pismo Beach and Avila Beach and soothing soaks at Sycamore Mineral Springs Resort. Wine country continues just over the mountains in unassuming Paso Robles.

CAMBRIA, SAN SIMEON, AND MORRO BAY

A monument to monumental wealth, hillside estate Hearst Castle draws the majority of visitors north along the Central Coast. It's definitely worth a visit, but allow time for the area's other pleasures as well, which are both more modest and more timeless. Cambria offers lovely Moonstone Beach and a low-key Main Street. Morro Bay and nearby Montaña de Oro State Park draw numerous outdoor enthusiasts, whether for kayaking, paddling, or hiking. Tiny Cayucos has a protected beach and a pier that feel like they exist in a time warp.

When to Go

During the summer, weather can be hit or miss. Sunny, postcard-perfect days are not uncommon, but the coastline can also be blanketed in fog. School vacations and local festivals draw visitors to the area. Crowds are larger, lines are longer, parking is more expensive, and services can be rushed. This is especially true in smaller towns like Solvang, Los Olivos, Cambria, and Morro Bay, which aren't as well equipped to deal with a crush of visitors.

Fall is the possibly the best time to visit. The summer crowds have thinned out, but the weather is still sunny and warm. Temperatures are still mild in winter, with

springtime in Ojai

average daily highs in the high 60s and nighttime lows no lower than the 40s. There's also occasional rain, more common in the northern towns like Cambria and San Luis Obispo. As a result, it's significantly less crowded. Winter is the best time for surfing because of the large northern swells that wrap around Point Conception and reel off Santa Barbara's point breaks. During the spring the land has been replenished by the rain and the hillsides are green. Open spaces are blanketed in wildflowers. Winds can be fierce, making outdoor activities like camping difficult.

sunset in Morro Bay

The Best of Santa Barbara and the Central Coast

The cultural, historic, and natural attractions of Santa Barbara can easily fill a long weekend of three or four days. Add another day or two each for nearby beach town Ventura and mountainside Ojai. Heading north along the coast to Hearst Castle and its charming beachside communities warrants a few days as well. Explore each region on its own or mix and match to fill a week-long vacation—five days off work with a weekend on each side.

Santa Barbara

DAY 1: SANTA BARBARA MISSION

Begin your day with a stop at State Street's Renaud's Patisserie & Bistro for coffee and croissants. Then take the short drive up to Mission Santa Barbara. No trip to Santa Barbara is complete without a visit to the "Queen of the Missions." Wander the courtyard, the museum, and the church itself. You're less than one mile from the excellent Santa Barbara Museum of Natural History, so stop to gawk at its worthy attractions, ranging from the remains of a pygmy mammoth to a massive blue whale skeleton.

Head down the hill and east to La Super-Rica Taqueria for lunch on gourmet-approved pork-stuffed pasilla peppers (or vegetarian rajas for the herbivores). Then head out into the sunshine for a relaxing afternoon at Leadbetter Beach, a perfect swath of sea and sand less than 10 minutes' drive away. End your day with dinner and cocktails at the Endless Summer Bar and Café, with a view of Santa Barbara Harbor.

Consider staying the night at The Presidio, a place right on State Street with a small fleet of beach cruisers for exploring. In the same price range is relatively inexpensive Hotel Santa Barbara. If you want to splurge, make a reservation at one of the luxurious garden cottages at the historic Simpson House Inn.

Santa Barbara Mission

Danish charm in Solvang

Simpson House Inn, Santa Barbara

A more modern option is the elegant Canary Hotel, with canopied beds and a rooftop pool with superb views of the city.

DAY 2: STATE STREET

Begin your day with a hearty Southern-meets-California breakfast at the Tupelo Junction Café, located right on State Street. Take advantage of your hard-won parking space and strike out on foot, with your destination an easy 0.25 miles away: the Santa Barbara County Courthouse, one of the finest examples of the city's distinctive Mediterranean architecture. Be sure to climb up to the top of the 85-foot-high Clock Tower for views of the city laid out between the Santa Ynez Mountains and the Pacific Ocean. Wander back down State Street, strolling on its wide brick sidewalk south toward the water. Take your time to enjoy the shops; maybe even poke into the Paseo Nuevo Shopping Center. If you're hungry, stop for a snack or lunch at any of the local eateries along the way, maybe a healthy salad or sandwich at The Natural Café. If you're feeling more energetic, follow State Street for one mile until it ends at

Stearns Wharf, the long wooden pier where you can enjoy the views and maybe sample a few wines at the Deep Sea Wine Tasting Room.

Now fueled up, head back up State Street, continuing for one mile to the Santa Barbara Museum of Art to spend the afternoon. Wander among the Monets, Asian artifacts, and terrific temporary exhibits. For dinner, treat yourself to an upscale Italian meal at Olio e Limone, just a block away. Try the rich homemade duck ravioli or the spaghetti with Dungeness crabmeat. If you have any more room or energy after dinner, head to The James Joyce for an Irish whiskey or a Guinness along with live music (bands play six nights a week).

DAY 3: BEACH TIME
SURFING IN CARPINTERIA

The pleasant beach town of Carpinteria, less than a 15-minute drive south of Santa Barbara on U.S. 101, is ideal for outdoor relaxation or recreation. Begin the morning by stopping in at The Garden Market, right off the Santa Claus Lane exit. Grab a breakfast

Gaviota State Park

ciabatta or a fruit smoothie to go. Then head south on U.S. 101 and exit at Bates Road to arrive at Rincon, one of California's premier surf breaks. Surfers can catch some waves, while spectators can head down to the cove to watch the action.

Once you're done with the surf scene, drive back to Carpinteria, just five minutes north, to Linden Avenue. Park at the end of the street and head to Carpinteria State Beach, billed as the "world's safest beach." Relax in the sand and enjoy the gentle waves. When hunger strikes, walk a few blocks up Linden Avenue to The Spot for a burger or shrimp po' boy sandwich. After lunch, stroll along Linden Avenue, visiting local shops like Robitaille's Candies and Whimsy, a vintage boutique. As the day winds town, log more beach time, or take a half-block detour off Linden Avenue to Island Brewing Company, where you can enjoy an Island Blonde or Paradise Pale Ale along with the ocean view from the deck. Plan for dinner at The Palms, a Carpinteria landmark where you grill your own steak or fish entrée. Load up on greens at the all-you-can-eat salad bar.

HIKING THE GAVIOTA COAST

If you like your beach a little less civilized, or prefer a good hike to watersports, the Gaviota Coast might be a better choice. Get yourself going with a coffee and pastry from State Street's The French Press and then head north on U.S. 101. After 20 miles, take the El Capitán State Beach exit and stop at Canyon Market to grab a sandwich to go. Continue 13 miles north to the main entrance to Gaviota State Park; About 2.5 miles north of the park's main entrance, exit off U.S. 101 to Highway 1 heading toward Lompoc. Take an immediate right at the exit and then another right to an unmarked parking area. This is where your hike begins. Follow the trail to the Gaviota Hot Springs, a warm, natural pool where you can enjoy a soak. Hardcore hikers can continue on to Gaviota Peak, a more involved six-mile round-trip hike that offers stunning views. Wherever you choose to end your hike, end your day at Refugio State Beach, 11 miles south of Gaviota State Park's main entrance on U.S. 101. Cool off with a plunge into Refugio's protected waters.

Ventura and Ojai

DAY 4: SURF VENTURA

The coastal city of Ventura is less than 30 miles south of Santa Barbara on U.S. 101. Start your visit by strolling the Ventura Pier, one of the longest wooden piers in the state. Surfers (or surf fans) will want to head a half-mile west on the paved beach walkway to C Street to take in the waves. After spending your morning beachside, plan on lunch at Beach House Tacos, right on the wharf. Try the ahi tacos or "The Combo."

Spend the afternoon on Main Street, filled with old-school beach-town character. Wander the unique shops like Le Monde Emporium and The Iron & Resin Garage. History buffs will want to see Mission San Buenaventura, founded in 1782. Plan on dinner on Main Street: seafood at either the popular Lure Fish House or the sophisticated, upscale Watermark on Main. Lay your head at the inexpensive Bella Maggiore Inn or the Best Western Plus Inn of Ventura; or splurge at Four Points By Sheraton Ventura Harbor Resort in Ventura Harbor Village.

DAY 5: OJAI, MOUNTAINSIDE RETREAT

Take Highway 33 north to Ojai (less than 30 minutes from Ventura; 45 minutes from Santa Barbara) to spend your morning hiking the surrounding national forest. Both Shelf Road and Gridley Trail, just west of town, offer short hikes with sublime views of the valley. Just north of town on East Ojai Avenue, the Ojai Ranger District Office is worth a stop for trail information, maps, and hiking guidebooks.

After working up an appetite, plan on lunch on Ojai Avenue. Jim & Rob's Fresh Grill serves an Ojai-healthy take on Mexican food. Or head north on Ojai Avenue and take a right on South Montgomery Avenue for a filling salad or sandwich at the Ojai Café Emporium. After lunch, wander the shops on Ojai Avenue, or walk two blocks over to Bart's Books, a sensational independent bookstore whose million-plus inventory now stretches outside the building. Then hop back into your car to drive north up Ojai Avenue to Meditation Mount. The meditation center, serene garden, and tranquil views will give you a sense of life in Ojai Valley, which has become a center of diverse spirituality.

Head back down the hill for dinner. Dine

Ventura Pier at sunset

ON A MISSION

Mission San Miguel

Twenty-one Spanish missions dot the length of California, providing a glimpse into the lives of early Spanish settlers and their interactions with the indigenous people. Six of the missions—including the most beautiful—are located along the Central Coast.

- **Mission Santa Barbara** (page 42) is the most beautiful mission and the best maintained, with lovely grounds and a nice museum. If you only visit one mission, this should be it.

- **Mission San Buenaventura** (page 161) in downtown Ventura is called the "Mission of the Sea." Its best features are its landscaped garden and tile fountain.

- **Mission Santa Inés** (page 119) is a relic of the Spanish past in Danish-themed Solvang. Its comprehensive collection of vestments includes one worn by the founder of the missions, Spanish missionary Junípero Serra.

- **Mission La Purisima Concepción** (page 143) in Lompoc is the most extensively restored mission. Located in a state park, it's surrounded by 25 miles of hiking trails. Its living history days recreate 1820s life.

- **Mission San Luis Obispo de Tolosa** (page 235), embedded in San Luis Obispo's picturesque plaza, hosts many community events. It's known for a room dedicated to the indigenous Chumash people.

- **Mission San Miguel** (page 267) is remote, worn, and quiet, with a dark history. Many of its original murals are intact.

the belltower at Mission San Buenaventura

outside, at informal Italian eatery Boccalli's, or try Azu for tapas and cocktails. If you want to spend the night in Ojai, consider the rustic yet hip Ojai Rancho Inn or spoil yourself at the Emerald Iguana Inn.

Santa Barbara Wine Country
DAY 6: SOLVANG AND WINE COUNTRY

The Santa Barbara Wine Country is just 45 minutes from downtown Santa Barbara and just over an hour from Ventura or Ojai. The region can be explored fairly extensively in a full day, depending on how much wine you drink (don't forget to designate a driver who won't be imbibing).

Head out early on Highway 154 west; after 24 miles turn left on Highway 246 west to Solvang. Stop in Solvang for breakfast at the Solvang Restaurant (try the Danish *æbleskiver*) or Birkholm's Bakery & Café. Walk off the sweets by exploring the kitschy Danish town on foot. Pop into the Hans Christian Andersen Museum or get a primer on Danish culture at the Elverhøj Museum of History and Art. If that's too much Danish culture for you, visit Mission Santa Inés, with its impressive collection of vestments.

Then drive six miles up Alamo Pintado Road to the tiny town of Los Olivos. Fortify yourself with lunch at Sides Hardware and Shoes, located right on the town's main street (get something topped with the restaurant's tasty house-made bacon). Then begin an afternoon of wine tasting at Carina Cellars, known for its syrahs, and continue on to the Carhartt Winery, a tasting room that claims to be the world's smallest. Other options include Beckmen Vineyards or Kalyra Winery. Drive back past Solvang a few miles to The Hitching Post II in Buellton for dinner. Featured extensively in the 2004 movie *Sideways,* The Hitching Post II serves superb grilled-to-order steaks. If you still haven't gotten your fill of wine, order a bottle of the homemade pinot noir. Then sleep it off—turn in at the sleek Hotel Corque or the Wine Valley Inn & Cottages.

North to Hearst Castle
DAY 7: SAN LUIS OBISPO
AND AVILA BEACH

Hearst Castle is one of the most popular destinations in the state; the coastal communities along the way are just as worthy

San Simeon's magnificent Hearst Castle

of exploration. From wine country, take Highway 154 west for 32 miles to U.S. 101 in Santa Barbara; then head north. It' another 57 miles to the pleasant, easygoing college town of San Luis Obispo (the drive is about an hour and 45 minutes).

Plan on lunch in downtown SLO on the outdoor deck at Novo, one of the city's most popular restaurants. Possible activities before or after lunch include browsing the shops on Higuera Street or visiting Mission San Luis Obispo de Tolosa, with its nice plaza out front. If you don't mind breaking a sweat, the four-mile round-trip hike to the summit of 1,546 foot-high Bishop Peak offers stunning views of the area.

When you're ready to move on, make the 15-minute drive to nearby Avila Beach, just seven miles south on U.S. 101 and three miles down Avila Beach Drive. End your day exploring the coastline, perhaps at Pirate's Cove just north of town, with an intriguing cavern and a beach popular with sunbathers (some without swimsuits). Book a cozy room, suite, or guesthouse at the Sycamore Mineral Springs Resort. Enjoy dinner at the on-site Gardens of Avila Restaurant, serving organic fare made from local ingredients. End your day with a relaxing soak under the stars in one of the resort's private hot springs tubs.

DAY 8: MORRO BAY
Head to Morro Bay, just 24 miles north of Avila Beach on Highway 1 and 12 miles north of San Luis Obispo. Fuel up at Frankie and Lola's, a breakfast spot right by the harbor (order a fried green tomato benedict). Spend the morning enjoying the picturesque coastline, whether snapping pictures at 576-foot-high Morro Rock or doing something more active like kayaking or hiking. To hit the water, stop in at one of the many kayak and paddleboard rental shops along the Embarcadero or head to Morro Bay State Park, which rents equipment right at the marina. If time allows, paddle over to the spine of dunes called the Morro Bay Sandspit, which separates the bay from the

the view from San Luis Obispo's Bishop Peak

ocean. Hikers will find nearly 50 miles of trails in Montaña de Oro State Park, just eight miles south. Four-mile round-trip Valencia Peak Trail offers sweeping views of the bay.

Plan on lunch on the Embarcadero: barbecued oysters or fish-and-chips at the Dockside Too Fish Market. Browse The Shell Shop or enjoy a glass of wine at the Stax Bar & Bistro. Sometime during the day, confirm the Hearst Castle tour you have planned for tomorrow (it's a good idea to book it at least a month in advance).

End the day with a fine sea-view dinner at Dorn's Original Breakers Café or The Galley Seafood Grill & Bar. Stay the night at Beach Bungalow Inn and Suites or in the El Morro Masterpiece Motel.

DAY 9: HEARST CASTLE
Hearst Castle is just a 45-minute drive north of Morro Bay on Highway 1. With an afternoon tour of the mansion on the hill booked, you have time for a morning detour to Cambria, 20 miles north of Morro Bay. Stop at The French Corner Bakery to grab coffee and pastries to enjoy on Moonstone

CHEAP EATS

tasty fish taco at Spencer Makenzie's Fish Company

Many places on the Central Coast offer elegant cuisine and fine wines, but not every meal requires a white tablecloth. Dine at these casual, creative eateries for under $10.

SANTA BARBARA

- **La Super-Rica Taqueria** (page 74) offers affordable Mexican dishes like pork-stuffed pasilla chilies, approved by foodie patron saint Julia Child.

- **Norton's Pastrami and Deli** (page 70) flies in the face of health-conscious Santa Barbara with heaps of pastrami and cheesesteaks.

- **Tinkers** (page 86) is famed for gut-busting burgers worth the 10-minute drive to Summerland.

- **Beach Liquor** (page 92), in Carpinteria, has a taqueria in back that's been hyped by the *New York Times*.

- **Jalama Beach Store and Grill** (page 102) produces an amazing third-pound burger. Your meal includes the thrill of satisfying your appetite in the middle of nowhere.

VENTURA

- **Beach House Tacos** (page 178), on Ventura Pier, puts creative spins on tasty tacos, like adding raisins or soy-ginger-lime sauce.

- **Spencer Makenzie's Fish Company** (page 178) makes tempura-battered sushi-grade fish tacos that may be the best on the Central Coast.

OJAI

- **The Farmer and the Cook Market & Cafe** (page 203) is the place to eat healthy, organic, and vegetarian with choices like swiss-chard enchiladas.

- **Jim & Rob's Fresh Grill** (page 203) serves an Ojai-healthy take on Mexican food.

CAMBRIA AND SAN SIMEON

- **Main Street Grill** (page 306) offers tri-tip steak sandwiches and burgers with more bang for the buck.

- **Sebastian's Store** (page 306) serves affordable burgers and roast beef in the shadow of Hearst Castle.

Beach, where you can also wander the scenic coastline dreaming of shimmering gemstones. Then continue 10 miles up Highway 1 to San Simeon. Allow time for lunch at Sebastian's Store, a casual eatery in a historic building. After lunch, just cross Highway 1 to make the drive up to Hearst Castle for your tour. First-timers will want to take the Grand Rooms Museum Tour. You'll also have time to wander the grounds and enjoy photo ops amid the opulence of a vanished era.

End your day back in Cambria with a seafood dinner at the cozy Sea Chest Oyster Bar, with its views of Moonstone Beach, or South of the Border lobster enchiladas at eclectic Robin's, just off Cambria's Main Street. Stay the night at Sand Pebbles Inn or its slightly more upscale neighbor, the Blue Dolphin Inn, where the crashing waves will lull you to sleep.

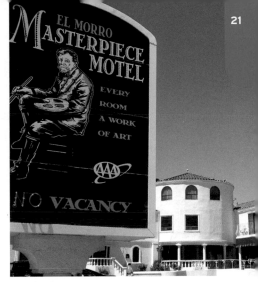

El Morro Masterpiece Motel

Wine Tasting

If it's not the coastline that draws you here, it may just be the wine. Once known as an up and-coming wine region, the Central Coast is becoming a respected one. Local craft breweries add a new twist to tasting trips.

Santa Barbara

Kalyra Winery tasting room on Lower State Street is decorated like a tiki bar. Sample the winery's extensive list of reds, whites, and dessert wines. Close to East Beach, the tasting room of Municipal Winemakers, is decorated in an ironic twist on its name, with old office furniture, filing cabinets, and trophies. Expect Rhône-style wines, including grenache, syrah, and a sparkling shiraz. Located on Stearns Wharf, the Deep Sea Wine Tasting Room pours Conway Family Wines, including the popular signature Deep Sea Red. The tasting room offers views of the harbor and the distant Channel Islands. Telegraph Brewing Company Tasting Room is located in a renovated World War II-era Quonset hut. Try the flagship California Ale or something from the experimental Telegraph Obscura line. In the heart of the surf town of Carpinteria, Right Island Brewing Company operates a tasting room from an industrial space that used to be a citrus packing house. Taste the fruits of the brewmaster's labors, including the popular Island Blonde and seasonal Avocado Honey Ale. The small patio offers views of the Pacific.

Santa Ynez Valley

The tasting bar at Sort This Out Cellars in Solvang is a hip throwback to the 1960s, with lots of shiny chrome and wine bottles adorned with pin-up girls. Sample merlot, syrah, sangiovese, sauvignon blanc, chardonnay, muscat, and the Elvira Macabernet—named for the horror movie hostess. Enjoy live music on Friday and Saturday. Just outside the tiny town of Los Olivos, bucolic Beckmen Vineyards allows you to take your glass along while wandering outside, where three gazebos overlook a duck pond. Their fine biodynamic wines include a variety of syrahs and a killer grenache. The beers of Figueroa Mountain Brewing Company, including the flavorful

Enjoy the view of Paso Robles' wine country.

Hoppy Poppy IPA, are served in restaurants and bars throughout the Central Coast. Sample the suds at their source: the brewery in Buellton. On weekends, the brewery hosts live bands and food trucks.

Beckmen Vineyards

Paso Robles

Off Highway 46, Eberle Winery was one of the first wineries in Paso Robles. Free daily wine-cave tours provide an overview of wine-making followed by sampling in the large tasting room. Choose from hearty, bold reds such as cabernet sauvignon, barbera, zinfandel, a few whites, and a few fabulous blends. Outside, a covered deck overlooks the vineyard-braided hillsides. Sample mourvèdres, merlots, petite sirahs, and chardonnays in the sculpture garden at Sculpterra Winery. Among the stunning sculptures are a 14-foot-tall bronze cat and a 15-foot-tall granite puma. Vina Robles has a comfortable tasting room with a large fireplace and couches. Sample from cabernet sauvignons, petite sirahs, zinfandels, port wines, and blends. You can also stick around for a concert in the 3,300-seat amphitheater. The Firestone Walker Brewing Company taproom serves beers brewed right next door, including the popular DBA British Ale and the rare Wookey Jack, a black IPA.

BEST BEACHES

remote Point Sal State Beach

- **Leadbetter Beach** (page 54) in Santa Barbara is big and wide, with rising cliffs and a grassy lawn. It's ideal for a day of sunning, swimming, and lounging.
- **Rincon** (page 89) in Carpinteria is one of California's most revered surf breaks, where waves wrap in from a distinct point and peel into a cove.
- **Refugio State Beach** (page 100) on the Gaviota Coast is a postcard-perfect finger of sand on a scenic cove shaded by towering palm trees. The water is calm enough for kids to splash around safely.
- **Jalama Beach** (page 102) on the Gaviota Coast offers the only access to the long, wild stretch of coastline near Point Conception. This remote county park has a playground and horseshoe pits, but its main draws are surfing, fishing, and beachcombing.
- **Point Sal State Beach** (page 144) is one of California's remotest public stretches of sand, undisturbed by footprints. It can only be reached via a strenuous 10-mile round-trip hike; access is governed by Vandenberg Air Force Base.
- **Pirate's Cove** (page 252), just south of Avila Beach, is where smugglers once dropped their illegal goods. Now this secluded beach is known for sunbathers who drop their clothes—all of them.
- **Moonstone Beach** (page 294) in Cambria consists of pockets of sand interspersed with jumbles of rocks offshore. Beachcombers can still find its namesake stones on this gem of a beach.

the boardwalk at Moonstone Beach

Coastal Recreation

Here are all the ingredients for serious recreation: mountains, streams, canyons, and certainly not least, the Pacific Ocean.

Hiking

Santa Barbara has superb hiking trails just miles from downtown. The four-mile round-trip hike to Inspiration Point rewards hikers with views of the ocean and the Channel Islands, while Seven Falls is a scramble to several pools of water. Just west of the city, Gaviota State Park has 2,000 acres to explore, including a 1.5-mile round-trip excursion to Gaviota Hot Springs or the more demanding six-mile round-trip climb to Gaviota Peak.

Ringed by mountains, Ojai is a superb spot for a hike. Both Shelf Road and Gridley Trail provide views of the Ojai Valley. San Luis Obispo County's most distinct geologic features are its nine volcanic peaks. The tallest is Bishop Peak, a 1,546-foot-high outcropping with superb views after a two-mile ascent.

Kayaking and Stand-Up Paddleboarding

The Channel Islands provide some of the state's best sea kayaking. On Santa Cruz, Cavern Point is honeycombed with holes in the cliffs accessible to paddlers, while the small islets of Anacapa are pocked with an astounding 130 sea caves.

Up the mainland coast, Avila Beach is protected from wind and large waves by Point San Luis, making it ideal for beginners. Morro Bay teems with wildlife, from herons to sea otters.

Surfing

Featured in many surf magazines and surf movies, Rincon is one of California's most revered surf breaks. Especially during the winter, the point creates long peeling waves that have inspired generations of surfers. Rincon hosts scores of other surfers on most days.

Whether you call it Surfer's Point or C Street, this Ventura point break is a magnet for surfers. Unlike Rincon, which has south swells blocked by the Channel Islands during the summer, Surfer's Point receives waves from the north, west, and south.

Scuba Diving and Snorkeling

The waters off the Channel Islands are littered with shipwrecks and host to a plethora of sealife. Santa Barbara Island has warmer waters as well as The Rookery, where you can dive with playful seals. The rocks off Anacapa and Santa Cruz Islands are dotted with sea urchins and swarmed with schools of fish.

Cycling

Backed by mountains and hugging the coast, Santa Barbara is a good place to hop on a street bike. The Mountain Drive Bike Route goes up into the hills, while the Coast Route is an easier ride along the shore. Meanwhile, mountain bikers can hit the single-track trails at Elings Park.

San Luis Obispo is also fine place for pedaling. The Madonna Inn Bike Trail runs from Marsh Street 0.75 miles to the kitschy tourist complex. Mountain bikers ride up and down Madonna Mountain, which has a fire road and a single-track trail.

riding a wave in Ventura

SANTA BARBARA

It's been called the American Riviera, with weather, community, and sun-drenched beaches reminiscent of the Mediterranean coast. In truth, Santa Barbara is all California.

It's one of the state's most picturesque cities, with a plethora of palm trees and chic, healthy residents. It's famous for its pleasant Mediterranean climate and Spanish Colonial Revival architecture. After a 1925 earthquake, the city rebuilt itself in the style of the Santa Barbara Mission, arguably the most beautiful of the California missions, with white stucco surfaces, red-tiled roofs, arches, and courtyards.

Nestled between the Pacific Ocean and the mountains, its copious sunshine, wide roads, warm sandy beaches, and challenging mountain trails inspire physical activity and healthy living. Along the waterfront, a paved path allows anyone on two feet, two wheels, or anything else that moves to enjoy the coastline alongside grassy areas with palm trees gently swaying in the breeze. At least five weekly area farmers markets make healthy produce abundant and accessible.

Santa Barbara is also where beach culture meets high culture. You'll find lots of museums, outdoor shopping areas, great restaurants, and four-star resorts; a growing young wine region thrives. But the pace of life is slow enough to make it a favorite escape for Southern California locals as well. It's not surprising that many of these refugees from Los Angeles decide to stay and become Santa Barbara residents.

HIGHLIGHTS

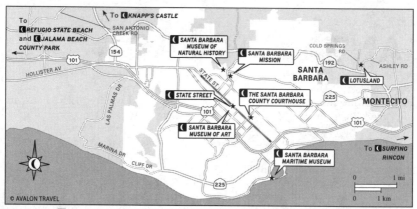

© AVALON TRAVEL

LOOK FOR 【 TO FIND RECOMMENDED SIGHTS, ACTIVITIES, DINING, AND LODGING.

【 State Street: It would be difficult to visit Santa Barbara without spending some time on State Street, lined with fine shops, bars, restaurants, and examples of Spanish Colonial Revival architecture (page 30).

【 Santa Barbara Museum of Art: This underrated gem has an impressive permanent collection that includes many French impressionist masterpieces (page 30).

【 Santa Barbara County Courthouse: This Spanish Colonial Revival courthouse is a flat-out gorgeous government building. Climb the stairs to the clock tower for great views of the city (page 37).

【 Santa Barbara Maritime Museum: Learn about the area's fascinating maritime history, from deadly shipwrecks to surfing innovations (page 40).

【 Santa Barbara Mission: There's a reason that Santa Barbara Mission is referred to as the "Queen of the Missions." This well-maintained site has beautiful buildings and a museum that feels more complete than most of the other missions (page 42).

【 Santa Barbara Museum of Natural History: View a giant blue whale skeleton and a pygmy mammoth specimen at this extensive facility, which includes a planetarium and a sea center (page 43).

【 Knapp's Castle: In the mountains above Santa Barbara, the remains of Knapp's Castle feel like the ruins of an ancient city. All that is left are stonework, archways, and sweeping views of the Santa Ynez Valley and Lake Cachuma (page 44).

【 Lotusland: Even if you're not a plant fanatic, it's worth it to take a two-hour tour of this 37-acre amusement park for gardeners and botanists (page 45).

【 Surfing Rincon: Just south of Carpinteria, this is one of the best surf breaks in California. Even if you're not a surfer, it's fun to watch them ride waves at this scenic point and cove (page 89).

【 Refugio State Beach: This palm-shaded crescent of sand on a usually tranquil cove is one the best beaches in California (page 100).

【 Jalama Beach County Park: This wild, windswept beach is popular with surfers, anglers, and anyone looking for an escape from civilization (page 102).

PLANNING YOUR TIME

Santa Barbara is fairly compact and can easily be enjoyed in a weekend, but to fully explore the city you'll need at least three or four days, especially if you want to enjoy water activities, hiking, or cycling. If you're the meandering type, the waterfront and State Street will suit you fine and can be explored in a weekend.

The ideal time to visit is from March to May, when everything is pristine after the mild winter rains. The temperatures are still moderate, the views are crystal clear, and the air is fresh and crisp. The June gloom kicks off summer, with lots of fog that sometimes doesn't burn off until early afternoon. October through December is also a great time. There are more chances of rain then, but it's not unusual to be able to spend Thanksgiving weekend at the beach, playing in the water and burning off all those calories.

The city's grid layout makes sightseeing easy; the majority of sights are within 12 blocks downtown, so walking is often preferable to constantly looking for parking. If you are an early riser, it's recommended to get to sights when they first open in order to avoid crowds. Everything gets progressively more crowded as the day wears on, but the early mornings, and even as late as 10am-11am, are reasonably crowd-free. Many visitors stay downtown or by the waterfront, and the city is an easy base for the sights you'll need to drive to, such as the mission, Montecito, and Carpinteria. Even the Santa Ynez Valley is only a 30- to 40-minute drive and is a great day trip. If you head to the valley for the day, drive up via the San Marcos Pass on Highway 154, over the mountains, and return to the city via U.S. 101 along the coast, or vice versa. That way you get the best of everything—mountains with killer views, lots of ocean, and ranchland.

ORIENTATION

Santa Barbara is defined by **State Street,** the main drag, which runs from the beach through the downtown area. There is only one major artery into and out of Santa Barbara, U.S. 101. Aside from Highway 154 through the San Marcos Pass, which heads from Santa Barbara over the mountains and into the Santa Ynez Valley, no other roads lead here. This can be a problem every once in a while: Fires can shut down U.S. 101, leaving Santa Barbara isolated from its neighbors. If there is a major traffic accident, there simply are no alternate routes.

Aside from that, getting around Santa Barbara is easy, as the city is laid out in a classic grid pattern. State Street does get congested during summer months; unless you enjoy sitting in your car and inching your way along, it's best to use other arteries on the weekends. The first street east of State Street is Anacapa Street, which runs one way to the ocean. Chapala Street, the first street west of State Street, runs one way toward the mountains. These two streets allow for quick travel through the city.

Although State Street is not a lengthy street, you will often hear people refer to the 400-600 blocks as "Lower State." The "upper" section of State Street has fewer visitors and less foot traffic, but it is worth a visit for a few restaurants that are popular with locals as well as several lodging options.

Besides downtown, Santa Barbara's **Waterfront** is very popular with visitors and includes attractions like the harbor, Stearns Wharf, and the Santa Barbara Zoo. One section of the Waterfront area east of State Street and west of U.S. 101 is a hip industrial landscape of wineries, art galleries, and surf shops that has become known as the **Funk Zone.**

The northern section of the city is often referred to by its main attraction: **the Mission,** although it's also called **the Riviera.** Other attractions here include the Santa Barbara Museum of Natural History. Continuing up into the **Foothills** of the Santa Ynez Mountain Range via Highway 154, you'll find more remote attractions like Knapp's Castle and the Chumash Painted Cave State Historic Park.

East of the city, **Montecito** is an affluent, unincorporated section of Santa Barbara County where you'll find upscale shopping and dining along **Coast Village Road** and attractions like Casa del Herrero and Lotusland.

The Mesa is a bench of elevated land just

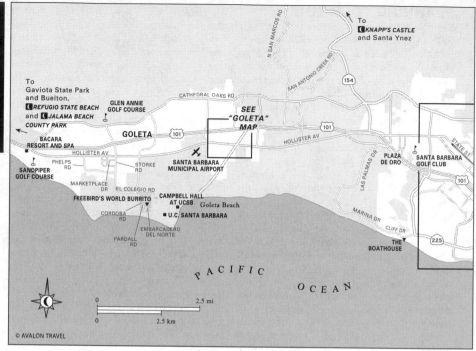

southwest of Santa Barbara's downtown. It is primarily a residential area with little interest for visitors, although it does have some restaurants that are worth the short 15-minute drive.

Just southeast of Santa Barbara, you'll find the distinct coastal communities of **Summerland** and **Carpinteria.** Carpinteria is a great little beach town to visit for a relaxed day of surf and sand.

West of Santa Barbara, **Goleta** is primarily residential; it's also home to the Santa Barbara Airport. Nearby **Isla Vista** is the location of the University of California and its thriving college community. To the far west, the **Gaviota Coast** is undeveloped, other than its worthwhile coastal parks.

HISTORY

Prior to the arrival of the Spanish on these lands in the mid-1500s, about 20,000 Chumash people lived between Malibu and San Luis Obispo and on the Channel Islands in self-sustaining and autonomous communities. There are still cave paintings, which are records of Chumash stories, scattered throughout the Central Coast region. In 1542 Juan Rodríguez Cabrillo sailed into the Santa Barbara Channel and, contrary to popular belief, didn't drop anchor near the mainland. He landed his ship at the Channel Islands, never having set foot in what is now Santa Barbara. But he put up a Spanish flag and claimed the region for Spain. It was Sebastián Vizcaíno, a cartographer for the Duke of Monte Rey, who landed in the Santa Barbara harbor 60 years later, on December 4, 1602, which happened to be the feast day of Saint Barbara. The flag was officially planted, and Santa Barbara was put on the map for the first time. Living on land claimed and named by Spain didn't really affect the Chumash people until the arrival of Spanish missionaries in the mid-1700s.

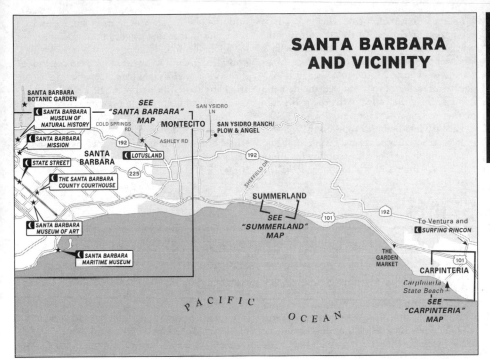

In need of defensible positions along the coast to secure its newly claimed territory, Spain established the very first presidio, a ramshackle wood structure, at Santa Barbara on April 21, 1782. The formal presidio, or fort, was constructed beginning in 1784, followed closely by the Santa Barbara Mission in 1786. Spain effectively ruled the region until the early 1820s, when Mexico fought for and won its independence from Spain. But Mexico's rule was short-lived as the United States declared war on Mexico in 1846 in order to expand its territories.

With the discovery of gold in Northern California in 1849, Easterners came west, and many of those looking for a new life ended up in Santa Barbara. The city's mild climate also began to draw people to the coast for health reasons. In the late 1880s Santa Barbara was considered a health resort, and reports of the day promoted the healing environment of the city's natural springs and mild climate. Of course, the arrival of the railroad in 1887 also helped the city grow. Many wealthy East Coast industrialists who could afford second homes on large swaths of land built estates in Montecito, just outside the city. But at the end of the 19th century, although there were large and impressive hotels like the Potter and Arlington that catered to the elite, the city was still relatively small. A 1925 earthquake decimated parts of Santa Barbara, and the fortuitous opportunity to reinvent the city is considered a seminal moment in its evolution. The city leaders saw a blank canvas and called on the town's original Spanish and Mexican influences to create a definable identity, still evident in the downtown of today. But even after World War II, Santa Barbara was considered a sleepy little beach community, not the destination it is now. There were iron oil derricks all along Summerland's beaches and blighting the Mesa.

Property values plummeted when a Japanese submarine fired a shell at the coast during the war. Since there were few viable businesses here, land was cheap. But it wasn't long before things started to change. More people began to recognize what the area had to offer, and demand increased. By the early 1990s, the real estate market was growing exponentially.

Part of Santa Barbara's appeal is the fact that its natural boundaries, created by the ocean and the mountains, leave little possibility for urban sprawl. (It's interesting to note that the tallest building is still only a mere eight stories, and there's just one at that height.) Preservationists have long held political power and have kept unbridled growth in check in order to control the city's overall visual theme. Considering the area's limited building potential, it's no wonder that land became a hot commodity. And its strong agricultural components, most notably the wine industry, avocados, broccoli, and strawberries, mean Santa Barbara is assured of being a desirable location for a long time to come.

Sights

Santa Barbara is a visually appealing city surrounded by extreme natural beauty. Many visitors come for the coastline, but also for the historical mission, the museums, and the amazing architecture, including Spanish buildings with wrought-iron rails, wooden porches, and copious colorful tile work; buildings from the 1880s, with their Western feel; and even the 1940s-influenced structures with an industrial motif.

DOWNTOWN

Downtown Santa Barbara covers about 12 blocks. The pedestrian-friendly area has more than enough places to grab a bite, window-shop, or find an ATM. There are even frequent recycling bins to keep the streets clean. What are lacking, however, are restrooms. Surprisingly, there is only one public restroom (914 State St.); most businesses reserve their facilities for customers only.

◖ State Street

Although **State Street** runs through different sections of Santa Barbara, the roadway through 12 blocks downtown is the heart of the city. With wide brick sidewalks on either side shaded by palm trees and decorated with flowers that give it a tropical feel, State Street is perfect for an afternoon stroll. Clothing stores, restaurants, and bars line the street along with popular attractions including the Santa Barbara Museum of Art and the Granada Theatre.

◖ Santa Barbara Museum of Art

The two-floor **Santa Barbara Museum of Art** (1130 State St., 805/963-4364, www.sbma.net, Tues.-Sun. 11am-5pm, adults $9, seniors, students with ID, and children $6) has an impressive art collection that would make some larger cities envious. Wander the spacious, well-curated museum and take in some paintings from the museum's collection of Monets, the largest collection of the French impressionist's paintings in the West. The museum also has ancient works like a bronze head of Alexander from Roman times and a collection of Asian artifacts including a 17th- or 18th-century Tibetan prayer wheel. There are interesting temporary exhibitions on display as well.

Santa Barbara Contemporary Arts Forum

Located in the Paseo Nuevo Mall, the **Santa Barbara Contemporary Arts Forum** (CAF, 653 Paseo Nuevo, 805/966-5373, www.sbcaf.org, Tues.-Sat. 11am-5pm, Sun. noon-5pm, free) showcases cutting edge art with exhibitions that may include sculpture, interactive installations, and works created with new technology. The CAF also hosts frequent events,

© STUART THORNTON

Downtown's State Street is the heart of Santa Barbara.

with art discussions, live entertainment, and video installations.

Brooks Institute Gallery 27

Aspiring photographers and those who appreciate photographic art should stop at the worthwhile **Brooks Institute Gallery 27** (27 E. Cota St., 805/690-4900, www.brooks.edu, Sat.-Thurs. 10am-9pm, Fri. 10am-5pm). The Brooks Institute was founded as a photography school in 1945, but now it also has programs in film production, visual journalism, design, and screenwriting. Gallery 27 showcases the photos of its students, faculty, and alumni along with the work of world-renowned photographers who include Keith Carter, Joyce Tenneson, and Rodney Smith.

El Presidio de Santa Bárbara State Historic Park

For some serious history, visit **El Presidio de Santa Bárbara State Historic Park** (123 E. Canon Perdido St., 805/965-0093, www.sbthp.org, daily 10:30am-4:30pm, closed major holidays, adults $5, seniors $4, children under 16 free, admission includes Casa de la Guerra), one of four former Spanish fortresses along the California coast. This two-acre site dates back to 1782 and includes two original sections: the family residence called El Cuartel and the Canendo Adobe. The Presidio was once the military headquarters and the government center for an area stretching from San Luis Obispo County to Los Angeles. Today, the white adobe buildings with red-tiled roofs encircle a dusty courtyard that gives a hint to what downtown Santa Barbara looked like over 200 years ago during the Spanish colonial period. Reconstructed rooms, including the *cocina* (kitchen), padre's quarters, and commander's quarters, appear as they would have during that time. There are also exhibits on everything from ceramics to a ledger of items the colonists requested from their native Spain. One exhibit that diverges from the site's Spanish colonial focus imparts information about a Japanese American community that resided here from 1900 to 1940.

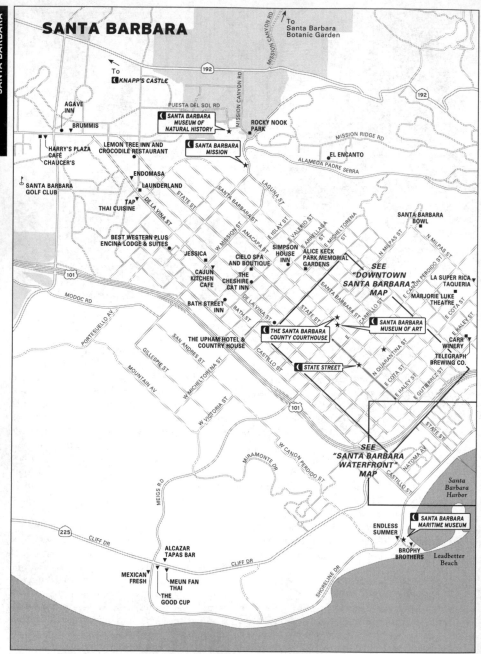

SANTA BARBARA

To Santa Barbara Botanic Garden

MISSION CANYON RD

To KNAPP'S CASTLE

192

192

PUESTA DEL SOL RD

MISSION CANYON RD

AGAVE INN

BRUMMIS

SANTA BARBARA MUSEUM OF NATURAL HISTORY

ROCKY NOOK PARK

MISSION RIDGE RD

HARRY'S PLAZA CAFÉ

CHAUCER'S

LEMON TREE INN AND CROCODILE RESTAURANT

SANTA BARBARA MISSION

EL ENCANTO

ALAMEDA PADRE SERRA

SANTA BARBARA GOLF CLUB

ENDOMASA

LAUNDERLAND

TAP THAI CUISINE

DE LA VINA ST

STATE ST

SANTA BARBARA ST

LAGUNA ST

SANTA BARBARA BOWL

N MILPAS ST

N MILPAS ST

W MISSION ST

ANACAPA S

E ISLAY ST

VALERIO ST

ARRELLAGA ST

E MICHELTORENA ST

BEST WESTERN PLUS ENCINA LODGE & SUITES

JESSICA

CIELO SPA AND BOUTIQUE

SIMPSON HOUSE INN

ALICE KECK PARK MEMORIAL GARDENS

N CANON PERDIDO ST

LA SUPER RICA TAQUERIA

101

MODOC RD

CAJUN KITCHEN CAFE

THE CHESHIRE CAT INN

DE LA VINA ST

SANTA BARBARA ST

SEE "DOWNTOWN SANTA BARBARA MAP

MARJORIE LUKE THEATRE

E COTA ST

BATH STREET INN

BATH ST

CARRILLO ST

E HALEY ST

PORTESUELLO AV

SAN ANDRES ST

THE UPHAM HOTEL & COUNTRY HOUSE

CASTILLO ST

STATE ST

THE SANTA BARBARA COUNTY COURTHOUSE

SANTA BARBARA MUSEUM OF ART

CARR WINERY

GILLESPIE ST

W MICHELTORENA ST

N QUARANTINA ST

E COTA ST

TELEGRAPH BREWING CO.

MOUNTAIN AV

STATE STREET

N QUARANTINA ST

E HALEY ST

E GUTIERREZ ST

101

W VICTORIA ST

STATE ST

MIRAMONTE DR

SEE "SANTA BARBARA WATERFRONT" MAP

MEIGS RD

W CANON PERDIDO ST

NATOMA AV

CASTILLO ST

Santa Barbara Harbor

225

CLIFF DR

SANTA BARBARA MARITIME MUSEUM

ENDLESS SUMMER

CLIFF DR

SHORELINE DR

BROPHY BROTHERS

Leadbetter Beach

ALCAZAR TAPAS BAR

MEXICAN FRESH

MEUN FAN THAI

THE GOOD CUP

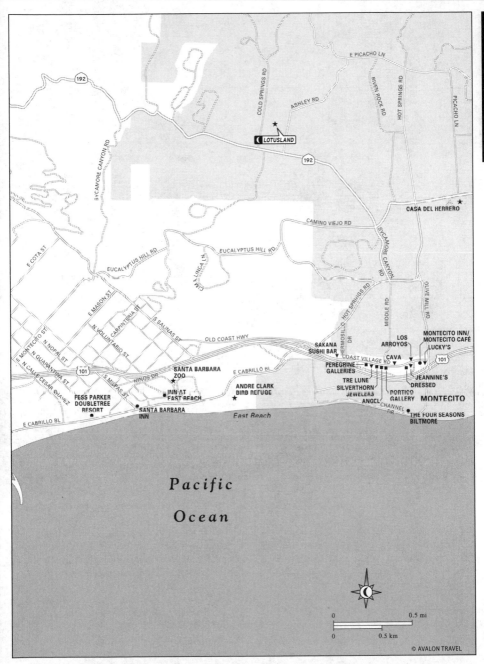

SANTA BARBARA

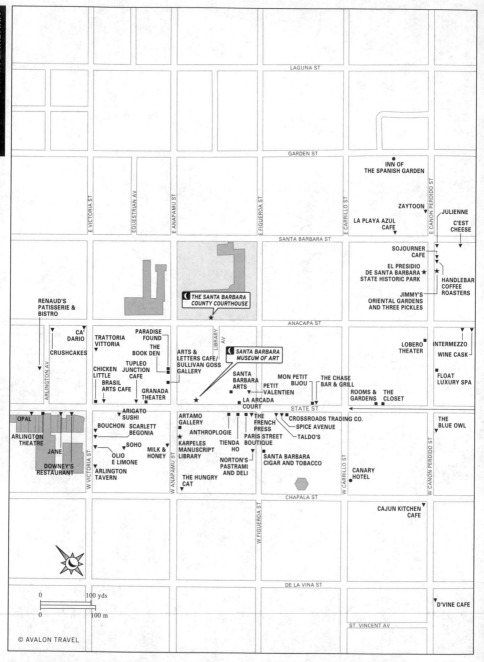

LAGUNA ST

GARDEN ST

INN OF
THE SPANISH GARDEN

E VICTORIA ST
EQUESTRIAN AV
E ANAPAMU ST
E FIGUEROA ST
E CARRILLO ST
E CANON PERDIDO ST

ZAYTOON

JULIENNE

LA PLAYA AZUL
CAFE

C'EST
CHEESE

SANTA BARBARA ST

SOJOURNER
CAFE

EL PRESIDIO
DE SANTA BARBARA ★
STATE HISTORIC PARK

★ HANDLEBAR
COFFEE
ROASTERS

RENAUD'S
PATISSERIE &
BISTRO

☾ THE SANTA BARBARA
COUNTY COURTHOUSE

JIMMY'S
ORIENTAL GARDENS
AND THREE PICKLES

ANACAPA ST

LIBRARY AV

CA'
DARIO

TRATTORIA
VITTORIA

PARADISE
FOUND

LOBERO
THEATER

INTERMEZZO
WINE CASK

CRUSHCAKES

THE
BOOK DEN

ARTS &
LETTERS CAFE/
SULLIVAN GOSS
GALLERY

☾ SANTA BARBARA
MUSEUM OF ART

ARLINGTON AV

CHICKEN
LITTLE

TUPLEO
JUNCTION
CAFE

FLOAT
LUXURY SPA

BRASIL
ARTS CAFE

GRANADA
THEATER

SANTA
BARBARA
ARTS

MON PETIT
BIJOU

PETIT
VALENTIEN

THE CHASE
BAR & GRILL

ROOMS &
GARDENS

THE
CLOSET

LA ARCADA
COURT

STATE ST

ARIGATO
SUSHI

ARTAMO
GALLERY

THE
FRENCH
PRESS

CROSSROADS TRADING CO.

SPICE AVENUE

THE
BLUE OWL

OPAL

BOUCHON

SCARLETT
BEGONIA

ANTHROPLOGIE

PARIS STREET
BOUTIQUE

TALDO'S

ARLINGTON
THEATRE

SOHO

MILK &
HONEY

KARPELES
MANUSCRIPT
LIBRARY

TIENDA
HO

JANE

OLIO
E LIMONE

SANTA BARBARA
CIGAR AND TOBACCO

CANARY
HOTEL

DOWNEY'S
RESTAURANT

ARLINGTON
TAVERN

NORTON'S
PASTRAMI
AND DELI

W VICTORIA ST
W ANAPAMU ST
W CARRILLO ST
W CANON PERDIDO ST

THE HUNGRY
CAT

CHAPALA ST

W FIGUEROA ST

CAJUN KITCHEN
CAFE

DE LA VINA ST

0   100 yds
0   100 m

ST. VINCENT AV

D'VINE CAFE

© AVALON TRAVEL

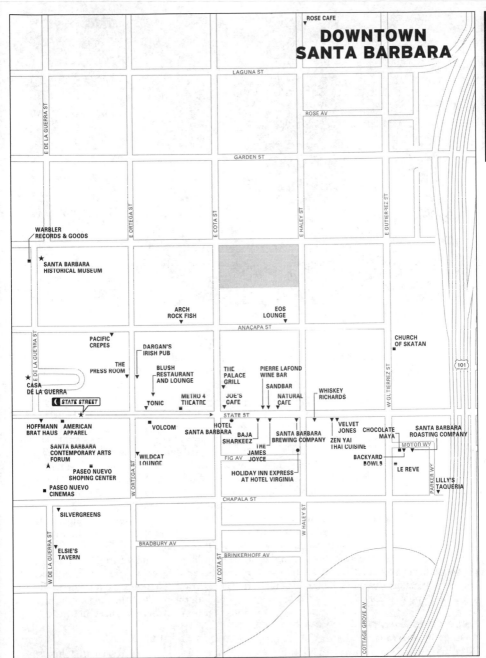

DOWNTOWN SANTA BARBARA

ROSE CAFE ▼

LAGUNA ST

ROSE AV

GARDEN ST

E DE LA GUERRA ST

E ORTEGA ST

E COTA ST

E HALEY ST

E GUTIERREZ ST

WARBLER
RECORDS & GOODS ■

★ SANTA BARBARA
HISTORICAL MUSEUM

ARCH
ROCK FISH ▼

EOS
LOUNGE ▼

ANACAPA ST

CHURCH
OF SKATAN

PACIFIC
CREPES ▼

DARGAN'S
IRISH PUB ▼

THE
PRESS ROOM ▼

BLUSH
RESTAURANT
AND LOUNGE

THE
PALACE
GRILL ▼

PIERRE LAFOND
WINE BAR ▼

SANDBAR ▼

WHISKEY
RICHARDS ▼

W GUTIERREZ ST

[101]

★ CASA
DE LA GUERRA

🚋 STATE STREET

TONIC ▼

METRO 4
THEATRE ▼

JOE'S
CAFE ▼

NATURAL
CAFE ▼

STATE ST

HOFFMANN AMERICAN
BRAT HAUS APPAREL

VOLCOM ■

HOTEL
SANTA BARBARA ▼

BAJA
SHARKEEZ ▼

SANTA BARBARA
BREWING COMPANY ▼

VELVET
JONES ▼

ZEN YAI
THAI CUISINE ▼

CHOCOLATE
MAYA ▼

SANTA BARBARA
ROASTING COMPANY ▼

SANTA BARBARA
CONTEMPORARY ARTS
FORUM ▲

WILDCAT
LOUNGE ▼

THE
JAMES
JOYCE ▼

FIG AV

MOTOR WY

BACKYARD
BOWLS ▼

W ORTEGA ST

PASEO NUEVO
SHOPING CENTER

HOLIDAY INN EXPRESS
AT HOTEL VIRGINIA

LE REVE ■

PARKER WY

PASEO NUEVO
CINEMAS ■

CHAPALA ST

LILLY'S
TAQUERIA ▼

W DE LA GUERRA ST

SILVERGREENS ▼

ELSIE'S
TAVERN ▼

BRADBURY AV

W COTA ST

BRINKERHOFF AV

W HALEY ST

COTTAGE GROVE AV

© STUART THORNTON

El Presidio de Santa Bárbara State Historic Park

Santa Barbara Historical Museum

The **Santa Barbara Historical Museum** (136 E. De La Guerra St., 805/966-1601, www. santabarbaramuseum.com, Tues.-Sat. 10am-5pm, Sun. noon-5pm, donation) details Santa Barbara's history from the days when the Chumash people were the lone residents to the devastating 1925 earthquake to the days of landscape painters like Carl Oscar Borg and beyond, providing context for the city we know today. Among the museum's 80,000 artifacts and art pieces is a shrine that was imported into the city's Chinatown in 1898. The museum is also home to the world's largest collection of the works of cowboy and Western artist John Edward Borein, which include etchings, watercolors, ink drawings, and oil paintings. In the **Gledhill Library** you can delve further into the region's rich history through some 5,000 books and 70,000 photographs.

Casa de la Guerra

Casa de la Guerra (15 E. De La Guerra St., 805/965-0093, www.sbthp.org, Sat.-Sun.

noon-4pm, adults $5, seniors $4, children free, includes admission to the Presidio) is the former home of the fifth Presidio commander, José de la Guerra. Constructed between 1819 and 1827, it was an integral part of civic and social happenings in Santa Barbara's early days. The family's importance in the community continued when De la Guerra's son Pablo entered politics becoming a state senator and the lieutenant governor of California. On the National Register of Historic Places, Casa de la Guerra was one of the models for the city's reconstruction after the 1925 earthquake. The whitewashed adobe building has 12 rooms around a courtyard. One room features a late-19th-century black horsehair sofa, one of the building's original furnishings. Other rooms have been repopulated with antiques from the period. There are also rotating exhibits, which in the past have focused on the missions that Junípero Serra founded in Mexico.

Jimmy's Oriental Garden

In the 1860s and 1870s, a small Chinese

population came to Santa Barbara, mostly to work on railroad and highway projects. They resided in the old adobes around the Presidio. At one point, Santa Barbara's Chinatown included a few stores, a school, a place of worship, several opium dens, and some gambling rooms. Today, the distinctive red-tiled roof and red doors of **Jimmy's Oriental Garden** (126 E. Canon Perdido St., 805/965-0093, http://sbthp.org), across from the Presidio, are all that remains. The Chung family lived and worked here for decades, starting in 1947. The Oriental Garden closed its doors in 2006; the space is currently rented by a sandwich shop, **Three Pickles** (805/965-1015, http://threepickles.com, Mon.-Sat. 11am-4pm, $6-11), but one of the building's rooms has some images and text on display that tell some of Santa Barbara's Asian American history.

◖ Santa Barbara County Courthouse

If only all government buildings could be as striking as the **Santa Barbara County**

Courthouse (1100 Anacapa St., 805/962-6464, www.santabarbaracourthouse.org, free docent-led tours Mon.-Tues. and Fri. 10:30am and 2pm, Wed.-Thurs. and Sat. 2pm). Constructed in 1929 after the devastating 1925 earthquake, the courthouse, which is actually four buildings that cover a whole city block, is one of the city's finest examples of Mediterranean architecture. The interior's high ceilings, tile floors, ornate chandeliers, and art-adorned walls give it the feel of a California mission. The old Board of Supervisors room is impressive, with 6,700 square feet of murals depicting the county's history and its resources. Also visit El Mirador, the clock tower, an 85-foot-high open deck that provides great views of the towering Santa Ynez Mountains and the Pacific Ocean, with the city's red-tiled roofs in the foreground.

Karpeles Manuscript Library

The computer guidance system used by the early Apollo moon missions and an original Stone copy of the Declaration of Independence are the highlights of the collection at the

© STUART THORNTON

the beautiful Santa Barbara County Courthouse

Karpeles Manuscript Library (21 W. Anapamu St., 805/962-5322, www.rain. org/~karpeles, Wed.-Sun. noon-4pm, free). Other exhibits focus on Mark Twain, the baseball's earliest days, and great moments in medical history. It's one of 12 Karpeles museums across the country that showcase the largest private holdings of original documents and manuscripts in the world. The library also presents frequent Sunday afternoon lectures.

Moreton Bay Fig Tree

Hovering over the intersection of Montecito Street and Chapala Street like a giant green cloud, the **Moreton Bay Fig Tree** (daily sunrise-half hour after sunset) is thought to be the largest such tree in the country. Born in 1876, this monster fig tree has a 38-foot trunk and rises 80 feet high. It's estimated that 16,000 people could stand in the shade of this tree. The gigantic tree has been designated a "tree of notable interest" by the city of Santa Barbara and is listed on the official registry of California Big Trees, which designates the largest specimens of tree species in the state.

WATERFRONT

The harbor and waterfront area stretches from East Beach west to Leadbetter Beach, encompassing the city blocks west of U.S. 101. In addition to the beaches are visitor favorites like the Santa Barbara Harbor, Stearns Wharf, and the Santa Barbara Zoo. A few blocks east of Lower State Street, a hip micro-neighborhood called the Funk Zone has sprouted up in a formerly industrial section of the city. Highlights include the Urban Wine Trail, artists' work spaces, surfboard-shaping warehouses, and cafés.

Urban Wine Trail

The wines of Santa Barbara County have been receiving favorable reviews in the national media. The area is known predominantly for wines made from pinot noir and chardonnay grapes, but with the diversity of microclimates, there are over 50 grape varietals grown here.

This means you can find traditional varieties like cabernet sauvignon, merlot, sauvignon blanc, and syrah along with sangiovese, dolcetto, viognier, cabernet franc, malbec, and others.

Not all wine tasting is done surrounded by vineyards. On the **Urban Wine Trail** (www. urbanwinetrailsb.com) you can sample some of the county's best wines without even seeing a vine. Near Lower State Street, a block from the beach, you can walk to six tasting rooms; visiting others that are part of the trail will require a little driving. Recent legislation means that some, but not all, wineries can now offer wines by the glass in addition to wine tasting, so if you sample something you like, you can purchase a glass to enjoy on the spot or a bottle to take with you.

Kalyra Winery (212 State St., 805/965-8606, www.kalyrawinery.com, Mon.-Fri. noon-7pm, Sat.-Sun. noon-8pm) is famous for having been featured in the 2004 movie *Sideways*. This tasting room wasn't in the film, but you can still sample the California and Australian wines made by Mike Brown, an Aussie and avid surfer, in a tiki-room setting. Kalyra started out making sweet wines, and still offers quite a few of them, but has a broad portfolio.

Once you're done at Kalyra Winery, walk a block down Yanonali Street to **Santa Barbara Winery** (202 Anacapa St., 805/963-3633, www.sbwinery.com, daily 10am-5pm), the oldest winery in the county, started in 1962. The chardonnay is delightful and truly expresses a Santa Barbara character with its bright citrus notes. Other varieties include pinot noir, sangiovese, and sauvignon blanc. If you are looking to sample a diverse array of wines, this is your best stop. The tasting bar is just a few feet from the barrel room, and there's a good-size gift shop.

Municipal Winemakers (22 Anacapa St., 805/931-6864, www.municipalwinemakers.com, Sun.-Wed. 11am-6pm, Thurs.-Sat. 11am-11pm, tasting $10) is in an unpretentious small space with an even smaller deck. Inside are rough wood ceilings and plain walls,

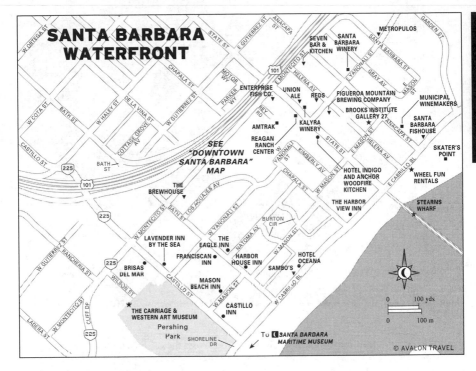

with a four-top table and standing room at the bar. This is a weekend venture for owner Dave Potter, who will answer your questions and pour his wines. The offerings are Rhône-style wines, including grenache, syrah, and a sparkling shiraz.

Carr Winery (414 N. Salsipuedes St., 805/965-7985, www.carrwinery.com, Sun.-Wed. 11am-6pm, Thurs.-Sat. 11am-8pm, tasting $10) focuses on small lots of syrah, grenache, cabernet franc, and pinot noir. The tasting room is in a World War II Quonset hut, with a bar up front and tables in the back. The wine bar features live music on Friday and house wines on tap.

Nothing improves a great glass of wine like a great view. The **Deep Sea Wine Tasting Room** (217 Stearns Wharf, 805/618-1185, www.conwayfamilywines.com, daily noon-7pm, tasting $8-20) takes advantage of this fact with a location right on Stearns Wharf, offering

views of the harbor, the shoreline, and the distant Channel Islands. Sample Conway Family Wines, including the popular signature Deep Sea Red, a blend of five grapes that are mostly syrah.

Stearns Wharf

Stretching 2,250 feet into the harbor, **Stearns Wharf** (State St. and Cabrillo Blvd., www.stearnswharf.org, parking $2.50 per hour, first 1.5 hours free with validation) was the longest deep-water pier between Los Angeles and San Francisco at the time of its construction by lumberman John P. Stearns in 1872. It has weathered many natural disasters, including storms and fires; a restaurant fire in 1973 caused its closure for almost nine years. Today it hosts seaside tourist favorites like fish-and-chips eateries, candy stores, and gift shops. It's also home to the **Ty Warner Sea Center** (211 Stearns Wharf, 805/962-2526, www.sbnature.

© STUART THORNTON

Stearns Wharf

org, daily 10am-5pm, multi-museum passes adults $8, seniors and teens $7, children $5), operated by the Museum of Natural History, with many interactive exhibits such as a live-shark touch pool and a 1,500-gallon surge tank filled with sea stars, urchins, and limpets.

Santa Barbara Maritime Museum

It's only fitting that the **Santa Barbara Maritime Museum** (113 Harbor Way, 805/962-8404, www.sbmm.org, Memorial Day-Labor Day daily 10am-6pm, Labor Day-Memorial Day daily 10am-5pm, adults $7, children and seniors $4, free for military personnel in uniform) sits right on the working harbor. Built as a Works Progress Administration project during the Great Depression, it served as a U.S. Navy training facility for more than 50 years. The city of Santa Barbara purchased the building in 1995, opening the museum in 2000. A dozen different exhibits touch on different aspects of local maritime history, including abalone diving, commercial diving, and surfing.

Don't miss the exhibits on shipwrecks, including the wreck of the steamship *Winfield Scott,* which struck the rocks off Anacapa Island in 1853, and the Honda Disaster of 1923, when nine U.S. Navy destroyers struck a reef near Point Conception. The Munger Theater screens high-definition educational films, and there is a fun hand's-on children's area. One popular exhibit simulates steering a boat into the harbor; another features a working periscope that peers outside the building at the wharf and the harbor. Other galleries focus on the local Chumash people, the whaling and fur-hunting eras, and modern oil drilling and commercial fishing. In September 2013 the museum acquired and began displaying the Fresnel lens of the Point Conception Lighthouse.

The Carriage and Western Art Museum

For those who long for the days of horse-powered transportation, **The Carriage and Western Art Museum** (129 Castillo St., 805/962-2353, www.carriagemuseum.org,

THE GREAT QUAKE: SANTA BARBARA REBORN

Santa Barbara's distinctive Spanish Colonial Revival architecture owes its existence to a natural disaster: a 6.8 magnitude earthquake that struck on the morning of June 29, 1925. The epicenter was right off the Santa Barbara coast. The quake was so powerful that it was felt from Paso Robles down to Orange County and east to Mojave.

One survivor described it as sounding "like a million dogs crunching bones." So much rubble was piled up on State Street that it became impassable. Walls crumbled from downtown hotels, leaving them with exposed rooms that made them look like dollhouses. Vital sections of the Southern Pacific Railroad were damaged, and several significant buildings were leveled, including the Arlington Hotel, the Californian Hotel, the San Marcos office building, and the Potter Theater. Thirteen people lost their lives.

In the aftermath of the quake, city officials enacted a strict building code for Santa Barbara's downtown that led to the city's rebirth. New structures had to adhere to Spanish Colonial Revival architectural style. The distinctive architecture—along with the temperate climate—are the main reasons Santa Barbara has become so popular as a vacation destination.

Mon.-Fri. 9am-3pm, docent tours third Sun. of every month 1pm-4pm, free) is worth a stop. In addition to stagecoaches and carriages, the museum features an extensive saddle collection, including saddles that once belonged to famous equine enthusiasts like Will Rogers, Clark Gable, and Jimmy Stewart. It also has a replica of the Senate Saloon, Santa Barbara's first bar.

Santa Barbara Zoo

The **Santa Barbara Zoo** (500 Ninos Dr., 805/962-5339, www.sbzoo.org, daily 10am-5pm, adults $14, children and seniors $10) shelters its critters in enclosures that resemble natural habitats. One multispecies habitat mimics an African savanna that with giraffes, tortoises, cranes, and meerkats, all carefully separated from the pride of lions next door. You can get close enough to the lions to hear them occasionally roar. This cool little municipal zoo also takes pride in its local endangered species, such as the foxes indigenous to the Channel Islands, just 20 miles away. The "California Trail" exhibit shows off still endangered California condors, one of the rarest birds in the country and the largest land bird on the continent. As you slowly stroll along the paths, you'll also see giant anteaters, huge elephants, monkeys, and snow leopards. One of the best-named kids' exhibits ever, "Eeeww!" showcases insects, reptiles, and wonderfully slimy amphibians.

You can rent strollers and wheelchairs just inside the zoo. Also close to the gate is the **Ridley-Tree House Restaurant,** which offers plenty of outside tables and a walk-up counter that sells sandwiches and burgers. There's also Mexican-inspired fare at **The Wave.** The gift shop offers cute souvenirs for both kids and adults.

Reagan Ranch Center

President Ronald Reagan had a strong connection to the Santa Barbara area, dating back to his 1974 purchase of Rancho del Cielo, a sprawling 688-acre ranch and vacation home in the Santa Ynez Mountains northwest of Santa Barbara. What became better known as the Reagan Ranch hosted foreign dignitaries that included British prime minister Margaret Thatcher and Soviet leader Mikhail Gorbachev. Two blocks from the beach, the **Reagan Ranch Center** (217 State St., 888/872-1776, www.yaf.org, tours Mon.-Thurs. 11am-4pm, free) offers an interpretive history of Reagan's days at the ranch with artifacts from the property and a 28-foot-long interactive timeline. The center also exhibits a 5,000-pound chunk of the Berlin Wall and the former president's Jeep Scrambler.

THE MISSION AND THE RIVIERA

The eastern portion of the city is nestled in the hills of the impressive Santa Ynez Mountains. Home to the Santa Barbara Mission, the Santa Barbara Museum of Natural History, and the Santa Barbara Botanic Gardens, it's also the best place to access the city's best hiking trails.

Santa Barbara Mission

It's easy to see why the **Santa Barbara Mission** (2201 Laguna St., 805/682-4713, http://santabarbaramission.org, daily 9am-4:30pm, self-guided tours adults $5, seniors $4, children $1, children 6 and under free, docent-guided tours Thurs.-Fri. 11am, Sat. 10:30am, adults $8, children free) is referred to as the "Queen of the Missions." Larger, more beautiful, and more impressive than many of the 20 other missions, it's second to none for its art displays and graceful architecture, all of which are complemented by the serene local climate and scenery. Unlike many of the California missions, the church at Santa Barbara remained in use

THE FROG SHRINE

Santa Barbara's Paterna Road has a curious attraction: a low rock wall crowded with frogs: stuffed frogs, plastic frogs, and ceramic frogs. The first frog appeared around 1989. Local legend says that within one of the frogs is a letter that curses anyone who removes a frog from the perch. As result, the frog population continues to grow. These days, the frog wall is popular enough to have its own Facebook page.

To find the Frog Wall from the Santa Barbara Mission, take Los Olivos Street up and then turn right on Alameda Padre Serra. Veer left on Lausen Road, and then bear right at the fork onto Paterna Road. The frogs begin after a few hundred yards.

after the secularization of the mission chain in the 19th century. When you visit, you'll find the collection of buildings, artwork, and even the ruins of the water system in better shape

"The Queen of the Missions"

© STUART THORNTON

than at the other missions. The self-guided tour includes a walk through the mission's striking courtyard, with its blooming flowers and towering palm trees, and entrance to the mission museum, which has, among other displays, a photo of the church after a 1925 earthquake toppled its towers as well as a collection of Chumash artifacts. The original purpose of the mission was to convert the indigenous Chumash people to Christianity. The mission's cemetery is the final resting place of more than 4,000 Chumash people.

◖ Santa Barbara Museum of Natural History

Continuing the outdoors theme that pervades Santa Barbara, the **Santa Barbara Museum of Natural History** (2559 Puesta del Sol, 805/682-4711, www.sbnature.org, daily 10am-5pm, adults $11, seniors and teens $8, children $7) has exhibits to delight visitors of all ages. Inside, visit the large galleries that display stories of the life and times of insects, mammals, birds, and dinosaurs. Of particular interest is a display showcasing the remains of a pygmy mammoth specimen that was found on the nearby Channel Islands. Learn a little about the human history of the Santa Barbara area at the Chumash exhibit. Head outdoors to circle the immense skeleton of a blue whale, and to hike the Mission Creek Nature Trail. If you're interested in the nature of worlds other than this one, go into the **Gladwin Planetarium** and wander the Astronomy Center exhibits. The Planetarium hosts shows portraying the moon and stars, plus monthly Star Parties and special events throughout the year.

If you're more interested in the Earth's array of sealife, head down to Stearns Wharf and visit the **Ty Warner Sea Center** (211 Stearns Wharf, 805/962-2526, www.sbnature.org, daily 10am-5pm, multi-museum passes adults $8, seniors and teens $7, children $5), which is operated by the Museum of Natural History. Check out the tunnel through the 1,500-gallon tide pool tank, touch a sea cucumber, examine microscopic sea creatures, and get involved in the science of oceanography.

© STUART THORNTON

the Ty Warner Sea Center on Stearns Wharf

Santa Barbara Botanic Gardens

The year-round perfect weather makes for a perfect spot to grow the gorgeous **Santa Barbara Botanic Gardens** (1212 Mission Canyon Rd., 805/682-4726, www.sbbg.org, daily 9am-5pm Nov.-Apr., daily 9am-6pm Mar.-Oct., adults $8, seniors and teens $6, children $4). The gardens focus solely on the indigenous plants of California, with plantings from the deserts, chaparral, arroyo, and more. The gardens spread out over many acres and cross several hiking trails. Check out the small stand of coastal redwoods, the centerpiece of the park, which remains shaded and cool even when the sun beats down in the heat of summertime. Another garden shows off the beauty of native California lilacs. The mission of the gardens encompasses conservation of California wilderness areas as well as the water and soil in developed areas. Visit the Home Demonstration Garden for an example of beautiful landscaping using California native species that are suited to the climate and conditions, and thus need less irrigation and chemical fertilizers.

Located in the mountains above Santa Barbara, Knapp's Castle has superb views.

Guided tours are offered Saturday and Sunday at 11am and 2pm with your admission ticket; join the standard tour or call ahead to arrange a private tour. You can take your own self-guided tour with a map and the advice of the docents. The shop offers books and garden-themed gifts, while the nursery sells native California plants. The garden does not have a restaurant or snack bar.

◖ Knapp's Castle

Coming up to the stone steps, archways, and fireplaces of **Knapp's Castle** feels like wandering into the ruins of an ancient city. They are all that remain of this structure, built by Union Carbide founder George Owen Knapp in 1916, that burned down in 1940. Beyond the stonework that remains, you'll find impressive views of the Santa Ynez Valley and Lake Cachuma below. Reaching Knapp's Castle is a bit of an adventure. From U.S. 101, take Highway 154 north and continue for 10 miles. Turn right onto East Camino Cielo Road and drive three miles. Look for a dirt pullout and a big red metal gate on a road to the left. Park your car and walk down the dirt road. You'll pass another metal gate with a sign announcing: "Right to pass revocable by owner" (the castle on a private parcel of land that is currently open to the public). It's a worthwhile 0.5-mile walk to Knapp's Castle and its fine views.

Chumash Painted Cave State Historic Park

More like a historic spot than a historic park, the **Chumash Painted Cave Historic Park** (805/733-3713, www.parks.ca.gov, daily dawn-dusk) offers an impressive example of rock art made by the indigenous Chumash people; the artwork here may date back to the 1600s. The cavern walls are decorated with black and white-striped human figures and wheel shapes. While the meaning of these distinct red and blue pictographs is unknown,

© STUART THORNTON

the people who created them may have been shamans who traveled to the cave for spiritual reasons or to seek power. To reach the park, take Highway 154 from Santa Barbara into the mountains and turn onto Painted Cave Road. Take Painted Cave Road two miles up a steep, narrow mountain road. There is only enough parking for one or two vehicles. Walk up just a few steps from the roadway to peer into the sandstone cave, where the art is protected by a locked metal gate. The winding mountain drive can be rough for those who get carsick.

MONTECITO

Just east of Santa Barbara, wealthy Montecito boasts many celebrity residents, including Oprah Winfrey. It's also the location of some of the most exclusive luxury resorts in the nation. Even if you aren't staying at the San Ysidro Ranch or the Four Seasons Biltmore, Montecito is worth a visit to take a tour of the stunning Lotusland, browse the upscale shops and restaurants along Coast Village Road, or to one of the area's finest meetings of sand and sea at Butterfly Beach.

【 Lotusland

A must-see for botanists and gardeners, **Lotusland** (695 Ashley Rd., 805/969-3767, www.lotusland.org, tours Feb. 15-Nov. 15 Wed.-Sat. 10am and 1:30pm, adults $35, ages 5-18 $10) is a 37-acre garden of over 3,000 plant species that were planted with an artist's touch. The amazing garden is the life's work of Ganna Walska, a Polish born former opera singer who spent over 40 years developing the intricate layers of plantlife on the land. Take in the world's second-largest collection of cycads, stout plants that can resemble flowering eggs or palm trees, one of the largest collections of aloe plants outside Africa, a cactus garden featuring creeping devil cacti that resemble large spikey worms, a topiary garden, and a lotus-filled water garden.

The only way to visit Lotusland is to reserve a spot on a two-hour docent-guided tour. You'll learn all about the unique characteristics of the plants and their shepherd, Walska, who proclaimed herself "the enemy of the average."

© STUART THORNTON

some of the striking plants in Montecito's Lotusland

Casa del Herrero

Casa del Herrero (1387 E. Valley Rd., 805/565-5653, www.casadelherrero.com, docent-led 1.5-hour tours Wed. and Sat. 10am and 2pm, over age 10 $20, reservations required) is Spanish for "House of the Blacksmith." It's a fitting name for the home and garden of George Fox Steedman, an industrialist and engineer who spent the last years of his life on this Montecito property doing silversmithing and metalworking. Steedman worked with architect George Washington Smith to design the home; he moved in on the same day that the 1925 earthquake toppled much of downtown Santa Barbara. Not a crack was found in Casa del Herrero. Today, it's one of the finest examples of the local Spanish colonial architecture. The 11-acre site, with a historic house museum and garden, is only accessible on a 90-minute docent-led tour by reservation.

Entertainment and Events

A wealthy town with close ties to cosmopolitan Los Angeles, Santa Barbara offers visitors a wealth of live cultural displays, from a symphony and an opera to a near-endless parade of festivals. The students of UCSB add a lively bit of zest to the town's after-dark scene.

BARS AND CLUBS

The proximity of the University of California to downtown Santa Barbara guarantees a livelier nighttime scene than you'll find elsewhere on the Central Coast. Check with the locals to discover the ever-changing hot spots. Bars cluster on State Street and beyond, and plenty of hip clubs dot the landscape.

The best place to start an evening out on the town is at **Joe's Café** (536 State St., 805/966-4638, www.joescafesb.com, daily 7:30am-11pm), a steak house and bar known for the stiffest drinks in town. Don't expect a fancy cocktail menu; just go with the classics in this historic establishment and its throwback feel, with checkered tablecloths, a tin-paneled ceiling, and framed black-and-white photos of mostly old men adorning the walls.

Tonic (634 State St., 805/897-1800, www.tonicsb.com, Thurs.-Sat. 8pm-1:30am) has a hipster feel, complete with exposed brick walls and a long glass bar. Top-flight DJs spin a mostly hip-hop or house groove, with the occasional mash-up for variety. Tonic also hosts college nights and ladies nights. Two lounges provide a respite from the partiers at the main bar and on the dance floor. To cool down, go outside to the huge outdoor patio, which has its own funky octagonal bar.

For a traditional Irish bar experience in downtown Santa Barbara, head to **The James Joyce** (513 State St., 805/962-2688, www.sb-jamesjoyce.com, daily noon-1:30am). Peanut shells litter the floor as locals sip Guinness at the bar or play competitive games of darts in the backroom. The James Joyce has live entertainment six days a week, including Irish music on Sunday.

Also on State Street, **Whiskey Richards** (435 State St., 805/963-1786, Tues.-Sun. noon-2am, Mon. 5pm-2am) has a slightly edgier feel than some bars on State Street, hosting punk bands, punk vinyl nights, and punk karaoke. College kids pack both the dance floor and the big outdoor seating area at **Sandbar** (514 State St., 805/966-1388, www.sandbarsb.com, Mon.-Fri. 11am-2am, Sat.-Sun. 9am-2am), especially near the end of the week. Young folks also party at **Baja Sharkeez** (525 State St., 805/845-9572, www.sharkeez.net/santa-barbara, Mon.-Fri. 11am-2am, Sat.-Sun. 9am-2am). This may be due in some part to its 84-ounce drinks, served in fishbowls, and its happy hour (Mon.-Fri. 3pm-7pm), where you can buy one drink and get another one for just $0.25.

Half a block off State Street, **The Press Room** (15 E. Ortega St., 805/963-8121, daily

© STUART THORNTON

Joe's Café

11am-2am) claims it has been the "unofficial British consulate since 1995," with great punk and indie bands playing on the jukebox and a Sex Pistols poster hanging in the men's room as evidence. Enjoy conversation along with a pint of Bass, Boddingtons, or the lesser-known Bombardier. Across the street from The Press Room, **Dargan's Irish Pub** (18 E. Ortega St., 805/568-0702, http://dargans.com, Sun.-Wed. 11:30am-1:30am, Thurs.-Sat. 11:30am-2am) has a couple ways to entertain you while you sip a pint, including pool tables and live music as well as traditional Irish music on Thursday and blues, rock, and country acts playing into the night on Saturday.

Elsie's Tavern (117 W. De La Guerra St., 805/963-4503, Mon.-Fri. noon-1:30am, Sat.-Sun. 4pm-2am, cash only) is tailor-made for hipster types, with old arcade games, board games, books for reading, and worn couches for lounging. The **Wildcat Lounge** (15 W. Ortega St., 805/962-7970, www.wildcatlounge.com, daily 4pm-2am) caters to a wilder college-aged

crowd of with red padded vinyl on its walls and cages for those who feel compelled to dance in captivity. An outside area with a pool table offers a breath of fresh air. DJs spin house music at the upscale, ultramodern **Eos Lounge** (500 E. Anacapa St., 805/564-2410, www.eoslounge. com, Wed.-Sat. 8pm-2am). Enjoy multiple bars and dance floors as well as an outdoor patio.

On the other side of the highway in the Funk Zone, **Seven Bar & Kitchen** (224 Helena Ave., 805/845-0377, www.sevensb.com, Mon.-Fri. 3pm-1am, Sat.-Sun. noon-1am) is a modern, arty lounge. The U-shaped bar dispenses fruit-infused cocktails, and there's a heated patio out back.

Another new addition to the Funk Zone is **Figueroa Mountain Brewing Company** (137 Anacapa St., 805/694-2255, www.figmtnbrew. com, daily 11am-9pm). This tasting room is decorated with Western country items like wagon wheels, saddles, and pitchforks as a reflection of the main brewery's location in the Santa Ynez Valley, where Figueroa's eight flagship beers are brewed. A handful of specialty beers are brewed on-site. Get started with a flight of four four-ounce tasters. Note that although the brewery's address is Anacapa Street, the door to the establishment is on Yanonali Street.

Also in the Funk Zone, **Telegraph Brewing Company** (418 N. Salsipuedes St., 805/963-5018, www.telegraphbrewing.com, tasting room Thurs. 4pm-6pm, Fri. 4pm-8pm, Sat. 2pm-6pm) is located in a renovated World War II-era Quonset hut. Up to 10 taps pour tastes of small batch beers, including the flagship California Ale, Stock Porter, and Cerveza de Fiesta, a pilsner-style lager, and the experimental Telegraph Obscura beers.

LIVE MUSIC

A great place to take in a concert during the warm summer and fall months is the ◖ **Santa Barbara Bowl** (1122 N. Milpas St., 805/962-7411, www.sbbowl.com), which has hosted concerts by artists such as Bob Dylan, Robert Plant, Mumford & Sons, and local girl Katy Perry. Built in 1936, it's the largest outdoor amphitheater in the county. The seats on the left side have the best views of the city below.

Founded in 1873, the **Lobero Theater** (33 E. Canon Perdido St., 805/963-0761, www.lobero.com) is the oldest continuously operating theater in the state. It once hosted entertainers like Tallulah Bankhead and Bela Lugosi but now welcomes jazz acts like Pat Metheny and Dianne Reeves along with indie-rock darling Jenny Lewis and jam band Chris Robinson Brotherhood. The medium-size theater has only one level, and it's filled with cushy red-velvet seats—perfect for a music-filled night out on the town. Check the website for shows coming up during your visit. You can buy tickets online, by phone, or at the box office.

Home to Opera Santa Barbara, the Santa Barbara Symphony, and the State Street Ballet, the **Granada Theatre** (1214 State St., 805/899-2222, http://granadasb.org) also hosts concert series, featuring acts like The Moody Blues, Big Bad Voodoo Daddy, and Bobby McFerrin.

If you prefer to dance and drink to live bands, head over to **Velvet Jones** (423 State St., 805/965-8676, www.velvet-jones.com, daily 9pm-2am). Artists as big as the Foo Fighters have performed at the venue in the last few years, although the venue usually has nationally touring rap, reggae, indie rock, and punk acts. Check the calendar on the website for upcoming events and shows.

Located upstairs, **Soho** (1221 State St., Suite 205, 805/962-7776, http://sohosb.com, daily from 5pm) has hosted big-time touring acts such as Jimmy Cliff, Donovan, and Built to Spill. It has live music seven nights a week. With its brick walls, Soho has a sophisticated New York City-type feel. Make reservations to have an organic dinner at the venue before taking in the evening's entertainment.

PERFORMING ARTS

The **Santa Barbara Symphony** (Granada Theatre, 1214 State St., 805/898-9386, www.thesymphony.org) aspires to compete with its brethren in Los Angeles and San Francisco. The symphony orchestra puts on seasons that pay homage to the great composers, plus the works of lesser-known talented artists. Whether you prefer Mozart or Mahler, you can listen to it at the concert hall at the Granada Theatre. Every seat has a great view of the stage, and the acoustics were designed with music in mind, making for an overall great symphony experience.

Opera Santa Barbara (OSB, Granada Theatre, 1214 State St., www.operasb.com) focuses on the classics and little-known works of the Italian masters, staging operas such as *Aida, Don Pasquale* and *Madame Butterfly* at the Granada Theatre.

Santa Barbara's longest running professional theater company, the **Ensemble Theatre Company** (805/965-5400, www.ensembletheatre.com) just moved into its new home in the **Victoria Theater** (33 W. Victoria St.) in the fall of 2013. Productions have included stage adaptations of Fyodor Dostoyevsky's *Crime and Punishment* and Joan Didion's *The Year of*

SANTA BARBARA SOUNDS

Santa Barbara boasts several chart-topping pop artists. Though folk pop strummer **Jack Johnson** is a Hawaii native, he first began performing by playing guitar with local party band Soil while attending UCSB. He ultimately graduated with a degree in film and music production.

Pop singer **Katy Perry** was born and raised in Santa Barbara. The high-profile celebrity's hometown visits have caused media frenzies, including in 2012, when she visited the Old Mission Santa Barbara with then boyfriend and fellow musician John Mayer.

Santa Barbara can also claim several bands from the 1990s, including alt-rock favorite **Toad the Wet Sprocket**, who reunited in 2010. Local punk band **Nerf Herder** earned a place in pop-culture history by providing the theme song for cult TV show *Buffy the Vampire Slayer*.

So take in some local music while you're in town. Who knows? Maybe you'll be the first to catch the next pop star.

Magical Thinking The **Center Stage Theater** (751 Pasco Nuevo, 805/963-0408, www.centerstagetheater.org) focuses on dance, including ballet and modern performances. A handful of local groups, including the Lit Moon Theatre and Out of the Box Theater Company, have also made the Center Stage their home, staging everything from plays with a formerly incarcerated cast to improv comedy. Located on the campus of Santa Barbara Junior High School, **Marjorie Luke Theatre** (721 E. Cota St., 808/884-4087, www.luketheatre.org) has a range of live performances that include concerts, ballet performances, and dance recitals.

CINEMA

With over 2,000 seats, the mission revival **Arlington Theatre** (1317 State St.,

805/963-4408, www.thearlingtontheatre.com) screens current movies as well as film premieres and Santa Barbara International Film Festival events. It also hosts dance performances, arts events, and occasional lectures.

Downtown on State Street, the **Metro 4 Theatre** (618 State St., 805/963-9503, www.metrotheatres.com) shows four first-run films most of the year and hosts some Santa Barbara International Film Festival events. Another spot to catch a movie downtown is **Paseo Nuevo** (8 E. De La Guerra Plaza, 805/963-9503, www.metrotheatres.com), located in the **Paseo Nuevo Shops & Restaurants** area. The **Metropolitan Plaza de Oro Theatre** (371 S. Hitchcock Way, 805/963-9503, www.metrotheatres.com) screens art-house films, indie flicks, and documentaries in two theaters.

FESTIVALS AND EVENTS
Year-Round

A great way to experience Santa Barbara's arts and culture is to take in the many happenings at **First Thursday** (downtown, downloadable map at www.downtownsantabarbara.com, first Thurs. of each month 5pm-8pm). The bounty of events includes art openings and receptions, lectures, live music, and wine tastings at downtown venues that include the Lobero Theater, the Santa Barbara Museum of Art, and Sullivan Goss: An American Gallery.

Inspired by European sidewalk art shows, the **Sunday Arts and Craft Show** (Cabrillo Blvd. from east of Stearns Wharf to Calle Cesar Chavez, 805/560-7557, www.santabarbaraca.gov, Sun. 10am-dusk) has 200 artists showcasing their paintings, sculptures, and crafts near East Beach every Sunday.

Nite Moves (Leadbetter Beach, 805/284-4720, www.runsantabarbara.com, May-Sept. Wed. 6pm) is a weekly open ocean swim and 5K run, followed by an after-race festival with food, beer, and music.

Spring

Painters use Mission Plaza as their canvas at the **I Madonnari Italian Street Painting Festival**

(805/964-4710, www.imadonnarifestival.com, late May, free), inspired by a similar event in Grazie di Curtatone, Italy. Participants and their sponsors buy sections of the street ($125-650), with proceeds benefiting the nonprofit Children's Creative Project.

The International Orchid Show (Earl Warren Showgrounds, 3400 Calle Real, 805/403-1533, www.sborchidshow.org, adults $12, students and seniors $10, children under 12 with adults free) has been celebrating the flowering plants annually for almost 70 years. Expect artworks and flower vendors as well as lots of orchids.

Summer

Fiesta (various venues in Santa Barbara, 805/962-8101, www.oldspanishdays-fiesta. org, some events free), also called Old Spanish Days, is Santa Barbara's biggest annual festival. Since 1924 it has paid tribute to the city's Spanish and Mexican heritage with parades, live music, horse shows, bull riding, and the erection of public marketplaces known as *mercados*. During Fiesta, hotel rooms are nearly impossible to find, with rare vacancies filled at premium rates.

For two days, the **French Festival** (Oak Park, 300 W. Alamar St., 805/963-8198, www. frenchfestival.com, weekend near July 14, free) offers a good excuse to eat French bread, pastries, crepes, quiches, and pâtés, all in an annual celebration of Bastille Day. You'll also find live entertainment on three stages and vendors selling French merchandise from berets to impressionist paintings.

The longest day of the year is celebrated at the annual **Solstice Parade** (805/965-3396, www.solsticeparade.com, free). This line of extravagantly dressed participants and colorful floats proceeds nine blocks down State Street and three blocks down West Micheltorena Street before ending in Alameda Park. The **California Wine Festival** (Chase Palm Park, 800/797-7753, www.californiawinefestival. com, $69-140) features a series of wine-tasting events in scenic seaside Chase Palms Park.

Fall

The **Santa Barbara Harbor and Seafood Festival** (Santa Barbara Harbor, 805/897-1962, www.harborfestival.org, Oct., free) is set to coincide with the start of lobster and fishing season. Seafood lovers can enjoy lobster, clam chowder, and fish tacos provided by local fishers and vendors. There are also presentations on maritime history and local ocean resources.

Runners come to town for the *Santa Barbara News-Press Half-Marathon* (805/967-8822, www.newspress.com/halfmarathon, $55-65), which benefits local student athletes. If you are not ready for a half marathon, opt for a 5K fun run. Another fall running event is the **Pier to Peak** (805/284-4720, www.runsantabarbara.com), a half marathon from Stearns Wharf up to La Cumbre Park, at an elevation of 3,996 feet.

Winter

The 11-day **Santa Barbara International Film Festival** (various venues, 805/963-0023, http://sbiff.org) showcases over 200 films and includes 20 world premieres, drawing big Hollywood names like Quentin Tarantino, Jennifer Lawrence, Daniel Day-Lewis, Amy Adams, and Ben Affleck.

Shopping

DOWNTOWN
Shopping Districts

In Santa Barbara, even the malls and shopping districts are visually interesting. They are all outdoor malls, but they are still fun for hanging out. If you're looking for a fairly standard shopping expedition, go to **State Street.** From end to end, this busy main drag hosts a nearly unbelievable array of mall-style stores, plus a few independent boutiques for variety. You'll find lots of lovely women's apparel, plenty of housewares stores, and all the usual stuff you'd expect to find in a major urban shopping center.

Explore the **Paseo Nuevo Shopping Center** (651 Paseo Nuevo, 805/963-7147, www.paseonuevoshopping.com, Mon.-Fri. 10am-9pm, Sat. 10am-8pm, Sun. 11am-6pm), a series of pathways off State Street that have clothing stores, including Nordstrom and Macy's, along with chain eateries like Chipotle and California

© STUART THORNTON

Paseo Nuevo Shopping Center

Pizza Kitchen. Also right off State Street is **La Arcada Court** (1114 State St., 805/966-6634, www.laarcadasantabarbara.com), a collection of shops, restaurants, specialty stores, and art galleries. Along the tile-lined walkways, playful humanlike sculptures appear in front of some of the shops.

Art Galleries

Find the work of modernist artist John Bernhardt and regional painter Grant Wood at the **Sullivan Goss Gallery** (7 E. Anapamu St., 805/730-1460, http://sullivangoss.com, daily 10am-5:30pm). Its inventory of over 3,000 American artworks includes paintings and sculptures. In an ideal location near the Santa Barbara Museum of Art, the **Artamo Gallery** (11 W. Anapamu St., 805/568-1400, www.artamo.com, Tues.-Sun. noon-5pm) features modern art with a focus on paintings, although it also includes prints, sculptures, photographs, and collages. Tucked into La Arcada Court, **Santa Barbara Arts** (1114 State St., Suite 24, 805/884-1938, www.sbarts.net, Mon.-Sat. 11am-6pm, Sun. noon-5pm) is a good place to browse through handmade jewelry, ceramics, sculptures, paintings, and wearable art—the work of 50 local artists.

Bookstores

The Book Den (15 E. Anapamu St., 805/962-3321, www.bookden.com, Mon.-Sat. 11am-6pm, Sun. 11am-5pm) has been around for 110 years and calls itself California's oldest used bookstore. It now carries new books as well. Right next door, **Paradise Found** (17 E. Anapamu St., 805/564-3573, http://paradisefoundsantabarbara.com, Mon.-Sat. 10am-6pm, Sun. noon-6pm) has a New Age selection, with books on self-help and Eastern religions. They also sell dream catchers, wind chimes, and candles. Up State Street a bit, **Chaucer's Bookstore** (3321 State St., 805/682-6787, www.chaucersbooks.com, Mon.-Sat. 9am-9pm,

Sun. 9am-8pm) sells new hardcovers, paperbacks, and magazines.

Children's Stores

If you are expecting or already have a wee one, **Chicken Little** (1236 State St., 805/962-7771, www.chickenlittlekids.com, Mon.-Sat. 10am-6pm, Sun. 10:30am-5:30pm) has what you need. We're talking car seats, strollers, nursery decor, and maternity clothing.

Mon Petit Bijou (1014 State St., 800/945-0015, www.monpetitbijou.com, Mon.-Sat. 10am-6pm, Sun. 11am-5pm) calls itself an "opulent baby boutique." That means they sell stylish linen pant sets and collectible toys, among other high-end items.

Clothing and Accessories

Tienda Ho (1105 State St., 800/962-3643, www.tiendaho.com, Mon.-Sat. 10am-6pm, Sun. 11am-6pm) carries women's clothes from Morocco, India, Indonesia, China, and South America. They also have home furnishings and accessories. The **Paris Street Boutique** (1103 State St., 805/568-0473, www.parisstreetboutique.com, Mon.-Sat. 10:30am-6pm, Sun. 10:30am-5pm) has clothes from France, specifically Paris street-style fashion.

You may find a slightly used Prada or Gucci product at **Jessica** (2008 De La Vina St., 805/687-2755, http://jessicaconsign.blogspot.com, Mon.-Sat. 11am-6pm), a store with fine women's apparel on consignment. Check the store's blog for the latest acquisitions. You could score a Marc Jacobs, Louis Vuitton, or Chloé product for more than half off the regular retail price at **The Closet** (920 State St., 805/963-8083, http://theclosetsb.net, daily 11am-8pm), a high-end women's resale boutique.

The popular national recycled men and women's clothing dealer **Crossroads Trading Co.** (1025 State St., 805/892-5700, http://crossroadstrading.com, Mon.-Sat. 11am-7pm, Sun. noon-6pm) also has a location on State Street. International "youth clothing" dealer **Volcom** (625 State St., 805/884-0346, www.volcom.com, Sun.-Thurs. 10am-8pm, Fri.-Sat. 10am-9pm) specializes in clothing for

the skater, surfer, or snowboarder in your life. Popular chain **Anthropologie** (1123 State St., 805/962-5461, www.anthropologie.com, Mon.-Sat. 10am-8pm, Sun. 11am-7pm) sells women's clothing and home decor. Find clothing for both men and women can at the Santa Barbara location of **American Apparel** (733 State St., 805/966-9299, www.americanapparel.net, Mon.-Thurs. 10am-8pm, Fri.-Sat. 10am-9pm, Sun. 11am-8pm).

Home Furnishings

Outfit your home with a bamboo bed or a braided sea-grass console at **Rooms & Gardens** (924 State St., 805/965-2424, www.roomsandgardens.com, Mon.-Sat. 10am-5:30pm, Sun. 11am-5pm), which sells shabby chic and artistically aged furniture and furnishings. Actress Mary Steenburgen was such a big fan of this store that she opened a location in Santa Monica. The **Steven Handelman Studios** (716 N. Milpas St., 805/962-5119, www.stevenhandelmanstudios.com, Mon.-Fri. 9am-5pm, Sat. 10am-3pm) makes wrought iron products and light fixtures with an artist's touch. Think ornate chandeliers and fancy mailboxes.

Surf and Skate

Santa Barbara surfboard shaper Al Merrick has shaped boards for the world's best surfers, including Kelly Slater, Tom Curren, Shaun Tomson, and Dane Reynolds, making his Channel Island Surfboards legendary. The **Channel Islands Surf Shop** (36 Anacapa St., 805/966-7213, www.cisurfboards.com, Mon.-Sat. 10am-7pm, Sun. 11am-5pm) showcases lots of Channel Islands's latest boards.

Skaters should make a pilgrimage to **Church of Skatan** (26 E. Gutierrez St., 805/899-1586, Mon.-Fri. 11am-6:30pm, Sat. 10am-6:30pm, Sun. 11am-5pm), a wholly unique skateboarding store housed in an old church with stained-glass windows. Racks of boards and T-shirts have replaced the church's pews.

Specialty Stores

Warbler Records & Goods (131 E. De La Guerra St., 805/845-5862, www.

warblerrecords.com, Mon.-Sat. 10:30am-6:30pm, Sun. noon-5pm) is a small store with an impressive selection of used and new records. They also sell CDs, cassettes (really!), turntables, and nonmusic items such as ceramics and lamps. **Santa Barbara Cigar and Tobacco** (10 W. Figueroa St., 805/963-1979, www.santabarbaracigars.com, Mon.-Thurs. 10am-6pm, Fri. 10am-8pm, Sat. 10:30am-8pm, Sun. 11am-6pm) is a popular stop for smoking aficionados.

Sweets

Swiss-born Maya Schoop-Rutten is serious about chocolates. She travels around the world to stock **Chocolate Maya** (15 W. Gutierrez St., 805/965-5956, www.chocolatemaya.com, Mon.-Fri. 10am-6pm, Sat. 10am-5pm, Sun. 10am-4pm) with only the best, including confections like ganaches infused with limoncello and rosemary-infused dark chocolates. Chocolate Maya also serves European style hot chocolates for those rare, chilly Santa Barbara days.

Farmers Markets

Its no surprise that Santa Barbara has two weekly farmers markets: **Saturday morning** (Santa Barbara and Cota St., 805/962-5354, www.sbfarmersmarket.org, Sat. 8:30am-1:30pm) and **Tuesday afternoon** (500-600 blocks of State St., 805/962-5354, www.sbfarmersmarket.org, Tues. 3pm-6:30pm).

MONTECITO

Montecito's tony **Coast Village Road** is lined with shops and boutiques.

Art Galleries

Peregrine Galleries (1133 Coast Village Rd., 805/969-9673, www.peregrinegalleries.com, daily noon-5:30pm) has a specific niche: early American paintings and vintage jewelry, including early Chanel. If you are looking for a landscape painting to decorate your home, stop in to the **Portico Gallery** (1235 Coast Village Rd., 805/695-8850, www.porticofineart.com, Mon.-Sat. 11am-5pm). Portico showcases the work of 22 local and national artists with a focus on landscapes. Portico also offers classes for aspiring artists.

Clothing and Accessories

Dressed (1253 Coast Village Rd., 805/565-1253, www.dressedonline.com, Mon.-Fri. 10am-6pm, Sat. 10am-5:30pm, Sun. 10am-4pm) and sister store **Ready** (1253 Coast Village Rd., 805/565-0819, www.dressedonline.com, Mon.-Fri. 10am-6pm, Sat. 10am-5:30pm, Sun. 10am-4pm) have women's clothing and accessories from designers like Alexander Wang and Vanessa Mooney. Designers, including Yigal Azrouel, sometimes come by the store.

Angel (1221 Coast Village Rd., 805/565-1599, daily 10am-7pm) is a contemporary clothing store highlighting the work of local and internationally known upscale designers. Expect luxury garments and accessories from Cynthia Vincent, Joie, and Vince. The people at **Silverhorn Jewelers** (1155 Coast Village Rd., 805/969-0442, www.silverhorn.com, Mon.-Sat. 10am-5:30pm) travel the world to find stunning rare gemstones; their team designs the perfect jewelry to highlight each gem.

Beaches

There's nothing easier than finding a beach in Santa Barbara. Just follow State Street to its end, and you'll be at the coast.

EAST BEACH

Named because it is east of Stearns Wharf, **East Beach** (1400 Cabrillo Blvd., www.santabarbaraca.gov, daily sunrise-10pm) is all soft sand and wide beach, with a dozen volleyball nets in the sand close to the zoo; if you look closely you can see the giraffes and lions. It has all the amenities a sun worshipper could hope for: a full beach house, a snack bar, a play area for children, and a path for cycling and in-line skating. The beachfront has picnic facilities and a full-service restaurant at the East Beach Grill. The **Cabrillo Pavilion Bathhouse** (1119 East Cabrillo Blvd.), built in 1927, offers showers, lockers, a weight room, one rentable beach wheelchair, and volleyball rentals.

WEST BEACH

On the west side of Stearns Wharf, **West Beach** (Cabrillo Blvd. and Chapala St., between Stearns Wharf and the harbor, daily sunrise-10pm) has 11 acres of picturesque sand for sunbathing, swimming, kayaking, windsurfing, and beach volleyball. There are also large palm trees, a wide walkway, and a bike path, making it a popular spot. Outrigger canoes also launch from this beach.

LEADBETTER BEACH

Considered by many to be the best beach in Santa Barbara, **Leadbetter Beach** (Shoreline Dr. and Loma Alta Dr., daily sunrise-10pm) divides the area's south-facing beaches from the west-facing ones. It's a long, flat beach with a large grassy area. Sheer cliffs rise from the sand, and trees dot the point. The beach, which is also bounded by the harbor and the breakwater, is ideal for swimming because it's fairly well protected, unlike the other flat beaches.

Many catamaran sailors and windsurfers launch from this beach, and you'll occasionally see surfers riding the waves. The grassy picnic areas have barbecue sites that can be reserved for more privacy, but otherwise there is a lot of room. The beach and the park can get packed during the many races and sporting events held here. There are restrooms, a small restaurant, and outdoor showers. Directly across the street is Santa Barbara City College. If you enter the stadium and walk up the many steps, you'll get some terrific views of the harbor, plus a workout.

ARROYO BURRO BEACH

To the north of town, **Arroyo Burro Beach** (Cliff Dr., 805/687-3714, www.sbparks.org, daily 8am-sunset), also known as Hendry's, is a favorite for locals and dog owners. To the right as you face the water, past Arroyo Burro Slough, dogs are allowed off-leash to dash across the packed sand and frolic and fetch out in the gentle surf. Arroyo Burro is rockier than the downtown beaches, making it less pleasant for games and sunbathing. But the rocks and shells make for great beachcombing, and you might find it slightly less crowded on sunny weekend days. You'll find a snack bar, restrooms, outdoor showers, and a medium-size pay parking lot. At peak times, when the parking lot is full, there's nowhere else to park.

The beach is flanked by large cliffs, one of which is home to the **Douglas Family Preserve.** The 70-acre, eucalyptus-studded, dog-friendly preserve is popular with local residents, but few visitors ever hear about it. The parcel was planned to be developed into housing, but a grassroots campaign raised awareness of the potentially destructive development, and fund-raising efforts to purchase it were bolstered when actor Michael Douglas made a substantial donation, allowing the parcel to remain undeveloped. He then named it after his father, actor Kirk Douglas.

BUTTERFLY BEACH

Butterfly Beach (Channel Dr., across from the Four Seasons Hotel, Montecito, daily sunrise-10pm) is accessed by a handful of steps leading to the narrow beach. Many people come here hoping to catch a glimpse of a celebrity from nearby Montecito, but chances are that won't happen. Butterfly is the most west-facing beach in Santa Barbara, meaning that you can actually see the sun set over the Pacific. To find it, take U.S. 101 to Olive Mill Road in Montecito (a few minutes south of Santa Barbara). At the stop sign, turn toward the ocean (away from the mountains) and follow it 0.25 miles along the coast; Butterfly Beach is on the left. The beach is packed most weekends and often weekdays too, and parking is limited. Park on either side of the street along the beach, or drive up Butterfly Road and park in the nearby neighborhoods. Bring your lunch, water, and sunscreen—there are no public facilities at this beach. Dogs roam freely.

Sports and Recreation

With the year-round balmy weather, it's nearly impossible to resist the temptation to get outside and do something energetic and fun in Santa Barbara. From golf to sea kayaking, there are plenty of options for recreation.

PARKS

Referred to as the "crown jewel" of the city's parks, the **Alice Keck Park Memorial Gardens** (1500 Santa Barbara St., 805/564-5418, www. santabarbaraca.gov, daily sunrise-10pm), includes a garden with a koi pond, a low-water demonstration garden, and 75 different tree and plant species. It was once the site of the El Mirasol Hotel, where wealthy Eastern families like the Vanderbilts, the Rockefellers, and the Guggenheims stayed. The hotel was destroyed by fire in 1966. The site was spared development in part by Pearl Chase, a pioneering local conservationist and preservationist. Adjacent to Alice Keck Park Memorial Gardens is **Alameda Park** (1400 Santa Barbara St., 805/564-5418, www.santabarbaraca.gov, daily sunrise-10pm), a two-block city park with rare trees and a gazebo along with a large playground with a play castle, swings, and slides.

The natural environment at 11-acre **Rocky Nook Park** (610 Mission Canyon Rd., 805/568-2461, www.countyofsb.org, daily 8am-sunset) includes a creek, trees, and sandstone boulders. There's also an area for picnicking. Birders should keep an eye out for the hepatic tanager, which has been spotted here for some years. The former home of botanist Francesco Franceschi, **Franceschi Park** (1501 Franceschi Rd., daily sunrise-30 minutes after sunset) unsurprisingly has its own rare botanical garden. The 18-acre site also provides fine views of the city, the ocean, and the Channel Islands. At 230 acres, **Elings Park** (1298 Las Positas Rd., 805/569-5611, www.elingspark.org, daily 7am-sunset) touts itself as the largest privately funded park in the nation. The grounds were used as trash dump before being reclaimed; they now host a wide variety of recreation options, with a BMX course, a hang gliding training hill, hiking trails, soccer fields, and softball and baseball diamonds.

The west side of **Chase Palm Park** (both sides of E. Cabrillo Blvd. from Stearns Wharf to East Beach, 805/963-0611, www.santabarbaraca.gov, daily sunrise-10pm) is a strip of open space, with giant palm trees towering over a bike path and walkway. The east side has fountains, grassy lawns, a duck pond, and Shipwreck Playground, designed to resemble an ocean schooner. The carousel ($2 per ride) dates to 1916. Located on the edge of Chase Palm Park, with a view of East Beach, **Skater's Point** (Cabrillo Blvd. at Garden St., daily 8am-30 minutes after sunset) is a skateboarder's dream, with a bowl, a half pipe, a launch ramp, rails, curbs, and banks. Even if you're not going to skate, it's fun to watch the skaters in action.

© STUART THORNTON

the carousel at Chase Palm Park

Situated above the harbor, **Shoreline Park** (Shoreline Dr. and La Marina, 805/564-5418, www.santabarbaraca.gov, daily sunrise-10pm) includes a whale-watching vista point next to a bronze whale-tail statue as well as a Japanese garden and a small playground. It also offers access to Mesa Beach, which becomes submerged during high tide.

BIRD-WATCHING

Santa Barbara's range of terrain draws a diversity of bird species. The website of **Santa Barbara County Birding** (http://sbcobirding.com) is a great resource for visiting birders.

One easily accessible spot to take in the city's resident and migratory birds is the **Andree Clark Bird Refuge** (1400 E. Cabrillo Blvd., 805/564-5418, www.santabarbaraca.gov, daily sunrise-10pm). The 42-acre city-run park, adjacent to the Santa Barbara Zoo, has a saltwater marsh and brackish lake that frequently hosts common gulls, ducks, and grebes. The lake's islands are sometimes home to roosting night herons, egrets, and cormorants.

Another option is to head above Santa Barbara into **Mission Canyon,** where nesting and seasonal birds include canyon wrens, cedar waxwings, and bad-tailed pigeons. It's also a good place to find hummingbirds and woodpeckers. To get to the Mission Canyon area, drive up Los Olivos Street and bear left as it becomes Mission Canyon Road. Options to bird here include **Rocky Nook Park,** the grounds of the **Santa Barbara Museum of Natural History,** and the **Santa Barbara Botanic Gardens.**

HIKING

The two-mile hike up to **Inspiration Point** (4 miles round-trip, moderate-strenuous) gives you access to the best vistas of the city, the ocean, and the Channel Islands. The uphill hike starts out paved, then becomes a dirt road, and then a trail. To reach the trailhead from the Santa Barbara Mission, head up Mission Canyon Road. At the stop sign, take a right onto Foothill Road. Take a left at the next stop sign on Mission Canyon Road, and stay left at the fork on Tunnel Road. Continue down Tunnel Road to the end, where there is a parking area.

Starting from the same spot, **Seven Falls** (3 miles round-trip, easy) begins as a hike but becomes a scramble up a creek bed to its namesake attraction, where bowls of rock hold pools of water. It's a good place to cool off on a hot day. Follow the paved road at the end of Tunnel Road; it's gated and locked against vehicle traffic but is accessible to hikers. After 0.75 miles, continue on the Tunnel Trail. When the trail dips down by the creek, head upstream. The hike requires some boulder hopping and mild rock climbing.

The **Rattlesnake Canyon Trail** (3 miles to intersection with Gibraltar Rd., moderate) takes hikers up into sage-covered hills and into a canyon with waterfalls and pools. This area was once where the Santa Barbara Mission got its water, and the remnants of a dam from the mission days survive on a side trail off the Rattlesnake Canyon Trail. To reach the trailhead from the Santa Barbara Mission, take Mission Canyon Road to Foothill Road, and then turn right. Take a quick left to keep following Mission Canyon Road. Continue on the road past Tunnel Road to Las Canoas. Turn right onto Las Canoas and travel for 1.5 miles to an open area in front of a bridge, where the trailhead is located.

One of the area's best waterfalls is **Tangerine Falls** (3 miles round-trip, moderate-strenuous). This 100-foot waterfall can be reached via trail hiking and a bit of rock scrambling. Take the **East Fork Trail** up 0.25 miles and turn onto the **West Fork Trail**. Go 0.5 miles on the path past a white sign, and take a right at the unmarked junction. Descend to creek and continue along the creek bank. You will have to do a bit of scrambling to reach the falls. The trailhead can be reached by taking U.S. 101's exit 94A onto Olive Mill Road. It turns into Hot Springs Road. Turn left onto Mountain Drive, and continue for one mile. Look for the trailhead on the right before the creek.

CYCLING

There are plenty of cycling opportunities in Santa Barbara, from flat leisurely pedals by the water to climbs up into the foothills. The **Santa Barbara Bicycle Coalition** (www.sbbike.org) has a set of downloadable do-it-yourself bike rides and maps. Another option for Santa Barbara cycling information is **Traffic Solutions** (805/963-7283, www.trafficsolutions.info). Visit the website to obtain a copy of the free Santa Barbara County bike map.

The **Mountain Drive Bike Route** is a 16-mile loop that starts at the dolphin statue in front of Stearns Wharf and climbs up State Street,

LOCAL VISION: PEARL CHASE

It seems in every town, there's someone who stops to preserve what's gone before us, even while everyone else hurries toward the future. In Santa Barbara, that person is Pearl Chase, who played an integral role in keeping the city's history alive, and in doing so shaped how it looks today.

Born in Boston in 1888, Pearl Chase first moved to Santa Barbara in 1900. Her early accomplishments included co-founding the local American Red Cross chapter and helping to shut down an illegal slaughterhouse. In the early 1920s, Chase embarked on her life's mission: civic beautification and historic preservation. She is remembered today for her successful efforts to preserve the historic Moreton Bay Fig Tree and the harbor front area that is now Chase Palm Park, which was named in her honor. In addition, she was an instrumental figure in the restoration of the Presidio.

Chase received many accolades, including being named the *Los Angeles Times* "Woman of the Year" in 1956. The National Trust for Historic Preservation awarded her its highest honor in 1973. She passed away a few years later, in 1979, but the non-profit **Pearl Chase Society** (www.pearlchasesociety.org) carries on her work today.

Sycamore Canyon Road, Stanwood Road, and El Cielito Road until it reaches Mountain Drive. It then takes riders down through Montecito and back along Cabrillo Boulevard to the starting point. This strenuous ride climbs some 800 vertical feet. A less demanding option is **The Coast Route,** which hugs the coastline from West Beach past Leadbetter Beach and Shoreline Park into Goleta and Isla Vista.

If you'd rather be pedaling the dirt rather than the pavement, Santa Barbara's mountainous and hilly terrain makes for good mountain biking. **Velo Pro Cyclery** (http://velopro.com) provides a fine introduction to the area's mountain biking resources.

Elings Park (1298 Las Positas Rd., 805/569-5611, www.elingspark.org, daily 7am-sunset) has single-track trails for beginners and intermediates. Just a few minutes from downtown Santa Barbara, it's perfect for a quick, no-hassle ride. **Romero Canyon Trail** (6-mile short loop, 11-mile round-trip long ride, moderate-difficult) is a little more involved. The ride begins with a four-mile climb up Romero Canyon Road, an old fire road. Keep to the right, and the road becomes a single-track trail. After crossing Romero Canyon, you can opt to drop down on the single-track trail for the short loop, or continue up to paved Camino Cielo Road for views of the area. To reach the trailhead, take the Sheffield exit from U.S. 101. Take Sheffield Road until it ends at East Valley Road; take a left on East Valley Road, and then a quick right onto Romero Canyon Road. Turn right onto Bella Vista Road and 0.25 miles to the trailhead.

If you need to rent a bike, **Wheel Fun Rentals** (23 E. Cabrillo Blvd.; 22 State St., 805/966-2282, www.wheelfunrentals.com) has two locations. Rent a surrey bike or a beach cruiser for an easy ride by the coast, or rent a road bike to head up into the foothills.

RUNNING

Santa Barbara's consistently pleasant weather makes it easier to opt for a run outdoors rather than a few hours in the gym. The **Cabrillo Waterfront Multi-Purpose Path** is a nice three-mile-long paved trail that covers the whole waterfront and harbor area from Leadbetter Beach to the Andree Clark Bird refuge. It's a great way to take in Santa Barbara's coastal scenery while getting a workout.

Another area ideal for lacing up the running shoes is the large open space at **More Mesa.** You can combine the trails here for a six-mile loop. To reach More Mesa, head north of Santa Barbara on U.S. 101. Take the Patterson exit and turn left toward the coast. Continue on the road past the bike path and the horse corral, and park on the left.

HANG GLIDING

Have you ever wanted to fly? Here's your chance. Santa Barbara's south-facing Santa Ynez Mountains and thermal updrafts make it ideal for hang gliders. The 200-foot-high training hill in Elings Park is touted as the best in the country.

Fly Away Hang Gliding (805/403-8487 or 802/558-6350, www.flyawayhanggliding.com, daily by reservation, $200) offers beginning lessons that start with a simulator and progress to a launch off the training hill at Elings Park. Most students will get to soar 50 to 100 feet by the end of their first three-hour or longer lesson. Fly Away also sells new and used hang gliding equipment. Advanced hang gliders should contact the **Santa Barbara Soaring Association** (www.sbsa.info) to find out about local sites and conditions, and to gain access to launch and landing zones ($10 usage fee).

SURFING

During the summer months, the Channel Islands block the south swells and keep them from reaching the Santa Barbara coastline. During fall and winter, the big north and northwest swells wrap around Point Conception, offering some of the best waves in the area and transforming places like Rincon in nearby Carpinteria into legendary surf breaks.

Beginners should head to **Leadbetter Point** (Shoreline Park, just north of the Santa Barbara Harbor), a slow, mushy wave that's also perfect for long-boarders. The locals are reasonably welcoming, and the small right break makes for easy and fun rides. For a bit more of a challenge, paddle out to the barrels at **Sandspit** (Santa Barbara Harbor). The harbor's breakwater creates hollow right breaks for adventurous surfers only. Be careful, though: Sandspit's backwash has been known to toss surfers onto the breakwater.

Looking for surfing lessons? Check out the **Santa Barbara Surf School** (805/745-8877, www.santabarbarasurfschool.com). The instructors have decades of surfing experience and pride themselves on getting beginners up and riding in a single lesson. They also offer five-day surf camps in the summer. **Surf Happens** (805/966-3613, http://surfhappens. com) has private and group lessons for beginning to advanced surfers. Surf Happens also offers the Ocean Divas program for women who want to learn how to ride the curl; check out Diva Intro Days on the third Saturday of every month. In the summer, Surf Happens posts up at the southern end of Santa Claus Lane in Carpinteria.

KAYAKING AND STAND-UP PADDLEBOARDING

You can see Santa Barbara Harbor and the bay under your own power by kayak or stand-up paddleboard. A number of rental and touring companies offer lessons, guided paddles, and good advice for exploring the region. **Channel Islands Outfitters** (117B Harbor Way, 805/617-3425, www.channelislandso.com, daily 7am-7pm) rents kayaks and paddleboards and also offers kayak tour of Santa Barbara Harbor and stand-up paddleboard tours of Goleta Point. More adventurous sea kayak tours focus on the nearby Channel Islands. Advance reservations are recommended, especially for summer weekends. **Stand Up Paddling Adventures** (805/881-2115, www. supadventuressb.com) offers a range of lessons, including a stand-up paddleboard immersion course ($200). They'll also drop off a board for you at Santa Barbara Harbor, Leadbetter Beach, Butterfly Beach, or at Santa Claus Lane

in Carpinteria so you don't have to haul it from their shop.

BOATING

Learn to sail, charter a sailboat, or rent a powerboat at the **Santa Barbara Sailing Center** (133 Harbor Way, 805/350-9090, http://sbsail.com), It also offers sailing excursions aboard a 50-foot catamaran, the *Double Dolphin*. Hop aboard the **Sunset Kidd** (125 Harbor Way, 805/962-8222, www.sunsetkidd.com, from $40) for a two-hour morning or afternoon cruise, or opt for the romantic sunset cocktail cruise.

Another way to get out on the water is to hitch a ride on the **Santa Barbara Water Taxi** (888/316-9363, www.sbwatertaxi.com, Fri. 1:30pm-5:30pm, Sat.-Sun. noon-5:30pm, adults $4, children $1). Painted yellow, black, and white to resemble a New York City cab, **Lil' Toot** departs from the harbor on the hour and the half hour and from the wharf at 15 minutes and 45 minutes past the hour. During your taxi ride, you'll see sealife and learn about harbor history. The taxi also has hour-long sunset cruises (adults $25, children $17).

WHALE-WATCHING AND FISHING

With its proximity to the feeding grounds of blue and humpback whales, Santa Barbara is one of the best spots in the state to go whale-watching. **Condor Express** (301 W. Cabrillo Blvd., 805/882-0088, www.condorexpress. com) offers cruises to the Channel Islands to see the big cetaceans feed (blue and humpback whales in summer; gray whales in winter). The 72-foot catamaran seats 127 people and has lots of outdoor deck space and plush amenities. Cruises depart almost daily year-round; call in advance to purchase tickets.

If you want to go fishing, give **WaveWalker Charters** (691 Camino Campana, 805/964-2046, www.wavewalker.com) a call. This private six-passenger charter boat rents for $960 for a three-quarters of a day—expensive unless you bring five friends along to split the cost. Bait and all tackle are included, but your fishing license is not.

SCUBA DIVING

Scuba diving in the Santa Barbara area is focused on the nearby Channel Islands, where jungles of kelp teem with sealife. **Truth Aquatics** (301 W. Cabrillo Blvd., 805/962-1127, www.truthaquatics.com) has a range of diving adventures, including a dive on the 1853 wreck of the SS *Winfield Scott* and spearfishing excursions.

BEACH VOLLEYBALL

East Beach (1400 E. Cabrillo Blvd., daily sunrise-10pm) has been called the epicenter of California beach volleyball; it's where Olympic gold medalists Phil Dalhausser and Todd Rogers trained for years. Over a dozen courts spread out across the beach. Courts are also available at **West Beach** (Cabrillo Blvd. and Chapala St., between Stearns Wharf and the harbor, daily sunrise-10pm) and **Leadbetter Beach** (Shoreline Dr. and Loma Alta Dr., daily sunrise-10pm). To reserve the East Beach and West Beach courts, contact the city's parks department (805/564-5422, www.santabarbaraca.gov).

GOLF

It might not get the most press of the many golf destinations in California, but with its year-round mild weather and resort atmosphere, Santa Barbara is a great place to play a few holes. There's everything from a popular municipal course to championship courses with views of the ocean from the greens.

If you're already interested in exploring Santa Barbara's wine country, consider reserving a tee time at **La Purisima Golf Course** (3455 Hwy. 246, Lompoc, 805/735-8395, $29-79). This golf course, built in 1986, gets high praise for its design and difficulty level—even if you're an expert golfer, "La Piranha" will test your skills. The par-72 course is a 45-minute drive from downtown Santa Barbara, but many locals think it's worth the trip. In addition to the 18 holes, you can access the grass driving range, the short-game practice area, and the pro shop. A number of PGA and LPGA golf pros are on hand to help you improve your game.

The **Sandpiper** (7925 Hollister Ave., 805/968-1541, www.sandpipergolf.com, $74-159, cart $16) boasts some of the most amazing views you'll find in Santa Barbara. The view of the Pacific Ocean is so great because it's right up close, and on several holes your ball is in danger of falling into the world's largest water trap. And hey, there's a great championship-rated 74.5, par-72, 18-hole golf course out there on that picturesque beach too. Take advantage of the pro shop and the on-site restaurant, but be aware of the semiformal no-denim dress code that Sandpiper enforces. It's not cheap, but a long walk on the beach with a great golf game in the middle of it seems well worth it to an endless stream of golfers who rank Sandpiper as one of their favorite courses. The land here used to be an oil-production facility before it was transformed into a golf course in 1972.

Santa Barbara Golf Club (3500 McCaw Ave., 805/687-7087, www.santabarbaraca.gov, Mar.-May daily 6am-7pm, June-Aug. daily 6am-8pm, Sept.-Oct. daily 6am-7pm, Nov.-Feb. daily 6am-5pm, greens fees $48-58) is an 18-hole, par-70 course with views of the foothills and the sea.

SPAS

Folks who can afford to live in Santa Barbara tend to be able to afford many of the finer things in life, including massages, facials, and luxe skin treatments. You'll find a wide array of day spas and medical spas in town.

If you prefer a slightly more natural spa experience, book a treatment at **Le Reve** (21 W. Gutierrez St., 805/564-2977, www.le-reve.com). Using biodynamic skin care products and pure essential oils, Le Reve makes good on the advertising that bills it as an "aromatherapy spa." Choose from an original array of body treatments, massage, hand and foot pampering, facials, and various aesthetic treatments. If you're up for several hours of relaxation, check out the spa packages that combine facials with massage and body treatments.

Cielo Spa and Boutique (1725 State St., Suite C, 805/687-8979, www.cielospasb.com)

prides itself on its warm, nurturing environment. Step inside and admire the scents, soft lighting, and the natural New Agey decor. Contemplate the colorful live orchids, feel soothed by the flickering candlelight, and get lost in the tranquil atmosphere. The menu of services has an almost Northern California flare, with signature champagne treatments and a focus on organics and natural lotions and potions. Check into the luxury packages that combine massages, facials, and more for a full day in the spa.

Located at Fess Parker's Doubletree Resort, the **Spa Del Mar** (633 E. Cabrillo Blvd., 805/884-8540, www.santabarbaraspadelmar. com, Mon.-Sat. 9am-6pm, Sun. 10am-4pm, massages $130-195) offers a unique massage

that was a favorite ritual of ancient Egyptian queen Cleopatra. Called **Cleopatra's Gold Massage** (one hour, $150), the relaxing, revitalizing massage uses an oil made with jasmine, rose, vanilla, and gold flakes. The Spa Del Mar also has massages, body treatments, and facials without utilizing the precious metal.

Float Luxury Spa (18 E. Canon Perdido St., 805/845-7777, http://floatluxuryspa.com, Mon.-Sat. 9am-7pm, Sun. 10am-6pm, massages $70-165) has an acu-massage, which is a combination of massage and acupuncture, along with other massages and facials. Before or after your treatment, relax in Float's private garden, adorned with reflection pools and fountains.

Accommodations

If you want a plush beachside room in Santa Barbara, be prepared to pay for it. Almost all of Santa Barbara's hotels charge premium rates, but there are a few charming and reasonably priced accommodations near downtown and other attractions.

DOWNTOWN

The great thing about staying downtown is that you don't need a car. Walk out your door and you're close to shopping, restaurants, galleries, and bars. On the flip side, weekend evenings can get noisy, and there's a lot of foot traffic on State Street.

$150-250

If you're walking down State Street, you can't miss the **Hotel Santa Barbara** (533 State St., 805/957-9300, www.hotelsantabarbara.com, $160-290), with its distinct green awning and international flags. The best thing about this no-frills hotel is its location, stumbling distance from State Street's bars and restaurants. It also features a spacious Mediterranean-style lobby with plants, couches, and chairs. The 75 guest rooms were remodeled in late 2013 with new

furniture, carpeting, fridges, and decor. Other pluses include an expanded continental breakfast where you can make your own waffles and valet parking for just $7 per night.

Reasonably priced **C The Presidio** (1620 State St., 805/963-1355, www.presidiosb.com, $150-250) is also close to the action. Its 16 guest rooms are clean and have been recently renovated. Second-floor guest rooms have vaulted ceilings, and every guest room has Wi-Fi and TVs with HBO. Other assets include the friendly staff, a sun deck, and a fleet of beach cruisers for motel guests.

The **Best Western Plus Encina Lodge & Suites** (2220 Bath St., 805/682-7277, www. encinalodge.com, $175-300) is tucked within a residential area three blocks off State Street. The guest rooms have fridges, coffeemakers, and flat-screen TVs with free movie rentals. Guest rooms are also stocked with fresh fruit and cookies to make you feel even more at home. Other features include a heated pool, a hot tub, and a bird aviary (not a common motel feature!). You can also enjoy meals onsite at the **Los Aves Café** (805/845-4263, daily 7am-9pm).

© STUART THORNTON

Hotel Santa Barbara is located right on State Street.

It's part of a chain now, but the **Holiday Inn Express at the Hotel Virginia** (17 W. Haley St., 805/963-9757, www.hotelvirginia.com, $170-275) has lots of history, dating back to 1916. Renovations have spiffed up the place without eradicating its historic charms, which include the terra-cotta tiled floor and a bright blue fountain in the lobby. Some of the guest rooms retain exposed brick walls. The smallish baths feature prized showerheads, the beds have both cotton and feather pillows, and all guest rooms have coffeemakers and flat-screen LCD TVs. The restaurants and shops of State Street are steps from the lobby, and the beach isn't too much farther.

The **Bath Street Inn** (1720 Bath St., 805/682-9680, www.bathstreetinn.com, $165-295) specializes in small-town charm and hospitality. It is large for a B&B, with eight guest rooms in the Queen Anne-style main house and another four in the more modern summerhouse. Each room has its own unique color scheme and style, some with traditional floral Victorian decor, others with elegant stripes. Some guest rooms have king beds, others have queens, and several have two-person whirlpool tubs. Despite the vintage trappings, you can expect a few modern amenities, including free Wi-Fi. But the inn has not entered the DVD era yet. All guest rooms have a TV and a VCR, and the common area has an extensive collection of movies on videotape. Early each morning, a sumptuous home-cooked breakfast is served downstairs. Choose between sharing your meal with your fellow guests in the dining room or escaping to the sunny garden patio for a bit of privacy.

Over $250

For a taste of Santa Barbara's upscale side, stay at the **Inn of the Spanish Garden** (915 Garden St., 805/564-4700, www.spanishgardeninn. com, $300-450). This small boutique hotel gets it right from the first glimpse; the building has the whitewashed adobe exterior, red-tiled roof, arched doorways, and wooden balconies characteristic of its historic Presidio neighborhood. Courtyards seem filled with lush greenery and tiled fountains, while the swimming pool promises relief from the heat. The pleasing setup of this luxury hotel definitely has something to do with the two owners' urban planning backgrounds. One of the owners is also the artist behind the hotel's paintings; these guys are talented. Inside, guest rooms and suites whisper luxury with their white linens, earth-toned accents, and rich, dark wooden furniture. Enjoy the benefits of your own gas fireplace, sitting area, balcony or patio, fridge, and minibar. The complimentary continental breakfast includes fresh-baked quiches and fruit smoothies on request. You can arrange for a massage or facial in the comfort of your room. The Spanish Inn is just three blocks from State Street, within walking distance of a number of theaters and historic Santa Barbara attractions.

If you're willing to pay a premium rate for your room, the **Cheshire Cat Inn** (36 W. Valerio St., 805/569-1610, www.cheshirecat. com, $219-409) can provide you with true luxury B&B accommodations. Each room has

©STUART THORNTON

the popular Inn of the Spanish Garden

an *Alice in Wonderland* name, but the decor doesn't really match the theme: Instead of whimsical and childish, you'll find comfortable Victorian elegance. Guest rooms are spread through two Victorian homes, the coach house, and two private cottages. Some suites feel like well-appointed apartments complete with a dining room table, a soaking tub, and a bookshelf stocked with a few hardbacks. Relax in the evening in the spacious octagonal outdoor spa, or order a massage in the privacy of your own room. Each morning, come downstairs and enjoy breakfast. In addition to the fine facilities, the Cheshire Cat's warm innkeepers will immediately make you feel at home.

The newest Santa Barbara luxury lodging establishment is the stylish, playful **C Canary Hotel** (31 West Carrillo St., 805/884-0300, www.canarysantabarbara.com, $295-675). Worth splurging on, the elegant guest rooms have wooden floors, extremely comfortable canopied beds, and giant flat-screen TVs, along with unexpected amenities such as a pair of binoculars for sightseeing and bird-watching

and a giant candle to set the mood for romantic evenings. While it may be difficult to leave such comforts, the hotel has a rooftop pool and lounge on its sixth floor that offer stunning views of the Santa Ynez Mountains and the red-tiled roofs of the beautiful city. Downstairs, the hotel restaurant and bar, Coast, serves breakfast, lunch, dinner, and a happy hour menu Monday-Friday 4pm-7pm.

Hosting guests since 1871, **The Upham Hotel & Country House** (1404 De La Vina St., 805/962-0058, www.uphamhotel.com, $235-475) has the distinction of being the oldest continuously operated hotel in Southern California. The historic hotel has a range of options that include guest rooms, cottages with gas fireplaces, and suites, including a two-bedroom suite for families. The Upham strives to keep you well fed during your stay with a continental breakfast in the morning, wine and cheese in the afternoon, and milk and cookies at night. If you're still hungry, **Louie's** (805/963-7003, www.louiessb.com, Mon.-Thurs. 11:30am-2pm and 5:30pm-9pm, Fri.

© STUART THORNTON

the rooftop pool at the Canary Hotel

11:30am-2pm and 5:30pm-10pm, Sat. 5:30pm-10pm, Sun. 5:30pm-9pm, $13-33) serves what it calls California comfort food with an elegant flair. The Upham also runs the **Country Home** ($200-475), a bed-and-breakfast with eight guest rooms located half a block from the main hotel.

The historic C **Simpson House Inn** (121 E. Arrellaga St., 805/963-7067, www.simpsonhouseinn.com, $230-610) is a wonderful place to spend an evening or two. The main house, constructed in 1874, is a historic landmark that withstood the 1925 earthquake. Stay inside one of the main building's six ornately decorated guest rooms or opt for one of the four guest rooms in the reconstructed carriage house. There are also four garden cottages. Whichever you choose, you will be treated to comfortable beds and a flat-screen TV with modern features that include Netflix, YouTube, and Pandora Radio access. The service is first-rate, and the staff are happy to help you get restaurant reservations or will deliver popcorn to your room on a silver platter if you opt to stay in with a

movie. In the morning, dine on a vegetarian breakfast in the main house's dining room or in your own room. The grounds include one acre of English gardens with fragrant flowers, gurgling fountains, fruit trees, chairs, tables, and the oldest English oak tree in Southern California.

WATERFRONT

With easy access to the harbor, beaches, and attractions like Stearns Wharf, the harbor and waterfront area is an ideal place to stay—if you can afford it. There are also several restaurant options within walking distance.

$150-250

A lovely little boutique hotel in a quiet residential neighborhood near the beach, the **Franciscan Inn** (109 Bath St., 805/963-8845, www.franciscaninn.com, $155-325) looks just like a Spanish Colonial Revival hacienda, with pale adobe-style walls and a traditional red-tiled roof. Guest rooms offer everything from cute, economical, double-bed rooms to

© STUART THORNTON

the relaxing grounds of the Simpson House Inn

rotating group of regional and local artists, many from the nearby Funk Zone micro-neighborhood. Upstairs is a vertical garden, two outdoor lounges, and a library filled with art books. The hotel is in a great location, one block from the beach and two blocks from Santa Barbara's downtown, although it's also near the train station, so expect to hear the occasional train roll by. In addition to its friendly staff, another asset of Hotel Indigo is its on-site **Anchor Woodfire Kitchen,** a creative new restaurant serving creative food.

A block from West Beach, the **Harbor House Inn** (104 Bath St., 805/962-9745, www.harborhouseinn.com, $150-335) will outfit you with beach chairs, beach towels, and umbrellas for a day on the sand. Afterward, retire to one of the 17 guest rooms and studios. All are furnished with comfortable antique furniture. Ask for a room with a full kitchen if you'll be in town for a few days. The Harbor House Inn also gives its guests a breakfast basket and the use of its three-speed beach-cruiser bicycles.

At the southern end of East Beach, the **Santa Barbara Inn** (901 E. Cabrillo Blvd., 800/231-0431, www.santabarbarainn.com, $189-289) is a boutique hotel with views of the beach and the surrounding palm trees. Every guest room has a private balcony or patio. Take a dip in the hotel's heated pool or soak in its jetted tub. In the morning, fortify yourself for a day at the beach with a light continental breakfast.

Another good value for its location, the **Mason Beach Inn** (324 W. Mason St., 805/962-3203, www.masonbeachinn.com, $139-309) has 45 guest rooms in a two-story red-tiled building. The courtyard includes a heated pool and jetted tub. Enjoy a continental breakfast in the inn's breakfast room or on the outdoor patio.

A block and a half from the harbor, **The Eagle Inn** (232 Natoma Ave., 805/965-3586, $192-350) includes both standard guest rooms and detached casitas. Half of the inn's guest rooms have fireplaces and whirlpool tubs for two. Meanwhile, the eight casitas—each named for a nearby island in the Channel Islands chain—have luxurious features that

luxurious multiple-room suites. The decor ranges from classic to modern. The largest suite sleeps seven comfortably; smaller guest rooms can sleep four if they're friendly. The amenities add to the charm: You can grab an item from the full continental breakfast and a cup of coffee in the morning, or a warm cookie in the afternoon. Take a swim in the heated pool, soak in the whirlpool tub, check your email with the free Wi-Fi, or even throw in a load of laundry at the on-site coin-op machines. Stearns Wharf and downtown are a short walk away.

Part of an international boutique hotel chain, **Hotel Indigo Santa Barbara** (121 State St., 805/966-6586, www.ihg.com, $189-289) opened in 2012. While the guest rooms are not spacious, they are artfully designed—clean and modern. Expect sleek, compact guest rooms with hardwood floors. The European-style collapsible glass shower wall is located right in front of the toilet. Some guest rooms also have small outdoor patios. The hotel's hallways are essentially art galleries showcasing a include fireplaces, whirlpool tubs, tiled baths, and patios or balconies. No matter where you stay at the Eagle Inn, you'll get a complimentary hot breakfast and free use of the inn's bicycles.

At **Brisas del Mar** (223 Castillo St., 805/966-2219, www.brisasdelmarinn.com, $170-300), two blocks from the harbor, you get to choose among guest rooms, suites, and penthouses with fully equipped kitchens. Amenities include a large heated pool, a whirlpool, and sun decks to take in views of the Santa Ynez Mountains. All guests are welcomed with a bottle of champagne.

The 23-room **Lavender Inn By The Sea** (206 Castillo St., 805/963-4317, www.lavenderinnbythesea.com, $236-266) is surrounded by lavender gardens, and all guest rooms have lavender-scented bath products. Lavender lovers and lavender likers can all enjoy the large heated pool, a whirlpool, a morning deluxe continental breakfast, and a bottle of champagne.

$250-350

If you're in Santa Barbara to soak up the sun on the sandy beaches, book a room at the **Inn at East Beach** (1029 Orilla Del Mar Dr., 805/965-0546, www.innateastbeach.com, $200-325). Unsurprisingly, it's just a block from East Beach, and a nice walk along the waterfront boardwalk will take you to Stearns Wharf and on to downtown. While it may look like a typical motel from the outside, the recently refurbished guest rooms are clean and stylish, with modern furniture and plants to give them a homey feel. The junior kitchen suites include a full kitchen with a large fridge, oven, and stove-top that are ideal for a longer stay. The guest rooms surround a courtyard with a heated kidney-shaped pool. Other amenities include continental breakfast, free parking, flat-screen TVs with 146 channels, and a shared washer and dryer for guest use. One-of-a-kind Hawaiian shirt-wearing general manager Frank Santana dispenses information about the area with a dollop of humor. If you will be visiting during the off-season, be

sure to check the hotel's website for promotional deals.

You pay for a great location just feet from the harbor at the **Castillo Inn** (22 Castillo St., 805/965-8527, $230-350). This boutique hotel has 20 redesigned guest rooms with free Wi-Fi and TVs with HBO. Guests come back for the clean rooms and friendly staff.

Fall asleep while staring out your window at the Pacific and Santa Barbara Harbor in an Ocean View King Room at **Hotel Oceana** (202 W. Cabrillo Blvd., 805/965-4577, www.hoteloceanasantabarbara.com, $180-431). Other guest rooms have flat-screen TVs and comfortable bedding. Enjoy Santa Barbara's renowned weather outdoors at Hotel Oceana's two heated pools and the pool deck with cabanas and a Ping-Pong table. Or hop on a complimentary beach cruiser for a two-hour ride.

Over $350

Are you ready and willing to pay premium prices for a luxury beachfront resort hotel room? If so, check out the **Harbor View Inn** (28 W. Cabrillo Blvd., 800/755-0222, www.harborviewinnsb.com, $325-795). This stunning Spanish colonial-style property is right across the street from the flat white sands of West Beach and steps from Stearns Wharf. Blooming flowers and bright ceramic tiles create beautiful outdoor spaces everywhere on the property. The pool is a focal point of the resort, with long hours and food and beverage service. The pool deck also features a kids pool, a hot tub, and a view of the nearby Pacific. Inside your lovely guest room, soft lighting and orange-and-red tones create a feeling of warmth. Suites offer palatial spaces and extra amenities. Every guest room also has a porch or balcony. If you want to enjoy a tasty meal without leaving the resort property, choose between room service and the on-site oceanfront restaurant **Eladio's** (805/963-4466, Sun.-Thurs. 7am-9pm, Fri.-Sat. 7am-9:30pm, $8-14). Eladio's is best known for its breakfasts but serves three meals each day and has a good list of wines that is heavy on the local vintages.

UPPER STATE STREET

On upper State Street, the **Lemon Tree Inn** (2819 State St., 805/687-6444, www.treesinn.com, $185-350) has nice landscaped grounds with fruit trees and flowers. Guest rooms overlook a courtyard with a saline pool and a spa. The Lemon Tree's friendly staff, good rates (for Santa Barbara), and excellent on-site **Crocodile Restaurant & Bar** make it easy to overlook some of the guest rooms, which can be a bit run down.

Also on Upper State Street is the **Agave Inn** (3222 State St., 805/687-6009, www.agave-innsb.com, $159-259), which has clean motel rooms with splashes of vibrant colors in the decor. Every guest room has microwaves, mini fridges, Wi-Fi, and iPod docks.

THE MISSION, THE RIVIERA, AND THE FOOTHILLS

In the hills above downtown Santa Barbara, **El Encanto** (800 Alvarado Place, 805/845-5800, www.elencanto.com, $375-905) completed a seven-year restoration in 2013. Each of the 92 individually designed bungalows has hardwood floors and a private patio or garden. Wander among seven acres of gardens, work out in the fitness studio or relax in an infinity pool with views of the Pacific. **The Spa at El Encanto** (massages $160-460) can further relax guests with massages, facials and pedicures, while **The Dining Room at El Encanto** (805/770-3530, Mon.-Sat. 7am-10:30am and 11:30am-2pm and 5:30pm-10pm, Sun. 11am-2pm and 5:30pm-10pm, $31-50) serves upscale contemporary American fare.

MONTECITO

Montecito has some of Santa Barbara's most luxurious—and expensive—accommodations, but these resorts also all have impressive histories.

Built in 1928 by Charlie Chaplin, the **Montecito Inn** (1295 Coast Village Rd., 805/969-7854, www.montecitoinn.com, $295-345) keeps the spirit of the silent movie star alive with movie posters decorating the hallways and a large library of complimentary

© STUART THORNTON

the historic Montecito Inn

Chaplin films for guests. Luxury guest rooms and suites also have fireplaces, heated bathroom floors, and steam showers. There's also a heated outdoor pool, a jetted tub, a spa, and the **Montecito Café** on the grounds. The inn is perched on one end of Coast Village Road, making it an ideal place to explore Montecito's upscale shops and restaurants.

Built in 1927 on the site of the former Santa Barbara Country Club, **The Four Seasons Resort Biltmore Santa Barbara** (1260 Channel Dr., 805/969-2742, www.foursea-sons.com, $495-3,000) has hosted politicians and celebrities that include President John F. Kennedy and Rock Hudson. Right across from Butterfly Beach, the luxury hotel has guest rooms with modern amenities such as plasma TVs, rain showerheads, and soaking tubs. The fern-shaded pool has music piped underwater so that you can listen while you're holding your breath. A stay at the Biltmore Santa Barbara includes use of the adjacent **Coral Casino Beach and Cabana Club,** which has its own Olympic-size heated pool, an oceanfront whirlpool, a deck with ocean views, and a state-of-the-art fitness center.

The **San Ysidro Ranch** (900 San Ysidro Lane, 805/565-1700, www.sanysidroranch.com, $700-5,500) might have the richest history and highest rates of any of Montecito's luxury resorts. It was a way station for Franciscan monks in the 1700s, then a citrus ranch in the 1800s, and started accommodating guests in 1893. This was where Laurence Olivier married Vivien Leigh, and future president John F. Kennedy honeymooned here with his wife, Jacqueline. The ranch has 41 private cottages and suites, each with a private deck or patio, a fireplace or stove, and heated bathroom floors. Some guest rooms also include private outdoor hot tubs and rain showers. The grounds include 17 miles of hiking trails, including one that leads to a waterfall. Two restaurants are also on-site: the upscale **Stonehouse** (Mon.-Wed. 6pm-10pm, Thurs.-Sat. 11:30am-2pm and 6pm-10pm, Sun. 10am-2pm and 6pm-10pm, $41-68) and the **Plow & Angel** (daily 5pm-10pm, $22-38).

Food

DOWNTOWN
Brazilian
A new addition to Santa Barbara's international food scene, the **Brasil Arts Café** (1230 State St., 805/845-7656, http://brasilartscafe.com, Mon.-Sat. 8am-9pm, $12-22) serves classics like white fish stew and meat dishes with rice and beans as well as *açaí* bowls and smoothies. Work off your meal by signing up for one of the samba or capoeira classes that take place in the restaurant's back studio.

Breakfast and Brunch
Breakfast spot **Scarlett Begonia** (11 W. Victoria St., Suite 10, 805/770-2143, www.scarlettbegonia.net, Tues.-Wed. and Sun. 9am-2pm, Thurs.-Sat. 9am-2pm and 5:30pm-9pm, $11-31) serves farm-to-table ingredients and free-range organic eggs. The breakfast menu is packed with singular options that include maple bacon biscuits, chipotle *chilaquiles* (a traditional Mexican dish with fried pieces of tortillas, eggs, salsa, cheese, and a choice of meat), breakfast pizzas, and shrimp and grits. After 10am, they add lunch fare that includes sandwiches and a burger. The Thursday-through-Saturday dinner menu expands further, with appetizers, salads, desserts, and entrées, including a fish of the day.

A chain with six locations from Ventura to Lompoc, the **Cajun Kitchen Café** (1924 De La Vina St., 805/687-2062, www.cajunkitchenca-fesb.com, daily 6:30am-2:30pm, $6.25-10.50) puts a New Orleans spin on typical breakfast dishes, with items such as gumbo omelets, Cajun *chilaquiles,* and jambalaya topped with two eggs. They also have beignets, New Orleans's take on the doughnut. There's a second location not far away (901 Chapala St., 805/965-1004, Mon.-Sat. 6:30am-3pm, Sun. 7am-3pm, $6.25-10.50).

Backyard Bowls (331 Motor Way, 805/845-5379, www.backyardbowls.com, Mon.-Fri. 7am-5pm, Sat.-Sun. 8am-5pm, $6-11) makes the kind of breakfasts you can feel good about eating. They take the pulp of the highly nutritious *açaí* berry—which is also high in antioxidants—and blend it with other fruits, and then top it with more fruit, granola, and honey.

Brewpubs

The **Santa Barbara Brewing Company** (501 State St., 805/730-1040, Mon.-Thurs. 11:30am-11pm, Fri.-Sun. 11:30am-midnight, $9-19) started brewing beer way back in 1995 before brewpubs and craft beers were as popular as they are now. They serve up pints of house-made Gold Coast Wheat, Rincon Red Ale, and State Street Stout. Pub food includes wings, burgers, and pizzas. In the back are pool tables, dartboards, and a shuffleboard table. In addition, catch your favorite sports team on one of the brewpub's 24 TVs.

California Cuisine

◖**Opal** (1325 State St., 805/966-9676, http://opalrestaurantandbar.com, Sun. 5pm-10pm, Mon.-Thurs. 11:30am-2:30pm and 5pm-10pm, Fri.-Sat. 11:30am-2:30pm and 5pm-11pm, $15) is a comfortable but lively local favorite. As a matter of fact, the menu points out local favorites, including the pesto sautéed bay scallop salad and the chili-crusted filet mignon. In addition to their eclectic offerings, most with an Asian twist, the stylish eatery serves up gourmet pizzas from a wood-burning oven and fine cocktails from a small bar. A quieter side room with rotating art is ideal for a more romantic meal.

Casual bar and eatery **Intermezzo** (819 Anacapa St., 805/966-9463, www.intermezzosb.com, Tues.-Sat. 4pm-11pm, $12-18) is run by the folks at the adjacent higher-end Wine

Cask Restaurant. Along with the bar atmosphere, expect a higher noise level and a shorter menu stocked with creative appetizers, burgers, and flatbreads-including a tasty one with prosciutto, arugula, Humboldt Fog cheese, and oven-dried tomatoes. The fried chicken and waffles appetizer basket is a nice twist on the Southern soul food staple, and comes with apricot marmalade dipping sauce. It's a nice place to unwind with specialty cocktails and moderately priced food to share.

Julienne (138 E. Canon Perdido St., 805/845-6488, www.restaurantjulienne.com, Tues.-Sat. 5pm-10pm, Sun. 5pm-9pm, $18-27) secures its ingredients locally from places like the Santa Barbara Farmers Market and the Santa Barbara Fish Market. The dinner menu changes; the small open kitchen offers dishes like grilled quail, stuffed rabbit, or pork belly. You can also opt for a three-, four-, or five-course tasting menu.

Jane (1311 State St., 805/962-1311, Mon.-Sat. 11:30am-2:30pm and 5:30pm-10pm, $13-26) is named after owner Margaret Huston's grandmother, who encouraged her to open her first restaurant, the Montecito Café. Photos of her grandmother also decorate the walls as a personal tribute. The menu includes steak, seafood, pasta and meal-size salad bowls.

You'll find fine and food cocktails in a sleek, modern environment at **Blush Restaurant and Lounge** (630 State St., 805/957-1300, www.blushsb.com, Mon.-Thurs. 11am-midnight, Fri. 11am-2am, Sat. 10am-2am, Sun. 10am-midnight, $19-34). The cocktails include barrel-aged Manhattans and margaritas with elderflower liqueur and other ingredients. The menu features entrées along with lots of shared plates like roasted marrow and lobster mac and cheese. Blush caters to late-night diners with a lounge menu served after 10pm.

The **Pierre Lafond Wine Bistro** (516 State St., 805/962-1455, www.pierrelafond.com, Mon.-Thurs. 11am-9pm, Fri.-Sun. 9am-close, $12-34) showcases the wines of the Santa Barbara Winery and the Lafond Winery. The bistro prepares meat and seafood dishes along with dishes featuring organic produce, grass-fed beef, organic poultry, and seafood from sustainable fisheries. You can also expect entrée-size-d salads, flatbreads, and several vegetarian options, including a farmers market vegetable risotto.

The **Arts & Letters Café** (7 E. Anapamu St., 805/730-1463, www.sullivangoss.com, daily 11am-2:30pm, $8-16) is a lunch spot in the courtyard connected with the Sullivan Goss art gallery. Dine in the outdoor courtyard, decorated with a fountain, flowers, and plants. Menu favorites include the pumpkin soup and the pork belly sandwich topped with apricot jalapeño preserves, cabbage, pickled red onions, and a poppy seed dressing.

Santa Barbara native Ron True cooked in New York City, San Francisco, and Philadelphia kitchens before returning to his hometown in 2012 to open the **Arlington Tavern** (21 W. Victoria St., 805/770-2626, http://arlington-tavern.com, restaurant Mon.-Sat. 5pm-10pm, Sun. 5pm-9pm, bar Mon.-Sat. 4pm-midnight, Sun. 4pm-10pm, $15-28). The dinner menu includes black cod, fried chicken, and filet mignon. Late diners can take advantage of a bar menu, with indulgent items like roasted bone marrow, crispy pork bellies, and fries and gravy, Monday-Saturday until midnight. A true tavern, the Arlington also offers a fine wine and beer list.

Cheap Eats

Not all Santa Barbara restaurants serve healthy food or fancy fare. Old school **Norton's Pastrami and Deli** (18 W. Figueroa St., 805/965-3210, www.nortonspastrami.com, Mon.-Fri. 10am-7pm, Sat. 10:30am-3:30pm, $5-9.50) serves gut busters like pastrami sandwiches, corned beef sandwiches, and Philly cheese steaks. Lunch is crowded; good luck finding a seat at the small countertop or in the small dining space. Fortunately, Norton's recently opened another location (226 S. Milpas St., 805/965-7575, Mon.-Sat. 10am-4pm, $5-9.50).

Is there anyplace better to order a grilled cheese sandwich than a gourmet cheese shop? Probably not. **C'est Cheese** (825 Santa Barbara St., www.cestcheese.com, Mon.-Fri. 10am-6pm, Sat. 8am-6pm, $6-9.50) carries 120 different types of cheeses from Spain, Italy, France, Holland, and the good old US of A. During lunch, they make BLT grilled cheeses, goat cheese grilled cheeses with chorizo, and their signature grilled cheese with four-year-aged cheddar, Scharfe Maxx, and mozzarella. They also have salads and soups if you are not feeling cheesy.

Another place for a fine sandwich is **Metropulos** (216 E. Yanonali St., 805/899-2300, www.metrofinefoods.com, Jan.-May Mon.-Fri. 8:30am-5:30pm, June-Dec. Mon.-Fri. 8:30am-6pm, $10). The sandwiches include a turkey and brie sandwich with cranberry fig confit and "The Little Piggie," where ham, bacon, cheese, and other toppings are stuffed between two pieces of toasted sourdough. Metropulos is also known for its morning breakfast wraps.

Locals are very passionate about their favorite sandwiches at the **D'Vine Café** (205 W. Canon Perdido St., 805/963-9591, www.dvine-cafe.com, Mon.-Fri. 8am-4pm, Sat. 11am-3pm, $5.50-9.25) Some advocate for the grilled caprese; some swear by the grilled tri-tip sandwich. Others say forget the hot sandwiches and go for the cheeseburger. After you decide on your sandwich, you can take it to go or scarf it down on the café's outdoor patio.

The Blue Owl (5 W. Canon Perdido St., 805/705-0911, www.theblueowlsantabarbara.com, Tues.-Thurs. 11am-3pm, Fri. 11am-3pm and 10pm-2:30am, Sat. 10am-3pm and 10pm-2:30am, $7-10) began as a pop-up restaurant in Zen Yai Thai. The popularity of its inexpensive Asian fusion menu quickly warranted a new space. The day menu includes a duck croissant, a crab melt, and a *banh mi* sandwich with roast beef. A special late-night menu on Friday and Saturday includes fried rice and a peanut butter burger, and a green curry patty with peanut tamarind sauce.

Coffee

A long, narrow coffee shop right on State

Street, **The French Press** (1101 State St., 805/963-2721, Mon.-Fri. 6am-7pm, Sat. 7am-7pm, Sun. 8am-7pm) is lined with hipsters and couples getting caffeinated and using the free Wi-Fi. As its name suggests, the very popular café serves individually prepared French press coffee and espresso along with other beverages that'll leave your body buzzing. Also on the drink menu is the Magic Bowl, which mixes steamed milk, chamomile, and honey. There's a small seating area out front and another out back on Figueroa Street, as well as a second location (528 Anacapa St.).

Former professional cyclists run the appropriately named **Handlebar Coffee Roasters** (128 E. Canon Perdido St., Suite A, 719/201-3931, http://handlebarcoffee.com, Mon.-Sat. 7am-5pm, Sun. 8am-1pm), where they roast their own coffee beans. Sip your coffee on the outdoor patio, which is shaded by umbrellas.

Buy a bag of beans or a freshly brewed cup of coffee at the **Santa Barbara Roasting Company** (321 Motor Way, 805/962-0320, www.sbcoffee.com, Mon.-Fri. 5:30am-9pm, Sat. 6am-9pm, Sun. 6:30am-9pm), which slow roasts small batch coffee. You can also purchase beans online.

Creole

The Palace Grill (8 E. Cota St., 805/963-5000, www.palacegrill.com, daily 11:30am-3pm and 5:30pm-10pm, Fri.-Sat. 5:30pm-11pm, $20-40) boasts of being one of Santa Barbara's most popular restaurants and a little piece of old New Orleans in sunny California. The atmosphere gets lively in the evenings, so this isn't the place to come for a quiet meal. Live entertainers delight the crowds several nights each week, and every once in a while a restaurant-wide sing-along breaks out. The food is pure Louisiana bayou; look for classically prepared étouffées, jambalaya, and gumbo ya-ya. The seafood is fresh, the steaks are aged to perfection, and much of the fresh finned fish and meat is served blackened and spiced in Cajun style. Even the appetizers and desserts drip creole and Cajun flavors. Start off with a house specialty cocktail or a glass of California wine.

While you dine, be sure to take a moment to appreciate the particularly fine service that is a staple of the Palace's reputation.

Desserts

Satiate your sweet tooth at **Crushcakes** (1315 Anacapa St., 805/963-3752, www.crushcakes.com, cupcakes and coffee daily 9am-6pm, café daily 8am-5pm, cupcakes $3). The namesake item is a red velvet cupcake with sour cream frosting. There are other creative cupcakes, full-size cakes, and other deserts. If you want to avoid a sugar rush, try a breakfast burrito, grilled panini, or a wrap.

Fine Dining

Of the many and varied high-end California cuisine restaurants that crowd Santa Barbara, **Bouchon** (9 W. Victoria St., 805/730-1160, www.bouchonsantabarbara.com, daily 5pm-10pm, $25-36) might be the best, priding itself on both creative cuisine and top-notch service every night. You'll pay a premium to dine here, but it's worth it for a special night out. Your server will be your guide, helping you make selections from the menu, recommending wine pairings with each course, and answering any questions you might have about the restaurant or the food. California style dishes are prepared with local and organic ingredients whenever possible, and the menu changes often based on what's available. The wine list is a special treat. It consists entirely of wines from Santa Barbara County. Servers have favorites, and they're generally great. The presentation of the food matches its quality. The dining room features romantic low lighting, smallish tables, interesting artwork, and an outdoor patio that's perfect for balmy summer nights.

The **Wine Cask** (813 Anacapa St., 805/966-9463, www.winecask.com, Tues.-Thurs. 11:30am-3pm and 5:30pm-9pm, Fri. 11:30am-3pm and 5:30pm-10pm, Sat. 5:30pm-10pm, Sun. 5:30pm-9pm, $24-38) serves items like braised lamb shank and duck cassoulet in a dining room with a fireplace and an old vaulted ceiling. The family crest of the De la Guerra family, one of the city's most important early families, is located above the fireplace.

Chef John Downey opened his namesake **Downey's Restaurant** (1305 State St., 805/966-5006, www.downeyssb.com, Tues.-Sun. 5:30pm-close, $30-39) in 1982. The UK native had already built up quite a resume, working under James Beard and cooking for Queen Elizabeth. Downey's is an intimate space with 14 white-clothed tables and paintings of local landscape on the walls. The menu focuses on fish and meat entrées, including the popular grilled duck in cabernet sauce. The wine list is heavy on the products of Santa Barbara and Central Coast wineries, making room for some Napa wines as well.

French

Renaud's Patisserie & Bistro (1324 State St., Suite N, 805/892-2800, www.renaudsbakery. com, daily 7am-3pm, $7-13) is a little French eatery that serves up breakfast and lunch items with big tastes. A bakery best known for its French pastries and cakes, Renaud's also has a small menu of sandwiches, salads, pastas, quiches, and *tartines*. The signature Renaud's salad is a healthy and tasty lunch option with greens, grilled chicken, gruyère cheese, and a hard-boiled egg. Just the half salad option is huge, so only order a full salad if you want to share.

Housed in a small space, **Petit Valentien** (1114 State St., 805/966-0222, Mon.-Fri. 11:30am-3pm and 5pm-close, Sat.-Sun. 11am-2:30pm and 5pm-close, $17-18) serves classic French cuisine, including frog legs, escargot, and steak au poivre. Ethiopian food is an unexpected addition to the weekend lunch menu.

Pacific Crêpes (705 Anacapa St., 805/882-1123, www.pacificcrepe.com, Mon.-Fri. 10am-3pm and 5:30pm-9pm, Sat. 9am-9pm, Sun. 9am-3pm, $9-16) specializes in—guess what?—crepes. Breakfast crepes can include eggs, bacon, or ham or both meats. Lunch and dinner versions include the Basque crepe, with ratatouille and prosciutto, and a vegetarian crepe with brie, chopped apples, walnuts, and leeks. *Bon appétit!*

German

The **Hoffmann Brat Haus** (801 State St., 805/962-3131, http://hoffmannbrathaus. com, Sun.-Thurs. 11am-10pm, Fri.-Sat. 11am-11pm, $7-9) limits its focus to gourmet sausages, which can be accompanied by Belgian fries, Belgian waffles, and German and Belgian beers. Opt for a traditional bratwurst, or get adventurous with a sausage made from rattlesnake and rabbit meat with jalapeños.

Healthy Fare

Whether you're a vegetarian or not, you'll find something delicious at the **Sojourner Café** (134 E. Canon Perdido St., 805/965-7922, www. sojournercafe.com, Sun.-Wed. 11am-10pm, Thurs.-Sat. 11am-11pm, $11). A select few dishes include a bit of lean poultry or fish in among the veggies. Sojourner features healthful dishes made with ingredients that showcase local organic and sustainable farms. Daily specials use ingredients that are fresh and in season, including some seafood. Lots of the cuisine blends ethnic flavors, from familiar Mexico to exotic India. If you're looking for something a little less healthy, you can choose a classic root beer float or chocolate milk shakes. Sojourner displays the work of local artists on a rotating schedule. If you fall in love with the wall art over your table, inquire with your server about purchasing it.

Also boasting a healthy menu is the **Natural Café** (508 State St., 805/962-9494, www.natu-ralcafe.com, daily 11am-9pm, $8). It's part of a small chain, but feels right at home on State Street. The mostly vegetarian menu features tofu hot dogs and an array of salads but makes room for healthy carnivore options like turkey burgers and chicken sandwiches.

The city's first certified green restaurant, **Silvergreens** (791 Chapala, 805/962-8500, www.silvergreens.com, Mon.-Fri. 7am-10pm, Sat.-Sun. 8am-10pm, $5.50-10) hones in on fresh local ingredients to make menu items you can feel good about eating. Lunch and dinner patrons can order salads, smoothies, pastas, sandwiches, and burgers with beef, turkey, or vegetarian patties. There's also an Isla Vista location (900 Embarcadero Del Mar, 805/961-1700, www.silvergreens.com, Mon.-Wed. 7am-1am, Thurs.-Fri. 7am-2am, Sat. 8am-2am, Sun. 8am-1am, $5.50-10).

Indian

A Bombay-born chef cooks up Indian cuisine and Pakistani fare at **Spice Avenue** (1027 State St., 805/965-6004, www.spiceavenuesb.com, Mon.-Thurs. 11:30am-2:30pm and 5:30pm-9:30pm, Fri.-Sun. 11:30am-3pm and 5:30pm-9:30pm, $12-18). Enjoy the daily lunch buffet or try the popular mixed grill of clay oven-cooked chicken, lamb, and shrimp.

Italian

If you want a superb Italian meal and sophisticated dining experience, **(Olio e Limone** (11 W. Victoria St., Suite 17, 805/899-2699, www.olioelimone.com, Mon.-Sat. 11:30am-2pm and 5pm-close, Sun. 5pm-close, $18-37) is the place to go in Santa Barbara. Chef Alberto Morello is a Sicily native who opened Olio e Limone in 1999. You'll be impressed by the artistic presentation of the dishes, which include homemade pasta. The duck ravioli with creamy porcini mushroom sauce ($24) is easy to rave about. Another standout item is the spaghetti with Dungeness crabmeat. Enjoy the impressive wine list or opt for a cocktail: the Italian mojito, spiked with prosecco, is worth a taste. The adjacent **Olio Pizzeria** (11 W. Victoria St., Suite 21, 805/899-2699, daily 11am-close, $15-20) is a more casual affair, focusing on brick-oven pizzas. They also have a detailed menu of antipasti with salamis, cheeses, and breads.

Family-friendly **Aldo's Italian Restaurant** (1031 State St., 805/963-6687, www.sbaldos.com, Mon.-Thurs. 11am-9:30pm, Fri.-Sun. 11am-10:30pm, $16-33) operates from a historic State Street restaurant site that dates back to 1927. Dine indoors among columns and Italian frescos or outdoors on a patio overlooking State Street. Expect hearty classics, including chicken parmesan and cioppino. One favorite is sushi-grade salmon topped with cilantro pesto. There are also vegetarian and gluten-free options. Cash-saving daily specials

Aldo's Italian Restaurant

include family-friendly Tuesday night, when any entrée comes with two kids meals for free.

Across the street from Aldo's is **The Chase Bar & Grill** (1012 State St., 805/965-4351, Sun.-Thurs. 11am-9pm, Fri.-Sat. 11am-10pm, $17-30), which claims to be the oldest Italian restaurant in Santa Barbara. The old Italian atmosphere, with vines and lights hanging from the ceiling, borders on kitschy. Sit at the bar or in booths to enjoy classic dishes like eggplant parmesan, homemade ravioli, and calamari steak *piccata*.

The owner of **Ca' Dario** (37 E. Victoria St., 805/884-9419, www.cadario.net, Mon.-Sat. 11:30am-10pm, Sun. 5pm-9:30pm, $15-32) learned how to make pasta, gnocchi, and sauces while growing up in his native Italy. The signature dish is ravioli al burro e salvia (filled with spinach and ricotta in a brown butter and sage sauce). Other options include baked chicken, roasted quail, and daily rotisserie and fish specials. While white tablecloths provide class, the tables are close together, making the atmosphere cozy and casual. Its popularity

SANTA BARBARA

© STUART THORNTON

The Chase Bar & Grill

warranted the opening of **Ca' Dario Pizzeria** (29 E. Victoria St., 805/957-2020, http://cadariopizza.net, Mon.-Sat. 11:30am-2:30pm and 5pm-9:30pm, Sun. 5pm-9:30pm, $9-15), down the street.

Indulge in classic homemade pasta dishes like veal tortellini and meat lasagna. **Trattoria Vittoria** (30 E. Victoria St., 805/962-5014, www.trattoriavittoria.com, Mon.-Thurs. 11:30am-2pm and 5pm-9pm, Fri. 11:30am-2pm and 5pm-10pm, Sat. 5pm-10pm, Sun. 5pm-9pm, $13-28). Sit at the bar at to watch bartender Ivo serve up drinks with flair.

Japanese

With a popular dining patio, **Arigato Sushi** (1225 State St., 805/965-6074, www.arigato-santabarbara.com, daily 5:30pm-close, special rolls $7-22) is known for its *nigiri* jalapeño yellowtail sushi. Unique starters include an oyster shot or sea urchin, both served with quail egg. If you are not in the mood for sushi, try steamed pot stickers, Kobe beef, or soft-shell crab.

Mexican

Have you ever wanted to know what true authentic Mexican food might taste like? **La Super-Rica Taqueria** (622 N. Milpas St., 805/963-4940, Sun.-Thurs. 11am-9pm, Fri.-Sat. 11am-9:30pm, $5) can hook you up. Be prepared to stand in line with dozens of locals and even commuters from Los Angeles and the occasional Hollywood celeb. All agree that La Super-Rica has some of the best down-home Mexican cuisine in all of SoCal. This was Julia Child's favorite taco stand, and it has been reviewed by the *New York Times*. Don't come for the ambiance; it's a taqueria in what feels like a beach shack. You also need to adjust your concept of Mexican food: If you're looking for a fast-food burrito supreme with chips and salsa, you'll definitely be disappointed (there's no burrito on the menu). But if you're ready for the real deal, you've found it. The corn tortillas are made fresh for every order, the meat is slow cooked and seasoned to perfection, and the house special is a grilled pork-stuffed pasilla chili pepper. Vegetarians can choose from a few delicious meat-free dishes, including the rajas, a standout with sautéed strips of pasilla peppers, sautéed onions, melted cheese, and herbs on a bed of two fresh corn tortillas.

Popular **La Playa Azul Café** (914 Santa Barbara St., 805/966-2860, www.laplayaazulcafe.com, Tues.-Sun. 11am-9pm, $9-17) is just a couple of blocks off State Street. The menu includes tostadas, burritos, and specialties like steak ranchero platters and *chile verde* entrées. Eat indoors or outside on a brick patio with a view of the Presidio.

The award-winning **Rose Café** (424 E. Haley St., 805/966-3773, www.rosecafe2.com, daily 8am-9pm, $3-13) is a diner that serves home-style Mexican food a few blocks from State Street. It's a local favorite; you won't find tourists sitting at the L-shaped counter or scattered tables and chairs. Try enchiladas in red or green sauce or the superb *chilaquiles* with chorizo.

Another popular player in Santa Barbara's terrific Mexican food scene is **Lilly's Taqueria** (310 Chapala St., http://lillystacos.com,

Sun.-Mon. and Wed.-Thurs. 10:30am-9pm, Fri.-Sat. 10:30am-10pm, all tacos $1.60), which has been written up by *Men's Health* and *Maxim*. This unassuming spot serves carne asada, but they also have the more unusual *ojo* (steamed beef eye) and *labio* (steamed beef lip). They recently added a veggie taco to the small menu: corn, zucchini, carrots, and green beans crowded onto a corn tortilla.

Middle Eastern

For a Middle Eastern feast, go to **Zaytoon** (209 E. Canon Perdido St., 805/963-1293, www.zaytoon.com, Mon.-Tues. 11:30am-11pm, Wed.-Sat. 11:30am-midnight, Sun. 5pm-11pm, $18), a great place to enjoy an evening out with a group of friends, sharing a hookah around the table, and appreciating the talents or shimmying belly dancers. The interior dining room is attractive, with potted palms and gauzy fabric draped from the ceiling. Try to get a table out on the garden patio, a large, softly lit space enveloped by a living green jungle, where you can order your own hookah. The menu has most standard Middle Eastern favorites, such as baba ghanoush, hummus, falafel, Greek salad, shawarma, and kebabs of many kinds.

Seafood

In downtown Santa Barbara, **The Hungry Cat** (1134 Chapala St., 805/884-4701, www.thehungrycat.com, Mon. 5pm-10pm, Tues.-Thurs. 11:30am-10pm, Fri. 11:30am-midnight, Sat. 11am-midnight, Sun. 11am-10pm, $10-27) is housed in a small but sleek modern space. This cat has the expected seafood options (fish tacos at lunch, peel-and-eat shrimp) as well as more exotic offerings (sturgeon caviar, local sea urchin). Try the house-made chorizo and clams with grilled bread ($22). Sit at the bar for happy hour specials (Mon. 5pm-6pm, Tues.-Fri. 3pm-6pm) to dine on a lobster roll or fried oysters while enjoying half-price cocktails and beers.

Named for a geological feature of Anacapa Island and appropriately located on Anacapa Street, **Arch Rock Fish** (608 Anacapa St., 805/845-2800, Sun.-Thurs. 11:30am-10pm, Fri.-Sat. 11:30am-11pm, $15-34) makes

The Hungry Cat

creative spins on seafood, from spaghetti with clams and bacon to miso cod with red chili and baby bok choy. On Monday and Tuesday, the restaurant hosts a crab feed ($14 pp) that includes a two-pound bucket of local crab, corn on the cob, potatoes, and bread.

Southern

The **Tupelo Junction Café** (1218 State St., 805/899-3100, www.tupelojunction.com, Tues.-Sat. 8am-2pm and 5pm-9pm, Sun.-Mon. 8am-2pm, $14) serves breakfast, lunch, and dinner, but it is the breakfast that shouldn't be missed. At this Southern-meets-Southern California restaurant, your juice or mimosa will be served in a mason jar. The collision between cuisines continues on the morning menu, which includes a breakfast wrap with Southern elements like andouille sausage mixed into a Mexican breakfast burrito with a tasty avocado salsa. Don't miss the half biscuit covered in spicy red sausage gravy. Despite all the Southern charm, the sleek interior will remind you that you're in Santa Barbara.

© STUART THORNTON

The Tupelo Junction Café serves terrific Southern food on State Street.

Tapas

If creative cocktails and clever snacks sound good, head to **Milk & Honey** (30 W. Anapamu St., 805/275-4232, http://milknhoneytapas. com, Mon.-Sat. 5pm-midnight, $8-17). People rave about the bacon-wrapped dates and avocado hummus. Other options include ceviche, ahi tartare, and paella. Cocktails range from the classics (mint juleps, Moscow mules) to the unexpected (an Irish whiskey shot laced with Sriracha hot sauce and pickle juice). Low lighting, deep red walls adorned with local art, and lots of wood and stone-work make this a good place for a romantic evening out.

Thai

People rave about the pumpkin curry at **Zen Yai Thai Cuisine** (425 State St., 805/957-1102, daily 11:30am-2pm and 5:30pm-10pm, $10-12). You can also expect other choice curries, noodles, and stir fries. You might want to make a reservation: The intimate, dimly lit space has just 10 tables.

WATERFRONT

It's not much of a surprise that a lot of Santa Barbara's seafood restaurants are located on or near the water. There are a few other worthy eateries in this region that make a trip to nearby downtown unnecessary when you are craving a great meal.

Breakfast and Brunch

This **Sambo's** (216 W. Cabrillo Blvd., 805/965-3269, daily 6:30am-3:30pm, $6-15) in Santa Barbara was the original breakfast restaurant that blossomed into a chain of 1,117 restaurants in 47 states by 1981. Although the founders, Sam Battistone and Newell "Bo" Bohnett, say Sambo's was named after them, the chain was controversial for utilizing racial stereotypes in its marketing. This location is now the last one standing; it's known for hearty breakfast fare like steak and eggs, chicken fried steak and eggs, and biscuits and gravy.

Brewpubs

Under the highway on the harbor side of State

Street, **Union Ale** (214 State St., 805/845-8243, http://unionale.com, daily 11am-midnight, $8-17) serves craft beers in a bar/restaurant decorated with wooden barrels and sports paraphernalia. They also have gourmet burgers, flatbreads, salads, sandwiches, tacos, and ribs to soak up the suds.

There's a lot going on at **Brewhouse** (229 W. Montecito St., 805/884-4664, Sun.-Thurs. 11am-11pm, Fri.-Sat. 11am-midnight). Let's start with the beer: Brewhouse brews its own beer in seven small barrels. The focus is on ales and lagers, with one belly-burning number called the Habanero Pilsner. The food menu has grilled pork chops, grilled steaks, and filet mignon enchiladas. Brewhouse also showcases local art on its walls and features live bands from Wednesday to Saturday. If you just want to try their beer, come in for the daily happy hour (4pm-6pm), when pints are just $3.50.

New American

Between the harbor area and downtown, the ☾ **Anchor Woodfire Kitchen** (119 State St., 805/845-0989, http://anchorwoodfirekitchen.com, Mon.-Thurs. 7am-11am and 5pm-10pm, Fri.-Sun. 7am-11am and 5pm-11pm, $14-40) use a wood-fired pizza oven for pizzas but also for dinner entrées that include a New York steak and a daily whole fish. This popular new spot has its own in-house charcuterie that makes delicious spreadable salami and a lineup of cocktails that combine liquors with ingredients obtained at the Santa Barbara Farmers Market. They also serve a fine breakfast that includes breakfast pizza, brioche french toast with bourbon maple syrup, and braised brisket with a poached egg. Be sure to try the housemade bacon, which is a seasoned slab of pork as thick as a smartphone.

Yes, they do mean *that* **Endless Summer** (113 Harbor Way, 805/564-4666, www.endlesssummerbarcafe.net, daily 11:30am-close, $10). When they decided to create a new restaurant in the harbor area, the owners went to Bruce Brown, a Santa Barbara resident and acknowledged creator of the "real" surfing movie genre, and asked him if he would mind having a restaurant named for his most famous film. Bruce thought it was a fine idea, and not only gave the project his blessing but quickly became a regular in the dining room. Photos of Bruce, other famous surfers, and lots of surfing paraphernalia—including framed movie posters from *The Endless Summer* and *The Endless Summer II*—deck the walls of this harbor-side bar and café. The menu has plenty of salads and sandwiches, includes a tasty Cajun-seared ahi appetizer with a terrific wasabi dipping sauce, and the restaurant also serves from the menu of the Waterfront Grill downstairs. Service is friendly, and the atmosphere tends toward casual local hangout. Many patrons know each other and the staff, and the bar gets crowded as the evening wears on.

Seafood

A Santa Barbara seafood staple since 1977, **Enterprise Fish Co.** (225 State St., 805/962-3313, www.enterprisefishco.com, Sun.-Thurs. 11:30am-10pm, Fri.-Sat. 11:30am-11pm) casts its nets wide to gather seafood from all over the globe, from British Columbia salmon to Idaho rainbow trout and Maine lobster. Save money by hitting their impressive happy hour (Mon.-Fri. 4pm-8pm, Sun. 5pm-close) where you can enjoy a $5 order of Cajun popcorn shrimp, a $1 oyster on the half shell, and a 20-ounce draft beer for $4.50.

The **Santa Barbara Fishhouse** (1101 E. Cabrillo Blvd., 805/966-2112, www.fishousesb.com, Mon.-Sat. 11:30am-9pm, Sun. 9:30am-9pm, $16-27) has popular halibut fish tacos with black beans, *pico de gallo*, garlic, cabbage, and avocado, drizzled with their own taco sauce. Local seafood options include an abalone appetizer, a red snapper ceviche, and seasonal California spiny lobster. The interior is decorated with a large aquarium and fishing poles. There's also a dog-friendly outdoor patio with a fire pit.

It isn't that often that you can find good seafood that locals enjoy on one of California's touristy wharfs, but the **Santa Barbara Shellfish Company** (230 Stearns Wharf, 805/966-6676, www.sbfishhouse.com, daily

11am-9pm, $10-19) is right on Stearns Wharf, and locals dine here. Owned by the same folks behind the Santa Barbara FisHouse and the Boathouse at Hendry's Beach, the Santa Barbara Shellfish Company is known for its market-price lobster tacos and clam chowder. In season, you can also dine on local spiny lobster or Dungeness crab.

It takes something special to make Santa Barbara residents take notice of a seafood restaurant, and **Brophy Brothers** (119 Harbor Way, 805/966-4418, www.brophybros.com, Sun.-Thurs. 11am-10pm, Fri.-Sat. 11am-11pm, $23) has it. Look for a small list of fresh fish done up California style with upscale preparations. The delectable menu goes heavy on locally caught seafood. At the clam bar, you can order some fresh steamed clams or oysters, a bowl of the house clam chowder, or a tasty seafood salad. With a prime location looking out over the masts of the sailboats in the harbor, it's no surprise that Brophy Brothers gets crowded at both lunch and dinner, especially on weekends in the summer. There's also a location in Ventura Harbor.

Tapas

Reds Bar & Tapas (211 Helena St., 805/966-5906, http://redsbarandtapas.wordpress.com, Tues.-Thurs. 3pm-midnight, Fri. 3pm-1am, Sat. 1pm-1am, Sun. 1pm-7pm, $5-17) is part tapas bar, part wine-tasting room, part local art showcase, and part music venue. The tapas include gruyère mac and cheese and tri-tip sliders. The happy hour (Tues.-Fri. 3pm-7pm) has discounted well drinks, house wines, beer, and tapas.

UPPER STATE STREET

Up and away from bustling downtown, Upper State Street has a few local favorites.

Classic American

Go back in time at classic Santa Barbara institution **Harry's Plaza Café** (3313 State St., 805/687-2800, www.harryssb.com, Sun.-Thurs. 11am-10pm, Fri.-Sat. 11am-11pm, $10-35), which hasn't changed much since it opened in 1968. You can still sink into a red leather booth, sip from a giant martini, and sink your teeth into prime rib. The burned-ends prime rib and tri-tip barbecue sandwich will take you back to the days before anyone worried about cholesterol (burned ends are the end pieces of barbecued meat that usually have a higher fat content).

German

German food is not the first thing that comes to mind when you think of Santa Barbara, but everyone in the city knows **Brummis** (3130 State St., 805/687-5916, Mon.-Sat. 5pm-9pm, $8-30) for its hearty German food and enthusiastic proprietor. The menu here offers all the Teutonic classics: bratwurst, spaetzle, and wiener schnitzel. Wash it all down with world-famous German beer.

Indian

From the outside, **Flavor of India** (3026 State St., 805/682-6561, www.flavorofindiasb.com, Mon.-Sat. 11am-3pm and 5pm-10pm, $6-18) doesn't look like much, but it's a longtime local's favorite because of its all-you-can-eat lunch buffet and classic menu that includes curries, vegetarian entrées, and chicken tikka.

Italian

How often do locals get excited by hotel restaurants? Not often, but the sleek, modern, and mirrored **Crocodile Restaurant & Bar** (Lemon Tree Inn, 2819 State St., www.tree-inns.com, daily 7am-2:30pm and 4pm-9:30pm, $12-28) is an exception. Expect Italian fare like chicken parmesan as well as burgers and healthier options like lemon chicken salad with artichokes and feta cheese.

Japanese

Craving a sushi roll around midnight? **Endomasa** (2710 De La Vina St., 805/687-0210, www.edomasasushi.com, Sun.-Thurs. 6pm-midnight, Fri.-Sat. 6pm-1am, $13.50) stays open late. Or dine early to take advantage of the daily dinner special (6pm-8pm, $13.50), a parade of food including a jumbo

California roll, shrimp tempura, vegetable tempura, chicken teriyaki, salad, miso soup, and rice. One of the most popular rolls is the buffalo volcano roll: a baked California roll with cream cheese and a spicy sauce. Dine at the sushi bar or at a private table.

Thai

TAP Thai Cuisine (2611 De La Vina St., 805/682-1114, www.tapthaicuisine.com, Tues.-Thurs. 11am-3pm and 5pm-9:30pm, Fri. 11am-3pm and 5pm-10pm, Sat. noon-9:30pm, Sun. 5pm-9:30pm, $8-14) puts a modern spin on traditional Thai food. The three owners, whose first initials spell out "TAP," artfully prepare dishes like the very popular drunken noodles and serve delicious Thai iced tea in mason jars. Black-and-white line drawings of food decorate the walls, contributing to the modern feel.

MONTECITO
Cafés

Busy **Jeannine's** (1253 Coast Village Rd., 805/969-7878, www.jeannines.com, daily 6:30am-4pm, $7.50-12) is a popular bakery and eatery for breakfast and lunch. The banana Kahlua french toast tops a list of locals' favorites. Lunchtime moves into salads, burgers, and sandwiches, but baked goods like scones, muffins, coffeecakes, and cookies are always available. A European I know swears by their tiramisu. There are two additional locations in Santa Barbara (15 E. Figueroa St., 805/687-8701, daily 6:30am-3:30pm; 3607 State St., Mon.-Fri. 6am-4pm, Sat. 7am-4pm, Sun. 7am-3pm).

Italian

Tre Lune (1151 Coast Village Rd., 805/969-2646, www.trelunesb.com, daily 7:30am-10pm, $15-37) feels like a classic, evoking the past with black-and-white photos of stars of the 1950s decorating the walls. The pizzas have three or four toppings, including Italian ingredients like prosciutto, pesto, and roasted eggplant, while the pastas might include ingredients like wild boar *ragù* or lobster. Breakfast

has lighter dishes, including frittatas or prosciutto and cantaloupe.

Latin American

The menu at **Cava Restaurant & Bar** (1212 Coast Village Rd., 805/969-8500, Mon.-Sat. 11am-10pm, Sun. 9am-10pm, $16-25) blends Mexican, Spanish, California, and South American flavors. Enjoy a homemade tamale trio, shrimp empanadas, posole, or grilled chicken in mole sauce. The outdoor patio overlooks West Coast Village Road, while the inviting dining room offers a fireplace for chilly nights.

Mexican

Perched right on Coast Village Road, **⟨ Los Arroyos** (1280 Coast Village Rd., 805/969-9059, www.losarroyos.net, Sun.-Thurs. 11am-9pm, Fri.-Sat. 11am-9:30pm, $9-17.50) is a semicasual Mexican restaurant. The menu goes far beyond taqueria fare, with crab enchiladas, seafood burritos, and rajas (tacos with grilled chilies, grilled onions, and cheese). The high-protein burrito is stuffed with lean filet mignon, avocado, and beans. Sit indoors at wooden tables or outside on the tiled patio.

New American

Located in the historic Montecito Inn, the **Montecito Cafe** (1295 Coast Village Rd., 805/969-3392, www.montecitocafe.com, daily 11:30am-2:30pm and 5:30pm-10pm, $10-28) makes everything in house—including the hamburger buns. People love the homemade lamb sausage and the goat cheese pancake appetizer with salmon and caviar. Other options include salad bowls, burgers, and pastas, along with seafood and meat entrées.

Treat yourself to a memorable meal at **The Stonehouse** (San Ysidro Ranch, 900 San Ysidro Lane, 805/565-1724, www.sanysidroranch.com, Mon.-Wed. 6pm-10pm, Thurs.-Sat. 11:30am-2pm and 6pm-10pm, Sun. 10am-2pm and 6pm-10pm, $41-68), the flagship restaurant of the San Ysidro Ranch luxury hotel. The dining room is located in a former 19th-century citrus packing building

SANTA BARBARA

© STUART THORNTON

Cava Restaurant & Bar

with an adjoining ocean-view deck. The small, elegant menu may include Maine lobster, herb-crusted rack of lamb, or local chanterelle mushrooms on house-made fettuccini.

Lucky's (1279 Coast Village Rd., 805/565-7540, http://luckys-steakhouse.com, Mon.-Fri. 5pm-10pm, Sat.-Sun. 9am-3pm and 5pm-10pm) is an old-school steak, seafood, and cocktails joint. The dinner menu starts with a $20 burger, hovers around $50 cuts of steak, and tops out with a $79 steamed Maine lobster. Most customers think the high price tag is worth it. Daily specials include meatloaf and filet mignon stroganoff.

Sushi

With colorful pools and drizzles of bright sauces, a plate of sushi at **C Sakana Sushi Bar & Japanese** (1046 Coast Village Rd., 805/565-2014, Sun.-Thurs. 5pm-9:30pm, Fri.-Sat. 5pm-10pm, sushi rolls $7.50-16.50) looks like a work of art. The sushi chefs are indeed artists, using unconventional ingredients like tempura snow crab legs and torched mozzarella while employing sauces like roasted jalapeño yogurt and basil coconut curry to ratchet up the flavor of their rolls. Located in a shoebox-size space in a Montecito strip mall, Sakana has wholly unique rolls like the habanero lobster melt, a baked flash of taste and mild heat caused by lobster tempura, mango, cilantro, spicy tuna, and avocado topped with truffle soy and creamy habanero sauce. They also offer "press boxes"—similar to sushi rolls but without the nori.

THE MESA

This neighborhood, east of downtown, is home to a handful of local favorites—restaurants that are worth the short drive.

Coffee and Tea

The Good Cup (1819 Cliff Dr., 805/963-8699, Mon.-Thurs. 6am-8pm, Fri.-Sun. 6am-6pm) is a favorite local hangout and coffee shop. Enjoy coffee, tea, blended drink, smoothie, sandwich, or, why not, a scoop of gelato while enjoying the free Wi-Fi and scouring the community bulletin board.

Mexican

Downtown Santa Barbara is not the only place with great taquerias. **Mexican Fresh** (315 Meigs Rd., 805/963-7492, www.mexicanfresh.com, daily 8am-9pm, $5-11) represents the Mesa with fresh ingredients. Go for the fish tacos, which use whatever has been recently caught. Other items include quesadillas, *tortas,* salads, and big meat and seafood plates. Dine in the restaurant's brightly colored interior or head out to their heated patio.

Seafood

The Boathouse (2981 Cliff Dr., 805/898-2628, www.sbfishhouse.com, Mon.-Fri. 7:30am-9pm, Sat.-Sun. 7:30am-10pm, $9-27) serves seafood staples like fried calamari, clam chowder, and oysters rockefeller just steps from the sand and surf of Arroyo Burro Beach (also known as Hendry's Beach). Entrée options include mesquite-grilled local white sea bass and *panko*-crusted Alaskan halibut. The seating is all about the views, from the outdoor patio

right on the beach or from the interior, where every seat offers a glimpse of the coast.

Spanish

Intimate and romantic, **Alcazar Tapas Bar** (1812 Cliff Dr., 805/962-0337, www.alcazartapasbar.com, Mon.-Wed. 5:30pm-10pm, Thurs.-Fri. 5:30pm-11pm, Sat. 8am-1pm and 5:30pm-11pm, Sun. 8am-1pm, $7-23) serves fine shareable plates and creative cocktails. The large list of veggie options includes tofu brioche, kale chips, and avocado hummus that are worth raving about. Bacon-wrapped dates, paella, and chicken mole will satisfy carnivores.

Thai

For a pad thai fix in the Mesa, visit **Meun Fan Thai** (1819 Cliff Dr., 805/882-9244, Mon.-Thurs. 11am-9:30pm, Fri.-Sat. 11am-10pm, Sun. 4pm-9:30pm, $9-16). This colorful and comfortable eatery also has spicy eggplant, broccoli beef, and three flavorful fish dishes. Lunch specials (Mon.-Fri. 11am-2:30pm) include an entrée, rice, and soup or salad. Paintings of Thailand decorate the walls.

Information and Services

MAPS AND VISITOR INFORMATION

The **Santa Barbara Conference and Visitors Bureau** (1601 Anacapa St., 805/966-9222, www.santabarbaraca.com) maintains an informative website and visitors center. The **Outdoor Santa Barbara Visitors Center** (Waterfront Center, 113 Harbor Way, 4th Fl., 805/884-1475, daily 11am-5pm) provides information about Channel Islands National Park, the Channel Islands National Marine Sanctuary, the Los Padres National Forest, and the City of Santa Barbara.

EMERGENCY SERVICES

Cottage Hospital (Bath St. and Pueblo St., 805/682-7111) is the only hospital in town and

has the only emergency room. In case of an emergency, call 911 immediately. The **Santa Barbara Police Department** (805/897-2335) is located at 215 East Figueroa Street.

NEWSPAPERS

As a major city, Santa Barbara has its own daily newspaper, the **Santa Barbara News Press** (www.newspress.com). Look for it in shops, on newsstands, and in your hotel or inn. Check the "Scene" and "Life" sections for information about entertainment, events, and attractions. The **Santa Barbara Independent** (www.independent.com) is the local free weekly that has a comprehensive events calendar.

LOCAL TV AND RADIO

KZSB (AM 1290) is the only local talk radio station, with a variety of local programming, traffic reports, local news, and world news from the BBC. Show topics include gardening, real estate, food, travel, and politics, all with a local perspective. **Channel 18** is the local community access TV channel, with way too much coverage of city hall meetings and various boards and commissions, like the Architectural Board of Review, but they also offer some local programming. **KEYT** (www.keyt.com) is the main TV station broadcasting from Santa Barbara (on channel 3 in town), where you can get the latest local, regional, and some national news, as well as local sports and weather. It is broadcast from what is called TV Hill, just above the harbor.

POSTAL SERVICES

The main branch of the **Post Office** (836 Anacapa St.) is located one block east of State Street. A second smaller **downtown branch** (1221 State St.) is in Victoria Court, at the back of the building. For those closer to Upper State is the **San Roque station** (3345 State St.). The main phone number for all three branches is 805/564-2226. With ongoing budget cuts, it's best to phone ahead to check on the ever-changing hours.

LAUNDRY

If the need arises, you can have your laundry done for you at **Launderland** (2636 De La Vina St., 805/687-8380) or use their coin-operated services. They have fast turnaround times and are very professional.

Getting There and Around

AIR

To reach Santa Barbara by air, fly into the **Santa Barbara Municipal Airport** (SBA, 500 Fowler Rd., 805/967-7111, www.flysba.com). A number of major commercial airlines fly into Santa Barbara, including United, Alaska/Horizon, Frontier, and American.

Airport Shuttles

Chances are you'll fly into Los Angeles or San Francisco and then connect to Santa Barbara. If you're coming in from LA and not connecting to Santa Barbara by air, the 90-mile drive takes about two hours. There are commercial shuttle vans and buses from LA, but keep in mind these will also take at least two hours, depending on traffic. **Santa Barbara Air Bus** (805/964-7759, www.santabarbaraairbus.com) runs between Los Angeles's LAX airport and Santa Barbara every day and will deliver you in comfort.

TRAIN

A more beautiful and peaceful way to get to Santa Barbara is by train. The **Amtrak** (800/872-7245, www.amtrak.com) *Coast* *Starlight* stops at the centrally located train station (209 State St.) daily in each direction on its way between Seattle and Los Angeles, and the *Pacific Surfliner* makes up to 10 stops daily on its route between San Luis Obispo and San Diego. Other Amtrak routes from points east connect to the *Coast Starlight* at Emeryville, in the Bay Area east of San Francisco, and to the *Coast Starlight* and *Pacific Surfliner* at Los Angeles.

CAR

Santa Barbara is located on U.S. 101, in this neck of the woods also known as the Pacific Coast Highway and El Camino Real. To head out to the Santa Ynez Valley and other local wine regions, take Highway 154 east of Santa Barbara. In Santa Barbara itself, expect fairly standard city driving, complete with traffic jams on weekdays and on beach access roads on weekends. Parking can be challenging, especially at the beach on sunny summer weekends. Expect to pay a premium for a good-to-mediocre parking spot, or to walk for several blocks. If possible, take the local public shuttle from the downtown area to the beach and leave your car elsewhere.

BUS

Greyhound (34 W. Carrillo St., 805/965-7551, www.greyhound.com) has a somewhat dingy terminal one block off State Street. It's convenient, however, as this is the main bus hub.

Santa Barbara has its own local transit authority. The **MTD Santa Barbara** (805/963-3364, www.sbmtd.gov, regular fare $1.75, waterfront service $0.25) runs the local buses, the Waterfront Shuttle, and the Downtown-Waterfront line. Have exact change to pay your fare when boarding the bus or shuttle; if you're going to change buses, ask the driver for a free transfer pass.

WALKING TOURS

Seeing Santa Barbara on foot is the best way to experience the city. The **Red Tile Walking Tour** (www.santabarbaraca.com) is a condensed 12-block self-guided tour of all the important buildings in town. You can download either a map version to print or a podcast version narrated by John O'Hurley of TV's *Seinfeld*. You'll see Casa de la Guerra, the County Courthouse, and the Presidio, among other defining buildings.

For a more structured tour, **Santa Barbara Walking Tours** (805/687-9255, www.santabarbarawalkingtours.com, $23) has a 90-minute docent-led tour of the visual art and history in town. It combines parts of the Red Tile tour but also shows you some of the beautiful paseos, tile work, and public art that's almost everywhere.

The **Architectural Foundation of Santa Barbara** (805/965-6307, www.afsb.org, $10) hosts two-hour-long docent-led tours of downtown Santa Barbara on the weekend, enlightening participants about the city's architectural styles, historic buildings, and landscape history. The **Saturday Tour** meets at the City Hall steps at De La Guerra Plaza at 10am and includes visits to the Casa de la Guerra, Lobero Theater, and the Hill-Carrillo Adobe. The **Sunday Tour** meets at the downtown library at 10am and goes to other architectural gems, including the Granada Theatre, the Arlington Theatre, and the U.S. Bankruptcy Court Building.

TROLLEY TOURS

If walking just isn't your thing, get an expanded overview of the city by riding through it. The best is the **Landshark** (805/683-7600, www.out2seesb.com, Nov.-Apr. daily noon and 2pm, May-Oct. daily noon, 2pm, and 4pm, adults $25, under age 10 $10), a live-narrated 90-minute tour on the Landshark, a 15-foot-high amphibious vehicle. You'll see most of the important buildings except the mission. On the plus side, on the last part of the tour the Landshark plunges into the ocean and turns into a boat, going past the breakwater for great views of the coast. It's fun and informative, and you can ask all the questions you want. More likely than not you'll see dolphins and seals at the very least. All Landshark tours depart from the entrance to Stearns Wharf.

The **Santa Barbara Trolley Company** (805/965-0353, www.sbtrolley.com, daily 10am-5:30pm, adults $19, under age 12 $8) offers another live narrated tour that includes the mission and other great locations like Butterfly Beach in Montecito and the bird refuge. Tours pick up and drop off at 15 different locations every 60 minutes; see the website for a comprehensive schedule.

TAXI CABS

Taxis are not abundant in town, nor are they in much of a rush; it's best to call for one. Assuming you do get a taxi, you're apt to get a leisurely cab ride to your destination. **Santa Barbara Checker Cab** (888/581-1110) is a safe bet.

STATE STREET TROLLEY

For just $0.25, you can ride the trolley the length of the waterfront or the length of State Street. Two electric shuttle bus routes (www.sbmtd.gov) serve the downtown corridor (State St.) and the waterfront (Cabrillo Blvd.) daily every half hour. Children under 45 inches tall can ride free, and free transfer is available between the Downtown Shuttle and the Waterfront Shuttle; just ask the driver.

Summerland

Located between Montecito and Carpinteria, Summerland clings to the side of sloping Ortega Ridge and offers views of the Pacific. Just an eight-mile drive from downtown Santa Barbara, it's a quiet community of just 1,500 residents that feels a world away from the nearby city. It's worth a morning or afternoon visit for a stroll down Lillie Lane, which has a handful of antiques stores and boutiques, and a visit to its underrated dog-friendly beach.

Founded in 1889 by spiritualist and entrepreneur H. L. Williams, Summerland at one time had its own community séance room, earning it the nickname "Spookville." Today, the only evidence of this era is Williams' abandoned yellow house, which—of course—is said to be haunted. The town's spooky bent changed in the 1890s when oil was discovered, and the Summerland Oil Field, the first offshore oil production facility in the western hemisphere, was built off the coast.

RECREATION
Summerland Beach (parking in Lookout Park) is a long, broad sandy beach that doesn't get as crowded as other Santa Barbara-area beaches. The Channel Islands block most of the ocean swells, so the water is ideal for waders and children. Summerland Beach is also dog friendly, which draws a lot of locals taking their pets for a walk. The packed sand at low tide is a great spot for an ocean-side run or jog.

The four-acre county-run **Lookout Park** (805/568-2465, www.countyofsb.org, daily 8am-sunset) is situated on a bluff over Summerland Beach. The grassy public space has a playground, a barbecue area, a sand volleyball court, and restrooms. A plaque explains the history of the oil production facility built offshore. To reach the park, take U.S. 101's Summerland exit and turn right into the park. From Lillie Avenue, head south on Evans Avenue until it runs into the park.

SHOPPING
Antiques
Summerland is known for its antiques stores. A good place to start browsing is the **Summerland Antique Collective** (2192 Ortega Hill Rd., 805/565-3189, daily 10am-5pm), a

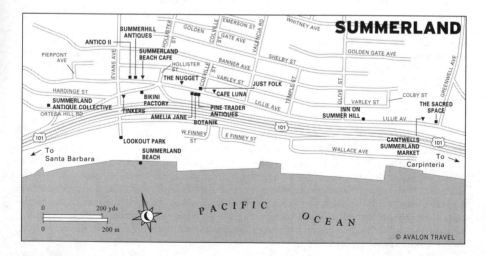

© AVALON TRAVEL

Summerland Beach is a great place to escape the crowds.

series of rooms showcasing the antiques of 30 collectors. Shop here for jewelry, furniture, knickknacks, and art.

If you want to focus in on European antiques, **Summerhill Antiques** (2280 Lillie Ave., 805/969-3366, www.summerhill-antiques. com, Mon.-Sat. 11am-5pm, Sun. noon-5pm) is the place for Old World chandeliers, furniture, and lamps. Upstairs from Summerhill Antiques, **Antico II** (2280 Lillie Ave., 2nd Fl., 805/565-4899, www.anticoii.com, Mon.-Sat. 11am-5pm, Sun. noon-5pm) specializes in French country furniture and clocks. The showroom at **Pine Trader Antiques** (2345 Lillie Ave., 805/845-2618, www.pinetrader. com, Tues.-Sat. 11am-5pm, Sun. noon-5pm) is set up to look like an immaculately decorated home. Come here for antique Irish and French country furniture. Sure, **Mediterranee Antiques** (2500 Lillie Ave., 805/695-0910, www.mediterraneeantiques.com, Tues.-Sat. 11am-4pm) has European antiques and art. But this shop distinguishes itself from other

Summerland antiques dealers with Latin American merchandise, from Peruvian gilded mirrors to Mexican fine art pieces.

Art Galleries

If you're interested in purchasing a saxophone made out of tin kitchen pieces or a bicycle from the 1800s, **Just Folk** (2346 Lillie Ave., 805/969-7118, www.justfolk.com, Wed.-Sat. 10am-5pm, Sun. 11am-5pm, Mon.-Tues. by appointment) is definitely worth checking out. Even if you're not, this two-floor gallery is worth visiting. It's like a museum of American folk art and outsider art. Pieces include the works of Howard Finster, an evangelical preacher who painted on wood, burlap, and metal and who gained some notoriety for creating album covers for rock bands R.E.M. and the Talking Heads. He was also the inspiration for the R.E.M. song "Maps and Legends."

Home Furnishings

Botanik (2329 Lillie Ave., 805/565-3831, www.

© STUART THORNTON

Summerland is known for its antique stores.

botanikinc.com, Mon.-Sat. 10am-5:30pm, Sun. 11am-4pm) is a home-furnishings and garden store located in a 1920s Victorian. It sells rattan furniture, rare orchids, and succulents as well as books. Next door, **Amelia Jane** (2325 Lillie Ave., 805/565-7766, www.littleameliajane.com, Mon.-Sat. 10am-5:30pm, Sun. 11am-4pm) specializes in vintage and eclectic decor, books, toys, and clothes for babies and toddlers.

Clothing and Accessories

"Bohemian elegance" is the goal at **Bonita** (2330 Lillie Ave., 805/565-3848, www.bonitasummerland.com, Mon.-Sat. 10am-6pm, Sun. 11am-5pm), according to its owner. The boutique focuses on women's clothing, jewelry, shoes, and accessories. **The Bikini Factory** (2275 Ortega Hill Rd., 805/969-2887, http://bikinifactory.com, Mon.-Sat. 10am-6pm, Sun. 11am-4pm) has hundreds of pieces of women's swimwear, including Brazilian brands, one pieces, and mix-and-match items.

Specialty Shops

The Sacred Space (2594 Lillie Ave., 805/565-5535, www.sacredspace.us, daily 11am-5pm) sells Asian artifacts, garden art, statues of deities, crystals, and candles. Even if you are not in the mood to shop, come visit for the hot tea and a relaxing walk around the garden with its tropical plants, sculptures, shrines, and peaceful waters.

ACCOMMODATIONS
Over $250

The only place to stay in Summerland is the **Inn on Summer Hill & Spa** (2520 Lillie Ave., 805/969-9998, www.innonsummerhill.com, $229-429). It's a nice place where every guest room is unique. Each has a gas fireplace, a soaking tub, and a balcony or patio with views of the ocean and the offshore Channel Islands. Canopy beds offer another layer of luxury. The spa offers massages and facials ($110-175), and there's an eight-person outdoor hot tub. The friendly staff serves a full hot breakfast in the morning and wine and appetizers in the afternoon. A king suite with two baths can accommodate groups of four or five. The downside of spending the night here is the noise from the nearby freeway.

FOOD

One of Santa Barbara County's most renowned burger joints, **Tinkers** (2275 Ortega Hill Rd., 805/969-1970, daily 11am-8pm, $4-9) is little more than a shack with a counter overlooking the grill and a small seating area out back. In addition to burgers, the menu has chicken sandwiches, tacos, fries, and onion rings, but by far the most popular item is the sourdough bacon cheeseburger, a delicious mess of beef, bacon, and cheese between two grilled slabs of sourdough, cut in half to make it more manageable. You'll still need a tree's worth of napkins to clean yourself up after this meal.

A local landmark for over 30 years, the **Summerland Beach Café** (2294 Lillie Ave., 805/969-1019, www.summerlandbeachcafe.

com, Mon.-Fri. 7am-3pm, Sat.-Sun. 7am-4pm, $8-13) serves hearty home-style breakfasts and lunches. Wake up with a crab-cake eggs benedict or an omelet. Breakfast is served all day; lunch options include salads, burgers, and sandwiches. Dine in one of the café's many rooms or on its multitiered front porch, where dogs are also welcome.

If you're looking for healthier fare, try **Café Luna** (2354 Lillie Ave., 805/695-8780, Mon.-Sat. 7am-5pm, Sun. 7:30am-5pm, $8-14). The range of vegetarian options includes a tabbouleh wrap and a hot portobello mushroom sandwich. Carnivores can opt for a salmon eggs benedict or a hot Cuban sandwich.

There aren't many options for dining in Summerland after dark. One is **The Nugget** (2318 Lillie Ave., 805/969-6135, Sun.-Thurs. 11am-9pm, Fri.-Sat. 11am-9:30pm, $9-23), an Old West saloon; Look for the wooden Indian statue out front. The bar and adjacent dining room are decorated with mounted animal heads that glare down on you as you eat your burger or pulled pork sandwich.

INFORMATION AND SERVICES
There aren't many services in Summerland, in part because it's so close to Santa Barbara. You can take advantage of **Cantwells Summerland Market** (2580 Lillie Ave., 805/969-5893, Mon.-Sat. 6:30am-8pm, Sun. 7am-7pm), which has a deli, and the local **Post Office** (2245 Lillie Ave., 805/565-7984, www.usps.com).

GETTING THERE AND AROUND
Summerland is less than 10 miles south of Santa Barbara on U.S. 101. There's only one exit for the community. The **Santa Barbara MTD** (805/963-3366, http://sbmtd.gov) has a Carpinteria-bound bus that makes a stop in Summerland at the corner of Lillie Avenue and Evans Avenue.

Summerland is small, so it's possible to park your car on Lillie Avenue and walk to all the antiques stores and restaurants. To get to Summerland Beach, take the Summerland exit from U.S. 101 and turn right into Lookout Park. From Lillie Avenue, head south on Evans Avenue until it runs into the park. There's a path from the park down to the beach.

Carpinteria

Twelve miles south of Santa Barbara, Carpinteria is a relaxed, unassuming beach town, one of the few in California that has managed to avoid overdevelopment and hold on to its unique character. It's centered around the palm tree-lined main thoroughfare, Linden Avenue, which leads right to the gentle sandy beach. The great thing about Linden Avenue is that it is not overrun with chain stores or upscale establishments. It still has its longtime eclectic mix of locally owned businesses that include The Spot, a burger shack, and The Palms, a unique steak house and bar that dates back to 1912. The town is also home to some naturally occurring tar pits, a harbor seal rookery, a fine state beach, and one of the state's most revered surfing spots, Rincon. It's a great place to come for a day of sun, waves, and beach life.

SIGHTS
Carpinteria State Beach
The shallow, gently sloping sands at **Carpinteria State Beach** (5361 6th St., 805/968-1033, www.parks.ca.gov, daily 7am-sunset, day-use $10, camping $35-65) have given it a reputation as "the safest beach in the world." With 4,000 feet of ocean frontage, the beach is broad and sandy on its west end and studded with rocks and tide pools as you head east. At the east end, tar drips down the hillsides like melted chocolate, leaving giant globs in the sand. The indigenous Chumash people

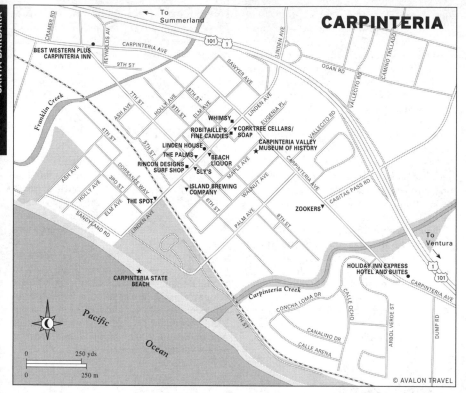

gathered these naturally occurring tar deposits to seal their canoes and water baskets (the activity that gave the area its name). Many plant and animal fossils have been found in these tar pits, and this tar was used to pave the region's first roads. Today, the beach is popular for tide-pooling, surfing, and surf fishing. It's also one of the most popular camping destinations in the California State Parks system.

Carpinteria Bluffs Nature Preserve

Once the site of a proposed oil refinery and then a housing development, this 52-acre parcel of land is now protected as the **Carpinteria Bluffs Nature Preserve** (end of Ballard Ave., www.carpinteriabluffs.org). Sandy paths lead around the bluffs to views of the Channel Islands. Located east of Carpinteria State

Beach, it's the largest undeveloped coastal space between Santa Barbara and the Ventura County line, and it's a popular spot for dog walking, bird-watching, strolling, and easy hiking. Hikers can walk from the Carpinteria Bluffs Nature Preserve to an overlook with views of the Carpinteria Seal Sanctuary.

Carpinteria Seal Sanctuary

One of only four harbor seal colonies in Southern California, the **Carpinteria Seal Sanctuary** is home to almost 100 adult seals. An overlook with a bluff-top bench offers views of the seals lounging on the beach below. Access the viewing area by walking in on the **Coastal Vista Trail** from Carpinteria State Beach to the north or from Carpinteria Bluffs Nature Preserve from the south. The beach is closed December 1-May 31, when the seals typically give birth to their young. Volunteers patrol the sanctuary to ensure the seals' safety.

Carpinteria Valley Museum of History

The **Carpinteria Valley Museum of History** (956 Maple Ave., 805/684-3112, www.carpinteriahistoricalmuseum.org, Tues.-Sat. 1pm-4pm, donation) tells the history of the region through three groups that settled here: the indigenous Chumash people, early Spanish and Mexican settlers, and American and immigrant pioneers. Museum exhibits display everything from Chumash artifacts to Victorian home furnishings.

SPORTS AND RECREATION
C Surfing

Carpinteria can lay claim to **Rincon** (U.S. 101 at Bates Rd., on the Ventura County-Santa Barbara County line), one of the most legendary surf breaks in all of California. Known as the "Queen of the Coast," it's considered California's best right point break, with long waves that hold up for as long as 300 yards. If it's firing, you'll also most likely be sharing Rincon with lots of other surfers. You might even see revered three-time world champion surfer Tom Curren in the lineup.

There are actually three waves at Rincon. The Cove is the very popular inside section that starts halfway up the point and can peel down the line all the way to the in-shore rocks. Less crowded, The Indicator is the slower moving wave at the top of the point. The Rivermouth is the unpredictable section that connects The Indicator wave to The Cove's wave. Unfortunately, the creek here has been known to dump polluted water into the lineup.

Rincon truly comes alive during the winter months when the large winter swells roll into the area. On these days, the surf gets as crowded as a Southern California freeway. If you have never been before, consider surfing Rincon first on an off-day (when the waves are smaller or the weather isn't the best) so that you don't have to deal with the crowds. Even nonsurfers will enjoy the scenic walk along

the small dirt path from the parking lot to the cove. Who knows? Maybe you'll see a pro surfer catching an amazing ride.

Not nearly as beloved as Rincon, **Tarpits** is an inconsistent beach and reef break at the southern end of Carpinteria State Beach, where naturally occurring tar seeps into the sand and bluffs. You can park in a state park parking lot right near the break.

Bird-Watching

Birders flock to the **Carpinteria Salt Marsh** (end of Ash St., http://carpinteria.ucnrs.org, free docent-led tours Sat. 10am), a 230-acre estuary that hosts some 200 bird species, including rarities like Belding's Savannah sparrow and the light-footed clapper rail. More than half of the land is owned by the University of California, while the other portion is owned and operated by the City of Carpinteria. The marsh is located just west of Carpinteria State Beach. To access it, drive down Linden Avenue toward the ocean. Turn right onto 3rd Street, and drive until it ends at Ash Avenue; turn left, and park on the street. The section of the marsh along Ash Avenue has nature paths, platforms, and interpretive plaques.

Spectator Sports

Believe it or not, Carpinteria is a wonderful place to take in the fast-moving sport of polo. The third-oldest polo facility in the country, **Santa Barbara Polo and Racquet Club** (3300 Via Real, 805/684-6683, www.sbpolo.com, Sun. 1pm and 3pm, $10), hosts ongoing polo tournaments from early May to mid-October. If one of the Sunday matches inspires you to learn how to play the team horseback game, contact the **Santa Barbara Polo School** (805/729-2812).

ENTERTAINMENT AND EVENTS
Bars and Clubs

Located in an industrial building by the train tracks, **Island Brewing Company** (5049 6th St., 805/745-8272, www.islandbrewingcompany.com, Mon.-Fri. 2pm-9pm, Sat.-Sun.

11am-9pm) is a craft brewery serving up five year-round beers, including the popular Island Blonde, as well as a few unique seasonal offerings like Avocado Honey Ale. The no-frills atmosphere, with the interior dominated by brewing equipment resting on a concrete floor, keeps the focus on the beer. You can also sip your suds on the outdoor patio, within view of passing trains and the ocean in the distance.

If you prefer wine to beer, head over to **Corktree Cellars** (910 Linden Ave., 805/684-1400, www.corktreecellars.com, Tues.-Thurs. 11:30am-9pm, Fri.-Sat. 11:30am-10pm, Sun. 10am-9pm), which serves eight different flights of wine. Each flight includes three three-ounce pours. Do your tasting at the concrete bar, the comfy couch area, or in the dining room, where you can also order up a sampling of artisanal cheeses, tapas, or an entrée.

Festivals and Events

The big annual event in Carpinteria is the **California Avocado Festival** (early Oct., 805/684-0038, http://avofest.com). The three-day festival celebrates the fruit and its significant place in local agriculture. Among the tasty offerings are a Best Guacamole contest and the creation of the world's largest vat of guacamole.

Local vendors sell fresh produce at the **Carpinteria Farmers Market** (800 block of Linden Ave., summer Thurs. 3pm-6:30pm, winter Thurs. 3pm-6pm), which takes over one block of Linden Avenue every Thursday.

SHOPPING

Linden Avenue is a pleasant place to sample from some of Carpinteria's homegrown businesses. **Robitaille's Fine Candies** (900 Linden Ave., 805/684-9340, www.robitaillescandies.com, Mon.-Sat. 10am-5:30pm, Sun. 10am-3pm) stocks chocolates, fudge, and brittles. They have the distinction of providing the mints for the 50th Presidential Inauguration. Turtles, caramels, clusters, molded chocolates, and 10 flavors of fudge are made on-site.

Another Linden Avenue original, **SOAP** (910 Linden Ave., 805/684-6695, http://soap-carpinteria.com, Mon.-Sat. 10am-5pm, Sun.

noon-4pm) brings an Asian flair to everything from bath products to kimono-style robes. Vintage boutique **Whimsy** (962 Linden Ave., 805/684-1222, daily 11am-5pm) specializes in shabby chic furniture and other antique finds. There's also a second Carpinteria location (5042 7th St., 805/684-7211, daily 11am-5pm).

Rincon Designs Surf Shop (659 Linden Ave., 805/684-2413, http://rincondesigns.net, Mon.-Sat. 9:30am-6pm, Sun. 10am-5pm) has been a Carpinteria fixture for over 30 years. Surfboard shaper Matt Moore makes his famous surfboards right in the back of the shop. Rincon Designs also rents boards and wetsuits.

CAMPING

With 216 campsites, **Carpinteria State Beach** (5361 6th St., 805/968-1033, www.parks.ca.gov, camping $35-65) is one of the most popular campgrounds in the California State Parks system. Reservations are necessary for the summer months along with weekends and holidays. Reservations for summer campsites may need to be made as far as seven months in advance. The park has four campground loops, with the tent sites just a bit more than arm's length from one another. The campground's amenities include picnic tables, outdoor showers, RV hookups, telephones, and close proximity to the beach; Linden Avenue, with its restaurants, shops, and a grocery store, is just a few blocks walk away. Everything you need is within walking distance. The only drawback is the nearby train tracks, which mean that trains occasionally rattle by.

ACCOMMODATIONS

Unfortunately, Carpinteria doesn't have any stellar lodging options. Possibilities in town include a few chain hotels and some local establishments with mixed reviews.

$150-250

The **Holiday Inn Express Hotel & Suites Carpinteria** (5606 Carpinteria Ave., 805/566-9499, www.ihg.com, $135-186) offers what you would expect from the chain, including studio suites and deluxe two-room suites with microwaves and fridges. Other features include an outdoor pool, a business center, a fitness room, and a complimentary breakfast bar. Another option is the **Best Western Plus Carpinteria Inn** (4558 Carpinteria Ave., 805/684-0473, http://bestwesterncalifornia. com, $130-250). guest rooms have fridges and coffeemakers, while the grounds feature a tropical courtyard, an outdoor heated pool, and a hot tub. If you are traveling with a large group, the **Linden House** (789 Linden Ave., 805/574-0031, $350) is a three-bedroom vacation rental that can accommodate six guests. A stay includes complimentary use of the house's beach cruisers.

FOOD

You can't complain if your steak is burned or seasoned wrong at **The Palms** (701 Linden Ave., 805/684-3811, http://thepalmscarpinteria.com, Mon.-Sat. 5pm-10pm, Sun. 4:30pm-9:30pm, $7-27). That's because since 1968, this one-of-a-kind steak house has allowed diners to order up a raw piece of steak, chicken, fish, or lamb, then season it themselves with a selection of sauces and spices before tossing it on the indoor grill. Sure, you can also get the staff to cook your food, but then you'd miss out on the experience of grilling your own dinner and bonding with your fellow diners by the grill. You can also take advantage of the $7 all-you-can-eat salad bar, with homemade croutons and sides like baked potatoes and beans. The Palms building has been a landmark in Carpinteria since 1912; it has served as a hotel, a restaurant, a beer bar, a bank, and a post office.

Another local favorite is **The Spot** (389 Linden Ave., 805/684-6311, Mon. 10am-6pm, Tues.-Thurs. and Sun. 10am-7pm, Fri.-Sat. 10am-8pm, $4-7). This shack serves up ever-popular burgers along with shrimp po' boys, tacos, chili cheese fries, and salads (which one of these things doesn't belong with the others?). Throwback restaurant and bar **Sly's** (686 Linden Ave., 805/684-6666, www.slysonline.com, Sun. 9am-3pm and 5pm-9pm, Mon.-Thurs. 11:30am-2:30pm and 5pm-9pm, Fri. 11:30am-2:30pm and 5pm-10pm, Sat. 9am-3pm and 5pm-10pm, $12-50) advertises its "seafood, steaks, and cocktails." Variations include steak tartare, chicken livers in marsala, and classic cocktail concoctions like sazeracs, sidecars, and gimlets. Blue-plate specials might include gumbo and bouillabaisse. Another Carpinteria mainstay is the oddly named **Zookers** (5404 Carpinteria Ave., 805/684-8893, Mon.-Thurs. 11:30am-3pm and 5pm-9pm, Fri.-Sat. 11:30am-3pm and 5pm-9:30pm, $10-27). The popular shrimp and scallop tostada is a standout on a dinner menu of seafood, meat dishes, pastas, and entrée-size salads. There's also a daily fresh fish special.

Just one exit north of Carpinteria, **The Garden Market** (3811 Santa Clause Lane, 805/745-5505, www.gardenmarketsb.com, Mon.-Fri. 8am-6pm, Sat.-Sun. 8am-10pm, $6-11) is worth a detour off U.S. 101. It's a market; it's a deli; it's a coffee shop; and it's an eatery with a dining spot on a patio in a succulent garden. Enjoy one of the market's breakfast *ciabattas,* tasty smoothies, lunch sandwiches, or salads to eat here or take out.

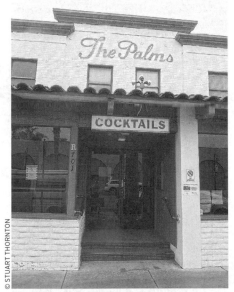

© STUART THORNTON

The Palms restaurant

Yes, **Beach Liquor** (794 Linden Ave., 805/684-2919, Sun.-Thurs. 8am-9pm, Fri.-Sat. 8am-10pm, $4-8) is a liquor store, but the counter in the back serves up some surprisingly great Mexican food. The burritos are so good that they have been hyped in the *New York Times*. Everything is freshly made, including tostadas, tacos, quesadillas, and fajitas. Come before noon for the superb breakfast burrito with meat, eggs, cheese, and mashed potatoes. It's the best I've ever had.

INFORMATION AND SERVICES

On weekdays, stop into the **Carpinteria Valley Chamber of Commerce** (1056-B Eugenia Place, 805/684-5479, www.carpinteriachamber.org, Mon.-Fri. 9am-4pm) for information, brochures, and guides.

Carpinteria is home to the outpatient health care provider **Samsun Clinic** (4806 Carpinteria Ave., 805/566-5080, www.sansumclinic.org). For serious injuries, head to the **Santa Barbara Cottage Hospital** (400 W. Pueblo St., 805/682-7111, www.cottagehealthsystem.org).

GETTING THERE AND AROUND

Carpinteria is just 12 miles south of Santa Barbara along U.S. 101. The *Pacific Surfliner* by **Amtrak** (800/872-7245, www.amtrak.com) also makes 10 stops daily at the platform (475 Linden Ave. at 5th St.) in Carpinteria headed to points both north and south.

Parking is relatively easy: Linden Avenue has lots of street parking, while the ocean end of the thoroughfare has a small free parking lot offering access to the beach. On crowded weekends, you might have to park away from the beach or Linden Avenue on a side street and walk to your destination.

Isla Vista and Goleta

The kids have definitely taken over Isla Vista, an unincorporated enclave located on a plateau above the beach. It's home to the University of California, Santa Barbara, and many of its students, so expect bookstores, bars, coffee shops, and restaurants focused on cheap staples like pizza, burritos, and sandwiches. The streets teem with bicycles and skateboards.

Nearby, Goleta is the less flashy, working-class brother of scenic Santa Barbara, eight miles to the east. Instead of Spanish Colonial Revival architecture and visitor-friendly attractions you'll find subdivisions, strip malls, and chain stores. Just incorporated as a city in 2002, Goleta is worth a visit for a handful of sights, including the Goleta Beach County Park, the Goleta Butterfly Grove, and the South Coast Railroad Museum.

Goleta is also home to the Santa Barbara Airport, and it has a handful of lodging options that can be less expensive than those in nearby Santa Barbara, even though it's just a 15-minute drive to State Street.

SIGHTS
University of California, Santa Barbara

The **University of California, Santa Barbara** (UCSB, 552 University Rd., 805/893-8000,

GOLETA

© STUART THORNTON

Isla Vista

www.ucsb.edu) has a student body of over 20,000 students on its 1,000-acre campus right on the Pacific. You can take a 1.5-hour campus walking tour weekdays at noon and 2pm by reservation. Another reason to visit the campus is the **Art, Design & Architecture Museum** (use Parking Structure 22, 805/893-2951, www.museum.ucsb.edu, Wed.-Sun. noon-5pm, free), which focuses on the development of Southern California architecture from the late 19th century to the mid-20th century. The museum draws from an archive of more than one million architectural drawings along with papers, photos, models, decorative objects, and furniture. Exhibits include vintage photographs and drawings from the Old Masters that date as far back as the 16th century. Past exhibits have focused on the works of Francisco Goya and local artist Channing Peake.

Rancho La Patera and Stow House

Tour Goleta Valley's rich agricultural heritage at the **Rancho La Patera and Stow House** (304 N. Los Carneros Rd., 805/681-7216, www.stowhouse.com, Sat.-Sun. 1pm-4pm, Mon.-Fri. by appointment, adults $8, under age 12 free), the former site of a ranch known for lemon trees, almonds, walnuts, and other crops. While much its 1,042 acres were subdivided and developed in the 1960s, the house, gardens, and other historic structures have been preserved by the Goleta Valley Historical Society. Take a guided tour of the house and wander through the garden, which includes exotic species like the lemon-scented gum tree, the wine palm, and giant bamboo. There's also a redwood tree that was planted on the grounds way back in 1874.

Goleta Monarch Butterfly Grove

Thousands of migrating monarch butterflies visit the **Goleta Monarch Butterfly Grove** (Sperling Preserve, Ellwood Mesa, 805/961-7500, www.goletabutterflygrove.com) each year between November and February. The grove owes its existence to the actions of one man: Olive oil producer Ellwood Cooper began growing and selling eucalyptus seedlings on this plot of land in the late 1800s. The remnants of his eucalyptus nursery created an ideal habitat for monarch butterflies. Today, docents are available (Nov.-Feb. Sat.-Sun. 11am-2pm) to answer questions about the orange-and-black insects. The 137-acre parcel also includes trails and beach access.

South Coast Railroad Museum

All aboard, railroad and train fans! Next stop is the **South Coast Railroad Museum** (300 N. Los Carneros Rd., 805/964-3540, www.goletadepot.org, Thurs.-Fri. 1pm-4pm, Sat.-Sun. 11am-4pm, free). Appropriately housed in an old railroad station, the museum focuses on the impact the railroad industry has had on the surrounding region. The star attraction is the miniature train ($1.50 per ride) that takes you on a 0.5-mile ride around the museum's grounds. Other highlights include a 300-square-foot model railroad exhibit and a theater that screens train-related films.

SHOPPING

Goleta's **Camino Real Marketplace** (7004 Market Place Dr., 805/685-3458) has all the big guys: Costco, Best Buy, and BevMo, as well as a movie theater and range of restaurants, including Chili's and the local brewpub Hollister Brewing Company. It also hosts the **Goleta Farmers Market** (Thurs. 3pm-6:30pm, Sat. 10am-2pm).

For over 30 years, **The Chocolate Gallery** (5705 Calle Real, 805/967-4688, http://chocolategallery.com, Mon.-Sat. 10am-6pm, Sun. noon-5pm) has been personalizing and crafting chocolate into novelty shapes, from baseball mitts to sports cars. It also sells congratulatory and birthday cards made entirely out of chocolate.

Miss Behavin' (6551 Trigo Rd., Isla Vista, 805/968-2840, www.shopmissbehavin.com, Mon.-Sat. 11:30am-7:30pm, Sun. noon-6pm)

is a small women's clothing and accessories store in Isla Vista. Stop in for floral shorts, summer dresses, and bikinis.

BEACHES

At the base of the UCSB campus, **Goleta Beach County Park** (5986 Sandspit Rd., 805/568-2461, www.countyofsb.org, daily 8am-sunset) is a long, sometimes kelp-strewn beach. A bike path connects it with nearby UCSB, making it a popular spot with students. There's a grassy area partially shaded by trees, with a small jungle gym for the kids. The 1,500-foot wooden pier is popular for fishing, and the low breaks make it an easy entry point for kayakers. You can also launch small boats from the pier on weekends, when a crane lowers boats into the water (there is no launch ramp). On the mountain-facing side along the bike path are a few platforms for viewing birds in the slough behind the beach. Facilities include picnic tables, barbecue pits, horseshoes, and multiple restrooms. Food is available on-site at the **Beachside Bar & Café** (5905 Sandspit Rd., 805/964-7881, www.beachside-barcafe.com).

SPORTS AND RECREATION
Surfing

Students at UCSB are lucky enough to have their own point break, **Campus Point.** It probably increases enrollment. It needs a big swell to break, but when it breaks, expect to see the student body hit the water; it's right across the street from the campus. At the UCSB entrance gate, take a left and park in the parking lot across from the dormitory, where you will be charged a small fee for parking.

In nearby Goleta, **Surf Country** (109 B Fairview Ave., 805/683-4450, http://surfcountry.net, Mon.-Sat. 10am-7pm, Sun. 10am-5pm) rents soft-top surfboards, regular surfboards, body boards, and wetsuits.

Golf

Before taking a swing, take in the magnificent view of the Pacific and the Channel Islands at the **Glen Annie Golf Club** (405 Glen Annie

Goleta Beach County Park

Rd., 805/968-6400, www.glenanniegolf.com, greens fees Mon.-Fri. $57, Sat.-Sun. and holidays $72), an environmentally conscious 18-hole course located due north of Isla Vista. The club has worked with Audubon International to create wildlife habitats on its land. Who knows what you might see when you're out walking the lush, hilly par-72 course? The on-site **Frog Bar & Grill** (Mon.-Fri. 11:30am-2pm, $8-14) draws any number of non-golfers up to Glen Annie for lunch, with California cuisine that's a far cry from most clubhouse fare. Come for the golf, stay for the food.

A less expensive option is the **Ocean Meadows Golf Club** (6925 Whitter Dr., 805/968-6814, www.oceanmeadowsgolfclub.com, greens fees Mon.-Fri. $20, Sat.-Sun. $22), with a nine-hole course that passes by a wetlands area.

Disc Golf

Toss the disc around at the 18-hole **Evergreen Disc Golf Course**, which winds through trees in a city park, the Evergreen Open Space (Evergreen Dr.). While there are no signs for the course in the park, a downloadable map (www.evergreendiscgolf.com) shows where the next tee is located. To reach the Evergreen Disc Golf Course, take the Glen Annie Road exit from U.S. 101 toward Storke Road. Then turn right on Glen Annie Road, followed by a left on Cathedral Oaks Road. Turn left again on Evergreen Drive before taking the first right onto Forest Drive. The course is on the left.

ENTERTAINMENT AND EVENTS
Bars

The **Old Town Tavern** (261 Orange Ave., 805/967-2403, Mon.-Tues. 11am-midnight, Wed.-Sat. 11am-2am, Sun. 10am-midnight) fills up with crowds of UCSB students on Wednesday, which is College Night. On other nights, this dive bar is a nice place to have a drink, play pool, or sit out front on the wooden deck. Beers are available on tap, with Colt 45 malt liquor and Schlitz High Gravity in cans for less discerning patrons or those who drink ironically.

If you want to avoid the rowdy college crowds, head to **Mercury Lounge** (5871 Hollister Ave., 805/967-0907, Mon.-Fri. 5pm-2am, Sat.-Sun. 7pm-2am), a comfortable, hip bar with a pool table and eclectic art hung on the walls for your appreciation. Recline on the couches indoors or head out back to the small smoker's patio. There are DJs spinning music every Thursday night, and the bartenders offer to hot microwave popcorn when you order your drinks.

Zodo's (5925 Calle Real, 805/967-0128, www.zodos.com, Tues.-Sat. 8:30am-2am, Sun.-Mon. 8:30am-midnight) is a brightly colored complex that can entertain kids of all ages for hours. This big, modern facility has an arcade for kids and a bowling alley for competitive types. Adults can enjoy the tap house, with an impressive list of 40 imported and craft beers on tap. Check out the two daily happy hours (4pm-7pm and 10pm-midnight). There's also a grill that serves half-pound burgers, sandwiches, and wraps.

Performing Arts

Like any respectable place of higher learning, the **University of California, Santa Barbara,** gets its share of arts and music events. On campus, **Campbell Hall** (Mesa Rd. and University Plaza, 805/893-3535, https://artsandlectures. sa.ucsb.edu) has had a range of events from concerts by blues legend Taj Mahal to lectures about food from Alice Waters.

Festivals and Events

Goleta can boast not one but two weekly farmers markets. One is on Thursday at the **Camino Real Center** (805/962-5354, www.sbfarmersmarket.org, 7004 Marketplace Dr., Thurs. 3pm-6pm), and the other is on Sunday at the **Camino Real Marketplace** (805/962-5354, www.sbfarmersmarket.org, Storke Rd. and Hollister Ave., Sun. 10am-3pm).

Goleta celebrates its famed local produce at the **California Lemon Festival** (Girsh Park, Phelps Rd., 805/967-2500, www.lemonfestival. com) each fall. Attractions include pie-eating contests, live music, plenty of vendors, and the popular **Goleta Fall Classic Car Show** (which hopefully doesn't include any lemons).

ACCOMMODATIONS

The accommodations in Goleta mostly consist of a few chain motels and hotels along U.S. 101 and near the airport. The exception is the upscale Bacara Resort & Spa.

Under $150

If you just need an inexpensive place to lay your head for an evening, the **Motel 6 Santa Barbara-Goleta** (5897 Calle Real, 805/964-3596, www.motel6.com, $80-125) has surprising ultramodern decor in the guest rooms. There's also a small pool and a laundry facility. It's next door to Zodo's bowling alley, arcade, and restaurant, if you feel like hitting some pins or downing some suds.

$150-250

The **Hampton Inn Goleta** (5665 Hollister Ave., 805/681-9800, http://hamptoninn1.hilton. com, $169-369) strives to make you feel right at home. In-room amenities include fridges, microwaves, and coffeemakers. There's also an outdoor pool and a fitness room. The **Best Western South Coast Inn** (5620 Calle Real, 805/967-3200, http://bestwesterncalifornia. com, $130-300) is a good bet for an overnight stay in Goleta. Take advantage of the pool, hot tub, and complimentary full breakfast with eggs. The hotel also offers a shuttle to the nearby Santa Barbara Airport.

Over $250

Once you check into the **Bacara Resort & Spa** (8301 Hollister Ave., 805/968-0100, www.bacararesort.com, from $450), there's little reason to leave. Spread out like a Mediterranean village over 78 acres of oceanfront property, Bacara has three heated saline pools, four tennis courts, four restaurants, a spa, and gardens.

There is also a cliff-top walking path and beach access. All of the luxury accommodations include deep soaking tubs, marble showers, and private balconies or patios, many with ocean views. The guest rooms are all an impressive 450 square feet in size, while the suites top out at a whopping 925 square feet.

The best known of Bacara's restaurants is **Miró** (805/571-3018, Sun.-Thurs. 7am-3pm and 5:30pm-9:30pm, Fri.-Sat. 7am-3pm and 5pm-9:30pm, $18-36), a stylish venue named for Joan Miró that displays two of the Spanish artist's original sculptures. In addition to its cuisine, Miró is known for its wine cellar, with over 12,000 bottles. The Sunday brunch (Sun. 10:30am-1:30pm, adults $60, ages 5-12 $30) is a monstrous buffet of seafood, egg dishes, waffles, desserts, and bottomless mimosas.

FOOD
Cafés
Fresco Café North (5940 Calle Real, 805/962-8999, www.fresconorth.com, Sun.-Thurs. 10:30am-8pm, Fri. 10:30am-9pm, $9-15) is a casual bistro serving healthy organic and natural food that will fill you up. The menu includes salads, tortilla wraps, and sandwiches like the ahi club triple decker with bacon and avocado.

Indian
The India Club (5701 Calle Real, 805/967-7171, daily 11:30am-3pm and 4:30pm-9pm, $10-14) is a casual Indian eatery in a strip mall where you order your meal at the counter. Some people rave about the lamb tikka masala, while others hype up the chicken malabar, a chicken dish with coconut, onions, and spices. They have mango *lassi* (a tasty Indian yogurt drink) as well as *boba* drinks (bubble tea), which aren't usually found in Indian restaurants.

Mexican
The best bet is ◖ **Pollofino** (6831 Hollister Ave., 805/685-1141, daily 11am-9pm, $5-24). Working out of a nondescript strip mall, these guys do taqueria food right. The meat is flavorful, and the multicolored salsas have kick. Try the marinated charbroiled chicken in secret sauce with beans, salsa, and tortillas. They also have full racks of barbecued ribs and cook up whole pounds of tri-tip.

Freebird's World Burrito (879 Embarcadero Del Norte, 805/968-0123, daily 24 hours, $5-14) is a popular spot in the heart of the Isla Vista college community. Order at the counter, deciding which ingredients you want inside your taco, burrito, or quesadilla. There's a small dining area inside and some picnic benches outside.

A more authentic Mexican taqueria, **Super Cucas Restaurant** (6527 Madrid St., 805/770-3806, www.supercucas3.com, Sun.-Wed. 7am-2am, Thurs.-Sat. 7am-4am, $3.50-10) is popular with the local college students for breakfast burritos served all day, which make a good late-night snack after a night on the town. I've definitely had better, but it does the job.

Pies
Fruit pies, pot pies, quiches: **Simply Pies** (5392 Hollister Ave., 805/845-2200, www.simplypiessb.com, Tues.-Fri. 7:30am-5:30pm, Sat. 10am-5:30pm, pies $11-30, entrées $6.50-12.50) is a purveyor of all sorts of pies. Regardless of the type, the pies are made from locally sourced organic ingredients. Peruse the simple lunch menu to pair a slice of quiche or a pot pie with a salad.

Seafood
Get your seafood fix at **Nikka Fish Market & Grill** (5722 Calle Real, 805/967-2600, www.nikkagrill.com, daily 10:30am-8pm, $8-13.50). Walk past the fresh seafood display case and up to a counter to order fresh ahi, snapper, salmon, or halibut, served in a variety of ways, including in a sandwich, in a taco, or on a platter.

INFORMATION AND SERVICES
The **Goleta Valley Chamber of Commerce** (805/967-2500, www.goletavalley.com) can provide information to visitors about Goleta and its attractions by phone or on their

SANTA BARBARA

© STUART THORNTON

the breakfast burrito at Isla Vista's Super Cucas Restaurant

website. If a medical emergency arises, **Santa Barbara Cottage Hospital** (400 W. Pueblo St., 805/682-7111, www.cottagehealthsystem.org) is just a few miles away.

GETTING THERE AND AROUND

Goleta is eight miles north of Santa Barbara on U.S. 101. Goleta is a bit spread out and is probably navigated most easily by car. Isla Vista is just a little farther west; it can be reached via Storke Road or South Los Carneros Road from Goleta. From Santa Barbara, take U.S. 101 north and take Exit 107 onto Los Carneros Road. If you are without a vehicle, the **Santa Barbara MTB** (805/963-3363, www.sbmtd.gov) has a few bus routes running through Goleta. Although the **Santa Barbara Municipal Airport** (SBA, 500 Fowler Rd., 805/967-7111, www.flysba.com) has a Santa Barbara address, it is surrounded by Goleta.

The Gaviota Coast

In some ways, the Gaviota Coast is Southern California's last major stand against the encroachment of urbanization. It acts as a soothing balm to residents from Santa Barbara south to the sprawling metropolis of Los Angeles who want to escape civilization for a weekend in nature. This stretch of coastline, between Goleta's Coal Oil Point and Vandenberg Air Force Base's Point Arguello and beyond to remote Point Sal, is unpopulated and only lightly touched by development.

It wasn't always this way. Before European settlers arrived, it was one of the most densely populated regions of California. The Chumash people lived here and harvested sustenance from the Santa Barbara Channel using canoes. Then the missionaries came and attempted major agricultural projects in now nearly unpopulated places, including Jalama and Honda Canyon. After the mission system collapsed, the area was divided into Mexican land grants before large ranches appeared. Some large ranching operations, such as the Hollister Ranch, still exist today.

It's a great place for a day trip from Santa Barbara—it's only 20 miles to the first park, El Capitán State Beach—for a day of relaxing on a beach, hiking, surfing, or stand-up paddleboarding. Even though this is a rural stretch of coastline, the area's three state parks—El Capitán State Beach, Refugio State Beach, and Gaviota State Park—are typically crowded during the summer months. It's also a great place to camp for the night.

Pockets of the Gaviota Coast are protected by the presence of El Capitán State Beach, Refugio State Beach, Gaviota State Park, and the impressive Jalama Beach County Park. But there's still a push by local conservation groups, including the Gaviota Conservancy, to designate this area a National Shoreline.

EL CAPITÁN STATE BEACH

Closest to Santa Barbara, **El Capitán State Beach** (10 Refugio Rd., Goleta, 805/986-1033, www.parks.ca.gov, $10) offers a narrow, rocky beach with tide pools and the largest campground of the three Gaviota Coast state parks.

On February 26, 1776, the Anza expedition camped in the area that would later become El Capitán State Beach. A day earlier, the priest Pedro Font wrote in his journal: "The people of the expedition, some of whom have never seen the ocean, have much to admire." There is still much to admire here: a nice but narrow strand of beach for sunbathing, surf fishing, a few infrequent waves offshore for surfers, and stands of sycamore and oak trees offering shade along El Capitán Creek. A stairway provides access from the bluffs to the beach area. Amenities include RV hookups, pay showers, restrooms, hiking and biking trails, a fabulous beach, a seasonal general store, and an outdoor arena. Many of the camping sites offer an ocean view.

Camping

El Capitán State Beach (10 Refugio Beach Rd., Goleta, 800/444-7275, www.reserveamerica.com, $45) is the largest of the state park campgrounds on the Gaviota Coast. It has 123 campsites strung along multiple loops in the shade or sun, depending on your preference—if you get here early enough. The sites offer a little more privacy than Refugio or Gaviota, and there is a walkway and stairs accessing the rocky beach below.

For the inexperienced camper, **El Capitán Canyon** (11560 Calle Real, 866/352-2729, www.elcapitancanyon.com, canvas safari tents from $155, cabins $225-795) offers several ways to ease into the outdoors. On 300 acres of land that includes private hiking trails and a spa, El Capitán Canyon is also a place for more experienced outdoors enthusiasts to pamper themselves. The accommodations here—some are far from camping—begin with canvas safari tents and yurts that include beds and furniture but have no running water, even though there are bathhouses nearby. The cedar cabins are available in a range of options, from a bunk cabin that is perfect for families to the property's priciest offering, the Safari Cabin, a two-bedroom suite with a loft and an ocean view. Most of the other cabins are like small wooden studio apartments complete with kitchenettes and, in some cases, deep soaking tubs. In front of each is a picnic table and fire pit for communing with nature. El Capitán Canyon's cabins appeal to couples seeking a restful, romantic retreat as well as families with children. Kids will love the heated pool and a short hike to a llama and goat enclosure.

On the grounds, the Canyon Market serves a nice selection of breakfast, lunch, and dinner options. They also will deliver barbecue kits to your cabin so you can prepare your meal on an open fire. These kits start at $60 for hamburgers, hot dogs, and veggie burgers, so expect more than Oscar Meyer wieners and Costco patties.

CRUSHED IN THE DEVIL'S JAW

A series of rock outcroppings and reefs off Honda Point on the Gaviota Coast have a dangerous reputation with a name to match: The Devil's Jaw. The most notable maritime tragedy occurred on September 8, 1923, when 13 U.S. Navy destroyers made their way around Point Conception. Due to a navigational error and some unusual currents, they thought they were farther south than they actually were. The ships headed east only to have their views obscured by a dense fog bank.

Suddenly, seven of the destroyers crashed onto the rocks and reefs in these treacherous coastal waters.

The sailors on the spared ships sprang into action to save the survivors on the sinking vessels, while local fishing boats picked up waterlogged sailors who were thrown onto the rocks. Some survivors were able to wade ashore. Still, the Honda Point Disaster resulted in the death of 23 men and the loss of seven ships. It is the U.S. Navy's largest peacetime tragedy.

⟨ REFUGIO STATE BEACH

If Gaviota State Park is the region's hiking hotspot, **Refugio State Beach** (10 Refugio Beach Rd., Goleta, 805/968-1033, www.parks.ca.gov, $10) is the best place for a beach day on the Gaviota Coast. This thin but long finger of beach is lined with scenic palm trees. Here, brave children plunge into the chilly waters and scream while their parents look on in the comfort of the sun.

In the late 1700s the land here was a cattle ranch called Nuestra Senora del Refugio. In 1798, José María Ortega took over the ranch and started to do a little smuggling on the side, trading with stocked foreign ships, which was forbidden by the ruling Spanish. These activities piqued the interest of the Monterey pirate Hippolyte de Bouchard, who traveled south to Refugio in 1818, hoping to score some of the smuggled goods. Even though Refugio's residents hid themselves and the loot, Bouchard took it upon himself to burn the ranch house and smuggling station before departing.

Today, the only ominous offshore presence is the hazy oil rigs in the distance that look like ghostly pirate ships. As for Refugio, the waters are way less scary. This is a well-protected cove for sea kayaking or stand-up paddleboarding. Refugio's park rangers also provide beginning and advanced kayak tours that include training in kayak usage.

Camping
Refugio State Beach (10 Refugio Beach Rd., Goleta, 800/444-7275, www.reserveamerica.com, $45) has 67 campsites to crash at after a day at the nearby beach, which is just feet away from some of the sites. In the summer, the sites, which are fairly close together, can feel a bit crowded, but this is a scenic campground shaded by trees.

Accommodations
OVER $250
Spread out for a couple of days at the **Circle Bar B Guest Ranch & Stables** (1800 Refugio Rd., Goleta, 805/968-3901, http://circlebarb.com, $292-754) in the hills above Refugio State Beach. Choose from spacious guest rooms, private cabins, creek-side cottages, and two-story units that sleep up to six. All overnight guests get three square meals a day along with use of the ranch's library, pool, and game room. The Circle Bar B also has horseback riding with a trail guide, available to nonguests as well. The Circle Bar B has been a guest ranch since 1941 and is still run by founder Florence Brown's family. Over the years, the ranch has expanded to include more acreage and additions, including a dinner theater.

GAVIOTA STATE PARK
Gaviota is the Spanish word for "seagull." In 1769, soldiers on the Portola Expedition killed

one of the birds while camping here, giving the park its name. Of the Gaviota Coast's three state parks, **Gaviota State Park** (10 Refugio Beach Rd., Goleta, 805/968-1033, www.parks.ca.gov, $10) is the place to go for hiking. The park has multiple trails leading into its 2,000 acres of oak woodland and chaparral backcountry.

Besides the hiking trails, Gaviota State Park has a nice little beach area under the shadow of an 811-foot-high train trestle. Just west of the beach is a fishing pier, where on crowded days the plethora of upright fishing poles stand like bristles off the wooden structure. It's known for being quite windy.

Hiking

One hike that allows you to see the sweep of the park and its coastline is the **Beach to Backcountry Trail** (3 miles round-trip, 700-foot elevation gain). To find the trailhead, turn right before the Gaviota State Park kiosk and follow the unsigned road. At the first bend in the road, park in the pullout. From here, you'll see the trailhead. The trail begins on a road before taking a left onto a multiuse trail. The path heads up past sandstone rock formations and a cave before reaching views of the coast.

Another popular trail is the 0.7-mile hike up to **Gaviota Hot Springs.** If you get lost easily, this mostly unsigned trail is going to be a challenge. The trailhead is actually about 2.5 miles north of the state park's main entrance; exit off U.S. 101 to Highway 1 heading to Lompoc. Take an immediate right at the exit and then another right to an unmarked parking area. From here, it doesn't get any easier. Take the unmarked trail about 0.5 miles up, and when the main trail veers left, go straight on what looks like a spur trail. A few hundred yards up is a pool of naturally occurring warm—not hot—water behind a little artificial dam made of rock and concrete. It can fit three or four people at a time, making it a good place for a relaxing soak.

More adventurous hikers can continue on the main path up to **Gaviota Peak,** a 2,458-foot summit that offers one of the best views of the Gaviota Coast. It's a strenuous three-mile hike one-way.

Camping

Gaviota State Park (10 Refugio Beach Rd., Goleta, 800/444-7275, www.reserveamerica.com, $45) has 39 campsites in a small loop by Gaviota Creek, just 100 yards from the beach. These sites are mostly open to the elements, including the wind that roars through Gaviota

THE UFOS OF THE GAVIOTA COAST

During a night camping at Jalama Beach County Park or another spot on the Gaviota Coast, you may look up and see a strange flying object overhead. Most likely it's not an alien craft searching for humans to probe but an unpiloted satellite or test missile launched from Vandenberg Air Force Base.

Encompassing over 99,000 acres of land on the elbow of the California coast by Point Conception, Vandenberg was initially an Army base called Camp Cooke. In 1965 the Air Force took over the sprawling base and began launching test missiles in reaction to Russia's *Sputnik* launch in 1957. The base has the distinction of being the place where the first polar-orbiting

satellite was sent into space in 1959. Vandenberg was also designed to be the space shuttle's West Coast launch and landing site, but the site's technical problems and the space program's decision to consolidate shuttle operations at Cape Canaveral in Florida led to the closure of the shuttle program at Vandenberg in 1989.

If you see a UFO in the sky while in the west section of Santa Barbara County, check out Vandenberg's launch schedule (www.vandenberg.af.mil) to see if it's a missile being tested or a satellite being sent into space. If it's not listed there, you may have seen a truly unidentified flying object.

Pass and the heat because there is little tree cover to block the sun.

🕊 JALAMA BEACH COUNTY PARK

The western portion of Santa Barbara County around Point Conception is mile after mile of desolate beach, uncrowded waves, and mostly uninhabited coastal bluffs. The best place to experience a truly wild patch of the Gaviota Coast is to head out to **Jalama Beach County Park** (9999 Jalama Rd., Lompoc, 805/736-3504, www.sbparks.org, day-use $10). It's the only public beach between Gaviota State Beach and the beach at the tiny town of Surf, a stretch of more than 48 miles. Jalama draws families camping far from cell phone service in first-come, first-served sites; surfers hoping to score uncrowded waves; anglers hoping to reel in a few fish; and beachgoers who like their beaches in an undeveloped state.

There have been some serious shipwrecks on this section of coast. In 1854 the steamship *Yankee Blade* hit some rocks and sank, killing 415 people. Later, in 1923, the largest peacetime loss of U.S. Navy ships occurred when seven destroyers ran aground and 23 people perished nearby at Honda Point.

If you are into out-of-the-way treasures, you'll know you are on the way to someplace special as you wind around on the 14.5-mile-long Jalama Road toward the park. Despite its remote location, Jalama is a park with some unexpected amenities, including a playground, a horseshoe pit, a basketball court, flush toilets, and the well-stocked **Jalama Beach Store and Grill.** The little store has almost all you could need, including canned goods, firewood, cold beer, cigars, and even DVD rentals. Meanwhile, the grill serves breakfast, lunch, and dinner, including their patented—seriously, the patent is displayed by the pickup window—Jalama Burger, a tasty third-of-a-pounder that'll make burger fans drool.

Jalama Beach County Park

While the park's facilities are impressive for its remote location, the coastline is the draw. Surfers can ride waves right out front while anglers cast off the beach for perch and rockfish. For the adventurous, it's a six-mile beach hike from Jalama east to Point Conception, one of California's best-known maritime landmarks. Check to make sure it's low tide before heading out.

Camping

Jalama Beach County Park (9999 Jalama Rd., Lompoc, 805/736-3504, www.sbparks. org, tent camping $20-40, RV camping with hookups $35-40) has 117 first-come, first-served campsites. There are 12 spots whose sites blend into the beach out front and a row of RV-friendly sites on a bluff with a view of the park below. The amenities here are surprisingly good, including clean restrooms with flush toilets, fire pits, picnic tables, and an outdoor shower for washing off after any ocean recreation. Be aware that the spring and early summer winds in this area can be quite fierce.

The park also offers seven popular cabins for rent (805/686-5050, $100-200) for those who want to experience the region's beauty without roughing it.

SANTA BARBARA WINE COUNTRY

At the heart of Santa Barbara's wine country are the towns of Santa Ynez, Los Olivos, Solvang, and Santa Maria. These small farming communities are often overlooked in favor of the surrounding beach communities. But underneath their small-town charm is a big equestrian history, rustic Western lifestyle, and even Prohibition-era ideals and temperance movements, ironic for an area with a thriving wine industry.

Solvang started in 1911 as a Danish retreat. It's still ripe with Scandinavian heritage as well as modern sensibility. In the 1950s, far earlier than other themed communities, Solvang decided to seal its fate by keeping a focus on Danish architecture, food, and style, which still holds an allure 50 years after its conception, although the theme park atmosphere is not lacking in kitsch. Easily walkable, Solvang is also home to Mission Santa Inés, bakeries, miles of rolling paved roads for bikers and cyclists (Lance Armstrong once trained here), oak-studded parks, wine-tasting rooms, and the well-known Solvang Theaterfest, an outdoor event and theater venue. Solvang is close to the now-famous ostrich farm from the movie *Sideways* as well as the Chumash Casino, if you need your one-armed-bandit fix.

Santa Ynez has always been a laid-back horse and farming community, unaffected by time. That it is now the gateway to the wine region does not detract from its agrarian roots. Los Olivos is an artist's enclave and a wine taster's dream. The central flagpole, sitting boldly on Grand Avenue, is the de facto rallying point for visitors, since there are still no stoplights in the area. Within a two-block radius of the flagpole

HIGHLIGHTS

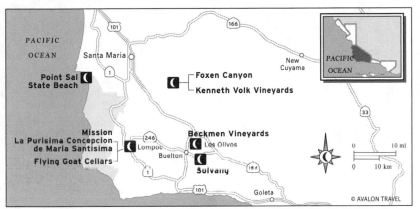

LOOK FOR ◖ TO FIND RECOMMENDED SIGHTS, ACTIVITIES, DINING, AND LODGING.

◖ **Solvang:** Long before thematic towns came into vogue, Solvang decided to stay true to its heritage. With Danish bakeries and restaurants, a Danish history museum, and excellent wineries, Solvang is unlike any other town on the coast (page 118).

◖ **Foxen Canyon:** Whether you drive with the top down or ride your bike, Santa Barbara wine country has beautiful scenic back roads. Foxen Canyon Road, beginning in Los Olivos and ending in Santa Maria, is one of the most popular routes, passing green rolling hills, farms, ranches, and vineyards (page 132).

◖ **Beckmen Vineyards:** This winery set the standard for sustainable farming using biodynamic methods. Not only are the wines terrific, but the planet is better off (page 134).

◖ **Mission La Purisima Concepción:** Sitting on 2,000 acres in Lompoc, Mission La Purisima is the most beautiful yet least visited mission on the Central Coast (page 143).

◖ **Point Sal State Beach:** Inaccessible to vehicular traffic since 1998, Point Sal can only be reached by an adventurous 10-mile round-trip hike. Experiencing the solitude of one of California's remotest beaches is worth the effort (page 144).

◖ **Flying Goat Cellars:** Pinot noir lovers should not miss a chance to taste the seductive wines at this simple tasting room. The dedication to the grape is evident in each sip (page 145).

◖ **Kenneth Volk Vineyards:** Taste award-winning wines, with a focus on chardonnay, pinot noir, and "heirloom" varietals, on 12 acres of serene land along Tepusquet Creek (page 146).

are a dozen tasting rooms, half a dozen excellent restaurants, and a few art galleries representing some of the best local artists. Unpretentious and simple, it's a perfect one-day getaway—unless you also use it as a base to explore Lake Cachuma, Figueroa Mountain, or the broader wine region, in which case you'll need several days.

Santa Maria is the workhorse of the agricultural area within Santa Barbara County. Driving through Santa Maria, you see fields and vineyards on both sides of the freeway, and it's easy to assume it's merely a farming region, but Santa Maria also has a strong Western history, not to mention the now famous Santa

WINE COUNTRY

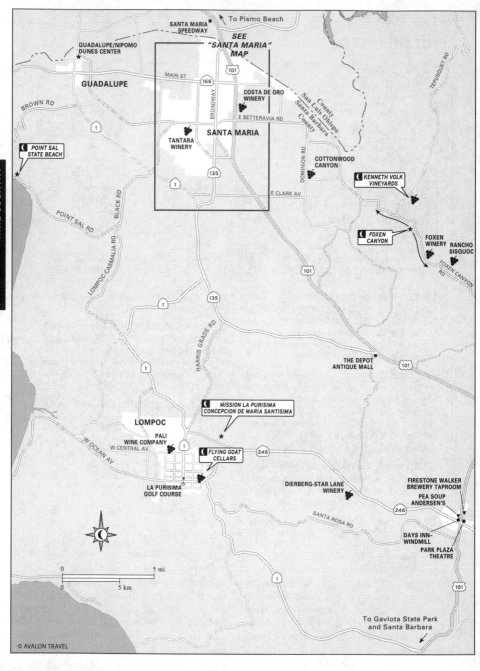

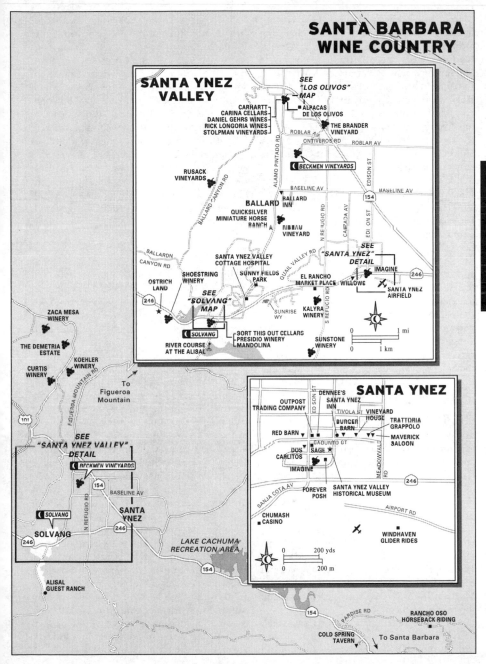

SANTA BARBARA WINE COUNTRY

SANTA YNEZ VALLEY

SEE "LOS OLIVOS" MAP

CARHARTT
CARINA CELLARS
DANIEL GEHRS WINES
RICK LONGORIA WINES
STOLPMAN VINEYARDS

ALPACAS DE LOS OLIVOS

THE BRANDER VINEYARD

ROBLAR AV
ONTIVEROS RD
ROBLAR AV

RUSACK VINEYARDS

BECKMEN VINEYARDS

ALAMO PINTADO RD

BASELINE AV
BASELINE AV

154

EDISON ST

BALLARD INN

BALLARD

QUICKSILVER MINIATURE HORSE RANCH

RIDEAU VINEYARD

CAJADA ST

EDISON ST

SEE "SANTA YNEZ" DETAIL

BALLARD CANYON RD

SANTA YNEZ VALLEY COTTAGE HOSPITAL

QUAIL VALLEY RD

BALLARDN CANYON RD

N REFUGIO RD

SHOESTRING WINERY

SUNNY FIELDS PARK

EL RANCHO MARKET PLACE

WILLOWS

IMAGINE

246

OSTRICH LAND

SEE "SOLVANG" MAP

SANTA YNEZ AIRFIELD

246

SUNRISE WY

KALYRA WINERY

S REFUGIO RD

ZACA MESA WINERY

SOLVANG

SORT THIS OUT CELLARS
PRESIDIO WINERY
MANDOLINA

SUNSTONE WINERY

1 mi

1 km

THE DEMETRIA ESTATE

KOEHLER WINERY

RIVER COURSE AT THE ALISAL

FIGUEROA MOUNTAIN RD

CURTIS WINERY

To Figueroa Mountain

101

SANTA YNEZ

SEE "SANTA YNEZ VALLEY" DETAIL

BECKMEN VINEYARDS

OUTPOST TRADING COMPANY

DENNEE'S

SANTA YNEZ INN

EDISON ST

TIVOLA ST

VINEYARD HOUSE

TRATTORIA GRAPPOLO

RED BARN

BURGER BARN

MAVERICK SALOON

154

BASELINE AV

DOS CARLITOS

CADURITO CT

SAGE

SOLVANG

SANTA YNEZ

N REFUGIO RD

246

IMAGINE

MEADOWLARK RD

246

FOREVER POSH

SANTA YNEZ VALLEY HISTORICAL MUSEUM

SOLVANG

246

SANJA COTA AV

AIRPORT RD

LAKE CACHUMA RECREATION AREA

CHUMASH CASINO

WINDHAVEN GLIDER RIDES

200 yds

200 m

154

ALISAL GUEST RANCH

RANCHO OSO HORSEBACK RIDING

154

PARDISE RD

COLD SPRING TAVERN

To Santa Barbara

WINE COUNTRY

Maria tri-tip barbecue. It's now built up with housing, but there are still small charming areas like the Far Western Tavern in Orcutt, the historic Santa Maria Inn, and one of the best missions on the Central Coast, Mission La Purisima. There is also Vandenberg Air Force Base, where you can watch missiles and rockets take off; wineries that produce some of the top-scoring and top-selling wine in the country; the Santa Maria Valley Strawberry Festival; and Point Sal State Beach, one of California's remotest beaches.

PLANNING YOUR TIME
This region has many small towns with distinct personalities and one major city, Santa Maria. Santa Ynez and Los Olivos can both easily be visited within a day from Santa Barbara. Solvang is a five-minute drive from Santa Ynez and Los Olivos, but it is suggested that visitors reserve an entire day for this town. Santa Maria is a 15-minute drive north of Solvang, and because it has a lot more outdoor recreational opportunities, it is best to reserve an entire day for a visit to this area as well. In a weekend, you can get a feel for all of the towns in the Santa Barbara Wine Country, but as always, more time is necessary if you really want to explore these areas in depth.

HISTORY
Today, we call it wine country, but this vast expanse in northern Santa Barbara County is really two valleys—the Santa Ynez Valley and the Santa Maria Valley—not originally known for grapes or wines. Santa Maria was originally farmland, and still produces strawberries and broccoli, among many other crops. Between 1869 and 1874, four of the valley's prominent settlers contributed the land where their properties met to form a town that became known as Grangerville. Centered on Main Street and Broadway, Grangerville was renamed Santa Maria in 1905; it is the agricultural heart and soul of the county.

The Santa Ynez Valley comprises Solvang, Santa Ynez, and Los Olivos; these towns formed out of necessity, as Los Olivos and Santa Ynez were stagecoach and rail stops. In the late 1800s the stagecoach from Santa Barbara stopped twice a day in Santa Ynez at the College Hotel, then proceeded down Edison Street toward the main stagecoach stop at Mattei's Tavern in Los Olivos, which eventually became a railroad stop. Solvang, which means "sunny fields," developed as a settlement for the Danish who migrated here in 1910. The town fathers bought 10,000 acres of land, and the town was created in 1911. The goal was to create a home away from Denmark; the first building to be built was the Lutheran Church, and the second was a Danish folk school, which still stands today as the Bit O' Denmark restaurant.

WINE HISTORY
The first documented viticulture in California dates from 1779 at Mission San Gabriel Arcángel in Southern California, and eventually grapes were grown throughout the mission system. The so-called "mission grape," a hybrid of different types, was high in sugar content, low in acid, and produced a thin, sweet wine that, by many accounts of the times, wasn't all that good. But this grape dominated the industry until the end of California's Mexican era in the late 1840s. By that time, wine and brandy production was a significant source of income for some of the missions. Old Mission Santa Barbara established a vineyard and winery around the 1830s. Grapes were used not only to make wine but also raisins, which were handy food for travelers. But grape production was not limited to the missions. About 1820, San Antonio winery was built in what is now Goleta. The lonely historic adobe winery is still standing nearly 200 years later, although it's on private property. Another commercial winery, the Packard Winery, was built in 1865, also in Santa Barbara, and in the late 1890s about 200 acres of grapes were being turned into wine on Santa Cruz Island. Near Mission La Purisima, grapes were also planted in the 1880s, and a few of those vines still survive today, also on private property.

In the 1960s and 1970s, when the first commercial grapevine plantings in the Santa Maria Valley since Prohibition were made, grape growers and vintners planted anything and everything, without regard to the end product. It has taken Santa Barbara vintners nearly 20 years to understand its soil, its climate, and what is best suited for the diverse growing regions and the American Viticultural Area's (AVA) federally recognized grape growing regions. It's one of the coolest viticultural areas in the state, and its unique east-to-west-oriented mountains allow for fog and ocean breezes to seep into the region and create nice microclimates for grape cultivation. Currently there are 54 different varieties of grapes planted throughout the Santa Barbara Wine Country on 20,000 to 26,000 acres. Pinot noir and chardonnay are the most widely planted varieties, with chardonnay commanding an astounding 40 percent of that acreage; pinot noir comes in at 25 percent. The wine industry in Santa Barbara County is thriving, in spite of the fluctuations of the economy, transitional markets, fickle consumers, and inconsistent harvests.

Santa Ynez Valley

The wine industry has dominated the region in the last 10 years, even though commercially planted grapes have been here for over four decades. With the success of the 2004 film *Sideways,* the area has received additional attention, helping to place a visit to this area on the list for wine lovers across the globe. Some areas, like Happy Canyon, have hotter temperatures and can produce cabernet sauvignon and sauvignon blanc; cooler growing regions like the Santa Rita Hills benefit from close proximity to the coast. There are cool- and warm-climate plantings of syrah and chardonnay, providing different styles and acid levels, and the diversity of the area is astounding. Every winery is doing something different, and it is this attitude of experimentation that has contributed to the valley's success. It also doesn't hurt that the Santa Ynez Valley is a beautiful place to spend time.

SANTA YNEZ

Named "The New Town" when it was founded in 1882, Santa Ynez retains its historical Western flavor, with some of its old storefronts and hitching posts still intact. By 1889 the town had become the focal point both socially and economically of the entire Santa Ynez Valley, complete with mercantile stores, blacksmith shops, garages, grocery stores, a barbershop, a harness shop, a millinery shop, and several saloons. The College Hotel was once the area's main lodging establishment, complete with a Victorian design and 16 roof turrets. The hotel, which stood on Sagunto Street just south of Edison Street, hosted guests from all over the world. These days Santa Ynez is a shadow of its former self, no longer the important hub it was, a quiet spot with a handful of businesses. And yet people still come to the valley from the world over to explore the region.

Sights and Drives

Santa Ynez is a very small town. There are only two hotels, not including the Chumash Casino resort, which is technically in Solvang despite being just down the road from Santa Ynez. One of the reasons people choose to stay in Santa Ynez is that it makes a good base from which to explore, and it is very quiet. If you don't want lots of people around in the morning or at night, it's ideal. You can walk the length of town in about 10 minutes, and there are a few sights and drives to check out.

Wine country is famous for long winding roads that pass vineyards, ranches, cattle, and old oaks. These roads are ideal for a drive, a bike ride, or even a run. Make sure you share the road and keep alert, as the beauty and serenity can sometimes lull you into a very calm state.

Directly off Highway 154 is an area known as **Happy Canyon,** the warmest grape-growing area in the entire valley. Take Highway 246 toward Happy Canyon from Santa Ynez. Highway 246 eventually connects with Highway 154, and near the intersection of Highways 154 and 246 is Armor Ranch Road. Follow Armor Ranch Road for about four miles; Happy Canyon Road is on the left. There are a lot of horses here, and if you take Happy Canyon Road toward the mountains, there is some beautiful scenery as it heads deeper into the low, flat region before it begins climbing into the mountains. Or simply stay on Armor Ranch Road and make a loop back to Highway 154. You'll join the highway south of where you entered, so turn right back on to Highway 154, then to get back to Santa Ynez, turn left onto Highway 246.

Santa Ynez is small, but the area has history, admirably presented at the **Santa Ynez Valley Historical Museum and Parks-Janeway Carriage House** (3596 Sagunto St., 805/688-7889, www.santaynezmuseum.org, Wed.-Sun. noon-4pm, adults $4, under age 16 free). There's a good-size diorama with a narrow-gauge train that makes its way around the track, showing how the train depot near Mattei's Tavern used to look back in the day. It's not high-tech, but it is fun. There are also small displays in the Valley Room showing the five original small towns: Solvang (founded in 1911), Santa Ynez (1882), Los Olivos (1887), Ballard (1881), and Buellton (1920). These are short histories but are part of the great development of the valley. The Pioneer Room is three rooms outfitted with turn-of-the-20th-century furnishings, many from local ranches.

The carriage house is an impressive collection of various types of carriages, surreys, and wagons, including an old popcorn wagon from 1909 that sold nuts and fresh popcorn, as well as an old fire wagon. These carriages are in fantastic shape; it is clear they have been well cared for. There is also a selection of tack and saddles.

Wine Tasting

There used to be a larger contingency of wineries in and near Santa Ynez, but the migration to Solvang and Los Olivos has left only a few. A short drive will get you to some wonderful area wineries.

IMAGINE

Imagine (3563 Numancia St., 805/688-1769, www.imaginewine.com, daily 11am-5pm, tasting $10) is one of the only tasting rooms in town, and it is staffed solely by the owners. The light wood-toned interior has a classic Victorian feel, and the room is spacious with lots of light. You'll get an average of six tasting samples to ponder, including viognier and chardonnay on the white side, and syrah, zinfandel, pinot noir, and merlot on the red side. The winery is an easy walk from anywhere in town; the space doubles as an art gallery.

KALYRA WINERY

Kalyra Winery (343 N. Refugio Rd., 805/693-8864, www.kalyrawinery.com, Mon.-Fri. 11am-5pm, Sat.-Sun. 10am-5pm, tasting $10-12) is famous for having been featured in the 2004 film *Sideways*. The building itself has been home to several other wineries prior to Kalyra moving in. The partial wraparound deck provides great views of the valley and mountains, and when the sun is setting and the golden hues hit the leafed-out vines, it's truly beautiful. The winery's interior is a nod to brothers Mike and Martin Brown's Australian roots and love of surfing. They initially started out producing sweet wines but have since expanded their portfolio to include a large number of red and white wines, including some made from Australian grapes.

RIDEAU VINEYARD

Rideau Vineyard (1562 Alamo Pintado Rd., 805/688-0717 www.rideauvineyard.com, Sun.-Fri. 11am-4:30pm, Sat. 11am-5pm, tasting $10) is housed in an 1884 two-story adobe, one of the few remaining in the state. The emphasis here is on Rhône-style varieties, namely syrah,

WINE TASTING 101

Tasting wine is not a science, but it's not a sport either. There are specific steps to follow in order to have the best possible experience and to fully enjoy and understand what the winemaker was trying to accomplish with the wine.

You may see both wine know-it-alls and sport tasters while you're out wine-tasting, but don't pay any attention to anyone who is arrogant, rude, or intoxicated. Wine-tasting is meant to be enjoyed, not endured. If a tasting room is crowded and there's no room at the tasting bar, move on to another one. If you see limos out front, that might also be a clue to avoid that particular tasting room, as often people hire a car and driver so that they can drink liberally.

· **Swirl:** First off, it's important to know that your nose is much more powerful than your taste buds. Swirling the wine in your glass might seem like a ridiculous custom, but this actually releases the esters, the aromatic compounds in the wine. The air interacts with the wine and enhances the scents.

· **Smell:** The second step is to smell the wine. Really get your nose in the glass and take a deep breath. Exhale and do it again. This sets the stage for your palate and will immediately give you clues and ideas about the wine. Frankly, there's no mystery here. It's no different than smelling anything—your food,

cologne, whatever—except that wine has many parts and layers that can be detected. Your nose will give you a greater understanding of the wine. As you smell it, ask yourself what specific scents you can identify.

· **Taste:** To spit or not to spit? That's a matter of preference. Part of wine-tasting is actually the tasting part, and fully experiencing a wine means swallowing it. As with any wine-tasting, though, most wineries will pour about six wines, and some may pour more than that. In California, the law allows a one-ounce pour. That may not seem like a lot, but if you sample six to eight wines, that's the equivalent of one glass at a restaurant. It's also important to plan out your trip. If you plan on visiting, say, four wineries, visit two, take a food break, and then visit two more. Alcohol is dehydrating, so always keep water with you to stay hydrated. It's easy to forget about water in a fun tasting-room atmosphere. It's also important to try new things. Some people say they only like a certain wine, but every winery produces their wines differently, and there is no standard recipe for anything. Be adventurous and sample. If you don't like it, spit it out. And never let anyone tell you that you should or shouldn't like a wine. It's ultimately a personal preference. Buy what you like, but try everything.

viognier, roussanne, and grenache, as well as blends and other wines like riesling and grenache blanc. The small gift shop has some New Orleans-inspired items, since owner Iris Rideau originally hails from Louisiana, and there are concerts several times each year where you'll find gumbo and other creole foods being served. It's a beautiful spot to relax and enjoy a picnic on the lush green back lawn. Tastings are done both inside and outside.

BRIDLEWOOD WINERY

As you drive up the long driveway of **Bridlewood Winery** (3555 Roblar Ave., 805/688-9000, www.bridlewoodwinery.com,

daily 11am-5pm, tasting $10), you'll come upon a long structure that looks like a mission, actually a former equestrian center; all Bridlewood's wines have a horse theme. The focus is on Rhône-style varieties, such as eight different versions of syrah as well as three different viogniers, which they do very well. Tossed in the mix is a bit of chardonnay, port, pinot noir, and zinfandel from vineyards up and down the state. The tasting room is a large facility that can accommodate big crowds, but you can also head outside and enjoy the surroundings. Removed from the main road, it's a peaceful spot, perfect for a picnic on the back veranda.

SUNSTONE WINERY

Just one mile from Kalyra Winery is **Sunstone Winery** (125 N. Refugio Rd., 805/688-9463, www.sunstonewinery.com, daily 11am-5pm, tasting $12-16), which has a Spanish and Tuscan vibe with mottled yellow walls suggesting an old estate in the countryside in Europe—it's not actually an old building, but it feels like it. Since its inception in 1990, the focus at Sunstone has been growing grapes without any pesticides, and they are certified organic growers. Probably best known locally for their merlot, they also produce Bordeaux-style blends and syrah, and their white wines include viognier and sauvignon blanc. This is a very popular spot and sometimes gets downright crowded.

Entertainment and Events

The land in Santa Ynez was home to the Chumash people long before grapes were ever planted. With the advent of the reservation system, Native Americans needed a source of viable revenue and a way to be self-sustaining, so the **Chumash Casino** (3400 E. Hwy. 246, 800/248-6274, www.chumashcasino.com, daily 24 hours) was created. For a long time it was housed in a tent structure, but they eventually petitioned the county to build a proper resort. This was met with local opposition, but the casino was eventually built. Now it is one of the largest draws in the area and one of the few places in the county to draw big-name performers. Additionally, the Chumash people have been actively involved in giving back to the community in various ways. The casino has 2,000 slots, a variety of poker options that include a 24-hour room, bingo large enough for 1,300 players, and blackjack. People are routinely bused in, so expect crowds. There are three restaurants in the casino, a 123-room hotel, a gift shop, and a 1,300-seat entertainment showroom bringing in a solid lineup of performers.

The **Maverick Saloon** (3687 Sagunto St., 805/686-4785, www.mavericksaloon.org, Mon.-Fri. noon-2am, Sat.-Sun. 10am-2am) has hardwood floors, dollar bills hanging from the

Santa Ynez Valley's Chumash Casino

ceiling, and every kind of sign you can imagine tacked to the walls. It gets loud and wild, especially on nights and weekends when the bar is packed—in part because there's not much else to do in the area. The outdoor patio seating is taken first, and then the bar becomes flooded with people. The stage area is a larger space for overflow, unless there's a band playing. Live bands from the region play on Friday night 8:45pm-11:30pm and on Saturday afternoon at 3pm. A $5 cover charge applies. There's also darts, pool, and a whole lot of that renegade, devil-may-care vibe.

Each May hundreds of people get ready for the **Wine Country Half Marathon** (starts on Sagunto St., www.runsantaynez.com), a 13.1-mile race through the wine country. Both individuals and teams can enter. If you enjoy running, this is a great way to see the valley, as it starts in Santa Ynez, winds through Los Olivos, traverses down Ballard Canyon, and ends in Solvang, passing vineyards and farms along the way. The plants are leafed out in May and the weather is nearly perfect. The after-race festival includes wine- and beer-tasting, music, food, and awards.

Held at Live Oak Camp each October, the **Chumash Intertribal Pow Wow** (www.santaynezchumash.org) is open to the public to watch traditional dances and drumming circles and learn about Native American culture via speakers and literature. There are also Native American arts and crafts for sale and the chance to expand your knowledge of Chumash and other cultures by conversing with members of various Native American groups. It's free to attend but there is a small fee for parking.

Sports and Recreation
LAKE CACHUMA RECREATION AREA
The **Lake Cachuma Recreation Area** (2225 Hwy. 154, 805/686-5055, www.countyofsb.org, day-use vehicle fee $8, day-use hiker $5, towing a boat $13) was built in 1953 to provide a reservoir for the region. The lake covers just over 3,000 acres and has 42 miles of shoreline. Because it is a source of drinking water, no swimming is allowed, and body contact with the water is not allowed. There is a fully stocked general store that has firewood, canned foods, clothing, and even a small selection of magazines and books. There's also a gas station, a coin laundry, hot showers, fishing piers, and plenty of hiking and biking trails.

Boating on the lake is simple. You can bring your own boat to the four launch ramps and small harbor located at the marina, or rent a boat on an hourly or daily basis. They have motorboats, patio deck boats, and kayaks. Daily rental rates range from $30 per hour with a two-hour minimum for a four-passenger rowboat all the way up to $370 per day for a pontoon boat accommodating 20 passengers. Early spring mornings are great if you bring hot cocoa and get out on the water before the sun rises to wait for the warmth of a new day.

The **Nature Cruises** (located at the marina, adults $15, ages 4-12 $7) are conducted by park employees and are a great way to see the lake and surrounding area without any effort. Two cruises are offered, each two hours long and held on a 30-passenger covered pontoon boat called the *Osprey*. A naturalist is on board and speaks about the environment and wildlife and answers any questions visitors may have. The **Wildlife Cruise** (Mar.-Oct. Fri. 3pm, Sat. 10am and 3pm, Sun. 10am) focuses on the plants and animals, such as deer and bears, that make the lake their home. It's a wonderful outing to get an up-close look at the shoreline and learn about the wildlife and history of the habitat, but make sure you bring a wrap as it can get cool on certain parts of the lake. The **Eagle Cruise** (Nov.-Feb. Fri.-Sat. 10am and 2pm, Sun. 10am) with a focus specifically on bald eagles and ospreys, both of which live at Lake Cachuma. You'll also see a greater concentration of migratory birds during these months.

Learn more about the area at the **Neal Taylor Nature Center** (Lake Cachuma Recreation Area, 805/693-0691, www.clnaturecenter.org, Tues.-Sat. 10am-4pm, Sun. 10am-2pm, free). The nonprofit center has exhibits on the construction of Bradbury Dam along with information on the area's fish, plant, and animal populations.

If **fishing** is your thing, Lake Cachuma is a good spot due to the lake bottom's rocks, shallow areas, and aquatic plant beds. During nondrought years the lake supports populations of largemouth and smallmouth bass, crappie, bluegill, red-ear sunfish, and rainbow trout. Catfish have been caught here that weigh up to 32 pounds. Carp, an invasive species, has taken over the lake, and in 2010 the county began allowing bow fishing for carp. A carp bow-fishing permit can be attained free of charge at the park entrance.

For those who prefer to camp, there are several choices for your **camping** experience. Single-family campsites are first come, first served. More than 400 campsites, 100 with full electrical, water, and sewer hookups, and 30 with electrical and water hookups, can accommodate any size RV. Each campsite contains a picnic table and fire ring, with showers, restrooms, and potable water nearby. An RV dump station is also available. It fill up early, so you'll need to plan ahead. The County Parks website (www.countyofsb.org) has detailed campsite information to view and download.

And then there are the popular **yurts** (reservations 805/686-5050, $60-85). A domed tent-like structure, the yurts at Cachuma feature platform beds that sleep up to six people. They have a lockable door, inside light and heat, and screened windows. Set on a bluff with access to the lakeshore, they have very nice views. The park now also has four **cabins** (www.countyofsb.org, $110) available for rent. The cabins have electricity, baths, kitchenettes, porches, picnic tables, and fire pits. Bring your own linens and towels.

GLIDER RIDES

Windhaven Glider Rides (Santa Ynez Airport, 900 Airport Rd., 805/688-2517, www.gliderrides.com, Sat.-Sun. 10am-5pm, $135-265) offers glider rides over the wine country. It's an amazing experience to float above the region and not only see the vineyards but get a better understanding of the topography of the land. Windhaven has been operating for 20 years and takes riders of any age. Flights last 15-30 minutes. A plane tows the glider up along with you and a pilot, then drops the towline so you're soaring above the earth without the noise of engines, making this a relatively quiet and very scenic experience. Of course, everything ultimately depends on the weather.

HORSEBACK RIDING

Sitting on 300 acres and a lengthy drive from anywhere, **Rancho Oso Horseback Riding** (3750 Paradise Rd., 805/683-5110, www.ranchooso.net, $45-120) offers a variety of horseback riding options. The one-hour trail ride starts at $45, and though your horse isn't roaming free, it's still a nice, if predictable, ride through the backcountry. You will cross streams and will see a few Chumash artifacts—this was a Chumash village site long ago—as you meander the lower canyons. There are also longer rides like the one on the Arroyo Burro Trail, which lasts for four hours.

SWIMMING HOLES

The Santa Ynez River has a few places to swim. The most popular is **Red Rock** (end of Paradise Rd., www.fs.usda.gov, adventure pass $5), where reddish rocks stud the jade-green river water. A lot of teenagers and young adults dive off the highest rocks, frequently resulting in injuries. To reach Red Rock, take Paradise Road from Highway 154 and drive east 11 miles to the parking area. On the way, you can pick up a $5 U.S. Forest Service Adventure Pass so that you can legally park at Red Rock. After parking, take the dirt road. You'll eventually get your feet wet on the nearly one-mile walk in.

Shopping

The few shops in Santa Ynez are all a stone's throw from each other, so you can easily browse all the shops in this area.

For 15 years **Dennee's** (3569 Sagunto St., 805/686-0842, Mon.-Sat. 9am-5pm, Sun. 11am-5pm) has provided lots of interesting home furnishings with a country and equestrian motif. The place is packed with large and small items, some from local craftspeople in town, and there's a large diversity of items such as leather couches, accent pieces, mirrors, and decorative items for your home. Think of it as high-end farm decor with a country twist. **Sage** (1095 Edison St., 805/688-0955, Mon.-Sat. 10am-5pm) features a wide variety of home items and decor, including imported furnishings, table linens, Italian dishware, books, candles, unique lamps, bath products, Egyptian cotton towels, soaps from Provence, wind chimes, and CDs.

Outpost Trading Company (3547 Sagunto St., 805/686-5588, Mon.-Wed. 10am-5pm, Thurs.-Sat. 10am-6:30pm, Sun. 11am-4pm) is an eclectic shop that sells Western wear, art, and home furnishings, couture clothing, hand-crafted items, and custom-made furniture and woven tack. **Forever Posh** (3583 Numancia St., 805/688-1444, Tues.-Fri. 10am-5:30pm, Sat. 10am-5pm) has trendy clothes and lounge wear for women, custom jewelry, sunglasses, and designer handbags as well as bridal gifts. The shop is small but offers expert help and a nice assortment of items.

Accommodations
OVER $250
Bed-and-breakfast **ForFriends Inn** (1121 Edison St., 805/693-0303, www.forfriendsinn. com, $250-320) emphasizes socializing. It's most apparent during the serving of daily wine and homemade appetizers in the rose garden, when the innkeepers perform pop songs and encourage the guests to sing along. The main house at ForFriends has five guest rooms with private balconies, jetted tubs, and gas fireplaces or stoves. There's also a private cottage for rent as well as a two-story suite with two fireplaces and a view of the valley. Mornings begin with a three-course breakfast. Guests also receive a "Friendship Pass" that allows complimentary tastings at 20 local wineries.

As you enter the elegant and opulent **☾ Santa Ynez Inn** (3627 Sagunto St., 805/688-5588, www.santaynezinn.com, $245-495), you're transported into the Victorian era. Think of it as a high-end bed-and-breakfast. The average room is about 600 square feet and

Santa Ynez's ForFriends Inn

WINE COUNTRY

© STUART THORNTON

Santa Ynez Inn

has a steam shower and heated tile floor. The guest rooms are large with beautiful antiques, and it's clear the owners have spent a good deal of time and money to make it all the highest quality possible. Breakfast is served each morning in the parlor, a lush wood-rich Victorian room that feels more like a museum than an inn. The grounds have an exercise room, a dry sauna, and a sun deck with an outside jetted tub. In the evening a wine and cheese reception is offered. There are only 20 guest rooms; it's a quiet place in a quiet town to enjoy a quiet experience.

Food

CLASSIC AMERICAN

Inside the 1907 **((Vineyard House** (3631 Sagunto St., 805/688-2886, www.thevineyardhouse.com, Mon.-Sat. 11:30am-9pm, Sun. 10am-9pm, $12-32), there is some magic at work. Creative, flavorful food comes out of this kitchen on a regular basis. The baked brie is always a treat, as is the crispy buttermilk chicken and hearty, thick venison chile verde.

They make their own soups and salad dressings as well as desserts like the eternally decadent and gooey molten chocolate cake. The interior is homey and intimate, but the prime seating on nice days is the deck overlooking Sagunto Street, where the pepper trees hang languidly over the tables.

Located at the Chumash Casino, **Willows** (3400 E. Hwy. 246, 805/686-9855, www.chumashcasino.com, Sun.-Thurs. 5pm-10pm, Fri.-Sat. 5pm-11pm, $32-98) is unexpectedly elegant, with white tablecloths in a room with narrow arches. There are private dining rooms on the outdoor terrace as well. The emphasis here is seafood and beef entrées. Side dishes are extra, so be prepared to throw down some cash. The only drawback is that you have to walk through the casino to get here, but once inside, the noise of clanging slot machines quickly fades.

The no-frills **Burger Barn** (3621 Sagunto St., 805/688-2366, daily 7am-3pm, $5-11) sates your hunger while leaving enough money for that nice bottle of wine. It's known for inexpensive but tasty burgers and salads. Very popular with visitors and locals in part because of the price, it can get very crowded. The outdoor area has plastic tables and chairs, and the interior isn't much better, but it's all about quick and easy food. There is also a breakfast menu that includes omelets and a rib-eye steak-and-egg platter.

((Cold Spring Tavern (5995 Stagecoach Rd., 805/967-0066, www.coldspringtavern.com, restaurant Mon.-Fri. 11am-3pm and 5pm-9pm, Sat.-Sun. 8am-3pm and 5pm-9pm, tavern daily noon-9pm, $21-31) was a former stagecoach stop when wagons and riders were the way to traverse the mountains from the valley to Santa Barbara. It was built in 1886 and hasn't changed much since. Rustic and secluded, it hosts live music every Friday-Sunday. A stream runs by the place, situated in a narrow canyon that can be cool even during the summer months. Motorcyclists, townies, and locals hang out in the bar area, and there is often dancing both inside and outside the bar. The on-site restaurant, in a separate building, is the place to find tri-tip sandwiches during the summers months, grilled outdoors over an open flame, as well as wild rabbit, venison, boar, and very good chili. A visit to the tavern is as much about the food as it is about enjoying the charming space. There's also an old jail on-site, a one-room wooden building that used to hold unruly customers.

Across Highway 154 is the **Paradise Store & Grill** (1 Paradise Rd., 805/967-3254, www.paradisestoresb.com, daily 9am-dusk, $6-10). This small country store, dating back to the 1950s, has blossomed into a grill, a small grocery, and a weekend concert venue. It has a menu that serves burgers and sandwiches, including the popular grilled tri-tip sandwich that comes with barbecue sauce and salsa. They also serve cold beer, which is crucial on hot valley days. A stone stage around back of the store hosts bands on Saturday and Sunday.

ITALIAN

The immensely popular Italian restaurant **Trattoria Grappolo** (3687 Sagunto St., 805/688-6899, www.trattoriagrappolo.com, Tues.-Sun. 11:30am-3pm and 5pm-10pm, Mon. 5pm-10pm, $15-30) serves pizzas, fresh fish, and tender roast chicken, all cooked in a wood-burning oven. Other specialties include carpaccio and the Rollino Veneto, a rolled-up pizza stuffed with smoked mozzarella and radicchio. Of course, there is also pasta, and a nice diverse selection of California and Italian wines is presented. The restaurant has a compact interior, so many people opt for the deck instead. It's not uncommon to see workers and winemakers from the vineyards show up in their cowboy boots and hats for authentic Italian cuisine in the sometimes loud space.

MEXICAN

Modern pueblo meets country at Mexican restaurant **Dos Carlitos** (3544 Sagunto St., 805/688-0033, www.doscarlitosrestaurant. com, daily 11am-10pm, $25), which boasts high vaulted ceilings and a nice outdoor patio. The furnishings were made in Mexico, and

there is an authentic feel to the place, although the authentic Mexican food comes with a steep price tag. The menu includes grilled *churrasco* rib-eye steak and grilled chicken breast in traditional mole. Diners also rave about the fresh lime margaritas. Sit at the copper-topped bar and try one of 50 tequilas by the shot ($25-75).

Information and Services
MAPS AND VISITOR INFORMATION
The lone option is the **Santa Ynez Valley Visitors Association** (www.syvva.com), which has a fairly comprehensive website covering much of the valley. Remember that many businesses here still don't have websites, only phone numbers, so getting specific information is often a challenge.

EMERGENCY SERVICES
The **Santa Ynez Valley Cottage Hospital** (2050 Viborg Rd., Solvang, 805/688-6431, www.cottagehealthsystem.org) offers emergency services. Should you have an emergency, dial 911 immediately. Police services are the **County of Santa Barbara Sheriff's Department** (1745 Mission Dr., Solvang, 805/688-5000, www.sbsheriff.org).

NEWSPAPERS AND MEDIA
The *Santa Ynez Valley News* (http://syvnews. com) covers the local angle and is published each Thursday. The *Santa Barbara News-Press* (www.newspress.com) is a daily newspaper covering all of Santa Barbara County, with the main office in Santa Barbara and another office in Lompoc. The alternative weekly *Santa Barbara Independent* (www.independent.com) covers the whole county, although the emphasis is on the city of Santa Barbara. New issues are available for free around the county starting on Thursday.

POSTAL SERVICES
Given the limited size of the **Post Office** (3564 Sagunto St., 805/693-9287, www.usps.com), it's advisable to call ahead for operating hours and services.

LAUNDRY

There are no laundry services in town; your best bet **is St. Paul Cleaners and Laundry** (1693 Mission Dr., Solvang, 805/688-9618), located a few miles down the road in Solvang.

Getting There

Santa Ynez is accessed via Highway 246, which cuts through the area. If you're arriving by car from the north, you can exit the highway and drive through Solvang, or take the Highway 154 exit and drive in the back way. Each route has its advantages. Driving through Solvang is great if you've never seen the town before, but on weekends the road is packed with slow-moving cars, buses, and RVs. The Highway 154 route, with scenic rolling hills and a few vineyards, can take you through Los Olivos or along Highway 154 until you turn right onto Highway 246. If you're driving from the south, take either U.S. 101 up through the Gaviota Pass and exit through Solvang, or drive through the San Marcos Pass on Highway 154, which can also be a long drive, depending on traffic. Here you'll pass Lake Cachuma, where you'll probably see deer and cattle strolling the oak-studded hillsides.

Small craft can land at the **Santa Ynez Valley Airport** (900 Airport Rd., 805/688-8390, www.santaynezairport.com), a tiny airfield right near town that serves the entire valley.

◖ SOLVANG

Solvang feels far from rural California. Windmills rise above the brick sidewalks, and European-style café seating spills out of charming restaurants. You'll also notice storks displayed above many of the stores in town; they're a traditional Danish symbol of good luck. Even the few chain restaurants like Subway are done up in the Danish style with a brick exterior and hanging plants. To some, the town might seem like Denmark on steroids, but the colorful and charming village is unlike any other; it's a great escape from the tedious mall architecture that dominates much of the United States.

Solvang originally looked like other towns of its day, with a Spanish theme punctuated by Western stores. The vision to create the Solvang we see today emerged after World War II. Long before thematic towns or city centers were in vogue, Solvang agreed on a unifying design theme, and that is part of the allure.

Solvang draws nearly two million visitors each year, and you'll still hear the muted strains of Danish spoken on occasion. During peak summer times and holidays, Solvang can be congested, with people clogging the brick sidewalks, riding rented surreys through the streets, and loitering in front of the bakeries and chocolate shops; it feels uncharacteristic of a small town. Try to visit during the off-season, when the simple joys of meandering among the lovely shops can still be enjoyed. It's at its best in the fall and early spring when the hills are verdant green and the trees in town are beautiful.

Sights and Drives
BALLARD CANYON

Ballard Canyon is not only a great local drive, it's also popular with cyclists and even runners. Just off the main street in Solvang, you can ride, drive, or run the canyon past vineyards, bison, and cattle; the road will take you out near Los Olivos. What makes this road so wonderful is the combination of straightaways mixed with gentle curves and occasional steep climbs, and of course the bucolic scenery from low in the canyon to high atop the ridge, which has views of the surrounding area. To access Ballard Canyon from downtown Solvang, head north on Atterdag Road. The road climbs the hill for a while, then drops you down into the canyon. Veer right onto Ballard Canyon Road, and follow it all the way through the canyon to Highway 246. To the right is Los Olivos; straight ahead is Foxen Canyon Road.

SANTA ROSA ROAD

Santa Rosa Road winds through the Santa Rita Hills, the best-known pinot noir-growing region in the county. The two-lane road meanders past a few wineries, old ranch houses, and lots of gentle sloping hills. Both cars and cyclists share this road, which eventually connects

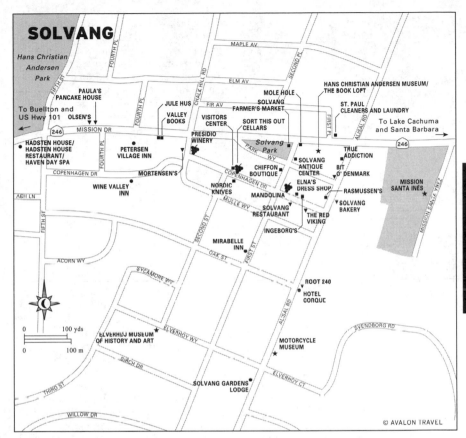

with Highway 1 south of Lompoc. The hills rise to the left; to the right are vineyards and farmland. Early morning and late afternoon are great times to be here as the sun gently bathes the hills and vineyards in a soft golden hue.

OSTRICHLAND

Made popular by the 2004 film *Sideways,* **OstrichLand USA** (610 E. Hwy. 246, 805/686-9696, www.ostrichlandusa.com, daily 10am-dusk, adults $4, under age 12 $1) is a farm on Highway 246 two miles before you reach Solvang from U.S. 101. At first glance, it seems somewhat prehistoric; you'll see massive birds wandering through the shrubs in the distance, their thin necks sporting small heads and big

eyes. They usually keep their distance and only approach when there is food to be had. Should you decide to feed them, you need to hold the food plate firmly in your hand, as they don't eat gingerly but attack the plate with fierce determination. If you have a loose grip on the plate, it will fly out of your hand with the first peck. Aside from feeding them, you can shop for ostrich eggs and ostrich jerky as well as emu eggs and ostrich-feather accoutrements.

MISSION SANTA INÉS

Established in 1804, **Mission Santa Inés** (1760 Mission Dr., 805/688-4815, www.mission-santaines.org, daily 9am-4:30pm, mass daily 8am, $5) has had its share of hardships, but

WINE COUNTRY

© STUART THORNTON

one of Solvang's windmills

it remains a working church to this day. It's named for Saint Agnes, in Spanish Santa Inés. The name of the town is spelled Santa Ynez, an Anglicization of the Spanish pronunciation. The interior is similar in size to the other missions. The long, tall, narrow church is more simply decorated, with hand-painted interiors and without much architectural detail. Of note is the large collection of about 500 church vestments, dating from the 15th to the early 18th centuries. Near the Stations of the Cross at the south end of the property are expansive views to the valley below, which used to be orchards for the mission. There is a back entrance that few people seem to find, through a parking lot at Mission Road and Alisal Road in Solvang. Behind the public restrooms, a brick walkway leads into the back side of the mission grounds.

The mission, established in 1804, was designed to be a stopping point between the missions at Santa Barbara and La Purisima in Lompoc. It was devastated by an earthquake in 1812 but was rebuilt; what is visible today is not original, with the exception of part of the original arch toward the south end of the property. The population of Chumash people living around the mission was reported to be close to 1,000 at its peak. After Mexican independence from Spain in 1821, secularization caused the departure of the Spanish missionaries and most of the Chumash people, and the mission declined until it was rescued by much-needed attention and money.

ELVERHØJ MUSEUM OF HISTORY AND ART

To fully understand Solvang, it's important to visit the **Elverhøj Museum of History and Art** (1624 Elverhoy Way, 805/686-1211, www.elverhoj.org, Wed.-Sun. 11am-4pm, $3), a delightful and surprisingly cool place. Not only does the museum offer tabletop and kitchen linens and local crafts, it presents a comprehensive history of the area, with nostalgic photos of the early settlers. Of particular note is the typical Danish kitchen, hand-painted in green with stenciled flowers everywhere and pine floors, countertops, and tables—it gives an idea of how creative the Danes made their homes, no doubt in an effort to brighten bleak winters. Those winters brightened considerably after they arrived in California, but it was a long journey. The museum also features exhibits of traditional folk art from Denmark, including paper-cutting and lace-making, which is clearly evident throughout town. There are displays of wood clogs and the rustic tools used to create them, and they offer rotating exhibits throughout the year that focus on the valley. It would be easy to dismiss the museum as just a novelty, but clearly the passion of the original settlers and their willingness to come to the New World and continue their way of life from the old country is something we can all learn from.

HANS CHRISTIAN ANDERSEN MUSEUM

The small **Hans Christian Andersen Museum** (1680 Mission Dr., 805/688-2052, www.bookloftsolvang.com, daily 9am-5pm, free) has a few Andersen artifacts, including the mold of

HANS CHRISTIAN ANDERSEN

© STUART THORNTON

Solvang's Hans Christian Andersen statue, by Danish sculptor Henry Luckow Nielsen

One way that Solvang celebrates Danish culture is by paying tribute to one of Denmark's most popular native sons, storyteller Hans Christian Andersen. He was born on the Danish island of Funen in 1805. He moved to Copenhagen at the age of 14 to embark on an acting career, but soon began writing. Although he authored poems, plays, and travel essays, he became best known for his fairy tales. He started by rewriting the fairy tales he had heard as a child, but soon had his greatest success with his own original stories, including *Thumbelina*, *The Little Mermaid*, *The Ugly Duckling*, and *The Emperor's New Clothes*.

Andersen wrote more than 160 fairy tales that have been translated into 125 languages. His stories continue to be adapted on the stage and screen today and are now a permanent part of our literary heritage and culture. As evidence of his continuing popularity, statues of the writer can be found in New York City's Central Park, Chicago's Lincoln Park, and, of course, Solvang's Hans Christian Andersen Park.

WINE COUNTRY

his head made for the bronze bust in the park on Mission Drive, first editions of his books from the 1830s in Danish and English, photographs, and a timeline chronicling his life, work, and impact on literature. It's easy to overlook Andersen as simply a writer of fairy tales, but Andersen also wrote novels, plays, and other works. Even a short visit will enlighten you about the prolific Dane.

MOTORCYCLE MUSEUM

The **Motorcycle Museum** (320 Alisal Rd., 805/686-9522, www.motosolvang.com, Sat.-Sun. 11am-5pm, Mon.-Fri. by appointment, $10) is truly a unique and interesting stop. Along the self-guided tour are 95 motorcycles, vintage and new, on display. Each bike has a description, and some are downright beautiful,

polished, and lovingly restored. There are bikes from the 1930s and 1940s, the earliest from 1903, and some are so cool that you'll want to strap on a helmet and take a ride. After 10 years in this spot they have amassed quite a private collection, with Ducati, Crocker, Matchless, Nimbus, and many more. Admission is not inexpensive compared to other things to do in town, but if motorcycles are your passion, you need to visit.

WILDLING ART MUSEUM

The **Wildling Art Museum** (1511 Mission Dr., 805/688-1082, www.wildlingmuseum. org, Wed.-Mon. 11am-5pm, adults $5, seniors $3.50, children $2) showcases the expansive beauty of the West: its landscapes, flora, and fauna. The Wilding's new location in Solvang, which opened in 2013, includes expanded exhibit space, an educational center, a research library, and a wilderness resource center that provides information about the county's natural areas. The large museum gift shop features books and other items focused on wilderness art. Each year the museum mounts four large exhibitions, which include lectures on art but also the preservation of diminishing Western wildlands.

QUICKSILVER MINIATURE HORSE RANCH

It's free to stop by the **Quicksilver Miniature Horse Ranch** (1555 Alamo Pintado Rd., 805/686-4002, daily 10am-3pm), a ranch that specializes in miniature horses for a growing list of customers from across the globe who desire these horses as pets. If you drive by the farm on almost any spring day, you may catch a glimpse of 25-30 newborn foals, measuring 20 inches tall, testing out their new legs as they attempt to leap and bound on the grass. Visitors can get up close with the newborns and the adults, but remember that this is not a petting zoo; it's a working ranch. There are usually about 90 horses on the ranch at any time.

NOJOQUI FALLS PARK

Walk off some of those Danish pastries at **Nojoqui Falls Park** (Alisal Rd., 7 miles south of Solvang, 805/934-6123, www.countyofsb. org, daily 8am-sunset). The star attraction in this county park is a seasonal waterfall that tumbles down a 164-foot-high moss-cloaked cliff face. The falls are reached by a 10-minute walk up a wide dirt path with bridges that cross several times over a small creek. During summer and dry times, the waterfall is little more than a series of droplets dripping down the rock formation. Still, it's an impressively steep box canyon. In addition to the falls, the park has ball fields, barbecue grills, a playground, restrooms and several picnic areas.

The falls were named for a Chumash village that once existed in the region, and there are two Native American legends concerning the falls. One details how a drought was devastating the Chumash crops, which caused a local chief to ask the gods for help. In the morning, a beautiful woman appeared, and she led the chief into the narrow canyon. She then floated up in the air and disappeared. Her clothes became a waterfall pouring down into the canyon. Another legend finds a couple of star-crossed lovers jumping off the falls together rather than becoming separated by their disapproving community.

Wine Tasting

There are no vineyards in Solvang, but there are tasting rooms, and they're all within walking distance of each other. Many people overlook Solvang tasting rooms because they assume that since it's a tourist spot, the wineries located here might be, shall we say, not as serious. Well, that's definitely not the case; there are some excellent wines represented locally that are worth seeking out.

PRESIDIO WINERY

Presidio Winery (1603 Copenhagen Dr., Suite 1, 805/693-8585, www.presidiowinery. com, daily 11am-6pm, tasting $16, includes a wine glass) is one of the few wineries on the Central Coast to be certified as a biodynamic winery. You'll see a small label on the back of the bottles that identifies the wine as having been approved by Demeter, the body that governs this farming method. Biodynamic methods go beyond organic farming and employ, ideally, a closed-loop farm system. Simply put, it's farming the best way to insure nonintrusive outside elements don't interfere with a healthy respect for the land. That aside, owner Doug Braun's wines are quite good, and his style of wine-making is more restrained than most others in the area. Chardonnay, pinot noir, syrah, and late-harvest wines are on offer at his tasting room on Copenhagen Drive at Mission Drive, in the heart of Solvang, a great place to begin your education about local wines and biodynamic farming methods.

MANDOLINA

Winemaker Megan McGrath-Gates produces some terrific white wines at **Tocatta** (1665 Copenhagen Dr., 805/686-5506, www.ll-wine.com, daily 11am-5:30pm, tasting $8-12), a bright and airy tasting room with exposed ceiling beams and a copper-topped wood bar. The focus here is on Italian varietals, including pinot grigio, barbera, nebbiolo, dolcetto, malvasia bianca, and sangiovese. There's a delicate touch to the wines due to Megan's sensibilities, and she studied in Italy to understand the Italian wine-making process-reflected in the wonderful wines she makes. The wines, especially the whites, are quite good and are sold at very reasonable prices.

SHOESTRING WINERY

Shoestring Winery (800 E. Hwy. 246, 800/693-8612, www.shoestringwinery.com, Fri.-Sun. 10am-4pm, tasting $10) is west of Solvang on the main road, just before you reach the town from U.S. 101. This winery started out when the owners migrated from Baltimore and bought 65 acres. Formerly adept at training racehorses, they still have a few on the property, but the focus is on wine. The early days were tight financially, and a shoestring budget allowed them to plant more and more vines. They still have a small production, but they offer merlot, syrah, sangiovese, rosé, and pinot grigio. The tasting room, in an old barn with a really cool floor made from wooden posts, feels more like a farm than polished and glitzy.

SORT THIS OUT CELLARS

Michael Cobb, owner of **Sort This Out Cellars** (1636 Copenhagen Dr., 805/688-1717, www.sortthisoutcellars.com, Sun.-Thurs. 10am-7pm, Fri.-Sat. 10am-10pm, tasting $5-15), decided to create a new type of winery that doesn't own any vineyards, land, or actual grapes, but instead simply buys the fruit. After all, you don't need a plot of land to make wine. The retro tasting room was inspired by an old photograph of the famed 1960s Rat Pack outside the Sands Hotel in Las Vegas. It has low-back bar stools at the tasting counter, lots of shiny chrome, and pinup girls on the wine labels. The ambience just might make you feel cool enough to sample their merlot, syrah, sangiovese, sauvignon blanc, chardonnay, muscat, and a super Tuscan blend. The Elvira Macabrenet is named for the campy 1980s horror movie hostess. Enjoy your wine while taking in live music on Friday and Saturday 6pm-10pm.

RUSACK VINEYARDS

Rusack Vineyards (1819 Ballard Canyon, 805/688-1278, www.rusackvineyards.com, daily 11am-5pm, tasting $9) is one of the best picnic spots in the valley. Bring your lunch and pick up a bottle of their sauvignon blanc, sangiovese, pinot noir, or their flagship Bordeaux-style wine called Anacapa, and lounge under the old oaks on the side deck. Ballard Canyon is mostly a quiet canyon, and the views of the other vineyards from the outside patio are wonderful. Around Halloween the canyon is dotted with bright pumpkins, and you'll occasionally see bison roaming the hills.

Entertainment and Events

It's important to understand that this part of the valley rolls up the sidewalks pretty early. There are events that take place, but there are few bars. For a full-on bar and club scene, you have to either drive 30 minutes south to Santa Barbara or 20 minutes north to Santa Maria. Businesses don't stay open late, and you'll be hard-pressed to find things to do when the sun goes down.

BARS

One option for an evening beer is the **Solvang Brewing Company** (1547 Mission St., 805/688-2337, www.solvangbrewingcompany.com, daily 11am-2am, dinner $12-23). It's easy to find under a windmill on Solvang's main drag, Mission Street. They brew their own beers with names that celebrate the town's Danish heritage, such as Windmill Wheat and Valhalla IPA. They also serve food, including burgers and entrées like Danish meatballs, and occasionally host live music.

CINEMA

Keeping in mind this is small-town USA, there's only one movie theater in the area, serving the southern part of the valley. The **Park Plaza Theatre** (515 McMurray Rd., Buellton, 805/688-7434, $9) is located right off U.S. 101 between Buellton and Solvang, sandwiched between the Marriot and the McDonald's. It has five small screens and comfortable seating. You're likely to find the latest films here and few crowds.

FESTIVALS AND EVENTS

The **Solvang Theaterfest** (420 2nd St., 805/688-1789, www.solvangtheaterfest.org) features semiprofessional theater, with both professional actors and local talent, at a beautiful outdoor venue. The Solvang group puts on four plays each year between June and October in a 700-seat venue originally built in 1974. There is a focus on musicals and lighter fare, and there has been great support for live theater in this small town. In a small compound of Danish-style architecture and beautiful old oak trees, this is a great summertime tradition.

Danish Days (www.solvangusa.com), held the third weekend in September, is a big draw. Started in 1936, it features clog-wearing Danes dancing in the streets, pastries and coffee everywhere, and even an *æbleskiver* (pancake) eating contest. It's Solvang's annual salute to its cultural heritage, and local women dress in traditional skirts, aprons, and caps despite the heat of the season. The men also wear their clogs and traditional outfits. The festival is referred to as Æbleskiver Days on occasion, and it has been a tradition for locals to serve *æbleskiver* from pans set up in the streets. There is also an afternoon of non-Danish entertainment when local rock bands perform adjacent to the Viking Beer Garden.

The food and wine event **Taste of Solvang** (www.solvangusa.com), held the third weekend in March, has been in existence for 20 years and keeps growing and becoming more sophisticated each year. It starts with a dessert reception, and considering the history of pastry and sweets among the Danes, that's enough right there. Following that is the walking smorgasbord, which features roughly 40 stops in town where you stop in and sample what they are serving—usually Danish food, though some restaurants and stores offer non-Danish food samples. Ten tasting rooms pour their vintages into your souvenir glass, and there's live entertainment in the park, where many people bring a picnic and relax. It's a five-day event that immerses you in the local culture and customs and the new crop of wineries.

The **Solvang Century** (800/548-4447, www.bikescor.com) is the best-known cycling race in the valley. Technically, it's not a race, it's a fund-raiser, but you still can't help but compete. They added a half-century race to accommodate riders who prefer the shorter distances, but there is still some pretty serious elevation gain, a minimum of 2,000 vertical feet, making this a challenging course. The money raised benefits heart-related diseases, since the founder of the event used cycling as a way to promote health after his own heart surgery.

Shopping
ANTIQUES

Solvang Antiques (1693 Copenhagen Dr.., 805/688-6222, www.solvangantiques.com, daily 10am-6pm) is home to some incredible antiques. In addition to a stellar collection of magnificent gilded antique clocks, there are music boxes, jewelry, watches, and gorgeous vintage telephones, from old candlestick models to the 1930s and 1940s designs. They also have artfully restored antique furniture. It's an expensive place but has such diversity that any antiques lover should stop in, even if just to browse one of the finest stores on the Central Coast.

In Los Alamos, 10 minutes north of Solvang, is a massive space filled with a vast collection of antiques, priced much lower than the Solvang Antique Center. **The Depot Antique Mall** (515 Bell St., Los Alamos, 805/344-3315, Mon.-Sat. 10am-5pm, Sun. 11am-4pm), once the depot for the Pacific

Coast Railway, now holds over 60 antiques vendors in three large rooms. Prices are reasonable on everything from vintage posters to an abundance of furniture to collectibles, and it's worth the short drive. Some items are knockoffs, but the wide selection rotates often, especially the larger furniture pieces.

BOOKSTORES

The Book Loft (1680 Mission Dr., 805/688-6010, www.bookloftsolvang.com, Sun.-Mon. 9am-6pm, Tues.-Thurs. 9am-8pm, Fri.-Sat. 9am-9pm) sells mostly new books, although there's a small section of used books as well. This over-40-year-old two-story store has a vast, well-organized selection, including local authors. The wooden stairs creak as you venture upstairs to see even more books. It has the feel of an old bookstore, not sanitized with fancy shelves; in fact, these shelves were all handmade. They also have a nice selection of antiquarian books, and upstairs is the Hans Christian Andersen Museum.

CLOTHING

Elna's Dress Shop (1673 Copenhagen Dr., 805/688-4525, www.elnas.com, daily 10am-5pm) is the place to go for handmade Danish dresses and costumes, as well as more contemporary but conservative and non-Danish-themed dresses for women. If you're searching for that perfect Danish outfit for a young one, you'll find it here. Aprons, caps, and brightly colored simple dresses, some with beautiful lace, are available off the rack, or they will make one for you. They have only a few Danish pieces for young boys, and they're pretty darn cute.

True Addiction (485 Alisal Rd., 805/686-2868, www.trueaddictionsolvang.com, Mon.-Tues. and Thurs. 9:30am-6pm, Wed. and Fri.-Sat. 9:30am-7pm, Sun. 10am-5pm) sells hip and trendy clothing for a younger crowd and includes a large section of shoes, boots, and jewelry. The stock rotates frequently, and in spite of being situated in a heavily touristed area, they have very reasonable prices and contemporary fashions.

SPECIALTY STORES

Mole Hole (1656 Mission Dr., 805/688-7669, www.moleholesolvang.com, daily 9:30am-5:30pm) is a gift shop with an emphasis on miniature collectibles as well as decidedly feminine and romantic items, many with a fairy theme or lots of lace. Upstairs is a humorous section of gifts for men—well, men heading over 50. Staff are extremely helpful, which has contributed to the store's success.

You'll feel a little better from the moment you enter **Jule Hus** (1580 Mission Dr., 805/688-6601, www.solvangchristmas-house.com, Mon.-Sat. 9am-5:30pm, Sun. 10am-5pm), where it's the holiday season all year long. They offer hand-carved wood ornaments, blown-glass ornaments, traditional Scandinavian ornaments, and stand-alone decorations, as well as a huge selection of nutcrackers. There are also traditional Danish quilts and lace items and plenty of trees fully decked out. Jule Hus has celebrated the Christmas spirit since 1967, and there are always people milling around searching for that ideal ornament. Other stores in town have small sections of Christmas items, but here it's all there is.

Rasmussen's (1697 Copenhagen Dr., 805/688-6636, www.rasmussenssolvang.com, daily 9am-5:30pm) opened in 1921 and is still going strong five generations later. It has everything Scandinavian: a one-stop shop for gifts, books, souvenirs, Danish packaged food items, and kitchen items.

Nordic Knives (436 1st St., 800/992-6574, www.nordicknives.com, Mon.-Fri. 10am-5pm) has more knives than you've probably ever seen in one place, including expensive high-end custom-made knives by well-known knife makers as well as jeweled, engraved, and one-of-a-kind knives. Many of them are very impressive. There are also hunting and kitchen knives with prices that are much lower than the custom blades. The shop has been in Solvang nearly 40 years, and they know their knives. Whether you need a simple knife or a traditional Swiss Army knife, they'll have it. The display case on the right-hand side as you enter

WINE COUNTRY

is worth a look, with beautiful knives of all types and pedigree.

Ingeborg's (1679 Copenhagen Dr., 805/688-5612, www.ingeborgs.com, daily 9am-5:30pm) has been making traditional Danish chocolates for over half a century. Over 70 varieties of chocolates, handmade on the premises, are sold. It isn't cheap, but it is Danish chocolate made by Danes. They also carry hard-to-find Dutch chocolates. Grab a seat at one of the six round red barstools and enjoy the ice cream.

Every Wednesday, year-round, rain or shine, fresh fruits, veggies, flowers, and local items from surrounding farms make an appearance at the **Solvang Farmer's Market** (Copenhagen Dr. and 1st St., 805/962-5354, summer Wed. 2:30pm-6:30pm, winter Wed. 2:30pm-6pm). This is not a major farmers market and takes up only two blocks, but the street next to the park is closed, and you can find fresh food harvested from local farms, many of them within a mile of town. It's hard to get much fresher than that.

Sports and Recreation
PARKS
At 15 acres, **Hans Christian Andersen Park** (633 Chalk Hill Rd., 805/688-7529, www.cityofsolvang.com) is the largest park in the area. Enter through a castle gate and you're amid pine and oak trees. Then you come to the skate park, which has cavernous half pipes and is actually well designed, though there are more cyclists who use it than boarders. There is a small wooden playground behind the skate park for the younger ones. If you continue driving through the park, you'll come to another playground with tall chute slides embedded in the sand. There are plenty of trees and picnic tables, all well groomed. Other unique features include a music-making station with chimes and a rock-climbing wall. If you drive all the way to the end, there are four tennis courts right next to a beautiful gnarled old oak tree. There are restroom facilities and drinking fountains.

Sunny Fields Park (900 Alamo Pintado Rd., 805/688-7529, www.cityofsolvang.com) is almost a pint-size Solvang. There's a Viking ship, swings, slides, and monkey bars, plus a gingerbread house, a faux windmill, and plenty of things to climb around on. Trees offer shade, as it gets hot during the summer. This is a great spot for little kids, and it's reasonably quiet, being just outside of town. There are drinking fountains and restrooms, plenty of parking, and a large, flat, grassy ball field.

GOLF
The 18-hole, par-72 **River Course at the Alisal** (150 Alisal Rd., 805/688-6042, www.rivercourse.com, greens fees $60-72) was featured in the 2004 movie *Sideways*. It's a beautiful course on the banks of the Santa Ynez River, punctuated with magnificent oak trees. Challenging and beautiful, it features four lakes, open fairways, tricky hazards, and large undulating greens accented by native sycamore trees. Elevated tees reveal some vistas and occasional vineyards, so bring your best game and your camera.

SPAS
Haven Day Spa (1450 Mission Dr., 805/686-1264, www.hadstenhouse.com, daily 9am-5pm, basic 1-hour massage $110) is hidden behind antique Asian doors. Beyond the doors the day spa reveals a quiet soft-toned interior for a mix of facials, massage, body wraps, and even tuning-fork therapy, which utilizes strategically placed tuning forks to bring harmony and balance back to the nervous system, muscles, and organs. The staff are knowledgeable and ready to accommodate.

Chiffon Boutique (475 1st St., 805/686-1155, www.chiffonboutique.com, Tues.-Fri. 11am-6pm, Sat. 10am-6pm, Sun. noon-4pm, basic 1-hour massage $70) is all about facials, waxing, nails along with haircuts, color, and styling. This small shop has quickly gained a reputation for having nice and trustworthy staff who listen. They contract out for massage services.

Accommodations

UNDER $150

Days Inn-Windmill (114 E. Hwy. 246, Buellton, 805/688-8448, www.daysinn.com, $80-140) was featured in the 2004 film *Sideways*—you can even stay in the same room where the main characters stayed in the film. The 108 guest rooms here are pretty standard and basic, with the best feature being the outdoor pool. It's right off U.S. 101, and you can't miss its namesake windmill. It's best to avoid the guest rooms fronting the freeway and go for an interior room to cut down on the noise. There are no views, but the rates are good. They also have Wi-Fi included in the rates and a continental breakfast for their guests.

Designed to resemble Denmark's Tivoli Gardens, the ◖ **Wine Valley Inn & Cottages** (1564 Copenhagen Dr., 805/688-2111, www.winevalleyinn.com, rooms $104-204, cottages $324-364) has courtyards, a European-style garden, and a working clock tower. All guest rooms have electric or free-standing fireplaces, and two units have large private patios. The six spacious one-bedroom cottages

© STUART THORNTON

Wine Valley Inn & Cottages

with kitchenettes have decor inspired by the C. S. Lewis fantasy novels *The Chronicles of Narnia* and European furnishings. Five of the six cottages include jetted tubs on private patios. Whether you stay in a cottage or in one of the inn's guest rooms, take advantage of the complimentary hot breakfast. The inn is right downtown, so you can get around without a car.

$150-250

◖ **Solvang Gardens Lodge** (293 Alisal Rd., 888/688-4404, www.solvanggardens.com, $169-229) is a 24-room delight on the edge of town. It feels like a small village. There are stone fireplaces and marble baths, and each guest room is unique and different. Some are decorated with a more modern theme, some have a traditional feel, but all are very well appointed. Beautiful gardens in both the front and center of the property give you a peaceful green space. The local owners will do everything they can to ensure your stay is the best it can be. It's quieter here since it's not on the main drag. In the morning you can walk into town or down to the dry riverbed.

The 42-room **Peterson Village Inn Solvang** (1576 Mission Dr., 805/688-3121, www.peterseninn.com, $150-350) has been around a long time and sees its share of return guests. It's traditional—maybe even a little stuffy—but it's in a great location on the town's main street, so you can simply walk outside into the thick of things. All guests get to enjoy the inn's European breakfast buffet.

◖ **Hotel Corque** (400 Alisal Rd., 800/624-5572, www.hotelcorque.com, $190-270) was originally a very Danish hotel, but an extensive renovation morphed it into a sleek and sophisticated venue catering to a younger crowd. It feels like it belongs in a major city, not a rural area, and that's part of its appeal. Although the 100 guest rooms and 17 suites are a tad small and the amenities are nothing unique, there's no disliking the decor—if you're looking for cool digs, you've found them. There's a pool, a jetted tub, and a fitness center on the grounds.

◖ **Hadsten House** (1450 Mission Dr.,

805/688-3210, www.hadstenhouse.com, $164-254) is a nonsmoking property, and one of the best places to stay in Solvang. French-style furnishings with custom mattresses, dark-toned furniture, and ample space pull you out of the Danish mentality and into a contemporary and sophisticated setting. A full breakfast and nightly wine and cheese are offered, as well as a heated indoor pool and outdoor hot tub. It's one of the closest hotels to U.S. 101 and the first you come to as you enter Solvang. Set in a square horseshoe pattern, it offers no views, but these are comfortable, well-appointed guest rooms with a European flair.

OVER $250

Mirabelle Inn (409 1st St., 800/786-7925, www.solvanginns.com, $250-295) is run by well-seasoned veterans of the hospitality industry. The 10 medium-size guest rooms decorated with antiques and lace are much more Victorian bed-and-breakfast in their feel; many have four-poster beds, and a few have sleigh beds. It's located in the heart of Solvang, so you can leave the vine-covered walls and go explore, then return to this other world. They have an in-house restaurant that serves wonderful food.

The **Alisal Guest Ranch** (1054 Alisal Rd., 805/688-6411, www.alisal.com, $515-680) dates back to 1946. The 73 guest rooms at this ranch retreat are all very large and have a strong Western and pueblo feel to them. Full breakfasts and dinners are included in the rates. And since this is considered a retreat, there are no TVs or telephones, but you do have access to Wi-Fi, tennis courts ($20 per hour), fishing in the ranch's lake (3-hour guided trip from $180), horseback riding ($50 per hour), and even archery ($35 per hour). The secluded and luxurious environment makes it possible for complete relaxation. But if you need to, you can walk into town.

Food

There are many places in town that serve traditional Danish food, which doesn't typically conjure up images of innovative global fare. But as Solvang is growing, with new hotels and wine-tasting rooms opening up, restaurants are looking to stand out from the traditional in what is becoming, albeit slowly, a true destination, with farm-fresh food and innovative ways of preparing it. But if you are looking for the traditional, you'll find it here too, occasionally with an accordion player outside the front door, enticing you to come in.

BAKERIES

Mortensen's (1588 Mission Dr., 805/688-8373, www.mortensensbakery.com, winter daily 7:30am-5:30pm, summer daily 7:30am-8pm) is one of the stalwarts of the Danish bakeries. It's best to visit the low-key interior for a strudel or éclair and a pot of tea or coffee and relax in the subdued environment. The Danish decor is not over the top, but it's still good Danish, and this is a great place to start your day.

Olsen's Danish Village Bakery (1529 Mission Dr., 805/688-6314, www.olsensdanishbakery.com, Mon.-Fri. 7am-6pm, Sat.-Sun. 7am-7pm) was established in Denmark way back in 1890, although this location isn't quite that old. They've been turning out homemade breads such as grain pumpernickel, sunflower seed pumpernickel, and Swedish cardamom, as well as cookies and all manner of sweets, for three decades.

Solvang Bakery (460 Alisal Rd., 805/688-4939, www.solvangbakery.com, Sun.-Thurs. 7am-7pm, Fri.-Sat. 7am-8pm) is a bright open space in a blue-and-white shop with an eye-catching array of gingerbread houses, Danish waffles, almond butter rings, and plenty more. They have been baking in Solvang for 30 years. Their onion cheese bread is a signature loaf.

Three generations have worked at **◖ Birkholm's Bakery & Café** (460 Alisal Rd., 805/688-8188, www.birkholmsbakery.com, Sun.-Thurs. 7am-6pm, Fri.-Sat. 7am-7pm), a local favorite since the 1950s. The friendly staff serves up Belgian waffles, Danish pastries, and butter cookies, all made from traditional family recipes. Sandwiches and salads are also available for lunch. Expect plenty of seating and Wi-Fi access with your purchase.

BREWPUBS

There are a couple of worthwhile brewpubs in nearby Buellton. **Firestone Walker Brewery Taproom** (620 McMurray Rd., Buellton, 805/225-5911, www.firestonewalker.com, daily 11am-9pm, tasting $6.50, food $12-24) features four Firestone Walker beers in addition to four alternating beers on tap. You can get it by the pint or by the mug, or try a sampler of four beers. They also offer food like pork chops, steaks, and burgers as well as beer-battered fish-and-chips. Firestone Walker is the best brewery on the Central Coast and right off U.S. 101, just north of Buellton. Grab a brew, and if your picky friend wants wine, well, they'll pour Firestone wines by the glass.

Learn about beer while you drink it at the **Figueroa Mountain Brewing Company Tasting Room** (45 Industrial Way, Buellton, 805/694-2252, www.figmtnbrew.com, Mon.-Thurs. 4pm-9pm, Fri.-Sun. 11am-9pm). The taproom is located in the main production facility, where you can ask the brewer questions while sipping the fruits of his labor, which include the popular Hoppy Poppy IPA along with the Danish Red Lager, Figueroa Mountain Pale Ale, and others. The tasting room hosts a trivia night every other Wednesday and live music on weekends.

DANISH

Year after year, **▮ Paula's Pancake House** (1531 Mission Dr., 805/688-2867, daily 6am-3pm, $7-12, www.paulaspancakehouse.com) is the top spot for Danish food. It can get very crowded, especially on the patio, so be prepared to wait during peak times. Their three-page breakfast menu is replete with huge plate-size pancakes of all types, including the Danish apple. Or go Dutch and try the Dutch sausage omelet. Lunches include traditional Danish foods as well as some Americanized items. The interior is casual, with more of a coffee shop feel, but it's also slightly Scandinavian. Note that breakfast and lunch are served but not dinner.

Bit O' Denmark (473 Alisal Rd., 805/688-5426, www.bitodenmark.com, daily 11am-9pm, $18-29) is known for their traditional smorgasbord as well as roasted duck and Monte Cristo sandwiches. It's the oldest restaurant in Solvang, housed in one of the very first buildings the original settlers built in 1911. It became a restaurant in 1929 and continues to cook up Danish ham, Danish pork, open-faced roast beef sandwiches, and the extensive smorgasbord ($20), which includes *medisterpølse* (Danish sausage), *frikadeller* (meatballs), *rødkål* (red cabbage), *spegesild* (pickled herring), and an array of cold salads. The room to the left as you enter is the best, with large curved booths.

Solvang Restaurant (1672 Copenhagen Dr., 805/688-4645, www.solvangrestaurant.com, Mon.-Fri. 6am-3pm, Sat.-Sun. 7am-5pm, $6-15.50) is well known for its *æbleskiver*, like doughnut holes drenched in warm raspberry jam. This diner with wooden beams decorated with Danish proverbs and wooden booths also has Danish items like creamed herring and Danish-style meatballs along with typical diner fare like burgers, tuna melts, and omelets. Don't be surprised to see a line out the door.

▮ The Red Viking (1684 Copenhagen Dr.,

The Red Viking restaurant

WINE COUNTRY

© STUART THORNTON

Pea Soup Andersen's

805/688-6610, www.theredvikingrestaurant. com, daily 8am-8pm, $8-17) rolls out Danish dishes such as *hakkebøf* (chopped sirloin and onion topped with a fried egg), wiener schnitzel (veal cutlet), an authentic Danish smorgasbord, and a line of Danish cheeses, hams, and beers. This is one of the top Danish food stops.

Pea Soup Andersen's (376 Ave. of the Flags, Buellton, 805/688-5581, www.peasoupandersens.net, daily 7am-10pm, $7-20) is the granddaddy of Danish restaurants, first opened in 1924. They serve American food, like burgers and milk shakes, and, of course, pea soup in a bread bowl. There's a small gift shop, a bakery with fresh daily sweets and fudge, a small art gallery upstairs, and best of all, a mini museum about Rufus T. Buell (as in Buellton), how he started the town, and how Andersen's came into being. It also chronicles some of the changes in the dining scene locally. It's just outside Solvang proper, located just off U.S. 101, and has the feel of a coffee shop. There are plenty of cans of soup for sale.

NEW AMERICAN

◖**Hadsten House Restaurant** (1450 Mission Dr., 800/457-5373, www.hadstenhouse.com, Sun.-Thurs. 5pm-9pm, Fri.-Sat. 5pm-10pm, $13-36) entered the dining scene in 2008 but immediately elevated the local culinary perspective. Dark and moody inside, it has a central fireplace that creates a hip urban environment, more metropolitan than rural. The short ribs have a demi-glace that will send your mind reeling, and the warm spinach salad is perfectly balanced. Or go for the Hadsten burger, which is piled with everything—including an egg. It's best to make reservations for this small space that produces some very fine food.

Sleek and sophisticated, **Root 246** (420 Alisal Rd., 805/686-8681, www.root-246. com, Mon.-Sat. 5pm-10pm, Sun. 10am-2pm and 5pm-10pm, $25-50), one of the newest additions to the dining scene, has upped the ante. It looks like it belongs in Hollywood, not in rural Solvang, but that's part of the evolution of Solvang and wine-country cuisine. Chef and consultant Bradley Ogden has started over 10 restaurants and knows how to create exciting food. The menu rotates often depending on seasonal ingredients. You'll find oysters, organic mushroom flatbread, and a variety of fish and game dishes. The lengthy creative cocktail list includes an *açaí* sour martini and a tequila drink that employs muddled sage and smoked sea salt. The crowd is young and urban; you won't see a lot of old-school Danish residents here.

Located in nearby Buellton, ◖**The Hitching Post II** (406 E. Hwy. 246, 805/688-0676, http://hitchingpost2.com, daily 5pm-9:30pm, $23-50) became famous after it was the setting of several scenes in the 2004 movie *Sideways*. Even before the movie, it was well known locally for its barbecued meats and homemade wines, especially the Pinot Noir Highliner, and its country restaurant feel. Start with the grilled artichoke appetizer, which comes with a tangy smoked-tomato pesto-mayo dipping sauce. You can watch your meat as it's grilled to order over a red oak fire. Meals come with a vegetable tray,

The Hitching Post II, in Buellton

garlic bread, a soup or salad, and a choice of rice pilaf, baked potato, grilled vegetables, or their very good crispy French fries. Get ready to loosen your belt!

GROCERIES

El Rancho Market Place (2886 Mission Dr., 805/688-4300, www.elranchomarket.com, daily 6am-10pm) is an upscale supermarket and features an old-fashioned full-service meat counter, fresh local organic produce, and a complete selection of local and international wines, champagnes, and spirits. They have very good hot and cold entrées, salads, and fresh-baked bread and pies—perfect for putting together a picnic. If you want something quick and easy, they have a great selection. There's some outdoor seating near the entrance, and on occasion they grill tri-tip outside.

Information and Services
MAPS AND VISITOR INFORMATION

The **Solvang Visitors Center** (1639 Copenhagen Dr., 800/468-6765, www.

solvangusa.com) is staffed by locals wearing red vests. They have comprehensive information not just on Solvang but the entire valley as well. They also print a free visitors guide to Solvang and the Santa Ynez Valley that you can find around town.

EMERGENCY SERVICES

The Santa Ynez Valley Cottage Hospital (2050 Viborg Rd., Solvang, 805/688-6431, www.cottagehealthsystem.org) offers emergency services. Should you have an emergency, dial 911 immediately. Police services are the **County of Santa Barbara Sheriff's Department** (1745 Mission Dr., Solvang, 805/688-5000, www.sbsheriff.org).

NEWSPAPERS AND MEDIA

The *Santa Ynez Valley News* (http://syvnews.com) covers the local angle and is published each Thursday. The *Santa Barbara News-Press* (www.newspress.com) is a daily newspaper covering all of Santa Barbara County, with the main office in Santa Barbara and another office in Lompoc. The alternative weekly *Santa Barbara Independent* (www.independent.com) covers the whole county, although the emphasis is on the city of Santa Barbara. New issues are available for free around the county starting on Thursday.

POSTAL SERVICES

Given the limited size of the **Post Office** (430 Alisal Rd., 805/688-9309), it's advisable to call ahead for operating hours and services.

LAUNDRY

If you need to do laundry on your trip, try **St. Paul Cleaners and Laundry** (1693 Mission Dr., 805/688-9618).

Getting There
CAR

Highway 246 bisects the town. Known as Mission Drive while it runs through town, Highway 246 connects to U.S. 101, the primary freeway on the Central Coast, and the small but still well-traveled Highway 154,

WINE COUNTRY

© STUART THORNTON

which connects to Santa Barbara in the south and U.S. 101 farther north. It's important to note that Solvang gets crowded on weekends, and getting in and out can be a slow proposition. But since you have little choice but to wait it out, just remind yourself how good a Danish cookie will taste when you finally arrive.

BUS

The **Clean Air Express** (805/692-1902, www.cleanairexpress.com, single ride $7) is a commuter bus that connects Santa Barbara and Solvang.

TRAIN

Amtrak (800/872-7245, www.amtrak.com) runs buses to Solvang from the train stations in Santa Barbara and San Luis Obispo. The bus stop is located at 1630 Mission Drive. Travel times for the buses is approximately one hour to Santa Barbara, 1.5 hours to San Luis Obispo.

Getting Around

While it's the largest of the small towns in the area, Solvang is still a very navigable town and can easily be explored on foot in less than a day.

TROLLEY

A horse-drawn trolley traverses the streets of Solvang, taking participants on a narrated tour on the Honen Streetcar, a replica of either a late 1800s or a 1915 streetcar, depending on whom you choose to believe. Two large horses will pull you around town as you learn the history and noteworthy spots of Solvang. The **Solvang Trolley & Carriage Co.** (805/794-8958, www.cleanairexpress.com, Thurs.-Mon. noon-6pm, adults $10, seniors $8, children $5) has tours that last about 25 minutes and run every 35 minutes. Board at the visitors center (Copenhagen St. and 2nd St.).

TAXI

Solvang Taxi (805/688-0069, www.solvang-taxi.com) operates daily 24 hours. You have to phone them, however, as you rarely see a taxi in town. Like many other vendors, they also offer wine transportation. **Promenade Cab**

Company (805/717-8400, http://valleypromenadecab.vpweb.com) also operates in Solvang.

BUS

Santa Ynez Valley Transit (805/688-5452, www.cityofsolvang.com) is a scheduled minibus serving Ballard, Buellton, Los Olivos, Santa Ynez, and Solvang, operating Monday-Saturday starting at 7am. The Chumash Casino also offers a shuttle service (800/248-6274) serving Goleta, Santa Maria, and Lompoc. Riders with a Club Chumash gaming card get preferred seating.

LOS OLIVOS

Tiny Los Olivos is marked by a flagpole that sits dead center on Grand Avenue, acting as a traffic circle. Most of the shops and other venues here are within two blocks of the flagpole, which is often used as a marker when locals are giving directions.

Los Olivos began as a town in 1861 with the establishment of the Overland-Coast Line Stage Station at Ballard. Actually, at the time, it was more a loose aggregate of residences; it wasn't until 1887 that Swiss-Italian immigrant Felix Mattei, anticipating the arrival of the Pacific Coast Railway, opened a hotel to accommodate rail and stage passengers making north and south connections in Los Olivos, and a semblance of an actual town began to form. The local streets were built by Chinese railroad workers, and following the first whistle of the engine in November 1887, Los Olivos, while still small, was finally put on the map. Today, it's a pleasant community with an offering of wine-tasting rooms, boutiques, art galleries, and restaurants for visitors.

Sights and Drives
◖ FOXEN CANYON

If there is any drive or ride that's important to Los Olivos, it's **Foxen Canyon**. It's the site of a wine trail but worth checking out even if you're not into wine; Foxen Canyon is a beautiful, meandering road, immensely popular with cyclists and perfect for a tour with the top down. Where Alamo Pintado Road ends

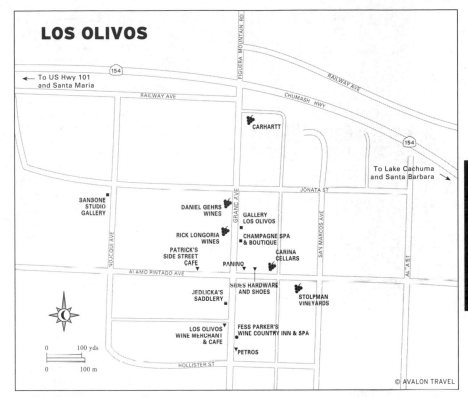

and turns into Highway 154 at the northern end of Los Olivos, Foxen Canyon Road Begins. You can take Foxen Canyon Road just south to Los Alamos or continue all the way into Santa Maria. Typical of the area, there are wineries, ranches, and farms populated with oak trees, cattle, deer, and hawks.

FIGUEROA MOUNTAIN
Figueroa Mountain's 4,528-foot crest is one of the shortest drives you can take to get the farthest away from the typical valley topography of chaparral-covered hills and oak trees. This is also where Michael Jackson's Neverland Ranch is located, but you can't see anything more than a rather nondescript gate. As Figueroa Mountain Drive peels off from Route 154 near Los Olivos and you make your way toward the foothills, the oak trees begin to be replaced by pine trees, wildflowers, and more pronounced rock formations. From the lookout tower located on top of the mountain, 360-degree views of much of the county greet you. The Santa Ynez Mountains are to the south, appearing as a sheer mountain wall from this perspective. On a clear day, typically between February and April, the Channel Islands shimmer on the horizon.

The foreground of this view is the Santa Ynez Valley. Above and to the west is Point Conception, a land revered by the Chumash people, the place of the setting sun, where they traditionally believed they would travel to in the afterlife. You can descend the way you came, or if you're adventurous (and depending on the type of car you have), you can continue on some bumpy roads and over streams to eventually merge with Happy Canyon Road,

© STUART THORNTON

WINE COUNTRY

Beckmen Vineyards

making this a 30-plus-mile loop. This is not a short drive, but it offers some spectacular scenery.

CLAIRMONT FARMS

Clairmont Farms (2480 Roblar Ave., 805/688-7505, www.clairmontfarms.com, Sat.-Mon. 10am-6pm, Sun. 11am-6pm, donation $3) is a family-owned and operated working organic lavender farm that has five acres of lavender, as well as 175-year-old olive trees originally planted by Catholic priests; it's part of the grove that gave Los Olivos its name. Visitors can observe the process of distilling lavender and learn all the ways this herb is being used, in essential oils or as a cooking herb. They sell oils, teas, honey, soaps, and more, all infused with lavender; there's even lavender shampoo for your dog. Not only is it informative, you'll also leave feeling totally relaxed.

Wine Tasting

Los Olivos has become a hub of wine-tasting rooms. Not long ago the area was mainly full

of art galleries and just a few wineries. Now with 30 wine-tasting rooms, Los Olivos has become a convenient stop to taste and shop for all things wine. This tiny hamlet can become quite packed during the high season: Parking is at a premium, tasting rooms can be full to over-flowing, and there are often waits at the few restaurants in town. Plan your trip to avoid the high season and you'll have a much better time.

◖ BECKMEN VINEYARDS

You'll need to drive to get to **Beckmen Vineyards** (2670 Ontiveros Rd., 805/688-8664, www.beckmenvineyards.com, daily 11am-5pm, tasting $10-15), since it is located in the middle of a residential district. The tasting room is in a red building, and there's a wooden deck out back with tables and chairs. There are also three gazebos overlooking a duck pond on the property. It's peaceful out here, and that's the point. Their grapes are biodynamically farmed, using no chemicals whatsoever, right by the tasting room and on a plot of land called Purisima Mountain, where the soil is ideal for grenache and syrahs. You'll see this name at many wineries in the valley; the Beckmen fruit is sold to other wineries and is very popular. Sauvignon blanc, cabernet sauvignon, marsanne, a killer grenache, and a range of syrahs are available to taste. This is one of the best wineries in the area, and they excel at most every wine they make. It's possible to get a great bottle of wine here for under $50.

CARHARTT

Carhartt (2990 Grand Ave., 805/693-5100, www.carharttvineyard.com, daily 11am-5pm, tasting $10) is the smallest tasting room in the valley, but the winery makes big wines. The tasting room, which looks like a wooden shack, can comfortably hold maybe six people, but it does have an outdoor area allowing for some elbow room—although people seem to like crowding themselves inside. The signature wines, merlot and syrah, come from Carhartt's own 10-acre estate, a former cattle ranch, and they buy fruit to produce sauvignon blanc,

KNOW YOUR GRAPES

Want to seem more knowledgeable about wine than you really are? Before you come to wine country, get to know your popular California grapes. While nearly every wine grape known to humankind is grown somewhere in the state, and different varietals go in and out of fashion almost as fast as clothing does, California has a few distinctive and easy-to-find grapes that are the foundation of wine-making in the state.

Chardonnay: Most of the white wine made and sold in California is chardonnay. The grapes grow best in a slightly cooler climate, which works well in vineyards closer to the coast. Most chardonnay wines are made from nearly 100 percent chardonnay grapes. Chardonnay is typically fermented in steel tanks, then poured into steel or oak barrels to finish fermenting and to age It Just a little bit. Most California chardonnays taste smooth and buttery and a bit like fruit; they often take on the oak flavor of the barrels they sit in. Chardonnay doesn't keep (age), so most chards are sold the year after they're bottled and consumed within a few months of purchase.

Sauvignon Blanc: This pale-green grape is used to make both sauvignon blanc and fumé blanc wines in California. Sauvignon blanc grapes grow well in warm-to-hot parts of the state. California sauvignon blanc wine has a "food friendly" reputation: It goes well with salads, fish, vegetarian cuisine, and even spicy foods. Sauvignon blanc has such a light, fruity, and floral taste that it almost seems to float away. The difference between a sauvignon blanc and a fumé blanc is in the wine-making more than in the grapes. Fumé blanc wines tend to have a strong odor and the taste of grapefruit. Fumés also pair well with fish dishes and spicy Asian cuisine.

Pinot Noir: Unlike the other California-favored red wine grapes, pinot noir grapes do best in a cool coastal climate with limited exposure to high heat. California vintners make single-varietal pinot noir wines that taste of cherries, strawberries, and smoke when they're great, and of mold and fish when they're not.

Zinfandel: A good California zinfandel is not what you think it is. For starters, it's not sweet and pale pink. A true zinfandel is a hearty deep-red wine. These grapes grow best when tortured by their climate, especially in the inland Central Coast. Zinfandel was one of the first types of grape introduced in California, and a few lucky vineyards have "old vines," zinfandel vines that have been producing grapes for nearly 100 years. A great zinfandel wine boasts the flavors and smells of blackberry jam and the dusky hues of venous blood. Zinfandel often tastes wonderful all by itself, but it's also good with beef, buffalo, and even venison.

Cabernet Sauvignon: If you spend any length of time in California's wine regions, you'll hear the phrase "cab is king." This always means cabernet sauvignon, a grape from the Bordeaux region of France that creates a deep, dark, strong red wine. The grapes that get intense summer heat make the best wine. In France, cabernet sauvignon grapes mix with several other varieties to create the famed Bordeaux blends. In California, winemakers use cabernet sauvignon on its own to brew some of the most intense single-grape wine in the world. A good dry cab might taste of leather, tobacco, and bing cherries. Harsh tannins can create a sandpapery feeling in the mouth and an unpleasant tree-bark flavor, making cabernet sauvignon difficult for newcomers to the wine world to enjoy. Cabs age well, often hitting their peak of flavor and smoothness more than a decade after bottling. By then, the tannins have mellowed and the wine tastes less like chewing on an oak branch.

sangiovese, and petite sirah from both Santa Barbara and Paso Robles.

CARINA CELLARS

Carina Cellars (2900 Grand, 805/688-2459, www.carinacellars.com, daily 11am-5pm, tasting $10) has made a name for itself with syrah, specifically syrah from the well-regarded Colsen Canyon vineyard. But they also have a blend, Iconoclast, that merges Napa Valley cabernet sauvignon with Santa Barbara syrah. Other wines in their portfolio include viognier, petite sirah, and red Rhône-style blends. The tasting room also features rotating art on the rustic-looking walls. Carina has expanded to two tasting bars inside to handle the influx of people. Located in downtown Los Olivos, this is one of the best and most consistent wineries.

STOLPMAN VINEYARDS

Stolpman's (2434 Alamo Pintado Ave., 805/688-0400, www.stolpmanvineyards.com, daily 11am-5pm, tasting $15) tasting room, in a late-1800s building with a red-painted board-and-batten exterior with white trim, was originally a private residence. The tasting room's interior was designed using recycled materials and a Tuscan-inspired tasting bar. Outdoors is a red brick patio for sipping wine. These days, lawyer turned vintner Tom Stolpman remains steadfastly focused on syrah and syrah blends as the flagship wines, but also includes sangiovese, roussanne, and sauvignon blanc. The tasting room also has a selection of crystal decanters and Stolpman's own estate olive oil. The wines are outstanding, though a little on the pricey side. Stolpman's also has a tasting room (2323 Ballard Canyon Rd., Solvang, 805/688-0400) in Solvang.

DANIEL GEHRS WINES

Housed in a 100-year-old home, **Daniel Gehrs Wines** (2939 Grand Ave., 805/693-9686, www.danielgehrswines.com, daily 11am-6pm, tasting $10) was a residence and then a doctor's office long before it became a wine-tasting room. There are several rooms packed with gift items, a small tasting bar in the front, and a nice patio in the back where they conduct wine-tastings during the summer months. Dan Gehrs has long been a fixture in the wine scene and was one of the first winemakers in the valley. Among their offerings are riesling, pinot noir, ports made with traditional Portuguese grapes, sangiovese, gewürztraminer, and a few of Dan's daughter's wines under the Vixen label.

RICK LONGORIA WINES

Like Daniel Gehrs, Rick Longoria has been involved in the wine industry for decades, and his winery, **Rick Longoria Wines** (2935 Grand Ave., 805/688-0305, www.longoriawine.com, daily 11am-4:30pm, tasting $10), is next door to Daniel Gehrs Wines. The small, narrow tasting room, originally a machine shop from the turn of the 20th century, carries chardonnay, pinot noir, and tempranillo, and Rick's locally well-known Blues Cuvée, a blend of predominantly cabernet franc with the addition of merlot and cabernet sauvignon. The Blues series of wines features labels portraying famous blues artists. The winery has a small partially shaded side patio with a few tables, and you can hear the two water fountains on the patio as you sample the wines.

KOEHLER WINERY

The **Koehler Winery** (5360 Foxen Canyon Rd., 805/693-8384, www.koehlerwinery.com, daily 10am-5pm, tasting $10-15) seems to have it all: It produces cabernet sauvignon, syrah, viognier, sauvignon blanc, and other wines in a very pretty hillside location. There are picnic tables outside, and since it's set back from the main road, it is quiet and serene here. Koehler also make pinot noir, which isn't grown on-site but is sourced from the Santa Rita Hills. Koehler wines have received outstanding reviews in the national press.

ZACA MESA WINERY

The **Zaca Mesa Winery** (6905 Foxen Canyon Rd., 805/688-9339, www.zacamesa.com, daily 10am-4pm, tasting $10) is one of the oldest wineries in the county and the very first to plant syrah grapes way back in the 1970s, long before most people even knew what syrah was. This has given them a leg up on working with the variety. Viognier, chardonnay, roussanne, and mourvèdre round out the offerings at this winery, which has a very cool large-scale chess set on the property. It's a great spot to picnic, as it's off the beaten path. The tasting room is midsize, meaning it can get crowded at peak times.

CURTIS WINERY
Curtis Winery (5249 Foxen Canyon, 805/686-8999, www.curtiswinery.com, daily 10am-5pm, tasting $10) has a thing for Hawaiian shirts, and that's pretty much the vibe here: low-key and fun. The emphasis is solely on Rhône-style wines like grenache, mourvèdre, syrah, roussanne, and viognier. It was actually one of the first wineries to focus on these grapes. Curtis routinely turns out some very fine wines that showcase the area, which leans toward bright, expressive fruit. There are also a lot of gift items and books, and a grassy area fronting the main road with picnic tables and views to the vineyards across the street.

THE BRANDER VINEYARD
The **Brander Vineyard** (2401 N. Refugio Rd., 805/688-2455, www.brander.com, daily 10am-4pm, tasting $10-15) facility looks like a small wine château in Europe—well, except for the pink walls. Surrounded by flowers and poplar, cottonwood, and redwood trees, and a rustic courtyard with picnic tables, this is a place known for sauvignon blanc. Brander is the undisputed king of that varietal in this area, having been making it since the 1970s. Equally impressive is a cabernet sauvignon—remarkable considering this is not the prime growing area for it. Rosé, syrah, and merlot round out the offerings.

DEMETRIA ESTATE
The **Demetria Estate** (6701 Foxen Canyon Rd., 805/686-2345, www.demetriaestate.com, by appointment only) features stellar pinot noir, syrah, pinot blanc, chardonnay, and a Rhône-style white blend. The vineyard is biodynamically farmed; the care given the vines is expressed in the beautifully crafted wines, which are not inexpensive. The wine-making facility is in a yellow mottled Tuscan building set on a hill overlooking acres of vines. Bring a picnic lunch, uncork a bottle, and relax.

Festivals and Events
The annual **Quick Draw and Art Walk** (http://santaynezvalleyarts.org) is held right across from the flagpole each August. Local artists race against the clock to complete a drawing, painting, or sculpture within 45 minutes. The works are then auctioned off in a live auction, and you can walk home with something hot off the press. There's also a silent auction and a barbecue in the park, artists hold demonstrations, and all the local galleries stay open late. They've been doing this for over a quarter of a century.

A celebration of all things olive-related, the **Los Olivos Jazz and Olive Festival** (www.jazzandolivefestival.org) takes place the second Saturday in June. It includes performances by jazz acts, an amateur-chef cook-off, and lots of local wines.

Shopping
ART GALLERIES
What once was an art destination with a dozen galleries has dwindled down to just two galleries now. The largest gallery in town these days is **Gallery Los Olivos** (2920 Grand Ave., 805/688-7517, www.gallerylosolivos.com, Feb.-Nov. daily 10am-5pm, Dec.-Jan. daily 10am-4pm), which is an artists' co-op, with the artists themselves running the show. They present over 40 regional artists from within Santa Barbara County, working with wood, acrylic, ceramic, and pastels to create original traditional and abstract works of art. They rotate monthly solo shows. The space is larger than you'd expect, with a lot of first-rate work.

At **Sansone Studio Gallery** (2948 Nojoqui Ave., 805/693-9769, www.sansonestudio.com, daily 11am-5pm), Joel and Pamela Sansone use the medium of vitreous enamel on copper to create vibrant work. Vitreous enamel is applied to a copper surface and then kiln-fired. The powdered glass becomes molten and fuses to the copper, making the colors extremely rich and deep. Their work is abstract in theme, and their small off-the-beaten-path studio is worth seeking out just to see their unique pieces.

CLOTHING

Jedlicka's Saddlery (2883 Grand Ave., 805/688-2626, www.jedlickas.com, Mon.-Sat. 9am-5:30pm, Sun. 10am-4:30pm) is all cowboy, all the time. Jeans, hats, boots—whatever you might need for actual cowboy work or pretend cowboy work is all here. Jedlickas's first opened in 1932 on the site of the town's turn-of-the-20th-century blacksmith shop. Western and English clothing, gear, and tack along with a large selection of clothing for kids keeps people coming back.

Spas

Champagne Spa & Boutique (2860 Grand Ave., 805/686-9202, www.fessparker.com, daily 10am-6pm, massages $75-225) is housed near the pool at the Fess Parker Inn, and you don't need to be a guest of the inn to partake of their services. Check out the deep-tissue massage or grape seed oil massage, or the full line of waxing and manicures. Facials for women, men, and kids are also offered.

Accommodations
OVER $250

Fess Parker's Wine Country Inn & Spa (2860 Grand Ave., 805/688-7788, www.fessparker. com, $345-705) was built by Fess Parker, the actor who played Davy Crockett and Daniel Boone in early TV shows. His mini empire included his own winery. Parker, who passed away in March 2010, was smart enough to get into land and real estate after his television days, and he was long a fixture of the valley. There's a wine store and a restaurant on the premises, and the feel of this traditional inn is changing to a more modern feel, letting go of the older Victorian trappings and replacing it with hipper and sleeker decor. But it still retains the elements people come for: small-town

hospitality, easy access to the wine country, and a Victorian and Western motif. Guest rooms are comfortable and large, have fireplaces, and surround a garden courtyard. This is the only hotel in Los Olivos, but Santa Ynez and Solvang are a short drive away.

Food

Panino's (2900 Grand Ave., 805/688-9304, daily 10am-4pm, $9-10.50) is all about sandwiches and salads. A small chain in the county, this outpost does very well. It's the perfect choice when you don't want a full sit-down meal but a quick bite to eat, or maybe something to take on the road. The sandwiches and salads are made to order, and there is a good selection of vegetarian options. The roast turkey and brie sandwich is a favorite, as is the avocado and provolone with fresh basil and honey mustard.

C Ballard Inn (2436 Baseline, Ballard, 800/638-2466, Wed.-Sun. 5:30pm-9pm, $30-34) is one of those restaurants where you wonder, How did they end up here, of all places? Chef-owner Budi Kazali has transformed Ballard into a destination—it's actually the only reason to stop in Ballard, a town sandwiched between Solvang and Los Olivos. There are only a dozen tables in this intimate space, and on busy weekend nights it can get loud. The menu rotates often to take advantage of the freshest ingredients Kazali can find. Most of the vegetables come from local farms, and the seafood is from Santa Barbara. On any given night you might find crispy barramundi, panko-crusted sweet breads, or a beef dish. You can be sure that whatever is presented on the small menu will be artfully prepared and exceptionally good.

Owned and operated by Jeff and Matt Nichols, **C Sides Hardware and Shoes** (2375 Alamo Pintado Ave., 805/688-4820, www. brothersrestaurant.com, Mon.-Thurs. 11:30am-2:30pm and 5pm-8:30pm, Fri.-Sun. 8am-11am, 11:30am-2:30pm, and 5pm-8:30pm, $20-34) is not a place to pick up a bucket of nails or get a pair of loafers. Rather, this unassuming restaurant—the waitstaff wear blue

© STUART THORNTON

Sides Hardware and Shoes restaurant, in Los Olivos

jeans and plaid shirts—serves up inspired American country cuisine that reflects Santa Ynez's fine wines and food. There's a nice list of Central Coast wines, including eight available by the glass. The lamb sirloin is tender and tasty, and there are also fish and vegetarian options. Any dish with the thick, almost candy-like house-made bacon is worth trying, and you will never have a better brussels sprout than those in the fried brussels sprouts appetizer.

Los Olivos Wine Merchant & Café (2879 Grand Ave., 805/688-7265, www.losolivoscafe.com, daily 11:30am-8:30pm, $14-29) has been plying its trade since 1995 and has always done well, but the 2004 film *Sideways* really cemented its popularity, and now it's nearly always packed. You can sit outside on the deck, inside at the tables, or at the bar. It has a wall of wine as part of its offerings, so if you find something you like with your lunch or dinner, you can buy a bottle or take one home with you. It gets noisy, and the service is usually strained because of the capacity crowds, but the café prepare wonderful food such as

parmesan gnocchi and pizzas, and the excellent house-made dipping oil for bread is sold by the bottle.

Petros (2860 Grand Ave., 805/686-5455, www.petrosrestaurant.com, Sun.-Thurs. 7am-10pm, Fri.-Sat. 7am-11pm, $16-36) is located inside the Fess Parker Inn. The Greek restaurant has a stunningly modern and hip decor in contrast to the conservative inn and the town, and it's a culinary change of pace unlike anything in the valley. Petros bakes its own pita, makes fresh yogurt, and serves predominantly small plates—perfect because there is an abundance of things to try, including sesame-crusted feta and spanakopita. There are full entrées as well, and many of the seasonings used are imported from Greece.

Los Olivos Grocery (2621 W. Hwy. 154, 805/688-5115, www.losolivosgrocery.com, daily 7am-6pm) is part grocery store and part deli. With an impressive selection of cheeses and a decent wine department, the full deli has picnic fixings, or the staff can assemble a picnic for you. Get the red-pepper hummus, the

Happy Canyon club sandwich, or a breakfast burrito to go. All of the produce in sourced from the area; you can dine on the covered patio or take it with you as you explore the wine country.

Information and Services

The website **Los Olivos California** (www.losolivosca.com) is the best source of information about the town, though it is by no means comprehensive.

EMERGENCY SERVICES

The Santa Ynez Valley Cottage Hospital (2050 Viborg Rd., Solvang, 805/688-6431) offers emergency services. Should you have an emergency, dial 911. Police services are the **County of Santa Barbara Sheriff's Department** (1745 Mission Dr., Solvang, 805/688-5000).

NEWSPAPERS AND MEDIA

The *Santa Ynez Valley News* (http://syvnews.com) covers the local angle and is published each Thursday. The *Santa Barbara News-Press* (www.newspress.com) is a daily newspaper covering all of Santa Barbara County, with the main office in Santa Barbara and another office in Lompoc. The alternative weekly *Santa Barbara Independent* (www.independent.com) covers the whole county, although the emphasis is on the city of Santa Barbara. New issues are available for free around the county starting on Thursday.

POSTAL SERVICES

Given the limited size of the **post office** (2880 Grand Ave., Suite B, 805/688-4573), it's advisable to call ahead for operating hours and services.

LAUNDRY

Since there are no services of this type in town, your best bet is **St. Paul Cleaners and Laundry** (1693 Mission Dr., Solvang, 805/688-9618), a few miles down the road in Solvang.

Getting There

Los Olivos is best accessed on Highway 154, just east of U.S. 101; Highway 154 runs through the town. The **Santa Ynez Airport** (900 Airport Rd., Santa Ynez) accepts small aircraft, and the **Santa Maria Public Airport** (SMX, 3217 Terminal Dr., Santa Maria, 805/922-1726, www.santamariaairport.com), with flights to Los Angeles and Las Vegas, is within a 20-minute drive.

Getting Around

Just like Santa Ynez, Los Olivos is a walking town. Only three blocks by two blocks, it is simple to get around. Some of the side streets don't have sidewalks, so be careful. It's also small enough that people simply wander the streets and cross whenever they feel like it, which is not safe—peak times bustle with traffic, and it's important to obey the traffic rules.

Santa Maria Valley

Stretching from the Santa Lucia Mountains toward the Pacific Ocean, the Santa Maria Valley used to be a stretch of lonely land populated by the Chumash people and lots of sagebrush, deer, bears, and rabbits. Today, Santa Maria is agriculture central. As you pass through on U.S. 101, you see fields and vineyards coupled with new housing developments. Most people assume this area is all about farming crops, but

Santa Maria also has a strong ranching history, with a namesake dish, the Santa Maria-style tri-tip. Although it doesn't have the idyllic charm of other towns along the Central Coast, it is a gateway to the wine industry, beaches, and some fabulous under-the-radar restaurants.

The Chumash people were the only residents until 1769, when an exploration party led by Gaspar de Portolà came through the

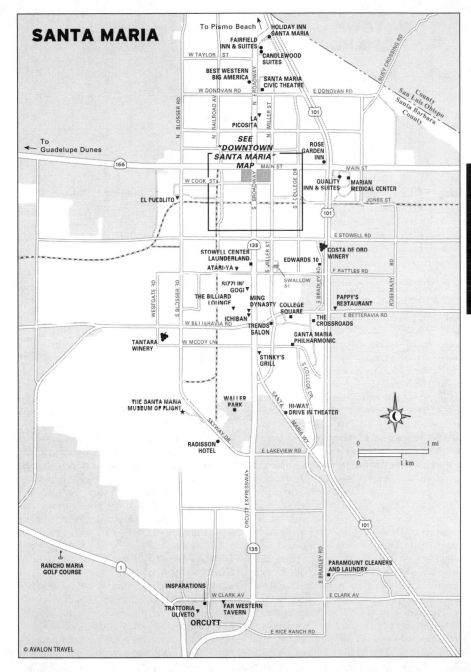

SANTA MARIA

To Pismo Beach

To Guadelupe Dunes

SEE "DOWNTOWN SANTA MARIA" MAP

HOLIDAY INN SANTA MARIA

FAIRFIELD INN & SUITES

CANDLEWOOD SUITES

BEST WESTERN BIG AMERICA

SANTA MARIA CIVIC THEATRE

LA PICOSITA

ROSE GARDEN INN

QUALITY INN & SUITES

MARIAN MEDICAL CENTER

EL PUEBLITO

STOWELL CENTER LAUNDERLAND

ATARI-YA

EDWARDS 10

COSTA DE ORO WINERY

SIZZLIN' GOGI

THE BILLIARD LOUNGE

MING DYNASTY

SWALLOW ST

PAPPY'S RESTAURANT

ICHIBAN

COLLEGE SQUARE

TRENDS SALON

THE CROSSROADS

SANTA MARIA PHILHARMONIC

TANTARA WINERY

STINKY'S GRILL

THE SANTA MARIA MUSEUM OF FLIGHT

WALLER PARK

HI-WAY DRIVE IN THEATER

RADISSON HOTEL

E LAKEVIEW RD

RANCHO MARIA GOLF COURSE

INSPARATIONS

PARAMOUNT CLEANERS AND LAUNDRY

TRATTORIA ULIVETO

FAR WESTERN TAVERN

ORCUTT

W TAYLOR ST

W DONOVAN RD

E DONOVAN RD

N BLOSSER RD

RAILROAD AVE

N BROADWAY

N MILLER ST

101

County San Luis Obispo

Santa Barbara County

SUEY CROSSING RD

MAIN ST

166

W COOK ST

S BROADWAY

S COLLEGE DR

JONES ST

101

E STOWELL RD

135

S MILLER ST

S BRADLEY RD

F RATTLES RD

ROSEMARY RD

W BETTERAVIA RD

E BETTERAVIA RD

W MCCOY LN

S COLLEGE DR

SANTA MARIA WY

WESTGATE RD

S BLOSSER RD

SKYWAY DR

ORCUTT EXPRESSWAY

135

1

S BRADLEY RD

W CLARK AV

E CLARK AV

E RICE RANCH RD

0   1 mi

0   1 km

© AVALON TRAVEL

WINE COUNTRY

DOWNTOWN SANTA MARIA

© AVALON TRAVEL

Santa Maria Valley, founding Mission San Luis Obispo de Tolosa in 1772 and Mission La Purisima in 1787. European settlers soon followed, looking for the possibility of free land. By the time California became a U.S. state in 1850, the Santa Maria River Valley was one of the most productive agricultural areas in California, and it is still a key component of the economy.

The Santa Maria Valley saw its share of oil exploration, beginning in 1888 and leading to large oil discoveries by the turn of the 20th century. In 1901, William Orcutt urged his company, Union Oil, to lease more than 70,000 acres here. For the next eight decades, thousands of oil wells were drilled and put into production, facilitating growth for the city of Santa Maria. By 1957 there were almost 1,800 oil wells in operation in the Santa Maria Valley, producing $60 million worth of oil. The city remained just four square miles until 1954, when annexations increased its size to about 22 square miles. You can still see some of the old wells, but more often you'll see vineyards and row crops, and chances are you'll eat and drink the bounty of Santa Maria wherever you dine.

SIGHTS
Santa Maria Museum of Flight
The **Santa Maria Museum of Flight** (3015 Airpark Dr., 805/922-8758, www.smmof.org, Fri.-Sun. 10am-4pm, adults $5, seniors $4, ages 12-17 $3, ages 7-11 $1) features displays of World War II and present-day aircraft and artifacts. The small but interesting museum is presided over by an all-volunteer staff. There are two hangars and a few old planes as well as a 3,000-volume library on aviation and a memorial garden highlighting the roles of women in aviation. The yearly air show, Thunder Over the Valley, is a huge draw each August. This is not a large museum, but the dedication of a few individuals makes this a great visit for aviation lovers.

Santa Maria Valley Discovery Museum
Santa Maria Valley Discovery Museum (705 S. McClelland St., 805/928-8414, www.smv-discoverymuseum.org, Mon.-Sat. 10am-5pm, $8) is a place for kids, and the emphasis is on education. They have a lot of small hands-on exhibits such as how a tractor works as well

as information about agriculture, how saddles are made, a boat and its terminology, and a 3,000-gallon tank with—you guessed it—sharks! If you're traveling with younger kids, this is a great stop. The museum do an admirable job with a diversity of things for kids to get involved in. The interior is brightly colored, enhancing stimulation.

◖ Mission La Purisima Concepción

Mission La Purisima Concepción (2295 Purisima Rd., Lompoc, 805/733-3713, www.lapurisimamission.org, self-guided tours daily 9am-5pm, free one-hour guided tours daily 1pm, adults $6, seniors $5) was founded on December 8, 1787, as La Misión de La Purísima Concepción de la Santísima Virgen María. The first mission was destroyed in an earthquake in 1812, and the priests then rebuilt the mission in a different spot; this is the current site that 250,000 annual visitors enjoy as a state historic park. Sitting on the 2,000 acres are trails for simple hikes and walks; many people bring picnics. You can examine the five-acre garden that shows indigenous and domesticated flora typical of a mission garden, including fig and olive trees and a wide variety of other plants that include sage and Spanish dagger. There are also mission animals typical of the times, including burros, horses, longhorn cattle, sheep, goats, and turkeys, which are displayed in a corral located in the main compound.

The mission is actually three buildings with well over a dozen rooms to explore, including the sleeping quarters of the soldiers, the weaving shop, the candle-making room, the simple church, a chapel, the priest's quarters, and a lot more. Many of the rooms still have their original dirt floors, and La Purisima, among all the missions, best provides a feel for daily life back then. There are also a few conical huts that the Chumash people lived in. Now a state park, this is one of the few missions that does not have religious services.

In 1785, Sergeant Pablo de Cota, stationed at Mission San Buenaventura in present-day Ventura, was ordered to find a location for a new mission that was roughly equidistant between the missions at San Luis Obispo and Santa Barbara. The Mission of the Immaculate Conception of the Most Blessed Virgin Mary was dedicated and construction began in the spring of 1788, after the winter rains. It was constructed in the traditional quadrangle shape, and Chumash people who had been converted by the missionaries lived outside the mission walls in their traditional dwellings.

On the morning of December 21, 1812, a major temblor stuck the coast. Two shock waves virtually destroyed the mission, and what was left of the shattered adobe walls dissolved in the heavy winter rains. When the priests decided to rebuild, the traditional design was abandoned; the new mission was built in a linear design, making it unique among the California missions.

But this mission would also fall into ruin, a victim of passing time and neglect. In 1824, La Purisima was at the center of a failed Chumash revolt. Soldiers guarding the mission were poorly paid, and the mission was waiting to receive money owed them from Spain. Spain didn't pay, and the soldiers turned their frustrations on the indigenous people. The Chumash people who lived at the three Santa Barbara missions rose up in armed revolt. Soldiers from the Presidio at Monterey took back the La Purisima mission by force; the attack left 16 Chumash people dead and several wounded. One of the Spanish priests negotiated surrender terms for the Chumash, but seven of the Chumash people who surrendered were executed; 12 others were sentenced to hard labor at the Santa Barbara Presidio.

Secularization in 1834 heralded the end for La Purisima. Religious services ceased in 1836, and the buildings fell into disrepair. In 1845 the mission was sold for a little more than $1,000, and the church was stripped of its roof tiles and timbers. The walls, exposed to the elements, crumbled. Eventually, the building was used as a stable. It was deeded to the State of California in 1934, and a subsequent restoration project became one of the largest of its kind in the nation.

Natural History Museum of Santa Maria

Learn about the animals that roam around Santa Maria at the city's **Natural History Museum** (412 S. McClelland St., 805/614-0806, www.naturalhistorysantamaria.com, Wed.-Sat. 11am-4pm, Sun. 1pm-4pm, free), including monarch butterflies, bats, owls, tule elk, mountain lions, and more. The museum's garden is home to the "Titans of the Pacific" exhibit, which has life-size statues of a killer whale, a great white shark, and a bottlenose dolphin.

◖ Point Sal State Beach

Also known as Paradise Beach or Paradise Cove, **Point Sal State Beach** (10-mile round-trip hike from the end of Brown Rd., moderate-strenuous, 805/733-3713, www.parks.ca.gov, daily sunrise-sunset, except for Vandenberg Air Force Base closures), is one of California's remotest and most rugged coastal areas, the rare beach public beach where you're unlikely

remote Point Sal State Beach

© STUART THORNTON

to see other people or even footprints in the sand. Located west of Santa Maria and tucked between Vandenberg Air Force Base and Guadalupe Dunes, Point Sal comprises 80 acres, including over 1.5 miles of oceanfront. The large, wide, golden-sand beach is ringed with steep, frequently sliding bluffs. Nearby are Point Sal and Lion Rock, a white-topped islet popular with roosting birds. The weather here changes more frequently than a model's outfits on a runway. The few souls who make the arduous trek here are looking for a deserted island experience—the chance to fish, beachcomb, picnic without another person in sight.

Of course, there's a reason Point Sal offers such solitude. Getting to Point Sal requires some serious effort. In 1998, severe winter storms destroyed sections of Point Sal Road, which previously offered the only road access. The road has been deteriorating ever since and hasn't been reopened to regular traffic, in part because it passes through a section of Vandenberg Air Force Base, which is frequently closed for military operations. Before heading out to Point Sal, visit the **Vandenberg Air Force Base website** (www.vandenberg. af.mil) to see if access is possible. Look under the "featured links" section and click on "Point Sal Access." If the beach is open, you can reach it from Highway 1 by taking Brown Road through farmland until it ends at a gate. There is parking on the dirt pullouts by the gate—which is a good thing, because this is where you leave your car behind. At the gate, continue on foot along Point Sal Trail, really an old road, that climbs up Point Sal Ridge through scenic hilly ranchland. At second large metal gate, you cross onto Vandenberg Air Force Base property. Signs warn you not to leave the road—the area is patrolled by working dog teams. The road then curves and descends steeply down to Point Sal State Beach. The hike is roughly five miles. Is the beach worth all that effort? You be the judge. Those who have experienced Point Sal would say "yes." Save energy and time for the steep, five-mile climb up hill back to your car at the end of the day.

WINE TASTING

The wineries in the Santa Maria area are spread out, requiring a car to visit even a few of them. Some are in industrial sections of the city, and some are among vineyards. Unlike Solvang, Los Olivos, and Santa Ynez, where it's easy to find several wineries along one road or right in the middle of the town, you have to plan your trips to these wineries. A great initial resource is the website of the **Santa Maria Valley Chamber of Commerce** (www.santamariawines.com).

◖ Flying Goat Cellars

The focus is on pinot noir at **Flying Goat** (1520 E. Chestnut Court, Unit A, Lompoc, 805/736-9032, www.flyinggoat.com, Thurs.-Sun. 11am-4pm, tasting $10). In addition to several iterations of beautifully seductive pinot noir, they are locally well known for Goat Bubbles, a light, delicate pinot noir sparkling wine. Owner Norm Yost goes for an uncommon restrained style with his wines, allowing the lush cherry and raspberry elements of the pinot noir grapes to express themselves and not be overwhelmed with too much oak. These are consistently excellent wines and avoid the bombastic and overripe characteristics that many pinot noirs tend to exhibit. As Norm has said, Why spend $4,000 a ton buying pinot noir fruit only to mask it behind oak? Ultimately he makes wine he would like to drink, and Norm steadfastly adheres to his principles. His tasting room is nothing more than a table at his small winery. This is a working facility and not a spot to lounge and look at pretty vineyards. In fact, the only wildlife you'll see will probably be Norm's dog.

Foxen Winery

Foxen Winery (7200 Foxen Canyon Rd., 805/937-4251, www.foxenvineyard.com, daily 11am-4pm, tasting $10) is known for its rustic wood tasting room that looks like a run-down shed. But the wines are a far cry from that image. Foxen also has a new solar-powered **tasting room** (7600 Foxen Canyon Rd., 805/937-4251, www.foxenvineyard.com, daily 11am-4pm, tasting $10) right down the road. In addition to chardonnay, syrah, cabernet sauvignon, and pinot noir, the winery is one of the few to produce chenin blanc, an underappreciated grape. Foxen has a long-standing reputation for producing some of the finest wines in the area, and the Foxen name goes back six generations. Their 10-acre vineyard is the only dry-farmed vineyard in the area, meaning that there is no irrigation; they simply rely on what Mother Nature provides.

Cottonwood Canyon

Cottonwood Canyon (3940 Dominion Rd., 805/937-8463, http://cottonwoodcanyon.com, Mon.-Thurs. noon-4pm, Fri.-Sun. 11am-5pm, tasting $10) started in 1988, and though it's just 10 minutes from downtown Santa Maria, this winery has managed to stay under the radar. After trying their wines, you'll wonder why you haven't heard of them. With a standard portfolio of wines that include six iterations of chardonnay, they also include a couple of sparkling wines and a dessert-style syrah as well as several pinot noirs. They farm 78 acres with the San Rafael Mountains as a backdrop. Winemaker Norm Beko also loves food, and many weekends he's grilling up something to share.

Tantara Winery

A dozen different pinot noirs are the flagship wines at **Tantara Winery** (2330 Westgate Rd., 805/938-5051, www.tantarawinery.com, by appointment only). There is also chardonnay and a syrah. These wines are sold directly at the winery since they have no tasting room, which is located at Bien Nacido Vineyards. The winemaking team of Jeff Fink and Bill Cates focuses on small lots of exceptional fruit, and they source pinot noir from some diverse growing areas along the Central Coast and Monterey and produce various expressions of those spots. Often they will pull barrel samples for visitors to taste. Their wines are not inexpensive, but this is the place if you're looking for beautiful high-end pinot noir.

Dierberg-Star Lane Winery

Dierberg-Star Lane Winery (1280 Drum Canyon Rd., Lompoc, 866/652-8430, www.starlanevineyard.com, daily 11am-5pm, tasting $10) has vineyards located in Happy Canyon, one of the warmest spots in the valley, which is why they can make exceptional cabernet sauvignon. The green-and-red barn tasting room is on the opposite side of the valley, however, and a little off the beaten path, but worth the drive for any serious wine lover. The Dierbergs operate three wine labels: Star Lane; their estate wines, called Dierberg; and Three Saints. All of these wines, at various price points, are excellent. The Star Lane sauvignon blanc is terrific, and the value-priced Three Saints wines, including merlot, cabernet sauvignon, and pinot noir, are best bets.

Pali Wine Company

Pali Wine Company (1036 W. Aviation Dr., Lompoc, 805/736-7200, www.paliwineco.com, by appointment, tasting $10) is located out in a warehouse-looking building in Lompoc, where you taste the wines next to the barrels, stacked cases of wine, and stainless steel fermentation tanks. Pinot noir from multiple vineyard sites across California is the specialty, showcasing how a single type of grape can be so different depending on where it was grown. They also make a killer grenache, chardonnay, and cabernet sauvignon. It's a younger winery, but they have produced impressive wines in part because they are dedicated to not taking shortcuts with their wines.

Scott Cellars

Owner Peter Scott Fraser does almost everything himself at **Scott Cellars** (316 N. F St., Lompoc, www.scottcellars.com, Fri.-Sun. 11am-4pm, tasting $7). With production of less than a thousand cases, this is a small operation, but a dream come true for Scott, a self-taught winemaker who started out with a tiny winery in Ventura. His wines include sangiovese, pinot noir, syrah, pinot gris, and chardonnay. Fraser also does a Cuvee J, a blend of zinfandel and syrah. He's usually here, brimming with enthusiasm and ready for conversation.

Kenneth Volk Vineyards

The owner of **Kenneth Volk Vineyards** (5230 Tepusquet Rd., 805/938-7896, www.volk-wines.com, daily 10:30am-4:30pm, tasting $10) was not initially into wine. At college in San Luis Obispo he pursued a degree in fruit science, imagining a future in an orchard or greenhouse. But in 1981 he established Wild Horse Winery & Vineyard in Templeton, and over the next two decades production soared from 600 to 150,000 cases. In 2003, Ken sold Wild Horse, and in 2004 he formed Kenneth Volk Vineyards in Santa Maria. He has won countless awards and makes damn good wines using as many diverse aspects of wine-making as possible. "Just as a rich stew or curry creates a more vivid culinary experience when it includes a complex combination of ingredients that harmonize, we seek to bring together complementary flavors for a richer wine experience," he says. In addition to the standard offerings like chardonnay, pinot noir, viognier, cabernet sauvignon, and merlot, he's been a champion of what are called heirloom varieties—funky, wonderfully oddball wines like malvasia, négrette, and trousseau. You won't regret the long trek to get to the tranquil 12-acre property along the Tepusquet Creek, surrounded by oak and sycamore trees.

Costa de Oro Winery

Costa de Oro Winery (1331 S. Nicholson Ave., 805/922-1468, www.cdowinery.com, Sat.-Thurs. 11am-6pm, Fri. 11am-8pm, tasting $10) started off as a farming operation with row crops; they then decided to plant grapes on a patch of land that wasn't working right. The grapes thrived, and now pinot noir and chardonnay are the main wines they produce from their 20 acres. There's usually something musical happening Friday night and Sunday at the tasting room, which is also the outlet for Costa de Oro's produce operation. Today, the tasting room, which opened in 2006, sits on the site of the Gold Coast strawberry stand, where you can also pick up fresh veggies and fruits in season. The wines offered at Costa de Oro include sauvignon blanc, three different versions of chardonnay, and three different versions of pinot noir, among others.

Rancho Sisquoc

Rancho Sisquoc (6600 Foxen Canyon Rd., 805/934-4332, www.ranchosisquoc.com, Mon.-Thurs. 10am-4pm, Fri.-Sun. 10am-5pm, tasting $8) is one of those spots where you really have to want to go there. Located out in the boonies, it's a beautiful spot and is probably best enjoyed by bringing a picnic. Their wood-sided tasting room is rustic but comfortable, more like an upscale barn. Grab a bottle of their silvaner, chardonnay, or merlot and sit outside with some food to enjoy wine country, looking out to a vast field with low hills in the distance. This is definitely a quiet place.

ENTERTAINMENT AND EVENTS
Bars

Yes, there's a bar in Santa Maria called **Stinky's Grill** (2430 S. Broadway, 805/614-9366, www.stinkysgrill.com, daily 11am-10pm). The folks at Stinky's insist there is not a stench in their bar; instead, they say, ask who would ever forget a bar named Stinky's. It's actually a sports bar that serves food and draft beers in 16- and 25-ounce versions. The **Olde English Tap Room** (801 S. Broadway Ave., 805/928-7777, www.santamariainn.com, Sun.-Thurs. 11am-10pm, Fri.-Sat. 11am-midnight) is an old-time establishment with a fireplace and wood floors located in the Santa Maria Inn. The Tap Room serves local craft beers and specialty cocktails and offers live music on weekends (Fri.-Sat. 8pm-11pm). For a little pool, check out **The Billiard Lounge** (1931 S. Thornburg St., 805/925-3780, daily 11am-2am, $8 per hour), which has plenty of regulation pool tables and a jukebox with all the old songs you thought you left behind in high school. Try karaoke if your pool game is off. The beer is cheap, which draws in a younger crowd. You might also be able to catch live music at **O'Sullivan's**

Pub (633 E. Main St., www.osullivanspub.net, Mon.-Wed. noon-10pm, Thurs. noon-midnight, Fri.-Sat. noon-2am, Sun. noon-8pm), an alternative twist on the traditional Irish pub. Even if you don't, you can still enjoy craft beer and local wines.

Performing Arts

Like its cousin in Solvang, the **PCPA Theaterfest** (800 S. College Dr., 805/922-8313, www.pcpa.org, tickets $15-32) is housed on the campus of Allan Hancock College and has been producing theater for 40 years. They have two stages: The Seversen Theatre is a theater in the round with seating on all sides, and the larger Marian Theatre has a traditional stage. They present mainly musicals and comedies—lighthearted theater to keep you happy.

Just up the road is the **Santa Maria Civic Theatre** (1660 N. McClelland, 805/922-4442, www.smct.org, tickets $14), an intimate 100-seat venue operating since 1959; though non-professional, it has kept a high standard of quality. Some of the shows are well-known theater pieces from the likes of Agatha Christie, while other works are less well known. Shows run only on Friday and Saturday evening.

The **Santa Maria Philharmonic** (120 E. Jones St., 805/925-0412, www.santamariaphilharmonic.org) presents various classical music performances at a variety of venues, so it's best to check with the website to see where they might be. Primarily they perform at **Grace Baptist Church** (605 E. McCoy Lane), but they also offer free concerts at malls and travel out of the county as well. Their current music director conducted for the London and Royal Philharmonic Orchestras before coming to Santa Maria.

Cinema

The **Edwards 10** (1521 S. Bradley Rd., 805/347-1164, www.regmovies.com) shows first-run films on 10 screens. Overall the seats are comfy and the drink holders work. The screens are a little small but standard. You can also enjoy a double feature from the comforts of your car at the **Hi-Way Drive In Theatre** (3085 Santa Maria Way, 805/937-9715).

Festivals and Events

Strawberries are a big crop in Santa Maria, and for over two decades they have celebrated the berry with more strawberries than you've ever seen at the annual **Santa Maria Valley Strawberry Festival** (Santa Maria Fair Park, 937 S. Thornburg St., 805/925-8824, www.santamariafairpark.com), held over three days in April. There are food booths, rides, live bands, an old-fashioned carnival, and the chance to sample different strawberry varieties and strawberry desserts while you learn about the strawberry industry, the valley's number-one crop. This is one of the most attended festivals in the county.

The **Celebration of Harvest** (Rancho Sisquoc Winery, 6600 Foxen Canyon Rd., www.sbcountywines.com, 1pm-4pm, $75) is an annual event held each October. In the past, the Chumash people had a harvest ceremony known as the Hutash, which lasted for several days; it inspired this event to drink wine, listen to bands, bid on silent auction items, see local artists, sample local food, and bask in the outdoor beauty of Rancho Sisquoc. The winery itself is located here, but it's also one of the few fields around that's large enough to accommodate 3,000 people. Almost every local winery attends with their wares, and frankly there's no way to sample everything. But if you're on the hunt for certain wines or specific varieties, this is a great place to get a feel for all of Santa Barbara County's wines.

SHOPPING

Santa Maria is mainly a mall town. Sure, there are still small shops that dot the main arteries, but almost everything is relegated to strip malls—quite lovely and large strip malls with a Spanish flair, but malls nonetheless—and new versions are popping up all the time.

Shopping Centers

Santa Maria Town Center East (371 Town Center E., 805/922-7931, www.

santamariatowncenter.com, Mon.-Fri. 10am-8pm, Sat. 10am-7pm, Sun. 11am-7pm) is the largest spot to shop in Santa Maria and the largest indoor mall on the Central Coast, with over 60 stores. Anchored by Sears and Macy's, it's a basic mall with standard shops like Bath & Body Works, Payless Shoes, Subway, and Foot Locker. There are plans for a movie theater with 10 screens, but that's still in the works. The interior is pleasant enough—light, bright, and airy—and there's free parking in a covered parking lot. You'll be able to find coffee, tacos, and cake here as well.

Across the street is **Santa Maria Town Center West** (Main St. and S. Broadway, 805/922-7931, www.santamariatowncenter.com, Mon.-Fri. 10am-8pm, Sat. 10am-7pm, Sun. 11am-7pm), which is a mix of older stores, like one of the few remaining JCPenneys, and places like Big Lots, Subway, Starbucks, and a few Mexican restaurants. With the construction of the new mall, Santa Maria Town Center East, this original site has been somewhat neglected, but new storefronts have been put up in parts that stand in stark contrast to the old portion of this outdoor strip mall. It's not nearly as busy as the other malls, but there's also plenty of parking to be found.

The Crossroads (2120 S. Bradley Rd.) is where Best Buy, Wal-Mart, and Home Depot all sit on what were once fields of beans. You can't miss the shopping center, as it is beside U.S. 101 at Betteravia Road. Home to heavyweights like PetSmart, Staples, and TJ Maxx, it's certainly well designed and attractive, as malls go, with a series of traffic circles on Bradley Road to connect to the various parking lots. It gets very busy because of the diversity of stores.

College Square (540 E. Betteravia Rd.) is home to Panera Bread, which has the best spot, dead center inside this strip mall. It's joined by Jamba Juice, Starbucks, Cycle Star Bicycles, See's Candies—all stores that you've probably seen before, but there's also a nail salon and a pizza joint.

Farmers Markets

There are two farmers markets in Santa Maria: **Wednesday** (location of the original town site, 100 S. Broadway at Main St., 805/305-9829, Wed. noon-4pm,), where there are the usual veggies and breads, pastries, plants, flowers, and lots of bee products, including pollen and honey. In Orcutt there is a market on **Tuesday** (Clark Ave. and Bradley Rd., Orcutt, Tues. 10am-1pm).

SPORTS AND RECREATION
Parks

Bounded by residential communities, **Waller Park** (3107 Orcutt Rd., 805/934-6211, www.countyofsb.org, daily 8am-sunset) is one of the loveliest parks you will encounter in Santa Maria. The 153 acres include two beautiful lakes with fountains, a grassy lawn, shady picnic areas, playgrounds, basketball and volleyball courts, and even a disc golf course, as well as barbecue grills and picnic tables, horseshoes, a small playground, and restrooms. A three-acre off-leash dog park is within the greater park and has canine drinking fountains.

Los Alamos Park (805/934-6211, www.countyofsb.org, daily 8am-sunset) is a county park located a bit out of town in the mouth of Drum Canyon. This 51-acre park has a softball field, horseshoe pits, biking trails, and hiking trails. To reach it, take Highway 135 from U.S. 101 and pass through Los Alamos. Then take Centennial Road. The park is on the left.

Golf

La Purisima Golf Course (3455 E. Hwy. 246, Lompoc, 805/735-8395, www.lapurisimagolf.com, daily 6:30am-dusk, greens fees $30-79) is an 18-hole, par-72 course designed by Robert Graves, who also designed Sandpiper in Santa Barbara and Hunter Ranch in Paso Robles. It's moderately priced and there is a small grill for food and a pro shop. This is a tough course, with a lot of hills and brisk, cool winds in the afternoon—in other words, "challenging" is an understatement. But if you're up for it, it will be worth your effort, in spite of its rather remote location. Like many courses on the Central Coast, there is an abundance of oak trees to contend with.

Rancho Maria Golf Course (1950 Casmalia Rd., 805/937-2019, www.ranchomariagolf.com, daily 6:30am-dusk, greens fees $20-35) is a rather unknown 18-hole, par-72 course even more secluded than Purisima. There are no parallel fairways and no houses to be seen on this remote course, but there are a lot of trees and a short elevation gain. They have a small coffee shop, putting green, and practice bunkers. The pricing is quite good for a municipal course.

Car Racing

Santa Maria Speedway (1900 Hutton Rd., Nipomo, www.racesantamariaspeedway.com) is located just off U.S. 101 and in addition to car races is home to tractor pulls—all of it loud, fast, and out of control. They also host occasional concerts. The 0.3-mile oval clay track has been operating since 1964, and though it's not large, it does see a steady stream of races. The crowds get pretty rowdy, as there's nothing else like it in the area.

Spas

InSpaRations (130 E. Clark Ave., Orcutt, 805/934-8682, www.insparations1.com, Tues.-Sat. 9am-7pm, 1-hour massage $65-75), located just south of Santa Maria in Orcutt, will do your hair or give you a pedicure, manicure, or massage. The bright, cheery space is enhanced by the sincere and knowledgeable staff. **Trends Salon** (338 E. Betteravia Rd., 805/349-9031, Mon.-Fri. 8am-7pm, Sat. 8:30am-5pm) is more about trendy hair than anything else, though they perform manicures and pedicures and an esthetician is on staff as well.

ACCOMMODATIONS
Under $150

The **Rose Garden Inn** (1007 E. Main St., 805/922-4505, www.pacifichotels.com, $70-85) is for the budget-conscious. The place is a little worn but offers a great value compared to most hotels in Santa Maria. Coffee is located in the lobby, as is Wi-Fi. Outside are a pool, a basketball court, and a tennis court. Rose Garden is a little farther from the shopping malls, so you'll need to drive to them or anywhere else.

At the **Quality Inn & Suites** (210 Nicholson Ave., 805/922-5891, www.qualityinn.com, $97-112), complimentary breakfast is served each morning. In addition to an outdoor pool, amenities include a spa tub and a children's pool, Wi-Fi, a coffee shop, and outdoor barbecue grills. There are 64 guest rooms in this two-story property, and the standard rooms feature fridges and coffee- and tea-makers.

Candlewood Suites (2079 Roemer Court, 805/928-4155, www.candlewoodsuites.com, $80-250) is a 72-room hotel with clean, comfortable, good-value accommodations. It's located in a more industrial area on the outskirts of town but benefits from close freeway access. There's a fitness area, a laundry facility, and a small business center.

The **Holiday Inn Santa Maria** (2100 N. Broadway, 888/465-4329, www.ihg.com, $100-150) offers some rooms with kitchenettes, which is why it's big with business travelers and for extended stays. The four-story hotel was renovated in 2008 and has 415 guest rooms and suites, which are the standard rooms you'd expect from Holiday Inn—nice, but nothing out of the ordinary. They have free Wi-Fi, a fitness room, and a swimming pool on the premises.

With an eye toward what they call early-American furnishings, **Best Western Big America** (1725 N. Broadway, 805/922-5200, www.bigamerica.com, $118-145) is one of the top-rated places to stay in Santa Maria. The 106 guest rooms, while a little dull and of the standard hotel type, are still large and clean, and there are a lot of amenities, including a 24-hour pool and hot tub and a continental breakfast each morning. It's located downtown right in the thick of things. They have an on-site restaurant and provide shuttle service to the airport.

$150-250

Santa Maria Inn (801 S. Broadway, 805/928-7777, www.santamariainn.com, $150-260), constructed in 1917, now has 164 good-size

Santa Maria Inn

guest rooms and 18 suites. You can choose to stay in the historic part of the hotel or one of the newer guest rooms. Either way, the feeling is turn-of-the-20th-century in the decor and Victorian-style furnishings. Located centrally in Santa Maria, the pet-friendly inn has an in-house restaurant and an old tavern on the premises. The rooms have coffeemakers, fridges, and blow-dryers, while some have soaking tubs and fireplaces. There are five acres of grounds for you to walk with your pet. You can also enjoy (without your pet) an outdoor pool, a heated spa, and a fitness center.

Radisson Hotel (3455 Skyway Dr., 805/928-8000, www.radisson.com, $120-200) is located near the airport and the southern portion of town. It's another standard hotel, although the guest rooms have been given a face-lift with brighter colors. There's an outdoor pool, a fitness center, and an in-house restaurant, which looks over the airstrip. Basic amenities and good pricing make this a worthwhile choice if you're searching for a reliable name.

Fairfield Inn & Suites (2061 Roemer Court, 805/925-8500, www.marriott.com, $100-250) is a newer four-story hotel that has 89 guest rooms from a trustworthy name. The guest rooms are nicely decorated, going for an upscale corporate feel. There's an indoor pool and continental breakfast, but it's a pretty basic hotel. It does not accept pets and is completely smoke-free. The entire hotel is wired for Internet as well as Wi-Fi.

Located 15 minutes' drive from Santa Maria in the tiny town of Los Alamos, the **1880 Union Hotel** (362 Bell St., Los Alamos, 805/344-2744, www.unionhotelvictmansion. com, $185-325) dates back to 1880, and it looks it, with an Old West feel and a downstairs saloon that serves the hotel's very own 1880 Ale on tap. You can play pool or shuffleboard in the bar. There are 14 guest rooms—nine with private baths—and two luxury suites. One room has the distinction of being where Paul McCartney and Michael Jackson's "Say Say Say" music video was filmed.

FOOD
Bakery

Voted the best in the area, **Gina's Piece of Cake** (307 Town Center E., 805/922-7866, www.ginaspieceofcake.com, Tues.-Fri. 7:30am-7pm, Sat. 7:30am-6pm, Sun. 11am-5pm, $3) is that great bakery where you can smell the sweet icing used for all the cakes they make. But more than just beautiful custom cakes, they bake brownies, cookies, muffins, éclairs, bagels, and breads in their little pink shop.

Chinese

Ming Dynasty (2011 S. Broadway, 805/928-6881, www.mingdynastysantamaria.com, Sun.-Thurs. 11am-9pm, Fri.-Sat. 11am-10pm, $9-18) is a hugely popular restaurant most notable for its buffet. Yes, it's kind of Americanized and has that usual Chinese decor that seems just slightly old, but it has great value, fresh and flavorful food, and it gets crowded. They do have à la carte options, but most diners heads for the all-you-can-eat lunchtime buffet.

Classic American

The Garden Room at the Santa Maria Inn (801 S. Broadway, 805/928-7777, www.santamariainn.com, Sun.-Thurs. 6am-2pm and 5pm-9pm, Fri.-Sat. 6am-2pm and 5pm-10pm, $25) is located on the first floor of the hotel. White tablecloths, lots of old wood, and a proper environment make it like your grandparents' house, a little stuffy but worth a stop, if only for the ridiculously decadent Vermont french toast. Tri-tip is on the menu, as is the very good signature tortilla soup. On nice food is served on the back patio, a sunny little spot away from the noise on the main street. A three-course dinner-at-dusk menu is offered every day 5pm-6pm for $22 pp.

Pappy's Restaurant (1275 E. Betteravia Rd., 805/922-3553, Mon.-Thurs. 6am-10pm, Fri.-Sat. 6am-11pm, Sun. 6am-9pm, $10-25) is more truck stop than sit-down formal. It opened in 1959, and frankly, not much has changed with the place. Old cowboy photos line the walls and it's very casual, with a counter facing the kitchen and basic booths and furniture. It's also one of the few places that's open late. Pappy's makes a great tri-tip, and the home fries are terrific. It's right off the freeway, and the large parking lot is convenient if you're towing something.

Italian

Housed in a little cottage, **Trattoria Uliveto** (285 S. Broadway, Orcutt, 805/934-4546, www.trattoriauliveto.com, Tues.-Thurs. 11:30am-2:30pm and 5pm-9pm, Fri. 11:30am-2pm and 5pm-10pm, Sat. 5pm-10pm, Sun. 5pm-8pm, $12-34) has warmth and charm from its hardwood floors to its soft wood and exposed-beam ceilings. Yet it still feels slightly sophisticated. The food is dependable and authentic, and it's one of the few Italian places in the area.

Japanese

It seems stunning that in the midst of a land of steaks and tacos is **Ichiban** (2011 S. Broadway, 805/614-9808, daily 11:30am-2pm and 5pm-9pm, $11-19), a very good, though pricey, Japanese restaurant in the middle of Santa Maria. They offer attentive service, and the quality of the fish is uniformly very high. They serve some of the best sushi on the Central Coast. Another option is **Atari-Ya** (1551 Stowell Center Plaza, 805/922-0025, http://atari-ya.net, Tues.-Thurs. 11:30am-2pm and 5pm-9:15pm, Fri.-Sat. 11:30am-2pm and 5pm-9:30pm, Sun. 5pm-9pm, $9-18), which has been going since 1984. They have almost 40 sushi rolls and entrées including chicken teriyaki and ginger beef, along with karaoke.

Korean

A sleek, modern Korean restaurant in Santa Maria? In the capital of tri-tip steak barbecue, the introduction of Korean barbecue at **SizzlinGogi** (1841 S. Broadway, 805/287-9760, Sun.-Thurs. 11:30am-9:30pm, Fri.-Sat. 11:30am-10:30pm, $9-18) makes perfect sense. The meats are cooked right at your table on gas grills. The short ribs are a favorite.

Mexican

El Pueblito (603 S. Blosser Rd., 805/349-1088, daily 6am-10pm, $10-20) has solid, dependable Mexican food made with real ingredients. Sometimes the food can be a little greasy, but the shrimp fajitas are excellent. The restaurant is small but spacious enough, and the prices are lower than most other spots. **Maya** (110 S. Lincoln St., 805/925-2841, Mon.-Thurs. 7am-9pm, Fri.-Sun. 7am-10pm, $12) has been faithfully serving Mexican food since 1966. The brightly painted wood chairs and tiled floors make it feel festive as well as intimate. In addition to the standard Mexican fare they offer slightly different items, including an adobo marinated half chicken entrée and salmon enchiladas. They also have a great seniors menu—a typical Mexican item, which includes rice and beans—for about six bucks. **La Picosita** (923 N. Broadway, 805/347-3333, Mon.-Thurs. 8am-1am, Fri.-Sun. 8am-3am, $5) has a small taqueria menu with big flavors. Get a traditional carne asada or *al pastor* or opt for the more adventurous *lengua* or *cabeza* burritos.

Steak Houses

Still run by the same family that opened it in 1958, the **Far Western Tavern** (33 E. Clark Ave., Orcutt, 805/937-2211, www.farwesterntavern.com, Mon.-Thurs. 11am-2pm and 4pm-9pm, Fri.-Sat. 11am-2pm and 4pm-10pm, Sun. 9am-2pm and 4pm-9pm, $19-57) moved to a new location in Orcutt in 2012. The Tavern is best known for its 14-ounce bull's-eye steak, but there are nods to the wine country with a pinot filet mignon and a tenderloin steak served over grilled polenta in a pinot noir reduction. The meats are grilled over red oak, which lends them a beautiful smokiness.

At **Shaw's Steak House & Tavern** (714 S. Broadway, 805/925-5862, Mon.-Fri. 11:30am-9pm, Sat. 4pm-10pm, Sun. 4pm-9pm, $20), old black-and-white photos line the walls of the heavily wooded interior. Your main courses are prepared in plain sight, meaning the oak-wood grill sits behind a window and is visible from just about every table. Best known for their tri-tip, this is the kind of comfortable

TASTY TRI-TIP

Kansas City is known for its sauce-drenched barbecued ribs and Memphis is known to carnivores for its barbecued pork. The northern Santa Barbara County city of Santa Maria has its own meaty claim to fame: the barbecued Santa Maria tri-tip.

The tri-tip was first developed by Santa Maria butcher Bob Schultz, who started cutting a 2- to 3-pound triangular piece of meat off his top sirloins. One of the best ways to cook the meat was found to be over a grill burning red-oak wood. Typically the dish has been served in the area with salsa and *piquito* beans. Although you can now find tri-tip and tri-tip sandwiches all over California, Santa Maria has the distinction of being the place where this culinary creation truly took flight. The best places to taste tri-tip today are local restaurants like Santa Maria's Shaw's Steak House & Tavern, Orcutt's Far Western Tavern, and Santa Ynez area's Cold Spring Tavern.

place where you're tempted to kick off your shoes and get totally relaxed. Shaw's has been a popular spot with locals for years, in part because the portions are large, and the tavern is often packed.

INFORMATION AND SERVICES
Maps and Visitor Information
The **Santa Maria Valley Chamber of Commerce and Visitor and Convention Bureau** (614 S. Broadway, 800/331-3779, www.santamariavisitor.com, Mon.-Fri. 9am-5pm) can help you get oriented.

Emergency Services
The **Marian Medical Center** (1400 E. Church St., 805/739-3000, www.marianmedicalcenter.org) offers emergency services. Should you have an emergency, however, dial 911. The police force in town is the **Santa Maria Police** (222 E. Cook St., 805/928-3781).

Newspapers and Media
There are two newspapers that compete for attention. The **Santa Maria Times** (805/739-2200, www.santamariatimes.com) is the daily paper available throughout Santa Maria. The **Santa Maria Sun** (805/347-1968, www.santamariasun.com) is the free alternative weekly, published on Thursday.

Postal Services
Santa Maria has two **post offices** (201 E. Battles Rd., 805/275-8777; at the Town Center Mall, 142 Town Center E., 805/922-2972). Due to budget cutbacks, it's advisable to call ahead for specific hours and services.

Laundry
Check out **Stowell Center Launderland** (1511 S. Broadway, 805/922-2628) or **Paramount Cleaners and Laundry** (400 W. Main St., 805/922-7734); both are on main thoroughfares.

GETTING THERE
Car
If you're driving, Santa Maria is located directly along U.S. 101. The major streets that have access from both northbound and southbound U.S. 101 are Betteravia Road, Main Street, and Stowell Road.

Bus
An unstaffed stop for **Amtrak** (800/872-7245, www.amtrak.com) buses that connect to Amtrak trains in Santa Barbara and Hanford is located in Santa Maria at the International House of Pancakes (205 Nicholson Ave. at Main St.), just off U.S. 101. Neither tickets, nor baggage, nor package shipments are handled here. The nearest Amtrak stations to Santa Maria offering these services are north in San Luis Obispo or south in Santa Barbara.

Train
The Amtrak *Surfliner* does not stop in Santa Maria. The closest Amtrak train stops are 10 miles south in Guadalupe, or 10 miles north in Grover Beach in San Luis Obispo County.

Air

The **Santa Maria Public Airport** (SMX, 3217 Terminal Dr., 805/922-1726, www.santamariaairport.com) is quite small, but a couple of airlines do fly here from Las Vegas and LAX in Los Angeles; it might be worth looking into if you can get a connection via one of those cities.

GETTING AROUND
Taxi

As spread out as Santa Maria is, you might find yourself in need of a taxi. The **Yellow Cab Company of Santa Maria** (805/347-0000, www.santamariayellowcab.com), and **Santa Maria Valley Taxi** (805/937-1121) are all available on short notice.

Bus

Bus services are provided by the **Santa Maria Area Transit** (805/928-5624, www.ci.santamaria.ca.us/3075.html), which can accommodate both bikes and wheelchairs. Visit the website for a complete schedule. Basic one-way fares are $1.25, and exact change is required.

VENTURA AND OJAI

Ventura County has long been a stopping-off point on the way from Los Angeles to Santa Barbara and points north, but the area has much more to offer. Yes, U.S. 101 bisects the county as it takes you north out of Los Angeles. But it's also an area rich in natural, cultural, architectural, and historical treasures, with rugged transverse mountain ranges and fertile valleys ranging down to a magnificent coastline. In recent years, Ventura has begun to develop a solid identity of its own, with a growing and impressive arts scene, antiques and thrift shops, and a thriving restaurant landscape. It even boasts its own wine trail, which intercepts day-trippers heading for the more established Santa Ynez and Santa Maria Valley wine regions. Ventura is also the gateway to the Channel Islands, a series of five undeveloped islands that still retain their primal beauty, with unique spots to hike, fish, scuba, snorkel, and kayak. Ventura has retained its seaside charm due in part to a healthy sense of indifference for its southern neighbor, metropolitan Los Angeles. There is little pretense in Ventura, where a whole world awaits discovery.

Just 16 miles up the road but a universe away is the small enclave of Ojai, a longtime mecca for the artistic crowd and a hub for meditation, spiritual retreats, New Age teachings—anything left of center. It will enchant you with its small-town feel, walkability, and beautiful setting. Used as the backdrop for the 1930s movie *Lost Horizon,* the once secluded town is today anything but hard to find. Summer sees flocks of visitors shopping and dining on Ojai Avenue, doing yoga, getting in touch with their

© STUART THORNTON

HIGHLIGHTS

◖ Main Street: Wander along Ventura's main drag, lined with both historic structures and new boutiques, restaurants, and stores (page 160).

◖ Mission San Buenaventura: One of the most prosperous of the Central Coast missions, pretty San Buenaventura was personally dedicated by Junípero Serra (page 161).

◖ Surfing C Street: White lines of peeling waves scratch the seas off popular California Street, also known as or Surfer's Point. Surf the consistent break or sit back and take in the action at this Ventura recreation hub (page 173).

◖ Ojai Avenue: Not much has changed on Ojai's main thoroughfare since it was built in 1917. With its Spanish-style arcade and impressive Post Office Tower, it's the heartbeat of Ojai (page 187).

◖ Meditation Mount: This peaceful, quiet spot offers the best view of Ojai valley and the mountains that protect it. The serene property has a meditation center, a tearoom, and a well-manicured public garden (page 189).

◖ Hiking in Ojai: Adjacent to the sprawling Los Padres National Forest, Ojai is one of the best places on the Central Coast to head out for a hike (page 195).

LOOK FOR ◖ TO FIND RECOMMENDED SIGHTS, ACTIVITIES, DINING, AND LODGING.

inner selves, or just escaping the hectic pace of somewhere else. Similar to Santa Barbara's renewal after the 1925 earthquake, Ojai created its current Spanish Revival appearance after a fire decimated much of the town in 1917. It also hosts annual festivals of playwrights, music, wine, and theater. Nearby Lake Casitas offers plenty of boating, swimming, and camping in a somewhat remote mountain setting.

Northeast of Ventura is the Heritage Valley, a string of small cities—Santa Paula, Fillmore, and Piru—surrounded by acres of citrus groves.

This former land of railroads and ranches, easily accessed via Highway 126, is a worthy side trip for those who want to dip into Southern California's past.

PLANNING YOUR TIME

It's nearly always sunny in Ventura. On average, there are over 250 days of sunshine annually, and 70-degree weather delights nearly year-round. Rain is sporadic, although most of it falls November through March. Summers certainly see an influx of people, and the

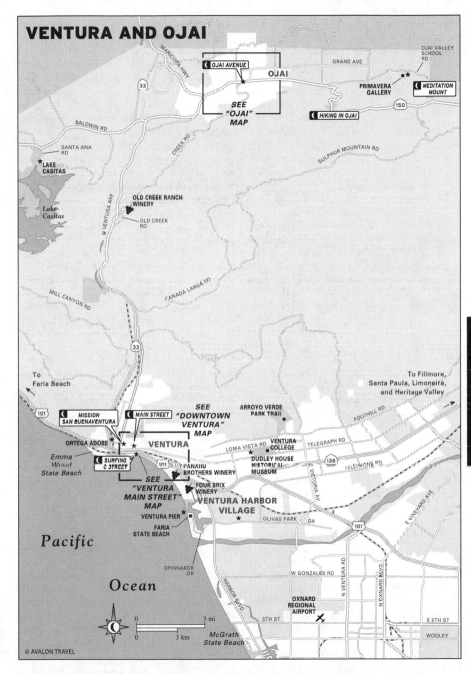

VENTURA AND OJAI

MARICOPA HWY

OJAI VALLEY SCHOOL RD

GRAND AVE

OJAI AVENUE

OJAI

33

PRIMAVERA GALLERY

MEDITATION MOUNT

SEE "OJAI" MAP

BALDWIN RD

HIKING IN OJAI

150

SANTA ANA RD

LAKE CASITAS

CREEK RD

SULPHUR MOUNTAIN RD

Lake Casitas

OLD CREEK RANCH WINERY

N VENTURA AVE

OLD CREEK RD

MILL CANYON RD

CANADA LARGA RD

33

To Faria Beach

To Fillmore, Santa Paula, Limoneira, and Heritage Valley

FOOTHILL RD

101

MISSION SAN BUENAVENTURA

MAIN STREET

SEE "DOWNTOWN VENTURA" MAP

ARROYO VERDE PARK TRAIL

VENTURA

ORTEGA ADOBE

LOMA VISTA RD

VENTURA COLLEGE

TELEGRAPH RD

126

TELEPHONE RD

Emma Wood State Beach

SURFING C STREET

101

DUDLEY HOUSE HISTORICAL MUSEUM

PANAHO BROTHERS WINERY

SEE "VENTURA MAIN STREET" MAP

FOUR BRIX WINERY

VENTURA HARBOR VILLAGE

VICTORIA AV

E VINEYARD AVE

VENTURA PIER

FARIA STATE BEACH

OLIVAS PARK DR

101

Pacific

SPINNAKER DR

W GONZALES RD

N VENTURA RD

N OXNARD BLVD

Ocean

OXNARD REGIONAL AIRPORT

5TH ST

E 5TH ST

WOOLEY

0   3 mi

0   3 km

HARBOR BLVD

McGrath State Beach

© AVALON TRAVEL

VENTURA AND OJAI

beaches teem with sun-worshippers. The best times to visit tend to be September-November and February-April, when the crowds are fewer and the weather, while perhaps a bit cooler than in summer, is clear and clean.

Downtown Ventura can be reasonably experienced within a day. If you intend to be outdoors, sailing, hiking, or heading to the islands, you'll need more time; a weekend at minimum. Add another day if you hope to visit Heritage Valley, as you need to factor in driving time.

Ojai is an ideal one-day trip from Ventura or Santa Barbara. But to fully experience the quiet town and absorb the tranquility of the area, a weekend is best. Summertime can get hot and crowded; the best times to visit this peaceful enclave are February-June, when the rains have usually passed and the hillsides are beginning to sprout with new life, and October-December, when the town is festively decorated for the holidays. Yes, it's a bit cooler then, but the crowds have thinned, and even though you won't have the place to yourself, it will feel like you do.

HISTORY

Ventura, now home to more than 100,000 residents, was originally—and is sometimes still—called San Buenaventura, which loosely translates from Spanish as "city of good fortune." The name is taken from the Spanish mission that was built here in 1782 by the missionary Junípero Serra.

Many cultural groups have inhabited the land where Ventura is now located. The earliest were the Chumash people, whose village here was called Shisholop. Archaeologists discovered even earlier cultures dating back as far as 10,000 years. Mission San Buenaventura brought the Chumash under the control of the Roman Catholic Church, encouraging them to establish a regimented life, learn new skills, and develop agricultural practices. Mission San Buenaventura, named for Saint Bonaventure, was the most successful and influential of the California missions founded by Serra.

Following the Central Coast earthquake of December 1812, the mission began a period of reconstruction to repair quake damage. Over time, due to diseases and a lack of funds, mission life declined, and in 1866 the City of San Buenaventura officially became part of Santa Barbara County. The majority of the residents were of Spanish, Mexican, and Native American origin. In 1873, Ventura County was formed, and San Buenaventura became a city within the new county.

The Northern California gold rush in 1849 brought many Easterners to California, and after the Civil War came another influx of new residents, who bought land from the Mexicans or simply squatted on property. Vast holdings were later acquired by Easterners, including railroad magnate Thomas Scott. Scott was impressed by a young employee named Thomas R. Bard who had been in charge of train supplies to Union troops; Bard was sent west to handle Scott's property. Bard is most often regarded as the father of Ventura. The Union Oil Company, located today as it was then in Santa Paula, was organized with Bard as president in 1890. The main Ventura oil field was drilled as early as 1914; at its peak it produced 90,000 barrels a day. For most of its history, Ventura has escaped the thrust of waves of immigration and has been able to enjoy its own more leisurely, less crowded way of life. At the same time, Ventura became prosperous. The city is located between two richly endowed valleys, the Ventura River valley and the Santa Clara River valley; the soil was so rich that citrus grew better here than anywhere else in the state. The growers along these rivers got together and formed Sunkist, now the world's largest organization of citrus production.

For most of the century that followed the incorporation of Ventura in 1866, it was pretty much isolated from the southern part of the state, and locals didn't seem to mind. Even from the north, entrance was by way of a single road along the beach, and stagecoach passengers either had to wait until low tide, when the horses could cross on the exposed wet sand at the Rincon, or go up the Ventura River Valley and then cross over the mountains to Santa Barbara via Casitas Pass, always a long

© STUART THORNTON

the rugged mountains above Ojai

and difficult trip. Inland, Ventura was hemmed in by Los Padres National Forest, comprising mountainous country, deep canyons, and peaks that rise as high as 8,831 feet at Mount Pinos. Ventura remained quite isolated until a narrow road, the Maricopa Highway, was built in the 1920s, but even then travel by car was slow and hazardous. Now there is direct access to the city, and the perilous journeys of long ago have been forgotten, thanks to the completion of the Ventura Freeway from Los Angeles to Ventura, the last link of which was finished in 1969.

Originally called Nordhoff, Ojai was mapped out in 1874, although the Chumash people had lived here for thousands of years prior to that. The area was part of a Spanish land grant to Fernardo Tico in 1837; Tico sold his vast holdings in 1853, and the land went through a series of landowners until, after some failed oil exploration, many of the settlers decided to form an actual town, and Nordhoff was born. You'll still see the name around town, such as Nordhoff High School. In the early 20th century a businessman from Toledo, Ohio, named Edward Libbey came to

Nordhoff and immediately fell in love with the place. In 1914 he unveiled grand plans to create a viable community, a cohesive town rather than the ramshackle stores and buildings that had congregated on the main street. In 1917 he got his chance, when a fire decimated much of the town and Libbey was handed a clean slate. A wealthy man who wanted his new adopted town to be distinctive, he financed much of the civic development to realize his dream. His work gives downtown Ojai its distinctive charm: a Spanish Colonial-style arcade along the main street, a post office tower designed after Havana's Campanile, and a pergola, the official entrance to Libbey Park. Today, Ojai's wealth is mostly apparent in large parcels of land and multimillion-dollar homes. But pretentiousness is not typical here, and Ojai retains a modest feel.

The name Ojai (pronounced O-high) is derived from the Chumash word *awhai,* which might mean "nest," or possibly "moon," depending on whom you ask. Much of the literature about Ojai claims one meaning over the other, but there is no definite proof of either.

Ventura

Ventura is short for San Buenaventura, which means "city of good fortune." There is much that is good about Ventura, including its weather (daytime temperatures average 70°F), consistent waves for surfers, and a historic downtown that includes a restored mission.

Downtown Ventura is compact and easy to walk around; it is three blocks from the beach and still feels somehow unfettered by "progress," with buildings that date to the 1800s (a long time by California standards). In recent years, the city has encouraged the growth of an impressive arts community and a thriving restaurant scene. A few blocks from Main Street is Surfer's Point, a coastal area also known as C Street. A ribbon of pavement by the ocean, the Omer Rains Bike Trail almost always hosts a collection of walkers, runners, and cyclists. Farther away, Ventura Harbor has a cluster of restaurants, bars, and hotels located around the harbor, which is the gateway to the nearby Channel Islands National Park.

SIGHTS
☾ Main Street

The seven-block section of Ventura's **Main Street** (Main St. between Ventura Ave. and Fir St.) combines the best of the city's past and present. Important cultural and historic sites include Mission San Buenaventura, the missionary Junípero Serra's ninth California mission, and the Ortega Adobe, where the Ortega Chile Packing Company originated. But Main Street is not stuck in the past; it's also home to stylish restaurants like the Watermark on Main, clothing boutique Le Monde Emporium, and the brick-and-mortar store for the popular online surf-culture retailer WetSand.

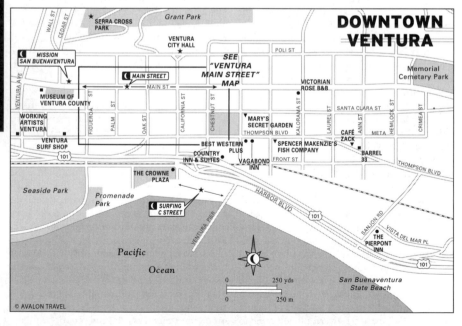

downtown Ventura's Main Street

©STUART THORNTON

🅒 Mission San Buenaventura

Referred to as the "mission by the sea," **Mission San Buenaventura** (211 E. Main St., 805/643-4318, www.sanbuenaventuramission.org, self-guided tours daily 10am-5pm, adults $4, seniors $3, children $1) is right on Ventura's Main Street and just blocks from the beach. It is just one of six missions that was personally dedicated by Junípero Serra, the founder of California's mission system.

A seven-mile-long aqueduct was built to bring water to the mission from the Ventura River. Because of its abundant water supply, Mission San Buenaventura became known for its lush orchards and gardens. Not that living at this mission was without hardships. Construction of the current mission began in earnest in 1792 after a fire burned the first church building. In 1812 a series of earthquakes and the resulting tidal wave forced the mission's inhabitants to escape inland. Later, pirate Hippolyte de Bouchard's threat to pillage the mission led to another temporary relocation.

Today, the mission is a peaceful remnant of California's past. Beautiful high ceilings and walls are decorated with paintings of Jesus at various Stations of the Cross, depicting the series of events before the Crucifixion. A one-room museum on the grounds displays the church's original doors and a collection of indigenous Chumash artifacts. Between the museum and the church is a scenic garden with a tile fountain, an old olive press, and a shrine.

Ventura City Hall

Like Santa Barbara's County Courthouse, **Ventura City Hall** (501 Poli St., 805/654-7800, www.cityofventura.net, Mon.-Fri. 8am-5pm) is both a government building and a stunning architectural treasure. The structure on a hill above downtown Ventura was built in 1912 to serve as the county courthouse. It was designed by famed architect Albert C. Martin, one of

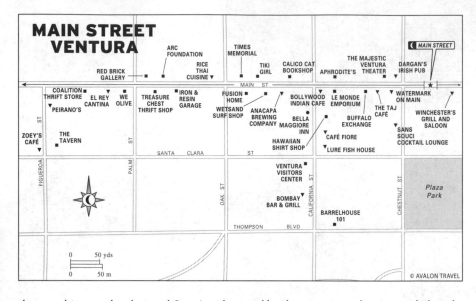

MAIN STREET VENTURA

ARC FOUNDATION
TIMES MEMORIAL
MAIN STREET
RED BRICK GALLERY
RICE THAI CUISINE ▼
TIKI GIRL
CALICO CAT BOOKSHOP
THE MAJESTIC VENTURA THEATER
APHRODITE'S
DARGAN'S IRISH PUB
MAIN ST
COALITION THRIFT STORE
EL REY CANTINA
WE OLIVE
TREASURE CHEST THRIFT SHOP
IRON & RESIN GARAGE
FUSION HOME
WETSAND SURF SHOP
BOLLYWOOD INDIAN CAFE
LE MONDE EMPORIUM
WATERMARK ON MAIN
PEIRANO'S
ANACAPA BREWING COMPANY
BELLA MAGGIORE INN
BUFFALO EXCHANGE
THE TAJ CAFÉ
WINCHESTER'S GRILL AND SALOON
ZOEY'S CAFÉ
THE TAVERN
HAWAIIAN SHIRT SHOP
CAFÉ FIORE
LURE FISH HOUSE
SANS SOUCI COCKTAIL LOUNGE
SANTA   CLARA   ST
FIGUEROA ST
PALM ST
OAK ST
VENTURA VISITORS CENTER
CALIFORNIA ST
CHESTNUT ST
Plaza Park
BOMBAY BAR & GRILL
BARRELHOUSE 101
THOMPSON   BLVD
0   50 yds
0   50 m
© AVALON TRAVEL

three architects who designed Los Angeles City Hall, in the French beaux arts style, with elegant features like neoclassic columns and arched windows. You'll notice the faces of 24 Franciscan friars amid the decor, along with some decorative lima-bean bouquets, a nod to the area's agricultural heritage. Highlights in the building's interior include its lobby, made of Italian marble, and its three stained glass domes.

Ortega Adobe

The 1857 **Ortega Adobe** (215 W. Main St., 805/658-4726, www.cityofventura.net, daily 9am-4pm) has a tasty history. In the late 1800s, Emilio Carlos Ortega started fire-roasting chilies in the adobe's kitchen, leading first to a Spanish chili sauce and later to the founding of the Ortega Chile Company, the first commercial food operation in California. Ortega's Mexican food products include peppers, beans, salsas, sauces, and taco shells; they can be found today in supermarkets all over the country. The adobe residence remained in the prominent Ortega family until 1905. By the late 1960s it was in danger of demolition, but was saved and restored by the city of Ventura

and local community volunteers, including the Daughters of the Golden West, whose efforts keep it open to the public today.

Museum of Ventura County

Need a little historical context for your Ventura vacation? The **Museum of Ventura County** (100 E. Main St., 805/653-0323, http://venturamuseum.org, Tues.-Sun. 11am-5pm, adults $4, seniors $3, children $1) exhibits some 30,000 objects and works of art that tell Ventura County's story. These include Chumash pieces, 200 historical figures created by Ojai artist George Stuart, and items related to the Saint Francis Dam disaster. Temporary exhibits have focused on the celebrity photography of Ojai photographer Guy Webster and the history of filmmaking in the county. The museum was initially opened in 1913 to showcase the collection gathered by Cephas Bard, a doctor who sometimes accepted historical artifacts in lieu of payment from his patients.

Dudley House Historical Museum

For a few hours each month, the **Dudley House Historical Museum** (197 N. Ashwood Ave., 805/642-3345, www.dudleyhouse.org, first

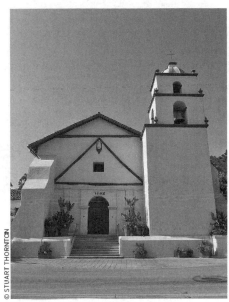

Mission San Buenaventura

Sun. of the month 1pm-4pm, free) offers a look back at the lives of a Ventura family who lived here from 1892 to 1930. Built by B. W. Dudley, the preserved Victorian farmhouse is furnished with its original furniture. Today, it's the setting for docent-led tours (by appointment) and open houses, where pre-1930s recordings are played to take your mind back in time. The adjacent lavender garden is one of the largest collections of the flowering plant in the state.

Serra Cross Park

Perched on a hill with fine views of Ventura and the sea, **Serra Cross Park** (www.serracrosspark.org) is home to a large wooden cross with a lot of history. The first cross on this site was built in the late 18th century to guide travelers to Mission San Buenaventura. Today's cross, mounted on a stone pedestal, is actually the third to stand here; it dates to 1912. Located in the larger Grant Park, the cross was sold to a nonprofit agency to prevent a possible constitutional conflict over the separation of church and state. Now that the cross has a

secure spot on the hill, people visit it to take in some local history along with panoramic views of the city and coastline below. It's also a popular spot for weddings. To reach Serra Cross Park from downtown Ventura's City Hall, take a left on Poli Street and then a right on the climbing Brakey Road. At the top of the hill, take a left, and then stay to the right until the parking lot.

C Street

California Street (end of Figueroa St. to the end of California St.), or **C Street,** hosted the world's first pro surfing event: 1965's Noseriding International. Today, extending 0.75 miles from Surfer's Point Park to the cove beside Ventura Pier, it's Ventura's recreation hub. Lines of white water streaming off the point entice surfers and stand-up paddleboarders while old long-boarders relive their glory days catching waves that can continue for 0.75 miles. You might see pro surfers like Ventura local Dane Reynolds out ripping apart the waves or practicing aerials. It's worth a visit even if you don't surf. The vibrant coastal scene includes the Promenade walkway, which bustles with joggers and power walkers, and the popular Omer Rains Bike Trail. Facilities include an outdoor shower, restrooms, and a picnic area. Parking can be challenging: There's a free lot that fills up quickly as well as a pay lot ($2 per day).

Ventura Pier

Stretching some 1,600 feet out into the ocean, the **Ventura Pier** (www.cityofventura.net) is one of the longest and oldest wooden piers in the state. After it was built in 1872, it served as a working pier for 40 years, shipping livestock, produce, and oil. A 40-mile pipeline brought oil down the Santa Clara Valley to a storage tank constructed beside the wharf. Disaster struck in 1889 when the *W. L. Hardison,* the world's first oil tanker, caught fire, setting off a series of powerful explosions at the wharf. Years later, in 1914, the wharf was split in half when storm swells sent the ship the SS *Coos Bay* crashing into the pier. The pier survived and

© STUART THORNTON

the Museum of Ventura County

was rebuilt, becoming a recreational center in 1936. Today, you'll find benches, interpretive panels, and the fantastic Beach House Tacos.

Olivas Adobe Historical Park

For a peek into California's 1800s rancho period, take a docent-led tour of **Olivas Adobe Historical Park** (4200 Olivas Park Rd., 805/658-4728, www.olivasadobe.org, guided tours Sat.-Sun. 11am-4pm, adults $5, family $10, seniors $3), owned by the City of Ventura. Constructed in 1847, the main house on the 4,693-acre Rancho San Miguel was home to Raymundo Olivas, his wife Theodora, their 21 children, and their employees.

The 45-minute tour illuminates what life was like during the ranch period, from how the adobe walls were constructed to how bread was baked in outdoor baking ovens. Stops include a bedroom that the eight Olivas daughters somehow managed to share and an impressive chapel on the second floor of the house. There are also some curiosities on display, including a desk made from an old piano, a wreath made of human hair, a Victorian-era mousetrap, and an upright barrel piano, a music box-like contraption that has figurines playing along to the music produced by a crank on the side of the machine.

Ventura Harbor Village

A collection of restaurants, art galleries, and shops has sprung up around the fairly large Ventura Harbor. **Ventura Harbor Village** (1583 Spinnaker Dr., 805/642-8538, www.ventura-harborvillage.com) hosts a comedy club and popular seafood eateries, including Andria's Seafood Restaurant & Market and Brophy Brothers. Just feet away from the village is the Harbor Cove Beach, a piece of shoreline popular with kayakers and kite fliers, and Surfer's Knoll Beach, where a wave breaks down the beach by the mouth of the Santa Clara River.

While a trip out of the harbor to visit the Channel Islands is highly recommended, the **Channel Islands Visitors Center** (1901 Spinnaker Dr., 805/658-5730, www.nps.gov, daily 8:30am-5pm) has some nice exhibits on

EL CAMINO REAL: THE KING'S HIGHWAY

As you drive U.S. 101 from Ventura up through Paso Robles and beyond, you'll begin to notice signs along the road that look like a shepherd's crook with a bell on it and the words "El Camino Real." The signs are peppered along a nearly 600-mile route in California. Here's why: At the same time that the American colonies were rebelling against England, a handful of Spaniards and Mexicans were establishing outposts up the California coast. In 1769, a fortress and the very first mission were established in San Diego. A footpath called El Camino Real, meaning "the king's highway," was created to connect each of the subsequent missions as they were constructed. The missions were situated in areas where large populations of indigenous people lived and where the soil was fertile enough to sustain a settlement. Each mission was designed to be a day's travel from the next—at least in theory—all linked by El Camino Real. As time progressed and more missions were built, the path became a roadway wide enough to accommodate horses and wagons. It was not, however, until the last mission was completed in Sonoma in 1823 that the little pathway became a major road. Ultimately, El Camino Real linked all 21 of California's missions, pueblos, and four presidios, from San Diego to Sonoma. In 1904 the El Camino Real Association was formed to preserve and maintain California's historic road. The first commemorative bell was placed in 1906 in front of the Old Plaza Church in downtown Los Angeles, and by 1915 approximately 158 bells had been installed along El Camino Real. The bells were made of cast iron, which encouraged theft, and the number of original bells plummeted to about 75. New bells made of concrete were installed in 1974. U.S. 101 loosely follows this original footpath.

the islands if you can't make the journey. The exhibits mostly focus on the islands' wildlife, with a stuffed golden eagle, a stuffed island fox, and a tide pool aquarium with live garibaldi damselfish, starfish, and kelp. There's also a diorama of the dig site on Santa Rosa Island where the remains of a pygmy mammoth was found. On a covered deck are some map displays of each island. Climb some stairs to the observation tower, which offers great views of the harbor and occasional views of the Channel Islands in the distance.

WINE TASTING

While it's not known as a wine destination, Ventura still has a handful of wineries. Visit the **Ventura County Winery Association** website (www.vcwines.com) for a rundown.

The folks at **Four Brix Winery** (2290 Eastman Ave., Suite 109, 805/256-6006, http://fourbrixwine.com, tasting room Fri. 4pm-8pm, Sat.-Sun. noon-5pm, tasting $10) know how to have fun. This urban winery hosts cellar concerts, blending parties, and tasting-room dinners. Oh, yeah, they produce wines on-site too. Although Four Brix does not have its own vineyard, it sources grapes from other Central Coast locations. The viognier and grenache blanc grapes come from Santa Ynez Valley, while the zinfandel and sangiovese grapes hail from Paso Robles. Their flagship wine is the Scosso, a blend of sangiovese, cabernet sauvignon, and merlot.

The **Panaro Brothers Winery** (451 Market St., Suite 7, 805/654-1577, http://panarobrotherswinery.com, tasting room Fri. 3pm-6pm, Sat.-Sun. 11am-6pm) is the product of an Italian American family that has been making wine for five generations. Their single-varietal and blended wines are made from Santa Barbara, San Luis Obispo, and Monterey County grapes.

ENTERTAINMENT AND EVENTS
Bars and Clubs

Filling multiple rooms in a house dating back to 1912, **The Tavern** (211 E. Santa Clara St.,

805/643-3264, http://thetavernventura.com, daily 5pm-2am) is quite a bar. Inside on a weekend night there may be two bands playing in two different rooms. If you're more interested in conversation, head for the room to the left upon entering, which has a fireplace and a couch, or opt for the large outdoor deck out back. The cocktails menu includes new spins on the classics, like the maple Manhattan. While sipping your spirits, be on the lookout for a spirit: they say the Tavern is haunted by the ghost of a young girl who died here in the late 1800s.

Winchester's Grill and Saloon (632 E. Main St., 805/653-7446, www.winchestersventura.com, Mon.-Fri. 4pm-1am, Sat.-Sun. 11am-11pm) is the place to go if you want something poured from a tap. Behind the 40-foot mahogany bar, bartenders serve up 36 beers, three ciders, and a root beer from Winchester's many taps. You can enjoy your beverage inside or on one of two heated patios. It can get loud and a little rowdy; people seem to step inside and become cowboys.

Dargan's Irish Pub (593 E. Main St., 805/648-3001, daily 11am-2am) feels like a mix of old and new. Classic Irish beer signs decorate the interior, but there are big-screen TVs over the bar playing the latest sporting events. Irish countryside scenes are painted on the wall, but modern hip-hop plays on the sound system. Order from a selection of Irish beers (Guinness, Murphy's, Smithwicks, Harp) and whiskies (Bushmills, Jameson, Tullamore Dew).

The cool retro lighted sign at **El Rey Cantina** (294 E. Main St., 805/653-1111, http://elreycantina.com, Tues.-Fri. 4:30pm-1:30am, Sat.-Sun. 11:30am-1:30am) draws people from Main Street to enjoy an extensive list of tequilas and Mexican cocktails (margaritas, sangria, and liquor-spiked *horchatas*).

If you'd rather enjoy a glass of wine (or share a bottle), head off to **Barrel 33** (1067 E. Thompson Blvd., 805/652-1810, Tues.-Sun. 5pm-11pm). They stock many regional wines alongside bottles from France, Italy, and Australia. You'll also find local beers on tap.

True beer connoisseurs flock to

Barrelhouse 101 (545 E. Thompson Blvd., 805/643-0906, www.barrelhouse101.com, Sun.-Mon. 11:30am-10pm, Tues.-Thurs. 11:30am-11pm, Fri.-Sat. 11:30am-midnight). The very impressive 101 beers on tap put them in the rarefied realm of legendary California beer joints. Beers from California and Belgium are strongly represented but Oregon and Delaware also make strong showings. During **happy hour** (Mon.-Fri. 4pm-7pm), draft beers are $1 cheaper.

Located in an industrial park southeast of downtown Ventura, **Surf Brewery** (4561 Market St., Suite A, 805/644-2739, www.surfbrewery.com, Tues.-Thurs. 4pm-9pm, Fri. 1pm-9pm, Sat. noon-9pm, Sun. noon-7pm) is the place to go to go for a pint of Mondo's Cream Ale, County Line Rye Pale Ale, or Oil Piers Porter. There's live music Saturday 6pm-8pm and brewery tours Saturday and Sunday at 3pm and 4pm.

By the end of the evening, a lot of people end up at dive bar **Sans Souci Cocktail Lounge** (21 S. Chestnut St., 805/643-4539, daily noon-2am), which stays open late. The small interior with red-couch seating can get a bit claustrophobic on crowded nights; escape to the semi-covered courtyard out front before it fills up with drinkers and smokers.

Live Music
The Majestic Ventura Theater (26 S. Chestnut St., 805/653-0721, www.venturatheater.net) gets a variety of pretty big national acts, including music icons Alice Cooper and Snoop Dogg—or should that be Snoop Lion?—along with newer acts the Dirty Heads and Dengue Fever. The 1,200-seat Mission-style theater opened in 1928 as a movie house; decades later it was converted into a concert venue. The old chandeliers still hang in the auditorium, and other remnants of the 1920s decor remain.

The **Bombay Bar and Grill** (143 S. California St., 805/643-4404, www.bombaybarandgrill.com, Wed.-Fri. 4pm-2am, Sat.-Sun. 11am-2am) has two stages and two dance floors for live bands and DJs. Expect entertainment five nights a week, including Wednesday-night

Located in Ventura's Livery Complex, the **Ventura Improv Company** (34 N. Palm St., 805/643-5701, www.venturaimprov.com, Fri.-Sat. 8pm) stages live comedy improv shows on Friday and Saturday nights. They also offer improv and movement workshops for those who dream of getting on stage.

Owned by two comedy pros, the **Ventura Harbor Comedy Club** (1559 Spinnaker Dr., 805/644-1500, http://venturaharborcomedy-club.com, shows Wed.-Fri. 8pm, Sat. 7pm and 9pm, Sun. 7pm, $15) hosts heavy hitters like Ron White and Bobcat Goldthwait. They also have open-mike nights if you want to test your material out on a live audience.

Festivals and Events

In the summer, Ventura's art studios and other venues open their doors for a weekend during the **Westside ArtWalk** (http://westsideartwalk.org). Some places that participate include the Museum of Ventura County and the Ventura Visitors Center. Other participating venues include restaurants, salons, antiques shops, unique boutiques, and coffee shops—almost any place with walls.

The **Ventura County Fair** (10 W. Harbor Blvd., 805/648-3376, www.venturacountyfair.org) goes down every summer on the Ventura County Fairgrounds, next to the city's main coastal recreation area. Expect the usual attractions: a Ferris wheel, cotton candy, and livestock exhibits. Live nightly entertainment often features 1980s acts like Bret Michaels and Joan Jett.

While it began as a chamber music festival, the **Ventura Music Festival** (805/643-3146, www.venturamusicfestival.org fest) has expanded to include jazz and crossover artists such as Branford Marsalis, Diane Schuur, Chris Botti, and Pink Martini. It takes place at the end of April and early May. **Ventura's First Fridays** (http://s232036650.online-home.us) is a monthly art walk showcasing the works of local artists; a map and a list of participating venues are available on the website. The **Ventura Harbor Summer Concert Series** (1583 Spinnaker Dr., 805/477-0470,

© STUART THORNTON

The Majestic Ventura Theater

blues jams. Bombay is also known for its Nacho Volcano Burger.

Zoey's Cafe (185 E. Santa Clara St., 805/652-1137, www.zoeyscafe.com) has live music and entertainment almost every night. The listening room hosts intimate acoustic performances, while the **Kenny Edwards Hall** holds up to 200 concertgoers. The range of performers stretches from pop princess Colbie Caillat to legendary punk band Black Flag. There are also bluegrass jams and comedy open mikes.

Performing Arts

The **Rubicon Theatre Company** (1006 E. Main St., 805/667-2900, www.rubicontheatre.org) stages plays in a 186-seat venue that was once a church. Expect classics like Thornton Wilder's *Our Town* as well as new works; there is usually one wholly original show each season. One of Rubicon's original plays, *Daddy Long Legs,* landed on the London stage. Rubicon has also begun performing some plays in Spanish with English subtitles.

VENTURA AND OJAI

www.venturaharborvillage.com, summer Sun. 1pm-4pm) brings pop, rock, and reggae bands to the harbor's Carousel Stage every Sunday afternoon.

SHOPPING
Shopping Malls and Districts

Main Street in downtown Ventura is home to a surprising number of unique local and specialty stores and has managed to retain a sense of individuality. For traditional shopping, visit the **Pacific View Mall** (Mills St. and Main St., 805/642-5530, www.shoppacificview.com, Mon.-Fri. 10am-9pm, Sat. 10am-8pm, Sun. 11am-7pm), with 140 stores and restaurants like Sears, Target, Old Navy, Gap, Ben & Jerry's, and many more. The two-story indoor mall offers Wi-Fi in the food court. Some of the restaurants have improved over typical fast-food joints, and occasionally chair massages are offered. There are several nail places, as well as familiar brand-name stores. It does get crowded on weekends, but it's pretty easy to get around midweek.

Farther south are the **Camarillo Premium Outlets** (740 E. Ventura Blvd., off Los Posas Ave., Camarillo, 805/445-8520, www.premiumoutlets.com, Mon.-Sat. 10am-9pm, Sun. 10am-8pm, holiday hours vary). Actually in the town of Camarillo, east of Ventura's southern neighbor Oxnard, there are 160 outlet stores peddling reduced-price brand-name merchandise, including Banana Republic and J. Crew.

Art Galleries

Ventura's strong arts scene has been overshadowed by Los Angeles, but that is beginning to change. **Red Brick Gallery** (315 E. Main St., 805/643-6400, www.redbrickart.com, Mon.-Thurs. 11am-6pm, Fri.-Sat. 10am-7pm, Sun. 11am-5pm) offers shows that rotate every six weeks. The gallery, lined with exposed redbrick walls, it represents about 150 artists working in paint, wood, glass, photography, and jewelry.

Known locally as WAV, **Working Artists Ventura** (175 S. Ventura Ave., 805/641-0400, www.wavartists.com) is an affordable living and workspace for artists in all media as well as dancers, musicians, writers, actors, and filmmakers. WAV opens its Theater Gallery to show off the work of its resident artists the first Friday of every month 6pm-9pm. **Art City Studios** (197 Dubbers St., 805/648-1690, www.artcitystudios.com, Wed.-Sun. 10am-5pm) is a workspace for 20 artists who create stone, wood, and bronze sculptures. They showcase their work in the on-site **Micro Gallery Showroom.**

Appropriately located in the Ventura Harbor Village, **Latitudes Fine Art Gallery** (1591 Spinnaker Dr., Suite 113, 805/642-5257, www.latitudesfineart.com, daily 11am-6pm) showcases photography with an emphasis on local coastal landscapes and animals. It was founded by photographers Steve Munch and Stephanie Hogue in 2010. Also in the harbor area, the **Ventura County Potters' Guild Harbor Gallery Store** (1567 Spinnaker Dr., Suite 105, 805/644-6800, www.vcpottersguild.com, Thurs.-Tues. 11am-6pm) displays the works of the local nonprofit Ventura County Potters Guild.

Thrift Stores

Ventura has long been known for a plethora of inexpensive thrift stores, but in recent years many have been converted into restaurants or bars. Still, there are bargains to be had. The inventory at the **Coalition Thrift Store** (270 E. Main St., 805/643-4411, Mon.-Sat. 9am-6pm, Sun. 10am-5pm) changes daily. Search for bargains on household items, furniture, shoes, clothes, and jewelry, and feel good about your purchases: the shop supports battered women and children's shelters. Other thrift store options include **Treasure Chest Thrift Shop** (328 E. Main St., 805/653-0555, daily 10am-7:30pm) and **The Arc Foundation of Ventura County Thrift Store** (265 E. Main St., 805/650-8611, Mon.-Sat. 9am-6pm, Sun. 10am-5pm).

Clothing

Specializing in trendy fashion, **Le Monde Emporium** (542 E. Main St., 805/648-7463,

A classic woody in downtown Ventura advertises The Hawiian Shirt Shoppe.

Mon.-Thurs. 10:30am-7pm, Fri.-Sat. 10:30am-10pm, Sun. 11am-7pm) has clothing in the latest colors and styles, appropriate for the beach or a night on the town. It's also open late on Friday and Saturday for fashion emergencies. **Aphrodite's Lingerie and Gift Gallery** (477 E. Main St., 805/652-0082, www.lingerieventura.com, Mon.-Tues. 10:30am-5:30pm, Wed.-Thurs. 10:30am-7pm, Fri.-Sat. 10:30am-9pm, Sun. 11am-6pm) highlights that it carries something for "every body." This means it has bustiers, dance wear, bras, and adult novelties ranging from petite to plus sizes.

Grab a complimentary cup of coffee and browse the "gently used" clothing for sale at **Harper Blue** (2415 E. Main St., 805/667-8167, www.harperblue.net, Tues.-Sat. 11am-6pm, Sun. 10am-5pm). This popular upscale consignment and resale boutique has received accolades from the *Ventura County Star* and *Huffington Post*. Although it started in Arizona, used men and women's clothing store **Buffalo Exchange** (532 E. Main St.,

805/648-6873, www.buffaloexchange.com, Sun.-Thurs. 11am-7pm, Fri.-Sat. 11am-8pm) has expanded to 45 stores in 17 states, including this one in Ventura. With a name like **Tiki Girl** (451 E. Main St., 805/643-4800, www.shoptikigirl.com, Mon.-Sat. 11am-6pm, Sun. noon-5pm), it should come as no surprise that this women's clothing store has a large bikini selection. It also carries dresses and accessories.

The Iron & Resin Garage (324 E. Main St., 805/643-0737, www.ironandresin.com, Mon.-Fri. 11am-7pm, Sat. 10am-7pm, Sun. 10am-6pm) is a clothing and accessory store for a particular type of man: guys who like surfing, motorcycles, hot-rodding, and rocking out. It also hosts art shows, motorcycle rides, and hootenannies. With vintage and modern aloha wear hanging on the walls, the **Hawaiian Shirt Shoppe** (40 S. California St., 805/643-8800, daily 11am-6pm) feels like a flowering tropical jungle in this small store. You'll also find other island items, including women's Hawaiian print dresses, leis, flip-flops, and hula dolls,

©STUART THORNTON

The Iron & Resin Garage is a hip men's clothing store.

and enjoy relaxing beach music playing while you're shopping.

Bookstores

If you're looking for your latest beach read, you can grab a used paperback classic at **The Calico Cat Bookshop** (495 E. Main St., 805/643-7849, Wed.-Sat. and Mon. 10am-6pm, Sun. noon-5pm). It's probably more worthwhile to browse the collectibles and antiquarian titles, including rare first editions and signed author copies.

Antiques

Attaboy Vintage (2478 E. Main St., 805/648-1668, Tues.-Fri. 11am-5pm, Sat. 11am-4pm, Sun. noon-4pm) is an antiques store for the hipster crowd. You might be able to find a retro looking toy robot, a View-Master, or an actual working typewriter. Shop for old toys, furniture, and vinyl records at **Times Remembered** (467 E. Main St., 805/643-3137, Mon.-Thurs. 10:30am-5:30pm, Fri.-Sat. 10:30am-9pm, Sun. 10:30am-5:30pm).

Home Furnishings

Fusion Home (418 E. Main St., 805/652-7017, http://fusionhomestore.com, Tues.-Fri. 11am-5pm, Sat. 11am-6pm) specializes in unique furnishings that are not mass-produced. This can include bamboo platform beds and cabinets made out of salvaged planks. Choose from a wide selection at **Elliot's Unfinished Furniture** (1501 Palma Dr., 805/639-9222, http://elliots.com, Mon.-Fri. 10am-5:30pm, Sat. 10am-5pm). Once you find the perfect piece for your bedroom, dining room, living room, or office, you get to choose what paint or finish you'd like. Elliot's can do the finishing in-house or you can do it yourself at home.

Specialty Stores

A veteran of Ventura Harbor Village for over 20 years, **Harbor Wind & Kite Co.** (1575 Spinnaker Dr., Suite 107B, 805/654-0900, www.harborwindkite.com, Sun.-Thurs. 10am-6pm, Fri.-Sat. 10am-7pm) has kites hanging everywhere, as well as every conceivable type of kite and kite accessory. Taste complimentary shooters of olive oil at **We Olive** (294 E. Main St., 805/648-6166, www.weolive.com, Mon.-Sat. 10am-6pm, Sun. 11am-5pm) tasting bar. The focus is the tasty cooking and dipping oil, but you'll also find other food and gift items as well.

Online surf supplier **WetSand Surf Shop** (446 E. Main St., 805/652-1706, www.wetsandsurfshop.com, Sun.-Thurs. 11am-5:30pm, Fri.-Sat. 11am-7pm) also has opened a brick-and-mortar store in Ventura. They carry surfboards in unorthodox shapes, bodysurfing planers, and clothing by brands like Deus Ex Machina and Brixton. **Ventura Surf Shop** (88 E. Thompson Blvd., 805/643-1062, summer Mon.-Sat. 9am-6pm, Sun. 9am-5pm, winter daily 9am-5pm) has been a local fixture since 1961. They carry over 90 used surfboards, along with new models by Campbell Brothers, Wayne Rich, and others.

Salzer's Records (5777 Valentine Rd., 805/639-2160, www.salzersstore.com, Sun.-Thurs. 10am-10pm, Fri.-Sat. 10am-11pm) is housed in a futuristic building that looks like

Fusion Home

it sprang out of an old episode of *The Jetsons*. Started back in 1966 by a Southern California music promoter, this fantastic store has the latest releases (on vinyl!) as well as a superb collection of used CDs, vinyl albums, and DVDs. They also stock unofficial concert CDs and DVDs that you won't find anywhere else.

Farmers Markets

Downtown Ventura County's Farmers Market (Santa Clara St. and Palm St., www.vccfarmersmarkets.com, Sat. 8:30am-noon) has produce stands along with vendors selling tamales and pot stickers. If you miss that one, there's still the **Midtown Ventura Market** (front west parking lot, Pacific View Mall, E. Main St. and Pacific View Dr., www.vccfarmersmarkets.com, Wed. 9am-1pm) on Wednesday.

BEACHES
San Buenaventura State Beach

San Buenaventura State Beach (San Pedro St., off U.S. 101, 805/968-1033, www.parks. ca.gov, day use $10) has an impressive two

miles of beach, dunes, and ocean. It also includes the 1,600-foot Ventura Pier, home to Eric Ericsson's Seafood Restaurant and Beach House Tacos. The historic pier was built way back in 1872. This is a safer place to swim than some area beaches. It doesn't get the breakers that roll into the nearby point. Cyclists can take advantage of trails connecting with other nearby beaches, and sports enthusiasts converge on the beach for occasional triathlons and volleyball tournaments. Facilities include a snack bar, an equipment rental shop, and an essential for the 21st-century beach bum—Wi-Fi, although to pick up the signal, you need to be within about 200 feet of the lifeguard tower.

Emma Wood State Beach

Emma Wood State Beach (W. Main St. and Park Access Rd., 805/968-1033, www.parks. ca.gov, day use $10) borders the estuary north of the Ventura River, and it includes the remnants of a World War II artillery site. There are no facilities, but a few minutes' walk leads to the campgrounds (one for RVs and one

Salzer's Records

group camp; first-come, first-served in winter, reservations required spring-fall). At the far eastern side of the parking lot is a small path leading out to the beach that goes under the train tracks. To the right are views up the coast to the Rincon. The beach itself has many rocks—some nearly the size of footballs—strewn about. It's a great spot for windsurfing, as the winds come off Rincon Point just up from the mouth of the Ventura River to create ideal windy conditions. There's a 0.5-mile trail leading through the reeds and underbrush at the far end of the parking lot; although you can hear the surf and the highway, you can't see anything, and you'll feel like you're on safari until you reach the beach where the Ventura River ends.

Harbor Cove Beach

Families flock to **Harbor Cove Beach** (1900 Spinnaker Dr., daily dawn-dusk), located directly across from the Channel Islands Visitors Center at the end of Spinnaker Drive. The harbor's breakwaters provide children and less confident swimmers with relative safety from the ocean currents. In addition, it's a great place to try your hand at stand-up paddleboarding. The wind can kick up at times, but when it's calm it's practically perfect. There's plenty of free parking, lifeguards during peak seasons, restrooms, and foot showers. Food and other amenities can be found across the street at Ventura Harbor Village.

Faria Beach

Farther north, the Ventura County-run **Faria Beach** (4350 W. U.S. 101, at the State Beach exit, 805/654-3951, daily dawn-dusk) is available for tent camping and has 15 RV hookups. The campground has a playground and horseshoe pits, barbecues, and shower facilities, but it's quite small. It's also very crowded with campers, trucks, and people during nice weather because of its proximity to the water. You might find you have more companions than you care for, but it's a long, flat beach, so you can spread out.

© STUART THORNTON

A surfer enjoys a wave at Ventura's C Street.

SPORTS AND RECREATION
Surfing

Ventura is definitely a surf town. The series of point breaks referred to as California Street, C Street for short, is the best place for consistent right breaks. There are three distinct zones along this mile-long stretch of beach. At the point is the Pipe, with some pretty fast short breaks. Moving down the beach is Stables, which continues with the right breaks with an even, low shoulder, and then C Street, breaking both right and left. The waves get mushier and easier for beginners the closer you get to Ventura Pier. There is a pay parking lot right in front of the break across the street from the Ventura County Fairgrounds (10 W. Harbor Blvd.).

Long-boarders and beginners should head to **Mondos** for soft peeling waves. It's a little north of town toward Santa Barbara; take U.S. 101 north to the State Beaches exit. Then head 3.5 miles north on the Pacific Coast Highway. Park in the dirt lot on the right side of the PCH.

South of downtown, **Ventura Harbor** has waves that refract off the harbor's jetties. Experts can attempt to ride the big waves of **Ventura Overhead,** off Emma Wood State Beach, but they occur infrequently, typically during winter's north and northwest swells.

SURF CLASSES

Surfclass (805/200-8674, www.surfclass.com, 2-hour session $90) meets at various beaches around Ventura, depending on weather and swells. They teach everyone from novice landlubbers to rusty shredders. The two-hour class rates are quite reasonable, and they limit class size for individual attention. They will also teach you surf etiquette and lingo.

Ventura Surf School (461 W. Channel Islands Blvd., 805/218-1484, www.venturasurfschool.com, private 2-hour lesson $125, 2 or more $80 pp, 4 or more $75 pp) can also teach you to surf, and they offer a weeklong surf camp and kids-only classes. Beginner lessons are at Mondos Beach.

SURF RENTALS

If you just need gear, swing by **Seaward Surf and Sport** (1082 S. Seaward Ave., 805/648-4742, www.seawardsurf.com, winter daily 10am-7pm, summer daily 9am-9pm, surfboard rental $15-50), which is the place to buy or rent almost anything for the water, including body boards and wetsuits. It's half a block from the beach, so you can head straight to the water.

All sorts of gear, including long boards and boogie boards, are available at **Beach Break Surf Shop** (1557 Spinnaker Dr., Suite 108, 805/650-6641, www.beachbreaksurfshop.com, daily 10am-6pm, all-day wetsuit rental $20). It's already at the harbor, so you can pick up your gear, cross the street, and hit the beach.

Ventura Surf Shop (88 E. Thompson Blvd., 805/643-1062, www.venturasurfshop.com, summer Mon.-Sat. 9am-6pm, Sun. 9am-5pm, winter daily 9am-5pm, board rental $30 per day, wetsuit $15 per day) rents surfboards, wetsuits, body boards, and a couple of stand-up paddleboards.

Whale-Watching

December-March is the ideal time to see Pacific gray whales pass through the channel off the coast of Ventura. Late June-late August has the narrow window for both blue and humpback whales as they feed offshore near the islands. **Island Packers Cruises** (1691 Spinnaker Dr., Suite 105B, 805/642-1393, www.islandpackers.com, $25-75) has operated whale-watching cruises for years and is the most experienced. It also runs harbor cruises with a variety of options, including dinner cruises and group charters. Most whale-watching trips last about three hours. Remember that whale-watching is weather-dependent, so cancellations can occur.

Sportfishing

Head out to sea with **Ventura Sportfishing** (1500 Anchors Way Dr., 805/676-3474, www.venturasportfishing.com, $80-425). Their half-day, full-day, and overnight excursions to the Channel Islands typically yield a bounty of yellowtail, rockfish, and lingcod.

For saltwater fishing gear and the latest fishing advice, stop by **Eric's Tackle Shop** (2127 E. Thompson Blvd., 805/648-5665, Mon.-Fri. 9am-6pm, Sat. 9am-5pm, Sun. 9am-5pm). The folks here can recommend numerous Southern California boat captains for fishing trips throughout the region.

Hiking

While Ventura is well known for its coastal recreation, there are also a few hikes in and around the city. The website www.venturacountytrails.org is a good reference for local hikes, with GPS coordinates and photos. Ojai, just 15 miles away, has a multitude of great hikes.

Northeast of the city center, **Arroyo Verde Park** (5000 Foothill Rd., 805/654-7800, www.cityofventura.net, Tues.-Sun. 6am-9pm, parking fees Sat.-Sun. and holidays $2 per hour, $5 per day) is popular with hikers, trail runners, and dog owners, since dogs are allowed on the trails. Its web of hiking trails wind up into the coastal sage and scrub-covered foothills. Begin on the **Jerry Revard Nature Trail** by the Arroyo Verde Center. The trail goes up and down like a roller coaster as it moves to the back of the canyon and eventually climbs up, offering views of the Channel Islands on clear days. Multiple spur trails offer a return route back to the parking lot; You can also opt to continue climbing by keeping to the right.

Ojai Valley produce used to be shipped to Ventura along the Southern Pacific Railroad line. The lower section of the former railroad is now the **Ventura River Trail** (805/654-7800, www.cityofventura.net), which runs 6.3 miles from Main Street to Ventura County's Foster Park. The fairly level trail passes through several ecological zones and goes past some important bird habitats. The natural beauty is augmented by seven art pieces that were commissioned by the city to convey the area's history. Along the way are several spur trails that lead to the river or an overlook. To reach the trailhead from downtown, take Main Street west and then turn right onto Olive Street. Take Olive Street one block, and then turn left on Dubbers Street.

© STUART THORNTON

Arroyo Verde Park

Cycling

The eight-mile-long paved **Omer Rains Trail** runs along Ventura's beachfront from San Buenaventura State Beach past the Ventura Pier and Surfer's Point to Emma Wood State Beach. **The Ventura River Trail** (Main St. and Peking St., www.ventura-usa.com) follows the Ventura River inland from Main Street just over six miles one-way, ending at Foster Park. From here it joins the **Ojai Trail,** a two lane bike path that follows Highway 33 into Ojai (16 miles one-way).

If you want to pedal it, **Wheel Fun Rentals** (850 Harbor Blvd., 805/765-5795, www.wheelfunrentals.com, Sat.-Sun. and holidays 10am-sunset) rents out beach cruisers, surreys, mountain bikes, and low-riding chopper bikes. Also, the **Ventura Bike Depot** (239 W. Main St., 805/652-1114, http://venturabikedepot.com, Mon.-Sat. 8:30am-7pm, Sun. 8:30am-6pm) rents mountain bikes, road bikes, hybrid bikes, beach cruisers, and surreys for two-hour, four-hour, and all-day stints.

Golf

Designed back in 1932, the city-owned **Buenaventura Golf Course** (5882 Olivas Park Dr., 805/677-6772, www.buenaventuragolf.com, green fees Mon.-Fri. $99, Sat.-Sun. and holidays $49) offers 18 holes with lots of challenging features, including trees and water. The grounds also have a putting course along with a grill. Hyped by *Golfweek Magazine* and *Golf Digest*, **Olivas Park Golf Course** (3750 Olivas Park Dr., 805/677-6770, www.olivaslinks.com, green fees Mon.-Fri. $49, Sat.-Sun. and holidays $59) is a challenging 18-hole course utilizing the natural habitat, including seaside grasses. Good for beginners, the **Saticoy Regional Golf Course** (1025 S. Wells Rd., 805/647-6678, www.saticoygc.com, green fees $8-20) is a nine-hole course near the Ventura hills. There's a lighted driving range for those who want to hit a few rounds after dark.

Horse Racing

Ventura does not have its own horseracing track, but it does have **The Derby Club at the**

Ventura County Fairgrounds (10 W. Harbor Blvd., 805/653-2533, www.venturacountyfair.org, Wed.-Mon., hours vary, $4-12). Wager on horse races beamed into the facility via satellite. Take in the action in the Derby Club's Shore Room, Surfside Room, or Island View Club. The facility also serves food and drink. There is free parking and free admission on Wednesday.

Circus and Acrobatics

Thinking of running away to join the circus? First you'd better learn the circus arts at **Airealistic Circus and Flying** (4476 DuPont Court, Suite B, 805/628-2777, http://ventura-circus.com, drop-in classes $15-35). They also offer traditional gymnastics, floor Pilates, Afro-Brazilian dance, and Aireal Yoga, where you hang off the ground in a hammock-like fabric.

Kart Racing

Try your hand at go-kart racing at **Jim Hall Kart Racing School** (10 E. Harbor Blvd., 805/654-1329, www.jimhallkartracing.com, $225-455). Hall is a former world kart championship racer. His 0.5-mile learning course in the Ventura County Fairgrounds lot will teach you how to handle the small, open four-wheeled vehicles.

Swimming

The **Ventura Aquatic Center** (901 S. Kimball Rd., 805/654-7511, www.cityofventura.net/aquatics, $5, call or visit website for hours) offers pools for workouts and for play. The facilities include a competition pool, a recreation pool, a water playground pool, and two water slides.

Spas

Owned by a husband and wife team, the **Michael Kelley Salon and Day Spa** (1895 E. Main St., 805/648-7743, www.michaelkelleysalon.com, Tues.-Sat. 8am-8pm, spa packages start at $185, 30-minute massage $45) has a range of relaxing options, from $1-per-minute massage chair to a six-hour treatment marathon that includes a massage, a facial, a manicure,

a pedicure, a scalp treatment, an aroma wrap, lunch, and a gift.

Celebrity stylist **Billy Yamaguchi's Innerchi Salon and Spa** (3383 Telegraph Rd., 805/658-7909, www.yamaguchibeauty.com, Mon. 9am-1pm, Tues. 8am-4pm, Wed.-Thurs. 11am-7pm, Fri.-Sat. 9am-5pm, 30-minute massage $40) uses the ancient art of feng shui to determine your hair and makeup. Spa treatments utilize Asian elements like bamboo and green tea.

It's easy to surrender a day to **Sweet Surrender Day Spa** (2713 E. Main St., 805/643-1772, www.sweetsurrenderspa.com, Mon.-Sat. by appointment only, body treatments $60-130). Owner Anna Maclaren does spray tans, facials, and body treatments, including a sweet chocolate body wrap. You can also get a makeover at **Bellissima Salon and Spa** (1786 E. Main St., 805/643-0388, www.bellissimasalonvta.com, Tues.-Fri. 10am-7pm, Sat. 9am-3pm), which specializes in hair, makeup, skin care, and waxes.

FOOD
Breakfast

Most mornings you'll have to wait to get inside the very popular **Pete's Breakfast House** (2055 E. Main St., 805/648-1130, www.petesbreakfasthouse.com, daily 7am-2pm, $5-12). Pete's fresh-squeezed orange juice, biscuits made daily, strawberry jam made in-house, pancakes, and omelets make it worth the wait. But the homemade corned beef hash and eggs are the real stars, inspiring breakfast lovers to drive all the way up from Los Angeles to spend the morning at Pete's.

Allison's Breakfast Café (3429 Telegraph Rd., 805/644-9072, www.allisonscountry-cafe.com, daily 7am-2am) is another hit with breakfast diners. Choose from a virtual United Nations of omelets (Italian, Greek, Mexican) alongside hearty fare like biscuits and gravy.

Brewpubs

The **Anacapa Brewing Company** (472 East Main St., 805/643-2337, http://anacapabrewing.com, Sun.-Wed. 11:30am-9pm, Thurs.-Sat. 11:30am-midnight, $14) looks like a brewpub should, with brick walls and beer-making vats behind the bar. Regulars drink the brewery's Pierpoint IPA at the long bar, while families eat burgers, salads, and pizza at booths and tables. The menu also has a few unexpected entrées like fried chicken and waffles.

Coffee

With coffee drinks, sandwiches, salads, and free Wi-Fi, The **Sandbox Coffeehouse** (204 E. Thompson Blvd., 805/641-1025, http://sandboxcoffeehouse.com, Mon.-Wed. and Fri. 7am-6pm, Thurs. 7am-10pm, Sat.-Sun. 8am-6pm) can satisfy a lot of your needs. There's a large outdoor patio out front for soaking up the sun. The Sandbox also supports the local arts. In addition to the art on the walls, it hosts live music, including an open-mike night on Thursday.

Healthy Food

◀ Mary's Secret Garden (100 S. Fir St., 805/641-3663, www.maryssecretgarden.com, Tues.-Thurs. 4pm-9:30pm, Fri.-Sat. 11am-9:30pm, $13) isn't just for vegetarians; it's for anyone who enjoys healthy dining. The prices are a bit steep, but the food is organic, vegan, and full of flavor. The secret burger, a veggie burger that can be ordered with fake bacon and avocado, evokes shades of its beefy counterpart but has its own tasty thing happening.

With windows looking out on Main Street and twirling ceiling fans, **Nature's Grill & Juice Bar** (566 E. Main St., 805/643-7855, www.naturesgrillventura.com, daily 11am-9pm, $6-11) is a great place to get a healthy meal after a day of recreation. The menu has a significant number of vegetarian options, including tempeh tacos and a veggie stir-fry. But there are also entrées with real meat, like the excellent seasoned chicken avocado sandwich with avocado slices and grilled onions.

Indian

There are several Indian restaurants on Ventura's Main Street. **The Taj Café** (574 E. Main St., 805/652-1521, www.thetajcafe-ventura.com, daily 11:30am-10pm, $9-19) specializes in the village cuisine of India, with crowd favorites like chicken tikka masala and more unusual items like *uttapam* (a griddle cake served with a coconut chutney) and Bombay frankies (similar to a burrito).

Named for India's booming film industry, the **Bollywood Indian Restaurant** (500 E. Main St., 805/648-2533, http://bollywood4.net, Mon.-Sat. 11am-2:45pm and 5pm-10:30pm, $11-15) presents chicken tikka masala and *saag paneer* (homemade cheese in chopped spinach) in starring roles. Sample the menu by ordering the vegetarian dinner or the mixed tandoori dinner for two.

Italian

Bolstered by a popular wood bar, **Café Fiore** (66 California St., 805/653-1266, www.fiorerestaurant.net, Mon.-Thurs. 11:30am-3pm and 5pm-10pm, Fri.-Sat. 11:30am-3pm and 5pm-11pm, Sun. 11:30am-3pm and 5pm-9pm, $16-32) is a hotspot for Ventura professionals grabbing a cocktail or meal after work. The food includes Italian favorites like cioppino, osso buco, and chicken parmesan, served in a sleek, high-ceilinged room decorated with furnishings that recall the interior of a Cost Plus World Market. Expect to wait a while for service on crowded nights and during happy hour.

Mediterranean

Located across the street from the San Buenaventura Mission, **Peirano's Restaurant** (204 E. Main St., 805/648-4853, Tues.-Thurs. 5pm-9pm, Fri. 5pm-10pm, Sat. 11am-4pm and 5pm-10pm, Sun. 11am-4pm, $16-38) is located in a historic market building that dates back to 1877. The menu skews Mediterranean, with appetizers like baba ghanoush, hummus, and stuffed dates, but the main dishes include braised short ribs, Kobe burgers, and pork chops. While enjoying your meal, you would never realize that the restaurant is also an archaeological site. Parts of the water system that served the mission and nearby Native American village have been unearthed beneath the building, along with artifacts from the city's early Chinese residents.

Mexican

In a prime spot on the Ventura Pier, ◖ **Beach House Tacos** (668 Harbor Blvd., 805/648-3177, Mon.-Fri. 11am-8pm, Sat.-Sun. 8:30am-8pm, $2.25-7.25) doesn't coast on its enviable location. Creative ingredients include soy ginger lime cream sauce-soaked ahi and ground beef tacos with raisins. Beginners can try "The Combo," a lump of grilled meat (chicken, carne asada, or pork) topped with melted cheese, grilled pasilla chilies, zucchini, and carrots. Order at a counter and dine on an enclosed seating section on the pier. Expect long lines on summer weekends.

While it's not in the most scenic section of Ventura, the **Cuernavaca Taqueria** (1117 N. Ventura Ave., 805/653-8052, Mon.-Fri. 10am-8:30pm, Sat.-Sun. 9am-7:30pm, $8) is worth traveling to for its tasty street-style tacos alone. This is a typical taqueria with an unassuming interior and soccer blaring on the television, but the tacos are a step above most others. The al pastor taco finds marinated pork shavings under chunks of pineapple on a tortilla bed. The al pastor taco alone was enough to inspire a glowing review from the *LA Weekly.*

Nearby, the equally revered **Taqueria Tepatitlan** (362 E. Ventura Ave., 805/653-0508, http://taqueriatepatitlan.com, Tues.-Fri. 9am-9pm, Sat.-Sun. 8am-3pm, $6.50-14) does the cuisine of northern Mexico right. Eight beers are on tap to wash down the burritos, *tortas,* and fish tacos (a favorite not on the printed menu).

New American

Watermark on Main (598 E. Main St., 805/643-6800, www.watermarkonmain. com, Tues.-Fri. 11:30am-2pm and 5pm-9pm, Sat. 5pm-10pm, Sun. 10am-2pm, $17-28) is housed in a distinctive historic building that dates back to 1907 and was previously home to a power company, a bank, and a jewelry store. The main dining room is a testament to the building's past with high, ornate ceilings and three hand-painted murals of El Camino Real, the road that linked California's missions. The dinner menu includes a list of beef, seafood,

poultry, and pork options with a choice of accompanying sauces like bourbon mustard, blue cheese demi-glace, and orange tamarind glace. The third floor's ocean-themed **W2O** (Thurs. 7pm-10pm, Fri.-Sat. 9pm-midnight, Sun. 1pm-4pm, $8-13) serves a tasty, less pricey bar menu, which includes Kobe sliders, pizzas, and tacos.

Located in a refurbished bungalow, **Café Zack** (1095 E. Thompson Blvd., 805/643-9445, www.cafezack.com, Mon.-Fri. 11:30am-2pm and 5:30pm-9pm, Sat. 5:30pm-9pm, $14-33) specializes in filet mignon, seafood, and wine. Don't overlook other menu items such as the seafood curry and a creative appetizer with sautéed lobster and corn served in black truffle oil.

Another eatery in a 1920s bungalow, **Café Nouveau** (1497 E. Thompson Blvd., 805/648-1422, www.cafenouveau.net, Wed.-Sat. 7am-2pm and 5pm-9pm, Sun.-Tues. 7am-2pm, $13-20) serves breakfast, lunch, and dinner on a heated garden patio surrounded by a garden. The creative, locally inspired menu includes meat, seafood, and vegetarian entrées, as well as appetizers like the ahi avocado roll.

Seafood

Housed in a building that resembles a boat, ◖ **Spencer Makenzie's Fish Company** (806 E. Thompson Blvd., 805/643-8226, www. smfishco.com, daily 11am-9pm, $5-12.50) is known for its giant fish tacos, a tasty fusion of Japanese and Mexican flavors. The sushi-grade fish is hand-dipped in tempura batter and then fried, while the white sauce, cabbage, and cilantro are traditional Baja ingredients. Choose from the array of homegrown sauces along the counter to add splashes of sweet and heat.

Right on Ventura Harbor, **Andria's Seafood Restaurant & Market** (1449 Spinnaker Dr., 805/654-0546, www.andriasseafood.com, Sun.-Thurs. 11am-9pm, Fri.-Sat. 11am-10pm, $11) is a local favorite for fresh seafood. With plastic trays and dingy furniture, Andria's feels like an old school cafeteria, but the seafood is good. A lot of the menu features fried fare—the fish-and-chips is recommended—but there are also items like a scallop stir-fry. It's a good place to get a casual seafood dinner without breaking the bank.

For a more sophisticated meal in Ventura Harbor, **Brophy Bros. Restaurant & Clam Bar** (1559 Spinnaker Dr., 805/639-0865, www.brophybros.com, daily 11am-10pm, $9-24) has seafood pastas, Cajun sea bass, and jumbo shrimp scampi, served with views of the harbor. They also serve up traditional clam chowder and fish-and-chips.

Sleek newcomer **(Lure Fish House** (60 California St., 805/567-4400, www.lurefishhouse.com, Sun.-Mon. 11:30am-9pm, Tues.-Thurs. 11:30am-10pm, Fri.-Sat. 11:30am-11pm, $15-25) is already a local favorite for seafood downtown. The menu focuses on charbroiled seafood, including fresh and sustainable wild local halibut, wild mahimahi, and other tasty morsels from the sea. They also do seafood pastas, cioppino, and live Maine lobster. You can also enjoy samples from the oyster bar or enjoy a cocktail.

Steak Houses

Prime Steakhouse (2009 Thompson Blvd., 805/652-1055, http://primesteakvc.com, Sun.-Mon. 5pm-9:30pm, Tues.-Thurs. 5pm-10pm, Fri.-Sat. 5pm-11pm, $10-30) is known for its extensive wine list, sophisticated atmosphere, and live entertainment. Expect classic steak house fare along with a few surprises, like a chili relleno stuffed with prime rib and cheese. Live music nights include the popular Frank Sinatra Tuesdays, when a local musician croons classic tunes popularized by Old Blue Eyes.

Thai

Every city needs a great Thai restaurant, and Ventura is no exception. **Rice Thai Cuisine** (387 E. Main St., 805/641-3573, www.riceonmain.com, daily 11:30am-3:30pm, Sun.-Mon. 5pm-9pm, Tues.-Thurs. 5pm-9:30pm, Fri.-Sat. 5pm-10pm, $9-17) does all the classics—curries, rice dishes, noodle plates—and branches out with salmon teriyaki, basil mussels, and Siamese spare ribs. Order beer, wine, or a *soju* cocktail to cool your mouth down after bites of the spicier dishes.

ACCOMMODATIONS
Under $150

The **(Bella Maggiore Inn** (67 S. California St., 805/652-0277, $75-175) has a great location a few blocks from the beach and just a block off Ventura's Main Street. Some of the guest rooms are no larger than a college dorm room, but there is a lobby with couches, Italian chandeliers, a piano, and a fireplace. Even better is a courtyard with a fountain and a dining area surrounded by vines. The moderate room rates include a tasty hot breakfast in the morning, with omelets, huevos rancheros, and french toast. Another asset of the Bella Maggiore is the free overnight parking behind the building.

The **(Best Western Plus Inn of Ventura** (708 E. Thompson Blvd., 805/643-3101, http://bestwesterncalifornia.com, $99-169) doesn't look like much at first. But this two-story U-shaped motel complex has a few pleasant surprises. Ten rooms have partial ocean views (albeit close to the railroad tracks). The clean guest rooms are all stocked with fridges and microwaves, and there's a guest laundry room. The hot breakfast buffet includes eggs, breakfast meats, and make-your-own waffles. There's a pool and a small hot tub. A jetted-tub suite is available for those who want to splurge. Across the street from grassy Plaza Park, and just a few blocks to downtown Ventura, it might be the best bang for your buck in the area.

Next door, the **Vagabond Inn-Ventura** (756 E. Thompson Blvd., 805/648-5371, www.vagabondinn-ventura-hotel.com, $74-140) also offers fridges and microwaves as well as a heated pool and a spa. The attached diner and old-school coffee shop even attract Ventura locals with their cheap breakfasts.

A few feet closer to the coast, the **Country Inn and Suites** (298 S. Chestnut St., 805/653-1434, www.countryinns.com, $134-170) has a variety of guest room types. Choose between standard guest rooms, guest rooms with balconies, guest rooms with fireplaces, and suites. Amenities include a heated outdoor pool, a whirlpool, a guest laundry facility, hot breakfast, and a complimentary pass to the Club Hollywood Fitness Center, located four blocks away.

The small 15-room **Viking Motel** (2107 E. Thompson Blvd., 805/643-3273, $80-150) offers something other area motels don't: full kitchenettes with stoves, fridges, and sinks. The guest rooms also have cable and wireless Internet. The two most expensive guest rooms have jetted tubs.

The **Harbor Inn Express Hotel & Suites Ventura Harbor** (1080 Navigator Dr., 805/856-9533, www.ihg.com, $125-175) offers a location on the harbor near its seafood restaurants. Many of the guest rooms have harbor views, and all have microwaves and mini fridges. There's also a business center and a daily breakfast buffet.

For a true bed-and-breakfast experience in Ventura, book one of the five guest rooms at the **Victorian Rose Bed and Breakfast** (896 E. Main St., 805/641-1888, www.victorianroseventura.com, $99-169). The historic structure dates back to 1880; its 96-foot-high steeple is visible from a few blocks away. Every guest room here offers different decor (for example, the Emperor's Bedroom evokes old China with its red and gold). But all the guest rooms have high ceilings, tile baths, and gas-burning fireplaces. The innkeepers serve a nice breakfast in the morning, and a spread of wine and snacks later in the day.

$150-250

If you are traveling to the Channel Islands National Park out of Ventura Harbor, the **C Four Points by Sheraton Ventura Harbor Resort** (1050 Schooner Dr., 805/658-1212, www.fourpoints.com, $145-175) is a great place to lay your head before an early-morning boat ride or to relax after a few days of camping on the islands. The guest rooms are clean and comfortable, with balconies and patios. With a gym, a tennis court, a pool, and a basketball court, there is a wide array of recreational opportunities available at the resort. For folks who have hiked all over the Channel Islands, Four

Points has a hot tub in a glass dome to ease your aching muscles.

A few hundred yards from the Ventura Pier and right by the beach, the **Crowne Plaza Ventura Beach** (450 E. Harbor Blvd., 800/842-0800, www.cpventura.com, $139-239) has guest rooms with ocean-view balconies if you get a room on the fifth floor or higher. It also offers pet-friendly guest rooms for $50 more.

Also on the coast, specifically near San Buenaventura State Beach, **The Pierpont Inn & Spa** (550 Sanjon Rd., 805/643-6144, www.pierpontinn.com, $119-299) is situated on some nice manicured grounds with grassy areas and flowers. The historic property, which dates to 1910, has guest rooms, suites, cottages, and a bungalow. In addition, there's a full-service spa on the grounds.

Another hotel close to San Buenaventura State Beach, the **Ventura Beach Marriott** (2055 E. Harbor Blvd., 805/643-6000, www.marriott.com, $179-329) is a four-story facility with kings, doubles, and suites with two baths. Outdoor amenities include a tropical courtyard, a pool, and a whirlpool. If you arrive late, you can grab a meal at the on-site **Pacifico Restaurant & Lounge** (daily 6am-10pm, $9-27).

INFORMATION AND SERVICES
Maps and Visitor Information

The **Ventura Visitors Center** (101 California St., 805/648-2075, www.ventura-usa.com, Mon.-Fri. 8:30am-5pm, Sat. 9am-5pm, Sun. 10am-4pm) occupies a big space in downtown Ventura and offers a lot of information, including a historic walking tour guide of the city.

Emergency Services

Community Memorial Hospital (147 N. Brent St., 805/652-5011, www.cmhshealth.org) has the only emergency room in the area. Police services are the **City of Ventura Police Department** (1425 Dowell Dr., 805/339-4400); in case of emergency, call 911 immediately.

Newspapers

The only local daily newspaper is the **Ventura County Star,** which can be found all over town. The alternative free weekly, published every Thursday, is the **Ventura County Reporter,** also available everywhere. They have good entertainment listings, including shows, concerts, theater, and film.

Local TV and Radio

KTVA (AM 1520) is the local talk-radio station, with a variety of local programming, traffic reports, local news and weather, jokes of the day, and national news; it covers the entire county.

Postal Services

With recent budget cuts, it is best to phone ahead for current hours of the main branch of the **post office** (675 E. Santa Clara St., 805/643-3057). There are two other branches (41 S. Wake Forest Ave., 805/642-1521, and 2481 Grand Ave., 805/643-3057).

Laundry

No one likes to do laundry, but if the need arises, you can head over to **Mission Plaza Laundry** (110 Olive St., 805/653-9077). They also offer pickup and delivery.

GETTING THERE AND AROUND

Los Angeles's **LAX** (1 World Way, Los Angeles, 310/646-5252, www.lawa.org) and **Burbank Airport** (BUR, 2627 N. Hollywood Way, Burbank, 818/840-8840, www.bobhopeairport.com) are the closest major airports. 1.5 hours south of Ventura. To get to Ventura from LAX without a vehicle, contact the **Ventura County Airporter** (805/650-6600, www. venturashuttle.com). The small and efficient **Oxnard Airport** (www.iflyoxnard.com) has no scheduled flights but welcomes private aircraft, and there are rental cars.

Traveling by car, Ventura is 65 miles north of Los Angeles and 34 miles south of Santa Barbara via U.S. 101. The nearest Greyhound bus station is in Oxnard, but the *Pacific Surfliner* by **Amtrak** (800/872-7245, www.amtrak.com) still stops in Ventura (Harbor Blvd. and Figueroa St.) several times each day in both directions on its runs between San Diego and San Luis Obispo.

Travel Ventura in a cab by calling **Gold Coast Cab** (805/444-6969, www.goldcoastcab.com). Open all the time, **Ventura Taxi Cab and Designated Drivers Service** (805/444-6969, www.venturataxiservice.com) covers the Ventura, Ojai, Santa Paula, and Fillmore areas. They also do wine tours and city nightlife outings.

Tours

Ventura Food Tours (805/295-8687, www. venturafoodtours.com, $59) fill people up with food and knowledge. The 3- to 3.5-hour long walking tours include sampling food at local downtown eateries, meeting local chefs, and learning about local history and culinary information.

The City of Ventura sponsors night-time **Ventura Ghost Tours** (805/658-4726, www. cityofventura.net, $25) by local historians during October-November. Other scary options include a ghost-hunting class for kids and a late-night séance in city hall.

Heritage Valley

Surrounded by acres of orange, lemon, and avocado groves, this string of agricultural communities along the Santa Clara River and Highway 126 is worth a visit to experience a bit of California history. Ride the vintage trains of the Fillmore & Western Railway, uncover information about California's natural gas industry in Santa Paula, or visit Piru's Rancho Camulos, the old ranch that inspired a popular late-1800s novel.

The largest city in Heritage Valley is Santa Paula, which claims to be the "citrus capital of the world." Santa Paula was also one of the most important centers of the state's early oil industry and the first headquarters of the Union Oil Company of California. Today, it sprawls a bit, with chain stores and restaurants radiating from its downtown Main Street area, which is home to a string of local businesses.

Ten miles from Santa Paula, Fillmore is half its size, with a small old town built up around a historic train depot. At the east end of the valley is the small, unincorporated town of Piru, where a handful of movies and TV shows have been filmed.

Heritage Valley's main sights are within 30 minutes' drive of Ventura, making it a pleasant afternoon trip—especially in winter, when the average daily temperatures hover around 70°F.

SIGHTS
Fillmore & Western Railway

Trains have become something of a novelty in the United States, especially on the West Coast. You can rediscover a way of life that's been lost by riding the rails at the **Fillmore & Western Railway** (364 Main St., Fillmore, 805/524-2546, www.fwry.com, call for weekend trains). It's an experience that train enthusiasts (and young fans of Thomas the Tank Engine) won't soon forget. The vintage trains have been beautifully restored and adorned with period furnishings. They lumber along pretty slowly; you could probably walk faster. But slowing down is actually a big part of the appeal. Nearby Hollywood film studios has taken advantage of the trains for several recent films (*Get Smart, Inception, Water for Elephants, Seabiscuit*).

Themed train rides include murder mysteries, the *Polar Express* for the holidays, and a July 4th firecracker and barbecue train. The most common outing is the **Weekend Scenic Excursion** (adults $24, seniors $22, ages 4-12 $14, under age 4 $10). This four-hour ride begins with a slow ramble out of Fillmore on the way to Santa Paula. On the way, the train passes rows of fruit orchards, waving motorists on nearby Highway 126, and a few ramshackle buildings. The train stops in Santa Paula next to the **Ventura County Agricultural Museum** for an hour. Then it makes the slow chug back to Fillmore with a stop at the **Loose Caboose Garden Center and Gift Emporium,** which also

a happy customer on the Fillmore & Western Railway

© STUART THORNTON

the California Oil Museum

has a fruit stand, a koi pond, a goat pen, and a rooster pen. It's worth noting that there's no air-conditioning, and the food and beverages are fairly inadequate, even though there is cold beer for sale.

California Oil Museum

The **California Oil Museum** (1001 E. Main St., Santa Paula, 805/933-0076, www.oilmuseum. net, Wed.-Sun. 10am-4pm, adults $4, seniors $3, children $1), located in Santa Paula, offers an important understanding of the early years of this area. Most people are surprised that Ventura and Santa Barbara are oil-rich lands. In fact, these two counties are home to the largest natural oil and gas seeps in the western hemisphere—seepages of tar and gas emissions, primarily from the ocean floor. The area's first inhabitants, the Chumash people, used the naturally occurring tar as a sealant for their wood boats, called *tomols,* which transported them between the Channel Islands and the mainland. Even now you can walk the coastline and occasionally smell the tar seeping up from

the ocean. Many "iron horses" are still visible pumping oil along the Central Coast today.

The museum offers overviews of oil exploration and the mechanics of how oil is drawn from underneath the ocean floor. There's an amazing display of three different drill bits used to penetrate the ocean's floor, alongside a number of vintage gas pumps. Upstairs you'll find the original 1890s offices of the Union Oil Company, restored to mint condition, exactly as they were at the turn of the 20th century; it's probably the finest commercial building restoration in the state. The nine offices include 10 tiled fireplaces, oak wainscoting, plaster archways, ceiling medallions, stained glass, and vintage lighting. The back building, known as the Rig Room, houses a full-size circa-1900 operating iron-and-timber drilling rig. Noisy and cumbersome, it's a fantastic reminder of just how far the technology of oil exploration has advanced in these days of geothermal computer mapping. It was slow, tedious, dirty, and dangerous work, with a high percentage of failure.

Limoneira

In the 1890s someone realized that the area near Santa Paula might make a great orchard, given the nutrient-laden soil, the vast amount of flat land, and the proximity to a viable water source, the Santa Clara River. Several companies moved in to grow citrus. **Limoneira** (1141 Cummings Rd., Santa Paula, 805/525-5541, www.limoneiratours.com, call for tours), founded in 1893, is still a powerhouse in the lemon and avocado business. You can visit their old goods store, which houses a museum chronicling the history of this lemon-producing area. Early farming techniques are explained, and antique equipment is on display. Visit the old packinghouse, still in use, and demonstration orchards of 300 citrus trees, with the beautiful scent of lemon in the air. Limoneira has incorporated a solar orchard on the property in an effort to reduce waste and harness the sun's energy; it also provides both school kids and adults with an opportunity to learn about green technologies. You may want to pack a lunch; there are picnic areas and boccie ball courts placed out among the orchards. It can get windy here, with breezes that run the length of the valley, but it's also peaceful and serene. Specialized tours can be arranged, including jeep tours and hot-air balloon rides over the orchards.

Santa Paula Art Museum

An art museum in an agricultural region? Yes: The **Santa Paula Art Museum** (117 N. 10th St., 805/525-5554, www.santapaulaartmuseum.org, Wed.-Sat. 10am-4pm, Sun. noon-4pm, adults $4, seniors $3, students free) is in the bottom floor of the standout historic Limoneira building in downtown Santa Paula. Most of the museum's collection is culled from plein air paintings that competed in the city's annual art show, which dates back to 1937. Rotating exhibits have appropriately included portraits of Santa Paula residents as well as artwork depicting agriculture.

Rancho Camulos

Just east of Piru is **Rancho Camulos** (5164 E. Telegraph Rd., 805/521-1501, www.rancho-camulos.org, tours Sat. 1pm, 2pm, and 3pm, adults $5, children $3), Ventura County's only National Historic Landmark. The 1,800-acre ranch was part of one of the largest Mexican land grants in Southern California, stretching from Piru to Valencia. In 1884 it inspired Helen Hunt Jackson's *Ramona,* an immensely popular novel about a mixed-race orphan girl who suffers discrimination and has a tragic love affair with a Native American man. The popularity of the novel caused fans to flood the ranch, and for a while there was a railroad depot here for all the visitors. Director D. W. Griffith filmed a 17-minute adaptation of the book, starring Mary Pickford, on the grounds. The hour-long tour takes you inside the main adobe, built in 1853 and currently being restored, and includes information about the Del Valle family, who resided here from 1853 to 1924, and the Rubel family, who have owned the ranch since 1924. Behind the sprawling adobe are a tiny, beautiful chapel about the size of a toolshed along with an elegant fountain.

ACCOMMODATIONS
Under $150

With its creaking boards and long, dark hallways, it doesn't take much imagination to conclude that the **Glen Tavern Inn** (134 N. Mill St., Santa Paula, 805/933-5550, www.glentaverninn.com, $59-109) might be haunted. That's probably why the hotel has been the site of the Ventura Paranormal Society's annual convention. Just feet away from the Santa Paula train depot, this distinctive Tudor and craftsman-style hotel has a colorful history perfectly suited for tales of lingering spirits. During Prohibition, the third floor was home to a brothel, a speakeasy, and a gambling parlor, where the rough social conditions of the Old West led some patrons to meet their ends. Saved from neglect in 2004, the inn now offers 36 fairly modern guest rooms, including six with soaking tubs. There is also a large lobby with a sitting area by a fireplace. On the bottom floor, **Enzo's** (805/933-5550, Tues.-Thurs. and Sun. 5pm-9pm, Fri.-Sat.

Rancho Camulos

5pm-10pm, $9-23) serves pizza, pasta, and Italian entrées.

Another choice in Santa Paula is the **Santa Paula Inn** (111 N. 8th St., Santa Paula, 805/933-0011, www.santapaulainn.com, $74-109), which, like the Glen Tavern Inn, harks back to the early 1900s and was once a brothel. A stay in one of the inn's 14 guest rooms includes continental breakfast.

FOOD

It's a pleasant surprise to find fine Cajun food in Santa Paula: **⟨ Rabalais' Bistro & Bakery** (861 E. Main St., Santa Paula, 805/525-2109, Mon. 6am-2pm, Tues.-Thurs. 6am-8pm, Fri. 6am-9pm, Sat. 7am-9pm, Sun. 7am-2pm, $10-20). Rabalais serves up tasty Cajun classics like po'boys, crawfish étouffée, gumbo, jambalaya, and shrimp and grits. At breakfast, go for the buttermilk biscuits drenched in crawfish

étouffée and beignets. The big elegant room is split between a bakery-café and a restaurant dining area.

There are lots of Mexican restaurants in Santa Paula; **La Terraza** (1000 E. Main St., 805/525-0528, Mon.-Fri. 9am-10pm, Sat.-Sun. 8:30am-10pm, $4-13) is a good choice. Opt to sit outside in the front courtyard or in the diner-style interior. The menu covers the basics: tacos, burritos and chiles rellenos. Brightly colored **El Pescador** (322 S. Peck Rd., 805/525-8846, www.elpescadorrestaurants.com, Mon.-Thurs. 8am-9pm, Fri. 8am-10pm, Sat. 7am-10pm, Sun. 7am-9pm, $5-18) serves up Mexican seafood dishes, including a fresh and tasty shrimp tostada. Other options include seafood cocktails and lobster dishes.

Santa Paula's only bar, **Garman's Restaurant & Irish Pub** (932 E. Main St., Santa Paula, 805/933-4600, www.garmanspub.

© STUART THORNTON

Santa Paula's Glen Tavern Inn

com, Mon.-Thurs. 11:30am-9pm, Fri.-Sat. 11:30am-10pm, $8-20) serves the Irish classics you would expect to find in a pub (shepherd's pie, corned beef and cabbage, bangers and mash) alongside dishes you might not (fish tacos, wraps). Enjoy eight beers on tap.

INFORMATION AND SERVICES

The website of the **Heritage Valley Tourism Bureau** (www.heritagevalley.net) has information about the region's attractions. If you're in Santa Paula on a weekday, stop in at the **Santa Paula Chamber of Commerce** (200 N. 10th St., Santa Paula, 805/525-5561, www.discoversantapaula.com, Mon.-Fri. 10am-2pm) for some tips.

Although it is close to Ventura, Santa Paula has its own hospital. The **Santa Paula Hospital** (825 N. 10th St., Santa Paula, 805/933-8632, www.vchca.org) has an emergency department.

Santa Paula has two **post offices** (111 S. Mill St., 805/933-0832; 950 W. Telegraph Rd., 805/926-0569).

The **Ventura County Star** (www.vcstar.com) covers the Heritage Valley. Out on Wednesday and Friday, the **Santa Paula Times** (www.santapaulatimes.com) focuses in on Heritage Valley news and concerns.

GETTING THERE

Heritage Valley is easy to get to by car from Ventura; take Highway 126 east for just 15 miles. Fillmore is another 10 miles. The **Ventura County Transportation Commission** (805/642-1591, www.goventura.org) has bus service to Santa Paula and Fillmore. They also have a Dial-A-Ride option for Santa Paula, Fillmore, and Piru. If you have your own plane, you can fly to the **Santa Paula Airport** (28 Wright Taxi Way, 805/933-1155, http://santapaulaairport.com).

Ojai

The indigenous Chumash people considered the Ojai Valley to be deeply spiritual. Today, you'll find plenty of other people who agree with that assessment. They come here to set up meditation centers, practice alternative healing arts, offer retreats, and generally engage in every mainstream and alternative soul-centered activity. The valley seems to draw a wide swath of religious thinkers. There's a relaxed, friendly "hippie" vibe that cannot be disassociated from Ojai. It makes a perfect getaway for people who want slow down and recharge, or stay put and detox.

Regardless of your belief system, you'll agree that Ojai is indeed a beautiful place. The surrounding mountains and rich agricultural lands provide a sense of verdant abundance. Topa Topa, the highest peak, which soars from near sea level to 6,244 feet, occasionally gets a dusting of snow. Hiking in the Los Padres Mountains is as close as a mile away. And the sunsets are stunning.

SIGHTS
◖ Ojai Avenue

Ojai Avenue is the main street and the lifeblood of Ojai. It was created as a boulevard in 1917 with a park on one side of the street, a Spanish-style arcade housing shops on the other, and the Ojai Post Office Tower and Portico, which was modeled after Christopher Columbus Cathedral in Havana, Cuba. It gives residents and visitors alike a sense of cohesion and an introduction to what Ojai is all about. This was the dream of Edward Libbey, an Ohio businessman who built a home in the valley and became

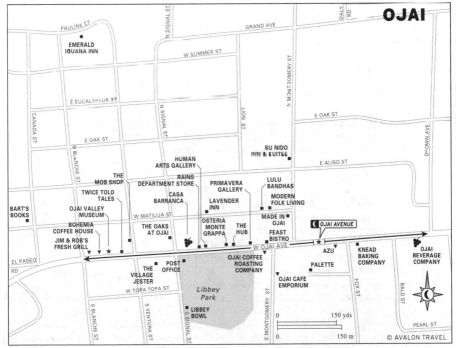

VENTURA AND OJAI

scenic downtown Ojai

an important civic leader in the town during the early 1900s. He presented his vision of the village to other civic leaders in 1914 and funded most of the projects that led to Ojai Avenue's distinctive look. Today, locals and visitors meander in and out of stores along **The Arcade,** along the 500 block of Ojai Avenue, which serves as a social gathering place. The Spanish arches shield the sidewalk, providing shade in the hot summers and shelter from foul weather.

Ojai Valley Museum

Ojai Valley Museum (130 W. Ojai Ave., 805/640-1390, www.ojaivalleymuseum.org, Tues.-Sat. 10am-4pm, Sun. noon-4pm, Wed. guided tours only, adults $4, ages 6-18 $1) is housed in an old Roman Catholic church that was rebuilt in 1918 after the devastating 1917 fire. From the outside you may not think it looks like a church at all. On the inside, the small museum, with an all-volunteer staff, presents permanent and rotating exhibits about the history and livelihood of the Ojai Valley. There's a mural of the Sespe Wilderness,

which serves as a backdrop of the backcountry of Ojai, complete with stuffed wildlife, on what was once the church altar. The museum holds a biannual sale of native plants. Behind the building is a small but intriguing Chumash Interpretative Garden of roughly 30 different plants that the Chumash people used for healing, tonics, food, and jewelry. Out front is an impressive life-size sculpture California condor to celebrate the recovering bird species that soars over the nearby mountains.

Krotona Institute of Theosophy

Spirituality and history come together at the **Krotona Institute of Theosophy** (2 Krotona Hill, 805/646-2653, Tues.-Fri. 10am-5pm, Sat.-Sun. 1pm-5pm), on a 115-acre wooded site. It has a meditation school, a library, and a bookstore. Theosophy is a set of beliefs that hold that true knowledge comes through spiritual means like meditation. While Theosophy dates back centuries, the Theosophy movement emerged in the United States in the 1870s. The Krotona Institute was originally located in Los

© STUART THORNTON

Ojai's Post Office Tower

Spanish varieties maximizes the flavors and complexities of their olive oils. On Wednesday from 1pm to 4pm and Saturday from 10am to 3pm, rain or shine, they welcome visitors to tour the farm's olive grove, explore the working ranch, and taste olive oils. Their tour begins outside with the history of the grove; an explanation of the different olive varieties, the maturing process, and the harvest, as well as a visit to the tree nursery. In addition to the variety of extra-virgin oils and flavored olive oils like rosemary, garlic, and mandarin, the farm produces products such balsamic vinegars, olive oil soaps, and face cream.

◖ Meditation Mount
Meditation Mount (10340 Reeves Rd., 805/646-5508, www.meditationmount.org, Wed.-Sun. 8:30am-sunset) has spectacular vistas of the orchard-dotted valley and the surrounding mountains banded with rock formations. Walk through the **International Garden of Peace,** a quiet, well-manicured garden with a century plant, cacti, rock roses, and wild buckwheat on the way to a view of the valley. This site was developed by a local nonprofit group in 1971 to encourage meditation in the service of humanity. Meditation Mount offers workshops and events, including full moon meditations and regular morning meditations (Wed.-Sun. 8:30am-9am).

To get here, drive east about three miles from downtown on East Ojai Avenue and turn left on Reeves Road. Continue through the orange groves until the road becomes a dead end at the parking area in front of the meditation center, tearoom, and library.

Angeles before migrating to Ojai in 1924. The grounds, in particular the mirror pools behind the library, are designed to encourage quiet contemplation. The library in the main building holds over 8,000 titles and is absolutely beautiful; it has a classic 1920s feel, with high bookshelves, a fireplace, lots of peace and quiet, and worn, comfortable chairs. The library's collection pertains largely to an understanding of spiritual subjects, including astrology, yoga, metaphysics, and reincarnation.

Ojai Olive Oil
Immigrants first planted Spanish olive trees in Ojai in 1880. Those trees still stand today, and **Ojai Olive Oil** (1811 Ladera Rd., 805/646-5964, www.ojaioliveoil.com, Wed. 1pm-4pm, Sat. 10am-3pm) still harvests them. Ventura County is on the same latitude as Casablanca in North Africa and enjoys an ideal Mediterranean climate in which to grow olive trees. In the last 12 years, the Asquith Family Farm has planted an astonishing 2,000 olive trees to complement the originals. Combining Italian, French, and

WINE TASTING
Casa Barranca
Casa Barranca (208 E. Ojai Ave., 805/640-1255, www.casabarranca.com, daily noon-6pm, tasting $10-15) is an organic winery. Visit their downtown tasting room to sample wines such as chardonnay, pinot noir, and various blends. The tasting room design echoes the Casa Barranca Estate house (not open to the public), which was designed by meticulous

VENTURA AND OJAI

© STUART THORNTON

Meditation Mount

craftsman architects Greene and Greene from Pasadena. The walls are decorated with murals of the area, and there are a few gift items on sale.

Old Creek Ranch Winery

The small family-owned **Old Creek Ranch Winery** (10024 Old Creek Rd., 805/649-4132, www.oldcreekranch.com, daily 11am-5pm, tasting $10) is located off Highway 33 on the way to Ventura. Turn off the highway eight miles north of Ventura between the communities of Casitas Springs and Oak View. Then continue down Old Creek Road 0.75 miles until the road ends. Cherry trees along the road lead up to the current winery, which is in front of the original 1880s building, still visible but in serious disrepair. The vineyard on the grounds was decimated in the 1980s by the bacterium that causes Pierce's disease. While

there are plans for a new vineyard, the grapes are currently sourced from Napa and Santa Barbara Counties. The small tasting room offers chardonnay, pinot noir, merlot, and cabernet sauvignon, as well as a few gift items. The tasting bar can get crowded, but the mood is always jovial.

Ojai Beverage Company

Ojai Beverage Company (655 E. Ojai Ave., 805/646-1700, www.ojaibevco.com, Mon. noon-9pm, Tues.-Wed. 11am-10pm, Thurs.-Sat. 11am-11pm, Sun. 11am-9pm) offers tastings and wines by the glass on a daily basis. While it's not affiliated with a winery, they have more wine than you can imagine, alongside a vast selection of over 300 whiskies, 200 tequilas, and 750 beers. You can always find a bottle of something unusual: wild strawberry sour mash, for example. The small tasting area in the back offers 20 beers on tap (five tastings $10, 15 tastings $25) and a side patio. They also serve a small menu that includes burgers and salads.

ENTERTAINMENT AND EVENTS
Bars and Clubs
There's not much of a nightlife scene in Ojai, but a few spots offer a bit of action or a place to grab a drink. Comfortable and neighborly, **The Hub** (256 E. Ojai Ave., 805/272-8344, http://thehubojai.com, daily noon-1am) feels like the last of a vanishing breed of low-key bars. It's definitely old-school (operating since 1948), with no pretension and no fancy drinks, but you can get beer in a can. It feels half built, with a lot of wood paneling, and one wall is lined with bookshelves and round barstools. There are pool tables in the back and a few games sitting around. There's live music on the weekends and some weeknights, mainly local bands with a flair for bluegrass, folk, and rock.

Located at the Ojai Valley Inn, upscale **Jimmy's Pub** (905 Country Club Rd., 805/640-2100, Sun.-Thurs. 11am-11pm, Fri.-Sat. 11am-midnight) is as far from a dive bar as you can get. The counterpoint to the Hub, Jimmy's has a wider selection of almost everything, including specialty cocktails, fine wines, and food. It's a comfortable and relaxing spot.

Located next door to the movie theater, **The Village Jester** (139 E. Ojai Ave., 805/640-8001, www.thevillagejester.com, Tues.-Thurs. 5pm-11pm, Fri.-Sat. 5pm-2am, Sun. noon-9pm) is a British pub serving across-the-pond beers like Boddingtons and Guinness. The high-ceilinged interior has two big TVs for showing sporting events. Out back is a large porch area. Expect live music on weekends.

Since 1932, **Deer Lodge** (2261 Maricopa Hwy., 805/646-4256, daily 11am-2am, www.ojaideerlodge.net, $20) has been drawing crowds with live music, beef and game dishes, and a pig roast every Sunday. You can find live music seven nights a week, including the Thursday night jamboree, where up to 20 local acts perform. A lot of bikers come here on the

weekend, but don't be intimidated by the line of Harleys out front; there's plenty of room for everyone here.

Performing Arts
The **Libbey Bowl** (210 S. Signal St., 805/646-3117, www.libbeybowl.org) is home to the popular Ojai Music Festival, the Storytelling Festival, plays, the Mexican Fiesta, free movie nights, and other community events. Located in Libbey Park, the 1,300-seat outdoor amphitheater was inaugurated with a performance by famed American composer Aaron Copland at the 1957 Ojai Music Festival. In 2008 the original bowl was abandoned due to a state of decay caused by wood rot and termite damage. The city and the Ojai Music Festival combined to construct the new venue; the current building opened in 2011. It also hosts touring acts such as alt-rock ensemble Edward Sharpe and the Magnetic Zeros and Eric Burdon, formerly of the Animals and War.

Since 2009 the **SENGA Classic Stage Company** (805/646-4885, www.franciscabeach.com) has staged classic American and European plays at the **Ojai Valley Grange** (381 Cruzero St.). Performances have included works by Anton Chekhov, George Bernard Shaw, Oscar Wilde, and a guy named Will Shakespeare.

Festivals and Events
The Ojai Music Festival (805/646-2053, www.ojaifestival.org), held the second week in June, began in 1947. Over the years this valley of olive trees and art galleries has played host to such distinguished visitors as Igor Stravinsky, Aaron Copland, The Bad Plus, and Kronos Quartet. The festival has earned a reputation as a breeding ground for eclectic new music emerging in the world. It's definitely worth a visit if you're in town, or make a special trip if this is music to your ears.

Over the course of 12 days in August, new playwrights, directors, dramaturges, actors, and technicians come together at the **Ojai Playwrights Conference** (805/640-0400, www.ojaiplays.org) to rehearse and present new, unproduced works of theater. Many of the plays developed at the conference go on to productions on stages in Los Angeles, Chicago, Seattle, Boston, and New York. But these are works in progress, and that's half the interest for the people attending. There are additional seminars and readings by well-known actors and directors, but the stars are the new works presented to an audience for the very first time. It all culminates with the five-day **Summer New Works Festival,** featuring readings of new works and special events.

Each June, close to 4,000 people enjoy the popular **Ojai Wine Festival** (11311 Santa Ana Rd., 800/648-4881, www.ojaiwinefestival.com) at nearby Lake Casitas. Over 60 vintners and 20 brewers from all over California offer samples of their creations at the one-day event. Arts and crafts vendors present their wares, food is sold, multiple bands play, and people break into spontaneous dancing. There are also free boat rides on the lake. Over 30 charity organizations benefit from the money raised. It gets crowded but it's a terrific event.

The annual **Holiday Home Look In** (www.ojaifestival.org), held the third weekend in November, right before Thanksgiving, benefits the Ojai Music Festival. Four private homes, works of art in their own right, are decorated and opened to the public. Many of the region's homes are hidden from sight on vast expanses of land, tucked into hillsides, down mountain sides, or off private roads, so this is a rare chance to see them. It's also a great way to experience a wide range of architectural styles—craftsman, mid-century modern, contemporary, and revivals of every ilk. This is a self-driving tour, so you can go at your own pace.

SHOPPING

There's not much to shopping in Ojai: You walk down Ojai Avenue and you've pretty much covered it all. On one side of the street are a few stores and the park; the other side is taken up with the Arcade, a long row of shops covered by a long archway, built in 1917. There are also some shops on the side streets, an easy, brief walk from the main drag.

Clothing

Owned by the former director of design at Patagonia, **Modern Folk Living** (306 E. Matilija St., 805/640-0678, http://modern-folkliving.com, Tues.-Sat. 11am-5pm, Sun. 10am-4pm) touts itself as an "eco-boutique." Browse the apparel, jewelry, and other gifts. **The Lennon Closet** (250B E. Ojai Ave., 805/640-3695, daily 10am-5pm) is a fine consignment store selling clothing and accessories. Some of the proceeds are donated to a charity dedicated to treatment of traumatic brain injuries.

Camping Gear

Ojai Surplus (952 E. Ojai Ave., 805/646-4064, www.ojaisurplus.com, Mon.-Sat. 9am-6pm, Sun. 9am-4pm) is the place to go for camping and hiking gear in Ojai. They stock cooking equipment, tents, backpacks, and a large selection of recreation gear, including firearms. There's also clothing for men and women, but it tends toward rugged and industrial gear (camouflage, jeans). The women's section also has dresses and jewelry.

Bookstores

Bart's Books (302 W. Matilija St., 805/646-3755, www.bartsbooksojai.com, daily 9:30am-sunset) was founded over 50 years ago by Richard Bartinsdale. His personal book collection was so big that he began displaying titles along the side of his house. Passersby browsed the shelves, making purchases by dropping money into a coffee can. While Bartinsdale no longer owns the store, the collection of mostly used titles has taken over the former owner's home and grounds. Bart's former kitchen now houses cookbooks, and the fiction section snakes around the building like a twisting hiking trail. Most of the store's one million books are stocked outside, making Bart's the largest independently owned and operated outdoor bookstore in the United States. There are tables and chairs outside where you can sit and read on a nice day.

Located next to the library, **Twice Sold Tales** (121 W. Ojai Ave., 805/646-4094, daily

Bart's Books

noon-5pm) sells used books from the library's collection. Paperbacks are just $0.50 and hard covers are $2. Although the shop is small, the selection is eclectic. Plus, the proceeds help the library, and who doesn't want that? Local artwork graces the walls.

Specialty Stores

One-of-a-kind **Rains** (218 E. Ojai Ave., 805/646-1441, www.rainsofojai.com, Mon.-Sat. 9:30am-6pm, Sun. 11am-5pm) is a modern rarity, an independent department store. The space dates back to 1874, when it was opened as a hardware store. Today, it fills all the needs of local residents, stocking kitchenware, local jams and jellies, clothing, appliances—you name it. They still sell hardware, too. This is not a massive warehouse space with industrial lighting and miles of endless volume but an intimate store reflecting simpler times.

Farmers Market

Ojai Farmers Market (300 E. Matilija St., 805/698-5555 www.ojaicertifiedfarmersmarket. com, Sun. 9am-1pm) is a cornucopia of abundance in all seasons. Vendors sell organic produce, eggs, honey, aromatics, homemade tamales, and much more near the Arcade Plaza. The market is also one of the better people-watching spots in town; you are likely to see a wide swath of humanity represented amid the small stalls that line the parking lot.

Art Galleries

Primavera Gallery (214 E. Ojai Ave., 805/646-7133, www.primaveraart.com, Mon.-Sat. 11am-5pm, Sun. noon-5pm) is without doubt the largest gallery in Ojai. For more than 25 years it has maintained an impressive collection of oil paintings, plein air, woodwork, glasswork, jewelry, and other American crafts. Many of the 100 artists represented have been with the gallery for decades; many also show internationally. This is an expensive place but the quality of the work is unmatched. There are multiple rooms with rotating work. Don't miss this visual treat.

Local, regional, and national artists are

represented at the large two-story **Trowbridge Gallery** (307 E. Ojai Ave., 805/646-0967, www.trowbridgeart.com, Thurs.-Tues. 11am-5pm), with a preference for plein air and traditional landscapes and still lifes. The unifying theme seems to be an expressive use of color. **Nomad: The Leslie Clark Gallery** (307 E. Ojai Ave., 805/646-1706, www.nomadgal.com, Wed.-Mon. 11am-5pm) exhibits the nomadic imagery of Africa as expressed in oil paintings, watercolors, *giclées,* and posters, mixed with items like masks and statues of fertility deities. It's an out-of-the-ordinary stop where you can also find men's and women's hand-embroidered shirts made by African artisans.

Palette (435 E. Ojai Ave., 805/640-8822, www.palette-gallery.com, hours vary) takes an innovative approach, creating a place where art, music, dance, and performance can meet. Openings are typically boundary-pushing themed events with DJs, stilt-walkers, hula-hoopers, live models, hand-drummers, projected video, performance artists, food,

wine—and, oh, yes, the art. There's a strong LA feel in the sculpture, painting, and commissioned work; it's showy but interesting and always entertaining.

Beatrice Wood Center for the Arts (8560 Ojai-Santa Paula Rd., 805/646-3381, www.beatricewood.com, Fri.-Sun. 11am-5pm) has a history in Ojai dating back to the 1940s. The space is named for a prominent artist and pottery maker who was part of the Dada art movement before moving to Ojai in 1948. Much of the work displayed is eclectic and modern, infused with an arts and crafts sensibility. There is sculpture, photography, all forms of painting, and occasionally some commissioned work. There are also artist workshops and occasional performances.

Part art gallery, part crafts store, **Human Arts Gallery** (246 E. Ojai Ave., 805/646-1525, www.humanartsgallery.com, Mon.-Fri. 11am-5pm, Sat. 11am-6pm, Sun. noon-5pm) has been in Ojai for over 35 years. It's like an adult playground: Much of what they sell has a whimsical, expressive flair. You might find

© STUART THORNTON

Human Arts Gallery

brightly painted furniture, hand-colored glass, or minutely detailed wood boxes.

Made in Ojai (323 E. Matilija St., 805/646-2400, www.madeinojai.com, daily 10am-6pm) operates as an artists' collective. All of the artists who sell their pieces at the store also work here. There's a wide range, and it's all quite impressive: fine art and prints, pottery, gemstone jewelry, custom leather boots, handmade teddy bears, and even hula hoops. You'll also find local olive oils, teas, lavender lotions, jellies, local honey, handmade soaps, and skincare products as well as books and music by local talent.

SPORTS AND RECREATION
Lake Casitas

For decades, **Lake Casitas** (11311 Santa Ana Rd., 805/649-2233, www.casitaswater.org, entrance fee Mon.-Thurs. $10 per vehicle, Fri.-Sun. and holidays $15 per vehicle) has been known for its fishing. Anglers flocked to the 2,700-acre artificial lake hoping to land a world-record catch. The photos at the bait shop near the marina proudly display some of the monster largemouth bass and trout that dedicated and patient anglers have pulled from these waters over the last 30 years. The lake is also stocked with rainbow trout, perch, and catfish.

With the popularity of sportfishing declining nationwide, the Casitas Municipal Water District hopes to draw in visitors by adding a little something for everyone, building the **Casitas Water Adventure** (adults $12, under age 12 free) water park and the adjoining **Lazy River,** a winding pool with water jets that push inner-tube riders along a 1,200-foot route. Just inside the park entrance is a spraying jungle gym set inside a large wading pool. A few feet away, a snaking concrete-lined waterway with a mellow current carries inner-tube riders in a circuitous route under waterfalls and cascading showers.

There are also boats for rent, plus camping, hiking, biking, and Frisbee golf, and the simple serenity of lounging or strolling by the water's edge. But because this is a reservoir,

swimming and wading in the water are not allowed. Amenities include coin-operated showers, on-site boat rental, a café with forgettable food, and a seasonal park store, should you have forgotten something. The lake is also a wildlife preserve and home to 65 species of birds, including herons and egrets, making it ideal for bird-watching. It's also common to see deer, coyotes, foxes, and other creatures.

The creation of this reservoir obliterated the Santa Ana Valley, which today lies below the 32-mile shoreline underneath 80 billion gallons of water. The dam that holds the water was completed in 1958. The federal government has spent $25 million to buy up land around the lake, which will be left as permanent open space to help keep the watershed clean.

Golf

The 18-hole, par-70 golf course at the **Ojai Valley Inn** (905 Country Club Rd., 800/422-6524, www.ojairesort.com, greens fees $180) was originally designed in the 1920s by George C. Thomas Jr., who also designed the Riviera, Bel Air, and Los Angeles Country Club courses farther south. He wanted every tee, fairway, and green to offer a different panorama, both beautiful and challenging. This course has hosted seven Senior PGA Tour events. The sheer beauty of the course, parts of which sit below the resort flanked by some of the surrounding mountains, is a treat in itself. There is also a driving range.

The par-71 **Soule Park** (1033 E. Ojai Ave., 805/646-5633, www.soulepark.com, greens fees $12-53) is an 18-hole regulation golf course with a medium-length layout that will reward good shots. It's mildly challenging, but only because of the back-to-back holes 14 and 15, where you have 400-plus yards into the wind. The fees are reasonable and the views are wonderful. There's a driving range and a small restaurant.

◖ Hiking

Ojai is ringed by impressive mountains, so it is no surprise that there are a lot of hiking options. The more than 300,000-acre **Ojai**

Ranger District of the Los Padres National Forest has 195 miles of trails at elevations ranging from 240 feet to 7,514 feet. The **Ojai Ranger District Office** (1190 E. Ojai Ave., 805/646-4348, www.fs.usda.gov, Mon.-Fri. 9am-12:30pm and 1:30pm-4pm) offers general information as well as an Ojai-area trail guide ($3).

A local favorite, **Shelf Road** (end of Signal St.) is an easy wide trail with minimal elevation gains and fantastic views of the valley; out and back is about four miles. You'll see walkers, runners, horses, and cyclists along the path. The trailhead starts high above downtown, nearly 1,000 feet above Ojai Avenue. The national forest is on one side and orange groves are on the other. The high point of the trail is only 150 feet higher than the actual trailhead, but the views open up to both sides of the valley; bring your camera. To get here from downtown, head north up Signal Street off Ojai Avenue and drive about one mile until you reach the end. Parking is available at the trailhead, which is marked by a gate. The trail takes you to another gate two miles away at Gridley.

Another popular path just outside downtown is the **Gridley Trail** (end of Gridley Rd., 6 miles), which offers fine views of the Ojai Valley and nearby avocado orchards. The rocky trail climbs from Gridley Road to Nordhoff Ridge, where, on clear days, you can make out the Channel Islands in the distance. To reach the trail, take a left of East Ojai Avenue onto Gridley Road. Park at the end of Gridley Road and then walk 50 feet down the road to the trailhead, on the north side of the street.

At the **Ventura River Preserve** (Rice Rd. near El Roblar Dr., www.ovlc.org), miles of well-marked trails weave through the riverbed, which is typically dry. A few natural springs on the preserve run year-round. The riparian habitat abuts the Los Padres National Forest and is home to 300 plant and animal species. Stay near the riverbed for a flat hike, or head up the fire road for a more strenuous workout. The preserve is accessed from the Riverview trailhead off Rice Road: Take Highway 150

a view of Ojai Valley from the Gridley Trail

© STUART THORNTON

toward Lake Casitas; shortly after the split from Highway 33, make a right at Rice Road and look for the preserve signs, about 0.5 miles up.

Located in the Sespe Wilderness, **Piedra Blanca** is about 20 miles from Ojai along Highway 33. You have to stop at **Wheeler Gorge Visitors Center** (17017 Maricopa Hwy., 805/640-9060) for a day-use pass. Continue up Highway 33 to the Rose Valley Road turnoff on your right and drive about 6.5 miles until it dead-ends at the parking lot. The white rock formations of Piedra Blanca are in front of you, just to the north. The trail is relatively flat, with an overall elevation gain of 300 feet. It's approximately 1.5 miles one-way, mostly through chaparral and manzanita with a few small creek crossings if there have been winter rains. The landscape then changes from thick brush to smooth sandstone, offering dramatic boulders to climb on.

Cycling

The **33 North/Ventucopa** is a challenging bike trail north along Highway 33, through Meiners Oaks, and toward the mountains—a climb of nearly 4,000 vertical feet with stunning vistas into the often unseen backcountry of the Los Padres Mountains. You can continue the ride well into the Carrizo Plain in Santa Barbara County, if you have the stamina; it's close to 60 miles one-way. The route vacillates between pine-covered mountains and the dry desertlike stretch toward the north near Cuyama. From downtown Ojai, simply take Highway 33 north and you'll be on your way.

West Ojai Avenue will take you toward Lake Casitas, a popular cycling route. Follow Ojai Avenue on the bike trail; once you reach the turnoff to the lake, Highway 150, follow the signs. There are some hills, but once you're outside town, there are vast meadows with panoramic views to the mountains. This can be a long ride, over 40 miles, or short, depending on when you decide to turn back. A good turn-around point is once you pass the lake and begin the mountain ascent. **East Ojai Avenue** runs flat on the opposite end of town toward orchards of citrus trees; then the road begins to climb toward Santa Paula and Highway 126. If you're not into the climbs, turn back toward Ojai after about four miles, and you'll have had a pleasant ride through the valley.

Located in an old gas station, **The MOB Shop** (110 W. Ojai Ave., 805/272-8102, www.themobshop.com, Mon. 1pm-6pm, Tues.-Fri. 10am-5pm, Sat. 9am-5pm, Sun. 9am-4pm,

---

THE PINK MOMENT

As the sun begins to set in Ojai, people come outside and gaze upward, seemingly transfixed. At first you might think that visitors from another planet are about to pay a visit, but everyone is actually looking toward the Topa Topa Mountains, where, when the atmospheric conditions are right, which usually means light cloud cover, the bluff above town will turn pink. The phenomenon is called the Pink Moment. When the moment comes, some claim to see the face of Chief Peak (Chief Peak is the high point on the ridge, where some see the head and bonnet, and there is indeed some resemblance to the outline of a sleeping Native American chief). Others say that a few times a year the entire valley, not just the mountains, glows with a pinkish hue. It has been suggested that this happens because Ojai is surrounded by an east- and west-facing mountain range, which is rare in California, where most ranges run north to south.

Whatever its cause, the Pink Moment does exist. It's a well-documented local experience; plenty of professional and amateur photographers have attempted to capture it, and others have tried to capitalize on the phenomenon. There's a Pink Moment Press, a novel called *Ojai: The Pink Moment Promises*, a chocolatier who has created Pink Moment Sweets, and doggie T-shirts promote the pinkness of your pet. Casa Barranca makes a local wine called the Pink Moment Rosé. Beyond the photos, trinkets, and anything else that sells the pinkness, is the reality; it's quite a beautiful sight to behold.

bike rentals $26-60 per day) rents out road bikes, full-suspension mountain bikes, and electric bikes for pedaling Ojai Valley and the nearby area. MOB also offers tours, including a 10-mile descent of Sulphur Mountain and a ride that takes you past the valley's alpaca farms.

Horseback Riding

Western Trail Rides (805/640-8635, www. westerntrailrides.org, Mon.-Sat. 10am-sunset, $35-60/hour) creates personalized trail rides for just an hour or a whole afternoon. You can choose to ride in the foothills and up to vistas or along cool mountain streams. Riding lessons are available for those who need a little more experience in the saddle. The **Ojai Valley Trail Company** (1290 Meyer Rd., 805/890-9340, www.ojaitrailrides.com, $40-120) offers river-valley and forest rides as well as pony rides for small children.

Hot Springs

For years it has been a poorly kept secret that hot springs exist in the mountains above Ojai. Most are only accessible to backpackers. Both **Willett Hot Springs** (9.5 miles' hike), which has springwater collected in a rubber tub, and **Sespe Hot Springs** (15.5 miles' hike), a few pools in Sespe Creek made with river rocks, can be reached on the **Sespe River Trail,** which starts at the **Piedra Blanca Trailhead.** To reach the trailhead, drive Highway 33 north from Ojai for 13 miles, and then turn right onto Rose Valley Road. Follow the road 5.5 miles to its end, where the trail begins

Popular **Matilija Hot Springs** (http://ojai-hotsprings.com) was closed to the public in May 2013 due to years of overuse. The non-profit Ecotopia hopes to reopen the springs in early 2014 with limited access. These springs can be found by driving north on Highway 33 from Ojai and turning left on Matilija Road.

Yoga

With a multitude of teachers, classes, and workshops, **LuLu Bandhas** (306 E. Matilija St., 805/640-7868, www.lulubandhas.com, classes

from $15) is almost like a yoga college. There are classes for beginners, including an introductory session for "stiff white guys," and regular practitioners, including courses on *vinyasa* and meditation. LuLu also offers online classes, DVDs, and books for the soul. **Sacred Space Studio** (410 Bryant Circle, Suite A, 805/646-6761, www.sacredspacestudio.com, drop-in class $20) has diverse course offerings, including yoga classes, belly dancing, West African dance, and aerial arts with trapeze rings.

Spas

Ojai Valley Inn and Spa (905 Country Club Rd., 888/697-8754, www.ojairesort.com, massages $145-350) consistently ranks among the top spas in the country. From traditional spa treatments to water therapy, dry steam rooms, eucalyptus hot tubs, and seasonal body scrubs, they offer it all, with aromatherapy, facials, and Kuyam, which they claim is the only treatment of its kind in the United States. It combines the therapeutic effects of desert clay, dry heat, inhalation therapy, and traditional Chumash guided meditation (Kuyam is a Chumash word that means "a place to rest together"). None of this comes cheap, of course, but you'll definitely feel pampered. The treatments take place in a striking Morocco-inspired building with a bell tower and an outdoor fireplace.

The **Day Spa of Ojai** (1434 E. Ojai Ave., 805/640-1100, www.thedayspa.com, daily 10am-5:30pm, 1-hour massage from $85) is housed in a beautiful old stone home on the outskirts of town. Simple hour-long treatments are available, but packages typically last 3-4 hours and include foot treatments followed by a massage and then a facial. The Day Spa also has wooden-barrel saunas and infrared saunas that penetrate more deeply for maximum relaxation. Chances are you'll be blissed out, so it might be best to arrange for a ride home.

Located inside a hotel, **The Oaks at Ojai** (122 E. Ojai Ave., 805/646-5573, www. oaksspa.com, massages $80-135) caters primarily to women, with traditional spa massages and scrubs. The Oaks also offers a lifestyle approach that goes beyond the typical hour-long session, and includes acupressure, a fitness regimen, and diet and health consultations.

ACCOMMODATIONS
Under $150
Casa Ojai Inn (1302 E. Ojai Ave., 805/646-8175, www.ojaiinn.com, $130-150) is a 45-room eco-sensitive lodging. "Green" touches include sink aerators, luxury low-flow showerheads, and efficient toilets. If you show up in an electrical or hybrid certified vehicle, they'll knock 5 percent off the cost of your stay. The craftsman-style furnishings are custom-made. Try a refreshing swim in the saltwater pool or enjoy the hot tub, then sunbathe on a spacious sundeck. Guests can enjoy discounts for spa services at the Ojai Day Spa or work out with complimentary passes to the Bryant Street Gym. The exterior looks more like a two-story motel, but don't let that put you off.

The **Ojai Serenity Suites** (1484 E. Ojai Ave., 805/646-9779, www.ojaicottage.com, $125-175) is a unique property located just outside downtown, with three distinct lodgings near the Soule Park golf course. The cottage is a 1,000-square-foot two-story stone structure with a two-person whirlpool tub and a full kitchen; it sleeps up to four people. The knotty pine walls make it feel like a secluded cabin. The loft has one bedroom and a bath plus a full kitchen and a small deck; it's not as charming as the cottage, but it's still very nice. The studio is a one-room space, nicely decorated with a small kitchenette. On-site diversions include a pool, a hot tub, croquet, and horseshoes.

The first thing you'll notice at the **☾ Blue Iguana Inn** (11794 N. Ventura Hwy., 805/646-5277, www.blueiguanainn.com, $129-249) is Iggy, the large mosaic iguana fountain out front. The building has a pueblo feel, with a dozen guest rooms and suites. Interior decor ranges from Spanish pueblo to craftsman. The grounds are relaxing, with lots of oak trees as well as a pool and several decks. The inn is close to downtown and right off the highway, so there can be some traffic noise when you're outside.

☾ Ojai Rancho Inn (615 W. Ojai Ave., 805/648-1434, http://ojairanchoinn.com, $89-209) seems tailor-made for a young, hip crowd. The owners say they were inspired by the summer camp atmosphere of the movie *Moonrise Kingdom*. The rustic decor of the guest rooms acknowledges the area's ranching past with stone floors, wood walls, and log frame beds. Handmade furnishings include indigo tie-dyed curtains and iPod docks and speakers embedded in a slab of found wood. In keeping with Ojai's spiritualism, guests receive a piece of *palo santo* wood to purify and cleanse their room during their stay. Lodging options include 4 guest rooms with kitchenettes, 10 guest rooms with jetted tubs, and a garden cottage. The grounds have a sunny space with a pool, barbecue grills, and a shuffleboard court. A wood sauna provides a place to unwind. Guests can borrow bicycles to ride the Ojai Bike Path, which is located right behind the property. There are even plans to build a stage out back for concerts and festivals.

$150-250
The **Lavender Inn** (210 E. Matilija St., 805/646-6635, www.lavenderinn.com, $145-300) is located just off Ojai Avenue in an 1874 building originally used as a schoolhouse and community center. Today, it offers intimate charm as a Victorian-style bed-and-breakfast. Each of the nine guest rooms is uniquely designed and offers mountain or garden views. The guest rooms are a bit small—or cozy, depending on your perspective. Enjoy a full breakfast each morning with herbs from the garden, a computer with Internet access for guest use, and a wine-and-cheese reception each evening. Two pet-friendly guest rooms are available for folks traveling with their furry pals.

The sister property of the Blue Iguana Inn, the **☾ Emerald Iguana Inn** (110 Pauline St., 805/646-5277, www.emeraldiguana.com, $179-319) is an oasis tucked into an Ojai neighborhood. The inn is surrounded by blooming flowers that include birds of paradise and star jasmine, and its architecture is inspired by the work of Spanish architect Antoni Gaudí. Inside,

© STUART THORNTON

Emerald Iguana Inn

each guest room has its own unique design features. Options include singles, a one-bedroom cottage with two floors, two balconies, a patio, and a full kitchen, and two-bedroom cottages that can accommodate six people. The focal point of the property is a sunny deck with a pool and a soaking tub. It's also where the continental breakfast is served every morning.

Su Nido Inn & Suites (301 N. Montgomery St., 805/646-7080, www.sunidoinn.com, $189-539) features mission revival architecture and nine guest rooms and suites ranging from 600 to 1,000 square feet in size. Even the smaller rooms are palatial, with tiled kitchens and baths, exposed-beam ceilings, and plush beds and sofas. They're so beautifully decorated that you'll feel like you're touring a model home. The staff is also exceptional. During the high season, a two-night stay is required on weekends.

Over $250

Located on 800 acres with its own golf course, spa, and tennis courts, the 308-room **Ojai**

Valley Inn and Spa (905 Country Club Rd., 855/697-8780, www.ojairesort.com, $313-789) seems more like a small village. The inn dates to 1922, when wealthy Ohio glass manufacturer Edward Libbey commissioned noted architect Wallace Neff to build a country club in Spanish colonial style, with features like tiled fountains and walkways, red-tile roofs, and a voluminous lobby. During World War II, the U.S. Army took over the resort as a training camp, stationing 1,000 troops here until 1944. The following year, the Navy occupied the resort as a rest-and-relaxation facility for their officers. The staff are professional, helpful, and genuinely friendly. It's a great spot for children and teenagers; on-site activities keep them occupied. Don't come expecting a secluded getaway—this place draws a crowd.

FOOD
Bakeries

The **Ojai Cafe Emporium** (108 S. Montgomery St., 805/646-2723, daily 6:30am-3pm) has a

Deer Lodge

small bakery fronting the street where you can pick up fresh scones, pastries, breads, and brownies made on-site daily. There's also a coffee bar with half a dozen options. **Knead Baking Company** (469 E. Ojai Ave., 310/770-3282, www.kneadbakingcompany.com, Wed.-Sun. 8am-4pm) is an artisanal bakery that utilizes local ingredients like orange-tangerine honey, fruit, vegetables, and herbs to create cakes, cookies, quiches, and breads. They also serve a café menu with breakfast and lunch items, including sandwiches and flatbread pizzas.

Breakfast
Few Ojai eateries open early or serve a hearty early breakfast, but **Eggs 'n Potatoes** (1103 Maricopa Hwy., 805/646-5346, http://eggsnpotatoes.net, daily 7am-2pm, $7.50-10) does both. The menu isn't too creative: Expect tried and true American breakfasts, with large portions served quickly. True to the restaurant's name, the fried potatoes are the standout.

Classic American
Located just three miles from downtown, **Deer Lodge** (2261 Maricopa Hwy., 805/646-4256, daily 11am-2am, www.ojaideerlodge.net, $20) is a rustic log cabin-style roadhouse, complete with animal heads on the walls. The menu has the expected barbecue tri-tip sandwiches, chili, and burgers, but given that this is Ojai, there are also vegetarian options like the veggie wrap and grilled lentil nut loaf.

Located in a former lumberyard, **Ojai Cafe Emporium** (108 S. Montgomery St., 805/646-2723, www.ojaicafeemporium.com, daily 7am-3pm, $6-14) looks and feels like a down-home diner inside. The choice seats are on the covered patio, which looks out to the parking lot. While the view may not be exciting, the food is. The quiche is a winner, as is their house specialty, the Topa Topa salad. Sunday brunch is usually packed.

Coffeehouses
The **Ojai Coffee Roasting Company** (337 E.

© STUART THORNTON

Boccali's restaurant

Ojai Ave., 805/646-4478, www.ojaicoffeero-astingco.com, Sat.-Mon. 5:30am-6pm, Sun. 5:30am-5pm) roasts 20 different coffees on-site. They also serve teas, baked goods (try a maple scone), and a few lunch items (sand-wiches and salads). The cozy, comfortable, but increasingly crowded little store also of-fers free Wi-Fi. The service is friendly and ef-ficient. The **Bohemia Coffee House** (214 W. Ojai Ave., 805/640-7210, daily 7am-10pm) has more than coffee, tea, pastries, and free Wi-Fi; it also showcases the works of local artists and hosts a popular open-mike night (Tues. 7pm-9pm).

Ice Cream
People have been stopping at **Ojai Ice Cream** (210 E. Ojai Ave., 805/646-6075, daily 11am-7pm) for over 30 years to enjoy the 32 flavors made on the premises, including Ojai Orange. They also serve yogurt, sorbet, and their own fudge in this small store that often gets crowded, especially during the summer.

Italian
Boccali's (3277 E. Ojai Ave., 805/646-6116, www.boccalis.com, Mon.-Tues. 4pm-9pm, Wed.-Sun. 11:45am-9pm, $10-17) has been lur-ing diners out to its location two miles east of downtown since 1986. This home-style Italian restaurant serves hearty pizza and pasta dishes in a small white building or out front on a nice alfresco dining patio. The food is tasty and the staff are friendly. While you'll fill up fast here, try to save room for the seasonal strawberry shortcake. In Ojai's covered Arcade, **Osteria Monte Grappa** (242 E. Ojai Ave., http://oste-riamontegrappa.com, Sun.-Thurs. 11:30am-8:30pm, Fri.-Sat. 11:30am-9:30pm, $11-36) utilizes local meats and sustainable seafood to create rustic dishes from northern Italy. Try the homemade pasta topped with a whole sautéed Maryland soft-shell crab.

Mediterranean
❰**Azu** (457 E. Ojai Ave., 805/640-7987, www.azuojai.com, lunch daily noon-3pm, dinner

daily 5:30pm-9pm, $14-36) is a great place to graze from the tapas menu. Choose from distinctive dishes such as Syrian chicken salad or seared sea scallops with a blood-orange chutney. For dessert, there's homemade gelato. There are always fresh flowers on the tables, and the hardwood floors and dark wood chairs contrast with the soft yellow walls and white linens for a sophisticated look. The service is prompt. Consider dropping in for happy hour (daily 5:30pm-7pm).

Mexican

For healthy, somewhat Americanized Mexican food, dine in or get takeout from the popular **Jim & Rob's Fresh Grill** (214 W. Ojai Ave., Suite 101, 805/640-1301, www.jimandrobsojai.com, Sun.-Wed. 8:30am-8:30pm, Thurs.-Sat. 8:30am-9pm, $10). The menu has tacos, taquitos, salads, and burritos, including citrus chicken and sautéed vegetable options. The tortillas and beans are lard-free.

Head to unpretentious **Los Corporales** (307 E. Ojai Ave., 805/646-5452, Mon. and Wed.-Thurs. 11am-9pm, Fri. 11am-2am, Sat. 9am-2am, Sun. 9am-9pm, $10-30) for chips and salsa and tequila shots. Stick with traditional Tex-Mex like the *chile verde* or inexpensive burritos with your choice of meat. The service can be slow at times, but you won't mind if you're sitting outside enjoying the view of Libbey Park.

New American

Feast Bistro (254 E. Ojai Ave., 805/640-9260, http://feastofojai.com, Tues.-Sat. 11:30am-2:30pm and 5:30pm-9pm, Sun. brunch 10:30am-3pm, $12-22) is a true bistro, packing a lot into a small space, including a wine, espresso, and tea bar, a cooking school, an open kitchen, and lively ambience. There's even a retail space stocked with olive oils and other condiments. Try the duck breast, daily frittata, or a veggie burger, and finish up with the olive oil cake, made from local olive oil. Wine-tastings, winemaker dinners, and cooking classes are scheduled intermittently.

[Suzanne's Cuisine (502 W. Ojai Ave., 805/640-1961, www.suzannescuisine.com, Wed.-Mon. 11:30am-2:30pm and 5:30pm-close, $25) has long had the reputation of being one of the best restaurants in town. The owners make daily trips to Los Angeles farmers markets to retrieve the best produce and freshest foods for their seasonal menu. You'll find dishes such as calf liver, pasta fettuccini with portobello mushrooms, a *chimichurri*-marinated prime rib, and four-egg omelets. But the true secret to Suzanne's success is the service—fierce dedication to creating the best possible dining experience. Reservations are recommended.

Vegetarian

With food fresh from the farm, **Farmer and the Cook Market and Cafe** (339 W. El Roblar Dr., 805/640-9608, www.farmerandcook.com, daily 8am-8:30pm, $7.50-12) feels like a glorified roadside stand, but they have organic, vegetarian, and some vegan options, with a swiss chard enchilada, handmade tamales, a salad bar, and even a wee bit of pizza and sushi. On Wednesday, try the rich vegetarian nut loaf. Or shop for organic fruits and vegetables in the market. **Hip Vegan Café** (928 E. Ojai Ave., 805/646-1750, www.hipvegancafe.com, daily 11am-5pm, $7-11) offers a lunch menu with all of the variety its name suggests: gluten-free and soy items, including mock-meat barbecue and Reuben sandwiches that employ seitan. Daily specials may include tortilla casseroles or eggplant parmesan.

INFORMATION AND SERVICES

Maps and Visitor Information

Located inside the **Ojai Valley Museum** (130 W. Ojai Ave., 805/640-1390, Mon.-Fri. 10am-4pm), the visitor information center is oftentimes understaffed. Thankfully, much of the information on Ojai is located in the foyer of the museum, so if the information center is closed, you can still grab all the literature you need. The **Ojai Visitors Bureau** (206 N. Signal

Farmer and the Cook Market and Cafe

© STUART THORNTON

St., Suite P, 888/652-4669, http://ojaivisitors.com, Mon. 9am-4pm, Tues.-Fri. 8am-5pm) has the latest information on Ojai's local events as well as maps and brochures for the area. The **Ojai Ranger District Office** (1190 E. Ojai Ave., 805/646-4348, www.fs.usda.gov, Mon.-Fri. 9am-12:30pm and 1:30pm-4pm) is the spot for information on hiking and backpacking.

Emergency Services

The **Ojai Valley Community Hospital** (1306 Maricopa Hwy., 805/646-1401, www.cmh-shealth.org) is the only hospital in Ojai and the only emergency room. In case of emergency, call 911 immediately. Police services are the **Ojai Police Department** (402 S. Ventura St., 805/646-1414).

Newspapers

The main newspaper is the *Ojai Valley News* (www.ojaivalleynews.com), published twice weekly on Wednesday and Friday; it can be found all over town. *The Ojai Post* (www.

ojaipost.com) is a local blog covering all of what's happening in town.

Postal Services

The main branch of the **post office** (201 E. Ojai Ave., 805/646-7904) is located on the main drag. This is a very small post office and is facing budget cuts like many others, so it is best to phone ahead to verify its hours.

Laundry

For laundry services, try **Ojai Valley Cleaners** (345 E. Ojai Ave., 805/646-2745).

GETTING THERE AND AROUND

If you're coming from Los Angeles, the drive is 60 miles (about 90 minutes). The most logical driving route is Highway 33, which leaves U.S. 101 at the coast near downtown Ventura. From Santa Barbara, drive southbound on U.S. 101, and near Carpinteria take Highway 150, which will eventually put you on Highway 33, where you will turn left to enter Ojai. There are two backcountry routes into Ojai as well: Highway 126 from Santa Paula and Highway 33 from the north. Both are accessed from I-5 and are long, arduous drives.

Gold Coast Transit (GCT, 201 E. 4th St., Oxnard, 805/487-4222 or 805/643-3158, www.goldcoasttransit.org) provides service to Ojai, specifically on Highway 6. One-way fares range from $0.75 for seniors to $1.50 for other adults. The Ojai-Main Street line, route 16, is available seven days a week except holidays. GCT connects to Amtrak trains, Greyhound buses, and LA-area Metrolink commuter trains at the Oxnard Transportation Center (201 E. 4th St., Oxnard). The red-and-green **Ojai Trolley Service** (805/646-5581, ext. 207, www.ojaitrolley.com, adults $1, seniors $0.50, under age 5 free) runs the length of the small valley.

Tours
The **Ojai Valley Museum Guided Historical Walking Tour** (805/640-1390, $10) is a great way to learn about Ojai's colorful past, get the lowdown on pioneer families, and check out architectural highlights and unique shops in town. The one-hour tours begin at the Ojai Valley Museum (130 W. Ojai Ave.), and a local museum docent leads the tour of the downtown area. Start times vary, so phone ahead. To explore the open spaces outside of town, opt for **Trails by Potter** (805/646-0382, www.hikingojai.com). In addition to hiking excursions, they also provide cycling tours and rock-climbing outings. **Cloud Climbers Jeep Tours** (805/646-3200, www.ccjeeps.com, $109) does a four-hour "all around Ojai" tour that includes climbing country roads and unwinding at a local winery.

THE CHANNEL ISLANDS

The Channel Islands sweep visitors back in time to a past when the California coastline was undeveloped. Only accessible by boat or plane, Channel Islands National Park is in the top 20 least crowded national parks due to its remote location. Those few who get to the five islands experience uncrowded trails, isolated beaches, and an extensive marine sanctuary. It's a place to experience the state in its purest, most natural form. Kelp forests offshore sway in the ocean's surge as pumpkin-colored garibaldi (the California state fish) swim past rocks dotted with multicolored sea urchins. Onshore, rare species, including the island fox and the Santa Cruz Island scrub jay, roam freely.

The islands have been federally protected for over 30 years. Long before they were a national park, they were ranchland. Santa Cruz Island, in particular, was prime grazing land in the 1800s for cattle and sheep, which were safe from the predators found on the mainland. Santa Cruz was also home to a winery, the remnants of which are still visible. Archaeological evidence suggests that the islands were inhabited by the indigenous Chumash people much earlier—as far back as 12,000 years ago.

The most visited of the park's islands are Anacapa, a dramatic five-mile spine jutting out of the sea, and Santa Cruz, California's largest island at 24 miles long and 6 miles wide. Sailing to the islands can take 3-4 hours; motorboats make the trip even faster, but exploring the islands isn't common. San Miguel, the farthest west, is not a short trip, nor is the small rock island of Santa Barbara. But Anacapa, Santa Cruz, and to a lesser degree Santa Rosa

HIGHLIGHTS

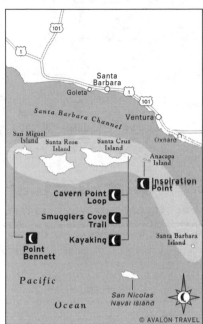

◖ Cavern Point Loop: Cavern Point offers cliff-top views of Santa Cruz Island's cave-riddled coast, the mainland, and migrating whales in season. The quick two-mile loop trail makes it possible to get to Cavern Point even if you only have a few hours on the island (page 216).

◖ Smugglers Cove Trail: This 7.5-mile round-trip hike starts at the Scorpion Anchorage and crosses the eastern tip of Santa Cruz Island to a scenic cobblestone beach cove (page 217).

◖ Kayaking: Both Santa Cruz Island and Anacapa Island are known for their abundance of sea caves. These beautiful caverns, which range from cathedral-size to small overhangs, are best explored by kayak (pages 218 and 222).

◖ Inspiration Point: Located on the west cliff edge of Anacapa Island, Inspiration Point has one of the most awe-inspiring views in the islands (page 221).

◖ Point Bennett: On rarely visited San Miguel Island, Point Bennett is home to one of the world's highest concentrations of seals and sea lions. Getting there involves a strenuous 16-mile round-trip hike guided by a park ranger (page 227).

LOOK FOR ◖ TO FIND RECOMMENDED SIGHTS, ACTIVITIES, DINING, AND LODGING.

can be visited as day trips, although only Santa Cruz and Anacapa trips are available year-round. There can be tough weather conditions: It's often very windy, and there's little shelter.

Inexpensive day trips allow visitors to explore, hike, kayak, snorkel, camp, and scuba dive at the islands. Multiday trips allow for extended camping excursions into the islands' interiors and for visiting several of the islands.

PLANNING YOUR TIME

A trip to the Channel Islands involves significant planning—especially if you are thinking of camping overnight. First off, when should you go? Every season has its positives and

negatives. During spring, the islands are colored with blooming wildflowers, but they are also frequently buffeted by winds. Summer finds warmer weather on the islands—there are also a fair number of foggy days—but this is also when most visitors head out to the park. Summer crowds fill the Island Packers Cruises boats that connect the mainland to Anacapa and Santa Cruz Islands. During a typical summer day, Island Packers takes 70 people out to Anacapa and 150 people out to Santa Cruz. But the islands themselves don't get too crowded: The National Park Service allows no more than 100 day visitors to East Anacapa Island and no more than 200 visitors to Santa Cruz

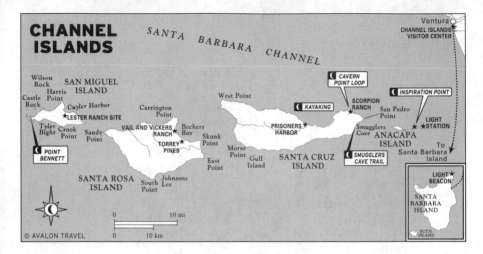

CHANNEL ISLANDS

Island's Scorpion Anchorage each day. With mild weather and calm seas, fall may be the all-around best option, although the Santa Ana winds can kick up in October. The winter months have cooler temperatures and occasional rainstorms but also offer dramatic sunsets and the chance of spotting migrating gray whales from December to April.

Each island within Channel Islands National Park offers different experiences and ranges of recreational opportunities. All of Anacapa Island and its two-mile trail system can be explored in an afternoon, making it a good day trip. In addition to its limited but worthwhile hiking options, the island is great for getting in the water for snorkeling or sea kayaking. Anacapa offers 30 sea caves to explore. As the largest island, Santa Cruz has the most opportunities for visitors. The island is a superb place for overnight camping and hiking. You can also go backpacking to the Del Norte backcountry campsite. In addition, Santa Cruz is superb for diving, snorkeling, and sea kayaking, especially right out front of the Scorpion Anchorage. Like Anacapa, Santa Cruz is known for its outstanding sea caves. David Bunnell, author of the *Sea Caves of Santa Cruz,* has mapped over 100 caves on the island. Approximately 35 sea caves are easily accessible from the Scorpion Anchorage. Santa Rosa's consistently strong winds makes

water recreation difficult, but as the second largest island, it has good hiking options, including a strenuous 13-mile round-trip hike through a canyon. Santa Rosa is also known for its vegetation, including one of the rarest pine trees in the world, the Torrey pine. Visitors are drawn to San Miguel Island by its exceptional wildlife, especially at Point Bennett, where there are an estimated 30,000 seals and sea lions. As the westernmost island, San Miguel is battered by strong winds, which render water sports unmanageable most of the time. There are a few hikes on the island as well. Farther south, Santa Barbara offers warmer water and excellent opportunities for swimming, diving, snorkeling, and kayaking. It's the smallest of the islands, meaning that the longest hike is a three-mile round-trip excursion.

In preparation for a trip to the islands, visit the **Channel Islands National Park Visitors Center** (1901 Spinnaker Dr., Ventura Harbor, 805/658-5730, www.nps.gov, daily 8:30am-5pm) in Ventura Harbor Village, where you'll find a bookstore, a display of marinelife, exhibits, and a 25-minute introductory film on the islands. Camping and renting kayaks or other equipment involves another layer of planning. Booking a campsite in Channel Islands National Park is easy by phone (877/444-6777) or through their reservation website (www.recreation.gov), but first you have to make sure transportation is available to take you there and back for the days you are out on the islands. The park suggests making reservations for camping during the summer as early as possible; reservations can be made as early as five months in advance. In addition, whether you bring your own kayak or rent one, if you are using Island Packers, you need to make sure that there will be room on the boat.

Getting There

The most popular way to get to the Channel Islands National Park is by hopping aboard a boat run by **Island Packers Cruises** (1691 Spinnaker Dr., Suite 105B, Ventura Harbor, 805/642-1393, www.islandpackers.com). Even the boat ride out to the islands is an adventure, with porpoises frequently racing beside the boats. There's also a snack bar on board selling what one crewmember calls "college food"— candy bars, beer, and salted snacks. Island Packers is a family-run business that has been taking people out to the Channel Islands since 1968. The staff are helpful and understanding even when the weather or other factors interfere with your planned trip. In addition to trips to the islands, Island Packers does wildlife cruises around the islands, whale-watching tours, and Ventura Harbor dinner cruises.

Trips to the most popular islands, Anacapa and Santa Cruz, are offered year-round, 5-7 days a week. Trips to the more far-flung islands are scheduled less frequently. Trips to Santa Rosa, San Miguel, and Santa Barbara are only possible from spring to fall. Island Packers visits Santa Rosa and San Miguel just 8-12 days a month during this time, while the three-hour one-way trip to Santa Barbara Island happens just four days a month from spring to fall. The most common landing at **Santa Cruz** (May-Oct. daily, Nov.-Apr. Tues. and Fri.-Sun., adults $56, ages 3-12 $39, over age 54 $51) is Scorpion Cove, with a crossing time of 90 minutes. Trips to **Anacapa** (year-round daily, adults $56, ages 3-12 $39, over age 54 $51), the closest island, take an average of 45 minutes. **Santa Rosa** trips (adults $78, ages 3-12 $62, over age 54 $70) take 2.5-3 hours and include stops at Santa Cruz. **San Miguel** day trips (adults $100, ages 3-12 $80, over age 54 $90) are uncommon due to the travel time of 3-4 hours. But there are a few days each year when you can do it, typically in September-October.

© GABRIEL SKVOR

Santa Cruz Island's Scorpion Anchorage

PACKING FOR THE CHANNEL ISLANDS

The Channel Islands National Park website says it best: "A visit to the Channel Islands is an exercise in preparation and self-reliance." There are no stores or vendors on the island, so you need to bring everything that you might need—but the packs you bring on the concessionaire transport can weigh no more than 45 pounds.

to pack a little bit more food and water. The only available water on the islands is located at Santa Cruz Island's Scorpion Ranch Campground and Santa Rosa Island's Water Canyon. Otherwise, you must have your own water. In addition, make sure that your food containers are island fox- and mouse-proof.

CLOTHING

The Channel Islands are susceptible to strong winds and can be covered in fog. Also, you might be pelted with sea spray on your boat ride out to the islands. It's a good idea to bring layers of clothes. Pack shorts and hiking shoes for warmer days, and be sure to include sweatshirts, windbreakers, hats, and sunscreen.

FOOD AND WATER

If you do an overnight trip to the Channel Islands, be sure to pack enough food and water. There is always a chance that your return transportation could be delayed, so make sure

ENTERTAINMENT

There is no TV or Internet on the islands. Luckily, there are many books about the Channel Islands. A great all-around primer is the multiple-author *Natural History of the Channel Islands*. To learn about living on the islands, check out Elizabeth Sherman Lester's *Legendary King of San Miguel* and Margaret H. Eaton's *Diary of a Sea Captain's Wife: Tales of Santa Cruz Island*. Scott O' Dell's *Island of the Blue Dolphins* is a popular children's novel set on the southern island of San Nicolas. For fiction, T.C. Boyle's *When the Killing's Done* and *San Miguel* are set in the Channel Islands.

Keep a close eye on the weather as your trip approaches. Gale-force winds have been known to spring up, and the seas can change quickly. You can call Island Packers (805/642-1393) the morning of your journey to make sure your trip is still happening.

If the high seas aren't your thing, go by air via **Channel Islands Aviation** (805/987-1301, www.flycia.com, half-day trip adults $160, children $135, deluxe day trip $220, camping trip $300, surf fishing trip $950), which flies from the Ventura County city of Camarillo out to Santa Rosa daily, weather permitting.

Kayaking Outfitters and Tours

To rent kayaks for a trip to Santa Cruz or Anacapa Island, contact **Channel Islands Kayak Center** (805/984-5995, www.cikayak. com, single kayaks $35, double kayaks $55), conveniently located next to Island Packers, who take you to the island (you'll also need to reserve a space for your rented kayak). You can rent kayaks for excursions or sign up for an

island cave tour (two-person tour $199 pp) out of Scorpion Anchorage.

The **Santa Barbara Adventure Company** (805/884-9283, www.sbadventureco.com, adults $199, children $170) runs day trips to the islands' sea caves from Santa Barbara Harbor. Possibilities include Painted Cave on Santa Cruz Island, cave tours that depart from Scorpion Anchorage, and infrequent trips to Santa Barbara Island for a five-hour guided paddle ($275). All-day excursions typically include breakfast and lunch in addition to the kayak tour of the cave and a snorkeling session.

Channel Islands Outfitters (805/899-4295, www.channelislandso.com, $125) offers a three-hour circumnavigation of Santa Barbara Island that involves a little sea cave exploration. Operating out of Oxnard's harbor, **Blue Ocean Kayaking** (3600 Cabezone Circle, Oxnard, 805/204-0977, www.blue-oceankayaking.com, $180 pp) specializes in kayaking tours of Anacapa Island. Their boat picks you up after kayaking so you get to see

© GRANT CUNNINGHAM, SANTA BARBARA ADVENTURE COMPANY

a Santa Barbara Adventure Company kayaking expedition

more of the island and never have to backtrack for the return trip.

Snorkeling and Diving Tours

Most dive operators are located in Ventura Harbor. **Peace Dive Boat** (1691 Spinnaker Dr., G Dock, Ventura Harbor, 805/650-3483, www.peaceboat.com, trips $105-525) plans trips to Santa Cruz and Anacapa for beginning and intermediate divers. They also offer lobster-hunting trips to Talcott Shoal at Santa Rosa for intermediate and advanced divers. **Cal Boat Diving** (805/486-1166, http://calboatdiving.com, trips $105-125, gear rental $45-65) also offers dives around Santa Cruz and Anacapa, along with gear rentals. Another option is Santa Barbara-based **Truth Aquatics** (301 W. Cabrillo Blvd., Santa Barbara, 805/962-1127, www.truthaquatics.com, $120-200), which schedules trips around Santa Cruz, Anacapa, Santa Rosa, and occasionally Santa Barbara Island. Based in San Pedro Harbor in Los Angeles, **The Great Escape** (866/348-3262, www.diveboat.com)

also guides dive trips out to southernmost Santa Barbara Island.

THE LANDSCAPE

Geography

The Channel Islands actually comprise eight islands off Southern California. The five northernmost islands—San Miguel Island, Santa Rosa Island, Santa Cruz Island, Anacapa Island, and Santa Barbara Island—are part of **Channel Islands National Park,** although the park owns and manages just one-quarter of the land on Santa Cruz Island; the **Nature Conservancy** owns and operates the western three-quarters of Santa Cruz Island land. The Channel Islands outside the national park's jurisdiction are San Nicholas, San Clemente, and Santa Catalina. Santa Catalina, located 22 miles off Los Angeles, has the only incorporated city on the archipelago: Avalon.

Geology

These islands are the result of a combination of volcanic action, plate tectonics, and changing sea levels that occurred millions of years ago. While the islands were never a part of the mainland, scientists believe that San Miguel, Santa Rosa, Santa Cruz, and Anacapa Islands were once part of a single larger island that they now refer to as Santarosae.

The popular **sea caves** of Anacapa Island and Santa Cruz Island are the result of waves crashing into the volcanic rocks of each island's coastline. Anacapa's shoreline in particular is decorated with arches, stacks, caves, surge channels, and blowholes caused by wave erosion.

One of the primary attractions on San Miguel Island is a geologic anomaly known as a **caliche forest.** It consists of calcified casts of ancient vegetation, which resemble stalagmites rising from the ground. They are the result of exposure to the island's persistent winds, which have blown away the topsoil.

Plants and Animals

Because of the Channel Islands' unique ecosystem, scientists have designated it the "Galapagos Islands of North America." The isolated landmasses are home to some 2,000 distinct plant and animal species, including 145 that are unique to the islands. These are known as endemic species, meaning that their populations are restricted to a particular region or location. These endemics have evolved because of the islands' isolation and relatively little contact with human populations.

The largest collection of endemics springs from a group of leaf succulents called **liveforevers.** Another interesting member of the Channel Islands' flora are the **island ironwood trees,** which are found on Santa Cruz Island, Santa Rosa Island, and farther south on San Clemente Island. These trees don't exist on the mainland today, but the discovery of fossils of the tree in Death Valley shows that they once grew there. The northeast side of Santa Rosa Island is home to a collection of **Torrey pines.** The only other place that this pine species occurs is in San Diego County's Torrey Pines State Reserve. Is has the smallest distribution of any pine species in the world.

Scientists have noticed that some plants and animals have evolved in response to their isolated environments. For instance, over many generations, some small animals seem to grow larger on the islands, while some larger plants and animals have become smaller. An example of a species becoming larger than their continental counterpart is the **giant coreopsis,** a member of the sunflower family that can be found on every island except San Clemente. A smaller coreopsis exists on mainland California and in Mexico's Baja Peninsula. The larger island version of the plant probably exists because there are fewer competitors and no grazing animals. Giant coreopsis is one of the most notable plants on Anacapa. It's a thick-stemmed, woody plant that can reach six feet in height. During spring, it turns green with yellow blossoms, while the rest of the year it is dormant. An example of dwarfism on the islands is the island fox, the largest native mammal on the archipelago. Smaller than its mainland relation, the gray fox, it's about the size of a domesticated cat. Its smaller size may be the result of the limited food options on the islands.

The population of **island foxes** has declined drastically, primarily due to predation by

---

WHICH ISLAND IS FOR YOU?

If you're interested in...

- **a day trip:** Anacapa or Santa Cruz
- **a weekend getaway:** Santa Cruz
- **hiking:** Santa Cruz or Santa Rosa
- **backpacking:** Santa Cruz
- **camping:** Santa Cruz
- **snorkeling or scuba diving:** Santa Barbara, Santa Cruz, or Anacapa
- **kayaking:** Santa Cruz or Anacapa
- **wildlife:** San Miguel or Santa Cruz
- **marinelife:** Santa Barbara, Santa Cruz, or Anacapa
- **plantlife:** Santa Rosa
- **solitude:** San Miguel

golden eagles. In 2004 the fox was designated an endangered species. A recovery program consists of captive breeding, reintroduction to the islands, and the removal of golden eagles from the area. Today, you may see island foxes roaming Santa Cruz Island's Scorpion Campground, scrounging for food.

The **island scrub jay** only lives in Santa Cruz Island's chaparral, woodland, and pine forests. It's the only endemic vertebrate species in the islands to be confined to just one island. The island scrub jay has a noticeably brighter blue plumage than other jays. It also uses different calls and lives longer than its mainland relatives. Birders frequently travel to Santa Cruz Island's Prisoners Harbor or Scorpion Ranch in an attempt to spot the rare bird.

The islands also boast rich marinelife. The tide pools and rocks are decorated with **starfish, sea urchins,** and **abalone.** Many species of fish inhabit the kelp beds and waters offshore, including bright **orange garibaldi,** vibrant **señoritas,** black-and-red **California sheephead,** and **eels.** Inhabitants of deeper waters around the islands include **sea otters, seals, sea lions, dolphins, whales,** and even **great white sharks.** A superb place to view seals and sea lions is San Miguel Island's Point Bennett. With 30,000 individuals from five species, it's one of the largest pinniped rookeries in the world.

HISTORY

Although the islands within Channel Islands National Park currently only have small human populations—mostly park employees and scientific researchers—the archipelago has a rich history. San Miguel Island has the richest paleontological and archaeological history, with over 500 Native American sites. The evidence found at Daisy Cave, located on the northeast side of the island, is substantial. A number of impressive artifacts, dating as far back 11,700 years, have been found here, including charred mammoth bones, primitive fishhooks, and part of a boat. There is evidence of humans living on Santa Rosa Island during the Pleistocene epoch, along with the animals they may have been hunting: pygmy mammoths.

The indigenous Chumash people used the Channel Islands as their hunting and fishing grounds. The Chumash built wooden canoes called *tomols* to travel back and forth to the mainland. Some Chumash settled on the islands, returning to the mainland to trade otter pelts and parts of marine mammals for edible plants that were unavailable on the islands. One Chumash legend says that the human race originated on Santa Cruz Island and then crossed a rainbow bridge to settle the mainland. Some of those early people fell off the rainbow into the ocean, where they became dolphins.

In 1542 the Portuguese explorer Juan Rodríguez Cabrillo visited the islands while exploring North America's west coast for Spain. The explorer and his crew tried to round Point Conception after their stay on San Miguel but were rebuffed by strong winds. They returned to San Miguel and anchored in Cuyler Harbor to repair damage to one of their ships. An unsubstantiated tale suggests that Cabrillo injured his leg from a fall on San Miguel and contracted gangrene, which caused his death, and that he was buried on the island. Another version of the story holds that the explorer was injured, died, and was buried on Santa Catalina Island. Today, a granite cross above San Miguel's Cuyler Harbor commemorates the explorer.

The European explorers introduced fatal diseases to the indigenous people while causing a depletion of natural resources on the archipelago. These two factors led to a drop the Chumash population on the islands. By 1822 the surviving Chumash people had moved to the mainland, many taken to the missions. The islands became home to Spanish ranching operations and fishing camps. Later, the U.S. military had outposts on Santa Rosa Island and Santa Barbara Island.

The march toward national park status began in 1938, when Anacapa and Santa Barbara became the Channel Islands National Monument. In 1980, San Miguel, Santa Rosa, Anacapa, Santa Barbara, and the eastern part of Santa Cruz were designated for protection as Channel Islands National Park.

Santa Cruz Island

Santa Cruz is the largest of the islands, and by far the most popular island to visit, in part because it most closely resembles the mainland. It's also the most hospitable: there are more buildings on this island than the others, and there is a campground near Scorpion Bay where you can pitch a tent, store your food in metal lockers, and explore on foot.

At the center of the island, the thick, dense vegetation feels almost prehistoric. The landscape is also marked by trees and dry creeks. The former grasslands are often barren, depending on the amount of rainfall each winter. This is also the only place in the world to see endemic species such as the Channel Islands fox and the island scrub jay. Large, beautiful ravens also make their homes here.

The Nature Conservancy, an environmental organization, owns 76 percent of the scorpion-shaped Santa Cruz Island, while the National Park Service maintains the remaining 24 percent. The two primary points of entry onto Santa Cruz are **Scorpion Anchorage** and **Prisoners Harbor.** The island has a range of hiking trails, snorkeling opportunities, two campgrounds, and an abundance of amazing sea caves that can be explored by kayak.

Before European colonization, Native Americans were a strong presence on Santa Cruz; it's believed that 1,000 Chumash people

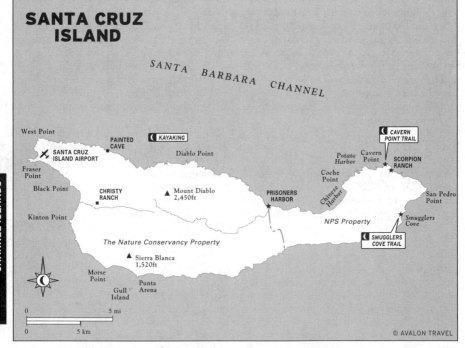

© GABRIEL SKVOR

the coastline of Santa Cruz Island

resided on the island in 11 villages. The island's name is said to have come from an interaction between the Chumash on Santa Cruz and members of the Portola expedition, the first recorded European exploration of California, in 1769. A member of the expedition, a priest named Juan Vizcaíno, visited the island that year and mistakenly left behind a staff topped with a cross. The friendly Chumash returned the staff to the Spanish, causing them to refer to the island as "La Isla de Santa Cruz," the island of the holy cross.

In the early 19th century, Santa Cruz was taken over by ranchers; early sheep ranchers were soon followed by cattle ranchers. One notable early rancher, Justinian Clare, planted vineyards on the island and produced a wine that was popular in the area until Prohibition. The Nature Conservancy took possession of most of the island in 1987. The National Park Service took over the east end of the island in 1997 and removed the last of the sheep.

Travel time to the island is 90 minutes, and travelers offload onto a short pier directly connected to shore, although shore landings from a skiff are sometimes done, depending on the conditions.

SIGHTS
Scorpion Ranch Complex

The extensive ranching operation that began on Santa Cruz Island in the mid-1800s continued until the 1980s. Today, the **Scorpion Ranch Complex** gives park visitors a glimpse into this isolated way of life. Farming equipment, some dating back to the 1880s, and wooden ranch structures are scattered around the complex in various states of decay. Today, the two-story Scorpion Ranch house, built in 1887, hosts a small visitors center downstairs with displays on threatened species, conservation, and the indigenous Chumash people. Another room is set up as a model ranch kitchen. The small caves in the nearby hillside, once used for

CHANNEL ISLANDS

© GABRIEL SKVOR

Santa Cruz Island has the most hiking trails of the Channel Islands.

storing dairy products, are now home to roosting Townsend's big-eared bats.

Prisoners Harbor

Prisoners Harbor is one of two entry points onto the island (the other is Scorpion Anchorage). It also offers access to the adjacent Nature Conservancy land. It was once the site of the island's second-largest Chumash village, called Xasas, that was occupied for over 3,000 years and had a population of 95-160 Chumash when Europeans first came to the region. Prisoners Harbor got its modern name from 30 or so criminals who were dropped off in the harbor by the Mexican government in 1830. Historians speculate that the prisoners attempted to escape from the island to the mainland using homemade rafts; some may have perished on the journey.

In the late 1800s, Prisoners Harbor was the main point of entry for the island's ranching operations, with a shipping center and warehouse. Although the main ranch house was torn down in 1968 after suffering flood damage, a warehouse from 1887, some ranching structures, and cattle corrals still exist in the area.

SPORTS AND RECREATION
Hiking

Santa Cruz Island has the most hiking trails of the Channel Islands, ranging from easy loops to more strenuous all-day hikes. Most hikes start from Scorpion Anchorage, where most visitors arrive on the island, but a few begin at the alternate landing site, Prisoners Harbor.

☾ CAVERN POINT LOOP

Cavern Point Loop (2 miles round-trip, moderate) starts at Scorpion Beach and offers superb views of the ocean, the island's rugged coastline, and on clear days without fog, the mainland. It leads to a cliff-top vista point where you can usually see soaring western gulls and pelicans dotting the sky or California sea lions and harbor seals in the ocean below. You may also spot migrating gray whales during the winter. Hike the loop

© GABRIEL SKVOR

Cavern Point

clockwise to avoid a steep climb by heading up from Scorpion Campground campsite 22 and looping back to the Scorpion Anchorage. Along the way, note the white chalky rocks coloring the hillsides. These light-colored deposits are skeletons of prehistoric diatoms, single-celled marine organisms. At Cavern Point, you can opt to continue two miles farther along the North Bluff Trail to reach Potato Harbor.

◀ SMUGGLERS COVE TRAIL
One of the best day hikes on the islands, the **Smugglers Cove Trail** (7.5 miles round-trip, moderate) starts at Scorpion Beach and follows an old ranch road that cuts across the island's eastern interior to a secluded cove. Begin at the Scorpion Anchorage basin and follow the single-track trail that originates on the left side of the canyon when you're facing west. Along the road, you'll notice an impressive stone retaining wall that was constructed during the island's ranching years. In the adjacent fields are piles of rocks that ranch workers created when

clearing the land for farming. Ascend until you connect to the old ranch road, known as Smugglers Road. After two miles you'll enjoy views of the island's eastern tip and Anacapa Island, jutting out from the sea like a giant shark fin. The descent on the way to the cove passes by an olive grove that was planted in the late 1800s. There are a few picnic tables and eucalyptus trees at the edge of the cove's scenic cobblestone beach. The west end has tide pools, where you can spot green anemones and, if you're lucky, rare black abalone. Save some energy for the hike back, which is steep at first. Also bring plenty of drinking water; none is available at Smugglers Cove.

SCORPION CANYON LOOP
Scorpion Canyon Loop (4.5 miles round-trip, moderate) starts at Scorpion Beach and treats you to a hike through a unique canyon, with a few stunning coastal views thrown in for good measure. Begin by taking the single-track trail out of the Scorpion Basin, on the left side of the canyon when you are looking west. Continue

on Smugglers Road toward the oil well. Instead of continuing left on the road to the cove, bear right, and then take another right that descends into Scorpion Canyon. Within the canyon is a range of vegetation that includes island scrub oaks, coast live oaks, island cherries, monkey-flowers, and lemonade berries. Look for the elusive island scrub jays in the oak, cherry, and toyon trees of the canyon's northwest fork. The canyon trail continues into the campground, where you can follow the road east out to the anchorage area.

POTATO HARBOR TRAIL

To view the section of north-facing coastline past Cavern Point, head out on the **Potato Harbor Trail** (5 miles round-trip, moderate), which starts at Scorpion Beach. Follow the road to the ranch area into the campground and continue to the upper section of the campground. Veer right onto the Potato Harbor Overlook Road. Continue until you arrive at the Potato Harbor overlook. While there's no access down to the harbor, you get a stunning view of the deep indentation in the steep coastline.

MONTANON RIDGE HIKE

The toughest day hike out Scorpion Anchorage is the **Montanon Ridge Hike** (8 miles round-trip, strenuous), starting at Scorpion Beach, which rewards you with true solitude and a superb view of the island's mountainous spine and the sea on either side. Hike up Smugglers Road, then take the route off to the right that leads toward the oil well and Montanon Ridge. The trail becomes steep as it climbs toward some radio towers in the distance. Keep going until you get to the 1,808-foot-high Montanon Peak.

PRISONERS HARBOR HIKES

More strenuous hikes for energetic, experienced hikers are available to and from the second landing at Prisoners Harbor. They appeal primarily to backpackers who want to camp in the backcountry and see as much of the island as possible. The long, challenging **Scorpion Beach to Prisoners Harbor Hike** (28 miles round-trip, strenuous) starts at Scorpion Beach and covers much of the eastern portion of the island. It's possible to hike just one way (14 miles) from Scorpion Beach to Prisoners Harbor if you arrange a boat pickup through Island Packers. Another option is to make a reservation to camp overnight at the Del Norte backcountry camp and hike the return trip to Scorpion Beach (14 miles) the next day.

Del Norte Camp Trail (7 miles round-trip, strenuous) starts at Prisoners Harbor and climbs up a historic ranch road through scrub brush and oak woodlands to the only backcountry campground on the islands. It's located in a shaded oak grove with views of the coastline. Bring drinking water; there is none at the campground.

You must make a reservation with Island Packers to land at Prisoners Harbor in order to hike the **Pelican Bay Trail** (4 miles round-trip, strenuous), which starts at Prisoners Harbor. You'll be accompanied by an Island Packers guide. It begins with a climb up a hill that offers views of Prisoners Harbor's pier. Then it passes from National Park Service land onto Nature Conservancy land to an overlook with views of Pelican Bay. Along the way, you'll pass through ironwood, oak, and pine forests.

◀ Kayaking

Santa Cruz Island is pocked with some of the world's largest and most incredible sea caves. The best way to explore them is by kayak. Some of the caves are as large as cathedrals—and even more breathtaking. The ocean surging in the cavernous depths creates a low rumble, and the walls are decorated with starfish and a sublime green glow. Outside the caves, sea lions and seals periscope their heads out of the water among mats of kelp.

The easiest caves to reach are right in Scorpion Bay. Paddle northwest (left if you are facing the water) out of Scorpion Anchorage toward **Cavern Point.** You will start spotting sea caves immediately. Far from Scorpion

© ST. ART THORN-ON

kayaking a sea cave on Santa Cruz Island

Anchorage, on the northwest side of the island, is **Painted Cave,** one of the largest and deepest sea caves in the world. The cave entrance is 160 feet high, large enough to admit a small boat, and the cavern extends 0.25 miles deep. In spring, a waterfall veils the entrance. The cavern is named for its vibrantly colored rocks and algae.

If you are serious about exploring Santa Cruz's sea caves by kayak, consider picking up a copy of David Bunnell's 1988 book *Sea Caves of Santa Cruz Island.*

Snorkeling and Scuba Diving

Just east and west of the Scorpion Anchorage Pier, where boats pull into the harbor, are kelp beds that are terrific for snorkeling and scuba diving. The wreck of the **USS** *Peacock,* a fairly intact World War II minesweeper, is located 50 yards off Scorpion Rocks, submerged in 40-60 feet of water.

To dive the island's other spots, you'll have to have your own boat or plan a trip with a dive operator out of Ventura Harbor. On the south-facing side of the island, just west of Smugglers Cove, **Yellow Banks** has four miles of extensive kelp forests and reefs in water 40-80 feet deep. You'll encounter diverse marinelife, including lobsters, sheephead, bat rays, barracudas, and blue sharks. Farther west, **Gull Island,** a state marine reserve, is centered on a small rock island one mile offshore. Exploring its thick kelp beds, you'll likely see blue coral, abalone, and even sea lions.

CAMPING

The most popular campground on Santa Cruz Island is the **Scorpion Ranch Campground** (877/444-6777, www.recreation.gov, $15), a short walk in from where the boat drops you off at Scorpion Anchorage. The lower campground (a 0.5-mile walk) has 22 sites in a eucalyptus-shaded canyon, while the upper loop has three regular sites and six group sites in a meadow. The upper loop is a nice spot but it's twice as far to lug your camping gear (a full mile). The campgrounds have a picnic table and a food storage box at every site. Pit toilets and water are also available.

There's also camping accessed from Prisoners Harbor; it's a strenuous 3.5-mile hike to the **Del**

Norte Backcountry Campsite (877/444-6777, www.recreation.gov, $15). It's a remote spot in an oak grove at 700 feet elevation. There are picnic tables and a pit toilet, but no drinking water is available, so you'll need to bring your own.

Anacapa Island

Anacapa actually comprises three islets. Together, they're 5 miles long and 0.25 miles wide. The land area of all three totals just one square mile. The island's name comes from the Chumash word for "mirage" or "ever-changing"—fitting adjectives for this small collection of islands that look like three long dashes on the horizon. Anacapa is wilder and more barren than nearby Santa Cruz Island. There are no trees here, and the island's low vegetation almost looks like a landscape recovering from fire. A coreopsis (tree sunflower) forest covers parts of the island. Resembling a charred Joshua tree most of the year, the coreopsis blossoms with yellow flowers for a few weeks every

March and April. From the end of April until early July, western gulls make their nests here. Thousands of the white birds line up on the island like scattered bowling pins. Protecting their eggs and newborn chicks, they squawk angrily and dive-bomb visitors in an attempt to drive them away. Keep your distance: These territorial birds will fly straight toward your head.

Visitors are able to access East Anacapa, a desertlike island with steep cliffs that is home to the stunning Inspiration Point, the Anacapa Lighthouse, and Arch Rock, a 40-foot-high rock window off the islet's eastern tip. There's also a two-mile trail system, a small visitors

© STUART THORNTON

Anacapa Island

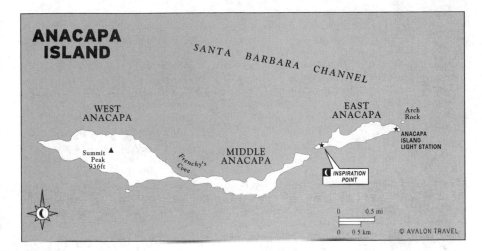

center, and a campground. Although there is a rangers residence and a few buildings on Anacapa, it is still a difficult place to sustain an existence. Supplies are hauled up out of the steep Landing Cove, a rocky inlet that serves as the island's point of entry. Electricity is provided by solar energy, while water has to come from the mainland and then be stored in the Water Tank Building, which has two 55,000-gallon redwood water tanks.

Even landing and disembarking from a boat onto Anacapa Island is a minor adventure. The boats back into tiny Landing Cove and up against the pier, where visitors exit the boat. Then they climb a metal staircase erected on the side of the steep shoreline. Travel time from the mainland is just 45 minutes.

SIGHTS
◖ Inspiration Point

If you have seen a photo of the Channel Islands on a calendar or a postcard, it's most likely the spectacular view from Inspiration Point. From this high vantage point on the west end of the island, Middle Anacapa Island and West Anacapa Island rise out of the ocean like a giant sea serpent's spine. Overhead and below, gulls soar and do aerial acrobatics. The healthy blue-green ocean is spotted with rust-colored kelp forests. The large mass of Santa Cruz Island

is visible in the distance, bulging out from behind the other Anacapa Islands. From the bench at Inspiration Point, you can sit and soak in the view and the solitude of the Channel Islands. Its name is the most apt description of Inspiration Point; in a word, it's inspiring.

Anacapa Island Light Station

Perched on the highest point of East Anacapa Island, this 39-foot tall white lighthouse tower looks like a chess piece surveying the rocky landscape. A number of ships have crashed here. One of the earliest wrecks was the steamship *Winfield Scott*. The boat was wrecked on the rocks of Middle Anacapa Island, but all 450 passengers and crewmembers survived. Shipping accidents continued until a 50-foot metal tower with a light on top was mounted on East Anacapa. The wrecks continued until the Bureau of Lighthouses finally allowed funding of a full light station with a fog signal and radio, which was constructed in 1932. The light station was staffed and maintained by a crew into the 1960s, when it was automated. The original Fresnel lens was replaced by a solar-powered acrylic lens in 1989 and moved to the small visitors center, where it's still on display.

There are no tours of the light station, but you can get a better view and a photo

a nesting western gull on Anacapa Island

opportunity by hiking the easy 0.5-mile round-trip trail from the visitors center.

SPORTS AND RECREATION
Hiking
INSPIRATION POINT LOOP

The easy, flat **Inspiration Point Loop** (1.5 miles round-trip, easy) starts at the visitors center and takes you around almost the entire island. On the way to stunning Inspiration Point, the trail includes stops at **Pinniped Point** and **Cathedral Cove,** where you can view sea lions stacked like sand bags on pocket beaches hundreds of feet below. The path also passes a Chumash midden, an archaeological site of broken seashells. In early spring you'll see a painter's palette of colorful wildflowers, while in late spring you'll dodge aggressive western gulls protecting their nesting sites.

Starting from the visitors center, the loop is easy to find and follow. A trail map is available outside the small visitors center for $1. Stay on the trails at all times to preserve this precious ecosystem—and to avoid falling from the edges of Anacapa's sheer cliffs.

◖ Kayaking

With 130 sea caves and numerous arches along its short coastline, Anacapa is ripe for exploration by sea kayak. Due to the islands' rugged cliffs, access to the water is only available from East Anacapa's Landing Cove. Bring your own gear or rent a kayak from **Channel Islands Kayak Center** (805/984-5995, www.cikayak.com, single kayaks $35, double kayaks $55). **Blue Ocean Kayaking** (3600 Cabezone Circle, Oxnard, 805/204-0977, www.blueoceankayaking.com, $180 pp) specializes in paddling tours of Anacapa Island.

The closest sea cave is located at the rear wall of Landing Cove. Another popular kayaking destination is the 40-foot-high **Arch Rock,** less than 0.25 miles east of the islet; Arch Rock is the official symbol of Channel Islands National Park. On the north end of the island, west of Landing Cove, is scenic **Cathedral Cove,**

© STUART THORNTON

Anacapa Island's breathtaking Inspiration Point

named for the impressive Cathedral Arch. It's a 0.6 mile paddle. **Cathedral Cave** has five entrances, all leading into an impressive chamber, one of the largest on Anacapa. During low tide, brightly colored sponges are exposed. For a longer paddle from Landing Cove, head to **Frenchy's Cove,** a long 3.75-mile paddle to the northeastern tip of West Anacapa Island. A hermit named "Frenchy" LaDreau lived here from 1928 to 1956, collecting drinking water from cavern seeps. Just west of the cove is Frenchy's Cave, where he stored liquor during Prohibition.

Snorkeling and Scuba Diving

Landing Cove ranges 10-50 feet deep. The reefs and kelp beds host calico bass, lobster, and abalone. At the east end of Landing Cove is an underwater arch at 30-50 feet deep that scuba divers can explore. Nearby **Cathedral Cove** is fairly shallow and usually calm (unless there are prevailing northwest winds), making it a good spot for beginning divers and snorkelers. Among the marinelife are reef fish, garibaldi, calico bass, and abalone, but the most popular animals are the playful sea lions. **Frenchy's Cove** has fairly shallow water, 10-35 feet deep, making it a good place for snorkeling; it also has a nice beach where you can take a break. Scuba diving is also possible on **Arch Rock,** where you can see kelp, a reef, anemones, and sea fans at 55-80 feet.

CAMPING

Without the protection of trees, the **Anacapa Campground** (877/444-6777, www.recreation.gov, $15) is very exposed to the sun and the wind. This primitive camping area has seven sites with flat spots and picnic tables. There are also some regularly serviced pit toilets. No drinking water is available. It can be reached from Landing Cove by a 0.5-mile hike that includes 154 stairs. The camping area is just a few feet off the Inspiration Point Loop Trail.

CHANNEL ISLANDS

Santa Rosa Island

At 53,000 acres, rugged, windy Santa Rosa is the second-largest island in Channel Islands National Park. Less visited than Anacapa or Santa Cruz, it boasts stunning white-sand beaches and coastal lagoons that seem virtually untouched. Its mountainous spine rises to 1,574 feet at Soledad Peak, offering beautiful views of neighboring Santa Cruz Island and the mainland in the distance.

While the western portion of the island is sandy without much elevation, the grassy rolling hills on the eastern end made it an ideal place to raise cattle. The Vail and Vickers Cattle Company ranched here from 1902 to 1998. During the 1920s, the Vail family also brought Roosevelt elk and mule deer to the island to be hunted for sport. While that big game operation ended in 2011, elk and deer still live on the island.

The end of ranching on Santa Rosa has been a positive development for the island's unique vegetation. It's home to about 500 plant species, including six endemic species that include the Santa Rosa subspecies of the Torrey pine. Santa Rosa also has protected archaeological sites dedicated to studying the artifacts of the indigenous Chumash people. The remains of a pygmy mammoth—just 4-6 feet tall—were discovered here in 1994.

Travel time from the mainland is about three hours by boat; you have to climb a 20-foot steel-rung ladder to reach flat land.

SIGHTS
Vail and Vickers Ranch Area

At one time there were over 9,000 cattle on Santa Rosa Island. Inland from the pier at Bechers Bay are remnants of the massive Vail and Vickers Cattle Ranch, which operated here from 1900 until 1998. In addition to the main ranch house, there are corrals, barns, a bunkhouse, a schoolhouse, and even an airstrip. Before Vail and Vickers came to the island, this was one of the largest sheep ranches in the state; Vail and Vickers transitioned from sheep ranching to cattle ranching. The company also ran a commercial hunting operation. Notable people such as California governor Earl Warren and entertainer Bing Crosby came to the island to hunt elk.

Torrey Pines

Torrey pines, some of the world's rarest pine trees, grow on the sandstone bluffs on the northeast end of Santa Rosa. In the early 1900s there were only 100 of these trees in the world. Today, due to conservation efforts, there are now more than 4,000. The only other Torrey pines are located on the mainland in San Diego County's Torrey Pines State Reserve. Santa Rosa's Torrey pines are a little smaller than the mainland version but have slightly larger cones. Torrey Pines can be reached by a moderate five-mile round-trip hike, starting from the boat pier and landing strip area.

Water Canyon Beach

Water Canyon Beach feels light years away from mainland Southern California's crowded seashores. Located in the middle of Bechers Bay, just over one mile from the Bechers Bay Pier, this two-mile stretch of scenic white sand is flanked by bluffs and the blue ocean. It's not unlikely that you'll have the beach all to yourself. It can get gusty: On a typical day, the island has winds of up to 20 knots. There are no facilities; potable water and an outhouse are available 0.5 miles away.

SPORTS AND RECREATION

Due to the frequent high winds, water sports are only recommended for those with significant experience. That said, Santa Rosa Island is the perfect place for anyone who wants to take a hike.

Hiking

If you don't mind sweating, Santa Rosa has a handful of hikes. All of these hikes start at the Bechers Bay Pier.

CHERRY CANYON TRAIL

The **Cherry Canyon Trail** (3.5 miles round-trip, moderate, start at the pier) provides a good introduction to the island. Hike inland from the pier through the Vail and Vickers Ranch complex, and then take a right on Soledad Road. Turn left into Cherry Canyon and look for island foxes wandering around in the canyon. The trail then rises to a ridge with views of Bechers Bay. To complete the loop, take a left on Telephone Road back toward the ranch and pier area.

LOBO CANYON

The **Lobo Canyon Trail** (13 miles round-trip, strenuous) starts at the pier and travels through a canyon sculpted by wind and water. At some points, the sandstone walls rise 100 to 300 feet. Some of the canyon's distinctive features are honeycombed rock formations known as tafoni. Other sections of the sandstone canyon walls are reminiscent of the U.S. Southwest. The canyon broadens at the far end, where the canyon's creek meanders into a secluded coastal cove.

BLACK MOUNTAIN TRAIL

The **Black Mountain Trail** (8 miles round-trip, strenuous) is a steep climb, starting at the pier, to the 1,298-foot summit of Black Mountain. On clear days you'll not only be rewarded with views of the rest of Santa Rosa but also glimpses of San Miguel Island, Santa Cruz Island, and the mainland. The mountain is home to unique plant species,

CHANNEL ISLANDS

including endemic island oaks and a small grove of Bishop pine. The vegetation on Black Mountain is known as a cloud forest because the vegetation absorbs moisture from the frequent fog. Hikers can make the journey a loop by combining it with the Cherry Canyon Trail, Telephone Road, and Soledad Road.

EAST POINT TRAIL

The **East Point Trail** (12 miles round-trip, strenuous) starts at the pier and covers a good portion of the island's northeast coast, including the rare Torrey pine forest and some unrestricted beaches. Its destination is East Point, home to multiple archaeological sites, mostly old Chumash campsites.

THE CHANNEL ISLANDS' SPECIAL SPECIES

© STUART THORNTON

an island fox

Where are you going to find the Santa Cruz Island scrub jay, the island fox, or the island night lizard? Only in the Channel Islands. Due to its remote location, the five islands of Channel Islands National Park have 23 endemic terrestrial animals and 11 land birds that are now island-only subspecies. These animals have evolved and changed from their counterparts on the mainland to adapt to the islands' unique natural habitat.

The island scrub jay has the smallest range of any North American bird species: 96-square-mile Santa Cruz Island. It's a brighter blue, has a bigger bill, and is larger than its mainland counterpart. Meanwhile, the island fox is the largest of the Channel Islands' native mammals. But

the animal is a third smaller than its relatives on the mainland. This doesn't mean that these special species are entirely safe, even on the isolated Channel Islands; in the 20th century, habitat destruction, predation by feral cats, and a 1959 wildfire led to the extinction of an endemic subspecies of song sparrow on Santa Barbara Island. Luckily, the island fox population has recovered since hitting a low of 100 animals on San Miguel, Santa Rosa, and Santa Cruz Islands in 1999. A captive breeding program has now stabilized the species' numbers, and if you camp in Santa Cruz Island's Scorpion Ranch Campground, be prepared to hide your food from the clever creatures.

Snorkeling and Scuba Diving

Diving off Santa Rosa Island is more difficult than Anacapa and Santa Cruz Islands. Among the many challenges are strong currents, large swells, limited visibility, and probably worst of all, frequent strong winds. It's not for beginners.

The anchorage at **Bechers Bay** is not known for its visibility, but it is possible to snorkel or dive here when it is calm. The eastern end has reefs where you can see lobsters, scallops, and anemones. It ranges 25-60 feet in depth. **Talcott Shoal,** off the island's northwest tip, is popular with advanced divers because 50-80 feet down, shale ledges host rockfish, sheephead, horn sharks, and most impressively, an abundant population of larger-than-average lobsters. It's best to plan a trip with a local dive operator such as the **Peace Dive Boat** (805/650-3483, www.peaceboat.com, $140) or **Truth Aquatics** (301 W. Cabrillo Blvd., Santa Barbara, 805/962-1127, www.truthaquatics.com, $120-200). Only very experienced divers should attempt the **East End Pinnacles,** formations that rise from the bottom of the ocean to within 40-50 feet of the water's surface off the island's east end. Fish and anemones can be found here. The visibility can be good, but the currents are strong.

CAMPING

Hike in 1.5 miles to reach **Water Canyon Campground** (877/444-6777, www.recreation. gov, $15), where you'll find 15 sites with picnic tables and pit toilets. No drinking water is available. **Backcountry camping** (805/658-5711, free) is also available on the beach mid-August-December. The East Point to South Point Beaches are open August 15-September 15. All beaches are open to backcountry camping September 16-December 31, except for those around Sandy Point and between Carrington Point and East Point.

San Miguel Island

Geographer D. L. Johnson called San Miguel "one of the windiest, most maritime, and wave-pounded areas on the west coast of North America." The westernmost of the park's islands, it's a remote and desolate place but offers stark beauty, such as the stunning beach at Cuyler Harbor and an alien-looking caliche forest. There are also more species of plants and animals here, including birds, than on the other islands. San Miguel also has the most paleontological and archaeological sites of any of the Channel Islands. There are over 500 Native American sites alone, including Daisy Cave, which has the oldest shell midden ever found in North America.

Due to fierce weather, sea kayaking, snorkeling, diving, and swimming are extremely limited on San Miguel. Hikers need to be accompanied by a ranger. Travel time from the mainland is about four hours. A skiff will usually run you to shore, but it depends on the weather conditions, which can be hit-and-miss.

SIGHTS
Cuyler Harbor

Most visitors arrive at **Cuyler Harbor,** a large half-moon bay on the northeast side of San Miguel. There are tide pools at the east end of the scenic two-mile-long white sand beach. Western gulls, California brown pelicans, cormorants, and Cassin's auklets nest on Prince Island, which sits in the mouth of the harbor.

On a bluff above the harbor, an inscribed stone cross is dedicated to Juan Rodríguez Cabrillo, the Portuguese explorer who navigated the California coast for Spain and anchored here in 1542 to make some repairs to his ships. Although there is no concrete evidence, Cabrillo is rumored to have died on the island during a return visit in 1543. He contracted gangrene in his leg following a fall.

◖ Point Bennett

The very few who make it to **Point Bennett** on San Miguel Island are treated to the sight

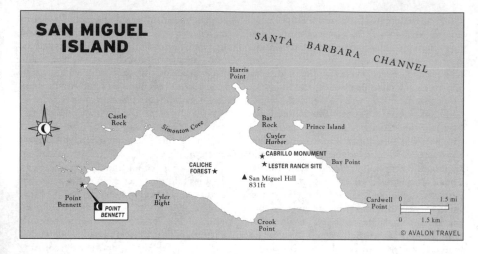

of one of nature's largest concentrations of marine mammals: an amazing array of some 30,000 pinnipeds in six species. It can only be reached by a **ranger-guided hike** (16 miles round-trip, strenuous). You can watch the sea mammals from the top of sand dunes as close as 20 feet away. California sea lions and northern elephant seals are the most plentiful, although there are often sizeable numbers of northern fur seals and harbor seals as well. It's rarer to spot northern sea lions and Guadalupe fur seals. To contact a ranger to accompany you to Point Bennett, call the park headquarters (805/658-5730), or from a boat use Marine Radio Channel 16.

Caliche Forest

Caliche is the sand castings of ancient vegetation. This forest of fossils resembles stalagmites protruding from the ground. It occurred when the root systems of the vegetation were replaced by sand that was later cemented by calcium carbonate; the roots were sheathed in caliche and then decomposed. You can only see these alien formations accompanied by a ranger on a **guided hike** (5 miles round-trip, strenuous) that starts at Cuyler Harbor and goes to

an overlook. To schedule a hike, call the park headquarters (805/658-5730), or from a boat use Marine Radio Channel 16.

Lester Ranch Site

Hike inland from Cuyler Harbor through a canyon (2 miles round-trip, moderate) with native vegetation to the **Lester Ranch Site,** where the Lester family lived from 1930 to 1942. Patriarch Herbert Lester proclaimed himself "king of San Miguel" and amassed a collection of shipwreck artifacts. His wife, Elizabeth Lester, educated their two daughters and later penned the book *The Legendary King of San Miguel* about her time on the isolated isle. The ranch house burned down in 1967; all that remains today are a cistern, a root cellar, and a pile of rubble that was once the living-room chimney.

Cardwell Point

If you want to catch a glimpse of sea lions but the thought of hiking 16 miles to Point Bennett exhausts you, hike to **Cardwell Point** (6 miles round-trip), starting from Cuyler Harbor. The Cardwell Point viewing area gets you as close to sea lions and seals as Point Bennett does, but

© FOLLIE RODRÍGUEZ

the monument to Portuguese explorer Juan Rodríguez Cabrillo

there are not nearly as many animals here. On clear days there are views of Santa Rosa Island in the distance.

HIKING

All of the hikes on San Miguel start from Cuyler Harbor. You're free to explore the two-mile Cuyler Harbor Beach, the one-mile hike to the ranger station, and the two-mile Lester Ranch Site Hike on your own. Hiking beyond the ranger station requires a permit and a ranger acting as your escort. That includes two of the most worthwhile hikes, to the Caliche Forest and to Point Bennett. Rangers or volunteers are always available to offer hikes when an Island Packers boat comes to San Miguel. To arrange for a hike prior to mainland departure, call the park headquarters (805/658-5730).

CAMPING

The nine primitive sites of the **San Miguel Campground** (877/444-6777, www.recreation. gov, $15) can be reached by a steep one-mile hike uphill. There are picnic tables and pit toilets. No drinking water is available, so you'll need to bring your own.

Santa Barbara Island

One-square-mile Santa Barbara Island is the smallest of the park's islands—little more than a small dome-shaped rock in the lonely Pacific, virtually impossible to see from the mainland. Secluded and lonely, it's a rare stop. As the southernmost island in the National Park, it has warmer waters, which offer some diving opportunities. Santa Barbara Island is also home to some impressive seabird colonies, including one of the world's largest colonies of Xantus's murrelets. There is also a sea lion rookery on the island.

Because this island doesn't have fresh water, it was probably never the site of a permanent Native American village, but there is evidence that early residents from the mainland used it as a stopping point on fishing trips. Spanish conquistador and explorer Sebastián Vizcaíno stopped on the island in 1602. The first known inhabitants were the Hyder family in the early 1900s. They erected 11 buildings here and raised crops. Later, between 1942 and 1946, the military occupied the islands, building barracks.

Travel time from the mainland is just over three hours; once here, you have to climb a steel-rung ladder from a skiff, then laboriously trudge up a 0.25-mile set of steps to reach the top.

SPORTS AND RECREATION
Hiking

The island has just over five miles of hiking trails, all starting from the visitors center. One of Santa Barbara Island's most distinct features is the 130-foot-high arch on its northern tip. It can be reached by the short **Arch Point Trail** (1 mile round-trip, moderate). Although you can't see the unique geologic feature from the trail, during the springtime it offers views of goldfields and coreopsis coloring the island a vibrant yellow. The **Elephant Seal Cove Hike** (2.5 miles round-trip, moderate) leads to a cliff edge looking down over a cove teeming with elephant seals. Similarly, the short **Sea Lion Rookery Hike** (2 miles round-trip, moderate) ends at a steep cliff looking down on a colony of sea lions. The Rookery is also a popular diving spot. The **Webster Point Hike** (3 miles round-trip, moderate) takes you to a mitten-shaped point on the west end of Santa Barbara Island. For a view of the whole island, take the **Signal Peak Hike** (3 miles round-trip, moderate) to its tallest point (634 feet). In spring, both are covered in wildflowers.

Snorkeling and Scuba Diving

Because it's the southernmost island, the waters off Santa Barbara Island are a little warmer for snorkeling and diving. Snorkelers in **Landing Cove** can view sea stars, sea urchins, lobsters,

SANTA BARBARA ISLAND

Arch Point

Shag Rock

LIGHT BEACON

Webster Point

Landing Harbor

▲ Signal Peak 634 ft

Sutil Island

0   0.25 mi

0   0.25 km

© AVALON TRAVEL

rockfish, and bright orange garibaldi in 20-40 feet of water. Perhaps the most popular dive site on the island is **The Rookery,** where a multitude of playful and curious seals interact with divers and snorkelers. The water is 20-35 feet deep. About 0.75 miles off Webster Point, **Arch Reef** is named for the 50-foot-wide underwater arch 70 feet below the surface. Swimming through the arch, you'll encounter rockfish, lingcod, and schools of mackerel. The arch itself is covered in anemones and starfish. **Shag Rock** is an islet located 200 yards off the island's north shore. The dive site is 30-50 feet deep, with reefs that extend into the sand. You may see bat rays, leopard sharks, and halibut.

Santa Barbara Island is some distance south of the other islands in Channel Islands National Park. Based out of San Pedro Harbor in Los Angeles, **The Great Escape** (866/348-3262, www.diveboat.com) does dive trips to the island. Santa Barbara-based **Truth Aquatics** (805/962-1127, www.truthaquatics. com, $120-200) also has the occasional Santa Barbara Island trip.

CAMPING

The **Santa Barbara Island Campground** (877/444-6777, www.recreation.gov, $15) has 10 primitive sites with pit toilets and picnic tables. No drinking water is available, so you'll need to bring your own. It can be reached after a steep 0.5-mile hike from the visitors center.

SAN LUIS OBISPO AND PASO ROBLES

Locals call San Luis Obispo by its nickname, SLO, and a visit to the city will immediately impress on anyone that "slow" is the order of the day. But the secret is out, and a burgeoning wine industry and excellent quality of life means that SLO is starting to speed up. With a beautiful downtown fronted by Higuera Street and the accompanying river walk, San Luis Obispo is beginning to receive attention for its idyllic way of life, proximity to the ocean and mountains, wide-open tracts of land, and nearly ideal weather.

Paso Robles, 30 minutes north of San Luis Obispo along U.S. 101, is the heart of the wine industry in San Luis Obispo County, and this cowboy town, home to fewer than 30,000 people, is garnering worldwide acclaim for its wines. Paso Robles is also a hop, skip, and a jump from the coast, where nearly one million people flock to the tiny hamlet of San Simeon on the rugged Pacific coast to visit Hearst Castle each year. But El Paso de Robles, known simply as "Paso" by locals, is slowly moving away from its Western roots and embracing a more cosmopolitan vibe. Artisanal cheese makers, high-end restaurants and wineries, and a thriving competitive olive oil industry share the downtown with renegade dive bars and local mom-and-pop venues. You're just as likely to see a tractor heading through town as you are a limo packed with eager wine tasters.

PLANNING YOUR TIME

Since San Luis Obispo is called SLO, that's really how it should be explored: slowly. You can get the feel of SLO in a weekend, but a long three-day

© STUART THORNTON

HIGHLIGHTS

place to stop for the night, a meal, a photo op—or even just to gawk (page 236).

◖ Higuera Street: Shaded by trees and lined with shops, restaurants, and bars, this lively one-way road is the center of San Luis Obispo (page 237).

◖ Bishop Peak: It's well worth the one-hour hike to the top of this 1,546-foot volcanic peak for the commanding views of San Luis Obispo and the surrounding area (page 246).

◖ Pirate's Cove and Cave: This scenic strip of beach on a small bay attracts sun-worshippers—with and without swimsuits (page 252).

◖ Kayaking and Stand-Up Paddleboarding: Shielded from the battering winds by Point San Luis, the waters off Avila Beach are ideal for a paddling excursion (page 255).

◖ Paso Robles Downtown Square and City Park: With trees, picnic tables, a gazebo, and even games of horseshoes, this grassy one-block town park is like something out of a Norman Rockwell painting (page 266).

◖ Eberle Winery: Enjoy complimentary tastings and wine-cave tours hosted by this pioneering winery, which produces bold red wines at moderate prices (page 274).

◖ Madonna Inn: Overrun with pink kitsch, this flamboyant roadside attraction is a unique

weekend is even better to explore, get into the groove of this laid-back town, stroll the streets, and see the variety of sights. The summer months see more visitors, but because the two local colleges aren't in session then, there are actually fewer people. Ideal times to visit are March-May and September-November due to the moderate weather that allows you to play outdoors, hike, cycle, and just hang out at the beach.

Paso Robles is farther inland, making the area much warmer during the summer months; triple-digit temperatures are common. Conversely, in the winter months temperatures dip down toward the freezing point. The best times to visit, unless you prefer the

heat of summer, are also around March-May and September-November. Keep in mind that September in Paso Robles is harvest time for the wineries. It's still usually quite warm, and oftentimes you can be where the wine-making action is when the wineries are busy crushing grapes. Paso Robles can best be explored over a weekend. If wine is a focal point, however, you'll want to visit for at least three or four days—or do a one-day wine tour for a quick overview of the wineries in the area. Weekends are the most crowded, so you may want to visit on a weekday. If you have a particular winery you're especially eager to visit, plan ahead and find out its hours.

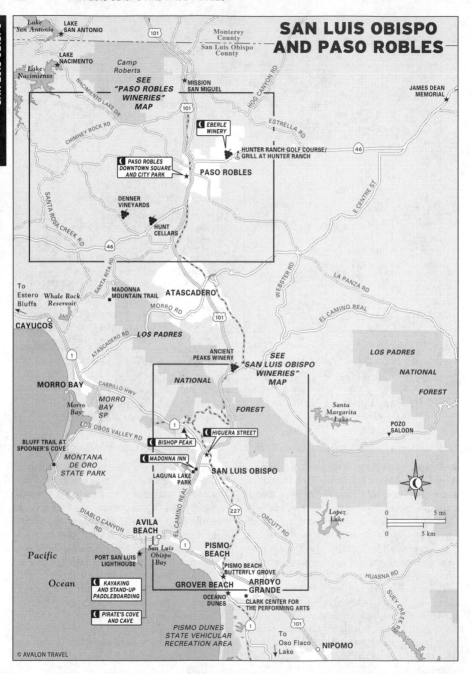

SAN LUIS OBISPO AND PASO ROBLES

Lake
San Antonio

LAKE
SAN ANTONIO

101

Monterey
County

San Luis Obispo
County

Lake
Nacimiento

LAKE
NACIMIENTO

Camp
Roberts

MISSION
SAN MIGUEL

HOG CANYON RD

JAMES DEAN
MEMORIAL

NACIMIENTO LAKE DR

SEE
"PASO ROBLES
WINERIES"
MAP

101

EBERLE
WINERY

ESTRELLA RD

CHIMNEY ROCK RD

HUNTER RANCH GOLF COURSE/
GRILL AT HUNTER RANCH

46

PASO ROBLES
DOWNTOWN SQUARE
AND CITY PARK

PASO ROBLES

E CENTRE ST

SANTA ROSA CREEK RD

DENNER
VINEYARDS

HUNT
CELLARS

46

SANTA RITA RD

MADONNA
MOUNTAIN TRAIL

ATASCADERO

WEBSTER RD

LA PANZA RD

To
Estero
Bluffs

Whale Rock
Reservoir

MORRO RD

101

EL CAMINO REAL

CAYUCOS

1

ATASCADERO RD

LOS PADRES

ANCIENT
PEAKS WINERY

SEE
"SAN LUIS OBISPO
WINERIES"
MAP

LOS PADRES

NATIONAL

MORRO BAY

CABRILLO HWY

NATIONAL

FOREST

Santa
Margarita
Lake

Morro
Bay

MORRO
BAY
SP

FOREST

POZO
SALOON

BLUFF TRAIL AT
SPOONER'S COVE

LOS OSOS VALLEY RD

1

BISHOP PEAK

HIGUERA STREET

MONTANA
DE ORO
STATE PARK

MADONNA INN

Laguna Lake
Park

SAN LUIS OBISPO

DIABLO CANYON RD

AVILA
BEACH

EL CAMINO REAL

227

ORCUTT RD

Lopez
Lake

0   5 mi

0   5 km

Pacific

PORT SAN LUIS
LIGHTHOUSE

San Luis
Obispo Bay

PISMO
BEACH

Ocean

KAYAKING
AND STAND-UP
PADDLEBOARDING

PISMO BEACH
BUTTERFLY GROVE

HUASNA RD

PIRATE'S COVE
AND CAVE

GROVER BEACH

ARROYO
GRANDE

OCEANO
DUNES

CLARK CENTER FOR
THE PERFORMING ARTS

PISMO DUNES
STATE VEHICULAR
RECREATION AREA

1

101

To
Oso Flaco
Lake

NIPOMO

SUEY CREEK RD

© AVALON TRAVEL

San Luis Obispo

Eleven miles inland from the coast, San Luis Obispo (SLO) is a worthy home base to explore nearby Montaña de Oro State Park and Morro Bay. Founded in 1772 by Junípero Serra, SLO is one of California's oldest communities. Despite this, the presence of the nearby California Polytechnic State University (Cal Poly) gives the small city a youthful, vibrant feel.

Higuera Street is a one-way, three-lane street lined with restaurants, clothing stores, and bars. Half a block away, restaurant decks are perched over the small San Luis Obispo Creek, a critical habitat for migrating steelhead. In front of the Mission San Luis Obispo de Tolosa is a plaza overlooking the creek with grassy lawn sections, plenty of benches, and a fountain with sculptures of bears, a fish, and one of the area's first human residents.

SIGHTS
Mission San Luis Obispo de Tolosa

The **Mission San Luis Obispo de Tolosa** (751 Palm St., 805/781-8220, www.missionsanluisobispo.org, summer daily 9am-5pm, winter daily 9am-4pm) was founded by the missionary Junípero Serra in 1772; it's the fifth mission in the chain of 21 California missions. The church is long and narrow, with exposed wooden beams on the ceiling. On the grounds is a small **museum** (805/543-6850, summer daily 9am-5pm, winter daily 9am-4pm, donation $3) with artifacts from the indigenous Chumash people and exhibits on the mission and the Spanish missionaries. A nice garden and the Mission Plaza in front of the mission complex are a nice place to spend the afternoon on a warm day.

© STUART THORNTON

Mission San Luis Obispo de Tolosa

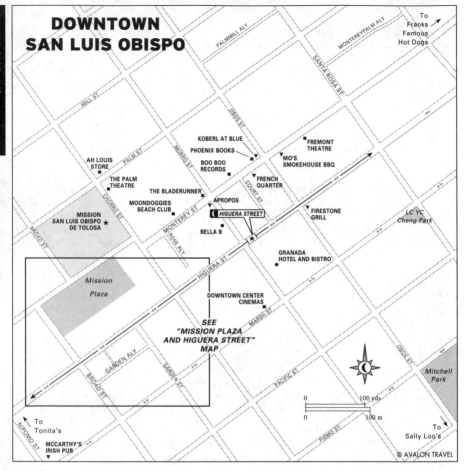

DOWNTOWN SAN LUIS OBISPO

To Franks Famous Hot Dogs

KOBERL AT BLUE
PHOENIX BOOKS
BOO BOO RECORDS
FREMONT THEATRE
MO'S SMOKEHOUSE BBQ
AH LOUIS STORE
THE PALM THEATRE
THE BLADERUNNER
FRENCH QUARTER
MOONDOGGIES BEACH CLUB
APROPOS
HIGUERA STREET
FIRESTONE GRILL
LC YC Cheng Park
MISSION SAN LUIS OBISPO DE TOLOSA
BELLA B
GRANADA HOTEL AND BISTRO

Mission Plaza

DOWNTOWN CENTER CINEMAS

SEE "MISSION PLAZA AND HIGUERA STREET" MAP

Mitchell Park

0   100 yds
0   100 m

To Tonita's
MCCARTHY'S IRISH PUB

To Sally Loo's

© AVALON TRAVEL

◖ Madonna Inn

The **Madonna Inn Resort & Spa** (100 Madonna Rd., 805/543-3000, www.madonnainn.com) is truly one of a kind. It's considered a pilgrimage site for lovers of all-American kitsch, but it wasn't planned that way. When Alex and Phyllis Madonna opened the inn in 1958, they wanted it to be different from a typical motel, and they made each guest room special. It started with 12 guest rooms; today there are 110 unique guest rooms, each decorated wildly differently to suit the diverse tastes of the road trippers who converge on the area. The creative names given to each over the years suggest what you will find inside: The Yahoo, Love Nest, Old Mill, Kona Rock, Irish Hills, Cloud Nine, Just Heaven, Hearts & Flowers, Rock Bottom, Austrian Suite, Caveman Room, Daisy Mae, Safari Room, Jungle Rock, and Bridal Falls. Then there is the famous men's restroom downstairs; the urinal is built out of rock and a waterfall flushes it. Men routinely stand guard so that their mothers, sisters, wives,

© ST JART THORNTON

The Madonna Inn is a San Luis Obispo landmark.

and female friends can go in to gawk at the unusual feature.

Much of the Inn has been custom-built. The leaded-glass inserts in the windowed area facing the large fireplace show Alex Madonna's enterprises: construction, lumber, and cattle. The Gold Rush dining room features a marble balustrade from nearby Hearst Castle. The 28-foot gold tree fixture in the main dining room was made from electrical conduit left over from building projects. A team of woodworkers carved the doors, beams, railings, and many other adornments by hand.

And there is pink, pink, pink everywhere—it was Alex Madonna's favorite color. The gregarious Madonna made his money in the construction business, something he learned when he served in the U.S. Army Corps of Engineers. After he left the service, his company built much of U.S. 101 along the Central Coast. He was known as flamboyant, effervescent, and larger than life, and he never shied away from the bold use of pink. Nowhere is

this more robustly expressed than the beyond-Vegas-style dining room. Most people who visit the Madonna don't stay here, which is a shame, since it's a really cool place to stay. The service is excellent. Even if you don't stay the night, stop by to marvel at the extravagant excess; you won't soon forget it.

Higuera Street

Similar to Santa Barbara's State Street, San Luis Obispo's **Higuera Street** is the heart of this pleasant city. For seven blocks, the one-way street is lined with restaurants, bars, gift shops, and lots of women's clothing stores. The clean sidewalks are perfect for a stroll under a canopy of ficus, carrotwood, and Victorian box trees.

Bubblegum Alley

Bubblegum Alley (Higuera St. between Broad St. and Garden St.) is a 70-foot-long alleyway whose walls are covered in pieces of chewed gum. The newly chewed chunks are bright

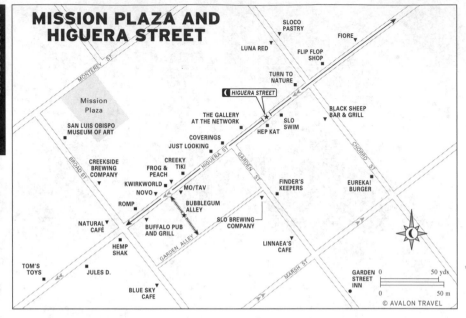

MISSION PLAZA AND HIGUERA STREET

green, red, and yellow, while the older pieces have turned a darker color. Some people have called this oddity an "eyesore," while others have touted it as one of the city's "special attractions." Regardless, Bubblegum Alley, which is rumored to have started as early as the late 1950s, is here to stay. Even after firefighters blasted the alleyway with water hoses in 1985, another layer of gum appeared shortly after.

Dallidet Adobe and Gardens

The **Dallidet Adobe and Gardens** (1185 Pacific St., 805/543-0638, ext. 10, http://historycenterslo.org, weather permitting Mar.-Nov. Fri. 10am-4pm, Sun. 1pm-4pm, tours can be arranged, free) date back to the 1850s, when the structure and grounds were home to Pierre Hypolite Dallidet, his wife, and their seven children. Dallidet was the first commercial vintner in the region. Though the original winery no longer stands, Dallidet's wine cellar is still intact. The one-acre gardens include plants from Dallidet's time and other native

species. Owned and operated by the History Center of SLO County, the Dallidet Adobe and Gardens are open for educational tours, events, and weddings.

San Luis Obispo Botanical Garden

Located in El Chorro Regional Park, the **San Luis Obispo Botanical Garden** (3450 Dairy Creek Rd., 805/541-1400, www.slobg.org, daily dawn-dusk, free) showcases the plants of the five major Mediterranean climatic regions. Walk on trails past aloe plants, trunks of elephant's milk brush, bruised blue rosemary bushes, and vibrant flame-like candelabra plants. The two-acre garden is scheduled to be expanded to 150 acres when funding permits.

Ah Louis Store

A distinct two-story building a couple of blocks from Higuera Street, the **Ah Louis Store** (800 Palm St.) was established in 1874 by Chinese pioneer Ah Louis to serve the local Chinese population. The first Chinese store

San Luis Obispo Botanical Garden

in the county, the structure also served as a bank, counting house, and post office, becoming a focal point for the Chinese community on the Central Coast. A lot of the customers were Chinese workers who had constructed the railroad tunnels for the Southern Pacific Railroad from 1884 to 1894. The history of the store is commemorated with a plaque out front, while a bronze bell hangs to the right of the store in remembrance of Ah Louis. Today, almost 150 years since it opened, the Ah Louis Store is still selling goods to the public. Its current resident is **Vintage Etc.** (805/594-1942, daily 11:30am-5pm), a gift store selling home and garden supplies.

San Luis Obispo Museum of Art

The **San Luis Obispo Museum of Art** (1010 Broad St., 805/543-8562, www.sloma.org, July 5-Labor Day daily 11am-5pm, Labor Day-July 3 Wed.-Mon. 11am-5pm, free) showcases the works of contemporary California artists working as painters, sculptors, printmakers, and photographers. Recent exhibits have focused

the historic Ah Louis Store

Paso Robles is the heart of San Luis Obispo County's wine industry.

on the social realism movement and pastel paintings.

WINE TASTING

Though Paso Robles is the undisputed leading wine region in the county, the San Luis area, which includes the Edna Valley and Arroyo Grande, has a diverse number of wineries. Don't dismiss this region in thinking that Paso has it all; there are some excellent wines coming out of San Luis Obispo, and any exploration of the wine region needs to include this area.

Edna Valley Vineyards

A stalwart of the area, **Edna Valley Vineyards** (2585 Biddle Ranch Rd., 805/544-5855, www.ednavalleyvineyard.com, daily 10am-5pm, tasting $10-20) benefits from its namesake region. The large tasting room and panoramic views to the hills (dormant volcanoes known as the Nine Sisters) in the distance with near views to the vineyards are stunning. They have a sizable number of gift items for sale in the large tasting room. There's also a demonstration vineyard out front, a place to examine different trellising techniques and how those methods affect how the grapes grow. Chardonnay, pinot noir, and limited-edition wines are the main products.

Talley Vineyards

The name Talley has been associated with farming in San Luis Obispo County since 1948. As you drive toward Lopez Lake you'll immediately notice **Talley Vineyards** (3031 Lopez Dr., 805/489-0446, www.talleyvineyards.com, daily 10:30am-4:30pm, tasting $8-15) on the left. The Mediterranean-Tuscan-style tasting room sits squarely in the middle of flat cropland, the surrounding hillsides covered in vines. A three-tiered fountain stands like a sentinel in the courtyard. The interior of the spacious tasting room features floor-to-ceiling glass, a horseshoe-shaped tasting bar, and high vaulted ceilings. You can often purchase some of the fruit and vegetables that grow on the property, including bell peppers, zucchini, tomatoes, and spinach. Pinot noir, chardonnay, syrah, cabernet sauvignon, and pinot gris are the main wines here, but they are best known for producing excellent chardonnay and pinot noir. Talley also has a second label, Bishop's Peak, a line of very good-value wines for under $20. For something special, Talley offers an **Estate Tour and Tasting** ($35), a 1.5-hour tour that includes private tastings and a tour of the historic El Rincon Adobe.

Saucelito Canyon Vineyard

Saucelito Canyon Vineyard (3080 Biddle Ranch Rd., 805/543-2111, www.saucelito-canyon.com, daily 10am-5pm, tasting $8) has one of those unique stories better suited to the History Channel than the pages of a guidebook. The parcel of land, located past Lake Lopez down a three-mile-long gated road, is so isolated that during Prohibition federal agents could never shut down the winery because they simply couldn't find it. The three acres of zinfandel, originally planted in 1880, are still producing fruit to this day. The tasting room is small, and though it's not made for more than 15 people, it has the necessary ingredients for a good time, namely friendly staff, very good wine, and a relaxed, intimate environment. There are even old photos from the turn of the 20th century showing the old-vine zinfandel and the homestead. Outside there are a few tables for relaxing. Zinfandel is king here, although other varieties, such as sauvignon blanc, tempranillo, merlot, and cabernet sauvignon, are made. Saucelito Canyon opens the historic vineyard property about once a year for the public to view the centuries-old vines. The canyon is remote, beautiful, and serene, and it pulsates with the history of men and women working the land.

Tolosa Winery

Imagine a tasting room designed for James Bond and you'll get an idea of what the interior of **Tolosa Winery** (4910 Edna Rd., 805/782-0500, www.tolosawinery.com, daily 11am-5pm, tasting $10) is like: cork floors, stainless steel ceilings, a glass bar, wood panels, and back lighting, all sleek and sophisticated. A plasma screen displays pictures of recent events and the

wine-making process, while another screen displays up-to-date specials and wine club information. There's even ambient music playing throughout the tasting room, patio, halls, and restroom. The tasting room looks out over the fermentation tanks of gleaming polished stainless steel. Guests can take a self-guided tour through the facility as well. Stay and picnic at their tranquil outdoor picnic area, or play a round of boccie ball as you soak in the peaceful surroundings. The focus is on chardonnay and pinot noir, but you'll also find merlot, syrah, viognier, and even grenache blanc.

Salisbury Vineyards

This 105-year-old schoolhouse, now a tasting room and art gallery, underwent a historic interior renovation and opened in the spring of 2005 with a new lease on life. As you enter the tasting room at **Salisbury Vineyards** (6985 Ontario Rd., 805/595-9463, www.salisburyvineyards.com, Mon.-Thurs. noon-5pm, Fri.-Sun. 11am-6pm, tasting $5), you're immediately struck by the openness of the space and the copious amount of wood, most notably the original hardwood floors. A sign by the front door warns that stiletto heels can have a detrimental effect on their old floors, and to walk gently, but that everyone is still welcome. Salisbury aims for the schoolhouse to serve a multitude of diverse functions, not simply as a tasting room. It's also part art gallery, presenting artwork from around the globe that rotates every 8-10 weeks. Pinot noir, syrah, a peach chardonnay, and a couple of wine blends are the main wines produced here.

Claiborne & Churchill

The **Claiborne & Churchill** (2649 Carpenter Canyon Rd., Edna Valley, 805/544-4066, www.clairbornechurchill.com, daily 11am-5pm, tasting $10) winery was started in 1983, inspired by the wines of Alsace in France, even though these types of wine were not often made in California, let alone San Luis Obispo County. Claiborne & Churchill decided to specialize in premium dry wines made from riesling, gewürztraminer, and pinot gris grapes as well as pinot noir from nearby vineyards. Not wanting to limit their portfolio, they also produce small lots of other wines, including a dry muscat, chardonnay, syrah, cabernet sauvignon, sparkling rosé, and a port-style wine. Claiborne & Churchill is still a small family-owned winery, and their facility is constructed out of straw bales and covered in plaster, making it unique among wineries in the United States. Using these sustainable materials has greatly reduced their cooling costs. However, when you visit the winery, you won't notice, as it looks like any interior. They do have a small section on part of a wall that shows how the bales fit together and gives more information about this unique architectural approach.

ENTERTAINMENT AND EVENTS
Bars and Clubs
As a college town, San Luis Obispo offers plenty of bars in the downtown area. A popular spot with the college students is **Mo/Tav** (725 Higuera St., 805/541-8733, www.motherstavern.com, daily 11am-1:30am), with two-for-one-drink nights, karaoke evenings, and weekend dance parties. Across the street is another popular drinking establishment called the **Frog & Peach Pub** (728 Higuera St., 805/595-3764, daily noon-2am). It has live music almost nightly, along with a back deck where you can have a drink on warmer evenings. A narrow bar with brick walls, the **Buffalo Pub and Grill** (717 Higuera St., 805/544-5515, daily 11am-2am) has beers on tap and happy hour every day (5pm-8pm).

Creeky Tiki (782 Higuera St., 805/544-2200, www.creekytiki.com, daily 11am-midnight) distinguishes itself from other Higuera Street bars with its surf theme. Surfboards and images of waves decorate the walls, and for warm nights there's a tiki bar out back. The bar has a water ski with four shot-glass holders, available on request, so that four pals can do a simultaneous shot of liquor together. The **Black Sheep Bar & Grill** (1117 Chorro St., 805/544-7433, www.blacksheepslo.com, daily 11am-2am) has a cozy pub feel on uncrowded

nights. This brick-walled, wood-floored tavern has a fireplace and a back patio. It also serves a burger basted in a Guinness beer reduction sauce.

Just a block off Higuera Street but a world away from the college bars there, **McCarthy's Irish Pub** (600 Marsh St., 805/544-0268, 8am-2am) is a dark, low-slung bar with loud music, friendly locals, and a shuffleboard table. Order up a draft Guinness, Smithwick's, or Magners Irish cider and get ready to make some new friends. **Creekside Brewing Company** (1040 Broad St., 805/542-9804, www.creeksidebrewing.com, Sun.-Wed. 11am-midnight, Thurs.-Sat. 11am-1:30am) is a small brewpub that serves a menu of 5-6 house-made beers. Sip brews like their popular IPA on a deck hanging over the creek or in the cavernous downstairs bar.

Live Music
SLO Brewing Company (1119 Garden St., 805/543-1843, www.slobrewingco.com, Tues.-Sun. 11:30am-2am, Mon. 3pm-2am) is a brewery, restaurant, bar, and music venue. Upstairs are pool tables and the dining area, while downstairs is a stage that has hosted acts like the Strokes, Green Day, and Snoop Dogg. Check the website for a list of upcoming acts. Another venue for live music, the **Performing Arts Center** (1 Grand Ave., 805/756-7222, www.pacslo.org), located on the California Polytechnic State University campus, also has live theater events, lectures, and comedy performances. The Madonna Inn has its own performance space: the 2,600-seat **Alex Madonna Expo Center** (100 Madonna Rd., 805/784-2410, www.madonnainn.com) has been booking big-name acts like Modest Mouse, The Postal Service, and Rebelution.

The **Steynberg Gallery** (1531 Monterey St., 805/547-0278, http://steynberggallery.com, 6am-7pm daily) is a coffee house, art gallery, and performance space in a 1930s art deco building. The gallery hosts music concerts by jazz and acoustic acts. Occasionally an established artist like Frank Black will grace the stage. Other nights might have poetry readings or open mikes. Another coffee shop and music venue, **Linnaea's Café** (1110 Garden St., 805/541-5888, http://linnaeas.com, Mon.-Wed. 6:30am-10pm, Thurs.-Fri. 6:30am-11pm, Sat. 7am-11pm, Sun. 7am-2pm) hosts folk and acoustic acts along with jazz jams and an old-timey jam. The **Frog & Peach Pub** (728 Higuera St., 805/595-3764, daily noon-2am) has live music from bar bands most nights.

East of San Luis Obispo, the **Pozo Saloon** (90 West Pozo Rd., Pozo, 805/438-4225, www. pozosaloon.com) is a historic watering hole dating back to 1858. It somehow pulls in acts like Willie Nelson, Dwight Yoakam, Snoop Dogg, and the Black Crowes to perform on its outdoor stage.

Cinema

The **Palm Theatre** (817 Palm St., 805/541-5161, www.thepalmtheatre.com) has the unique distinction of being the first solar-powered movie theater in the country. The Palm frequently screens independent, foreign, and art-house films. The **Fremont Theatre** (1035 Monterey St., 805/541-2141, http://themovieexperience2.blogspot.com) is an art deco movie house from 1942 that shows new films as well as classic movies. Another old-school option is to take in a drive-in movie at the **Sunset Drive-In Theater** (255 Elks Lane, 805/544-4475). Choose between a couple of first-run movies. For traditional films in a traditional setting, the seven-screen **Downtown Center Cinemas** (888 Marsh St., 805/564-8600) are located below the mall. This is the spot for current releases and blockbusters.

Festivals and Events

The **San Luis Obispo Farmers' Market** (Higuera St. between Osos St. and Nipomo St., www.slocountyfarmers.org, http://downtownslo.com, Thurs. 6:10pm-9pm) is a true phenomenon. One of the largest farmers' markets in the state, this weekly gathering has the goods of 70 farmers and lots of live music. Every March, the **San Luis Obispo International Film Festival** (805/546-3456, http://slofilmfest.org) screens a range of films

at the city's Palm Theatre (817 Palm St.) and Fremont Theatre (1035 Monterey St.) along with other venues around the county, including Paso Robles and Avila Beach. The five-day fest draws film folks like Josh Brolin and John Waters. **Festival Mozaic** (various locations, 805/781-3009 or 877/881-8899, www.festivalmozaic.com) has a winter concert series and a summer music festival. It features chamber music, orchestra performances, and educational events in venues that include Mission San Luis Obispo de Tolosa and Hearst Castle.

Similar to its cousin in Santa Barbara, the **I Madonnari Italian Street Painting Festival** (805/541-6294, www.imadonnarifestival.com) festival appears each year in September at the plaza of the Old Mission downtown, which is transformed with colorful large-scale street paintings. The 200 squares are divvied up and the labor-intensive work of chalk painting commences. Festival hours are daily 10am-6pm, and admission is free. Street painting has a long tradition in cities in Western Europe and probably started in Italy in the 16th century. The artists who use chalk to draw on the street are known as *madonnari*, or "Madonna painters," because they originally reproduced icons of Virgin Mary.

The **City to the Sea Half Marathon** (www. citytothesea.org) is still the best running event in SLO. It starts in downtown SLO and heads all the way to the ocean in Pismo Beach each October, when the weather is just about perfect for a long run. This is one of the largest races in the area and draws all manner of runners, from experienced to novice, to attempt the 13-mile route.

SHOPPING

There's lots of shopping to be done in San Luis Obispo. The profusion of shops along Higuera Street includes various local businesses as well as chains like Gap and Victoria's Secret.

Bookstores

Phoenix Books (990 Monterey St., 805/543-3591, Mon.-Wed. 10am-9pm, Thurs.-Sat. 10am-10pm, Sun. 11am-9pm) has piles of used

Fiore Boutique

© STUART THORNTON

books scattered on shelves and tables throughout a honeycomb of rooms. The subject matter covers the full range, including child psychology, art, and fiction.

Clothing and Shoes

Clothing stores lines Higuera Street, most specializing in women's fashion. They often stay open later on Thursday evenings to take advantage of the farmers market crowds. **Coverings** (760 Higuera St., 805/549-8373, Mon.-Wed. and Fri.-Sat. 11am-7pm, Thurs. 11am-8pm, Sun. 11am-6pm) sells women's clothing, shoes, and boots. **Fiore Boutique** (865 Higuera St., 805/541-6710, Mon.-Wed. and Fri.-Sun. 10:30am-7pm, Thurs. 10:30am-9pm) is a women's boutique with a range of handbags, jeans, and tops. Stock up on women's clothes, shoes, handbags and jewelry at **French Quarter** (969 Monterey St., 805/544-1415, www.shopfrenchquarter.com, Sun.-Wed. 10:30am-9pm, Thurs.-Sat. 10:30am-10pm). **Apropos** (1022 Morro St., 805/784-0664, www.shopapropos.com, Mon.-Sat. 10am-6pm, Sun. noon-4pm)

stocks "clothing to fit real women." That means Johnny Was items, Jag Jeans, and Color Me Cotton garments in sizes 2 to 18. Yet another women's boutique, **Bella B** (1023 Morro St., 805/547-8700, www.bellab.com, Sun.-Wed. and Fri.-Sat. 10am-8pm, Thurs. 10am-9pm, Sun. 10am-7pm) sells women's apparel, accessories, and shoes.

Multitaskers can get their hair done and score some hip clothes at **Hep Kat Clothing & Beauty Parlor** (785 Higuera St., 805/547-0777, www.hepkatclothing.com, daily 10am-8pm). The clothing section carries rock-and-roll-inspired accessories like spiked collars and black skull scarfs. One of six stylists can give you a matching rocking hairstyle in the adjacent salon. Save a few dollars by shopping for designer labels including Chanel, Gucci, Prada, and Louis Vuitton at **Finder's Keepers** (1124 Garden St., 805/545-9879, Mon.-Sat. 10am-5pm), an upscale consignment store. Focusing on sustainable fashion, the **Hemp Shak** (1115 Broad St., Mon.-Wed. and Fri.-Sat. 10am-6pm, Thurs. 10am-8pm, Sun. 11am-6pm) carries the latest men's and women's hemp clothing along with organic cotton and soy products.

Before hitting nearby beaches, get a new swimsuit at **SLO Swim** (795 Higuera St., 805/781-9604, www.sloswim.com, Fri.-Wed. 11am-5:30pm, Thurs. 11am-6pm), which boasts the largest selection of women's swimwear on the Central Coast. **Moondoggies Beach Club** (837 Monterey St., 805/541-1995, www.moondoggiesbeachclub.com, Mon.-Wed. 10am-7pm, Thurs. 10am-9pm, Fri.-Sat. 10am-8pm, Sun. 10am-6pm) outfits the local surf crowd. You'll see examples of their extensive surf-wear line if you spend any significant time on the Central Coast. Fashion-conscious men get the goods at **Jules D.** (1129 Garden St., Suite A, 805/781-0722, www.jules-d.com, Mon. 11:30am-5:30pm, Tues.-Sat. 10am-5:30pm, Sun. 11am-5pm). The store carries jackets, hats, shoes, and jewelry.

Flip Flop Shops (858 Higuera St., 805/548-1858, www.flipflopshops.com, Sun.-Wed. 10am-7pm, Thurs. 10am-9:30pm, Fri.-Sat. 10am-8pm) stocks 22 different flip-flop brands, including Sanuks, O'Neill, Roxy, and Volcom, ranging in price from $12 to over $100. Instead of flying to Rome to go shoe shopping, stop in at **!Romp** (714 Higuera St., 805/545-7667, www.rompshoes.com, Mon.-Sat. 11am-6pm, Sun. 11am-5pm), which focuses on European footwear, especially Italian brands. In addition to shoes, the store stocks handbags and jewelry.

Specialty Stores

If you need a quirky gift like a mustache-themed flask or a middle finger air freshener, stop into **Kwirkworld** (766 Higuera St., 805/544-4222, www.kwirkworld.com, Mon.-Wed. and Sat. 10am-8pm, Thurs.-Fri. 10am-9pm, Sun. 10am-7pm). **Turn to Nature** (786 Higuera St., 805/540-3395, www.turntonature.com, Sun.-Mon. 10am-5pm, Tues.-Wed. 10am-6pm, Thurs.-Sat. 10am-8pm) is a gift store with a nature-and-science theme. Pick up wind chimes, thumb pianos, rocks, and gems.

Boo Boo Records (978 Monterey St., 805/541-0657, www.booboorecords.com,

Boo Boo Records

Mon.-Wed. 10am-8pm, Thurs.-Sat. 10am-9pm, Sun. 11am-6pm) is San Luis Obispo's independent record store. Music lovers can browse through new and used CDs and vinyl. There are also turntables and amplifiers for sale if you want to set up your own sound system at home. Another place to stock up on music is **Cheap Thrills Records** (563 Higuera St., 805/544-0683, www.squaredealonline.com, Mon.-Sat. 10am-9pm, Sun. 11am-5pm), which carries a selection of used CDs, LPs, tapes, computer games, and movies. Kids will love **Tom's Toys** (682 Higuera St., 805/541-2896, Mon.-Wed. and Fri.-Sat. 9:30am-6pm, Thurs. 9:30am-8:30pm, Sun. 11am-6pm), which offers two stories filled with rubber-band guns, Rubik's cubes, Transformers, Power Rangers, and Lego.

Art Galleries

The **Just Looking Gallery** (746 Higuera St., 805/541-6663, www.justlookinggallery.com, Mon.-Wed. and Fri.-Sat. 10am-6pm, Thurs. 10am-8pm, Sun. noon-5pm) features the prints, sculptures, and paintings of local and regional artists. Going strong for over a decade, **The Gallery at The Network** (778 Higuera St., Suite B, 805/788-0886, www.galleryatthenetwork.com, Mon.-Sat. 11am-6pm, Sun. 11am-5pm) features the work of 45 regional artists. Browse through jewelry, ceramics, woodwork, and photographs.

SPORTS AND RECREATION
Parks

Located between San Luis Obispo and Morro Bay, **El Chorro Regional Park** (Hwy. 1 and Dairy Creek Rd., 805/781-5930, ext. 4, www.slocountyparks.com, daily 7am-dusk, $3 entrance fee charged Apr.-Sept. Sat.-Sun. and holidays only) was once the home of a U.S. Army training camp. Now it's a county park with more than 700 acres of recreational opportunities, including a campground with 63 sites, barbecue facilities, volleyball courts, softball fields, an off-leash dog park, and hiking trails. Chorro is also home to the San Luis Obispo

Botanical Garden and the Dairy Creek Golf Course.

Laguna Lake Park (504 Madonna Rd., 805/781-7222, www.slocity.org, daily dawn-dusk) is a city park with a lake for boating and fishing. The adjacent land has a volleyball court as well as barbecue and picnic areas. **Meadow Park** (2333 Meadow St., 805/781-7222, www.slocity.org, daily dawn-dusk) is a 14-acre city park with sand volleyball courts, a basketball court, a softball field, and a playground. There is also a picnic and barbecue area.

Hiking
◖ BISHOP PEAK

Just north of San Luis Obispo, the 1,546-foot-high **Bishop Peak** (trailheads at the end of Highland Dr. and off Patricia Dr., 805/781-7300, www.slocity.org) is the city's natural treasure. A four-mile round-trip hike to the rocky crown of Bishop Peak offers commanding views of San Luis Obispo and the surrounding area. Named by Spanish missionaries who thought the mountain resembled a bishop's hat, Bishop Peak is the tallest of the *morros* or "Nine Sisters," a chain of nine volcanic peaks stretching from San Luis Obispo up to Morro Bay. In addition to the fine views, Bishop Peak teems with wildlife, especially birds that float on the mountain's thermals. You might see golden eagles, bald eagles, hawks, owls, vultures, or kestrels. The hour-long hike passes through a forest, past Volkswagen Beetle-size boulders, and into a series of exposed switchbacks. Bring water! Just below the peak are a couple of benches, a water bowl for dogs, and a peak journal, in a metal box, that you can sign.

EAGLE ROCK

One of the most popular trails in **El Chorro Regional Park** (Hwy. 1 and Dairy Creek Rd., 805/781-5930, ext. 4, www.slocountyparks.com) is the 1.4-mile round-trip hike to **Eagle Rock**. It travels past ancient Native American grinding holes in rocks before offering views of the area's famous volcanic peaks known as the Nine Sisters of the Morros.

© STUART THORNTO

the view from Bishop Peak

Boating and Fishing

With water temperatures rising to around 70°F in the summer, the **Lopez Lake Recreation Area** (6800 Lopez Dr., 805/788-2381, www.slocountyparks.com) is perfect for fishing, boating, skiing, sailing, windsurfing, and canoeing. The 1,000-acre lake is a great place to cast a line for sunfish, bass, or crappie. Lopez Lake is also a wildlife hot spot, drawing over 150 bird species. The recreation area has a boat launch and boat rentals through **Invert Sports** (888/205-7119, www.invertsports.com).

Cycling

San Luis Obispo offers both urban bike paths and mountain trails. Completed in 2011, the **Madonna Inn Bike Trail** (www.madonnainn.com) allows riders to pedal 0.75 miles from Marsh Street to the Madonna Inn. **Madonna Mountain** (begins at Hwy. 1's Marsh St. exit) has a two-mile fire-road ride to its summit. Advanced riders can opt to take the **Rock Garden Trail** on the way down; it eventually connects with the single track **Lemon Grove**

Trail. The **Johnson Ranch Loop** (South Higuera St. and Ontario Rd., 805/781-7300, www.slocity.org) is a 3.5-mile-long trail that is perfect for a short mountain bike ride.

The **San Luis Obispo Bicycle Club** (805/543-5973, www.slobc.org) organizes weekly rides and has a wealth of information on local routes. If you need to rent a bike while in San Luis Obispo, consider **Wally's Bicycle Works** (306 Higuera St., 805/544-4116, Mon.-Fri. 10am-6pm, Sat. 10am-5pm).

Spas

If you need to clean yourself up, **The Bladerunner Salon & Day Spa** (894 Monterey St., 805/541-5131, www.thebladerunner.com, Mon. and Sat. 9am-5pm, Tues.-Wed. and Fri. 9am-6pm, Thurs. 9am-7pm, Sun. 11am-4pm) is a great place to do it. Their staff of almost 30 does hairstyling, nail services, airbrush tans, mud wraps, massages, and facials. The Madonna Inn has gone upscale with **The Spa at Madonna Inn** (100 Madonna Rd., 805/543-3000, ext. 474, www.madonnainn.

com, Sun.-Thurs. 9am-6pm, Fri.-Sat. 9am-7pm, $120-390). Treat your body to a facial, a massage, or tasty-sounding packages that include the Citrus Immersion and the Chocolate Meltdown.

Golf

The City of San Luis Obispo operates the 10-hole **Laguna Lake Golf Course** (11175 Los Osos Valley Rd., 805/781-7309, daily 7am-dusk, $8.25-12). Another option is the **Dairy Creek Golf Course** (2590 Dairy Creek Rd., 805/782-8060, www.slocountyparks.com, $34-43), a 6,548-yard, par-71 course within El Chorro Regional Park.

ACCOMMODATIONS
Under $150

Hostel Obispo (1617 Santa Rosa St., 805/544-4678, www.hostelobispo.com, dorm rooms $25-28, private rooms $65-75) is a short walk to downtown and the Amtrak station. There's a fully equipped kitchen and a pancake breakfast. Just know that you have to bring your own towel, and you have to hit the streets when the hostel is closed daily from 11am to 4:30pm.

A superb value, the **C Peach Tree Inn** (2001 Monterey St., 800/227-6396, http://

THE NINE SISTERS

One of the distinctive features of San Luis Obispo County is the nine ancient volcanic peaks known as the Nine Sisters of the Morros. These range from the prominent 576-foot Morro Rock of Morro Bay 14 miles south to 775-foot Islay Hill, located in the City of San Luis Obispo. The Nine Sister's highest peak is 1,559-foot Bishop Peak. The top portion is part of the 360-acre Bishop Peak Natural Reserve and is a popular spot for hikers and rock climbers. The Nine Sisters also create unique animal and plant habitats. Morro Rock is a nesting place for peregrine falcons, while Hollister Peak hosts a colony of black-shouldered kites.

peachtreeinn.com, $69-150) has nice guest rooms, friendly staff, and complimentary breakfast. The finest guest rooms at the Peach Tree are the Creekside Rooms, each with their own brick patio. Next to the lobby is a large common room with a back deck and rocking chairs to enjoy San Luis Obispo's frequently pleasant weather. The Peach Tree is located on the Old SLO Trolley route and is an easy one-mile walk to San Luis Obispo's downtown.

Just across the street from the Peach Tree, the **La Cuesta Inn** (2074 Monterey St., 805/543-2777, www.lacuestainn.com, $125-165) has reasonably priced guest rooms right near U.S. 101. All guest rooms have microwaves and fridges. This privately owned hotel has a small heated kidney-shaped pool and a hot tub. In the morning, a deluxe continental breakfast is served; coffee and juice are available in the lobby at any hour.

$150-250

Also in this cluster of accommodations is the **Apple Farm Inn** (2015 Monterey St., 805/544-2040 or 800/255-2040, www.applefarm.com, $129-269), which has more upscale guest rooms in the inn ($189-269) and less expensive rooms in the surrounding Trellis Court ($129-189). The inn guest rooms are twice the size of the Trellis Court rooms and are decorated like traditional bed-and-breakfast offerings, but all the Trellis Court guest rooms have gas fireplaces. On the grounds are a heated pool, a soaking tub, and the Apple Farm Restaurant & Bakery.

If you want to feel like you're spending the night in a cave, on safari, or on a showboat, stay at the **C Madonna Inn** (10 Madonna Rd., 805/543-3000, www.madonnainn.com, $189-459). An under-hyped asset on Madonna Inn's 2,200 acres is its deck with a large heated pool, two hot tubs, a poolside bar, and a view of an artificial cascade tumbling down the hillside.

The **Granada Hotel & Bistro** (1126 Morro St., www.granadahotelandbistro.com, $130-300) is a 17-room boutique hotel located just half a block off Higuera Street. The 1920s hotel has been renovated and modernized, with exposed brick walls, steel-framed windows, and hardwood floors. Most guest rooms also have fireplaces. On the second floor is a comfortable indoor and outdoor lounge area. Attached to the hotel is the **Granada Bistro** (Mon.-Thurs. 11:30am-3pm and 5pm-10pm, Fri. 11:30am-3pm and 5pm-11pm, Sat. 10:30am-3pm and 5pm-11pm, Sun. 10:30am-3pm and 5pm-10pm, $16-31), which serves Spanish-inspired cuisine from paella to squash-potato tacos.

The Sanitarium (1716 Osos St., San Luis Obispo, 805/544-4124, www.thesanitarium-spa.com, $190-390) is different. You can tell by the strange guest room names, which include Epiphanization and Tranquilibrium, and the mention of a salon for creative pursuits like painting and music. Every guest room is decorated with antique furniture and original art, while most have nice amenities that include soaking tubs, wood-burning fireplaces, and balconies.

Right downtown, the **Garden Street Inn** (1212 Garden St., 805/545-9802, www.garden-streetinn.com, $150-230) is a bed-and-breakfast housed in an 1800s Victorian, with nine guest rooms and four suites. In an homage to its past, the Garden Street Inn offers claw-foot tubs in a handful of its guest rooms, while others come without TVs.

Near Laguna Lake Park, the **Best Western Royal Oak Hotel** (214 Madonna Rd., 800/545-4410, www.royaloakhotel.com, $150-300) has guest rooms with private balconies, fridges, and microwaves. It also offers a pool, a fitness room, and complimentary breakfast.

FOOD

San Luis Obispo restaurants take advantage of their location near farms and wineries. The big college presence means that even the higher-end establishments keep things casual.

Barbecue

The owners of **Mo's Smokehouse BBQ** (1005 Monterey St., 805/544-6193, www.smokinmosbbq.com, Sun.-Wed. 11am-9pm, Thurs.-Sat. 11am-10pm, $10-20) researched barbecue restaurants in the U.S. barbecue belt before opening its doors. The result is flavorful shredded pork, tri-tip, hot-link sandwiches, and ribs.

Classic American

Being inside **Franks Famous Hot Dogs** (950 California Blvd., 805/541-3488, daily 6:30am-9pm, $2-5) feels a bit like you've time-traveled back to the 1950s. College students from nearby Cal Poly sit in the red-and-white booths snacking on Franks's daily handmade burgers, fries, or steamed hot dogs. Whether you get a chili cheese dog or a monster burger, the super low prices recall another era. It's rumored that they have a great breakfast burrito as well.

Although it's located in a neighborhood a few blocks from downtown, **High Street Deli** (350 High St., 805/541-4738, www.highstdeli.com, daily 9am-5:30pm, $6-8.50) is worth seeking out if you are a sandwich enthusiast. The California Turkey is a heated slab of tastiness with roasted turkey, an Ortega chili, slices of avocado, and more on toasted sourdough slices. They also sell Italian subs, hot pastramis, and meatloaf sandwiches. After ordering, hunker down on a stool at one of the barrel tables to eat these creations while they're still warm.

Hearty home-style food can be had at the **Apple Farm Restaurant** (2015 Monterey St., 805/544-6100, www.applefarm.com, daily 7am-9pm, $12-24). Breakfast, lunch, and dinner is served daily in a colorful dining room decorated with produce signs. Mornings feature omelets and chicken fried steak, while dinner adds steak and seafood entrées. The **Firestone Grill** (1001 Higuera St., 805/783-1001, http://firestonegrill.com, Mon.-Wed. and Sun. 11am-10pm, Thurs.-Sat. 11am-11pm, $5-18) creates a masterpiece of meat in its tender and tasty tri-tip sandwich. Locals swear by it. Brought to you by the same folks behind Cambria's Main Street Grill, the Firestone Grill also serves pork ribs, burgers, and salads.

A great concept done well, **◖ Eureka!Burger** (1141 Chorro St., 805/903-1141, www.eurekaburger.com, daily 11am-midnight, $9-23) is a small chain that focuses on gourmet burgers and craft beers. This popular two-story restaurant has some unique takes on the American classic, including a fig marmalade burger and a jalapeño egg burger. The meat is juicy, tasty, and cooked to order. They also have a range of microbrews on tap, including Scrimshaw, Racer 5, and Stone Pale Ale. A trip to the Madonna Inn is always worthwhile. Its over-the-top dining room, the **Gold Rush Steakhouse** (100 Madonna Rd., 805/784-2433, www.madonnainn.com, daily 5pm-10pm, $25-98), serves steaks of the filet mignon, New York, and top sirloin varieties. If you are not feeling like red meat, they also have Australian lobster tail and Cayucos abalone.

Contemporary and Fusion

The menu items at **Koberl at Blue** (998 Monterey St., 805/783-1135, www.epkoberl.com, restaurant daily 5pm-10pm, bar Sun.-Wed. 4pm-midnight, Thurs.-Sun. 4pm-2am, $23-48) are designed to be paired with a glass of wine. So whether you get the tempura fried oyster appetizer or the sautéed veal liver entrée, be sure to order wine, whether it's a Paso Robles cabernet or a Bordeaux from France.

On a nice day, **Novo** (726 Higuera St., 805/543-3986, www.novorestaurant.com, Mon.-Sat. 11am-close, Sun. 10am-2pm, $16-32) has a collection of decks overlooking San Luis Obispo Creek for dining and drinking. Novo serves tapas, including fresh shrimp avocado spring rolls and full-on entrées like lavender lamb chops. International flavors creep into the menu on items like pork *carnitas sopes,* Thai curries, and a stir-fried noodle dish.

Luna Red (1023 Chorro St., 805/540-5243, www.lunaredslo.com, Mon.-Sat. 11am-close, $15-32) is in an enviable location between Mission Plaza and bustling Higuera Street. With ample outdoor patio seating, Luna Red serves what it calls "an amalgamation of world cuisines." This claim is supported with a menu that includes sashimi, ceviche, lamb kebabs, and a hummus platter.

For something different but worthwhile, stop into the **SloCo Pasty Co.** (1032 Chorro St., 805/540-7278, www.slocopastyco.com, Sun.-Thurs. 11am-9pm, Fri.-Sat. 11am-10pm, $9-10). This unique eatery, with a small indoor dining area and a small patio out front overlooking Chorro Street, is all about Cornish meat pies. There are the traditional English offerings, including versions of bangers and mash and chicken potpie. But this being California, there are creative takes like a chicken curry pie, a carne asada pie, and "aporkrodite," a rich and tasty pie filled with pork loin, feta cheese, gorgonzola cheese, cream cheese, bacon, and chives. Delicious!

Italian

For over 30 years, **Café Roma** (1020 Railroad Ave., 805/541-6800, www.caferomaslo.com, Mon.-Thurs. 11:30am-2pm and 5pm-9pm, Fri. 11:30am-2pm and 5pm-9:30pm, Sat. 5pm-9:30pm, Sun. 5pm-8:30pm, $9-32) has been stuffing San Luis Obispo residents with Italian food. In Railroad Square, Café Roma has pizzas, pastas, steak, and seafood on the menu, but they do some interesting items like a gnocchi with wild boar *ragù.*

Vegetarian and Healthy Food

Another worthy place for dinner or lunch is the Rachael Ray-approved **Blue Sky Café** (1121 Broad St., 805/545-5401, www.bigskycafe.com, Mon.-Thurs. 7am-9pm, Fri. 7am-10pm, Sat. 8am-10pm, Sun. 8am-9pm, $9-22). There are plenty of options for carnivores, but Blue Sky has some vegetarian entrées, including a plate of local vegetables served in a variety of preparations. **The Natural Café** (698 Higuera St., 805/546-9200, www.thenaturalcafe.com, $5-10) offers up healthy salads, sandwiches, burgers, and a range of vegetarian items in an airy interior with lots of plants. This small chain with two locations in Santa Barbara has a menu that will make both your vegetarian and meat-eating friends happy.

INFORMATION AND SERVICES

Information about sights and lodging in San Luis Obispo County can be obtained at the

San Luis Obispo Chamber of Commerce Visitors Center (895 Monterey St., 805/786-2673, www.slochamber.org, Sun.-Wed. 10am-5pm, Thurs.-Sat. 10am-7pm). San Luis Obispo has its own daily newspaper, *The Tribune* (www.sanluisobispo.com), and its own free weekly newspaper, the *New Times* (www.newtimesslo.com).

San Luis Obispo is a city with most basic services. There are two branches of the post office (893 Marsh St., 805/543-5353; 1655 Dalidio Dr., 805/543-2605). In case of emergencies, San Luis Obispo is home to two hospitals: Sierra Vista Regional Medical Center (1010 Murray Ave., 805/546-7600, www.sierravistaregional.com) and French Hospital Medical Center (1911 Johnson Ave., 805/543-5353, www.frenchmedical-center.org).

GETTING THERE AND AROUND

Both Highway 1 and U.S. 101 run through San Luis Obispo. From the south, use the Highway 1/U.S. 101 combined freeway into town. Amtrak (800/872-7245, www.amtrak.com) has a San Luis Obispo station (1011 Railroad Ave.); the *Coast Starlight* train stops here once daily in each direction on its way between Seattle and Los Angeles, and SLO is the northern terminus of the *Pacific Surfliner,* with several departures daily on its route to San Diego. There are scheduled flights from Los Angeles, San Francisco, and Phoenix to the San Luis Obispo County Regional Airport (SBP, 901 Airport Dr., 805/781-5205).

The regional bus system, the RTA (805/541-2228, www.slorta.org), connects San Luis Obispo, Morro Bay, Cayucos, Cambria, and San Simeon. Fares range $1.25-2.50.

Avila Beach

The Chumash people referred to Avila Beach as the "hole in the sky" because it somehow doesn't get the fog that socks in the other Central Coast beaches. You'll get more great beach days here than elsewhere in San Luis Obispo County. Tucked between San Luis Obispo and Pismo, Avila Beach is sheltered from northwest winds by nearby Point San Luis, which makes it warmer than other towns along the coast. All of this makes Avila Beach an ideal getaway.

The beachfront includes two public piers, an aquarium, a historic lighthouse, a popular community beach, a dog beach, and a famed nude beach called Pirate's Cove. Another natural asset is its hot springs, which offer relaxing soaks at places like Avila Hot Springs and the Sycamore Springs Resort & Spa. The town itself is only about five blocks long and two blocks wide, with wine-tasting rooms, gift shops, and a few restaurants just footsteps from the beach. All of the buildings look clean and new, giving it the feel of an amusement-park

version of a California beach resort, but the real reason the community looks the way it does is because the town was completely rebuilt after an oil spill by Unocal that was discovered in 1988.

SIGHTS
Avila Beach

The heart of the community is the Avila Beach Promenade (www.avilabeachpier.com), a pedestrian-only section of Front Street right on the popular 0.5-mile main beach. On sunny days, the promenade bustles with beachgoers. It's also the location for events like farmers markets and arts showcases. Wide, golden Avila Beach is perfect for sunbathing. Placid San Luis Bay is a great place for kids and adults who want to wade or take a quick dip. The beach also has a few swing sets and a sliding board for the wee ones. Bisecting the beach, 1,685-foot-long Avila Beach Pier entertains anglers and pedestrians. At the end of the pier, Zippy's at the Pier (805/709-4828, summer

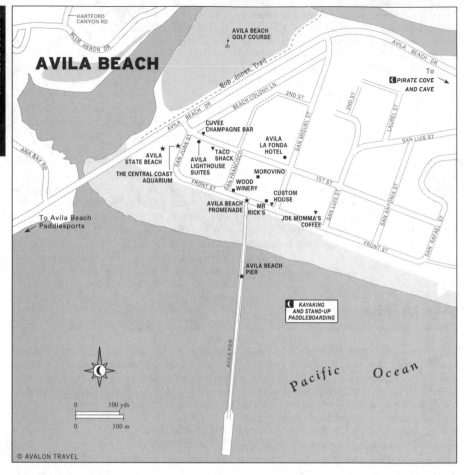

daily 10am-6pm, winter Sat.-Sun. 10am-6pm) rents out fishing poles and crab nets so you can try your luck at nabbing one of the halibut, croaker, or rock crabs that populate the water. Zippy's also sells hot coffee and cold beer. On Avila Beach Drive between Avila Beach and the Port San Luis Harbor, **Fishermen's Beach** is a wide, sandy beach where you can bring your dog for a walk.

Pirate's Cove and Cave

Pirate's Cove and Cave (end of Cave Landing Rd.) has always been one of the Central Coast's

most notorious beaches. It was once a secret spot for smugglers furtively unloading liquor from boats. Today, this 3,000-foot-long fingernail of beach is popular with naturists (meaning nudists). Even if you're not willing to shed your swimsuit, Pirate's Cove is worth a visit. Its scenic slice of coastline faces a gentle, almost tropical little bay. On crowded weekends, you'll see as many suited sunbathers as nudists, but as you head farther south, there will be more bare bodies than bikinis. You may even run into a spirited game of all-nude beach volleyball.

The cove can be found at the end of Cave

© STUART THORNTON

Avila Beach

Landing Road, which is just off of Avila Beach Road. Stop at the large dirt parking lot and walk the 0.5-mile dirt path down to the water. On the way down to the cove, be sure to detour to Pirate's Cave, which is off to the right and marked by a sign. The cavern's graffiti-covered walls open to a wonderful cliff edge view of the Pacific Ocean. Watch your step; the cave floor is often littered with broken bottles.

Despite the beach's popularity, Pirate's Cove lacks any facilities. In spring 2013, the San Luis Obispo County Parks Department acquired the land and it plans a new parking lot, restrooms, and an improved trail.

Point San Luis Lighthouse

Likely due to its remote location and relative inaccessibility, the **Point San Luis Lighthouse** (805/540-5771, www.sanluislighthouse.org) is not as well-known as other lighthouses that dot the California coastline. After it was completed in 1890, the lighthouse cast red and white flashes of light 17 miles out to sea to warn oncoming ships. During World War II, a radio listening station was constructed in front of its beacon. In 1969, its Fresnel lens was retired, and five years later, the facility was shuttered by the Coast Guard. The nonprofit San Luis Lighthouse Keepers took it over in 1995, and the group offers limited access. A visit to the light station is worth the effort on a spring day, when the coastal bluffs are colored with wildflowers.

The easiest way to reach the lighthouse is on a **trolley tour** (855/533-7843, Sat. noon, 1pm, and 2pm, Wed. noon, $20). The departure point is a parking lot located on the east side of Avila Beach Road, across from Port San Luis. roughly a half mile outside of town. Another option for large groups (20-50 people) is to reserve a Sunday group tour (805/540-5771, $25 pp, with lunch $35 pp). Eight-mile docent-led hikes to the lighthouse (Wed. and Sat. 9am, adults $5, under age 12 free) are also offered. The hikes leave from Port San Luis Harbor and takes the narrow, strenuous **Pecho Coast Trail** to the light station. The 3-4 hour **Point San Luis Lighthouse Adventure Tour** offered by

SAN LUIS OBISPO

© STUART THORNTON

Pirate's Cove

Avila Beach Paddlesports (3195 Avila Beach Dr., 805/704-6902, Fri. and Sun. by reservation) also includes the light station.

Central Coast Aquarium

Get insight into the marinelife in the local waters at the **Central Coast Aquarium** (50 San Juan St., 805/595-7280, www.centralcoast-aquarium.org, winter Sat.-Sun. 11am-4pm, adults $5, children, students, and seniors $3). It offers touch pools, marine exhibits, and classes on everything from knot tying to squid dissection.

WINE TASTING

Taste wine and watch the sunset at the **Wood Winery** (480 Front St., 805/595-9663, www.wildwoodwine.com, Mon.-Thurs. 11am-5pm, Fri.-Sat. 10:30am-6pm, Sun. 10:30am-5pm, tasting $5) on Avila Beach boardwalk, one of the few oceanfront tasting rooms in the state. It offers patio seating, cheese plates, and wines by the glass, with lovely syrahs as well as a wide selection of sangiovese, cabernet sauvignon,

chardonnay, and zinfandel. The room is decorated with soft aquatic tones and local artwork, but you'll likely be enjoying the ocean view. It's so relaxing here you may not want to leave. Located in the alley-like Landing Passage, **Morovino** (76 Landing Passage, 805/627-1443, http://morovino.com, Sun.-Tues. and Thurs. noon-5pm, Fri.-Sat. noon-6pm) focuses on Italian-inspired wines including pinot grigio and a dolcetto.

ENTERTAINMENT AND EVENTS

On summer Fridays, the **Avila Beach Farmers Market** (Apr.-Sept. Fri. 4pm-8pm) takes over the Avila Beach Promenade with produce vendors and live music. Saturdays bring **Art on the Beach** (June-Oct. Sat. 10am-5pm, www.elcaminoartassoc.com), exhibiting the work of local artists. For over 20 years, the **Avila Beach Blues Festival** (Avila Beach Golf Resort, 6464 Ana Bay Rd., 805/595-4000, www.otterproductionsinc.com) has been drawing big acts like the Steve Miller Band

© STUART THORNTON

the Point San Luis Lighthouse

and the Elvin Bishop Band to this little beach community each May.

Bars and Clubs

Mr. Rick's (404 Front St., 805/393-7423, www.mrricks.com, Mon.-Thurs. noon-close, Fri.-Sun. 11am-close) is the only real bar in Avila Beach. On sunny days, the patio out front is packed with drinkers taking in the sun and the views of the nearby Pacific. Inside, the bar is decorated with fish and nets, and the bartenders serve 16 beers on tap. There's a pool table and a stage for bands. Wednesday is karaoke night, while most weekend nights have live bands.

If you enjoy your wine with bubbles, be sure to visit the **Cuvée Bistro & Champagne Bar** (550 1st St., 805/595-2245, www.cuveechampagnebar.com, summer Mon. 11am-6pm, Wed.-Thurs. 1pm-7pm, Fri.-Sat. 11am-9pm, Sun. 11am-6pm, winter Wed.-Thurs. 1pm-7pm, Fri.-Sat. noon-9pm, Sun. 1pm-6pm). They have a list of champagne and bubbly wines to sip, along with a few beers, red wines,

and white wines. Cuvée also offers a snack menu that includes tapas, antipasti, paninis, and some sweet stuff.

SPORTS AND RECREATION
Fishing

You can fish right off Avila Beach Pier for halibut in the summer and croaker in the winter. Rent fishing poles or crab nets from **Zippy's at the Pier** (805/709-4828, summer daily 10am-6pm, winter Sat.-Sun. 10am-6pm). If you'd rather head out into deep waters, contact **Patriot Sportfishing** (805/595-7200, www.patriotsportfishing.com, full-day adults $82, full-day under age 12 $52). Their specialty is fishing for rock cod.

Kayaking and Stand-Up Paddleboarding

Protected from big waves by Point San Luis, Avila Beach and neighboring Port San Luis Harbor are ideal for kayaking and stand-up paddleboarding. The enthusiastic and informative team at **Avila Beach Paddlesports**

kayaking Avila Beach's Fossil Point

© VINCENT SHAY

(3195 Avila Beach Dr., 805/704-6902, www. avilabeachpaddlesports.com, daily 9am-5pm, single kayaks and stand-up paddleboards $17 per hour, double kayaks $23 per hour) rent kayaks and stand-up paddleboards for exploring the region's waters. From April to October they also rent out their equipment right on Avila Beach. If you really want a great introduction to the Avila Beach area, ask about the **Port San Luis Harbor Adventure** (2-3 hours, reservations required, $70), a kayak tour that provides a wealth of information on the harbor's wildlife, geology, and history. You'll see floating sea otters, lounging Port San Luis s, pillow basalt shore rocks, the Point San Luis Lighthouse, and Smith Island, a tiny rocky islet in the harbor that was once home to 14 whalers. The more adventurous should consider the **Fossil Point Adventure Tour** (2-3 hours, reservations required, $70) that explores the coastline between Avila Beach and Pirate's Cove, which is honeycombed with sea caves. You'll be required to duck into caves, navigate between tight rocks, and ride the waves. Other tours

include the **Shell Beach Cave Adventure** (2-3 hours, reservations required, $70) and history-heavy **Point San Luis Lighthouse Adventure Tour** (2-3 hours, Fri. and Sun. only, reservations required, $70) for lighthouse buffs. The outfitter will document your adventures and present you with a disc of photos when you return to dry land.

Hiking

Avila Beach's most popular walk is the 2.5-mile stroll along the **Bob Jones Trail** (www.bobjonestrail.com). This paved path starts at a parking lot right off U.S. 101 and runs along San Luis Obispo Creek all the way to Avila Beach. It's also a favorite of joggers and bikers.

Golf

The **Avila Beach Golf Course** (6464 Ana Bay Dr., 805/595-4000, www.avilabeachresort.com, greens fees $30-68) is a 6,500-yard, par-71 championship course. Challenges include the hilly terrain of the front nine and the tidal estuary crossings of the back nine.

a seal in Port San Luis Harbor

Spas

In addition to its sunny weather, Avila Beach has another natural asset: mineral springs in the valley just to the east. The best place for a soak is at **Sycamore Mineral Springs Resort** (1215 Avila Beach Dr., 805/595-7302, ext. 375, daily 8am-midnight, $13.50 pp per hour Mon.-Thurs., $17.50 pp per hour Fri.-Sun.). About 20 private tubs filled with the warm mineral waters are clustered on a hillside under oak and sycamore trees.

Next door is **Avila Hot Springs** (250 Avila Beach Rd., 805/595-2359, www.avila-hotsprings.com, Sun.-Thurs. 8am-8pm, Wed. and Fri.-Sat. 8am-9pm, adults $10, children and seniors $8). It's part of an RV resort but open to the general public. The admission fee offers access to a two-foot-deep hot mineral water soaking pool and a heated pool with sliding boards.

ACCOMMODATIONS
$150-250

For a rejuvenating stay in a natural setting, head to ◖ **Sycamore Mineral Springs Resort** (1215 Avila Beach Dr., 805/595-7302, www. sycamoresprings.com, $129-279), located in a tranquil canyon two miles from Avila Beach. Amenities on the grounds include a yoga dome, a labyrinth, a wellness center, a restaurant, and sulfur mineral springs, which can be enjoyed in hillside hot tubs. The Bob Jones Trail offers a paved two-mile walkway that connects the resort to Avila Beach. Lodging options range from cozy guest rooms to a two-story guesthouse with three bedrooms and three baths. Up on stilts, the West Meadows Suites include a living room with a gas fireplace and a bedroom with a four-poster king bed. The back decks include large soaking tubs that can be filled with fresh mineral water.

Another tempting option is the ◖ **Avila La Fonda Hotel** (101 San Miguel St., 805/595-1700, www.avilalafonda.com, $200-500), a block from Avila Beach. It resembles a 19th-century Mexican village, with a small grouping of Mexican casitas and indoor fountains. All guest rooms have two-person soaking tubs,

© STUART THORNTON

the unique Avila La Fonda Hotel

thermostat-controlled fireplaces, and heated towel racks. Your stay will be punctuated by edible goodness: You'll be welcomed with a snack-filled gift basket, chocolate-chip croissants and coffee are served every morning, a nacho bar is set up in the downstairs common area, and afternoon wine receptions are followed by freshly baked pies and cookies in the evening.

Over $250
Families will love the **Avila Lighthouse Suites** (550 Front St., 805/627-1900, www.avilalighthousesuites.com, $319-739). Enjoy the heated pool, hot tub, and family play area, which includes a putting green and an oversize checkers game. Parents and couples can relax in the spacious two-room units, each with a private patio or balcony.

Camping
There are a couple of camping areas in Avila Beach. **Avila Hot Springs** (250 Avila Beach Rd., 805/595-2359, www.avilahotsprings.com, tent camping $30, RV camping $35-45,

cabins $100-150) offers tent sites, RV sites, and cabins with kitchens. The **Port San Luis RV Campground** (805/903-3395, www.portsanluis.com, $40/dry sites, $60/full hookups) has first come, first served sites overlooking Port San Luis Harbor.

FOOD
The **Custom House** (404 Front St., 805/595-7555, www.oldcustomhouse.com, Sun.-Thurs. 8am-9pm, Fri.-Sat. 8am-10pm, $15-38) is located in a big airy building right on the Avila Beach Promenade. The seafood-heavy menu includes wild king salmon and cioppino; carnivores will favor the bacon-wrapped twin petite filet mignons and St. Louis-style barbecue pork ribs. The outdoor patio is packed on sunny days.

Located at the Sycamore Mineral Springs Resort, the **Gardens of Avila** (1215 Avila Beach Dr., 805/595-7365, www.sycamoresprings.com, Mon.-Thurs. 8am-2pm and 4pm-9pm, Fri.-Sat. 8am-9pm, $24-30) showcases local ingredients and organic produce, such as locally foraged chanterelles and roasted organic chicken. A five-course tasting menu ($55 pp) is also available.

Tiny **Taco Shack** (86 Landing Passage, 805/627-1707, Mon.-Tues. and Thurs.-Sun. 9am-8pm, $7-9) serves street-style tacos with meat, diced onions, and cilantro on corn tortillas as well as quesadillas, burritos, and other Mexican standards. **Joe Momma's Coffee** (310 Front St., 805/627-1500, www.joemommascoffee.com, Mon.-Thurs. 6:30am-6pm, Fri.-Sat. 6:30am-7pm) brews up tasty cups of Intelligentsia coffee. The modern two-story coffeehouse doesn't have Wi-Fi but does offer views of Avila Beach and the ocean, which are much more gratifying.

GETTING THERE

Avila Beach is located 10 miles south of San Luis Obispo on U.S. 101; take the Avila Beach Road exit. Parking can be a challenge during the summer and on weekends; there's a pay lot one block from the beach. Catch a free ride from Pismo Beach to Avila Beach on the **Avila Beach Trolley** (805/781-4472, www. slorta.org/avila, Memorial Day-Labor Day Thurs.-Sun., Labor Day-Memorial Day Sat.-Sun., free).

Pismo Beach

Walking around Pismo Beach, it feels like you've stepped back in time to a Southern California beach town from 50 years ago. With its long sandy beach studded with lifeguard stands and volleyball courts, the coastline in front of this community could be in Los Angeles or Orange County. The main attraction besides the surf and sand is the 1,200-foot-long Pismo Pier. On either side of the pier, surfers ride peaky waves. Meanwhile, anglers dangle their fishing poles off the side, hoping to land a perch or a smelt. Formerly known as the "Clam Capital of the World," Pismo used to be the best place to gather the famous Pismo clam, an edible bivalve that can be found on sandy beaches from Half Moon Bay to Baja California. Nowadays, due to overharvesting and sea otters munching on lots of the tasty bivalves, the clam population is so low that there is no more clamming in Pismo.

Getting to Pismo Beach is very easy; take the exits from U.S. 101. The town's one-way Pomeroy Avenue is lined with beachwear shops, candy stores, and fish-and-chips restaurants. Unique attractions include the Oceano Dunes State Vehicular Recreation Area and the Pismo Beach Monarch Butterfly Grove. It's also an ideal place to simply enjoy the beach.

SIGHTS
Pismo Pier

The first **Pismo Pier** (end of Pomeroy Ave.) was built for shipping back in 1881. That pier and another were destroyed by storms, and the third version, built in 1985-1986, still stands today. Walking out on the pier is a great way to get an eyeful of the far-ranging Pismo Beach and the Oceano Dunes to the south. A small concession shack on the pier sells snacks and rents body boards and fishing rods.

Oceano Dunes State Vehicular Recreation Area

It's a rare treat to be able to drive on one of California's beaches, and that is possible, as long as you have the right type of vehicle, at **Oceano Dunes State Vehicular Recreation Area** (3 miles south of Pismo Beach, off Hwy. 1, 805/473-7220, www.parks.ca.gov, day-use 6am-11pm, $5 per day per vehicle). There are 3,600 acres of dunes, beach, wetlands, lakes, and riparian areas to explore by four-wheel drive, dune buggy, four-wheeler, or on foot. In the 1930s and 1940s, the dunes were home to the "Dunites," a collective of mystics, nudists, writers, and artists who believed that the dunes were a center of creative

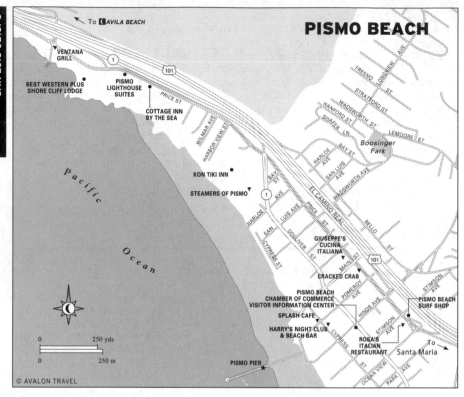

energy. Be careful if you decide to drive on the beach without the proper vehicle. Getting your car stuck in the sand can make for a long afternoon. You can also rent ATVs for the dunes at **B.J.'s ATV Rentals** (197 Grand Ave., Grover Beach, 805/481-5411, www.bjsatvrentals.com) and **Arnie's ATV Rentals** (311 Pier Ave., Oceano, 805/474-6060, http://pismoatvrentals.com).

If you want to explore the dunes but you don't have the proper vehicle, the **Oceano Dunes Preserve Trail** (2 or more miles round-trip) allows hikers to experience the region without fear of getting run over. Another hiking highlight is **Oso Flaco Lake** (end of Oso Flaco Lake Rd.), which has a 1.5-mile-long boardwalk trail that crosses the lake, heads into the dunes, and ends at a viewing platform of the nearby coast.

Pismo Beach Monarch Butterfly Grove

Sure, beachgoers and anglers flock to Pismo Beach, but the coastal community's most popular visitors are the thousands of monarch butterflies that take over a forest of eucalyptus and pine trees in the **Pismo Beach Monarch Butterfly Grove** (North Beach Campground, Hwy. 1, south end of Pismo Beach, 800/443-7778, www.monarchbutterfly.org) between November and February. During this time, docents and volunteers are onsite to answer questions daily 10am-4pm.

Guadalupe/Nipomo Dunes Center

Guadalupe/Nipomo Dunes Center (1065 Guadalupe St., Guadalupe, 805/343-2455, www.dunescenter.org, Sat.-Sun. 10am-4pm) is housed in a 1910 craftsman-style house, still beautiful inside with built-in bookshelves that hold the research library. Staff can guide you as to how best to explore the 18 miles of coastline and the 22,000 acres of the dunes complex, whether you're a bird-watcher or an off-roader, or you just want to walk the beach. Upstairs is a small exhibit space that includes a vertebra from a whale, a brief history of the area and dunes, and most visited of all, the history of the set of the 1923 film *The Ten Commandments,* which was filmed at the dunes.

Dinosaur Caves Park
Dinosaur Caves Park (Cliff St. and Shell Beach Rd., 805/773-4657, www.pismobeach.org, daily sunrise-sunset, free) is not a typical city park. This 11-acre city-run spot has a serious play area for the wee ones, with concrete dolphins, an orca, and best of all, a friendly-looking dinosaur and three cracked dinosaur eggs.

ENTERTAINMENT AND EVENTS
Harry's Night Club & Beach Bar (690 Cypress St., 805/773-1010, www.qualitysites.com, daily 10am-2am) has live bands every night except Thursday, which is karaoke night. Expect most of the acts to be classic rock cover bands. Harry's also has big-screen TVs for taking in sporting events and three pool tables for those who'd like to shoot a game or two.

The **Pismo Beach Clam Festival** (805/773-4382, www.pismochamber.com) honors the beach town's clamming past every fall with a clam chowder cook-off and a clam dig. The fest also highlights other aspects of Pismo with surf lessons, live music, and a wine walk. In June, one of California's largest car shows takes over downtown Pismo and the pier during the **Classic at Pismo Beach Car Show** (866/450-7469, http://thepismobeachclassic.com). Over 1,000 show vehicles are displayed at this free event.

SHOPPING
There is shopping to be done in Pismo Beach. To save money on some big-name clothing brands, head to the **Pismo Beach Premium Outlets** (333 Five Cities Dr., 805/773-4661, www.premiumoutlets.com, Mon.-Sat. 10am-9pm, Sun. 10am-7pm), where Levi's, Lane Bryant, PacSun, and others have outlet stores.

SPORTS AND RECREATION
Fishing
Anglers can try their luck at trying to snag a big one from the **Pismo Pier** (end of Pomeroy Ave.). The pier is the most heavily fished and the second-most productive pier on the Central Coast. If you didn't bring a rod, you can rent one from the small shack on the pier. No license is required for fishing from the pier.

Surfing
On either side of the Pismo Pier, waves consistently break for surfers. One of the best aspects of surfing the pier is that the surf is less susceptible to being destroyed by the winds that wreck waves at other local breaks. Rent a board from **Pismo Beach Surf Shop** (470 Price St., 805/773-2089, www.pismobeachsurfshop.com, half day $18-35, full day $35-50).

Kite Surfing and Stand-Up Paddleboarding
One way to experience the ocean at Pismo is to ride on a board powered by the wind or a paddle. **California Kiteboarding** (695 Price St., Suite 103, 805/550-3768, www.pismobeachkiteboarding.com) offers lessons on how to kite surf (3-hour lesson $240) and how to stand-up paddleboard (2-hour private lesson $85, 2-hour group lesson $65).

Horseback Riding
Exploring the coastline just south of Pismo Beach on horseback is possible through the **Pacific Dunes RV Resort and Riding Stables** (1205 Silver Spur Place, Oceano, 805/489-7787 or 888/908-7787, $50). One-hour rides go between dunes and out to the beach.

ACCOMMODATIONS

Pismo Beach's best lodging options are located on bluffs north of the pier and in the small downtown area.

Under $150

The exteriors of the buildings at the **Cottage Inn by the Sea** (2351 Price St., www.cottage-inn.com, $99-359) are meant to conjure up images of the English countryside. All of the guest rooms have gas fireplaces, fridges, and microwaves. The Cottage Inn also has a heated pool and a hot tub. Past the small pool deck is a spot on the bluffs over the beach with chairs and tables set up. It's a perfect location to take in the sunset or the stars with the Pismo Pier in the distance.

$150-250

Every guest room at the moderately priced **Kon Tiki Inn** (1621 Price St., 805/773-4833, www.kontikiinn.com, $170-200) has a sweeping view of the ocean as well as a patio or balcony. In front of the large hotel is a heated pool, hot tubs, and a staircase to the beach below. One perk of staying at the Kon Tiki is that guests get full use of the adjacent Pismo Beach Athletic Club, which offers Zumba classes and has an indoor lap pool.

For families or even couples who want to stretch out a bit, the ◖ **Pismo Lighthouse Suites** (2411 Price St., 805/773-2411, www.pismolighthousesuites.com, $229-429) all have two rooms and two baths, which is a rare hotel luxury. In addition, the suites have nautical decor, like lamps designed to resemble lighthouses and paintings of sea scenes, while the oceanfront suites each include a balcony or patio to take in the fine views of the Pacific or Pismo Beach. Kids will love the family play deck that has a small mini golf course, Ping-Pong tables, a badminton course, and a giant chess and checkers set. In addition, there's a heated pool, a spa, and beach access.

Right next door to the Pismo Lighthouse Suites is the **Best Western Plus Shore Cliff Lodge** (2555 Price St., 805/773-4671, www.shorecliff.com, $239-329). Every guest room

Best Western Plus Shore Cliff Lodge

© STUART THORNTON

Dolphin Bay Resort & Spa

at this recently renovated hotel has an ocean view and a patio or balcony to take in the scenery. The Shore Cliff Lodge has a large pool deck with a swimming pool and a soaking tub. Out front of the hotel buildings is a large grassy bluff with a gazebo on its tip that offers views of Pismo Beach and Pismo Pier. The Shore Cliff also has seven pet friendly guest rooms for those traveling with their four-legged friends.

Over $250

Upon entering your suite at the ⓒ **Dolphin Bay Resort & Spa** (2727 Shell Beach Rd., 805/773-4300, www.thedolphinbay.com, $400-1,000), it will be hard to stifle a gasp. The luxury suites are bigger than some homes, and the two-bedroom offerings can be up to 2,400 square feet. All the suites at Dolphin Bay have fully equipped kitchens with designer appliances and granite fireplaces. In addition, the suites have their own private terraces, most with an ocean view. It may be difficult to leave your room, but it is worth it to experience the

gem of the grounds: a pool deck inlaid with an infinity saline pool and a soaking tub. Some of the many perks of staying at Dolphin Bay include complimentary use of bicycles and a DVD library. The resort is also the home of the **La Bonne Vie Spa** (805/773-5003, Mon.-Fri. 10am-6pm, Sat. 9am-6pm, Sun. 9am-5pm, massages $110-320), which specializes in massages, facials, pedicures, and manicures. Last but not least, Dolphin Bay is located just a few hundred yards from the stairs that lead down to scenic Shell Beach.

CAMPING

Pismo State Beach has two campground options. The **Oceano Campground** (555 Pier Ave., Oceano, 800/444-7275, www.parks.ca.gov, tents $35, RVs $50) is ideal for birders. It's adjacent to a migratory bird habitat surrounding a lagoon. Also in the park is the **North Beach Campground** (Hwy. 1, Pismo Beach, 800/444-7275, www.parks.ca.gov, tents $35) that is in close proximity to the Pismo Beach Monarch Butterfly Grove.

FOOD
Deli
In nearby Shell Beach, wine shop 【 **DePalo & Sons** (2665 Shell Beach Rd., Shell Beach, 805/773-1589, daily 7am-10pm, sandwiches $6-13) is a wonderful place to stock up on picnic provisions. The deli counter displays a variety of premade food including pesto artichoke chicken breasts and roasted garlic bulbs. Wholly original and terribly tasty sandwiches include the Tuscan roasted sirloin steak sandwich, the Avila crab sandwich, and the pancetta BLT with a slab of homemade mozzarella and pesto mayo.

Italian
Giuseppe's Cucina Italiana (891 Price St., 805/773-2870, www.giuseppesrestaurant.com, Mon.-Thurs. 11:30am-3pm and 4:30pm-10pm, Fri. 11:30am-3pm and 4:30pm-11pm, Sat. 4:30pm-11pm, Sun. 4:30pm-10pm, $12-32) began as the senior project of a Cal Poly student. Now, almost 25 years later, the restaurant is still highlighting the cuisine of the Apulia region of Italy with pastas, meat dishes, and wood-fired pizzas, including one topped with clams.

An older crowd dines fills the multiple dining rooms and heated patio at **Rosa's Italian Restaurant** (491 Price St., 805/773-0551, www.rosasrestaurant.com, Mon.-Fri. 11:30am-2pm and 4pm-close, Sat.-Sun. 4pm-close, $9-16), another longtime Pismo Beach Italian favorite. The atmosphere is nice, with white tablecloths, but it doesn't feel too fancy. The menu is pasta-heavy, with fettuccine alfredo, cannelloni, and eggplant parmesan.

Markets
Like most California coastal towns, Pismo Beach has its own weekly **farmers market** (Pismo Pier, end of Pomeroy Ave., 805/773-4382, www.pismochamber.com, Wed. 3pm-6pm) on Wednesday afternoon.

Mexican
Near the string of hotels on Price Street, the sleek, stylish 【 **Ventana Grill** (2575 Price St., 805/773-0000, http://ventanagrill.com, Mon.-Thurs. 11:30am-9pm, Fri.-Sat. 11:30am-10pm, Sun. 10am-9pm, $14-39) serves up tasty California-Mexican dishes with ocean views. Menu items include entrées like tequila lime chicken, Alaskan halibut ceviche, and crab-encrusted mahimahi. Ventana also has some darn good margaritas in unique flavors like prickly pear and pineapple.

Away from the tourist strip in Shell Beach, **Zorro's Café & Cantina** (927 Shell Beach Rd., 805/773-9676, daily 7:30am-9pm, $10-18) serves Mexican- and American-style breakfast, lunch, and dinner. Breakfast has unique offerings like chiles rellenos and eggs, while dinner has more typical items such as fajitas and burritos.

Seafood
On most days a line snakes out of the brightly colored 【 **Splash Café** (197 Pomeroy Ave., 805/773-4653, www.splashcafe.com, Sun.-Thurs. 8am-8:30pm, Fri.-Sat. 8am-9pm, $5-10). People are willing to wait for a taste of rich, buttery clam chowder. It's not health food, but the chowder, served in a cup, a bowl, or a bread bowl, utilizes three different types of clams and hits the spot on a chilly day or after spending some time in the nearby Pacific. They also serve fish tacos, burgers, and fried seafood.

For a more sophisticated menu and better views, dine at **Steamers of Pismo** (1601 Price St., 805/773-4711, www.steamerspismobeach.com, Mon.-Thurs. 11:30am-3pm and 4:30pm-9pm, Fri. 11:30am-3pm and 4:30pm-10pm, Sat. 11:30am-3pm and 4pm-10pm, Sun. 11:30am-3pm and 4pm-9pm, $16-33). The menu has deep-fried seafood and chips platters, shrimp jambalaya, and chorizo and clam linguine. Steamers' happy hour (Sun.-Thurs. 3pm-7pm, Fri.-Sat. 3pm-6pm) offers a sampler of steamed clams, a fish taco, and a cocktail for the price of a dinner entrée.

It's not a good idea to wear your best clothes to the **Cracked Crab** (751 Price St., 805/773-2722, www.crackedcrab.com, Sun.-Thurs. 11am-9pm, Fri.-Sat. 11am-10pm, $12-53). The signature dish is a bucket for two of three kinds

Pismo Beach's popular Splash Café

of shellfish steamed with Cajun sausage, red potatoes, and corn. You are given a mallet, a crab cracker, and a bib. If that sounds like too much work, order a seafood sandwich or another entrée such as grilled albacore.

INFORMATION AND SERVICES

There's a **California Welcome Center Pismo Beach** (333 Five Cities Dr., Suite 100, 805/773-7924, www.visitcwc.com, Mon.-Sat. 10am-9pm, Sun. 10am-7pm) located at the Pismo Premium Outlets. In the center of Pismo Beach, the **Pismo Beach Chamber of Commerce Visitor Information Center** (581 Dolliver St., 805/773-4382 or 800/443-7778, www.pismochamber.com, Mon.-Fri. 10am-5pm, Sat. 10am-2pm) has pamphlets, maps, and information. There are a few banks in Pismo Beach along with a **Post Office** (100 Crest Dr., 805/481-5971, www.usps.com, Mon.-Fri. 9am-5:30pm, Sat. 9am-2pm). The nearby **Arroyo Grande Community Hospital** (345 S. Halcyon Rd., 805/489-4261, www.arroyograndehospital.org) has services for emergencies.

Paso Robles

As an up-and-coming wine-growing region, Paso Robles has become a familiar destination and appellation for state residents as well as a popular side trip from nearby Cambria. Huge crowds do not descend on Paso every weekend as they do in the more popular wine regions. You can still find room at the tasting bars, engage with knowledgeable tasting-room staff, occasionally meet a winemaker tending bar, and enjoy a friendly country atmosphere. For the best tasting experience, visit the Paso region over the weekend—many of the smaller winery

tasting rooms are open only Thursday-Monday or sometimes only Friday-Sunday. Most tasting fees are waived with a wine purchase.

SIGHTS
◖ Paso Robles Downtown Square and City Park

Mature oaks and sycamore trees dot the interior of the one-block **Downtown Square and City Park** (Spring St. and 12th St.) in downtown Paso Robles, the focal point of the city. There is a gazebo, a playground, a horseshoe pit, and

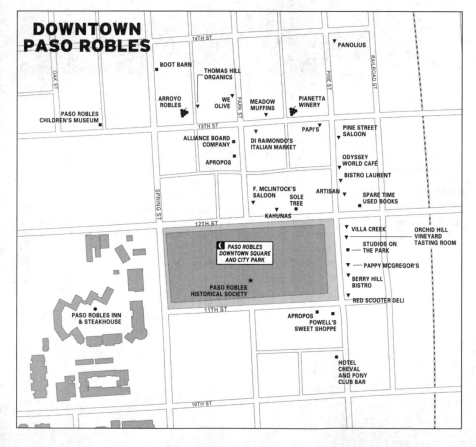

DOWNTOWN PASO ROBLES

Downtown Square and City Park

plenty of grass to stretch out on. Free concerts are offered, and the majority of the festivals and the farmers market are held here. In the center is the old original Carnegie Library, which has a sister in San Luis Obispo. Between 1883 and 1919, philanthropist Andrew Carnegie spent vast sums to help fund libraries around the world, nearly half of them located in U.S. towns. The library has a new life as a fully restored and beautiful history museum. Most of Paso Robles fans out from the City Park: wine-tasting rooms, restaurants, lodging, bars, a movie theater, antiques stores, and clothing stores. It's easy to spend an entire day within the few blocks that make up this downtown area.

Paso Robles Children's Museum

A good spot for younger kids is the **Paso Robles Children's Museum at the Volunteer Firehouse** (623 13th St., 805/238-7432, www.pasokids.org, Thurs.-Fri. and Sun. 11am-4pm, Wed. and Sat. 10am-4pm, adults $7, children $6, seniors $5). As much a playground as a museum, the space offers themed interactive exhibits with a slight educational bent for toddlers and elementary school-age children. There's even a simulated grape-stomp ball pit. Kids can draw, paint, climb, jump, play, and learn in one of the few spots in Paso Robles dedicated entirely to the younger set.

Paso Robles Pioneer Museum

The **Paso Robles Pioneer Museum** (2010 Riverside Ave., 805/239-4556, www.pasoroblespioneermuseum.org, winter Thurs.-Sun. 1pm-4pm, summer Thurs.-Fri. and Sun. 1pm-4pm, Sat. 10am-4pm, donation) celebrates the settlement of San Luis Obispo County. Exhibits have a distinctly Western Americana flavor and include some larger displays of carriages, farm equipment, and even an old one-room schoolhouse.

Mission San Miguel

Not as well-known as the Santa Barbara Mission, **Mission San Miguel** (775 Mission St., San Miguel, 805/467-2131, www.

© STUART THORNTON

Mission San Miguel

missionsanmiguel.org, daily 10am-4:30pm, self-guided tour $2), founded in 1797, has a rough-and-tumble history that includes madness, possible poisonings, and a documented murder. Mission San Miguel had an inauspicious beginning when one of its first friars was removed and sent back to Mexico after being found insane. A few years later, in 1801, it was suspected that three friars had been poisoned; it now seems more likely that they were sickened by drinking tainted mescal.

The Roman Catholic Church eventually abandoned the mission, and it passed into the hands of Petronillo Ríos and William Reed, who, along with his family, ran the mission as an inn. The most gruesome chapter in Mission San Miguel's history came in 1848, when a band of five bandits killed Reed. Their goal was to steal gold that William Reed often bragged about, but it was never found and likely never existed. This set off a rampage that ended with 11 people dead, including Reed's pregnant wife and a four-year-old boy. The bandits were captured six days later; two were killed in the gun

battle, and the other three were executed by firing squad.

After being damaged in 2003 by a 6.5-magnitude earthquake at San Simeon, Mission San Miguel reopened in 2009. Today the grounds include a cemetery, a small museum with Native American and mission artifacts, and a series of rooms that depict mission life. The long, narrow church is known for its altar, with a symbol meant to represent the "All-Seeing Eye of God." It's also the only California mission with its original murals still intact.

Charles Paddock Zoo

It's not the biggest or most diverse, but you'll have fun exploring the **Charles Paddock Zoo** (9100 Morro Rd., Atascadero, 805/461-5080, www.charlespaddockzoo.org, Nov.-Mar. daily 10am-4pm, Apr.-Oct. daily 10am-5pm, adults $5, children $4). Plan an hour or two to take a leisurely tour of the funky prehensile-tailed porcupines and the famous slender-tailed meerkats. You can also visit the aviary to enjoy the twitters and squawks of more than a dozen

JAMES DEAN: DEATH ON THE HIGHWAY

In the 1950s, James Dean was fast becoming a well-known movie star, and he loved making films. He also loved his car, a silver Porsche 550 Spyder that he nicknamed Little Bastard. In the early afternoon of September 30, 1955, Dean and Porsche factory mechanic Rolf Weutherich were on their way to an auto rally in Salinas, California. Dean was pulled over for speeding by a Bakersfield police officer, who issued a citation for driving 65 in a 55 zone and cautioned Dean to slow down and be careful. Dean and his companion continued on their way toward Paso Robles, with plans to spend the night, then leave the next morning for Salinas.

Around the same time, 23-year-old Cal Poly student Donald Turnupseed was heading home in his 1950 Ford Tutor. He made a left turn at the intersection of Highway 41 onto Highway 466 (later renamed Highway 46), unaware of the approaching Spyder. Contrary to reports that have since stated Dean's speed was in excess of 80 miles per hour, California Highway Patrol officer Ron Nelson, one of the first law enforcement officers on the scene, said the wreckage and the position of Dean's body "indicated his speed at the time of the accident was more like 55 mph." The two vehicles met nearly head on. Little Bastard crumpled and spun around, coming to rest near a telephone pole about 15 feet off the road. Rolf was thrown from the car and suffered a broken leg and serious head injuries, but he survived. Amazingly, Donald Turnupseed escaped the accident with only a gashed forehead and a bruised nose. But

James Dean suffered fatal injuries, including near decapitation. The coroner listed Dean's injuries as broken neck, multiple fractures of the upper and lower jaw, multiple fractures of the left and right arm, and other internal injuries caused by the two-car collision. James Dean was 24 years old.

In 1977 a James Dean memorial was erected near the site of the crash. The stylized sculpture is composed of concrete and stainless steel around a tree in a place called Cholame. Today, the Jack Ranch Café sits nearby, all that's left of the little town of Cholame. The sculpture was made in Japan and transported to Cholame, accompanied by the project's benefactor, Seita Ohnishi. Ohnishi chose the site after examining the location of the accident, now little more than a few road signs and flashing yellow signals. This is not the exact spot where the crash occurred; it was 900 feet northeast, before the highways were realigned. In September 2005, the intersection of Highways 41 and 46 in Cholame was dedicated as the James Dean Memorial Highway as part of the commemoration of the 50th anniversary of his death. Donald Turnupseed went on with his life, forming a fairly successful electrical contracting business and trying to avoid the spotlight, refusing all interview requests. He died in 1995. The site still draws visitors and curiosity seekers, though not as many as it used to. Dean only made three films: *Rebel Without a Cause*, *East of Eden*, and *Giant*, but his legacy lives on

varieties of common and exotic birds. The Zoo makes a fun destination if you've brought your kids to the largely adult playground that is Paso Robles.

Paso Robles Area Historical Society

The **Paso Robles Area Historical Society** (800 12th St., 805/238-4996, www.pasorobleshistoricalsociety.org, Tues. and Thurs.-Sun. 10am-4pm, donation) is a nice place to hide from the heat on a warm day. This small

museum is housed in the old Carnegie Library, which served the city from 1908 to 1995, and is located smack-dab in the middle of city park. Old bookshelves are filled with historical photos, and rotating exhibits highlight some facet of local history.

Franklin Hot Springs

Franklin Hot Springs (3015 Creston Rd., 805/712-5372, www.franklinhotsprings.com, Mon.-Thurs. 8am-10pm, Fri.-Sun. 8am-midnight, adults $7, under age 14, military, and

Franklin Hot Springs

seniors $5) is not a fancy mineral springs retreat. This local-favorite soaking spot is located on a ramshackle farm just east of town. If you can get past the rusting farm equipment and trailers on the property, you can relax in a concrete pool with a natural bottom. The 97°F water spills out of pipes at one end of the pool, and spills into a lake at the other end. There's a good chance you'll be sharing the waters with some ducks and a few grizzled locals.

WINE TASTING

The hills outside Paso Robles are braided with rows of grape vines, evidence of the growth of the local wine industry in recent years. The region now boasts more than 200 wineries, over 100 of which have tasting rooms open to the public. The sprawling landscape can be divided into four easily navigable parts: Highway 46 west of town, Highway 46 east of town (which does not directly connect to West Highway 46), downtown Paso Robles, and the remote areas north of town, where several roads branch off U.S. 101.

West Highway 46

The densest concentration of wineries cluster along Highway 46 west of Paso Robles and the little roads that spring off this main thoroughfare. Many intrepid wine tasters never make it past this short and easy-to-travel stretch, which locals refer to as the Westside.

ROTTA WINERY

Rotta Winery (250 Winery Rd., 805/237-0510, www.rottawinery.com, daily 10:30am-5:30pm, tasting $5) has been making wine in the region since 1856. It's best known for its estate zinfandel and black monukka desert wine, which is sweet but not cloying.

HUNT CELLARS

One of the best wineries in these parts is **Hunt Cellars** (2875 Oakdale Rd., 805/237-1600, www.huntcellars.com, daily 10:30am-5:30pm, tasting $5-10). Friendly and intensely knowledgeable staff members pour some of the best wines in Paso at this midsize informal tasting room. You enter a building that looks more like

SAN LUIS OBISPO

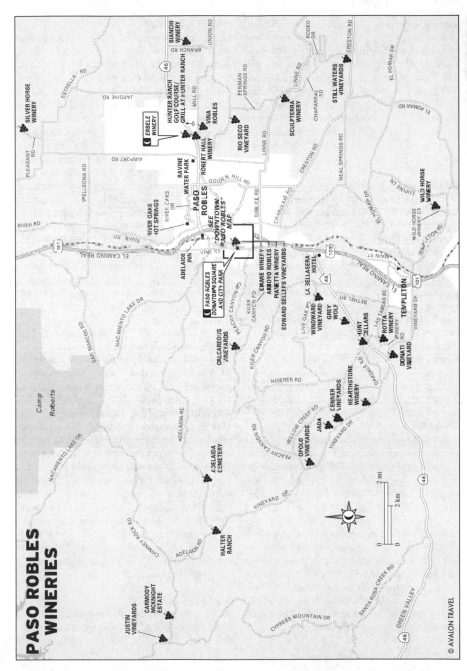

PASO ROBLES WINERIES

© AVALON TRAVEL

a house than a winery, then choose the regular or reserve tasting. Also be sure to check the chalkboard behind the bar for the day's specialty offerings. Almost all of the wines at Hunt are grown in the family-owned Destiny Vineyard. The specialty of the house is cabernet sauvignon, and Hunt makes some of the best in California. You'll also get to taste a few chardonnays, other red varietals, some red blends, and the famed (and expensive) port and dessert wines.

DARK STAR CELLARS

If you favor small wineries that only produce tiny runs of wine, **Dark Star Cellars** (2985 Anderson Rd., 805/237-2389, www.darkstarcellars.com, Fri.-Sun. 10:30am-5pm, tasting $10) is perfect for you. Be sure to ask at the bar about the "synthetic gravity" that is so important to the slow fermentation process used at Dark Star. You'll taste about 10 vintages here—all red wines of the Bordeaux and Rhône tribe. Most visitors think that the best of the lot is the much-lauded Ricordati, a Bordeaux-style blend that wins international awards year after year. Perhaps the nicest surprise of all comes when you've picked your favorites; prices at Dark Star range up to about $35 a bottle, and many are under $30.

EDWARD SELLERS

Edward Sellers wanted to make wine in spite of his moniker (yes, that's his real name, not a marketing gimmick). With a production of 5,000 cases and using exclusively Paso Robles fruit, the **Edward Sellers** (1401 W. Hwy. 46, 805/239-8915, www.edwardsellers.com, daily 11am-5pm, tasting $6) winery specializes in viognier, rosé, syrah, and various blends, and these are uniformly some of the best Rhône-style wines coming out of Paso Robles. Winemaker Amy Butler possesses an uncanny ability to make her wines both lush and restrained. In fact, she gets many compliments from fellow winemakers. With wines like these, you don't need much else.

HALTER RANCH

A long drive on curved roads under a canopy of oaks leads up to the old property known as **Halter Ranch** (8910 Adelaida Rd., 805/226-9455, www.halterranch.com, daily 11am-5pm, tasting $10). The 1880 Victorian house and old silo and barn seem perfectly suited to the spot. By contrast, the tasting room, built in 2005, is modern, with a curved bar, warm wood tones, and hip track lighting embedded in the wood beams. Halter Ranch is a 2,000-acre vineyard with 280 acres of grapes, mostly dedicated to Rhône and Bordeaux varieties. They also make rosé, sauvignon blanc, and syrah. A selection of cheeses, cured meats, dipping oils, and crackers are for sale and are perfect for a spontaneous picnic outside under the olive trees, or near the outdoor fireplace on the flagstone. Fresh bread is brought in on Friday. Halter Ranch honey is also available. The vineyard offers weekend winery and cave tours (Sat.-Sun. 11am and 1pm).

JADA

Wines at **Jada** (5620 Vineyard Dr., 805/226-4200, www.jadavineyard.com, daily 11am-5pm, tasting $10-15) go by unique names like XCV, a white blend of viognier, roussanne, and grenache blanc; Mirror, a mix of syrah and petit verdot; Hell's Kitchen, another blend of syrah, grenache, mourvèdre, and tannat; and Jack of Hearts, a Bordeaux-style blend of cabernet sauvignon, petit verdot, and merlot. The stacked stone walls and arched iron gate that fronts the highway will lead you alongside a line of mature purple-leafed plum trees. Inside the tasting room, the ceiling narrows, and the windows behind the tasting bar have beautiful views to the vineyards. The viewing deck, an expansive area of tables and chairs, also provides views of the vines and nearby properties. The facility has a hip, modern design juxtaposed with the earthy rolling hills.

DONATI VINEYARD

All of the wines at **Donati Vineyard** (2720 Oak View Rd., 805/238-0676, www.donatifamily-vineyard.com, daily 10am-5pm, tasting $5) come from Paicines, a mostly unknown area in a remote part of Monterey County. The majority of the production is red wine, especially cabernet sauvignon, which is made into a single varietal wine and which is also blended into claret, Meritage, and merlot. There are also limited quantities of syrah, cabernet franc, and malbec. As for the white wines, they produce pinot blanc, chardonnay, and pinot grigio. The tasting room is housed in a European-looking white building off Highway 46. The interior is modern with a sleekly styled tasting bar, in contrast to the Old World feel of the exterior. They make some wonderful wines, and it's a worthy stop.

GREY WOLF

The tasting room at **Grey Wolf** (2174 Hwy. 46, 805/237-0771, www.greywolfcellars.com, daily 11am-5pm, tasting $5) is inside a restored 60-year-old farmhouse, a great backdrop for tasting the wines. Grey Wolf was established in 1994 with the main goal of red wine production. They use only French and American oak in their barrel program, which supports their big reds, including zinfandel, syrah, petite sirah, cabernet sauvignon, and an excellent Meritage blend. There are one or two white wines, but those are produced in small quantities and usually sell out quickly.

DENNER VINEYARDS

At **Denner Vineyards** (5414 Vineyard Dr., 805/239-4287, www.dennervineyards.com, daily 11am-4pm by appointment, tasting $10), it's all about Rhône-style wines, with the lone exception of zinfandel. Syrah, mourvèdre, grenache, viognier, and roussanne are the grapes of choice, blended into seamless plush and sensuous wines. It's a state-of-the-art modern winery with a curvilinear design to match the rolling hillside. The tasting room, with expansive views to the surrounding vineyards, feels more like Napa Valley than Paso Robles. But it's all wonderfully executed, and from the wines to the building it is a sophisticated and beautiful experience.

CALCAREOUS VINEYARDS

Calcareous Vineyards (3430 Peachy Canyon Rd., 805/239-0289, www.calcareous.com, daily 11am-5pm, tasting $10) is named for the calcareous limestone soil that is rich with calcium and magnesium and pretty much defines this region's dirt. With over 400 acres, they are able to make an impressive array of wines, from cabernet sauvignon and petit verdot to pinot noir, chardonnay, viognier, and lots of blends. The beautifully manicured lawn at the front and back of the tasting room gives nice views of the gentle surrounding hills, and there are tables to relax at.

OPOLO VINEYARDS

Opolo is the name of a blended rosé-style wine from the Dalmatian coast bordering the Adriatic Sea in Croatia. Yes, it's far from Paso Robles, and **Opolo Vineyards** (7110 Vineyard Dr., 805/238-9593, www.opolo.com, Sun.-Fri. 10am-5pm, Sat. 10am-5:30pm, tasting $10) doesn't even make the opolo wine. They do, however, make lots of other wines, nearly 40,000 cases of 30 different varieties, including the standard zinfandel, cabernet sauvignon, chardonnay, merlot, and syrah. They also produce lesser-known wines like roussanne, malbec, grenache, and petit verdot. There are three walking trails that meander through the vineyards, so everyone can experience firsthand the beauty and tranquility of the vines. Tables are placed strategically along the trails for impromptu picnics.

HEARTHSTONE WINERY

At **Hearthstone Winery** (5070 Vineyard Dr., 805/260-1945, www.hearthstonevineyard.com, Thurs.-Mon. 11am-5pm, tasting $5), the tasting room, in a modest building in some of Paso's prime wine-growing region, has postcard views from the back deck of the verdant rolling hills the area is known for. The warm earthy tones of the interior make you feel like you're safe and secure, like being protected by rock and earth, which is exactly what the name Hearthstone was meant to imply. The 40 planted acres have a shallow clay top layer, perfect for stressing the vines, and are dotted with chunks of limestone rocks. One of the wines, Slipstone, a blend of syrah and grenache, received its moniker when the earthquake that hit Paso Robles in 2003 dislodged a large limestone rock that tumbled down the mountain and hit the grenache vines. It's still there to this day. Cabernet sauvignon, sangiovese, syrah, pinot noir, roussanne, and rosé round out the offerings. Hearthstone also has vineyard tours for two people with a private tasting (email josslyn@hearthstonevineyard.com, $62).

CARMODY MCKNIGHT ESTATE
The **Carmody McKnight Estate** (11240 Chimney Rock Rd., 805/238-9392, www.carmodymcknight.com, daily 10am-5pm, tasting $5) is one of those spots you just don't want to leave. As you're tasting the wines, you have a view onto a little pond with a small boat on it; it provides the feeling that you could get in it and lounge the day away. And then there's the art gallery, located inside the tasting room; much of the art finds its way onto the labels, and most of it is done by the owner himself. The wines are wonderful, restrained, balanced, and elegant. You will find pinot noir, cabernet franc, and four versions of chardonnay, among others.

JUSTIN VINEYARDS
Up the road from Carmody McKnight Estate is **Justin Vineyards** (11680 Chimney Rock Rd., 805/238-6932, www.justinwine.com, daily 10am-4:30pm, tasting $10). Justin has become known as one of the best wineries in the area, crafting Bordeaux-style blends, including Isosceles and Justification, that almost always score well in the national wine press. Once inside the tasting room, the plush rich wood tones of the bar and remote setting make it hard to leave and drive back down the mountain.

WINDWARD VINEYARD
Windward Vineyard (1380 Live Oak Rd., 805/239-2565, www.windwardvineyard.com, daily 10:30am-5pm, tasting $10) is something

of an anomaly. Normally pinot noir grows better in cooler weather, often near coastal influences. Windward is in Paso Robles, which is hot in the summer and downright cold in the winter. But this small parcel of vines is situated in a pocket of land that protects it. All they make is pinot noir, and they usually have several vintages out for tasting to compare and contrast. Windward sits among other vineyard neighbors, and their wood-paneled tasting room, though small, occasionally has artworks on the walls.

East Highway 46
Not as crowded as Highway 46 west of Paso Robles, Highway 46 east of town still has plenty of great wineries. You might even recognize one or two names out in the Eastside.

CELLAR 360 PASO ROBLES
One of the biggest winemakers to maintain a tasting room in the Paso region is **Cellar 360 Paso Robles** (7000 Hwy. 46 E., 805/226-7133, www.meridianvineyards.com, Fri.-Sun. 10am-5pm, tasting $5) at Meridian Vineyards. You've no doubt seen these wines on many menus and countless supermarket shelves. They make all the classic California varietal vintages, with best-sellers in chardonnay and cabernet sauvignon. Check out the Limited Release list for, well, more of the same plus a few slightly less common wines like a gewürztraminer and a sangiovese. Meridian's deli and store provide a perfect place to gather everything you need for the perfect wine picnic.

◖ EBERLE WINERY
It might not be the biggest, but ◖ **Eberle Winery** (3810 Hwy. 46 E., 3.5 miles east of U.S. 101, 805/238-9607, www.eberlewinery.com, fall-spring daily 10am-5pm, summer daily 10am-6pm, tasting free) is one of the pioneers of the Paso wine region. Gary Eberle has been making wine here for more than 25 years and winning a passel of gold medals over that time. Be sure to get a spot on a cave tour while you're visiting, then head to the light-wood tasting room. The free cave tour is a great

way to escape the heat on a hot summer's day. You'll learn about the wine-making process as you walk past barrels of wine stacked up like giant logs along the cave's walls. Despite the fun statuary and the great caves at Eberle, the star attraction here is the wine. The medium-size list features mostly hearty, bold red wines such as cabernet sauvignon, barbera, zinfandel, and a few fabulous blends. A few whites find their way to the bar, such as the Paso favorite viognier and the lesser-known roussanne. Taste as many as you possibly can; you may be surprised at how many bottles you'll want to walk away with. With most vintages selling for $15-25, you might be able to afford a few extras.

ROBERT HALL WINERY

Robert Hall Winery (3443 Mill Rd., 805/239-1616, www.roberthallwinery.com, daily 10am-5pm, tasting $5-10) is a massive complex; as you enter the tasting room you realize how small you are in contrast. The chandelier alone is huge. The tasting bar sits in the center, and the perimeter is full of products and gift items. They offer a wide selection of wines, from everyday inexpensive wines like their chardonnay and sauvignon blancs to their higher-end reserve syrah, cabernet sauvignon, and vintage ports. Robert Hall wines are widely distributed. Part of that is marketing, but part of that is due to the talent of winemaker and Texas native Don Brady. The grapes are sourced from the Paso Robles region in part to demonstrate how wonderful the produce of a region like Paso Robles is. Robert Hall made enough money doing diverse entrepreneurial things to be able to secure a prime plot of land here in the early 1990s, and today, he has one of the largest wineries in Paso Robles and is a stalwart promoter of the area.

VINA ROBLES

At **Vina Robles** (3700 Mill Rd., 805/227-4812, www.vinarobles.com, summer daily 10am-6pm, winter daily 10am-5pm, tasting $5-12), the centerpiece of the tasting room is the large fireplace surrounded by comfy sofas. This is a voluminous space with stone walls and eclectic artwork. The massive arched window looks out to the vineyards and the small lake. The wines comprise cabernet sauvignon, petite sirah, zinfandel, petit verdot, port wines, and blends of these grapes. They source fruit from other counties as well, notably Monterey County. The estate wines are well priced, most under $20. Just a few hundred feet from the tasting room, the outdoor Vina Robles Amphitheatre has hosted acts like Lyle Lovett, Los Lobos, and Tony Bennett.

BIANCHI WINERY

The tasting room at **Bianchi Winery** (3380 Branch Rd., 805/226-9922, www.bianchiwinery.com, daily 10am-5pm, tasting $5), off East Highway 46, has a small lake that hugs the exterior patio, surrounded by vines. The interior is beautifully designed, a melding of natural stone, expansive windows, and an inviting fireplace. The curved bar has an etched glass countertop, and the vibe inside is modern and hip, a juxtaposition with the rural surroundings. Bianchi produces about 15,000 cases and has the standard offerings of pinot noir, chardonnay, cabernet sauvignon, and others, with a nod to Bianchi's Italian heritage with wines like sangiovese, barbera, and refosco, an obscure oddball grape from northern Italy.

STILL WATERS VINEYARDS

Still Waters Vineyards (2750 Old Grove Lane, 805/237-9321, www.stillwatersvineyards.com, Thurs.-Mon. 11am-5pm, tasting $5) produces very small lots of wine, at most 200 cases of chardonnay, viognier, merlot, malbec, and cabernet sauvignon, at their out-of-the-way property. Since there was a 100-year-old olive grove on the property, they naturally decided to make olive oil as well, which is becoming more common in the Paso Robles area. A somewhat under-the-radar winery, Still Waters makes some very nice wines.

SCULPTERRA WINERY

At first glance, **Sculpterra Winery** (5125 Linne Rd., 805/226-8881, www.sculpterra.com, Fri.-Sun. 10am-5pm, tasting $5) seems more like a gimmick than a serious winery. Huge sculptures like a 10-ton puma and an 8-ton mammoth, all designed by local Atascadero artist John Jagger, greet visitors. The gardens are great for picnicking near these pieces after you've sampled mourvèdre, merlot, petite sirah, and chardonnay. While you're visiting, try the pistachios that grow on the property. Their wines are well balanced, achieving acidity with fruit ripeness, and their blends are quite nice.

RIO SECO VINEYARD

At **Rio Seco Vineyard** (4295 Union Rd., 805/237-8884, www.riosecowine.com, daily 11am-5pm, tasting $5), you'll realize that baseball has nothing in common with wine—unless you're owner Tom Hinkle. Tom was once a baseball scout, visiting high school, college, and semi-pro games to find the best young talent throughout the country. Then he retired and went into the wine business. The tasting room is unimpressive, a metal and wood building whose former owner was growing marijuana in the barn, but the wines Tom makes, like zinfandel, viognier, cabernet sauvignon, cabernet franc, and syrah, are inexpensive and unpretentious, just the sort of wine you'd have with pizza or burgers.

Downtown Paso Robles

Many wineries have set up tasting rooms right in downtown Paso.

ORCHID HILL VINEYARD

Orchid Hill Vineyard (1140 Pine St., 805/237-7525, www.orchidhillwine.com, daily noon-6pm, tasting $5) offers a small list of varietals, including viognier, syrah, sangiovese, and zinfandel. Visitors also spend some time gaping at the walls, which bear original artworks by local artists.

PIANETTA WINERY TASTING ROOM

The Pianetta Winery's vineyards are 14 miles north of town, but the **Pianetta Winery Tasting Room** (829 13th St., 805/226-4005, www.pianettawinery.com, Sun.-Thurs. noon-6pm, Fri.-Sat. 11am-7pm, tasting $5) is right in the heart of Paso Robles. The Pianetta Winery is known for its cabernet sauvignons.

ARROYO ROBLES

Arroyo Robles (1317 Park Ave., 877/759-9463, www.arroyorobles.com, daily 11am-7pm, tasting $5) is located a block and a half from Paso Robles's downtown historic City Park. Arroyo Robles offers wine, of course, but also a plethora of other items in their well-stocked tasting room, including books, gift items, maple syrup, and pancake mix, a sort of homage to a property the owners once had back in Vermont. Even now they offer a pancake breakfast before some of the major wine festivals in town. A broad portfolio of wine is made here, including the standard offerings like chardonnay, zinfandel, and syrah; they have also branched off into viognier, tempranillo, rosé, and several ports. Not willing to rest on their laurels, they also produce two sparkling wines, one of which is a sweet almond sparkler, and they are starting production on apple and pear hard cider.

Remote Wineries

To the north of Paso Robles, several roads branch off U.S. 101 leading to more remote wineries—and even better, their tasting rooms.

ADELAIDA CELLARS

Even if you don't love wine, it's worth the trip up to **Adelaida Cellars** (5805 Adelaida Rd., 800/676-1232, www.adelaida.com, daily 10am-5pm, tasting $10). You'll get stunning views of Adelaida's mountain vineyards and down to the valley below. Adelaida wines are made mostly with grapes grown on the estate vineyards, and the results can be fabulous. Adelaida takes advantage of its high elevation and difficult soil to raise grapes that produce small lots of top-tier boutique wines. Their signature wine is the pinot noir. The winery produces vintages under four labels; the Reserve and Adelaida labels run toward the higher end, while the SLO and Schoolhouse labels provide tasty and affordable table wines suitable for everyday drinking.

TABLAS CREEK VINEYARD

A local producer with prestigious founders and backers, **Tablas Creek Vineyard** (9339 Adelaida Rd., 805/237-1231, www.tablascreek.com, daily 10am-5pm) specializes in varietals and blends in the Rhône and Châteauneuf-du-Pape styles. Taste from the longish list of current commercial and winery-only vintages. Tablas Creek takes its wine-making seriously, maintaining its own grapevine nursery, keeping its vineyards organic, and using only its own yeasts created on-site. If such practices interest you, call in advance to get a spot on the vineyard and winery tours (daily 10:30am and 2pm). End your survey of this showplace with a visit to the dark bar and bright artwork of the tasting room. You'll find many uncommon for California blends and varietals, and the Tablas Creek bar staff can help you expand your palate and your knowledge of wine.

HALTER RANCH VINEYARD

Halter Ranch Vineyard (8910 Adelaida Rd., 805/226-9455, www.halterranch.com, daily 11am-5pm, tasting $10) sits on a 1,000-acre ranch property once owned by a pioneer of the Paso Robles area. In 2000 the ranch was bought by a Swiss emigrant who planted almost 280 acres of grapes from the Bordeaux and Rhône varietal families. All the vineyards are farmed using organic and sustainable methods, which combine with the limestone-rich soil and unique climate to help create intensely flavorful wines. The ranch is fronted by a charming white Victorian farmhouse, and tours (call in advance) take you around both this house and the other historic buildings on the property as well as the two wine-making facility structures. This newish winery has a small list from which to taste and purchase; its flagship vintages are syrah and cabernet sauvignon, but the less expensive ranch red and ranch white blends are also good buys.

KIAMIE WINERY

Kiamie Winery (9750 Adelaida Rd., 805/226-8333, www.kiamiewines.com, daily 11am-5pm, tasting $5) is a newer addition to the Paso Robles wine scene. The emphasis is on Rhône- and Bordeaux-style blends. Their grapes come from the Westside region, and all the vineyards they source are within close proximity of each other, lending to the balanced nature of their wines.

SILVER HORSE WINERY

The first thing you notice as you step out of your car onto the bluff-top tasting room of **Silver Horse Winery** (2995 Pleasant Rd., San Miguel, 805/467-9463, Fri.-Sun. 11am-5pm, tasting $7) is how quiet it is. Then you notice the views of the vast sky and the simple rolling hills into the distance. The Silver Horse portfolio includes only one white wine, albariño, as well as cabernet sauvignon, merlot, petite sirah, and several blended wines. The interior of the Spanish-style tasting room is comfortable, with a vaulted ceiling, a wood-burning fireplace, and leather club chairs. Autumnal tones and Southwestern art creates a warm, relaxed vibe. On either side of the tasting bar, window cutouts allow for views into the barrel room. Outside are boccie ball courts and, fittingly, horseshoes.

WILD HORSE WINERY

Wild Horse Winery (1437 Wild Horse Winery Court, 805/788-6310, www.wildhorsewinery.com, daily 11am-5pm, tasting $5) has long been one of the leading wineries on the Central Coast. They produce nearly 200,000 cases each year, and few wineries in California source fruit from such a broad spectrum of vineyards, which has allowed Wild Horse to select grapes from the specific areas they feel best showcase a particular wine. For example, they produce a pinot noir from one growing region in San Luis Obispo and two distinct growing regions in Santa Barbara. Viognier, chardonnay, and a malvasia bianca, a perennial favorite, are just some of their white wines. Syrah, cabernet sauvignon, merlot, and their flagship pinot noir are the reds. When you visit, be certain to try the heirloom varietals they have become known for, including blaufränkisch and verdelho. When in season, the grapes hanging from the arbor at the entrance are tantalizing fruit that you're encouraged to sample. There are plenty of picnic tables out front on the grass. The tasting room is small with a low bar on one side of the room and frankly isn't interesting. Like many tasting rooms, the decor is not really the point; it's the wines. Wild Horse is located near Templeton, and it's a quiet drive through rolling hills to get here.

POZO VALLEY WINERY

Pozo Valley Winery (2200 El Camino Real, Santa Margarita, 805/438-3375, www.pozovalley.com, Fri.-Sun. noon-5pm, tasting free) is not actually located in Pozo Valley, which might arguably be a good thing. The town of Pozo is 18 miles southeast of Santa Margarita, but the Pozo Valley Winery tasting room is just 1.5 miles off U.S. 101 in Santa Margarita. The tasting room is rustic, with much more of a cowboy feel than the flashy architecture of Napa Valley. An old wooden wine press sits in the corner, a reminder of earlier days. Zinfandel, cabernet sauvignon, and merlot are the inexpensive offerings, and they work well with food.

ANCIENT PEAKS WINERY

Ancient Peaks Winery (22720 El Camino Real, Santa Margarita, 805/365-7045, www.ancientpeaks.com, Thurs.-Mon. 11am-5:30pm, tasting $5) is located just one mile off U.S. 101 in Santa Margarita. The vineyards are located at the southernmost part of the Paso Robles growing area, and the unique soils, formed from the floor of an ancient ocean, are what makes their wines different, along with the talent of the winemaker. The soil nutrients found in this uplifted seabed are like nothing else in the entire region. You really need to sample the wines yourself to understand their uniqueness. The tasting room is all polished wood with a pleasing rustic charm, and they pour sauvignon blanc, merlot, cabernet sauvignon, and zinfandel with bottle prices usually under $20.

Wine Tours

If you prefer not to do your own driving on your wine-tasting excursions (something to consider if everyone in your group enjoys wine), take one of the many available wine tours. **The Wine Wranglers** (866/238-6400, http://thewinewrangler.com, $90-120, depending on pickup location) offers daily group tours, plus customized individual tours for a higher fee. Experienced guides will take you to some of the biggest and best wineries in the region. Group tour guests ride in the comfort of a small luxury bus; buses pick up tasters from Cambria, San Luis Obispo, Morro Bay, Pismo Beach, Paso Robles, and a number of other towns in the county. A picnic lunch in one of the vineyards is included, as are all tasting fees at the wineries you visit. If you know the region, feel free to request a stop at your favorite winery.

To taste at your own pace, contact **The Wine Line** (805/610-8267, www.hoponthewineline.com, from $60), where a chauffeured van will drop you off and pick you up at your choice of 60 wineries. In addition to information on Santa Margarita Ranch's sustainable wine-making practices, **Margarita Adventures** (22719 El Camino, 805/438-3120, www.margarita-adventures.com, adults $99, children $79) provides you with an overview of the ranch—from four zip lines 1,300 feet above the valley; it's not your average wine tour.

ENTERTAINMENT AND EVENTS
Live Music

Located on the grounds of the popular winery, the 3,300-seat outdoor **Vina Robles Amphitheatre** (3800 Mill Rd., 805/286-3680, www.vinaroblesamphitheatre.com, concert season May-Nov.) hosts performances by internationally known acts, including Lyle Lovett, Los Lobos, and Tony Bennett.

BARS

The **Firestone Taproom** (1400 Ramada Dr., 805/225-5911, www.firestonebeer.com, daily 11am-9pm) offers an airy, industrial bar where you can sample the Firestone Walker Brewing Company's beers, including the popular DBA

© STUART THORNTON

Firestone Walker Brewing Company

British Pale Ale and taproom-only brews that include a hoppy pilsner or a brown ale brewed with hemp seeds. Enjoy pub fare like burgers, pizzas, and steak ($12-24) at the U-shaped bar or the adjacent dining area.

The **Pony Club Bar** (1021 Pine St., 805/226-9995, www.hotelcheval.com, Sun.-Thurs. 5pm-10pm, Fri.-Sat. 5pm-11pm) in the upscale Hotel Cheval serves wine, beer, and *soju* cocktails indoors both at a horseshoe-shaped zinc bar and on an outdoor patio. Locals stop in for the popular happy hour (5pm-7pm) when all glasses of wine are $7 and all beers are half price.

The local chain **F. McLintocks Saloon** (1234 Park St., 805/238-2233, www.mclintocks.com, Mon.-Thurs. 11am-9pm, Fri. 11am-10pm, Sat. 8am-10pm, Sun. 8am-9pm) is a pseudo-Old West bar where the cocktails come in mason jars and mounted game heads and cattle brands decorate the walls. Hearty saloon fare includes steaks, ribs, burgers, and pastas.

Pappy McGregor's (1122 Pine St., 805/238-7070, www.pappymcgregors.com, daily 11am-1am) will satisfy those who want an Irish pub experience. Drink Guinness or a Paso black and tan (Guinness mixed with local favorite Firestone DBA) in one of the two bar areas or in the outdoor beer garden.

A true dive bar, the **Pine Street Saloon** (1234 Pine St., 805/238-1114, www.pinestreet-saloon.com, daily 11am-2am) is housed in an old building with history both as a hotel and later as a brothel. Enjoy live music or try your hand at karaoke or pool. There's a smoking and drinking corral out back.

Festivals and Events
SUMMER
The biggest annual event in Paso Robles is the **California Mid-State Fair** (2198 Riverside Ave., 805/239-0655, www.midstatefair.com, adults $10, children $6, seniors $8). The 11-day fair, which takes place every July, draws people from all over the state for its agriculture, livestock, and flower displays along with food and games. The biggest draws are the many music concerts at the fair: Performers have included

John Mayer, Rascal Flatts, Matchbox Twenty, and Tim McGraw.

At the **Winemakers' Cookoff** (Paso Robles Event Center, 2198 Riverside Ave., 877/264-6979, www.wincmakerscookoff.com, $75), 30 local winemakers offer tastes of their food and wine menus in a competition that raises money for local youth scholarships.

SPRING
Paso Robles celebrates a certain robust red-wine varietal in mid-March with the **Zinfandel Weekend** (805/239-8463, www.pasowine.com); 130 wineries participate in events over three days, including barrel tastings, wine-maker dinners, vineyard tours, and barbecues.

The simply named **Wine Festival** (805/239-8463, www.pasowine.com), featuring 60 wineries, includes a reserve event and a grand tasting in Paso Robles's downtown City Park.

FALL
Harvest Wine Weekend (805/239-8463, www.pasowine.com) celebrate the harvest every October with three days of events at 120 local wineries.

SHOPPING
Shopping Malls
There are two malls in three areas near downtown. Nibblick Road, off Spring Street and U.S. 101, bisects **Woodland Plaza** (180 Nibblick Rd.). This large outdoor mall includes Kohl's, Staples, Big 5, a pharmacy, a grocery store, JCPenney, Wal-Mart, the usual food joints, smaller specialty stores, and plenty of parking. Right across the street, where Nibblick and South River Road meet, is the smaller **The Highlands** (Oak Hill Rd. and Nibblick Rd.).

Clothing
Alliance Board Company (1233 Park St., 805/238-2600, Mon.-Sat. 10am-6pm, Sun. 10am-5pm) sells a small collection of surfboards along with snowboarding and skateboarding gear and some worthy surf-wear brands. The sunglasses section is extensive. **Kahunas** (817 12th St., 805/238-3214, www.

kahunassurf.com, Mon.-Sat. 10am-6pm, Sun. 10am-5pm), on the city square, also focuses on beachwear. There are no surfboards here, but surf accessories and sandals are for sale. Right down the street from Kahunas, **Sole Tree** (835 12th St., 805/238-7653, www.thesoletree.com, Mon.-Sat. 10am-6pm, Sun. 11am-4pm) offers Frye boots, Miz Mooz footwear, and a variety of handbags. On the other side of the city park, **Apropos** (840 11th St., Suite 103, 805/239-8282, Mon.-Sat. 10am-6pm, Sun. noon-4pm) sells women's apparel, including brands like Johnny Was, Amma, and Komarov as well as vintage-style jewelry.

Art
The nonprofit **Studios on the Park** (1130 Pine St., 805/238-9800, Thurs. and Sun. noon-6pm, Fri.-Sat. noon-7pm) showcases work by local artists. The **Meadow Muffins Mercantile & Artisan Cooperative** (811 13th St., 805/423-3632, www.mymeadowmuffins.com, Mon.-Sat. 11am-5pm, Sun. 11am-3pm) is an artists collective that sells all locally made products, from jewelry to cowboy-inspired art.

Books
You'll find shelves of used paperbacks, including westerns, romance, and mysteries, at **Spare Time Used Books** (945 12th St., 805/237-1140, Mon.-Thurs. 10:30am-5pm).

Specialty Food
Powell's Sweet Shoppe (840 11th St., Suite 101, 805/239-1544, Mon.-Sat. 10am-9pm, Sun. 10am-8pm) specializes in all kinds of sweet indulgences, with candy bins, gelato, and even chocolate-covered bacon on a stick. The first cheese shop in Paso Robles, **Di Raimondo's Italian Market & Cheese Shop** (822 13th St., 805/238-1268, www.pasocheese.com, Mon.-Sat. 10am-5pm, Sun. 11am-3pm) is still going strong. It's worth a stop at this tiny store just to sample the selection of mostly Italian cheeses and meats. Another nice spot for nibbling is **We Olive** (1311 Park St., 805/239-7667, www.weolive.

© STUART THORNTON

Powell's Sweet Shoppe

com, Mon.-Sat. 10am-6pm, Sun. 11am-4pm). Everything is available to sample, including a jalapeño olive oil and a fresh garlic olive oil.

SPORTS AND RECREATION
Lakes
Fifteen miles from Paso Robles, **Lake Nacimiento** (10625 Nacimiento Lake Dr., 805/238-3256, www.nacimientoresort.com) has 165 miles of shoreline perfect for water-skiing and bass fishing. Boat rentals are available, with options ranging from an eight-person pontoon boat to a 15-foot fishing vessel ($100-425 per day). You can also stay overnight in a campsite ($30-40) or in a lodge unit or separate cabin ($230-340). A little farther north, **Lake San Antonio** (74255 San Antonio Rd., 805/472-2311, www.lakesanantonioresort.com) also has opportunities for boating and fishing. Rent a ski, fishing, or pontoon boat ($100-425) for the day. Then stay the evening in a south-shore modular cabin ($195-340) or a north shore cottage ($235-265).

Water Park
Cool off at **The Ravine Waterpark** (2301 Airport Rd., 805/237-8500, www.ravinewaterpark.com, summer usually daily 10:30am-6pm, hours vary so phone ahead, adults $20, children under 48 inches tall $15, seniors $11) with flume slides, enclosed tube drops, and a wave pool. There's also a wading pool for kids.

Horseback Riding and Stagecoaches
Harris Stage Lines (5995 N. River Rd., 805/237-1860, www.harrisstagelines.com) offers more than the typical trail rides. In addition to climbing on the back of a horse, you can take a ride in a refurbished historic stagecoach or wagon. There are even a couple of Hollywood-built Roman chariots. Call in advance to arrange the outing of your choice. If you're really into the historic vehicle scene, you can even book a private driving lesson.

Ballooning
Paso Robles sits in a pretty valley that's perfect

for a romantic ballooning jaunt. **Let's Go Ballooning!** (Rio Seco Winery, 4295 Union Rd., 805/458-1530, www.sloballoon.com, $189 pp) can take you on a one-hour ride up over the vineyards any day of the week. You'll meet early at the Rio Seco Winery and spend 2-3 hours with your pilot, preparing and learning about how to ride safely.

Golf

Choices for hitting the ball around include **Hunter Ranch Golf Course** (4041 E. Hwy. 46, 805/237-7444, www.hunterranchgolf.com, daily 6:30am-dusk, greens fees $47-79) and **River Oaks** (700 Clubhouse Dr., 805/226-7170, www.riveroaksgolfcourse.com, daily 8am-dusk, greens fees $18-24).

Hiking

From the summit of 2,624-foot **Cerro Alto**, a high peak, you can view the volcanic peaks of the Nine Sisters between Paso Robles and Morro Bay. It's a 2.75-mile hike to the top. The trailhead, signposted "Cerro Alto Trail 12E01," is at campsite 18 in the **Cerro Alto Campground** (end of Cerro Alto Rd., 805/434-1996, www.fs.usda.gov, $5). From Paso Robles, head 12 miles south on U.S. 101 to the town of Atascadero, and take Highway 41 southwest for eight miles Cerro Alto Road. Continue one mile to the campground.

Cycling

Central Coast Outdoors (805/528-1080, http://californiabicycletour.com, $111-179) offers morning and afternoon bike tours. Spend the morning riding on the coast from Ragged Point to Cambria; after that you'll get transported to Paso Robles to visit a handful of wineries. Every Memorial Day Weekend, cyclists take over Paso Robles for the **Great Western Bicycle Rally** (562/455-0157, www.greatwesternbicyclerally.com). The main event is the century ride from Paso Robles to Morro Bay and Cayucos. There are also shorter scenic rides, including a geocache ride, a mountain biking excursion, and a winery tour ride.

Spas

You'll smell the sulfur as you drive up to the **River Oaks Hot Springs & Spa** (800 Clubhouse Dr., 805/238-4600, www.riveroakshotsprings.com, Tues.-Sun. 9am-9pm, $12-16 per hour), several minutes' drive from downtown Paso. Located on country club land, the sulfur-heavy mineral springs include outdoor and indoor open-air hot tubs, some with views of the thick gardens, which screen the spas from the adjacent golf course. Several packages are available, with some including massages, facial treatments, and wine service.

ACCOMMODATIONS

Accommodations around Paso Robles tend toward upscale wine-themed B&Bs. There are also a couple of unique hotels in downtown Paso Robles.

Under $150

The family-owned and operated **⟨ Adelaide Inn** (1215 Ysabel Ave., 805/238-2770, www.adelaideinn.com, $93-145) offers nice details that other motels of the same size and price range don't. Unexpected features include a koi pond, a barbecue area, and mini golf greens located by the pool and the outdoor hot tub. The guest rooms are clean and modern with fridges and coffeemakers. Adelaide Inn is located near the junction of U.S. 101 and East Highway 46, about 12 blocks from downtown Paso Robles.

The **Best Western Black Oak** (1135 24th St., 805/238-4740, www.bestwestern-blackoak.com, $125-200) has renovated guest rooms with microwaves and fridges. The King Jacuzzi Suite is perfect for drinking wine in a private full-size soaking tub. The grounds include a sauna, a heated pool, and a hot tub. Across from the Paso Robles Event Center, the **Holiday Inn Express Hotel & Suites** (2455 Riverside Dr., 805/238-6500, www.hixpaso.com, $120-250) has a range of guest rooms, from standard rooms to suites with jetted tubs. Amenities include a fitness center, a heated indoor pool, an indoor spa, and a morning hot breakfast bar.

$150-250

The **Orchard Hill Farm Bed & Breakfast** (5415 Vineyard Dr., 805/239-9680, www.orchardhillbb.com, $230-285) has the feel of an English country manor house. Each of the luxurious guest rooms has a balcony and top-tier amenities, including a gourmet breakfast. The attractive grounds are great for walking and lounging. **The Canyon Villa** (1455 Kiler Canyon Rd., 805/238-3362, www.thecanyonvilla.com, $235-285) is built in the Mediterranean style that suits this area so well. The decor of the four guest rooms continues the Italianate theme, while the oversize spa tubs, plush linens, private balconies, and gas fireplaces create a feeling of lush comfort. If you can't get enough of Paso Robles' vineyards, spend some time at the **Seven Quails Vineyards Bed and Breakfast** (1340 Valley Quail Place, 805/712-8574, www.sevenquails.com, $180-305), which is perched on a hilltop looking over rows of grapevines. Seven Quails has just two luxury suites. Guests can relax in their rooms or in a large common area with a fireplace or outdoors on a patio.

Over $250

Luxury and comfort can be found at the ◖ **Hotel Cheval** (1021 Pine St., 805/226-9995, www.hotelcheval.com, $330-475), a 16-room boutique hotel just half a block from City Park. The large guest rooms all have oversize showers, comfy California king beds, and baths with stone floors. Some guest rooms also have soaking tubs and gas fireplaces. All of the guest rooms face a sun-dappled courtyard with fireplaces, chairs, and tables for taking in the sun. Complimentary continental breakfast is served in the Pony Club bar.

Dating back to 1891, the **Paso Robles Inn** (1103 Spring St., 800/676-1713, http://pasoroblesinn.com, $251-409) taps into Paso's naturally occurring hot springs. Its deluxe spa rooms have a private mineral tub, either in the room or on the outdoor deck. Outside, there are gardens, a heated pool, and a spa.

Out in the wooded region between Paso and

Hotel Cheval

© STUART THORNTON

the coast, the **Chanticleer Vineyard Bed and Breakfast** (1250 Paint Horse Place, 805/226-0600, www.chanticleervineyardbb.com, $255) offers relaxed vacationing. Each of the three guest rooms includes an iPod dock, organic spa toiletries, a fresh seasonal breakfast, vineyard views, and access to the house stock of cute fuzzy animals.

La Bellasera Hotel and Suites (206 Alexa Court, 805/238-2834, www.labellasera.com, $250-480) offers wine-country luxury, with 13 different types of guest room. Enjoy the swimming pool, whirlpool, fireside cabana, and fitness center.

FOOD
California Cuisine

The culinary epicenter of Paso Robles is ◖ **Artisan** (843 12th St., 805/237-8084, www.artisanpasorobles.com, Mon.-Thurs. 11am-2:30pm and 5pm-9pm, Fri.-Sat. 11am-2:30pm and 5pm-10pm, Sun. 10am-2:30pm and 5pm-9pm, $28-34), near the city square. The white tablecloths, bustling open kitchen, and numerous wine glasses hint at the high-class cuisine to come. Most of the ingredients come from local sources, including abalone from Cayucos and greens from Los Osos. Dinner entrées change seasonally but may include wild boar tenderloin, lacquered duck breast, or a whole *branzino* fish. Unsurprisingly, an extensive local wine list complements the food.

Near the city park, **Villa Creek** (1144 Pine St., 805/238-3000, www.villacreek.com, daily 4pm-10pm, $19-28) has been serving dishes made with local produce since 1998. The L-shaped bar and restaurant are a comfortable place to sample chef Tom Fundaro's creations, from fennel-crusted salmon to the popular "Not Nachos," which is a shared plate of duck confit, mole negro, *cojita,* and raw corn relish. The owners branched out into the wine business in 2001, opening Villa Creek Cellars; you can taste their wines at the restaurant.

Contemporary and Fusion

A small eatery adjacent to the city park, **Red Scooter Deli** (1102 Pine St., 805/237-1780, http://redscooterdeli.com, Mon.-Thurs. 8am-6pm, Fri.-Sat. 8am-8pm, Sun. 9am-4pm, $6-9.75) serves salads as well as hot and cold sandwiches. Try the turkey bacon melt, a tasty mess of turkey, bacon, Ortega chilies, melted pepper jack cheese, and chipotle sauce. Dine on the popular deck, which overlooks the park.

The dining area of the **Berry Hill Bistro** (1114 Pine St., 805/238-3929, www.berryhillbistro.com, daily 11am-9pm, $18-27) is decorated with colorful umbrellas. The lunch menu includes paninis and salads along with a popular raspberry chipotle chicken sandwich. Dinner includes selections like chicken marsala and pan-roasted halibut.

The farm-fresh ingredients on the menu at **Thomas Hill Organics Market Bistro & Wine Bar** (1305 Park Ave., 805/226-5888, www.thomashillorganics.com, Mon. and Wed.-Thurs. 11am-3pm and 5pm-9pm, Fri.-Sat. 11am-3pm and 5pm-10pm, Sun. 10am-3pm

and 5pm-9pm, $25-35) come from a 10-acre farm just east of town. Meal options change weekly, with dinner items that include pan-seared scallops and jerk-marinated duck. The **Odyssey World Café** (1214 Pine St., 805/237-7516, daily 11am-9pm, $16-22) promises "a world tour for your palate." Stops include a long stay in the Mediterranean for pastas and a quick trip to the East for stir-fries and rice bowls. Dine indoors or outside on the garden patio.

French

While it's not fancy, **Panolivo** (1344 Park St., 805/239-3366, www.panolivo.com, daily 7:30am-8:30pm, $17-28) serves some of the tastiest cuisine in town. The breakfast sandwich, with cheese, ham, and chives, is a great way to start the day. Dinner items range from lobster ravioli to boeuf bourguignonne.

Upscale **Bistro Laurent** (120 Pine St., 805/226-8191, Tues.-Sat. 11:30am-2pm and 5:30pm-10pm, 4 courses $51, 5 courses $67) offers a tasting menu with possibilities like lamb sirloin or roasted duck breast. Chef-owner Laurent Grangien made a name for himself in France before turning his attention to the California coast.

Mexican

Like the best taquerias, **Papi's** (840 13th St., 805/239-3720, daily 11am-9pm, $10) offers big portions and a mean salsa. Prices may be a bit higher than at some other taquerias, but the casual atmosphere and tasty tacos and *tortas* make up for it.

INFORMATION AND SERVICES
Maps and Visitor Information

A visit to the **Paso Robles Visitors Center** (1225 Park St., 805/238-0506, Mon.-Fri. 8:30am-5pm, Sat.-Sun. 10am-2pm) will provide you with all the necessary materials to make your stay perfect. The **Paso Robles Chamber of Commerce** (1225 Park St., 805/238-0506, www.pasorobleschamber.

com, Mon.-Fri. 8:30am-4:30pm, Sat.-Sun. 10am-2pm) also offers a guide to Paso Robles along with specific dining, lodging, and winery information.

Emergency Services

For medical attention, the nearest hospital is **Twin Cities Community Hospital** (1100 La Tablas Rd., Templeton, 805/434-3500, www.twincitieshospital.com) in nearby Templeton. Police services are the **Paso Robles Police Department** (1220 Paso Robles St., 805/237-6464), located right downtown.

Newspapers and Media

The *Paso Robles Press* (www.pasoroblespress.com) comes out every week and also has an online version. It's all local information, including high school sports scores and local politics. *The Tribune* (www.sanluisobispo.com) is the daily paper that covers the county.

Postal Services

The **post office** (800 6th St., 805/237-8342) is located in downtown Paso Robles.

Laundry

The **6th Street Laundromat** (719 6th St., 805/237-9255, daily 6am-10pm) has an attendant on duty and provides fluff-and-fold services as well as coin-operated machines.

GETTING THERE AND AROUND
Car

U.S. 101 runs north-south through Paso Robles. From California's Central Valley (Fresno and Bakersfield), Paso Robles can be accessed via Highway 46, which leads directly into the city. It's a two-lane road with occasional passing lanes; if you get stuck behind a camper, RV, or someone towing a boat, which is very common, relax and enjoy the ride and pass only when it's safe to do so. **Paso Robles Cab** (805/237-2615) has rates at about $3 per pickup and $2 per mile.

Bus

The City of Paso Robles is the official agent for **Greyhound** (805/238-1242, www.greyhound.com), with the depot located at the Transit Center (800 Pine St.). Greyhound operates Monday-Saturday 8:30am-4:30pm. The local buses, **Paso Express** (805/239-8747, www.pasoexpress.com), have fixed routes within the city. Buses are equipped with lifts for those with disabilities; they also feature bicycle racks. **Dial-A-Ride** (805/239-8747, www.pasoexpress.com) is an on-demand public transit service that provides curb-to-curb service anywhere within city limits, also with lift-equipped vehicles. One-way fares for both types of buses are $1.50, but a variety of money-saving passes are available.

Train

The *Coast Starlight* train makes one daily northbound and one daily southbound stop at the Transit Center (800 Pine St.) on its way between Los Angeles and Seattle. There are no ticket sales at the transit center; you'll have to buy tickets in advance from **Amtrak** (800/872-7245, www.amtrak.com).

Air

The **Paso Robles Airport** (4912 Wing Way, 805/237-3877, www.prcity.com) is on the outskirts of town. There are no scheduled passenger flights, but charter services are available. There are scheduled flights from Los Angeles, San Francisco, and Phoenix to the **San Luis Obispo County Regional Airport** (SBP, 901 Airport Dr., San Luis Obispo, 805/781-5205), 35 miles south.

Shuttle

The **Wine Line** (805/610-8267, www.hoponthewineline.com) is one of the few companies to offer a hop-on, hop-off option. For about $50 they'll pick you up at your hotel, and you can use three vans that operate on a figure-eight route from downtown to both Eastside and Westside wineries, running about every

40 minutes. They provide water and a small bags of chips; you'll have to get more substantial food on your own. This is not a tour, but merely a shuttle service operating to and from some of the wineries. The best part is that at the end of the day, they'll drop you back at your hotel.

Breakaway Tours (179 Nibblick Rd., 800/799-7657, www.breakaway-tours.com), on the other hand, is a full-service operation that covers wine-tasting, basic ground transportation, airport shuttles, group tours—virtually anything. They'll even drive all the way to Los Angeles to pick you up from the airport. They've been operating for 15 years and know the area well, and they're happy to customize a day or weekend event for you. Frankly, anything you throw at them, they can handle. They also operate out of San Luis Obispo and Santa Barbara.

CAMBRIA, SAN SIMEON, AND MORRO BAY

As you travel north, the soft wide beaches of Santa Barbara and San Luis Obispo Counties recede and the landscape becomes more rugged. The coastline twists and turns through Morro Bay and onward to Cambria and San Simeon. There's much more open space and you begin to see pine trees.

The hills to the east contain this small coastal region, keeping it distinct both naturally and culturally. These towns have remained relatively unspoiled, not only in their natural beauty but in the old-fashioned simplicity of the homes and businesses that adorn their streets. Morro Bay still looks much like it did decades ago, a small beach community that fronts the Pacific Ocean, its namesake Morro Rock standing guard at the mouth of the bay. Within the bay is an active fishing fleet as well

as a rebounding local sea otter population. Cayucos is an unassuming little beach town with a popular beach and a pier that dates back to the 1800s. Just north of Cayucos, Cambria still has many 1880s storefronts and a feel of yesteryear.

But when it comes to this area, there is only one true sight: palatial Hearst Castle, located about seven miles north of Cambria in San Simeon. Once functioning mainly to service the palatial estate's inhabitant, millionaire William Randolph Hearst, San Simeon hasn't grown much since the turn of the 19th century.

PLANNING YOUR TIME

These beachside communities are all located along Highway 1. The big draw in this region—and one of the most visited attractions

HIGHLIGHTS

© AVALON TRAVEL

LOOK FOR ◖ TO FIND RECOMMENDED SIGHTS, ACTIVITIES, DINING, AND LODGING.

◖ **Hearst Castle:** Opulent, erratic, and ultimately all-American, this massive, lavish compound built on a remote hill is the closest thing to a true castle in California. Media mogul William Randolph Hearst spared no expense to construct the ultimate playground for the wealthy elite (page 291).

◖ **Moonstone Beach:** This stretch of beach exemplifies the beauty of this rugged area. It's named for the semi-clear stones that you can find on the sand here (page 294).

◖ **Piedras Blancas Elephant Seal Rookery:** Every winter elephant seals show up north of San Simeon to birth their pups. The males spar, the females wean their newborns, and the people get a free show (page 294).

◖ **Morro Rock:** Primal, austere, and endlessly photogenic, this ancient dormant volcano is a refuge for endangered falcons, a home to native Indian lore, and a traveler's delight (page 319).

◖ **Montaña de Oro State Park:** With 7 miles of coastline and almost 50 miles of trails, the park is a great place for wildlife lovers and outdoor recreation enthusiasts (page 321).

◖ **Kayaking and Stand-Up Paddleboarding:** The best way to explore Morro Bay's namesake estuary is by water. Kayaking and stand-up paddleboarding allow you to see the wildlife up close and reach natural attractions like the impressive dunes of the Morro Bay Sandspit (page 328).

in California—is Hearst Castle. Most visitors plan their itineraries around touring the immense mansion, including visits to its gateway towns, Cambria and Morro Bay. There's no advantage to planning to spend the night specifically in Morro Bay or Cambria, since they are only 15 miles apart. If you're heading north, it makes more sense to stop in Morro Bay and work your way up the coast, finding

accommodations in Cambria; the reverse is true when heading south.

You can stop off at Hearst Castle for the day as part of a longer road trip, but seeing all the area has to offer requires a weekend. One day and a night is enough time to get a feel for Cambria and San Simeon. Similarly, one day and a night can be perfect for just Morro Bay. The village of Cambria can be scouted out in

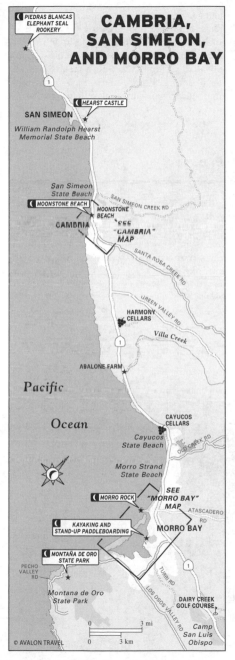

CAMBRIA, SAN SIMEON, AND MORRO BAY

PIEDRAS BLANCAS ELEPHANT SEAL ROOKERY

1

HEARST CASTLE

SAN SIMEON

William Randolph Hearst Memorial State Beach

San Simeon State Beach

MOONSTONE BEACH

SAN SIMEON CREEK RD

MOONSTONE BEACH

CAMBRIA

SEE "CAMBRIA" MAP

SANTA ROSA CREEK RD

GREEN VALLEY RD

HARMONY CELLARS

Villa Creek

1

ABALONE FARM

Pacific

Ocean

CAYUCOS CELLARS

Cayucos State Beach

OLD CREEK RD

Morro Strand State Beach

MORRO ROCK

SEE "MORRO BAY" MAP

ATASCADERO RD

KAYAKING AND STAND-UP PADDLEBOARDING

MORRO BAY

1

MONTAÑA DE ORO STATE PARK

PECHO VALLEY RD

TURRI RD

Montana de Oro State Park

DAIRY CREEK GOLF COURSE

LOS OSOS VALLEY RD

0   3 mi

0   3 km

© AVALON TRAVEL

Camp San Luis Obispo

a day, and you'll leave with an appreciation for the area, though you'll undoubtedly want to return. Morro Bay and nearby Cayucos can also be explored relatively well in a day and a night. But these places beg for leisure time: the ability to wander the beaches, the hillsides, and the streets with no agenda, which makes for a restful weekend getaway.

HISTORY

Surprisingly, in 1880 Cambria was the second-largest town in San Luis Obispo County, but by 1894 the railroad cut through San Luis Obispo, bypassing Cambria and shifting the economic base inland. Cambria survived, however, as a quiet, isolated farming community. The advent of the automobile in the 1920s led to improved roads being built to Cambria, which in turn brought land developers. The Cambria Pines Lodge was built so that prospective land buyers would have a place to stay as they scoped out potential building sites. Then, in 1958, Hearst Castle became a state park and opened its doors to the public. This brought throngs of visitors and gave quiet Cambria a new life, although it has managed to remain unspoiled.

San Simeon was once a vital whaling port, specifically around where the pier was built. There were homes near the point and plants to process the harvested whales. After the decline of the whaling industry and despite mining activity in the area, San Simeon slowed down. Today, it's a service-oriented place that predominantly serves visitors to Hearst Castle.

Morro Bay was first seen by nonnatives when Juan Rodríguez Cabrillo explored the area and called the rock El Morro. It has always been a fishing village; abalone was abundant here and in neighboring Cayucos until overfishing took its toll and depleted the resource. Even today, fishing and tourism are the main industries of the town. The layout for Morro Bay was planned as far back as 1872, when the town began to take a formal shape. There was a bit of drama during Prohibition, when out-of-work fisherfolk turned to running Canadian whisky near the rock. The Embarcadero, today the most popular spot in the city, didn't exist then;

it was created on landfill during World War II by the Navy. These days people flock here to spend time in the mild weather and enjoy the views, the rock, the shopping, and perhaps to get a drink or two.

Cayucos has always been a small town. Established primarily as a shipping port, this old Spanish land grant has never grown much, in part because its seclusion made it hard to get here by land. With the advent of the Pacific Coast Highway, people came, but they tended to drive right by, either staying in Morro Bay or heading to Hearst Castle. Even now it's uncrowded, although there are a surprising number of second homes here, as virtually every residence in this tiny enclave has views of the water.

Cambria and San Simeon

Cambria, originally known as Slabtown, retains nothing of its original if uninspired moniker. Divided into east and west villages, it is a charming area of low storefronts, easily walkable with moss-covered pine trees as a backdrop. Typically you'll see visitors meandering in and out of the local stores, browsing art galleries or combing Moonstone Beach for souvenir moonstone rocks. The really great thing about Cambria is that, aside from the gas stations, you won't find any chain stores—not one—in town, and Cambrians, and most visitors, like it that way. It truly is an idyllic spot, even during bustling summer months when the

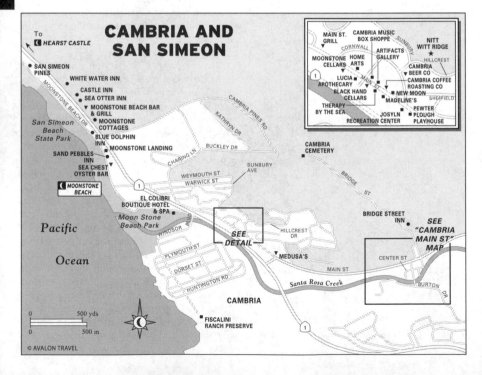

Hearst Castle's amazing Neptune Pool

crowds swell dramatically. Many of the buildings are original, dating to the 1880s.

There is only one true sight in this area. Cambria owes much of its prosperity to the immense mansion on the hill, Hearst Castle. Located about seven miles north in San Simeon, Hearst Castle, quite frankly, *is* San Simeon; the town grew up around it to support the overwhelming needs of its megalomaniacal owner and never-ending construction. The town dock provided a place for ships to unload tons of marble, piles of antiques, and dozens of workers.

Today, San Simeon is less a town and more a stopping point for visitors heading to Hearst Castle. Stores, hotels, and restaurants flank both sides of Highway 1. The general store and post office acted as a central gathering place for the community, and you can still walk up the weathered wooden steps and make a purchase here, whether it's a tasty sandwich from Sebastian's Store or a bottle of wine from the Hearst Ranch Winery. Around the corner at the building's other door, you can buy a book of stamps or mail a letter at the tiny operating post office.

If there's any strolling to be done, it's along the bluffs or on the rocky beaches. Set amid incredible open space between the hills and the ocean, San Simeon is truly a paradise of natural beauty, with stunning coastlines and gorgeous sunsets with amber light casting warm tones on the craggy rocks at the surf line.

SIGHTS
◖ Hearst Castle

There's nothing else in California quite like **Hearst Castle** (Hwy. 1 and Hearst Castle Rd., 800/444-4445, www.hearstcastle.org, tours daily 8:20am-3:20pm). Newspaper magnate William Randolph Hearst conceived the idea of a grand mansion in the Mediterranean style on land his parents bought along the central California coast. His memories of camping on the hills above the Pacific led him to choose the spot where the castle now stands. He hired Julia Morgan, the first female civil engineering graduate from the University of California,

JULIA MORGAN:
A WOMAN OF INDEPENDENT MEANS

Best known for designing and building Hearst Castle over a 21-year period, architect Julia Morgan designed more than 700 buildings in an illustrious career that spanned nearly 50 years. At 5 feet, 2 inches tall, she was a petite woman, but never one to be underestimated. On a cool spring morning in 1919, William Randolph Hearst swaggered into Julia Morgan's office in San Francisco. "Miss Morgan, we are tired of camping out in the open at the ranch in San Simeon, and I would like to build a little something," Hearst said in his high-pitched voice. And that set in motion events that would catapult her into architectural history.

Julia Morgan never married; she was devoted to her work and carved out a lasting legacy for women everywhere. She was the first woman to graduate from the prestigious Ecole des Beaux-Arts in Paris and was one of the first graduates, male or female, from the University of California, Berkeley, with a de-gree in civil engineering. Her notable California projects include not only the enduring Hearst Castle, but also the Bavarian-style **Wyntoon,** also for William Randolph Hearst; **Asilomar,** located in Pacific Grove; the **Los Angeles Herald Examiner Building** in Los Angeles; the **Margaret Baylor Inn** in Santa Barbara; and a plethora of commercial buildings, YWCAs, private residences, apartments, churches, and educational facilities.

Julia Morgan ultimately gave hope to women and girls everywhere, living a life that proved to them that their vision could someday be realized. Today the **Julia Morgan School for Girls,** an all-girls middle school in Berkeley, provides girls with education and empowerment. Morgan died in 1958 at the age of 85. In 1957 she granted her one and only press inter-view, stating simply and succinctly: "My buildings will be my legacy. They will speak for me long after I am gone."

Berkeley, to design and build the house for him. She did a brilliant job with every detail, despite the ever-changing wishes of her employer. By way of decoration, Hearst assisted in the relocation of hundreds of European medieval and Renaissance antiquities, from tiny tchotchkes to whole gilded ceilings. Hearst also adored exotic animals, and he created one of the largest private zoos in the nation on his thousands of Central Coast acres. Most of the zoo is gone now, but you can still see the occasional zebra grazing peacefully along Highway 1 south of the castle, heralding the exotic nature of Hearst Castle ahead.

The visitors center is a lavish affair with a gift shop, a restaurant, a café, a ticket booth, and a movie theater. Here you can see the much-touted film *Hearst Castle—Building the Dream,* which will give you an overview of the construction and history of the marvelous edifice, and of William Randolph Hearst's empire. After buying your ticket, board the shuttle that takes you up the hill to your tour. No private cars are allowed on the roads up to the castle. There are five tours to choose from, each focusing on different spaces and aspects of the castle.

THE TOURS

Expect to walk for at least an hour on whichever tour you choose, and to climb up and down many stairs. Even the most jaded traveler can't help but be amazed by the beauty and opulence that drips from every room in the house. Lovers of European art and antiques will want to stay forever.

The **Grand Rooms Museum Tour** (45 minutes, 106 stairs, 0.6 miles, adults $25, under age 13 $12) is recommended for first-time visitors. It begins in the castle's assembly room, which is draped in Flemish tapestries, before heading into the dining room, the billiard room, and the impressive movie theater, where you'll watch a few old Hearst newsreels. The guide then lets you loose to take in the swimming pools: the indoor pool, decorated in gold and blue, and the stunning outdoor Neptune Pool.

For a further glimpse into Hearst's personal life, take the **Upstairs Suites Tour** (45 minutes, 273 stairs, 0.75 miles, adults $25, under age 13 $12). Among the highlights are a stop within Hearst's private suite and a visit to his library, which holds over 4,000 books and 150 ancient Greek vases. At the end of this tour, you can explore the grounds, including the Neptune Pool, on your own.

Epicureans should opt for the **Cottages & Kitchen Tour** (45 minutes, 176 stairs, 0.75 miles, adults $25, under age 13 $12). Visit the wine cellar first, where there are still bottles of wine, gin, rum, beer, and vermouth along the walls. (After a visit here, actor David Niven once said that "the wine flowed like glue.") Then take in the ornate guest cottages Casa Del Monte and Casa del Mar, where Hearst spent the final two years of his life. The tour concludes in the massive castle kitchen, with its steam-heated metal counters, before leaving you to explore the grounds on your own.

The seasonal **Evening Museum Tour** (100 minutes, 308 stairs, 0.75 miles, adults $36, under age 13 $18) is only given in spring and fall. Volunteers dress in 1930s fashions and welcome guests as if they are arriving at one of Hearst's legendary parties.

Buy tour tickets at least a few days in advance, and even farther ahead on summer weekends. Wheelchair-accessible Grand Rooms and Evening Tours are available for visitors with limited mobility. Strollers are not permitted. The restrooms and food concessions are all in the visitors center. No food, drink, or chewing gum are allowed on any tour.

Nitt Witt Ridge

While William Randolph Hearst built one of the most expensive homes ever seen in California, local eccentric Arthur Harold Beal (a.k.a. Captain Nit Wit or Der Tinkerpaw) got busy building the cheapest "castle" he could. **Nitt Witt Ridge** (881 Hillcrest Dr., 805/927-2690, tours by appointment) is the result of

© STUART THORNTON

Nitt Witt Ridge

five decades of scavenging trash and using it as building supplies to create a multistory home like no other on the coast. The rambling structure is made of abalone shells, used car rims, and toilet seats, among other found materials. Today, you can make an appointment with owners Michael and Stacey O'Malley to take a tour of the property, but don't just drop in. It's weird, it's funky, and it's fun—an oddly iconic experience of the Central Coast.

Cambria Cemetery

Artsy isn't a word that's usually associated with graveyards, but in Cambria it fits. The **Cambria Cemetery** (6005 Bridge St., 805/927-5158, www.cambriacemetery.com, daily 9am-4pm) reflects the artistic bent of the town's residents in its tombstone decor. Unlike many cemeteries, at Cambria the family and friends of the deceased are allowed to place all manner of personal objects at their loved ones' graves. You'll see painted tombstones, beautiful panes of stained glass, unusual wind chimes, and many other unique expressions of love, devotion, and art as you wander the 12 wooded acres.

Moonstone Beach

Known for its namesake, a shimmering gemstone littering the shore, **Moonstone Beach** (Moonstone Beach Dr.) is a scenic pebbly slice of coastline with craggy rocks offshore. Huts constructed from driftwood can be found on some sections of the beach, and there is plenty more than just moonstones to find washed up on the shoreline. There is also a wooden boardwalk that runs along the top of the bluffs above the beach to take in the scenery and watch moonstone collectors with buckets wander below in the tideline. Access is at Leffingwell Landing, Moonstone Beach Drive, and Santa Rosa Creek.

Piedras Blancas Light Station

First illuminated in 1875, the **Piedras Blancas Light Station** (tours meet at the Piedras Blancas Motel, 1.5 miles north of the light station on Hwy. 1, 805/927-7361, www.

piedrasblancas.gov, tours mid-June-Sept. Mon.-Sat. 9:45am-11:45am, Sept.-mid-June Tues., Thurs., and Sat. 9:45am-11:45am, adults $10, ages 6-17 $5, under age 6 free) and its adjacent grounds can be accessed on a two-hour tour. The name Piedras Blancas means "white rocks" in Spanish. In 1948 a nearby earthquake caused a crack in the lighthouse tower and the removal of a first-order Fresnel lens, which was replaced with an automatic aerobeacon. Since 2001 the lighthouse has been run by the federal Bureau of Land Management.

Piedras Blancas Elephant Seal Rookery

Stopping at the **Piedras Blancas Elephant Seal Rookery** (Hwy. 1, 7 miles north of San Simeon, 805/924-1628, www.elephantseal.org, free) is like watching a nature documentary in real time. On this sliver of beach, up to 17,000 elephant seals rest, breed, give birth, or fight one another to mate. The rookery is right along Highway 1: Turn into the large gravel parking lot and follow the boardwalks north

the boardwalk above Moonstone Beach

or south to viewing areas where informative plaques give background on the elephant seals; volunteer docents are available to answer questions (daily 10am-4pm). The beaches themselves are off-limits to humans; they're covered in the large marine mammals. In the fall, most adult seals head out to sea, returning in early to mid-December. Most of the seal births occur between the end of December and the middle of February.

Fiscalini Ranch Preserve

A terrific place to take in Cambria's natural assets, the **Fiscalini Ranch Preserve** (www.ffrpcambria.org, daily dawn-dusk, free) is home to abundant plants and animals, including one of the last three remaining native Monterey pine forests and 25 special-status species like American peregrine falcons, western snowy plovers, and California red-legged frogs. Birdwatchers have spotted at least 182 bird species here. The preserve is actually two parcels of land on both the east and west side of Highway 1; head for the 364-acre western portion.

The preserve is named for the Fiscalini family, who started a cattle ranch and dairy farm on the land back in the mid-1850s. A housing development was planned here in the 1980s until an organization was formed to maintain the ranch as public open space. The land was finally purchased and preserved in 2000. The **Friends of Fiscalini Ranch Preserve** (www.cambriaranchwalks.com) also offer free monthly docent-guided walks.

William Randolph Hearst Memorial State Beach

Down the hill from Hearst Castle is **William Randolph Hearst State Beach** (750 Hearst Castle Rd., 805/927-2020, www.parks.ca.gov, daily dawn-dusk), with kelp-strewn sand along a protected cove. The 795-foot-long pier is great for fishing and strolling, and the **Coastal Discovery Center** (805/927-2145, Fri.-Sun. 11am-5pm, free), run by California State Parks and Monterey Bay National Marine Sanctuary, warrants a stop. It focuses on local natural history and culture, with exhibits on shipwrecks,

© STUART THORNTON

William Randolph Hearst State Beach

THE HEARST LEGACY

William Randolph Hearst: The name conjures images of wealth beyond belief. And with great wealth comes great responsibility. The William Randolph Hearst Foundation was established by its namesake, publisher William Randolph Hearst, in 1948 under California nonprofit laws, exclusively for educational and charitable purposes. Since then, the Hearst Foundations have contributed more than $735 million in the areas of education, health care, social services, and the arts in every state.

Since Hearst owned 26 newspapers at the height of his power, the foundation has always had a strong affinity for the written word. The **Hearst Journalism Awards Program** was founded in 1960 to provide support, encouragement, and assistance to journalism education at the college and university level. The program awards scholarships to students for outstanding performance in college-level journalism. The 50th annual program, which offered more than $550,000 in awards in 2010, consisted of six monthly writing competitions, three photo-journalism competitions, four broadcast news competitions (two in radio and two in television), and a multimedia competition.

Hearst also had political ambitions. His father was a state senator, and thus the foundation also funds programs for service in the public interest. The **United States Senate Youth Program** was established in 1962 by a U.S. Senate resolution. It's a unique educational experience for outstanding high school students interested in pursuing a career in public service. Two student leaders from each state, the District of Columbia, and the Department of Defense Education Activity spend a week in Washington DC experiencing their national government in action. Student delegates get the chance to hear major policy addresses by senators, cabinet members, officials from the Departments of State and Defense, and directors of other federal agencies. The students also participate in a meeting with a justice of the U.S. Supreme Court.

a display on elephant seals, and an interactive tide pool. This beach is also an ideal place to try kayaking.

WINE TASTING

Cambria has a handful of tasting rooms showcasing wines made here and in nearby Paso Robles.

Moonstone Cellars

Moonstone Cellars (801 Main St., Suite C, 805/927-9466, www.moonstonecellars.com, daily 11am-5pm, tasting $5-7) is an appropriate name for this little Cambria winery: Father and son Muril and Todd Clift began their wine-making careers producing wine in a basement near Moonstone Beach. They showcase their passion in the tasting room by pouring two chardonnays, a viognier, a cabernet sauvignon, a merlot, and a zinfandel.

Black Hand Cellars

Although the tasting room of **Black Hand Cellars** (766 Main St., Suite B, 805/927-9463, www.blackhandcellars.com, daily 11am-5pm, tasting $5) is in Cambria's west village, the vineyard is located northwest of Paso Robles. The focus is on syrahs, but they also do Rhône-style blends, Bordeaux-style blends, a grenache, and a dessert wine.

Twin Coyotes Winery

Twin brothers run **Twin Coyote Winery** (2020 Main St., 805/927-9800, www.twincoyotes.com, Fri.-Sat. noon-6pm, Sun.-Mon. noon-5pm, tasting $6), which offers a wide range of reds and some whites, including a cabernet sauvignon, a petite syrah, a merlot, a tempranillo, a primitivo, a chardonnay, and a dessert wine. They use sustainable means to farm grapes in their vineyard in Paso Robles.

Hearst Ranch Winery

The **Hearst Ranch Winery** (442 San Simeon Rd., 805/927-4100, www.hearstranchwinery.com, daily 11am-5pm, tasting $10) shares the historic 1852 general store in old San Simeon with the post office the popular Sebastian's Store Restaurant. This cool little tasting room pours a range of wines, including the award-winning Pico Creek Merlot and the Glacier Ridge Chardonnay.

SHOPPING
Antiques

Antiques on Main (2338 Main St., 805/927-4292, daily 10am-5pm) has three floors of everything from fossils to furniture. The **Country Collectibles Antiques Mall** (2380 Main St., 805/927-0245, daily 10am-6pm) has all kinds of small collectibles, including comic books, French pottery, and Disney memorabilia. In the Redwood Center shopping strip, **Rich**

Man Poor Man Antiques Mall (2110 Main St., 805/203-5350, www.richmanpoormanantiques.com, daily 10am-5pm) has two floors of high-quality antiques and collectibles from over 30 dealers, selling everything from furniture to estate jewelry.

Art Galleries

For over 30 years, the owners of the **Seekers Glass Gallery** (4090 Burton Dr., 800/841-5250, www.seekersglass.com, daily 10am-10pm) have worked with nationally known artists to secure the finest glass art. Works include vases, bowls, sculptures, and jewelry.

The **Vault Gallery** (2289 Main St., 805/927-0300, www.vaultgallery.com, daily 10:30am-6pm) displays the work of Central Coast photographers, painters, and sculptors, with a large collection of plein air paintings.

A large bronze sculpture out front welcomes visitors to the **Artifacts Gallery** (775 Main

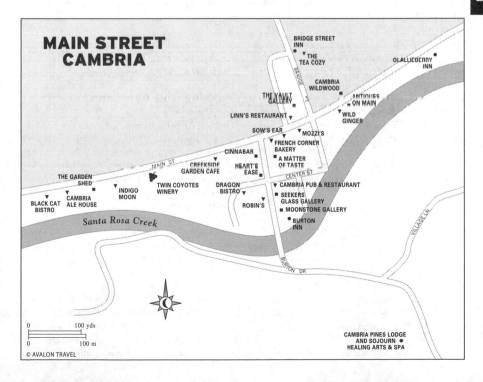

MAIN STREET CAMBRIA

CAMBRIA AND SAN SIMEON

© STUART THORNTON

Lucia Apothecary

St., 805/927-4465, www.artifactsgallery.com, daily 10am-6pm), which displays oil paintings, bronze sculptures, and fine art reproductions. The two-story building includes an in-house framing studio.

The **Moonstone Gallery** (4070 Burton Dr., 805/927-3447, www.moonstones.com, summer daily 10am-10pm, winter Sun.-Thurs. 10am-9pm, Fri.-Sat. 10am-10pm) specializes in moonstone jewelry, but they also showcase sculptures, kaleidoscopes, metal art, and hardwood jewelry boxes.

Bath and Beauty
The **Lucia Apothecary** (746 Main St., 805/927-1831, www.luciacompany.com, Sat. and Mon. 10am-5pm, Sun. 10am-4pm, Tues.-Fri. 11am-5pm) has body oils, scrubs, creams, washes, and mists in 19 scents inspired by California locales. The most popular is the Ojai, a mixture of viognier and apricot scents.

Heart's Ease (4101 Burton Dr., 805/927-5224, www.heartseaseshop.com, daily 10am-5pm) is located in a historic 1870s cottage, stocked with fragrances, soaps, and housemade potpourris. There's also a garden with plants for sale.

Clothing and Accessories
New Moon (777 Main St., 805/927-4496, Sat.-Thurs. 10am-6pm, Fri. 9:30am-6pm) has an array of high-end casual wear for women, with brands like Natural Fibers, Cut Loose, Citron, Rico, and Tribal Sportswear. Also take a look at their outlet shop, **Half Moon,** a few doors down.

Cambria Wildwood (4210 Bridge St., 805/924-0901, http://wildwoodcambria.com, Sun.-Fri. 10am-6pm, Sat. 10am-7pm) is a two-level store with apparel for men and women. Check out the large selection of Brighton jewelry as well as over 400 styles of hats.

Farmers Market
Stock up on produce, fruit, and honey at the food-only **Cambria Farmer's Market** (Veterans Hall Parking Lot, 1000 Main St., www.cambriafarmersmarket.com, summer Fri. 2:30pm-5:30pm, winter Fri. 2:30pm-5pm).

San Simeon's Brooks Gallery

Gifts

The **Cambria Music Box Shoppe** (778 Main St., 805/927-3227, www.cambriamusicbox. com, daily 10am-6pm) not only sells music boxes; it can also customize a music box just for you. You can also browse other music makers such as chimes, gongs, bells, and musical clocks.

Home Furnishings

Located in a beautiful old building that was a blacksmith shop in the 1800s, **Cinnabar** (4121 Burton Dr., 805/395-4111, http://cinnabaronline.com, Mon.-Thurs. 11am-6pm, Fri. 11am-8pm, Sat. 11am-9pm, Sun. 11am-5pm) has unique folk art pieces, home decor, and furnishings, including pieces made from reclaimed wood and even lamps made out of tree leaves. Another nifty shop in a historic building,

The Garden Shed (2024 Main St., 805/927-7654, www.cambriagardenshed.com, Sun.-Thurs. 10am-5pm, Fri.-Sat. 10am-6pm) is in a 19th-century former creamery. Here you'll find everything for your garden, including tools, books, gloves, and art.

Home Arts (727 Main St., 805/927-2781, www.home-arts.com, daily 10am-6pm) sells functional arty furniture like knotty pine coffee tables and reclaimed wood shutters. There's also a section dedicated to ocean-themed decor.

Occupying an old arcade building in San Simeon, along the strip of businesses on the west side of Highway 1, the **Brooks Gallery** (9255 Hearst Dr., San Simeon, 805/924-1506, www.brooksgalleryonline.com, Thurs.-Mon. 11am-3pm) showcases furniture made from salvaged wood as well as paintings by local artists.

Kitchen Supplies

A Matter of Taste (4120 Burton Dr., 805/927-0286, www.amatteroftastecambria.com, daily 10am-5pm) has all the supplies for a well-stocked kitchen: cookware, cookbooks, gadgets, and even superb ingredients like designer vinegars, jams, and jellies. It also hosts cooking classes taught by local chefs to show you how to put your new supplies to use whipping up tasty dishes at home.

Wine

Fermentations (2306 Main St., 805/927-7141, www.fermentations.com, daily 10am-8pm, five tastes $5) has moved into a larger space, allowing for an even larger selection of gourmet food and wines, with a focus on the products of nearby Paso Robles vineyards. They also sell olive oil and vinegar and host dip tastings.

SPORTS AND RECREATION
Surfing

Cambria is not a popular surfing destination, but there can be waves to ride if you have a board with you. The north end of the strip of businesses in San Simeon is where you'll find **Pico Creek,** a reef break off the spot where Pico Creek goes into the ocean. Just south of the creek is a beach where there can be peaky beach break waves. Park in the cul de sac at the western end of Pico Avenue. Another option is **Santa Rosa Creek,** at the southern end of Cambria's Moonstone Beach. This is a beach break littered with a few rocks. To get here, turn left into the public parking lot off Moonstone Beach Drive.

Kayaking

William Randolph Hearst State Beach (750 Hearst Castle Rd., 805/927-2020, www.parks.ca.gov, daily dawn-dusk) offers a protected cove that's ideal for kayaking. You may see sea otters, seals, and sea lions while paddling. Located right on the beach, **Sea For Yourself Kayak Outfitters** (805/927-1787, http://kayakcambria.com, mid-June-early Sept. daily 10am-4pm, single kayak $10 per hour, double kayak $20 per hour, stand-up paddleboard $15 per hour) rents out equipment right here. They also offer two- to three-hour kayak tours of San Simeon Cove ($50 pp). Other tours include fishing excursions and paddles along Cambria's coastal terrace or Moonstone Drive ($95-110).

Lawn Bowling

The **Joslyn Recreation Center** (950 Main St., 805/927-3364, Mon., Wed., and Fri.-Sat. 8:30am-noon, donation) has a large artificial turf field for lawn bowling. Lawn bowling is similar to boccie, where you try to roll balls closest to a target ball. If you don't know how to play, someone at the recreation center will be able to show you the basics.

Hiking

Fiscalini Ranch Preserve (www.ffrpcambria.org, daily dawn-dusk, free) is a wonderful place to take a walk. Hike the **Bluff Trail** (2 miles round-trip, easy, trailheads at the end of S. Windsor Blvd. and N. Windsor Blvd.) to view wildflower-colored bluffs and rocky shoreline, which includes tide pools and attracts relaxing sea lions. Monterey pines crown the ridgeline above. Multiple spur trails branch out to the bluffs' edge. A wooden boardwalk protects some sensitive areas, while arty driftwood benches provide places to sit and enjoy the scenery. The Bluff Trail can become a two-mile loop by taking the **Marine Terrace Trail** back. This wider trail is higher up on the hill. When you return to the South side of the preserve, you'll have to walk a block down on Wedgewood Street to return to the South Windsor Boulevard parking area.

In **San Simeon State Park** (500 San Simeon Rd., www.parks.ca.gov, daily dawn-dusk), the **San Simeon Creek Trail** (3.5 miles round-trip, moderate) goes through the park's wetlands, up to a grassy ridge with studded with Monterey pines. To reach the trailhead, park in the Washburn Day Use Area. Walk east on the service road, and take the trailhead on the right.

Horseback Riding

Explore Cambria's hills and forests via horseback with **Outback Trail Rides** (805/286-8772, www.outbacktrailrides.com, May-Sept., $55-85). Three possible rides include two that take in the pastoral landscape of working ranches and another that leads to an ocean view.

© STUART THORNTON
Fiscalini Ranch Preserve's Bluff Trail

Spas

Therapy By the Sea (816 Main St., 805/927-2956, http://therapybythesea.com, Mon.-Sat. 8am-7pm, Sun. 10am-5pm) offers a range of massages ($70-85 per hour), including Swedish, Reiki, warm stone, and pre-natal. They also provide facials and other relaxation packages. In the Cambria Pines Lodge, the **Sojourn Healing Arts & Spa** (2905 Burton Dr., 805/927-8007, www.sojournspa.com, by appointment) offers similar massage treatments ($90 per hour) that also include warm stones and aromatherapy.

ENTERTAINMENT AND EVENTS
Nightlife

If touring Hearst Castle leaves you thirsty for a beer, Cambria has a few different options. **Mozzi's** (2262 Main St., 805/927-4767, http://mozzissaloon.com, Mon.-Fri. 1pm-midnight, Sat.-Sun. 11am-2am) is a classic old California saloon—there's been a bar on this site since 1866. Old artifacts like lanterns and farm equipment hang from the ceiling above the long redwood bar, jukebox, and pool tables in this historic watering hole.

The **Cambria Ale House** (2084 Main St., 805/395-1295, Mon.-Thurs. 1pm-9pm, Fri.-Sat. noon-10pm, Sun. 1pm-8pm) is a tiny beer bar with a rotating selection of six unique microbrews on tap and a fridge stocked with bottle beers that you can purchase to go. Most nights you can sit on a couch or at the small bar to listen to live music from local singer-songwriters.

Cambria Pines Lodge Fireside Lounge (Cambria Pines Lodge, 2905 Burton Dr., 805/927-4200, www.cambriapineslodge.com, Mon.-Fri. 3pm-midnight, Sat.-Sun. noon-midnight) has live music nightly, performed on a stage to the right of a big stone fireplace. Enjoy a cocktail, beer, or wine seated at one of the couches or small tables.

Local craft brewery the **Cambria Beer Company** (821 Cornwall St., 805/203-5265, http://cambriabeerco.com, Mon.-Thurs. noon-7pm, Fri.-Sat. noon-8pm, Sun. noon-6pm) has

© STUART THORNTON

the Cambria Ale House

anywhere from two to nine beers on tap, with unique offerings like an olallieberry sour, orange wheat, vanilla bourbon porter, and chocolate mole stout. The most popular is the Old Number 23 Porter. Get a sampler flight with four samples for $6. The tasting room feels like a small cottage, with local art and vintage Pearl Jam posters on the walls.

The downstairs pub at **The Cambria Pub & Restaurant** (4090 Burton Dr., 805/927-0782, www.thecambriapub.com, Mon.-Tues. and Thurs. 11am-9pm, Fri.-Sat. 11am-10pm, Sun. 11am-9pm) is a fine spot for a cold beer. Enjoy one of 12 beers on tap, including local favorites like Firestone and Figueroa, while taking in the latest sporting event on the pub's four TVs.

Performing Arts

Cambria has its own little theater, the **Pewter Plough Playhouse** (824 Main St., 805/927-3877, www.pewterploughplayhouse.org, tickets $15-25). Its 59 seats are named for legendary stars of the stage like Laurence Olivier, Noël Coward, and Vivien Leigh. The theater does a wide range of shows. Catch a murder mystery like *Audience with a Murder,* a one-man tribute to Mark Twain, or a contemporary drama like *The Weir.* Enjoy a drink before or after the show at the piano bar off the lobby.

Festivals and Events

Sample wines from over 35 local wineries, as well as wine and food pairings, at the **Cambria Art and Wine Festival** (805/927-3624, www.cambriaartwine.org, $25-35) in January. The popular three-day event has been known to sell out. It also includes an art show and silent auction. The Old Western grounds, next to the Veterans Memorial building, announce **Pinedorado Days** (www.pinedorado.com), a community celebration that's occurred here every Labor Day weekend since 1949. Expect a parade and a car show along with barbecues, live music, kids' games, art shows, and food booths. During the month of October, the Cambria Historical Society sponsors

© STUART THORNTON

Mozzi's saloon

Cambria Scarecrow Festival (805/927-2891, www.cambriascarecrows.com), with creative scarecrows lining the streets of town.

ACCOMMODATIONS

Many of the accommodations in Cambria are along the small town's Hotel Row, a.k.a. Moonstone Beach Drive. San Simeon has a small strip of hotels on either side of the highway south of Hearst Castle.

Under $150

Located next to a church, the **[C Bridge Street Inn-HI Cambria** (4314 Bridge St., 805/927-7653, http://bridgestreetinncambria.com, $28-80) used to be the pastor's house. Now it's a clean, cozy hostel with a dorm room and four private rooms. The kitchen has a collection of cast-iron kitchenware, and there's a volleyball court out front. Part of Bridge Street's appeal is its enthusiastic young owner, Brandon Follett, who sometimes books live bands to play at the hostel. Even if there's no band scheduled to play, it doesn't take much to entice Brandon

to grab his acoustic guitar and play an eclectic song for his guests.

Her Castle Homestay Bed and Breakfast Inn (1978 Londonderry Lane, 805/924-1719, www.hercastle.cc, $120-160) is a bit different from your average B&B, with only two guest rooms available and lots of personal attention from the owners. When you make your reservations, ask about a half-day wine tour or dinner reservations. Her Castle can be the perfect hideaway for two couples traveling together who desire the privacy of "their own house."

One of San Simeon's best lodging options, **The Morgan** (9135 Hearst Dr., 800/451-9900, www.hotel-morgan.com, $119-250) is named for Hearst Castle architect Julia Morgan, paying tribute to her with reproductions of her architectural drawings in all of the guest rooms. The rooms are clean and well appointed, and some have partial ocean views; eight rooms come with soaking tubs and gas fireplaces. The Morgan also has a wind-sheltered pool and deck. A complimentary continental breakfast is served every morning. **The Massage Center at The Morgan** (805/927-3878, massages $90-145) offers massages, aromatherapy, warm stone therapy, and hand and foot scrubs.

Although it was established in 1957, **Cambria Palms Motel** (2662 Main St., 805/927-4485, www.cambriapalmsmotel.com, $89-139) has been remodeled and modernized; the 18 guest rooms have free Wi-Fi and cable TV. Some guest rooms also have private patios, and pet-friendly guest rooms are available. The family-friendly **Castle Inn** (6620 Moonstone Beach Dr., www.cambriainns.com, $144-169) has a great location, right across the road from Moonstone Beach, offering great ocean views. Guest rooms are unassuming, with wooden bed frames, coffee pots, fridges, and flat-screen TVs. The heated pool and hot tub are sheltered from the coastal winds. A basic continental breakfast is served in the morning.

$150-250

For a great selection of anything from economical standard rooms up to rustic cabins with king beds and a fireplace, pick the **Cambria**

© STUART THORNTON

CAMBRIA AND SAN SIMEON

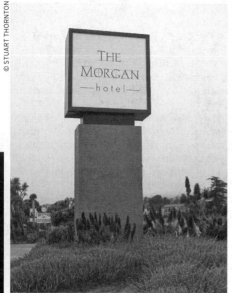

The Morgan hotel

Pines Lodge (2905 Burton Dr., 800/445-6868, www.cambriapineslodge.com, $139-300). All guest rooms have plenty of creature comforts, including TVs, private baths, and, in some cases, fireplaces. There's also a nice garden area with flowering plants, benches, and sculptures.

A favorite even among the many inns of Cambria, the **Olallieberry Inn** (2476 Main St., 888/927-3222, www.olallieberry.com, $150-225) is in a charming 19th-century Greek Revival home and adjacent cottage. Each of the nine guest rooms features its own quaint Victorian-inspired decor with comfortable beds and attractive appointments. A full daily breakfast, complete with olallieberry jam, rounds out the comfortable personal experience.

A pebble's throw from Moonstone Beach, the **◖ Sand Pebbles Inn** (6252 Moonstone Beach Dr., 805/927-5600, www.cambriainns.com, $194-294) is a two-story gray building where most guest rooms have glimpses of the ocean through bay windows. The clean, tastefully decorated guest rooms have comfortable beds, mini fridges, and microwaves. The six

guest rooms facing west have full ocean views, while the bottom three have patios. Expect nice little amenities such as welcome cookies, a better-than-average continental breakfast, coffee and tea served in the lobby, and a lending library of DVDs. Owned by the same family, the adults-only **◖ Blue Dolphin Inn** (6470 Moonstone Beach Dr., 805/927-3300, www.cambriainns.com, $199-349) offers slightly more upscale guest rooms than its neighbor. The six full ocean-view rooms come with fireplaces, Keurig coffeemakers, robes, and slippers. Breakfast is delivered to your room every morning.

Located on the north end of Moonstone Beach, the **White Water Inn** (6790 Moonstone Beach Dr., 805/927-1066, www.whitewaterinn.com, $169-289) is a small family-run hotel. The distinct yellow building looks like a collection of connected cottages, with 15 guest rooms and two mini-suites. All of the guest rooms have gas fireplaces; the mini suites have spas on private patios. The service is notable—continental breakfast is delivered to your room on china, and they'll even clean your car's windshield before your drive home.

Also by Moonstone Beach, **The Fogcatcher Inn** (6400 Moonstone Beach Dr., www.fogcatcherinn.com, $188-368) feels like something out of old Britain, with a thatched roof and brick paths. But it also has modern conveniences like Wi-Fi, microwaves, and temperature-controlled fireplaces. Dip in the heated pool or relax in the spa. Fill up at the hot breakfast buffet in the morning. The family suites can accommodate six people.

Just across the street from Moonstone Beach, the quaint **Sea Otter Inn** (6656 Moonstone Beach Dr., 800/927-5888, www.seaotterinn.com, $139-319) focuses on seaside charm. Standard guest rooms have fireplace heaters, microwaves, fridges, and DVD players. Upgrade to enjoy a whirlpool tub and a view of the ocean.

The sleek, modern **El Colibri Boutique Hotel & Spa** (5620 Moonstone Beach Dr., 805/924-3003, www.elcolibrihotel.com, $159-241) offers a wine bar in the lobby and a spa

Sand Pebbles Inn

on-site. All 34 guest rooms have fireplaces and soaking tubs.

The **Fog's End Bed and Breakfast** (2735 Main St., 805/927-7465, www.fogsend.com, $175-195) offers just five guest rooms on an eight-acre spread just outside Cambria's East Village. The gracious hosts spoil guests with a full breakfast in the morning along with appetizers and wine at night. Play boccie ball or horseshoes on the lawn or enjoy a game of pool in the barn.

The **Best Western Cavalier Oceanfront Resort** (9415 Hearst Dr., San Simeon, 805/927-4688, www.cavalierresort.com, $206-352) occupies a prime piece of real estate in San Simeon on a bluff above the ocean just south of Pico Creek. The highest-priced rooms are oceanfront offerings with wood-burning fireplaces, soaking tubs, and private patios. The grounds include a pool, an exercise room, a day spa, and a restaurant.

Moonstone Landing (6240 Moonstone Beach Dr., 805/927-0012, www.moonstone-landing.com, $150-295) provides inexpensive partial-view guest rooms with the decor and amenities of a mid-tier chain motel as well as oceanfront luxury guest rooms featuring porches with ocean views, soaking tubs, and gas fireplaces.

The **Burton Inn** (4022 Burton Dr., 805/927-5125, www.burtoninn.com, $150-350) offers apartment-size accommodations, some decorated in ornate English style and others with a casual beach feel. The tall-ceilinged family suites have multiple bedrooms that can sleep six while promoting both togetherness and privacy.

Over $250

One of the cuter and more interesting options on Moonstone Beach Drive, **Moonstone Cottages** (6580 Moonstone Beach Dr., 805/927-1366, http://moonstonecottages. com, $259-329) offers peace and luxury along the sea. Each of the three cottages includes a fireplace, a marble bath with a whirlpool tub, a flat-screen TV with a DVD player, Internet access, and a view of the ocean. Breakfast is delivered to your cottage each morning.

FOOD
Asian
Dragon Bistro (2150 Center St., 805/927-1622, www.dragonbistro.biz, daily 11am-9pm, $12-19) does Chinese food without the high sodium, fat, or sugar content. The restaurant uses fresh seafood, meat, and vegetables in traditional dishes like orange chicken and black pepper beef. The Treasures of the Sea is a hot platter with a fishing net of shrimp, scallop, fish, and clam. The generous lunch menu (11am-3pm) will leave you stuffed.

One of the best bargains in town is **Wild Ginger** (2380 Main St., 805/927-1001, www.wildgingercambria.com, Mon.-Wed. and Fri.-Sat. 11am-2:30pm and 5pm-9pm, Sun. 5pm-9pm, $15). This tiny pan-Asian café serves delicious fresh food like Vietnamese caramelized prawns and eggplant curry. There's also an array of take-out fare. Come early for the best selection.

Bakeries
The French Corner Bakery (2214 Main St., 805/927-8227, www.frenchcornerbakery.com, daily 6:30am-6pm, sandwiches $7) offers a selection of fresh-made bread and pastries behind a glass counter and a large mural of Paris. There's also a small menu of lunch options, including cold deli sandwiches, Mexican *tortas,* and hot offerings like an Italian meatball sandwich.

Breakfast and Brunch
Take in a hearty breakfast or lunch on the outdoor patio at the family-owned **Creekside Garden Café** (2114 Main St., 805/927-8646, www.creeksidegardencafe.com, Mon.-Sat. 7am-2pm, Sun. 7am-1pm, $5-10). Fuel up with omelets, scrambles, or pancakes.

Cheap Eats
Although Cambria and San Simeon have more than their fair share of fine dining, the places to get a burger or sandwich are actually some of the best and most popular eateries in the area. The best spot to fuel up for a Hearst Castle tour is easily **(Sebastian's Store** (442 Slo San Simeon Rd., San Simeon, 805/927-3307,

OLALLIEBERRIES

You'll see the name olallieberry around Cambria, perhaps spelled differently each time. Part loganberry, part raspberry, this berry grows in and around Cambria, but it was actually created in a laboratory. The original cross was made as early as 1935 as a joint project between Oregon State University and the U.S. Department of Agriculture. Selected in 1937 and tested in Oregon, Washington, and California and referred to as Oregon 609, it was eventually named Olallie and released in 1950. While developed in Oregon and planted there, it has never been very productive in that environment and is primarily grown in California. It has usually been marketed as olallieberry, just as Marion is sold as marionberry. The name means "berry" in Native American languages. The taste and structure is similar to a blackberry but a little milder. Make sure you try it while you're in town, or pick up a jar to take with you as a souvenir for people back home, who have probably never heard of it before.

Wed.-Sun. 11am-4pm, $7-12). Housed alongside the Hearst Ranch Winery tasting room and the tiny San Simeon post office, this small eatery showcases tender, juicy beef from nearby Hearst Ranch in burgers, french dips, and unique creations like the Hot Beef Ortega Melt. This is a popular place, and the sandwiches take a few minutes to prepare, so don't stop in right before your scheduled Hearst Castle tour.

The **(Main Street Grill** (603 Main St., 805/927-3194, http://firestonegrill.com, daily 11am-8pm, $4-18) is a popular eatery housed in a cavernous building located on the way into Cambria. The tri-tip steak sandwich—tri-tip drenched in barbecue sauce and placed on a French roll dipped in butter—is the favorite, even though the ABC burger, with avocado, bacon, and cheese topping the meat, puts most burger joints to shame.

© STUART THORNTON

Sebastian's Store

Coffee and Tea

Enjoy sophisticated afternoon tea at **The Tea Cozy** (4286 Bridge St., 805/927-8765, www. teacozy.com, daily 11am-4pm, $15): a whole pot of tea served with a three-tiered tray crammed with sweets and finger sandwiches. They also serve decidedly less dainty fare like tri-tip chili and a stilton cheeseburger. Built in the late 1870s, the building was once the residence of the Piedras Blancas Light Station's keeper. The **Cambria Coffee Roasting Company** (761 Main St., 805/927-0670, www. cambriacoffee.com, daily 7am-5:30pm) roasts their own beans. Head upstairs to stretch out and enjoy the free Wi-Fi.

Mexican

Every town in California has a taqueria, and Cambria is no different. **Medusa's** (1053 Main St., 805/927-0135, http://medusascambria. com, Mon.-Sat. 7am-8pm, $5-12) offers the usual tacos, burritos, and enchiladas as well as an extensive breakfast menu that includes *chilaquiles,* huevos rancheros, and chorizo and eggs. Get it to go or dine inside under a mural of a jungle pyramid.

New American and Fusion

One of the most popular restaurants in Cambria is the **Black Cat Bistro** (1602 Main St., 805/927-1600, www.blackcatbistro. com, Thurs.-Mon. 5pm-close, $18-30). The interior is homey, with a fireplace and wood floors. The ever-changing menu features farm-fresh ingredients in creative combinations like crab rellenos and chipotle shrimp pasta.

Part of an expansive local family business, **Linn's Restaurant** (2277 Main St., 805/927-0371, www.linnsfruitbin.com, daily 8am-9pm, $14-32) serves tasty, unpretentious American favorites in a casual family-friendly atmosphere. Save room for the olallieberry pie—or purchase a ready-to-bake pie, jam, or even vinegar to take home.

Madeline's Restaurant and Wine Shop (788 Main St., 805/927-4175, www.madelinescambria.com, daily 5pm-9pm) pours local wines by day (tasting room 805/927-0990,

CAMBRIA AND SAN SIMEON

© STUART THORNTON

Linn's Restaurant

daily 11am-5pm) and serves French-influenced dinner fare by night, with entrées like seafood gumbo, pan-seared duck, and vegetarian polenta.

The Sow's Ear Café (2248 Main St., 805/927-4865, http://thesowsear.com, daily 5pm-close, $17-39) breathes new life into comfort-food classics. The pot pies are stuffed with lobster, while the macaroni and cheese is spiked with sausage and smoked chicken. The chicken-fried steak and chicken and dumplings hew to classic rib-sticking recipes.

Indigo Moon (1980 Main St., 805/927-2911, www.indigomooncafe.com, daily 10am-9pm, $17-35) is another worthy dining destination. The menu is a fusion of American, European, and Asian influences, with entrées like the perfectly breaded calamari *piccata* with a tasty red curry sauce. Dine inside the historic cottage or out on the covered garden patio. Indigo Moon also sells artisanal cheeses and bottles of wine, so it's a good place to stop for picnic supplies.

The eclectic menu at **❰ Robin's** (4095 Burton Dr., 805/927-5007, www.robinsrestaurant.com,

daily 11am-9pm, $16-26) has cuisine from around the world, including Thailand (tofu pad thai, Thai green chicken), India (a selection of curries, tandoori chicken), the Mediterranean (meze plate), Mexico (lobster enchiladas), and the old US of A (flat-iron steak, burgers). What makes it so impressive is that they do it all so well. Start with the signature salmon bisque or the grilled naan pizzette of the day. The menu also has a number of vegetarian and gluten-free dishes. The setting is a historic building erected by Heart Castle's construction foreman as his own residence, with a large dining room and an outdoor deck decorated with hanging vines. Expect fine service from a staff that's proud of their product.

Seafood

If the smell of the salt air on Moonstone Beach leaves you longing for a seafood dinner, head for the **❰ Sea Chest Oyster Bar** (6216 Moonstone Beach Dr., 805/927-4514, daily 5:30pm-9pm, $20-30, cash only). No reservations are accepted, so expect a long line

Robin's restaurant serves favorites from around the world.

out the door at opening time, and prepare to get here early (or wait a long while) for one of the window-side tables. The wait is worth it. The restaurant is located in a wooden cottage with great ocean views. Framed photographs on the walls and books on bookshelves add to the homey feel of the place. Sit at the bar to watch the cooks prepare the impressive dishes like halibut, salmon, and cioppino, which is served in the pot it was cooked in. The menu of oyster and clam appetizers includes the indulgent Devils on Horseback, a decadent dish of sautéed oysters drenched in wine, garlic and butter and topped with crispy bacon on two slabs of toast. Yum!

An unassuming steak and seafood restaurant attached to San Simeon's Quality Inn, the family-owned **Manta Rey Restaurant** (9240 Castillo Dr., 805/924-1032, www.mantarey-restaurant.com, daily 5pm-9pm, $16-40) pleasantly surprises with its artfully done and tasty seafood dishes. Items like sand dabs, salmon, oysters, and sea bass come from nearby Morro Bay when in season. A good place to start is with Manta Rey's oysters Rockefeller appetizer ($14), a rich mix of baked oyster, bacon, cheese, and spinach in an oyster shell. The perfectly breaded sand dabs in a creamy basil and sherry sauce are a recommended entrée, especially if it's caught fresh in nearby Morro Bay. The decor here is basic—white tablecloths, flowers on the table—and there is a view of the highway and the ocean in the distance from the porthole-like windows. Being near Hearst Castle, there is frequently an international clientele. Every day, Manta Rey has an early bird special (5pm-6pm) so that you can save a few dollars on select entrées.

At the very least, the **Moonstone Beach Bar & Grill** (6550 Moonstone Beach Dr., 805/927-3859, www.moonstonebeach.com, Mon.-Sat. 11am-9pm, Sun. 9am-9pm, $20-31) is a great place for a drink. The deck out front—always crowded on summer days—has a nice view of the beach. It's ideal for a late-afternoon beer, local wine, or specialty cocktail. The dinner menu is heavy on grilled seafood, while lunch has a wide variety of sandwiches.

INFORMATION AND SERVICES
Maps and Visitor Information

The **Cambria Chamber of Commerce** (767 Main St., 805/927-3624, www.cambria-chamber.org, Mon.-Fri. 9am-5pm, Sat.-Sun. noon-4pm) is probably the best resource for information on the area. It also provides a free annual publication that lists many of the stores, restaurants, and lodgings in the area. Be sure to pick up a trail guide for additional hikes and walks—Cambria has great places to roam. The **Cambria Public Library** (900 Main St., 805/927-4336, Tues.-Sat. 11am-5pm) offers additional information and local history, including a map for a self-guided historical walking tour.

Emergency Services

Cambria is served by three facilities: **Twin Cities Hospital** in Templeton, 25 miles inland, and **Sierra Vista Regional Medical Center** and **French Hospital,** both in San Luis Obispo, 37 miles south. Cambria and San Simeon are policed by the **San Luis Obispo Sheriff's Department** (800/834-3346). If you have an emergency, dial 911.

Newspapers and Media

The Cambrian (2442 Main St., 805/927-8652) is the local paper, published each week on Thursday; copies cost $0.50. KTEA (103.5 FM) is the local radio station.

Postal Services

There is a **post office** (4100 Bridge St., 805/927-8610) currently open Monday-Friday 9am-5pm in Cambria, and postal services are available in San Simeon at **Sebastian's General Store** (444 S. San Simeon Rd., 805/927-4156, Mon.-Fri. 9am-5pm).

GETTING THERE AND AROUND
Car

Cambria and San Simeon are located directly along Highway 1 and are only accessible by this road, whether you're coming from the north or the south. You can access Highway 1 from U.S. 101 via scenic Highway 46, which connects to Highway 1 just south of Cambria. if you use Cambria as a base to explore the Paso Robles wine area, or even for excursions to Morro Bay (15 miles), a car will be necessary. The only available taxi service is **Cambria Cab** (4363 Bridge St., 805/927-4357).

Bus

The regional bus system, the **RTA** (805/541-2228, www.slorta.org), connects San Luis Obispo, Morro Bay, Cayucos, Cambria, and San Simeon. Fares range $1.25-2.50. The **Cambria Otter Bus** is a red-and-green trolley that runs through Cambria Friday-Sunday 10am-5:50pm. It runs the length of Main Street and heads out to Moonstone Beach Drive. Each ride costs $0.50.

Train

There is no rail service to Cambria or San Simeon; the nearest Amtrak train station is located in San Luis Obispo, 35 miles south of Cambria.

Air

There are scheduled flights from Los Angeles, San Francisco, and Phoenix to the **San Luis Obispo County Regional Airport** (SBP, 901 Airport Dr., San Luis Obispo, 805/781-5205), which is 35 miles south of Cambria.

Cayucos

Just 13 miles south of Cambria along Highway 1, Cayucos is one of California's best little beach towns. There are no real attractions here except for the small strip of a beach between open hillsides and the Pacific, but there are a good number of nice restaurants and places to stay, so it makes a nice, less touristy place to spend the night while visiting the area's attractions, including Hearst Castle, 30 miles north.

Cayucos is named after the indigenous Chumash people's word for kayak or canoe. One of the early proponents of the town was Captain James Cass, who, with a business partner, built the pier, a store, and a warehouse in the late 1800s. Today, the long, narrow pier still stands, while the warehouse is the town's

community center and home of the Cayucos Art Society Gallery.

RECREATION
Beaches

The major attraction of Cayucos is **Cayucos State Beach** (Cayucos Dr., 805/781-5930, www.parks.ca.gov) and the pier, which was built way back in 1875 by Captain James Cass. The beach has volleyball courts, swing sets, and lifeguard stands, which are staffed during the summer months. The pier is lit at night for night fishing. Cayucos is not known for consistent surf, but rideable waves can occur on the south side of the pier. This is a usually mellow beach break spot good for beginners. The relatively calm waters off Cayucos Beach

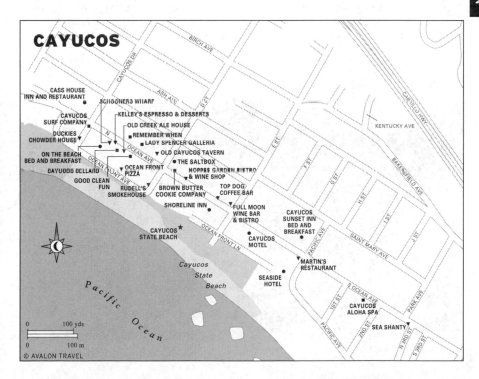

are a good place to try kayaking or stand-up paddleboarding.

Just a few feet from the beach, **Good Clean Fun** (136 Ocean Front Lane, 805/995-1993, http://goodcleanfunusa.com, daily 9am-6pm) rents out surfboards, wetsuits, body boards, stand-up paddleboards, and kayaks. They also have surf lessons, a surf camp, kayak tours, and kayak fishing outings. Another place to pick up beach equipment is the **Cayucos Surf Company** (95 Cayucos Dr., 805/995-1000, www.cayucossurfcompany.com, winter daily 10am-5pm, summer daily 9:30am-7pm). They have wetsuits, surfboards, body boards, and stand-up paddleboards for rent. They also offer private and group surfing lessons.

Hiking

The oceanfront land between Cayucos and Cambria is mostly undeveloped because it's preserved as part of the state park system. The 355-acre **Estero Bluffs State Park** (west of Hwy. 1 from N. Ocean St. to Villa Creek, www.slostateparks.com) is a coastal terrace that offers trails into intertidal areas. It includes a pocket cove and a beach at Villa Creek, which is also an important habitat for the endangered snowy plover.

The 784-acre **Harmony Headlands State Park** (Hwy. 1, 5 miles north of Cayucos, 805/772-7434, www.slostateparks.com, daily 6am-sunset, vehicles $3) was ranch and dairy land until the mid-1960s, and it opened as a state park in 2008. The only real way to experience this park is the 1.5-mile hike from the small 10-car parking lot out to the coast. The trail is a mostly flat dirt road. As it begins, it passes over a bridge where you may be able to look down and spot southwestern pond turtles. The trail continues through grasslands and hugs the side of a scenic ravine, then runs north along a marine terrace. It ends at a small rocky finger that juts out into the between rocks and tide pools. In the spring, wildflowers such as morning glories, California buttercups, and lupine color the grasslands. There are no facilities except for a portable toilet located next to a ranch house just a few minutes

Harmony Headlands State Park

into the trail, on a short side-spur trail to the right.

Spas
After a tough day of relaxing on Cayucos Beach, you deserve a massage. The **Cayucos Aloha Spa** (196 S. Ocean Ave., 805/995-2222, www.cayucosalohaspa.com, by appointment) has you covered with massages ($65 per hour), pedicures, manicures, and "bacials" (a facial treatment for your back).

Wine Tasting
Cayucos Cellars (131 N. Ocean Ave., 805/995-3036, www.cayucoscellars.com, winter Wed.-Mon. 11:30am-5:30pm, summer daily 11:30am-5:30pm, tasting $10) is a true family affair. All the employees are members of the Selkirk family. Cayucos Cellars produces just 500 to 800 cases of wine per year, including zinfandels and cabernet sauvignons. The winery is in an old barn in the Cayucos hills, but the tasting room is in the bright-blue building on the town's main drag.

ENTERTAINMENT AND EVENTS
Bars
The **⬛ Old Cayucos Tavern** (130 North Ocean Ave., 805/995-3209, daily 10am-2am) is a classic Western saloon, with a poker room in the back and a bar up front. In the barroom, over 10 beers are available on tap, and topless cowgirl paintings adorn the walls. There are also two pool tables and a shuffleboard table for those who want to play games without the fear of losing their money in the card room. Western scenes decorate the walls and wooden barrels serve as tables. Live bands perform on weekends.

The **Old Creek Ale House** (123 N. Ocean Ave., 206/794-6461, daily noon-midnight) is serious about beer, with 18 rotating taps of fine craft brews. To sample a good variety, ask the bartender for a four- or eight-sample tasting flight ($8-12). The space is decorated with keg taps and beer signs. There's even a beer fridge where you can get great cold beer to go.

the Old Cayucos Tavern

If you want to sample some local wines, the **Full Moon Wine Bar and Bistro** (10 North Ocean Ave., Suite 212, 805/995-0095, www.fullmoontastingroom.com, Thurs.-Sat. 4pm-10pm, Sun.-Mon. 1pm-8pm) has a heavy selection of wines from nearby Paso Robles, Monterey, and Santa Barbara as well as Europe. Full Moon serves soups, salads, dips, tapas, sandwiches, and deserts, all with an ocean view.

Festivals and Events
The **Independence Day Celebration** (http://cayucos-lions.org, July 4) is a big deal, with a serious sand sculpture contest on the beach, a parade, a barbecue, and a fireworks show from the pier. On New Year's Day, join the locals for the **Carlin Soule Memorial Polar Bear Dip** (Cayucos Pier, www.cayucoschamber.com, New Year's Day noon). It began with just seven brave souls (including founder Carlin Soule) hopping into the frigid Pacific without wetsuits. Bravery must be contagious; today, there are over 1,000 participants.

CAMBRIA AND SAN SIMEON

LIVING IN HARMONY

The population of Harmony has fluctuated throughout the years.

In the mid-1800s the hilly land around the present-day community of Harmony was settled by Swiss immigrants interested in dairy farming. The first cheese factory was established in the area in 1869. After that, this portion of San Luis Obispo County became known for its cheese- and butter-making, becoming home to companies like the Excelsior Cheese Factory and the Diamond Creamery. William Randolph Hearst traveled to Harmony to get his milk. Eventually, tensions grew between competing dairy farmers, which led to a feud and a murder. After peace was restored and a truce was made, the farmers decided to name the town Harmony in 1907 to reflect their newly adopted situation.

In 1958, Harmony ceased its cheese- and butter-making. The population of the town dropped until the 1970s, when some of the old dairy buildings were occupied by artists studios, galleries, and shops. The new influx of residents didn't quite restore Harmony to its former glory of the dairy days. In 1997, the entire town, including its buildings and 2.5 acres of land, was put up for sale for $1.49 million. The town never sold, and now a sign along Highway 1 announces a community with a population of 18 residents.

Currently, Harmony is primarily known for **Harmony Cellars** (3255 Harmony Valley Rd., 805/927-1625, www.harmonycellars.com, fall-spring daily 10am-5pm, summer daily 10am-5:30pm, tasting $5), a winery that makes both reds and whites, and **Harmony Glassworks** (2180 Old Creamery Rd., 805/927-4248, http://harmonyglassworks.com, daily 9am-5:30pm), a glass art gallery, studio, and school. Harmony is also home to the **Harmony Chapel** (805/927-1028, www.harmonychapel.net), a recording studio and café.

SHOPPING

Remember When (152 N. Ocean Ave., 805/995-1232, daily 10am-5pm) is home to antiques and collectibles. The **Lady Spencer Galleria and Distinctive Gifts** (148 N. Ocean Ave., 805/995-3771, www.ladyspencer.com, Mon.-Tues. and Thurs.-Sat. 10am-5pm, Sun. 10:30am-4pm) carries all sorts of unique items from barbed-wire earrings to soy candles and glass tableware.

Located in a two-story red building on Cayucos' main drag, **Brown Butter Cookie Company** (98 N. Ocean Ave., 805/995-2076, www.brownbuttercookies.com, daily 9am-6pm) bakes and sells original cookie creations, including the original brown-butter sea-salt cookie and more recent recipes such as coconut lime and cocoa mint. Witness the delectable creative process right behind the counter. Cayucos has its own **farmers market** (Cayucos Vet's Hall parking lot, 10 Cayucos Dr., 805/296-2056, June-Aug. Fri. 10am-12:30pm).

ACCOMMODATIONS
Under $150

The **Seaside Motel** (42 South Ocean Ave., 805/995-3809 or 800/549-0900, www.seasidemotel.com, $110-160) has brightly colored and uniquely decorated guest rooms with names like The Birdhouse and Sunflower. Some guest rooms have kitchenettes; all have flat-screen TVs and Internet access. Suites are available for larger groups.

True to its name, the **Shoreline Inn** (1 N. Ocean Ave., 805/995-3681, www.cayucosshorelineinn.com, $139-189) is right on the beach. All of the guest rooms have impressive beach and pier views as well as access to the beach and beachside showers. Everyone also gets a mini fridge, a microwave, free Wi-Fi, and a flat-screen TV with a DVD player. Start the morning with a deluxe continental breakfast, and snack on complimentary cookies in the afternoon.

The **Cayucos Motel** (20 S. Ocean Ave., 805/995-3670, www.cayucosmotel.com, $105-135) is also all about the beach, with beach

CAMBRIA AND SAN SIMEON

Brown Butter Cookie Company

access, an outdoor shower, and body-boards and beach towels that guests can check out to further enjoy the surf and sand. Each of the eight guest rooms is different; some have private patios. The outdoor deck includes a barbecue grill and a Ping-Pong table. Did I mention the continental breakfast? It's good value for the price.

$150-250

Located right behind the Brown Butter Cookie Company, **❮ The Saltbox** (150 D St., 800/995-2322, www.thesaltbox.com, $150-220) makes a superb home base while you're exploring the coast. The historic blue building, constructed by a ship's captain in the 1880s, is split into three units, each with fully equipped kitchens, private entrances, and a deck or patio. The ground-floor Captain's Quarters can accommodate six to eight people with three bedrooms, two bathrooms, and an enclosed brick patio area. It's a perfect fit for three couples or a big family. The Crow's Nest is an upstairs apartment with two bedrooms that can accommodate four people and has a nice view of the sea and the pier. The Carriage House is a small studio in the shade of the main house. The place is a bit dated (there's a VCR and a tape player in the Crow's Nest), but that is outweighed by lots of character, a great location, and fair rates.

The **Cayucos Sunset Inn Bed and Breakfast** (95 S. Ocean Ave., 805/995-2500 or 877/805-1076, www.cayucossunsetinn.com, $229-349) has five two-room suites with private balconies, soaking tubs, and fireplaces. The innkeepers provide breakfast in the morning as well as milk and cookies delivered to your room every evening. The modern rooms at **On the Beach Bed & Breakfast** (181 N. Ocean Ave., 805/995-3200, www.californiaonthebeach.com, $179-299) have gas fireplaces, private balconies, and jetted tubs. The rooftop hot tub offers views of the ocean and pier. Wake up to complimentary breakfast in the morning.

© STUART THORNTON

The Saltbox

Over $250

The **◖Cass House Inn and Restaurant** (222 N. Ocean Ave., 805/995-3669, http://casshouseinn.com, $225-325) offers five comfortable guest rooms in the old house of Captain James Cass, who basically founded Cayucos. Although the building was built in 1867, the guest rooms have modern, even luxurious amenities, including Anichini bed and bath linens, Wi-Fi, flat-screen TVs, and Tivoli radios. Cass House is just a block from the beach, so the crashing waves will lull you to sleep. The tasty breakfast includes bacon cured on-site and fresh-pressed orange juice.

FOOD
Coffee and Tea

Grab your morning caffeine jolt at **Top Dog Coffee Bar** (12 N. Ocean St., 805/900-5194, daily 6am-4pm) or **Kelley's Espresso & Desserts** (155 N. Ocean Ave., 805/995-2980, Mon.-Fri. 7am-2pm, Sat.-Sun. 7am-5pm).

Fine Dining

The **Cass House Restaurant** (222 N. Ocean Ave., 805/995-3669, http://casshouseinn.com, Thurs.-Mon. 5pm-8:30pm, 4-course meal $72) occupies a room in the bottom floor of the historic house. The menu changes daily and may include items like local grass-fed beef or truffle polenta. Everything is seasonally inspired, locally sourced, and made in-house—even the butter.

Hoppe's Garden Bistro and Wine Shop (78 N. Ocean Ave., 805/995-1006, www.hoppesbistro.com, Wed.-Sun. 11am-2pm and 5pm-close, $14-60) serves French-inspired cuisine in a building that dates to 1876. It was once the old Cottage Hotel, where the Hearst family sometimes dined before they built the castle up the road. The popular outdoor dining area utilizes 20,000 bricks. Dinner entrées include meat options like roasted pheasant, vegetarian offerings like grilled polenta, and a range of seafood dishes like sautéed abalone.

Mexican and Italian

If you can't decide between Mexican and Italian food, head to **Martin's Restaurant** (49 S. Ocean St., 805/995-2626, www.martinsrestaurantcayucos.com, daily 8am-9pm, $9-17); they do both. Fish tacos, shrimp enchiladas, tostadas, and burritos appear on the menu alongside pizza, calzones, and full entrées like chicken parmesan and salmon fettuccine.

Pizza

A blue building just a few feet from Cayucos Beach, **Ocean Front Pizza** (156½ Ocean Front Ave., 805/995-2979, daily 11:30am-8:30pm, $10-22) offers classic pizza combos, build-your-own pies, specialty pizzas like pesto and Thai, and barbecued chicken. All feature hand-tossed dough and homemade sauce.

Seafood

Cayucos is a place for seafood, and there is probably nothing in town as revered as **◖Rudell's Smokehouse** (101 D St., 805/995-5028, www.smokerjim.com, daily 11am-6pm, $4-11). Rudell's is nothing more than a little shack near the beach, but this place serves some of the tastiest fish tacos you'll ever eat, including salmon and albacore variations. The seafood is smoked, and the unexpected but welcome presence of chopped apples gives the fixings a sweet crunch. The seating options are limited to a few outdoor tables, so plan on taking your taco to the nearby beach.

Living up to its name, **Schooners Wharf** (171 N. Ocean Ave., 805/995-3883, Mon.-Thurs. 11am-9pm, Fri. 11am-10pm, Sat.-Sun. 8am-10pm, $9-28) has a serious nautical theme going: It's a two-story compound of corrugated metal and wood decorated heavily with marine flotsam and jetsam. The menu here is seafood-heavy, with a range of items from hearty lobster macaroni and cheese to a teriyaki shrimp stir-fry. But the burgers, made with nearby Hearst Ranch beef, are also worthy of your attention. If you are looking for somewhere to eat in Cayucos later at night, Schooners will probably be the only option.

At **Duckies Chowder House** (55 Cayucos Dr., 805/995-2245, daily 11am-9pm, $6-12.50), you can get your chowder New England

© GABRIEL SKVOR

the Sea Shanty

or Manhattan style and served in a cup, bowl, or bread bowl. Other seafood options are mostly fried; there are also salads and sandwiches on the menu. Pitchers of beer and the company of friends make it all go down easy.

The **Sea Shanty** (296 S. Ocean Ave., 805/995-3272, www.seashantycayucos.com, winter daily 8am-9pm, summer daily 8am-10pm, $10-25) serves gut-busting portions for breakfast, lunch, and dinner. The carb-loaded Cayucos Breakfast is biscuits drenched in eggs and gravy alongside a small mound of diced Swiss sausage. Lunches focus on charbroiled and fried seafood. Noteworthy desserts include a range of pies and cobblers. Dine inside under hundreds of hanging baseball caps—or better yet, sit outside on the covered wooden deck.

INFORMATION AND SERVICES

Before visiting, the website **Cayucos by the Sea** (www.cayucosbythesea.com) has information on everything from the town's history to its current lodging and restaurant options. The website of the **Cayucos Chamber of Commerce** (www.cayucoschamber.com) is also a good source of visitor information.

Cayucos has a few basic services, including **Mid-State Bank** (107 N. Ocean Ave., 805/995-3671), which has an ATM, and the **Post Office** (97 Ash Ave., Mon.-Fri. 9am-4pm). The **Cayucos Super Market** (301 Ocean Ave., 805/995-3929, daily 8am-8pm) has all the basic supplies you'll need. It's also home to the **Cayucos Sausage Company** (www.cayucossausagecompany.com), which has an array of homemade sausages.

Morro Bay

The picturesque fishing village of Morro Bay is dominated by Morro Rock, a 576-foot-high volcanic plug that looms over the harbor. In 1542, Juan Rodríguez Cabrillo, the first European explorer to navigate the California coast, named the landmark Morro Rock, because he thought it appeared to resemble a moor's turban.

With a view of the rock, the small city's Embarcadero is a string of tourist shops, restaurants, and hotels strung along Morro Bay, a large estuary that includes the harbor, the Morro Bay State Marine Recreational Management Area, and the Morro Bay State Marine Reserve. Uphill from the water, more restaurants, bars, and stores are located in Morro Bay's Olde Towne section.

With natural attractions that include the stunning Montaña de Oro State Park just miles from town and with a nice waterfront focus, Morro Bay is a worthy destination or detour for a weekend, even though a lot of the area's lodgings fill up during high-season weekends.

SIGHTS
◖ Morro Rock

It would be difficult to come to the town of Morro Bay and not see Morro Rock (www.slostateparks.com). The 576-foot-high volcanic plug, which has been called the "Gibraltar of the Pacific," dominates the town's scenery, whether you are walking along the bayside Embarcadero or beachcombing on the sandy coastline just north of the prominent geologic feature. The rock was an island until the 1930s, when a road was built connecting it to the mainland. The area around the rock is accessible, but the rock itself is off-limits because it is home to a group of endangered peregrine

© STUART THORNTON

Morro Rock

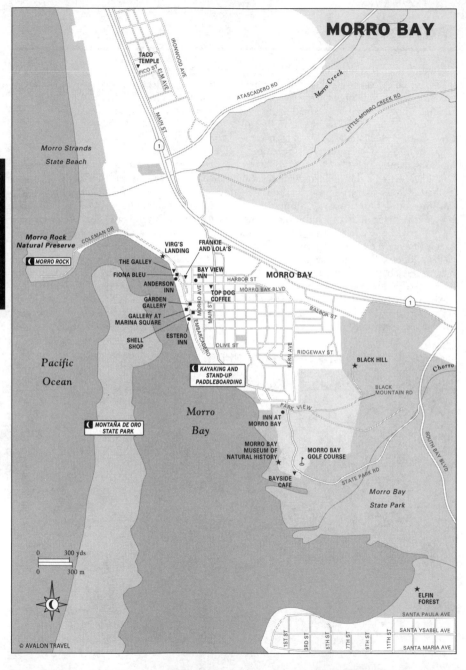

MORRO BAY

TACO TEMPLE
PICO ST
ELM AVE
IRONWOOD AVE
MAIN ST
ATASCADERO RD
Morro Creek
LITTLE MORRO CREEK RD

Morro Strands
State Beach

COLEMAN DR

Morro Rock
Natural Preserve

☾ MORRO ROCK

VIRG'S LANDING
FRANKIE AND LOLA'S

THE GALLEY
BAY VIEW INN
MORRO BAY
HARBOR ST
FIONA BLEU
ANDERSON INN
TOP DOG COFFEE
MORRO BAY BLVD
MORRO AVE
GARDEN GALLERY
BALBOA ST
GALLERY AT MARINA SQUARE
MAIN ST
EMBARCADERO
SHELL SHOP
ESTERO INN
OLIVE ST
KERN AVE
RIDGEWAY ST

BLACK HILL

Chorro

☾ KAYAKING AND STAND-UP PADDLEBOARDING

Pacific
Ocean

BLACK MOUNTAIN RD

PARK VIEW

☾ MONTAÑA DE ORO STATE PARK

Morro
Bay

INN AT MORRO BAY

SOUTH BAY BLVD

MORRO BAY MUSEUM OF NATURAL HISTORY

MORRO BAY GOLF COURSE

BAYSIDE CAFE

STATE PARK RD

Morro Bay
State Park

0   300 yds
0   300 m

ELFIN FOREST

SANTA PAULA AVE

SANTA YSABEL AVE

1ST ST
3RD ST
5TH ST
7TH ST
9TH ST
11TH ST

SANTA MARIA AVE

© AVALON TRAVEL

falcons. Indeed, a multitude of birds always seems to be swirling around the rock they call home.

[Montaña de Oro State Park

Montaña de Oro State Park (Pecho Rd., 7 miles south of Los Osos, 805/528-0513, www. parks.ca.gov) is for those seeking a serious nature fix on the Central Coast. This sprawling 8,000-acre park with seven miles of coastline has coves, tide pools, sand dunes, and almost 50 miles of hiking trails. A great way to get a feel for the park's immense size is to hike up the two-mile **Valencia Peak Trail** (4 miles round-trip). In springtime the sides of the trail are decorated with blooming wildflowers, and the 1,347-foot-high summit offers commanding views of Montaña de Oro's pocked coastline and Morro Rock jutting out in the distance. From this vantage point in spring, the park's sticky monkey flower, wild mustard, and California poppies dust the hillsides in gold. The hike is steep and exposed, so make sure to bring plenty of water on warm days.

For a feel of the coast, park right in front of **Spooner's Cove** and walk out on its wide coarse-grained beach. On the cove's north end, Islay Creek drains into the ocean. There's also a picturesque arch across the creek in the rock face on the north side. The **Spooner Ranch House Museum** informs visitors about early inhabitants of the park's land, the Spooner family. There are also displays about the area's plants, mountain lions, and raptors in the small facility.

Morro Bay State Park

Morro Bay State Park (Morro Bay State Park Rd., 805/772-2560, www.parks.ca.gov) is not a typical state park. It has hiking trails, a campground, and recreational opportunities, but this park also has its own natural history museum, a golf course, and a marina. Located just south of town, the park is situated on the shores of Morro Bay. One way to get a feel for the park is to hike the **Black Hill Trail** (3 miles round-trip), which begins from the campground road. This climb gains 600 vertical feet and passes

© STUART THORNTON

Montaña de Oro State Park

through chaparral and eucalyptus on the way to the 640-foot-high Black Hill, a part of the same system of volcanic plugs that produced nearby Morro Rock. From the summit, you can see the estuary below and part of Montaña de Oro State Park in the distance. Also on Black Hill is a forest of Monterey pine.

One unique aspect of Morro Bay State Park is the **Morro Bay Museum of Natural History** (Morro Bay State Park Rd., 805/772-2694, www.slostateparks.com, daily 10am-5pm, adults $3, under age 17 free). Small but informative, the museum has displays that explain the habitats of the Central Coast and some interactive exhibits for kids. An observation deck hanging off the museum allows for a great view of Morro Bay and has binoculars so that you can spot wildlife. Beside the museum is a garden that shows how the area's original inhabitants, the Chumash people, utilized the region's plants.

Another way to experience the park is to play a round of golf at the **Morro Bay State Park Golf Course** (201 State Park Rd., 805/782-8060, www.slocountyparks.com, Mon.-Fri. $43, Sat.-Sun. $48), or head out on the water in a kayak or canoe rented from the **Kayak Shack** (10 State Park Rd., 805/772-8796, www.morrobaykayakshack.com, $12-16 per hour).

Morro Bay Harbor Walk

The **Morro Bay Harbor Walk** (0.5 miles, easy) is a great way to take in Morro Bay's Harbor. Beginning at the north end of the Embarcadero, the boardwalk and bike trail runs along the harbor to towering Morro Rock. The harbor views are nice, and you can get some scenic photos of the picturesque harbor town and the hills behind it. You may also spot some sea otters in the water. Along the way, the walk passes through **Coleman Park,** a small city park with a picnic area, a basketball court, and a swing set for kids.

One way to do the Morro Bay Harbor Walk is by pedal power. Located near the start of the bike trail is **Farmer's Kites** (1108 Front. St., 805/772-0113, daily 9am-6pm). This kites store rents beach cruisers ($10 per hour) along with two-person and four-person surrey bikes ($20-30 per hour).

Giant Chessboard

Morro Bay's most unusual sight is the 16- by 16-foot **Giant Chessboard** (Centennial Pkwy., 805/772-6278). The waist-high chess pieces used in the game weigh as much as 30 pounds. Four picnic tables adjoin the Giant Chessboard; each has a chessboard where the local chess fiends play. You can reserve the giant board for a small fee.

Morro Bay Estuary Nature Center

Run by the Morro Bay National Estuary Program, the **Morro Bay Estuary Nature Center** (601 Embarcadero, Suite 11, 805/772-3834, www.mbnep.org, Mar.-Dec. daily 10am-6pm, Jan.-Feb. daily 10am-5pm) explains the significance of the 2,300-acre estuary that is a focal point of the town. A watershed exhibit shows where rainfall goes, while an aquarium has live steelhead trout. Another aquarium houses eelgrass along with hermit crabs and anemones. There are also windows looking out on the estuary, where you may be able to spot sea otters, harbor seals, and sea lions in the water.

Morro Bay Skateboard Museum

California is the birthplace of skateboarding, and the **Morro Bay Skateboard Museum** (601 Embarcadero, Suite 4, 805/610-3565, www.mbskate.com, Mon.-Fri. noon-5pm, Sat.-Sun. 10am-6pm, donation) celebrates skating with a collection of over 200 boards dating from the 1950s to the present. There are homemade boards, boards autographed by skate pros, a Budweiser promotional board, and several boards that have been ridden all the way across the country. Scooters and framed skateboarding trading cards are also on display. The small one-room museum also sells skateboards, skate shoes, and T-shirts.

SPAS

The **Bay Beauty Spa** (1140 Front St., Unit C, 805/772-5038, www.baybeautyspa.com, daily 9am-5pm) offers several massage options ($75-150), including popular couples massages and HydroMassage, which employs jets of hot water

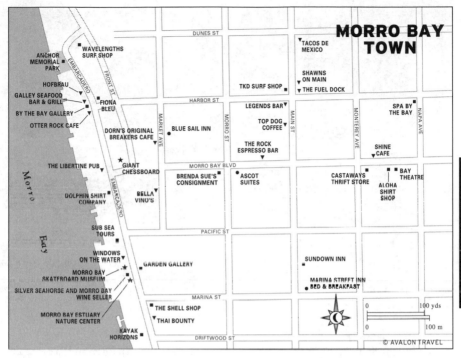

beneath a cushioned mattress. It's like a soak in a whirlpool tub, but you can do it fully clothed and stay completely dry. Other procedures include pedicures, facials, microdermabrasion, and waxing. The location has a nice view of the harbor. **Spa By the Bay** (895 Napa Ave., Suite A1, 805/234-6922, http://spamorrobay.com, Mon.-Sat. by appointment) provides massages ($65-130) in a relaxing, Asian-influenced setting. Their signature Coastal Massage utilizes stretching, acupressure, and hot rocks.

ENTERTAINMENT AND EVENTS
Bars

With old gas and oil cans hanging from the ceiling, **The Fuel Dock** (900 Main St., 805/772-8478, daily noon-2am) lives up to its name. Behind the bar is a good selection of liquor and beer to act as social lubricants. The front room has a stage that hosts live bands on weekends, while the back room has a couple of pool tables. Across the street, **Legends Bar** (899 Main St., 805/772-2525, daily 11am-2am) has a red pool table and a giant moose head poking out from behind the bar. Grab a drink and look at the framed historic photos covering the walls.

Down on the Embarcadero, ◖ **The Libertine Pub** (801 Embarcadero, 805/772-0700, Mon.-Fri. 3pm-midnight, Sat.-Sun. noon-midnight) is the place for the discerning beer drinker, with 20 rotating craft beers on tap and a selection of over 80 bottled beers. One of the beers on tap will always be a sour. Friday-Sunday an upstairs section features high-end bourbons and beers known as "whales": rare, highly coveted beers. You can also order craft cocktails (a basil bourbon drink that counts marmalade as one of its ingredients) and food (including clams, burgers, and *moules frites*). The bartenders also act as DJs, playing selections from the Libertine's stash of vinyl.

© STUART THORNTON

the Morro Bay Harbor Walk

◖ **Stax Wine Bar & Bistro** (1099 Embarcadero, 805/772-5055, Mon.-Thurs. noon-8pm, Fri.-Sat. noon-10pm, Sun. noon-8pm) has a nice sidelong view of the harbor. Sit at the long black granite bar or at the handful of tables to sample the selection of over 100 wines, many from local wineries. Five to eight rotating wines are served by the glass. The small food menu includes crostinis, paninis, salads, cheese plates, and local oysters.

Located up the hill from the Embarcadero, **Bella Vino's** (783 Market Ave., 805/225-1600, www.bellavinoswine.com, Tues.-Sun. 4:30pm-10pm) has fine views of the bay and rock and a sophisticated setting, with a fireplace and lots of dark leather and wood. Choose from a range of wine tastings: standard (five pours $9), reserve (five pours $14), and premium (five pours $22).

Borderline kitschy, with marine decorations that match it's harbor-side location, The **Otter Rock Café** (885 Embarcadero, 805/772-1420, www.otterrockcafe.com, Mon.-Fri. 10am-midnight, Sat.-Sun.

8am-midnight) draws a crowd that knows how to have fun. Tuesday and Wednesday karaoke nights are a prelude to Thursday's open jam sessions. The outdoor seating offers views of the harbor and the rock.

Cinema
There's only one movie house in town, the **Bay Theatre** (464 Morro Bay Blvd., 805/772-2444), and it has only one screen, so you're pretty limited unless you drive 20 minutes south to San Luis Obispo.

Festivals and Events
Strong winds kick up on the Central Coast in the spring. The **Morro Bay Parade and Kite Festival** (800/231-0592, www.morrobay.org) takes advantage of these gales with pro kite fliers twirling and flipping their kites in the sky. The festival also offers kite-flying lessons.

For over 30 years, the **Morro Bay Harbor Festival** (800/366-6043, www.mbhf.com) has showcased the best of the region, including

© STUART THORNTON

CAMBRIA AND SAN SIMEON

Libertine Pub

wines, seafood, live music, and a clam chowder contest.

Bird-watchers flock to the **Morro Bay Winter Bird Festival** (3rd Mon. in Jan., 805/275-4143, www.morrobaybirdfestival.org, free-$90). Some 200 species are typically spotted during the three-day event, which includes birding classes and tours of local birding spots.

The **Avocado and Margarita Festival** (714 Embarcadero, 805/772-4467, http://avomargfest.com, $2) celebrates great food and drink, all complementing and inspired the ever-popular locally grown avocado. The festival includes live music performances, a sombrero contest, and a raffle for a year's supply of avocados.

The motto of the **Central Coast Oyster Festival** (Morro Bay Golf Course, 805/459-0701, http://centralcoastoysterfestival.com, $24-28) in October is "Shuck Yeah," a reference to the centerpiece oyster-shucking contest. Oysters are provided by the Morro Bay Oyster Company. There's also beer, wine, cocktails, and music.

The **Rock to Pier Run** (805/772-6278,

$50-70) is an annual beach run in July from Morro Rock to Cayucos Pier and back.

SHOPPING
Antiques

Antiques are the main draw at **Brenda Sue's Consignment** (248 Morro Bay Blvd., 805/772-7226, daily 10am-5pm), but you'll find a little bit of everything: clothes, home decor, books, cameras, DVDs, and vinyl records.

Art Galleries

Since **By the Bay Gallery** (895 Embarcadero, 805/772-5563, www.bythebaygallery.com, daily 10am-6pm) opened in 1988 to sell the owner's woodcarvings, it has expanded to include American-made crafts, jewelry, sculptures, and ceramics. The gallery shares a building with the Anderson Inn and the Galley Restaurant.

Run by a community of artists, the **Gallery at Marina Square** (601 Embarcadero, Suite 10, 805/772-1068, daily 10am-6pm) showcases local art: the work of sculptors, photographers,

Stax Wine Bar

jewelry makers, glass workers, and wood workers. A public reception on the second Friday of every month (5pm-8pm) celebrates a member artist and a guest artist.

Clothing

Find clothes and gifts for kids at the **Silver Seahorse** (601 Embarcadero, 805/772-1336, www.silverseahorse.com, winter daily 10am-6pm, summer Sun.-Thurs. 10am-6pm, Fri.-Sat. 10am-8pm). The brightly colored options include bonnets, ballet shoes, tutus, and hats that look like birthday cakes.

Up from the Embarcadero, the **Queen's Closet** (325 Morro Bay Blvd., 805/772-4288, www.queenscloset.net, Mon.-Sat. 10am-5pm, Sun. noon-3pm) hopes to fill your closet with brands like Alfred Dunner, WeBeBop, and Cathy Daniels.

Poppy (911 Embarcadero, 805/771-9750, daily 10am-6pm) is stocked with accessories, jewelry, soaps, and candles.

Hit the beach with a tropical shirt from the **Aloha Shirt Shop** (458 Morro Bay Blvd.,

805/772-2480, www.alohashirtshop.com, daily 10am-4pm). This 4,000-square-foot retail center imports colorful island wear directly from Hawaii.

Farmers Market

Morro Bay has two weekly farmers markets: the **Thursday farmers market** (Spencer's Fresh Markets parking lot, 2650 Main St., Thurs. 3pm-5pm) and the **Saturday farmers market** (Main St. and Harbor St., 805/602-1009, Sat. 3pm-6pm).

Gifts and Accessories

Need a souvenir for that person who didn't make the trip? The **Dolphin Shirt Company** (715 Embarcadero, 805/771-9599, daily 10am-6pm) has you covered with T-shirts, sweatshirts, hats, art, and gifts.

Home and Garden

The **Garden Gallery** (680 Embarcadero, 805/772-4044, Mon.-Fri. 11am-5pm, Sat.-Sun. 10am-5pm) occupies a two-story building designed and built by one of its owners. The indoor and outdoor area is filled with cacti and other succulents, along with garden decorations like fountains and pottery and indoor items like clocks and candles.

Splash your home with color after stopping by **Fiona Bleu** (900 Embarcadero, 805/772-0541, www.fionableu.com, daily 10am-6pm). It's part art gallery, part home decor store. Brighten your living space with vivid ocean paintings, bright glass art, and colorful lamps.

Specialty Stores

Wavelengths Surf Shop (998 Embarcadero, 805/772-3904, daily 9:30am-6pm) has a good selection of new surfboards, skateboards, wetsuits, and surf wear, including hoodies and

T-shirts. Browse the outlet store located right across the street to find deals on used boards and wetsuits. It's also where you can rent a surfboard or wetsuit.

The "TKD" in **TKD Surf Shop** (911 Main St., 805/772-1211, daily 10am-6pm) stands for "totally killer deals," and it's true: You'll find real savings on surf wear and gear, including body boards, soft-top surfboards, and wetsuits. TKD also rents out wetsuits ($10 per day) and soft-top surfboards ($10 per day).

Since 1955, **The Shell Shop** (590 Embarcadero, 805/772-8014, daily 9:30am-5pm) has imported shells from over 22 countries. Beautiful marine items on sale include nautilus shells, abalone shells, and decorative pieces of coral as well as seashell jewelry.

Vinyl Isle (740 Morro Bay Blvd., 805/772-1103, Tues.-Sat. 11am-6pm, Sun. noon-5pm) has over 5,000 records with a heavy emphasis on jazz and 1970s rock. You'll also find used turntables, cassette tapes, and—believe it or not—eight-tracks.

Thrift Stores

Browse vintage clothes, vinyl records, and a selection of over 4,000 used DVDs at **Castaways Thrift Store** (410 Morro Bay Blvd., 805/772-6180, daily 10am-6pm).

Wine Stores

Stock up on Central Coast wines at the **Morro Bay Wine Seller** (601 Embarcadero, Suite 5, 805/772-8388, www.morrobaywineseller.com, Sun.-Thurs. 10am-6pm, Fri.-Sat. 10am-8pm, tasting $5). They also have beer, cheese, and wine accessories.

SPORTS AND RECREATION
Beaches

There are several beaches in and around Morro Bay. Popular with surfers and beachcombers, **Morro Rock Beach** (west end of Embarcadero, 805/772-6200, www.morro-bay.ca.us) lies within the city limits, just north of Morro Rock. The **Morro Bay Sandspit** (www.slostateparks.com) is a four-mile-long line of dunes and beach that separates Morro Bay from the

---

WATER FARMS

Aquaculture is the practice of farming aquatic organisms. The Cambria and Morro Bay area has two fine examples of aquaculture operations. The **Morro Bay Oyster Company** (805/234-7102, http://morrobayoysters.pinnaclecart.com) uses environmentally sustainable techniques to raise Pacific Gold oysters in the cold, nutrient-rich waters of Morro Bay. The oysters start off as small as a pencil eraser in mesh nets and are "farmed" for 12 to 24 months until they have developed into tasty bivalve mollusks with a shell. Farther up the road in Cayucos, **The Abalone Farm** (805/995-2495, www.montereyabalone.com) is the largest aquaculture facility in the nation. They produce an impressive 100 tons of California red abalone per year. The natural California red abalone population was decimated by years of overharvesting, so the Abalone Farm is a way for seafood lovers to once again dine on the large edible sea snail. Though there are currently no tours available for visitors to view these facilities, seafood enthusiasts can seek out these tasty, sustainably farmed products while dining at local restaurants.

The Shell Shop

ocean. The northernmost mile is within city limits, while the southern portion is located in Montaña de Oro State Park. You can access this area by walking in from the state park or by paddling across Morro Harbor to the land south of the harbor mouth.

Just north of town is **Morro Strand State Beach** (Hwy. 1, 805/772-2560, www.parks. ca.gov). The three-mile strand of sand is popular with anglers, windsurfers, and kite fliers. **North Point** (Hwy. 1 at Toro Lane) is a blufftop city park with a stairway to the beach and great tide pools. From here, you can also walk north all the way to Cayucos or head south toward looming Morro Rock. The wetlands at **Cloisters Park** (San Jacinto St. and Coral St.) are home to fish and birds. This city park also offers access to the beach.

Surfing

Morro Rock Beach (west end of Embarcadero, 805/772-6200, www.morro-bay.ca.us) has a consistent beach break. It's a unique experience to be able to stare up at a giant rock

while waiting for waves. **Wavelengths Surf Shop** (998 Embarcadero, 805/772-3904, daily 9:30am-6pm, board rental $20 per day, wetsuit rental $10 per day), on the Embarcadero on the way to the beach, rents boards and wetsuits, as does **TKD Surf Shop** (911 Main St., 805/772-1211, daily 10am-6pm, soft-top surfboard rental $10 per day, wetsuit rental $10 per day).

Kayaking and Stand-Up Paddleboarding

Paddling the protected scenic waters of Morro Bay, whether you're in a kayak or on a stand-up paddleboard (SUP), is a great way to see wildlife up close. You might see otters lazily backstroking in the estuary or clouds of birds gliding just above the surface of the water.

Paddle over the **Morro Bay Sandspit,** a finger of dunes located in the northern section of Montaña de Oro State Park that separates the bay from the ocean. Then beach your vessel and climb over the dunes to the mostly isolated beach on the ocean side. Parts of the dunes can be closed to protect the snowy plover. Away

Explore Morro Bay by kayak or paddleboard.

from the harbor area, the estuary can be very shallow; plan your paddling at high tide to avoid too much portaging.

Central Coast Stand-Up Paddling (1215 Embarcadero, 805/395-0410, www.central-coastsup.com, daily 9am-6pm) rents stand-up paddleboards ($18 per hour) and offers a 2.5-hour Morro Bay Tour ($75 pp). **Kayak Horizons** (551 Embarcadero, 805/772-6444, www.kayakhorizons.com, daily 9am-5pm) rents kayaks ($12-18 per hour) and paddleboards ($12 per hour) and hosts a three-hour paddle around the estuary ($59). **Central Coast Outdoors** (805/528-1080, www.centralcoastoutdoors.com, kayak tours $55-110 pp) has a range of kayaking tours that depart from the **Morro Bay State Park Marina** (100 State Park Rd.). Options include short paddles, sunset paddles, full-moon paddles, half-day paddles, and a kayak trip to the sandspit for a dinner in the dunes. Visit their website for more information. In Morro Bay State Park, you can secure a canoe or kayak from **A Kayak Shack** (10 State Park Rd.,

805/772-8796, www.morrobaykayakshack.com, summer daily 9am-6pm, winter Fri.-Sun. 9am-4pm, stand-up paddleboards $12 per hour, single kayaks $12 per hour, double kayaks $16 per hour).

Boat Tours

Sub Sea Tours (699 Embarcadero, 805/772-9463, www.subseatours.com, adults $14, seniors and students $11, children $7) is like snorkeling without getting wet. The yellow 27-foot semi-submersible vessel has a cabin outfitted with windows below the water. The 45-minute tour takes you around harbor is search of wildlife. Expect to see sea lions sunning on a floating dock and sea otters playing in the water. At a much-touted secret spot, fish congregate for feeding. You'll typically see smelt, appearing like silver splinters, but may also catch a glimpse of salmon, lingcod, perch, and sunfish. The captain may even cue up the Beatles' "Yellow Submarine" on the sound system. Kids will love it. Sub Sea Tours also schedules 2-3.5-hour **whale watching excursions**

(adults $40, seniors and students $35, under age 12 $30) to see California gray whales and humpback whales.

If you'd rather cruise the bay with the benefit of adult beverages, try **Lost Isle Adventure Tours** (Giovanni's Fish Market, 1001 Front St., 805/771-9337, http://baycruisers.com, adults $10, under age 13 $5), which take place on a ramshackle floating tiki bar. **Chablis Cruises** (800/979-3370, http://chabliscruises.com) are held on a two-story riverboat with a rooftop deck. Options include a two-hour **weekly champagne brunch excursion** (11am, adults $42, under age 12 $21) and **murder mystery dinner cruises** ($55). **Virg's Landing** (1169 Market Ave., 805/772-1222, http://virgslanding.com, $49-89) sends four boats out for daily fishing trips, searching for rock cod, albacore, king salmon, and halibut. They also offer whale-watching excursions from December to April.

Bird-Watching

Morro Bay is one of California's great birding spots. **Morro Bay State Park** is home to a **heron rookery,** located just north of the Museum of Natural History. At **Morro Rock,** you'll see endangered peregrine falcons, ever-present gulls, and the occasional canyon wren. On the northwest end of **Morro Bay State Park Marina Area** (off State Park Dr.) birders can spot loons, grebes, brants, and ducks; you may also see American pipits and Nelson's sparrows. The cypress trees host roosting black-crowned night herons.

In **Montaña de Oro State Park,** along the **Sandspit,** you might find wrentits, blue-gray gnatcatchers, and California thrashers. **Islay Creek** hosts gulls at the beach in the winter. Farther upstream, clay-colored sparrows, chipping sparrows, and rare migrating warblers have been spotted. The region can be accessed via the park's **Islay Creek Trail.** The **Morro Coast Audubon Society** (805/772-1991, www.morrocoastaudubon.org) conducts birding field trips to local hotspots; check their website for information on the upcoming field trips.

Hiking

Morro Bay State Park (Morro Bay State Park Rd., 805/772-2560, www.parks.ca.gov) has 13 miles of hiking trails. One of the most popular is the **Black Hill Trail** (3 miles round-trip, moderate), which begins from the campground road. This climb gains 600 vertical feet and passes through chaparral and eucalyptus on the way to the 640-foot-high Black Hill, part of the same system of volcanic plugs that produced nearby Morro Rock.

Montaña de Oro State Park (Pecho Rd., 7 miles south of Los Osos, 805/528-0513, www.parks.ca.gov) has almost 50 miles of hiking trails. Take in the park's coastline along the **Montaña de Oro Bluffs Trail** (4 miles round-trip, easy). The trailhead begins about 100 yards south of the visitors center and campground entrance and runs along a marine terrace to the park's southern boundary. On the way it passes **Corallina Cove,** where you may see harbor seals and sea otters. Starting at the parking area just south of the visitors center, **Valencia Peak Trail** (4 miles round-trip, moderate) leads to its namesake 1,347-foot-high peak, which offers a nice view of the coastline spread out below. The **Hazard Peak Trail** (6 miles round-trip, moderate-strenuous) starts at Pecho Valley Road and climbs to the summit of 1,076-foot Hazard Peak, with unobstructed 360-degree views. The **Islay Canyon Trail** (6 miles round-trip, moderate) takes you through the park's inland creek beds and canyons. Starting at the bottom of Islay Creek Canyon, this wide dirt path is popular with birders because of the 25 to 40 different bird species that frequent the area. An abandoned barn makes a good marker to turn back toward the trailhead.

Just south of Montaña de Oro State Park, the **Point Buchon Trail** (3.5 miles round-trip, easy, Apr.-Oct. Thurs.-Mon. 8am-5pm, Nov.-Mar. Thurs.-Mon. 8am-4pm) leads along pristine shoreline, passing a natural sinkhole and jagged sea-sculpted cliffs. The trail begins at Montaña de Oro State Park's Coon Creek Parking Lot. It's located on a parcel of land owned by utility company PG&E. In order to preserve the area's natural resources, the number of hikers each day is limited; make a reservation via the PG&E website (http://pge.modwest.com/pgereservations).

Located in nearby Los Osos, the **Elfin Forest Boardwalk Trail** (0.75 miles, easy, www.elfinforest.org, daily dawn-dusk) offers an easy boardwalk trail through 90 acres of marsh, dune scrub, and pygmy oak woodland. While some California live oaks reach heights of 50 feet, the persistent winds and poor soil keep these tiny specimens just 4-20 feet tall. Parking is off any of Los Osos's 11th to 17th Streets, which end at the edge of the forest. The 16th Street entrance offers the best access for people using wheelchairs or strollers.

Horseback Riding

No Worries Trail Rides (805/286-1338, http://jennerroscranch.webs.com) offers one-hour ($74), two-hour ($90) and all-day ($150) rides on Montaña de Oro State Park's trails and beaches. You meet your horse for the day at the park. Your transportation will be one of the rare horse breeds fostered at Jenner Rose Ranch, including haflingers, gypsy horses, and friesians.

City Parks

A couple of small city parks appeal to families or those who want a break from browsing in the Embarcadero's shops. Tiny **Anchor Memorial Park** (931 Embarcadero, 805/772-6278, www.morro-bay.ca.us) is dedicated to local people who have been lost at sea on fishing boats. This bay-front space has an anchor statue and nifty benches that resemble boat cleats. Two-acre **Tidelands Park** (300 Embarcadero to 394 Embarcadero, 805/772-6278, www.morro-bay.ca.us) has a kid's play area with a pirate ship and some seal statues. A staircase leads to the mudflats below. There's also a fish-cleaning station.

Golf

How many state parks have their own golf course? People call the **Morro Bay Golf Course** (201 State Park Rd., 805/782-8600, www.slocountyparks.com, greens fees Mon.-Fri. $43,

Sat.-Sun. $48) the "poor man's Pebble Beach," probably because of the hilly terrain and great ocean views. It also has a driving range, rental clubs, a pro shop, and a bar and grill.

ACCOMMODATIONS
Under $150

The **Sundown Inn** (640 Main St., 805/772-3229 or 800/696-6928, http://sundowninn.com, $139-149) is a well-priced motel within walking distance of Morro Bay's downtown and waterfront areas. Guest rooms have fridges, microwaves, and—here's something different—coin-operated vibrating beds.

The owners of the **Marina Street Inn Bed & Breakfast** (305 Marina St., 805/772-4016, www.marinastreetinn.com, $125-145) honeymooned here, so they know what visitors want. The four suites are individually decorated: one has a nautical theme; another features a willow-limb bedpost and a birdhouse table. Each suite shares a balcony or porch with the adjoining room. The hot breakfast may include a crustless quiche or buttermilk waffles.

Just up from the Embarcadero, the **Blue Sail Inn** (851 Market Ave., 805/772-2766, www.bluesailinn.com, $109-205) is another relatively inexpensive place to lay your head. Most guest rooms include balconies; there's also a hot tub and complimentary continental breakfast.

The 16-room **Back Bay Inn** (1391 2nd St., Los Osos, 805/528-1233, www.backbayinn.com, $110-190) is located in a scenic setting on the south end of the estuary in Los Osos, about three miles from the Morro Bay Embarcadero. Most guest rooms have a view of the bay; the second-floor units come with a balcony or fireplace. There is also a cottage, a loft, and a studio for rent. All guests receive an evening wine reception and a hot breakfast.

Located just inside Morro Bay State Park, the recently renovated **Inn at Morro Bay** (60 State Park Rd., 805/772-5651, http://innatmorrobay.com, rooms $119-239, cottage from $299) offers easy access to the golf course and the Museum of Natural History. The Cape Cod-style guest rooms offer views of the bay. The bed-and-breakfast special includes breakfast

El Morro Masterpiece Motel

for two. There's also a spa (805/772-5651, massages $55-120) with a range of treatments.

$150-250

The 🄲 **El Morro Masterpiece Motel** (1206 Main St., 805/772-5633, www.masterpiece-motels.com, $149-269) is a great place to stay for art enthusiasts and lovers of quirky motels. Each guest room is decorated with framed prints from master painters, and the hallways also have prints of paintings by Henri Matisse, Vincent Van Gogh, and Norman Rockwell. There's also a large indoor spa pool decorated like a Roman bathhouse that further differentiates this motel from other cookie-cutter lodging options.

Built in 1939, the bright 🄲 **Beach Bungalow Inn and Suites** (1050 Morro Ave., 805/772-9700, www.morrobaybeachbungalow.com, $159-279) have been extensively renovated. The 12 clean, spacious, and modern guest rooms have hardwood floors, local art on the walls, and flat-screen TVs. Eleven of the guest rooms have gas fireplaces. Family suites accommodate

four people, while king deluxe suites have full kitchens. Two bicycles are available for cruising around town. Guests receive a voucher for a meal at a local restaurant (including Frankie & Lola's, The Hungry Fishermen, Mi Casa, Giovanni's Fish Market, or Stax Wine Bar).

The unique **Front Street Inn and Spa** (1140 Front St., 805/772-5038, www.frontstreetinn. net, $199) offers just two large guest rooms that share a floor with a spa. The spacious high-ceilinged guest rooms are oriented around large windows, with superb views of the harbor and the rock. The two units are all about the view, with their furniture facing the large windows. Both have deep soaking tubs, fridges, and gas fireplaces. Expect to wake to the aroma of the bakery on the first floor. The adjacent **Bay Beauty Spa** (805/772-8548, www.baybeautyspa.com, massages $75-150) is known for its couples massages.

From the outside, the **Ascot Suites** (260 Morro Bay Blvd., 805/772-4437, www.ascot-suites.com, $149-259) resembles an English countryside inn. The theme continues in the guest rooms with English country fabrics and fireplaces. A rooftop garden showcases views of Morro Rock and the bay. Deluxe guest rooms include jetted tubs. Expect an expansive continental breakfast as well as a complimentary afternoon wine tasting.

All of the 33 guest rooms at the recently renovated **Embarcadero Inn** (456 Embarcadero, 805/772-2700, www.embarcaderoinn.com, $145-450) have at least a partial view of the bay. Many also include a private balcony and a fireplace. The family suite comes with two bedrooms and a fully equipped kitchen. Other amenities include a spa room with a hot tub and complimentary continental breakfast.

The **Estero Inn** (501 Embarcadero, 805/772-1500, www.esteroinn.com, $159-279 is located right on the waterfront. All eight guest rooms are suites with microwaves and fridges. Continental breakfast is served in the morning.

Over $250

The family-run **Anderson Inn** (897 Embarcadero, 805/772-3434, www.andersoninnmorrobay.com, $239-349) is an eight-room boutique hotel located right on Morro Bay's busy Embarcadero. Three of the guest rooms are perched right over the estuary with stunning views of the nearby rock. Those premium guest rooms also include fireplaces and jetted tubs.

CAMPING

Located a couple of miles outside downtown Morro Bay, the **Morro Bay State Park Campground** (Morro Bay State Park Rd., 800/444-7275, www.parks.ca.gov, tents $35, RVs $50) has 140 campsites, many shaded by eucalyptus and pine trees; right across the street is the Morro Bay estuary. Six miles southwest of Morro Bay, **Montaña de Oro State Park** (Pecho Rd., 7 miles south of Los Osos, 800/444-7275, www.parks.ca.gov, $25) has more primitive camping facilities. There are walk-in environmental campsites and a primitive campground behind the Spooner Ranch House that has pit toilets.

FOOD
Breakfast and Brunch

❰ **Frankie and Lola's** (1154 Front St., 805/771-9306, www.frankieandlolas.com, Sun.-Wed. 6:30am-2:30pm, Thurs.-Sat. 6:30am-2:30pm and 5pm-8pm, $4-13) does breakfast right. Creative savory dishes include the fried green tomato benedict topped with creole hollandaise sauce and tasty, colorful *chilaquiles* with red chorizo, avocado, and tomatillo salsa. Lunch focuses on burgers and sandwiches, while dinner is a little heartier, with options like bacon-wrapped meatloaf or chorizo-stuffed chicken.

The Coffee Pot Restaurant (1001 Front St., 805/772-3176, http://morrobaycoffeepot.com, daily 7:30am-2pm, $7-13) has been serving up breakfasts since 1960, an impressive career for any restaurant. They also make more than just traditional fare: try an omelet drenched in enchilada sauce and or french toast stuffed with cream cheese, walnuts, and marmalade.

On the road toward Montaña de Oro State Park, **Celia's Garden Café** (1188 Los Osos Valley Rd., Los Osos, 805/528-5711, http://celiasgardencafe.com, daily 7:30am-2:30pm, $9-12) is an ideal place to fuel up for a day of hiking. Fill up on a pork chop and eggs or the chicken-fried steak. Other options include omelets, benedicts, and hotcakes. Located in a plant nursery, the café has an indoor dining room and a dog-friendly outdoor patio.

Cheap Eats

In the mood for a darn fine hamburger? In nearby Los Osos, **Sylvester's Burgers** (1099 Santa Ynez Ave., Los Osos, 805/528-0779, www.sylvestersburgers.com, daily 11am-9pm, $5-8) attracts carnivores with juicy beef slathered in signature sauce. The yellow shack has a range of juicy, tasty, never frozen beef burgers, including The Sylvester Burger, a pound of beef topped with cheddar cheese, onion rings, bacon—and of course, Sylvester's sauce. Four beers are available on tap to wash it down. Eat on the outdoor deck or inside, where the walls are decorated with photos of the regulars.

La Parisienne (1140 Front St., 805/772-8530, Wed.-Mon. 7:30am-5pm, $4-7) is a

CAMBRIA AND SAN SIMEON

© STUART THORNTON

Frankie and Lola's

bakery that also serves a lot of inexpensive sandwiches. The breakfast sandwiches can be served on a baguette or a croissant, while the lunch menu includes sandwiches, salads, and burgers.

Classic American

The giant parking lot outside **Carla's Country Kitchen** (213 Beach St., 805/772-9051, $9) attests to the popularity of this breakfast and lunch spot. With blue-and-white checkered tablecloths, Carla's serves heaping portions of breakfast classics, including scrambles and omelets, along with sandwiches and burgers. The Pooney scramble is a tasty mess of spinach, cheeses, eggs, bacon, and mushrooms, although the accompanying biscuits—which looked amazing—were a bit dry.

Within Morro Bay State Park, the **Bayside Café** (10 State Park Rd., 805/772-1465, www.baysidecafe.com, Mon.-Wed. 11am-3pm, Thurs.-Sun. 11am-8:30 or 9pm, $8-25), true to its name, is right by the bay. The lunch menu skews toward burgers and fish-and-chips, while dinner features fancier fare such as lobster scampi.

For a slightly more upscale option, head downtown to **Shawns On Main** (912 Main St., 805/772-1059, Thurs.-Mon. 5pm-9pm, $12-21), an intimate two-room restaurant with local art decorating the walls. The small menu includes appetizers like panko-crusted local abalone and entrées like shrimp jambalaya and pork ribs.

Locals head to **The Hungry Fisherman** (399 Beach St., 805/772-3444, daily 6am-9pm, $10-30) for budget breakfasts and hearty egg dishes. At night there's classic diner fare like fried chicken and chicken fried steak as well as seafood.

Coffee and Tea

Popular **Top Dog Coffee** (857 Main St., 805/772-9225, www.topdogcoffeebar.com, daily 6am-6:30pm) is the place to get caffeinated, with all of the usual options as well

© STUART THORNTON

Bayside Café

as a few creative beverages like mango chai and Mexican mocha. The coffee beans are roasted right here. For lunch (6:30am-4pm), they also serve café fare: bagels, burritos, paninis, and sandwiches. There are tables inside and out front on the sidewalk. Right around the corner, **The Rock Espresso Bar** (275 Morro Bay Blvd., 805/772-3411, Mon.-Fri. 6:30am-5:30pm, Sat.-Sun. 7:30am-5pm) makes espressos, cappuccinos, lattes and mochas. Enjoy the cottage-like interior or the garden out back. They also sell 20 kinds of coffee beans.

German

The roast beef brings people back to the **Hofbrau** (901 Embarcadero, 805/772-2411, www.hofbraumorrobay.com, daily 11am-9pm, $7-15). It has been serving up popular half-pound hand-carved roast beef sandwiches au jus since 1971. The informal waterfront eatery also cooks up clam chowder, burgers, and fish-and-chips alongside German fare like bratwurst and sauerkraut. There's also a salad bar to balance your meat intake.

Mexican

People worship the crab cake and fish tacos at **Taco Temple** (2680 N. Main St., 805/772-4965, Mon.-Sat. 11am-9pm, Sun. 11am-8:30pm, $5-22, cash only). Housed in a big multicolored building east of Highway 1, where colorful surfboards hang on the walls, this is not the standard taqueria. Their California take on classic Mexican dishes includes sweet potato enchiladas and tacos filled with soft shell crab or calamari. The tacos are served like salads, with the meat and greens piled on tortillas. The chips and salsa are terrific.

You'll find a more traditional taqueria fare at **Tacos de Mexico** (980 Main St., 805/772-5796, Mon.-Thurs. 8am-9pm, Fri.-Sun. 8am-10pm, $4.50-7.50). The menu includes tacos, of course, as well as wet and dry burritos, with options like *chile verde* and *chile colorado*. The large tostadas are popular with the local crowd.

Taco Temple

Seafood

Seafood is the way to go when dining in the fishing village of Morro Bay. An unassuming fish house with views of the fishing boats and the bay, **Tognazzini's Dockside Restaurant** (1245 Embarcadero, 805/772-8100, www.bonniemarietta.com, summer Sun.-Thurs. 11am-9pm, Fri.-Sat. 11am-10pm, winter Sun.-Thurs. 11am-8pm, Fri.-Sat. 11am-9pm, $18-27) has an extensive seafood menu as well as art depicting sultry mermaids hanging on the wall. Entrées include albacore kebabs and wild salmon in a unique tequila marinade. If you're an oyster lover, you simply can't go wrong with Dockside's barbecued oysters appetizer, which features the shellfish swimming in garlic butter studded with scallions. Behind the main restaurant is the **Dockside Too Fish Market** (summer daily 10am-8pm, winter Sun.-Thurs. 10am-6pm, Fri.-Sat. 10am-8pm), a local favorite with beer, seafood, and live music.

Giovanni's Fish Market & Galley (1001 Front St., 805/772-2123, www. giovannisfishmarket.com, market daily 9am-6pm, galley daily 11am-6pm, $5-10) is a real working market, with live abalone and sushi-grade fish pulled right out of the bay. The fish-and-chips wins raves, and the clam chowder wins awards. Try the barbecued oysters in garlic or Sriracha butter, or Rockefeller-style with bacon and jalapeños. During summer months, expect long lines to dine on the outdoor patio.

Located on a hill above the Embarcadero, **Dorn's Original Breakers Café** (801 Market St., 805/772-4415, www.dornscafe.com, daily 7am-9pm, $13-30) offers a great view of Morro Rock from its dining room. It has been family-owned and operated since 1942. Dinner begins with bread and a dish of garlic, olive oil, vinegar, and cheese. The large menu of seafood and steak includes fresh daily specials like snapper, petrale sole, salmon, and halibut from local waters.

Elegant **Windows on the Water** (699 Embarcadero, Suite 7, 805/772-0677, www. windowsmb.com, Sun.-Thurs. 5pm-8:30pm,

Fri.-Sat. 5pm-9pm, $23-39) showcases local seafood like abalone, oysters, halibut and sand dabs. The wine list is heavy with local vintages.

The upscale **Galley Seafood Bar & Grill** (899 Embarcadero, 805/772-7777, http://galleymorrobay.com, daily 11am-2:30pm and 5pm-close, $18-46) is popular for items like pan-seared scallops. The menu changes daily depending on the fresh catch.

Thai
Thai Bounty (560 Embarcadero, 805/772-2500, http://thethaibounty.com, Thurs.-Tues. 11am-9pm, $11-14) won second place for their oyster entry in the Central Coast Oyster Festival, so the chefs know seafood. They take advantage of the local bounty—both fresh seafood and vegetables and herbs from their own garden—to create daily specials with preparations like panang curry, garlic pepper, and spicy stir fry. Dine indoors or out on the patio.

In nearby Los Osos, **Noi's Little Thai Takeout** (1288 2nd St., 805/528-6647, Mon.-Fri. 11am-7:30pm, $8-13) is a local favorite. They have a different curry dish for every day of the week along with noodle and rice plates.

Vegetarian
Run by the folks who own the adjacent Sunshine Health Foods store, the **Shine Café** (427 Morro Bay Blvd., 805/771-8344, www.sunshinehealthfoods-shinecafe.com, Mon.-Fri. 11am-5pm, Sat. 9am-5pm, Sun. 10am-4pm, $4.50-11) is a vegetarian's dream, focusing on local and organic ingredients in their smoothies, sandwiches and salads. The BLT uses bacon-flavored tempeh, and the namesake hummus wrap is big enough to sate even a carnivore's appetite. Gluten-free tempeh tacos are a house specialty. Order at the inside kitchen counter, then dine indoors under local art or out at sidewalk tables.

INFORMATION AND SERVICES
Maps and Visitor Information
The **Morro Bay Chamber of Commerce** (845 Embarcadero, Suite D, 800/231-0592, www.

morrobay.org) has a wonderful visitors center overlooking the bay at the end of a small boardwalk. It has a vast array of printed material you can take with you.

Emergency Services
French Hospital Medical Center (1911 Johnson Ave., San Luis Obispo, 805/543-5353, www.frenchmedicalcenter.org) is the closest hospital. If you have an emergency, dial 911. The local police are the **Morro Bay Police Department** (870 Morro Bay Blvd., 805/772-6225).

Postal Services
To access the **post office** (898 Napa Ave., 805/772-0839), you'll need to leave the Embarcadero area and head uptown.

Laundry
American Cleaners & Laundry (805/772-6959) has two locations in Morro Bay (365 Quintana Rd.; 1052 Main St.). They can provide pickup and delivery.

GETTING THERE
Car
As with most towns on the Central Coast, U.S. 101 cuts through Morro Bay. If you're traveling south from San Francisco, take U.S. 101 south to Atascadero, take Highway 41 west, and then head south on Highway 1. Exit at Main Street in Morro Bay. If you're traveling from Los Angeles, the best route is U.S. 101 north to San Luis Obispo, and then head north on Highway 1 to Morro Bay; take the Morro Bay Boulevard exit into town.

Bus
There is no direct bus service to Morro Bay, although **Greyhound** (805/238-1242, www.greyhound.com) travels along U.S. 101 and stops at San Luis Obispo Transit Center (800 Pine St., San Luis Obispo). From there you'll need to connect with **Regional Transit Authority** (805/781-4472, www.slorta.com) buses to get to Morro Bay. There are various

weekday and weekend routes. A door-to-door general public transit system, **Dial-A-Ride** (535 Harbor St., 805/772-2755, Mon.-Fri. 6:45am-6pm), established in 1977, operates within the city limits.

Trolley

The **Morro Bay Trolley** (595 Harbor Way, 805/772-2744, Mon. 11am-5pm, Fri.-Sat. 11am-7pm, Sun. 11am-6pm, over age 12 $1 per ride, ages 5-12 $0.50) operates three routes. The **Waterfront Route** runs the length of the Embarcadero, including out to Morro Rock. The **Downtown Route** runs through the downtown (as in uptown) area all the way out to Morro Bay State Park. The **North Morro Bay Route** runs from uptown through the northern part of Morro Bay, north of the rock, along Highway 1. An all-day pass (not a bad idea if you plan on seeing a lot of sights) is $3.

BACKGROUND

The Land

GEOGRAPHY

California's diverse coastal communities are the result of many different natural forces. Tectonic and volcanic activity over the past 250 million years created our coastal mountain ranges. The Channel Islands are the result of a similar geologic process. Coastal streams and rivers, along with wind and rain, helped shape and tear down these mountains through constant erosion. The beautiful though powerful ceaseless waves of the Pacific Ocean also cut into the coastal mountain ranges and helped carve vertical cliffs, terraces, and bluffs into the rock. Elsewhere along the California coast,

debris from wave erosion and sand deposited by streams and rivers began to accumulate and form the one thing we all seem to love, California's sandy beaches. Even inland, where windblown sand from the beaches collects, you can find fragile systems of coastal dunes unlike anything else in California. Coastal rivers and streams eventually meet with the salty waters of the Pacific and create marshes, lagoons, and estuaries that constitute the Central Coast's prime coastal wetlands. In other areas, abrasive sand and wave motion cut grooves and pockets into the rock where intertidal communities and tide pools formed. And even below the Pacific

Ocean's waters, geologic forces continue to act, through many of the same processes, on the sea floor.

CLIMATE

Santa Barbara, Ventura, and San Luis Obispo Counties all have a semi-arid climate, moderate and pleasant year-round. Summer at the coast means just a handful of triple-digit days, with temps otherwise in the low to mid-70s. There is always the possibility of cool marine fog rolling onto the coast during the summer months, which creates overcast conditions. The valleys, however, like Paso Robles and Santa Ynez, will see much hotter weather for a longer period of time and significantly less coastal fog, although when the sun sets, it cools off quickly. In the fall and winter it's still nice, with temperatures averaging in the mid-60s. Most of the rain falls between November and April; historically, the region sees less than 15 inches each year.

ENVIRONMENTAL ISSUES

In January 1969 an environmental disaster occurred in the Santa Barbara Channel when an offshore oil platform suffered a blowout and 200,000 gallons of crude oil escaped into the ocean over a period of 11 days. The oil created an 800-square-mile slick that impacted all of the northern Channel Islands and mainland beaches along the Central Coast. Thousands of seabirds and marine mammals died. Concurrently, scientists were becoming aware of a serious decline in the breeding success of California brown pelicans: The prehistoric-looking birds were unable to nest successfully because their eggshells were too thin to withstand the incubation period and were crushed in the nest. For several years, the pelicans suffered near total reproductive failure. In 1970 only one chick was successfully raised on Anacapa Island, historically the largest breeding colony for California brown pelicans on the West Coast. The cause of the failed pelican breeding was determined to be the pesticide DDT. High levels of DDT residue caused the eggshells to become thinner over time, and

DDT similarly affected bald eagles and peregrine falcons.

Fortunately, the American public and the government reacted reasonably swiftly to the loss of wildlife and to the egregious pollution of the environment. Many consider the publicity surrounding the Santa Barbara oil spill and the fate of the California brown pelican a major impetus for the environmental movement. Just one year later, in spring 1970, Earth Day was born. Ever since, people in Santa Barbara have been leading proponents for conservation. At a minimum, State Street offers green recycling cans so you can properly dispose of your water bottles and other recyclables.

Beyond the simple importance of personal responsibility, in light of the aforementioned incidents, one would think that people in the region, with its proximity to the ocean, would be environmentally responsible. But pollution of creeks remains an issue here, and in the three counties covered in this book, most notably Santa Barbara, the problem is severe. There are creek and beach cleanup days in all three counties that you may be able to participate in while you're here. Disturbingly, people still leave their debris all along the beaches, in the creeks, and in parks, though ironically, Santa Barbara's State Street is cleaner than most of the natural riparian corridors. Tainted creeks, unfortunately, lead to occasional beach closures; signs are posted at the beach if there are extremely unsanitary conditions. Beach water samples are collected weekly at Central Coast beaches and examined to identify microbe levels that could pose a threat to swimmers and beachgoers. As a general rule, it's always best to avoid swimming in the ocean, especially near creek terminations, within 72 hours after rains, as that water will probably contain higher levels of bacteria washed into the ocean from creeks and rivers.

Fresh water is the other major ecological issue facing the Central Coast; there simply isn't that much of it. The reality is that this is a semiarid climate with little rainfall two out of every three years. In Cambria, water is so scarce that businesses can be fined for going over their

ETHICAL TRAVEL

© GABRIEL SKVOR

As the sticker on the sign says, no one likes a dirty beach.

There are basic principles that apply no matter where you travel, and the Central Coast is no exception. Consider the following ideas as you explore the Central Coast, as doing so will enhance your experience.

· **Minimize your environmental impact:** Travel and camp on durable surfaces, dispose of waste properly, and recycle. There are green recycle bins all along State Street in Santa Barbara. Make sure your hotel recycles too. Respect wildlife and don't feed animals. Feeding wildlife damages their health, alters natural behaviors, and exposes them to predators and other dangers. Always follow designated trails, especially on the Channel Islands. Do not disturb animals, plants, or their natural habitats. Learn about and support local conservation programs and organizations working to preserve the environment.

· **Leave what you find:** Take only photographs. Leave only footprints. The impact of one person may seem minimal, but the global effect of removing items from their native

place can be decimating. This is certainly true of beachcombing. People always seem to want to take souvenirs from the beaches on the Central Coast, but the beaches, and the Channel Islands, should be left in their natural state.

· **Support the local economy:** Be aware of where your money is going by supporting locally owned businesses. To avoid buying products made from endangered plants or animals, see "Know Before You Go" at www.cbp.gov for the U.S. Customs list of restricted items. Bargain fairly: Remember the economic realities of your new currency. When bargaining, do so with respect for the seller and decide on a mutually beneficial price. Doing so contributes to the local economy, while an unfair price may contribute to a region's poverty.

This copyrighted information has been reprinted with permission from the Leave No Trace Center for Outdoor Ethics. For more information or materials, visit www.lnt.org or call 303/442-8222.

allotment. Historically, urban centers have been located along the area's coastal lowlands, with agriculture concentrated in valley-floor areas and grazing and natural lands occupying the surrounding foothills. But as more people discover the Central Coast and decide to relocate here, population pressures increase, and growth and development have expanded from urban centers to adjacent farmlands and rural areas both on the coast and in the interior. Along with population growth, the greatest threats to regional wildlife diversity are expansion of intensive types of agriculture, invasions by exotic species, and overuse of regional water resources.

Flora

TREES
The California Oak

The Central Coast is home to the protected California Oak, the signature tree that defines the region. There are 20 species of oaks native to California, roughly one-third of the 60 species scattered throughout the United States. But mainly you'll see the two species of massive oaks that grow on the valley floors, hillsides, and ridge tops: the **valley oak** (*Quercus lobata*) and the **blue oak** (*Quercus douglasii*).

The leaves of valley oaks are gracefully sculpted into a series of deep, rounded lobes, much like those hanging from our ears. Leaves on blue oaks have scalloped edges. Both trees can grow straight and tall; some have a classic vase shape while others spread widely with wandering horizontal branches. The mighty oak lives upward of 200 years, although it grows sparsely and independently, not in traditional thick forests. As you drive along U.S. 101 or travel through the region by train, you'll see

a California Oak

© JOSEPH SOHM/123RF.COM

the oak, twisted and fierce against a backdrop of agriculture and development, virtually everywhere. The oak tree is a sacred tree, at least to the area's indigenous residents, the Chumash people, who plucked the acorns from the oaks to make flour. Traditionally they used rock grinders (you can still see many natural grinders in rock formations around the area) to break open the acorns and grind the kernels, and would then rinse the meal to wash away its bitterness.

Eucalyptus

In addition to the sparse beauty of oak trees, the **eucalyptus** (*Eucalyptus globulus*) grows along much of the Central Coast. In the 1850s, eucalyptus trees were brought to California during the gold rush by Australians, since much of California has a climate similar to parts of Australia. By the early 1900s, thousands of acres of eucalyptus trees were planted; this was even encouraged by the state government. It was hoped that these trees would provide a renewable source of timber for construction, furniture making, and more importantly, railroad ties. It was soon discovered, however, that eucalyptus was particularly unsuitable for rail use, as ties made from the trees had a tendency to twist and buckle while drying, and the dried ties were so tough that it was nearly impossible to hammer rail spikes into them. One way in which the eucalyptus proved valuable in California was as a windbreak for highways, orange groves, and farms in the mostly treeless central part of the state. There are spots along U.S. 101 where this is clearly evident.

Avocado

One of the Central Coast's most populous trees, the **avocado** (*Persea americana*) is grown in orchards and backyards everywhere. Avocados were introduced to California in 1871 by Judge R. B. Ord of Santa Barbara, and today the majority of avocados for sale in the United States come from California. Santa Barbara is currently the third-largest avocado producer in North America, and Carpinteria has a yearly avocado festival to celebrate all things avocado.

Pine

As you move north, the pine tree becomes more prevalent. The **Monterey pine** (*Pinus radiata*) is the most common tree in Paso Robles and Cambria, usually covered with moss, giving it an almost Southern look. There is even a subspecies of the **Torrey pine** (*Pinus torreyana* subsp. *insularis*) that grows only on Santa Rosa Island.

FLOWERS

The **poppy** (*Eschscholzia californica*) is the California state flower, and in periods with a lot of rain you'll see the small simple orange-gold flower everywhere. Near the Santa Ynez Valley they can fully populate entire hillsides. They are also coastal, and Montaña de Oro State Park has lots of poppies as well. The poppy is hardy, growing at elevations as high as 6,000 feet. Fields of **lupine** (*Lupinus*) are also everywhere on rolling hills, and the coastal **fiddleneck** (*Amsinckia menziesii*) is another species found throughout the region. Many people consider it to be a weed, but its tiny yellow flowers add a dash of color to the area.

Fauna

MARINE MAMMALS

Warm-blooded creatures inhabit much of the Central Coast, and not just on land. In the ocean, **Pacific gray whales** (*Eschrichtius robustus*), often misidentified as California gray whales, are the most common whales you will see December-March on whale-watching exhibitions. Summer often brings the **humpback whale** (*Megaptera novaeangliae*), **orcas** (*Orcinus orca*), **blue whales** (*Balaenoptera musculus*), and their cousin, **fin whales** (*Balaenoptera physalus*), which are less visible. Overall there are 30 different species of whales that ply the waters of the Central Coast. Getting to see one is mostly a matter of opportunity and awareness, constantly scanning the horizon for that telltale sign of water shooting up from the surface. Nearly every year there is a whale, usually a baby, that loses its way through the channel and comes very close to shore in Santa Barbara.

Besides whales, there are dolphins, porpoises, **California sea lions** (*Zalophus californianus*), **elephant seals** (*Mirounga angustirostris*), **harbor seals** (*Phoca vitulina*), **northern fur seals** (*Callorhinus ursinus*), and adorable **sea otters** (*Enhydra lutris*) that all are part of the vast circle of life. They're less visible in Ventura, and as you move up coast there tends to be greater concentrations.

SEALIFE

Unless you dive into the temperate waters, chances are that any fish you see will be in a book or dead on a pier with a hook through its lip. Oddly, there are no great aquariums here. The two best are in Long Beach and Monterey, which bookend the Central Coast. Regardless, if you scuba or snorkel, chances are you'll see the **garibaldi** (*Hypsypops rubicundus*), which is the California state marine fish. Bright orange and similar in size to bass, they are curious and very territorial. Garibaldi are actually harmless if you see them while scuba diving, although they will come right up to you to protect their turf, acting all macho. You will see them even while kayaking at the Channel Islands, where pristine water allows 30-40 feet of visibility.

The area is also home to **spiny lobsters** (*Panulirus interruptus*), crabs, and **ridgeback shrimp,** all of which will probably end up on your plate for lunch or dinner. There are far too many fish to list, but when diving you can reasonably expect to see **sheepshead, halibut, sea urchins,** and **sea bass.** There are also **sharks** in the waters, and occasionally they come reasonably close to shore. The best place to experience this sealife is in the waters around Channel Islands National Park, specifically off Anacapa Island and Santa Cruz Island.

BIRDS

You can't miss the waterbirds along the Central Coast, including the **brown pelicans** (*Pelecanus occidentalis*), **cormorants** (*Phalacrocorax auritus*), **seagulls** (*Larus californicus*), **sandpipers, cranes, blue herons** (*Ardea herodias*), and **sanderlings** (*Calidris alba*), which scurry around in large groups around the surf on the beach. There are a plethora of **loons** (*Gavia immer*), **egrets** (*Ardea alba*), and **mallards** (*Anas platyrhynchos*), which are everywhere and seem to dominate the skies. Over 300 species of birds have been identified along the Central Coast, hugging the coastline and meandering through the sloughs and inland waterways; the coastal birds also help to define the region. The **black phoebe** (*Sayornis nigricans*) is amazing to watch as it catches insects in midair.

As you move inland you'll see **red-tailed hawks** (*Buteo jamaicensis*) often sitting above the freeway on an exit sign or languidly floating on thermal air pockets, searching for food. There are **turkey vultures** (*Cathartes aura*) in abundance as well. Near Lake Cachuma are small pockets of **bald eagles** (*Haliaeetus leucocephalus*) and **ospreys** (*Pandion haliaetus*), although they are somewhat shy and it takes a lot of patience to find them. Morro Rock

© HENRIK LEHNERER/123RF.COM

brown pelicans

is a known **peregrine falcon** (*Falco peregrinus*) nesting area. In addition, it's possible to find **California condors** (*Gymnogyps californianus*) soaring above the mountains near Ojai. The nearby Los Padres National Forest's Sespe Condor Sanctuary was the first place where captive raised condors were released into the wild back in 1992. The state bird, the **California valley quail** (*Callipepla californica*), occasionally runs across the roads, mainly in northern Santa Barbara County and into San Luis Obispo County, predominantly on forested back roads.

Then there is the funky oddball **black oystercatcher** (*Haematopus bachmani*), which is a stunning sight to see when you first lay eyes on one. They are black with a long bright-orange beak; they frequent beaches and the Channel Islands. There are far too many **crows** (*Corvus brachyrhynchos*), but should you get to the Channel Islands, you'll get the chance to see quite a few common **ravens** (*Corvus corax*) and maybe an **island scrub jay** (*Aphelocoma insularis*) if you are lucky. There is a vast world of birds on the Central Coast, and even if you're not a bird-watcher, a little understanding of these magnificent creatures will go a long way.

REPTILES

Snakes have always been a part of California, and there are 10 snakes in particular that make their home on the Central Coast. Most snakes, such as the **gopher** (*Pituophis catenifer*) and **garter** (*Thamnophis atratus*), are harmless and are about 3-4 feet in length. The **western rattlesnake** (*Crotalus viridis*) is venomous and potentially dangerous. The distinctive horny rings on the end of their tails and that unmistakable rattle sound mean that you should immediately leave the area. When you're out and about in wild areas, like Black Hill in Morro Bay, More Mesa on the bluffs above Santa Barbara, or along Moonstone bluffs in Cambria, you will probably come across snakes. They love to bask in the warm sun, so you're likely to cross paths with a snake when it's hot out, whether on a coastal trail, a mountain trail, or even in downtown parks. Always exercise caution. There is nothing to be afraid of, and most snakes have no more interest in getting close to you than you have in them. The bottom line is to leave them alone and move along. You will also see the ubiquitous **western fence lizard** (*Sceloporus occidentalis*).

AMPHIBIANS

The Central Coast is suitable for animals that want to spend time in the water and on land, and there are many amphibious creatures here. Of particular note are the **tiger salamander** (*Ambystoma californiense*), a four-inch-long black-coated guy with yellow spots and bars who lives primarily underground, and the **red-legged tree frog** (*Rana draytonii*), measuring about five inches or so. Its abdomen and hind legs are, you guessed it, red. There are other frogs, toads, and newts present, but these two amphibians in particular have the ability to halt development in the area. Since the tiger salamander and red-legged tree frog are federally protected by the U.S. Fish and Wildlife Service, the sighting of one of these little critters will

bring out conservationists, and there will be delays and possibly lawsuits regarding any proposed construction.

INSECTS AND ARACHNIDS

One of the beauties of the Central Coast is that we don't see too many pesky insects that torture innocent travelers with copious bites. Fall is spider season on the Central Coast and in many other areas of California as well. The most obviously active spiders during this season are the **garden spiders,** which weave large circular webs between bushes, trees, and vines to catch insects. Known generally as **orb-weavers** (Araneidae), this family contains over 1,500 local species. Female spiders make the webs to catch insects so they can produce a sac containing several hundred eggs before they die in early winter. Garden spiders make enough venom to kill their prey, but there is no threat to people. These spiders tend to be shy and will quickly retreat to a hiding place when encountered. Keep in mind that spiders are beneficial because they eat moths, wasps,

© JEFFREY BANKE/123RF.COM

A monarch butterfly rests on a eucalyptus branch.

flies, and other flying insects. If the spider is spinning its web in an inconvenient location, catch it and move it to an out-of-the-way spot where it can weave another web without being in your way. There are also **tarantulas,** which belong to the group of primitive spiders called Mygalomorphae. These beautiful large and hairy spiders are often seen in mountain regions, scrambling across the asphalt along the wine country back roads.

Butterflies of all types are common on the Central Coast, specifically the **monarch** (*Danaus plexippus*), which occupies groves in Goleta, just north of Santa Barbara, and in Pismo Beach. Both locations are eucalyptus groves. In addition to the monarch there are hundreds of **swallowtails** (Papilionidae), **skippers** (Hesperiidae), and the **radiant whites** and **sulphers** (Pieridae). The Santa Barbara Natural History Museum runs an occasional program called Butterflies Alive, a highly successful exhibition devoted to these beautiful winged creatures. Despite its rather hideous name, the California dogface butterfly, the state insect, is in reality a beautiful yellow and black butterfly.

History

Many people mistakenly believe that California has limited history, and that real American history all happened on the East Coast. Certainly the early European settlements like Jamestown are all back east. But while our ancestors wrestled with creating a democracy, the West Coast and the Central Coast were living their own history.

NATIVE AMERICANS

Prior to the arrival of the Spanish, roughly 15,000 **Chumash people** inhabited the coast, interior valleys, and the Channel Islands from Malibu, north of Los Angeles, to just north of San Luis Obispo. The **Salinan people** lived in parts of Paso Robles and north of Morro Bay. These two nations were hunter-gatherers, not warriors, and were oriented toward the ocean for their livelihood. They had comparatively advanced food-processing techniques and transportation, and they were friendly people, which hastened the destruction of their communities. They were known to make the arduous channel crossing in *tomols,* plank boats they constructed. Leadership of their autonomous villages was hereditary. The Chumash people were known for the quality of their tools and baskets, woven tight enough to hold water. This type of handiwork is reflected in the construction and detailing of the missions, since the majority of these buildings were built by indigenous people forced into laboring for the missionaries.

THE SPANISH AND THE MISSIONS: 1769-1821

Beginning in 1769 the Spanish, who had claimed this region as far back as the 1500s, established four royal presidios—forts, really—and founded 21 Franciscan missions along the California coast. In part, these establishments were built to ward off Russian traders who were working their way down the coast and who had established Fort Ross, north of Bodega Bay in Northern California. The last presidio was dedicated in Santa Barbara on April 21, 1782, by Governor Felipe de Neve, the missionary leader Junípero Serra, and Captain José Francisco Ortega, who was the first commander of the presidio. There were a mere 42 soldiers with them at the time. Spain ruled the area both in terms of the military presence and the socioeconomic and religious presence. The missions were the only industries of Alta California, and trade with ships of other nations eventually began, especially in hides, tallow, grain, brandy, olive oil, and leatherwork. New England merchants became the biggest customers for trade with the missions

Mission Santa Barbara is one of 21 missions built along the California coast.

by the 1820s and 1830s, popularizing news of this area on the East Coast.

THE MEXICAN PERIOD: 1821-1849

In 1821, Mexico achieved its independence from Spain, but the political unrest didn't end. Mexico passed a law abolishing slavery in 1829, directly aimed at stemming the missions' power and freeing the Native Americans. By 1833 a law was finally passed in Mexico that secularized the missions entirely. This meant that the lands held in trust for the Native Americans were to revert immediately to them, which in reality did not happen. Unscrupulous men and women took advantage of the difficulty in enforcing the law, as this region was still far from central Mexico and its authority. Suffering from internal political divisions, the Mexican government struggled to maintain control over the vast expanses of land it had inherited from Spain following the long war, and it lacked the resources to expand settlement of much of the territory.

The United States, fueled by technological breakthroughs and innovation and inspired by the concept of Manifest Destiny, was expanding its territories westward. Between 1846 and 1848 the United States went to war with Mexico. It was a defining event for both nations, transforming a continent and forging a new identity for its peoples. By the end of the war, Mexico had lost nearly half its territory—the modern-day U.S. Southwest from Texas to California—and the United States had become a major power. The Central Coast did not see fighting or bloodshed during the war but certainly felt its effects.

THE YOUNG STATE: 1850-1920

In 1848 gold was discovered at Coloma in Northern California, and a huge influx of Americans came to settle or make their fortunes in California. By September 1850, California was a state. By acts of Congress in the 1850s and 1860s, the U.S. government returned some of the mission lands and buildings to the Roman Catholic Church. But the old missions began to fall into disrepair, and struggling parishes sold off buildings, which were turned into inns, stores, bars, and stables. The tile roofs were sold to pay debts, which opened the adobe walls of the buildings to deterioration from rain and moisture.

And so California and the Central Coast became part of the United States. As Easterners made their way here, two spots in particular caught their attention: Santa Barbara and Paso Robles, which were recognized as places for natural healing. With the arrival of the railroad in the late 1880s, wealthy Easterners bought up land at rock-bottom prices to create vast estates, as is evidenced in Santa Barbara's Montecito and Hope Ranch communities. These were second homes for many of the landowners, and few of them actually lived here year-round. But for the most part the Central Coast remained an aggregate of sleepy little towns, while Los Angeles and San Francisco continued to grow. In part, this was due to the fact that even though the railroad allowed access to the area, the Central Coast still lacked proximity to larger metropolitan areas where goods could be obtained cheaply and conveniently.

THE EMERGING CENTRAL COAST: 1920-TODAY

In the 1930s the Great Depression struck and the Dust Bowl began to decimate the lower Midwest. Many economic refugees came to California, especially to the Central Coast, where farming and agriculture was still major

industries, to seek out new opportunities. When the Rincon section of U.S. 101 was built in the 1930s, it marked the first time you could drive to Santa Barbara along the coast, although this did little to increase commercial or residential development. World War II had little direct impact on this area, with the exception of a Japanese submarine that actually fired on Santa Barbara, although there was no damage, as well as the sinking of an oil tanker off the Cambria coastline by another Japanese submarine.

In the 1990s, land prices began to rise exponentially, and people began to realize how desirable the area was. With the realization that there is only so much oceanfront property available, prices climbed rapidly and demand exceeded available housing. Part of the region's success is that it has remained small and not overbuilt. Many people moved here because they wanted out of hectic and congested metropolitan areas.

Part of the area's growth can be attributed to the wine industry. From 1920 to 1933 Prohibition shut down nearly all of the wineries operating along the Central Coast, and it wasn't until 1962 that Santa Barbara Winery planted its first commercial grapevines, which eventually led to the beginnings of a new industry that now brings over a million visitors to the Central Coast annually. Today, the Central Coast is widely recognized for what it has long been: a beautiful landscape flanked by oceans and mountains with a relaxed way of life that is envied by many.

Government and Economy

The form of government in California's three Central Coast counties resembles other communities in the United States. Republicans and Democrats hold the majority of elected offices, with a handful of independents. In broad terms, the city of Santa Barbara tends to be more liberal with a greater concentration of Democrats in leadership, while conservatives and liberals are more evenly matched in the rest of the Central Coast's cities and towns.

The greatest issue these counties struggle with is growth, and that is the dominant political issue almost anywhere. The Central Coast has limited natural resources, and though it doesn't appear that way, chief among them is water. These counties have historically been slow- or no-growth oriented. The lack of congestion and the lack of problems inherent in too many people occupying too little space are what people love about living here. In one sense

people want to limit growth as much as possible to retain the way of life everyone seems to enjoy, and NIMBY ("not in my backyard") politics are alive and well as the local populace frequently shows up to contest new development. On the other hand, without growth there is limited economic expansion, and that can lead to long-term economic problems. Part of the issue is that many people who choose to live here already have plenty of money, and therefore have no interest in seeing anything change. For the rest of the population, who depend on this area for their livelihood, the goal is intelligent growth that lays out a reasonable future for the region and the limited resources we all must share.

The economy on the Central Coast is defined by tourism, the wine region, and agriculture. Tourism is by far the major economic engine of the region. Santa Barbara, the wine

© ASPENROCK/123RF.COM

a San Luis Obispo vineyard

regions, and Hearst Castle are important tourist draws, and large numbers of potential visitors live within a few hours' drive of the Central Coast. Second to them, European travelers flock here in droves. They commonly fly into Los Angeles or San Francisco, drive the California coast, and fly out of the city at the opposite end. Because the Central Coast is unlike the major metropolitan areas of San Francisco and Los Angeles and is known for its sublime coastline and intact towns, this area is often visited by people who want a unique and quintessentially California experience.

The wine regions are booming, bringing in not only agricultural revenue but also tourism dollars. In retrospect, the wine regions of Santa Barbara, Paso Robles, and to a lesser degree San Luis Obispo, the Edna Valley, and Ventura, have not been widely known. But that is changing, and there is strong demand for a wine country experiences.

Education is also a big economic force, with major educational institutions such as Cal Poly San Luis Obispo and the University of California, Santa Barbara (UCSB), as well as smaller but equally important institutions like Santa Barbara City College, Brooks Institute, and Westmont, all in Santa Barbara; Allan Hancock College in Santa Maria; Cuesta College in San Luis Obispo; and Ventura College and Channel Islands College in Ventura.

People and Culture

The population along the Central Coast is dominated by Caucasians and Latinos, with small pocket communities of other ancestries, such as Chinese and Japanese. The Central Coast is not an inexpensive place to live, which results in an even greater divide between the upper class and working class residents than you might find in other parts of the country. Regardless, the people who live in the Central Coast tend to be very accepting. People pretty much go about their business and allowing you to go about yours.

A broad spectrum of religious groups are represented on the Central Coast, including Muslims, Buddhists, Jews, Mormons, Protestants and a preponderance of Roman Catholics—a result of the historical Spanish and Mexican influence in the region. This area seems to be tolerant of differing religious beliefs and lacks the heated religious debates common in other places. One has to wonder if the subdued climate and easygoing pace makes people feel more kindly toward each other.

English is the dominant language along the Central Coast, but you will frequently hear Spanish as well. This is a heavily agricultural region; the majority of agricultural workers are Latino. Roughly 30 percent of families speak Spanish at home.

THE ARTS

Santa Barbara, in particular, has a thriving arts scene, in part because there is money here to support artistic endeavors. Opera, the symphony, live-theater venues, concerts, art galleries, and lectures are supported by patrons with deep pockets. UCSB and its Arts and Lectures Series also brings talent to appear and perform. To a lesser extent San Luis Obispo and Ventura have noteworthy arts representation, with venues like the Rubicon Theatre in Ventura and the Clark Center for the Performing Arts in Arroyo Grande.

Literature

The Central Coast, specifically Santa Barbara and San Luis Obispo, has long been a haven for writers. The area seems to be an ideal environment in which to write, with inspiring natural surroundings and so many local things to write about. **Sue Grafton** (*A is for Alibi, C is for Corpse*) has used Santa Barbara as a backdrop for her alphabet series featuring the character Kinsey Millhone, who lives in the fictional

Santa Teresa. Multiple prizewinner **T. C. Boyle** (*The Road to Wellville, Tortilla Curtain, Riven Rock*) also resides in Santa Barbara, in a Frank Lloyd Wright-designed home. His 2011 *When the Killing's Done* and 2012 *San Miguel* are set in the Channel Islands. Other well-known area writers include **Fannie Flagg** (*Fried Green Tomatoes*) and **Ross MacDonald,** whose Lew Archer crime novels *The Moving Target* and *The Drowning Pool* were both made into films starring Paul Newman. **Erle Stanley Gardner,** who created Perry Mason (*The Case of the Velvet Claws,* and well over 40 others) resided in Ventura. **Jack Kerouac** lived in San Luis Obispo in 1953, which some claim was the beginning of his best creative period; it might be hard to believe that working on the local railroad stimulated his creativity. Comic novelist **Christopher Moore** set his novels *Practical Demonkeeping, Lust Lizard of Melancholy Cove,* and *The Stupidest Angel* in Pine Cove, California, which is said to be a fictional stand-in for Cambria. Lesser-known writers and journalists carve out great stories each week for the local newspapers and for regional magazines such as *805 Living* (www.805living.com) and *Santa Barbara Magazine* (www.sbmag.com).

Visual Arts

Public art is supported in Santa Barbara, Ventura, and San Luis Obispo, which is not to say everyone likes what they see, but at least it creates discussion. The Central Coast has long been a haven for artists, and there are hundreds of art galleries showcasing plenty of local art. Wherever you go in the area, you'll most likely see painters setting up canvases near the missions or along bluff tops near the ocean to capture the mountains at sunset. Mission scenes are ubiquitous in local art, as are vineyard landscapes, but there are also pockets of experimental and contemporary art.

The **Santa Barbara Arts District** is mostly centrally located in the 800-1200 blocks of State Street. Santa Barbara has long had rotating public art displayed on State Street (www.sbartscommission.org), sometimes to rave reviews. In addition, the city's First Thursday (first Thurs. of every month 5pm-8pm) is a downtown showcase of the city's art and entertainment.

In San Luis Obispo there is no specific arts district but there are galleries dotting the city, and the website of the **San Luis Obispo Art Center** (www.sloartcenter.org) links to a wide variety of artists working in the area. **Ventura's ArtWalk** (www.artwalkventura.org), held each summer, has over 200 artists represented and shows off what is happening art-wise countywide. The **Ventura Public Art Program** (www.cityofventura.net/publicart) was started in 1991, and a seven-member board oversees projects in a variety of media. A map of current public art can be downloaded from their website. Similarly, the **Cambria Chamber of Commerce** (www.cambriachamber.org) has a fairly comprehensive listing of artists working in the small enclave.

Music and Dance

It's a simplistic notion to assume that small towns produce little talent; nothing could be further from the truth. Aside from well-known musicians who got their start on the Central Coast, including Katy Perry, Dishwalla, and the Mad Caddies, there is a strong dance community, covering hip-hop, flamenco, ballet, *folklórico,* and much more. **Rhythm Dance and Fitness Studios** (805/965-0444, www.dointhemost.com) is Tamarr Paul's nearly packed studio for hip-hop and more in Goleta. The **Linda Vega Dance Studio** (805/963-0073, www.vegaflamenco.com) is well known for flamenco and has been one of the premier dance studios in Santa Barbara; students routinely perform at Old Spanish Days Fiesta each August.

The **Arlington Theatre** (805/963-4408, www.thearlingtontheatre.com) and the **Lobero** (805/963-0761, www.lobero.com) in Santa Barbara are home to traveling musical and dance shows, as is the **Clark Center for the Performing Arts** (805/489-9444, www.clarkcenter.org) in Arroyo Grande and the **Performing Arts Center** (805/756-4849, www.pacslo.org) in San Luis Obispo. The

Majestic Theater (805/653-0721, www.venturatheater.net) in Ventura sees lots of musical acts but not as much dance.

Architecture and Design

Santa Barbara, and to a degree Ventura and San Luis Obispo, are predominantly defined by Spanish colonial architecture. The Spanish colonized the region and brought with them a mix of traditional Spanish and Persian designs. Most of downtown Santa Barbara and parts of San Luis Obispo and Ventura still have Spanish Colonial Revival as their identifying architecture, and this is what people expect to see when they visit.

In contrast are the towns of Paso Robles, Cambria, Arroyo Grande, Santa Ynez, and Los Olivos, identified by their Western-style storefronts. There are also pockets that are unique and different from anything else in the area, such as Solvang's Danish village and Santa Maria's blocky big-box stores.

ESSENTIALS

Getting There and Around

While not exactly remote, the Central Coast has the distinction of being sandwiched between two major cities that get all the attention, which is actually just fine with many locals. U.S. 101 slices through parts of the Central Coast, but that doesn't mean that getting to your ultimate destination is as easy as getting off a plane and hopping in a taxi.

AIR

Los Angeles International Airport (LAX, 310/646-5252, www.airport-la.com) and **San Francisco International Airport** (SFO, 800/435-9736, www.flysfo.com) are the two major airports that bring people to the Central Coast. **Santa Barbara Municipal Airport** (SBA, 805/681-4803, www.flysba.com) opened a new terminal in 2011 to receive more commercial traffic, and **San Luis Obispo County Regional Airport** (SBP, 805/781-5205, www.sloairport.com) is slowly adding more flights to its limited and small airport.

CAR

The most effective way to get around the Central Coast is by car. Driving is simple here, and it's not that easy to get lost. It's important to note that on peak summer days, main streets in the larger cities—Main Street in Ventura, State Street in Santa Barbara, and Higuera Street in San Luis Obispo—can get congested, although Higuera Street is less so, as it's a one-way street. Aside from that, drives from community to community are easy. The U.S. 101 freeway gets backed up most afternoons about 4pm with traffic heading south from Santa Barbara toward Ventura, and perpetual freeway construction slows things down, but it's usually only a 10-minute slowdown that picks up quickly.

Car Rentals

Renting a car is easy on the Central Coast, and it's a good idea since driving is the best way to see the sights. It's always best to compare rates. Make certain it includes unlimited mileage; the drive from Los Angeles to Ventura is 90 miles, but if you plan on getting to the far reaches of Cambria, for example, you'll start to rack up the miles. Some of the major car rental carriers are: **Enterprise** (www.enterprise.com) in Ventura (805/648-2882), Santa Barbara (805/966-3097), and San Luis Obispo (805/545-9111); **Avis** (www.avis.com) in Ventura (805/339-2260), Santa Barbara (805/964-4848), and San Luis Obispo (805/544-0630); **Hertz** (www.hertz.com) in Ventura (805/339-0585); and **Budget** (www.budget.com) in San Luis Obispo (805/541-2722).

BUS

Greyhound (800/231-2222, www.greyhound.com) is the most common way of arriving on the Central Coast by bus. There are major stops in Santa Maria, downtown Santa Barbara, downtown San Luis Obispo, and Paso Robles. Oddly, there isn't a Greyhound stop in the city of Ventura; the closest stop is in Oxnard, 25 minutes south of Ventura. To access beach areas like Lompoc, Guadalupe, Morro Bay, or Cambria, you will need to take a regional bus once you get off the Greyhound bus.

The bus systems on the Central Coast are well designed to help you move around within the cities. **Gold Coast Transit** (SCAT, 805/643-3158, www.goldcoasttransit.org) has bus service in western Ventura County as well as a connection to Ojai and is available seven days a week, except holidays. In Santa Barbara, you can ride the length of the waterfront, or the length of State Street, for just $0.50, on two daily electric shuttle routes (www.sbmtd.gov). The **Santa Ynez Valley Transit** (805/688-5452, www.syvt.com) is a scheduled minibus serving Ballard, Buellton, Los Olivos, Santa Ynez, and Solvang. The **San Luis Obispo Regional Transit Authority** (805/781-4472, www.slorta.org) covers the entire county.

TRAIN

Amtrak (800/872-7245, www.amtrak.com) is the only train service that operates along the Central Coast. The *Pacific Surfliner* runs from San Diego to San Luis Obispo several times daily in both directions, with stops in Ventura, Carpinteria, Santa Barbara, Goleta, Lompoc (listed as Surf), Santa Maria, Pismo Beach (listed as Grover Beach), and San Luis Obispo. The *Coast Starlight* runs once daily in each direction between Los Angeles and Seattle, with stops in Santa Barbara, San Luis Obispo, and Paso Robles. You cannot take the train to the coastal areas of Morro Bay and Cambria.

You might want to consider using the train for part of your trip. Stops in Santa Barbara, Ventura, and Paso Robles mean you can get off the train and walk to the downtown areas. The Santa Barbara stop lets you off on State Street a block from the beach. The Paso Robles stop is a two-block walk to the downtown square. San Luis Obispo's stop is a bit farther from downtown, so you'll need a car or taxi. Taking the train can make for a great day trip if you're short on time. For example, you could hop the train in San Luis Obispo and head to Ventura to explore the downtown, and then return to SLO by train, leaving your car parked all day.

BICYCLE

Getting around on a bike is easy, and all three counties have well-integrated bike lanes and paths. There's nothing like cruising along the beachfront or on country back roads. Contact **Traffic Solutions** (805/963-7283, www.

trafficsolutions.info) to obtain a copy of the free and most excellent Santa Barbara County bike map. You can rent bikes in Santa Barbara at **Wheel Fun Rentals** (23 E. Cabrillo Blvd. and 22 State St., 805/966-2282, www.wheelfunrentals.com). Be advised that the law in Santa Barbara County is that cyclists under age 18 must wear a helmet or be subject to a $70 fine.

For a great ride in Ventura, head to **Wheel Fun Rentals** (850 Harbor Blvd., 805/765-5795, www.wheelfunrentals.com) or the **Ventura Bike Depot** (239 W. Main St., 805/652-1114, http://venturabikedepot.com). In Ojai, try The **MOB Shop** (110 W. Ojai Ave., 805/272-8102, www.themobshop.com). For a languid ride in Santa Ynez wine country, check out **Surrey Cycle Rentals** (475 1st St., Solvang, 805/688-0091). San Luis Obispo offers **Wally's Bicycle Works** (306 Higuera St., 805/544-4116). In Morro Bay, **Farmer's Kites** (1108 Front. St., 805/772-0113) has the equipment for cruising the Morro Bay Harbor Walk.

Cycling Safety

Maybe it's the alluring near-perfect weather and sunshine, but far too many cyclists ride around without helmets. The Central Coast is a bike-friendly region, but sharing the major roads with cars without being protected is not a good idea. Helmets save lives. If you rent a bike, rent a helmet, or head to a cycle shop and buy one. At the very least check out **Play It Again Sports** (www.playitagainsports.com), which has stores in Ventura, Santa Maria, and Santa Barbara and sells used sports equipment, including helmets—it's better than having nothing on your head.

Although you'll see people riding without helmets, the police, normally pretty laid-back in these areas, will cite cyclists for moving violations. The congested State Street in Santa Barbara specifically is a place where you need to abide by the rules of the road. In Santa Barbara County, any cyclist under the age of 18 is required by law to wear a helmet; there's a $70 fine if you don't.

TAXIS

Taxis are not prevalent on the Central Coast, and are in fact few and far between once you leave Ventura and the city of Santa Barbara, although every city has them. In Santa Barbara, **Checker Cab** (805/966-6666) is a safe bet. In Ventura, there is **Yellow Cab of Ventura** (805/437-7977). Ojai has only **Topa Topa Taxi** (805/312-2288). Serving the entire Santa Ynez Valley, **Solvang Taxi** (805/688-0069) operates 24 hours a day. From San Luis Obispo to Pismo Beach, try **234 Taxi** (805/234-8294). The **Yellow Cab of SLO County** (805/543-1234) covers the Paso Robles area. **Yellow Cab** (805/489-1155) is the place to call for a ride in Cambria.

Tips for Travelers

BUSINESS HOURS

For all of its seeming dependence on tourism, it's an interesting phenomenon that all of the Central Coast, including larger towns like Santa Barbara and Ventura, still has a small-town feel. It's not uncommon for businesses to step away during "regular business hours" and place a hand-written note on the door saying they'll be back in a few minutes. A large number of business don't really have set hours; they might stay open later, or close early—it all depends on variables only they know. If there is a place you absolutely need to visit, it's advisable to call first to make certain they will be open.

ACCESS FOR TRAVELERS WITH DISABILITIES

Several years ago, a certain individual took it upon himself to frequent Central Coast wineries, hotels, and restaurants with the sole aim of suing anyone who was not in compliance with the disabled-access rules in the Americans with Disabilities Act (ADA). Though perhaps he was right in highlighting the issue, his aim was to extort money from small business in the area. Sadly, several business were forced to close down due to unreasonable demands and legal fees, and ultimately he filed more than 40 lawsuits, more to line his own pockets than to effect change. Eventually a federal judge put a stop to his egregious actions.

On the positive side, the region has become more aware of ADA issues, and that has made traveling along the Central Coast easier for anyone with a disability. All buses are wheelchair accessible, for example, and on major streets there are audible pedestrian signals and tactile guide strips for the visually impaired. The **Braille Institute** (www.brailleinstitute. org) has great programs in the Central Coast; contact the local field services coordinator in Santa Barbara and Ventura Counties (805/682-6222) and in San Luis Obispo County (805/462-1225). **Accessible Journeys** (www. disabilitytravel.com) has great pointers and information about traveling with a disability and can put you in touch, through their network of resources, with the right information to fit your needs.

TRAVELING WITH CHILDREN

Assuming your kids like the outdoors, there's plenty to keep them busy with bike paths, hiking, plenty of parks, and tons of beach activities, and it's all relatively inexpensive. Consider a surfing class, tide-pooling, kayaking, and definitely think about a day trip to the Channel Islands. The Central Coast has children's museums and other spots like natural history museums to keep little ones occupied without boring them. Near Ventura, in Oxnard, is **Gull Wings Children's Museum** (418 W. 4th St., Oxnard, 805/483-3005, www.gullwings.org). In San Luis Obispo is the **San Luis Obispo Children's Museum** (1010 Nipomo St., 805/544-5437, www.slocm.org), located just off Higuera Street downtown. Santa Maria has the **Santa Maria Valley Discovery Museum** (705 S. McClelland St., 805/928-8414, www.smvdiscoverymuseum.org) and Paso Robles offers the **Paso Robles Children's Museum** (623 13th St., 805/238-7432, www.pasokids.org).

WOMEN TRAVELING ALONE

For both men and women, traveling alone has its perks and its downsides. In general, people along the Central Coast are friendly, and they're likely to offer help if you look like you need it. Women traveling by themselves will find a helpful populace. The website **Journeywoman** (www.journeywoman.com) is a site devoted to women traveling solo, and it offers some great advice. Of course, it's always best to use common sense and to listen to your gut instincts if something or someone seems amiss. At area clubs and bars there have been reported cases of dosings, when someone slips some kind of drug, such as the "date rape" drug, into your drink when you're not looking, so it's always important to be alert and never leave your purse or your drink unattended. If there is a problem, ask for help.

SENIOR TRAVELERS

The Central Coast is a fantastic spot for seniors to visit. The roads are flat and walkable in every community, with very few strenuous hills. The website **Senior Journal** (www.seniorjournal. com) offers senior travel tips, suggestions, and even itineraries. The locally based website **Silver Years** (805/405-3164, www.silveryears.net) also provides more detailed regional information. There are often senior discounts available at sights and events; fewer hotels and restaurants offer senior discounts, but it never hurts to ask. Most movie houses offer senior discounts, as do the buses and the trolley.

GAY AND LESBIAN TRAVELERS

The Central Coast is a mix of liberal areas like Santa Barbara and pockets of more conservative values. That said, there are virtually no tensions between gay and straight people here, who tend to coexist very peacefully. In Santa Barbara, the **Pacific Pride Foundation** (www.pacificpridefoundation.org) has been around since 1974 and is an invaluable resource when visiting the area. In San Luis Obispo, the **Central Coast Gay and Lesbian Alliance** (www.ccgala.org), which incorporated as a nonprofit in 1994, covers that county. The **Pacific Pride Festival** (www.pacificpridefestival.org) is held on Santa Barbara's Leadbetter Beach each July and is the largest gathering of its kind on the Central Coast. Do keep in mind that the Central Coast is still a small-town region. Outside the major cities of Ventura, Santa Barbara, and San Luis Obispo, communities are relatively isolated. However, the upside of places that rely on tourism is that businesses rarely discriminate against anyone; this is still California.

TRAVELING WITH PETS

Pet-friendly hotels and establishments are abundant along the Central Coast, as are dog parks.

Not all beaches and parks, however, have off-leash areas, so it's important to note the signs posted at each recreation spot. Citations for not leashing your dog can and will be written, so pay attention; it's best to play by the rules. Many restaurants will allow pets on their patios, and a few establishments even allow pets inside. It's not uncommon to see a plethora of dogs on any major street, be it Main Street in Ventura, State Street in Santa Barbara, and Higuera Street in San Luis Obispo. The website **DogFriendly.com** (www.dogfriendly.com) is a fairly comprehensive source for pet-friendly accommodations, though not everything is listed. If you're not sure about a hotel, it's best to call in advance to find out about their pet fees and restrictions.

Health and Safety

EMERGENCY SERVICES

These are the main police contacts for the Central Coast. In an emergency, call 911.

- **San Luis Obispo Sheriff's Department** (1585 Kansas Ave., San Luis Obispo, 805/781-4550)

- **San Luis Obispo Police Department** (1042 Walnut St., San Luis Obispo, 805/781-7317)

- **Morro Bay Police Department** (850 Morro Bay Blvd., Morro Bay, 805/772-6225)

- **Ojai Police Department** (402 S. Ventura St., Ojai, 805/646-1414)

- **Paso Robles Police Department** (900 Park St., Paso Robles, 805/237-6464)

- **Santa Barbara Police Department** (215 E. Figueroa St., Santa Barbara, 805/897-2300)

- **Santa Maria Police Department** (222 E. Cook St., Santa Maria, 805/928-3781)

- Santa Ynez Valley: **County of Santa Barbara Sheriff's Department** (1745 Mission Dr., Solvang, 805/686-5000)

- **Ventura Police Department** (1425 Dowell Dr., Ventura, 805/339-4400)

HOSPITALS

These are the main hospitals on the Central Coast. For emergencies, always call 911.

- Cambria: **Twin Cities Community Hospital** (1100 Las Tablas Rd., Templeton, 805/434-3500)

- Morro Bay: **Twin Cities Community Hospital** (1100 Las Tablas Rd., Templeton, 805/434-3500)

- Ojai: **Ojai Valley Community Hospital** (1306 Maricopa Hwy., Ojai, 805/646-1401)

- Paso Robles: **Twin Cities Community Hospital** (1100 Las Tablas Rd., Templeton, 805/434-3500)

- San Luis Obispo: **French Hospital Medical Center** (1911 Johnson Ave., San Luis Obispo, 805/542-6378) and **Sierra Vista Regional Medical Center** (1010 Murray Ave., San Luis Obispo, 805/546-7600)

- Santa Barbara: **Cottage Hospital** (400 W. Pueblo St., Santa Barbara, 805/682-7111)

- Santa Maria: **Marian Regional Medical Center** (1400 E. Church St., Santa Maria, 805/739-3000)

- Santa Ynez Valley: **Santa Ynez Valley Cottage Hospital** (2050 Viborg St., Solvang, 805/688-6431)

- Ventura: **Community Memorial Hospital** (147 N. Brent St., Ventura, 805/652-5011)

PHARMACIES

These are the main pharmacies within the Central Coast. There's a **Rite Aid** (740 Quintana Rd., Morro Bay, 805/772-6198, www.riteaid.com) right off the U.S. 101 freeway in Morro Bay, and the **Ojai Village Pharmacy** (202 E. Ojai Ave., Ojai, 805/646-7272) has been around over 100 years. In Paso Robles there's a **CVS** (187 Nibblick Rd., Paso Robles, 805/238-2815, www.cvs.com). In San Luis Obispo there is a **CVS** (3960 Broad St., San Luis Obispo, 805/783-2903), and in Santa Barbara there is a **Rite Aid** (825 State St., Santa Barbara, 805/966-2760) right on State Street. Cayucos has the **Cayucos Pharmacy** (124 N. Ocean Ave., Cayucos, 805/995-3538). In Santa Maria there is a **Rite Aid** (2405 S. Broadway Ave., Santa Maria, 805/925-6404). Serving the Santa Ynez Valley, there's a **Rite Aid** in Solvang (616 Alamo Pintado Rd.), Solvang, 805/686-0016) in the Neilson's Shopping Center. The **Ventura Rite Aid** (131 W. Main St., Ventura, 805/643-1121) is in the Mission Plaza shopping center.

WATER SAFETY
Riptides

Remember that the ocean is a force greater than you, and there are occasional riptides and undercurrents along the calm, serene beaches of the Central Coast. Signs are posted when weather conditions warrant it. It's always best to swim with a buddy, or at the very least have someone waiting on shore for you.

Sailing

Sailing is a fantastic way to spend the day, but sailing requires wind. During the summer months the wind is predominantly from the west to northwest. The winds tend to be funneled around Point Conception, where the coastline turns north, and are accelerated along the north side (mainland-facing) portion of the Channel Islands. This area is referred to as "windy lane" and it can get extremely windy. This effect is strongest toward the west end of the channel and decreases as you move east. The winds tend to blow strongest in the afternoon and evening.

Be aware that this is a shipping channel, and many tankers and cargo ships move briskly through the waters. They have the right of way. They are huge, but they move fast, over 20 knots. So if you're heading to or back from the islands and you see a tanker in the water, know that they probably can't see you—and even if they can, it's impossible for them to change course; they'll be near you faster than you can imagine. Never try to outrun one of them.

Also be on the lookout for dive flags while you're sailing or boating. Divers are required to post a flag that sits atop a buoy; it is a red block with a white diagonal line through it. If you see one, avoid the area, as you could inadvertently cut an oxygen supply line. Also keep in mind that in the water, boats under sail have the right of way over motorboats.

EARTHQUAKES

Should a temblor occur while you are visiting, remain calm and follow these instructions. If you are inside, take cover by getting under a sturdy table or other piece of furniture, and wait until the shaking stops. If there isn't a table or desk near you, cover your face and head with your arms and crouch in an inside corner of the building where the building supports are the greatest (freestanding walls fall easily). Stay away from glass, windows, outside doors and walls, and anything that could fall, such as light fixtures or furniture. Use a doorway for shelter only if it is in close proximity to you and you know that it's a strongly supported, load-bearing doorway. Stay inside until the shaking stops and it's safe to go outside. Research has shown that most injuries occur when people inside buildings attempt to move to a different location inside the building or try to leave altogether. Be aware that the electricity may go out or the sprinkler systems or fire alarms may turn on. Do not use the elevators!

If you are outside, stay there; move away from buildings, streetlights, and utility wires and wait until the shaking stops. The greatest danger exists directly outside buildings. Many of the 120 fatalities from the 1933 Long Beach earthquake occurred when people ran outside, only to be killed by falling debris from collapsing walls. Ground movement during an earthquake is seldom the direct cause of death or injury.

If you're driving, stop as quickly as safety permits and stay in the vehicle. Avoid stopping near or under buildings, trees, overpasses, and utility wires. Proceed cautiously once the earthquake has stopped. Avoid roads, bridges, or ramps that might have been damaged by the earthquake.

CRIME

Crime in Ventura, Santa Barbara, and San Luis Obispo Counties is relatively low, according to recent reports by the Office of the Attorney General for the State of California. By comparison to the other 58 counties in the state, the Central Coast falls in the lower middle. However, it's an interesting trend that overall crime rates were higher in Ventura County, lower in Santa Barbara County, and even lower in San Luis Obispo County. Draw what

conclusions you will. Always lock your car and never leave valuables in plain sight; items such as a GPS units, cell phones, laptops, and cameras should either be taken with you or locked in the car's trunk.

There has been an increase in gang activity, unfortunately, and it is clearly charted as being worse in Ventura, and lessening farther north up the coast. Santa Barbara has had several high-profile gang stabbings and incidents, one in particular in broad daylight right on State Street. Task forces have been set up to grapple with these problems.

HOMELESSNESS

It's a sad commentary on our culture that we have mostly allowed the issue of homelessness to be ignored. In all three counties you will see panhandlers, with a greater concentration in Ventura and Santa Barbara. Task forces have been set up to deal with this issue too. Local businesses don't want potential customers accosted on State Street or Main Street, but it does happen, and it will continue to occur. Most panhandlers are not aggressive, though there has been an increase in the public's complaints about their assertive practices.

TRAINS

Given the fact that trains run through all three counties, it's important to know that incidents of people walking along the tracks or trying to outrun an oncoming train have been increasing. Granted, many of the deaths are of homeless men and women who are under the influence of drugs and alcohol, but there have also been cases of people just not paying attention. The active train lines are not separated in any way, meaning that anyone, including children, can walk onto the tracks at virtually any point in this region. Always use caution when crossing train tracks. If the crossing arms are down and the red lights are flashing, do not attempt to save time by cutting across the tracks before the train passes.

Information and Services

MONEY

All prices on the Central Coast are in U.S. dollars. Current sales tax rates vary from 7.5 to 8 percent, depending on where you are. Santa Barbara, for example, is at 8 percent, and most of Ventura County, with the exception of the Navy areas, is 7.5 percent. Similarly, in San Luis Obispo, the county overall is at 8 percent. It may not seem like much, but half a percent can add up, depending on the length of your trip. If you spend $2,000 on your trip that half percent is $10—and that's lunch.

All major banks will exchange foreign currency, and they tend to have better rates than small currency traders. In Santa Barbara you might consider **Montecito Bank & Trust** (1000 State St., Santa Barbara, 805/963-7511) or **American Riviera Bank** (1033 Anacapa St., Santa Barbara, 805/965-5942). In Ventura there is **Pacific Western Bank** (480 S. Mills Rd., Ventura, 805/658-1936), and in San Luis Obispo there is **Founders Community Bank** (863 Marsh St., San Luis Obispo, 805/543-6500). There are, of course, also larger banks like Bank of America and Rabobank. For international travelers, **XE** (www.xe.com) can provide exchange rates relating U.S. dollars to other currencies. Always check rates prior to your arrival to avoid unnecessary costs and fees.

COMMUNICATIONS AND MEDIA

Phones and Area Codes

Many visitors to the Central Coast are surprised that there is just one area code for all three counties; it's **805.**

Internet Services

Most hotels on the Central Coast, and an abundance of coffee shops, now offer free wireless Internet (Wi-Fi) connections. Additionally, it's becoming increasingly easy to pick up unsecured Wi-Fi signals in a variety of areas. If you don't have a computer, many hotels have a business center with one or two computers for guest use. Another option is to use the public computers at the libraries.

Mail Services

With **U.S. Postal Service** (www.usps.com) budget cuts, it is advisable to phone the post office branch to check their operating hours in case you need to buy stamps or mail something on a specific day. The main branches of the area's post offices are: **Ventura** (675 E. Santa Clara St., 805/643-3057), **Ojai** (201 E. Ojai Ave., 805/646-7904), **Santa Barbara** (836 Anacapa St., 805/564-2226), in the **Santa Ynez Valley** (430 Alisal Rd., Solvang, 805/688-9309), **Santa Maria** (201 E. Battles Rd., 805/922-0321), **San Luis Obispo** (893 Marsh St., 805/541-9138), **Paso Robles** (800 6th St., 805/237-8342), **Cambria** (4100 Bridge St. 805/927-8610), and **Morro Bay** (898 Napa Ave., 805/772-0839).

Newspapers and Periodicals

Major daily newspapers include the *Santa Barbara News-Press,* the *Ventura County Star,* and the *San Luis Obispo Tribune.* The weekly free alternative papers, which also provide good coverage of events and some insightful articles on local politics, include the *Ventura County Reporter* in Ventura, *The Santa Barbara Independent* in Santa Barbara, and the *New Times,* covering San Luis Obispo and Paso Robles. These papers publish each Thursday and are free at a multitude of locations.

Radio and Television

Keeping abreast of current events is important when you're traveling. The main radio stations that will provide you with important information in terms of local politics, talk, and current events are: in Ventura, KVTA (AM 1520), in Santa Barbara, KZSB (AM 1290); in the Santa Maria Valley, KSMA (AM 1240); for

San Luis Obispo, KYNS (AM 1340); and for Paso Robles, Morro Bay, and Cambria, KKAL (FM 92.5).

Local television in the area includes channels from Los Angeles, most notably KNBC. But for local news, weather, sports, and events, the three best stations are KEYT (www.keyt.com), which has the most comprehensive media coverage of the Central Coast, followed by KCOY (www.kcoy.com) and KSBY (www.ksby.com).

MAPS AND VISITOR INFORMATION

The **Santa Barbara Chamber of Commerce Visitors Center** (924 Anacapa St., Santa Barbara, 805/965-3023, www.sbchamber.org, Feb.-Oct. Mon.-Sat. 9am-5pm, Sun. 10am-5pm, Nov.-Jan. Mon.-Sat. 9am-4pm, Sun. 10am-4pm) has books and maps on the area. **Ventura Visitors Center** (101 S. California St., Ventura, 805/648-2075, www.ventura-usa.com, summer Mon.-Sat. 9am-5pm, Sun. 10am-4pm, winter Mon.-Sat. 9am-4pm, Sun. 10am-4pm) is located right downtown and is packed with everything you could want to know about Ventura. They have a surprisingly large amount of information in their large digs and the staff is eager to help. The beach town of Carpinteria has a place for visitors to get information at the **Carpinteria Valley Chamber of Commerce** (1056-B Eugenia Place, Carpinteria, 805/684-5479, www.carpinteriachamber.org, Mon.-Fri. 9am-4pm).

Located inside the **Ojai Valley Museum** (130 W. Ojai Ave., 805/640-1390, Mon.-Fri. 10am-4pm), the visitor information center is oftentimes understaffed. You can also try the **Ojai Visitors Bureau** (206 N. Signal St., Suite P, Ojai, 888/652-4669, http://ojaivisitors.com, Mon. 9am-4pm, Tues.-Fri. 8am-5pm), which has the latest information on Ojai's local events as well as maps and brochures for the area. The **Solvang Visitors Center** (1639 Copenhagen Dr., Solvang, 805/688-6144, www.solvangusa.com, daily 9am-5pm) is staffed by locals wearing red vests. They have comprehensive information not just on Solvang, but on the entire valley as well, including quarterly publications, local newspapers and newsletters, and maps. Although Los Olivos is just small enough that it doesn't have a visitors center, there is a small but functional website (www.losolivosca.com).

The **San Luis Obispo Visitors Center** (895 Monterey St., San Luis Obispo, 805/781-2777, www.visitslo.com, Sun.-Wed. 10am-5pm, Thurs.-Sat. 10am-7pm) recently moved to a new downtown location. They have maps and specific guides for restaurants, wineries, and the like. A popular place for travelers, Pismo Beach has a **California Welcome Center** (333 Five Cities Dr., Suite 100, Pismo Beach, 805/773-7924, www.visitcwc.com, Mon.-Sat. 10am-9pm, Sun. 10am-7pm), located at the Pismo Premium Outlets. They also have the downtown Pismo Beach **Chamber of Commerce Visitor Information Center** (581 Dolliver St., Pismo Beach, 805/773-4382 or 800/443-7778, www.pismochamber.com, Mon.-Fri. 10am-5pm, Sat. 10am-2pm), which has pamphlets, maps, and information.

The **Paso Robles Visitors Center** (1225 Park St., Paso Robles, 805/238-0506, Mon.-Fri. 8:30am-5pm, Sat.-Sun. 10am-2pm) will provide you with all the necessary materials to make your stay perfect. The **Cambria Chamber of Commerce** (767 Main St., Cambria, 805/927-3624, www.cambriachamber.org, Mon.-Fri. 9am-5pm, Sat.-Sun. noon-4pm) is probably the best resource for information on the area. The **Morro Bay Chamber of Commerce** (845 Embarcadero, Suite D, Morro Bay, 800/231-0592, www.morrobay.org, Mon.-Fri. 9am-5pm, Sat. 10am-4pm) has a wonderful visitors center overlooking the bay at the end of a small boardwalk. They offer a vast array of printed material you can take with you.

RESOURCES

Suggested Reading

NONFICTION

Beilharz, Edwin A. *Felipe de Neve: First Governor of California.* San Francisco: California Historical Society, 1971. This long-forgotten book gives a great historical account of the formation of California in the 1770s, including the missionary leader Junípero Serra and the missions up and down the coast, with a special emphasis on Santa Barbara. It's a tad dry in parts but is comprehensive in its understanding of the Spanish and their impact on the Central Coast.

Boutelle, Sara Holmes. *Julia Morgan, Architect.* New York: Abbeville Press, 1988. With projects in Santa Barbara, San Luis Obispo, and San Simeon, Julia Morgan had a major impact on the look and feel of the Central Coast. This definitive study of the reclusive Morgan is replete with color photos and drawings and has an abundance of information on Hearst Castle.

Bunnell, David Edward. *Sea Caves of Anacapa Island.* Santa Barbara: McNally & Loftin Publishing, 1993. If you are interested in exploring the sea caves of Anacapa Island, try to get your hands on this softcover book, a guide to the island's 135 sea caves that even includes maps of their interiors. Be aware that it has been over 20 years since Bunnell did his cave research.

Bunnell, David Edward. *Sea Caves of Santa Cruz Island.* Santa Barbara: McNally & Loftin Publishing, 1988. What author David Edward Bunnell did for the sea caves of Anacapa Island he does again with this look at Santa Cruz Island's caverns, with a good overview and maps of cave interiors.

California Coastal Commission. *Beaches and Parks from Monterey to Ventura.* Berkeley: University of California Press, 2007. This guide covers 310 coastal beaches, with color photographs as well as topographical maps and other useful information.

Castle, Rodger, and Gary Ream. *Morro Bay: Images of America.* Mount Pleasant, SC: Arcadia Publishing, 2006. Written by members of the Morro Bay Historical Society, this book gives a comprehensive history of this seaside town. The old photographs provide visual cues to how the town has changed.

Dana, Richard Henry. *Two Years Before the Mast.* New York: Barnes & Noble Classic Series, 2007. This personal journal chronicles Dana's life aboard a sailing trade ship in 1836. He visited Santa Barbara and other ports in California and talks about trading with the missions and the Native American way of life. He gives an excellent look into the Mexican period on the Central Coast. Perhaps the best quote, given the current boom on the Central Coast, is, "The Californians are an idle, thriftless people and can make nothing for themselves." If only he could revisit today.

Gardner, Theodore Roosevelt. *Lotusland: A Photographic Odyssey*. Santa Barbara: Allen A. Knoll, 1995. Packed with colorful photographs, this book sets out the rich botanical history of Lotusland in stunning visual detail. Once you see the photos, you'll want to visit.

Gray, Mary Taylor. *Watchable Birds of California*. Missoula, MT: Mountain Publishing, 1999. This is one of the most definitive guides to bird-watching, broken down by seacoast, inland, freshwater, and high-country birds. It has color photos to help with identification.

Gruver, Kathy. *The Alternative Medicine Cabinet*. West Conshohocken, PA: Infinity Publishing, 2010. Santa Barbara author Kathy Gruver uses area parks and agriculture as a springboard to discuss natural health issues common to the Central Coast and everyone else, including avoiding pesticide-laden foods and searching for healthy alternatives.

Hammond, Norm. *The Dunites*. Arroyo Grande, CA: South County Historical Society, 1992. Published by the South County Historical Society, this book details the eclectic arts community that sprung up in the Pismo Beach dunes during the 1920s and 1930s.

Lester, Elizabeth Sherman. *Legendary King of San Miguel*. Santa Barbara: McNally & Loftin Publishing, 1974. The author spent 12 years on remote San Miguel Island with her husband and their two daughters. Their experiences there form the basis of this book.

Masson, Kathryn. *Santa Barbara Style*. New York: Rizzoli, 2001. Santa Barbara never looked so good. This book includes photos of many Santa Barbara landmarks and Montecito estates, both interiors and exteriors, and shows all the details of what good decorating can do for a home.

Schoenherr, Allan A., C. Robert Feldmeth, and Michael J. Emerson. *Natural History of the Islands of California* Berkeley: University of California Press, 2003. This 500-page tome covers all the islands off California's coast with extensive information about the islands that make up Channel Islands National Park. The book has the most complete picture that I've found of the island's unique plant and animal life along with its little-known human history.

Various authors. *Ventura County—Looking Back: The Early Years*. Seattle: Pediment Publishing, 2009. More than 350 historical black-and-white photos are presented in this coffee-table book, spanning the 1870s to the 1920s, that shows how Ventura weathered many changes. This book celebrates the good, the bad, and the everyday.

FICTION

Boyle, T. C. *Riven Rock*. New York: Penguin Books, 1998. Boyle's seventh novel transforms two characters straight out of Montecito history. The people and place are real, and Boyle blends them into a complex novel about a mentally ill millionaire locked up in his own Santa Barbara estate in the early 1900s.

Boyle, T. C. *When the Killing's Done*. New York: Penguin Books, 2012. The Santa Barbara resident's 13th novel pits a national park employee against an environmentalist in a fight over what to do with the invasive species on Anacapa Island and Santa Cruz Island.

Grafton, Sue. *Q is for Quarry*. New York: Ballantine, 2003. The murder in this book, part of the Kinsey Millhone series, was based on a real homicide that occurred in Santa Barbara in 1969, unfortunately still unsolved; other characters in this particular book are also based on people in the sheriff's department, one of whom went on to become the police chief of San Luis Obispo.

Moore, Christopher. *Practical Demonkeeping*. New York: William Morrow Publishing, 2004. Christopher Moore's debut comic novel finds a man keeping a demon in a quirky California coast town called Pine Cove, actually a stand-in for Cambria.

Internet Resources

VISITOR INFORMATION

San Luis Obispo Visitors and Conference Bureau
www.visitsanluisobispocounty.com
Also available in Spanish, German, and French. They now have an insiders' blog.

Santa Barbara Conference and Visitors Bureau
www.santabarbaraca.com
A terrific comprehensive website that covers everything you can think of and offers many Internet specials and deals on lodging and food. The website provides information about the Santa Ynez Valley as well.

Ventura Visitors and Convention Bureau
www.ventura-usa.com
A comprehensive site about Ventura with a nice collection of photographs and videos. They also have their own series of videos on their own YouTube channel.

WINERIES

The Paso Robles Wine Country Alliance
www.pasowine.com
The single best website for researching the wines of Paso Robles. If only all wine websites were like this one. It has an extensive list of wineries and vineyards. In addition, they have a map that can show where the wineries are that produce specific types of wine.

The San Luis Obispo Vintners Association
www.slowine.com
Covers the reasonably small area south of Paso Robles, including the Edna Valley. It has a nice printable map of the wineries around the City of San Luis Obispo.

The Santa Barbara County Vintners Association
www.sbcountywines.com
The authoritative website for most of the wineries and growers in Santa Barbara County also lists upcoming special events at each winery and has downloadable maps. It also has a free touring guide.

The Santa Barbara Urban Wine Trail
www.urbanwinetrailsb.com
This small area is in downtown Santa Barbara and not in the grape-growing region of the valley, but the Urban Wine Trail is thriving. There's also a place where you can read blogs from the wineries on the Santa Barbara Urban Wine Trail.

Index

QR

S

List of Maps

www.moon.com

MOON.COM is ready to help plan your next trip! Filled with fresh trip ideas and strategies, author interviews, informative travel blogs, a detailed map library, and descriptions of all the Moon guidebooks, Moon.com is all you need to get out and explore the world—or even places in your own backyard. While at Moon.com, sign up for our monthly e-newsletter for updates on new releases, travel tips, and expert advice from our on-the-go Moon authors. As always, when you travel with Moon, expect an experience that is uncommon and truly unique.

KEEP UP WITH MOON ON FACEBOOK AND TWITTER

JOIN THE MOON PHOTO GROUP ON FLICKR

MAP SYMBOLS

▨▨▨	Expressway	【	Highlight	✗	Airfield	⚲	Golf Course
─────	Primary Road	○	City/Town	✗	Airport	🅿	Parking Area
═════	Secondary Road	◉	State Capital	▲	Mountain	🛆	Archaeological Site
═ ═ ═	Unpaved Road	⊛	National Capital	✚	Unique Natural Feature	⚑	Church
─ ─ ─	Trail	★	Point of Interest			🕆	Gas Station
···········	Ferry	•	Accommodation	⚑	Waterfall	◌	Glacier
══════	Railroad	▾	Restaurant/Bar	▲	Park		Mangrove
▨▨▨	Pedestrian Walkway	▪	Other Location	◨	Trailhead		Reef
▥▥▥	Stairs	Λ	Campground	✗	Skiing Area		Swamp

CONVERSION TABLES

°C = (°F - 32) / 1.8
°F = (°C x 1.8) + 32
1 inch = 2.54 centimeters (cm)
1 foot = 0.304 meters (m)
1 yard = 0.914 meters
1 mile = 1.6093 kilometers (km)
1 km = 0.6214 miles
1 fathom = 1.8288 m
1 chain = 20.1168 m
1 furlong = 201.168 m
1 acre = 0.4047 hectares
1 sq km = 100 hectares
1 sq mile = 2.59 square km
1 ounce = 28.35 grams
1 pound = 0.4536 kilograms
1 short ton = 0.90718 metric ton
1 short ton = 2,000 pounds
1 long ton = 1.016 metric tons
1 long ton = 2,240 pounds
1 metric ton = 1,000 kilograms
1 quart = 0.94635 liters
1 US gallon = 3.7854 liters
1 Imperial gallon = 4.5459 liters
1 nautical mile = 1.852 km

**MOON SANTA BARBARA &
THE CENTRAL COAST**

Avalon Travel
a member of the Perseus Books Group
1700 Fourth Street
Berkeley, CA 94710, USA
www.moon.com

Editor: Kevin McLain
Series Manager: Kathryn Ettinger
Copy Editor: Christopher Church
Graphics and Production Coordinator: Elizabeth Jang
Cover Designer: Elizabeth Jang
Map Editor: Albert Angulo
Cartographers: Stephanie Poulain, Brian Shotwell,
   Albert Angulo
Indexer: Rachel Kuhn

ISBN: 978-1-61238-699-7
ISSN: 2156-8596

Printing History
1st Edition – 2010
2nd Edition – April 2014
5 4 3 2 1

Front cover photo: lily pond at Mission Santa Barbara
© Jerry Moorman/Getty Images

Title Page: birds on Morro Rock © Stuart Thornton

Interior color photos: p. 4 the famous Cayucos Saloon
© Gabriel Skvor; p. 5 the Madonna Inn in San Luis
Obispo © Stuart Thornton; p. 6 (top left) a seal in
Port San Luis Harbor © Stuart Thornton, (top right)
a windmill in Solvang © Stuart Thornton, (bottom)
Anacapa's iconic Arch Rock © Stuart Thornton; p.
7 (top) sign at Avila Beach's Pirate's Cove © Stuart
Thornton, (bottom left) doors of Mission Santa
Barbara © Steven Heap/123rf.com, (bottom right)
Neptune Pool at Hearst Castle © Stuart Thornton/
Courtesy Hearst Castle®/California State Parks;
p. 8 a wave on a Santa Barbara beach © David
Schrader/123rf.com; p. 9 (top) seals at San Simeon
© Stuart Thornton, (bottom left) a happy passenger
anticipates a ride on the Fillmore & Western Railway,
(bottom right) the Point San Luis Lighthouse ©
Stuart Thornton; p. 11 © James Mattil/123rf.com;
p. 12 (top) © Visions of America LLC, (bottom)
© John Roman/123rf.com; p. 13 © Claudine Van
Massenhove/123rf.com; pp. 14 - 15 © Stuart Thornton;
p. 16 © James Nagy/123rf.com; p. 17 (top) © Stuart
Thornton, (bottom) © Henrik Lehnerer/123rf.com;
p. 18 © Stuart Thornton/Courtesy Hearst Castle®/
California State Parks; pp. 19 - 21 © Stuart Thornton;
p. 22 (top) © James Mattil/123rf.com, (bottom) ©
Stuart Thornton; pp. 23 - 24 © Stuart Thornton

Printed in Canada by Friesens

KEEPING CURRENT

If you have a favorite gem you'd like to see included in the next edition, or see anything
that needs updating, clarification, or correction, please drop us a line. Send your com-
ments via email to f   e.

32953012512218